HUDSON'S

BUILDING
AND ENGINEERING
CONTRACTS

AUSTRALIA
The Law Book Company
Brisbane · Sydney · Melbourne · Perth

CANADA
Carswell
Ottawa · Toronto · Calgary · Montreal · Vancouver

AGENTS
Steimatzky's Agency Ltd., Tel Aviv;
N.M. Tripathi (Private) Ltd., Bombay;
Eastern Law House (Private) Ltd., Calcutta;
M.P.P. House, Bangalore;
Universal Book Traders, Delhi;
Aditya Books, Delhi;
MacMillan Shuppan KK, Tokyo;
Pakistan Law House, Karachi, Lahore

HUDSON'S

BUILDING
AND ENGINEERING
CONTRACTS

Including the Duties and Liabilities of

ARCHITECTS, ENGINEERS AND SURVEYORS

ELEVENTH EDITION

BY

I.N. DUNCAN WALLACE Q.C., M.A. OXON.
of the Middle Temple, Barrister-at-Law

VOLUME 2

**LONDON
SWEET & MAXWELL
1995**

First Edition (1891) By Alfred Hudson
Second Edition (1895) By Alfred Hudson
Third Edition (1906) By Alfred Hudson
Fourth Edition (1914) By Alfred Hudson
Fifth Edition (1926) By Alfred Hudson K.C.
Sixth Edition (1933) By Lawrence Mead
Seventh Edition (1946) By Lawrence Mead
Eighth Edition (1959) By E.J. Rimmer Q.C., and
I.N. Duncan Wallace
Ninth Edition (1965) By I.N. Duncan Wallace
Tenth Edition (1970) By I.N. Duncan Wallace

Published in 1994 by
Sweet & Maxwell Limited, of
South Quay Plaza
183 Marsh Wall, London E14 9FT
Phototypeset by
MFK Typesetting Ltd.,
Hitchin, Herts.

Printed in Great Britain by
The Bath Press
Bath, Avon

A catalogue record for this book is available from the British Library

ISBN 0 421 33260 3

No natural forests were destroyed to make this product.
Farmed timber was used and replanted.

TABLE OF CONTENTS

VOLUME 1

(For a more detailed Table of Contents please see Volume 1)

VOLUME 2

Para.

9. TIME FOR PERFORMANCE

10. PENALTIES AND LIQUIDATED DAMAGES

11. VESTING AND SEIZURE OF MATERIALS AND PLANT

12. FORFEITURE AND DETERMINATION

13. SUB-CONTRACTS

14. ASSIGNMENT

15. INSURANCE AND INDEMNITIES

16. BANKRUPTCY AND LIQUIDATION

17. BONDS AND GUARANTEES

18. ARBITRATION

TABLE OF CASES

(References are to Paragraph numbers with those in bold referring to Illustrations)

xv

TABLE OF STATUTES

(References are to Paragraph numbers)

TABLE OF STATUTORY INSTRUMENTS

(References are to Paragraph numbers)

RULES OF THE SUPREME COURT

(References are to Paragraph numbers)

TABLE OF REFERENCES TO RIBA CONTRACT FORM CONDITIONS

(References are to Paragraph numbers)

TABLE OF REFERENCES TO ICE CONTRACT FORM CONDITIONS

(References are to Paragraph numbers)

ci

CHAPTER 9

TIME FOR PERFORMANCE

(1) Generally

Contracts of all kinds commonly specify a date for the performance of **9·001** some obligation. Even if no date is specified, or if a contractual date for performance has lapsed due to prevention or breach by the other party, or as a result of election to keep the contract in being (that is, waiver), there will be an implied requirement to perform the obligation within a reasonable time. In both cases it will be a question of construction, usually depending on the subject-matter of the particular promise and its relevant importance to the transaction viewed as a whole, whether the obligation is a condition, so that failure to meet the date is a fundamental breach, preventing enforcement of the contract (or recovery of price, for example) while entitling the other party to treat the contract as repudiated—in traditional legal parlance whether time is of the essence. If time is not of the essence the promisor in delay can enforce his own rights and the injured promisee has his remedy in damages, but no more. The question, though not of course its answer, will apply equally to both parties' respective obligations under the contract, as, for example, between buyer and seller, charterer and ship owner, purchaser and vendor, and contractor and owner.[1]

The principle has been well stated in an Australian case, where the particular obligation under review was that of the owner in a construction contract to make the site available to the contractor for a start of work by a named date:

---

[1] For a valuable discussion of the subject as a whole see Stoljar "Untimely Performance in Contract" in (1955) 71 L.Q.R. 527 and for building contracts in particular, *ibid.* at pp. 553–556.

"Where a contract contains a promise to do a particular thing on or before a specified day time may or may not be of the essence. If it is, the promisee is entitled to rescind, but he may elect not to exercise the right and an election will be inferred from any conduct which is consistent with the contract remaining in being. If not of the essence or no longer of the essence because of election, rescission is generally only permitted after giving a notice requiring performance within a specified reasonable time, and after non-compliance with the notice".[2]

The courts in other fields, particularly sale of goods, have often differed and have had considerable difficulty in rationalising a coherent guideline or principle for deciding whether a particular obligation is to be regarded as a condition precedent, so that failure to meet the named date or reasonable time requirement will be a fundamental breach justifying the other party in treating the contract as repudiated. The important practical point is that if time is not of the essence the injured party will be limited to his remedy in damages and may not withdraw from or cancel the contract.

9·002   Time may be of the essence in this special sense either as a matter of presumed intention after examination of the contract as a whole, together with its commercial background; or because the parties may have expressly so provided; or because, as the above quotation from the *Carr* case indicates, time not originally of the essence can, in a case of unreasonable delay, be rendered of the essence by notice. This latter doctrine appears to have originated in contracts for the sale of land, where post-contractual co-operation will be required in regard to matters such as giving title and completion.[3] While its precise legal basis may not be entirely clear, since it involves post-contractual and unilateral action by one party, it is submitted that this particular rule can be justified on the basis that where there is an obligation to perform by a named, or reasonable date, a failure to do so can continue so long, and in such circumstances as to evince an intention no longer to be bound by the contract, and when the period and circumstances give rise to any doubt, a notice to complete the promised act within a further reasonable time will serve, first, to show that any previous express or implied waiver has been withdrawn, and, secondly, to give the party concerned an opportunity to show that he does regard himself as bound. If he does not then comply with the notice, he will be evincing an intention no longer to be bound by the contract, or an inability to perform it, and the other party can elect to treat the contract as repudiated on ordinary general principles.[4]

9·003   In extreme cases even notice will not be required, if intention no longer to be bound can already be inferred from the conduct of the defaulting party.[5] Thus, in the case quoted above it was held that the

---

[2] *Carr* v. *J. A. Berriman Pty. Ltd.*, (1953) 27 A.L.J. 273 High Court of Australia, illustrated *ante*, Chap. 4, para. 4·212.
[3] *Stickney* v. *Keeble* [1915] A.C. 386.
[4] As to which see *ante*, Chap. 4, paras. 4·205 *et seq.*
[5] See, *e.g.* the case of *Kingdom* v. *Cox* (1848) 5 C.B. 522, see *infra*, Subsection (4), para. 9·020 where no notice is referred to in the report or appears to have been considered necessary, and *Carr's* case illustrated *ante*, para. 4·212. See also, *per* Lord Parker in *Stickney* v. *Keeble* [1915] A.C. 386, 416.

owner's failure to remedy his breach after the due date continued for so long and in such circumstances that, notwithstanding the absence of notice, the contract had been lawfully determined. Obviously, however, in all cases of delay, and even of total cessation of work, notice by the innocent party is a wise precaution. Notice is clearly also especially necessary wherever there has been an earlier election by the innocent party to treat the contract as subsisting after initial delays by the other party, as will very often happen in practice in construction contracts, while the owner is still hoping for an improvement in progress by the contractor.[6]

Much of the present Chapter will be directed to a contractor's or subcontractor's obligation in a construction contract to complete his work by a named or reasonable date, although, as stated, similar problems may arise in regard to the owner's obligations, such as those in regard to affording possession,[7] or in regard to payment of the price, or instalments of the price.[8] This particular question of interpretation, as previously stated, can be a difficult one, and in the case of instalment contracts for the sale or delivery of goods (with which construction contracts have points of resemblance) the 1893 Sale of Goods Act, recognising a previously confused case law, deliberately abstained from laying down any general rule where either buyers or sellers failed to perform their respective obligations promptly with regard to a first or later instalment,[9] and a Court of Appeal in 1931 suggested, as a criterion for deciding whether such a breach constituted a repudiation of the whole contract or merely a severable breach giving rise to damages, "the quantitative ratio which the breach bears to the contract as a whole and the degree of probability that such breach will be repeated".[10]

However, in examining a contractor's obligation to complete his work **9·004** to time, construction contracts differ very markedly from nearly all others in that the contractor can be expected to have expended very heavily in performing the contract prior, for example, to a relatively trivial delay after completion, and also that upon fixing of the work to the soil the property in it will have passed to the owner irrespective of the degree of payment, thus conferring a major and irretrievable benefit on the owner as against a possibly only minor or nominal loss suffered by him. No doubt for these reasons the courts have shown an exceptional assiduity in avoiding a time of the essence interpretation of the contractor's completion obligation in construction contracts,[11] it would seem even in cases where

---

[6] See, *e.g.* the case of *Pigott Construction Ltd.* v. *W. J. Crowe Ltd.* (1961) 27 D.L.R. (2d) 258 Canada, illustrated *ante*, Chap. 4, para. 4·158 and see the discussion *ante*, Chap. 4, Section 3(1), paras. 4·205–4·214, and the case of *Felton* v. *Wharrie* (1906) Hudson, *Building Contracts* (4th ed.), Vol. 2, p. 398, illustrated *infra*, Subsection (5), para. 9·023.

[7] As in *Carr's* case *supra*, and see *ante*, para. 4·147.

[8] As to this see *ante*, Chap. 4, Section 3(1)(*e*), paras. 4·221–4·222.

[9] See section 31(2) of the 1983 Act, and see Stoljar, *op. cit.*, pp. 540–544.

[10] *Maple Flock Company* v. *Universal Furniture Products Ltd.* [1931] 1 K.B. 148.

[11] *Lamprell* v. *Billericay Union* (1849) 3 Exch. 283, illustrated *infra*.

express language has been used in the contract.[12] Though there appears to
be a lack of authority in the Commonwealth, even express "time of the
essence" wording might well be regarded as overridden by or inconsistent
with other contract wording, quite apart from election or waiver arguments preventing its enforcement.[13]

There is a further aspect of construction contracts which has tended to
be overlooked by the courts, and which may explain the comparative
rarity of the case law on this subject. This is the practical consideration
that an obligation to complete by a certain date (even if coupled with liquidated damages provisions) is in reality of little value to an owner, for example where serious and unacceptable delays by a contractor are often
seen to develop during the construction period well before the completion
date, which indicate clearly that completion by that date is never going to
be attained. The overriding necessity to take much earlier action, and the
widespread use of express terms requiring due diligence by the contractor
throughout the construction period, enforceable by the owner through
termination clauses expressly conditioned on a failure of such diligence,
does much to explain the comparative rarity of case law on rescission or
termination for late completion.

9·005   Indeed, it may be convincingly argued that liquidated damages or
similar express provisions are remedies deliberately evolved for situations
where the degree of delay under contemplation is such that the owner will
prefer to allow the contractor to complete and accept damages as compensation. As will be seen, the presence of a liquidated damages clause has
sometimes been held to be inconsistent with a time of the essence
interpretation of the completion obligation,[14] but no such inconsistency
arises, it is submitted, with the implication of a due diligence obligation
enforceable, whether by way of damages or rescission, at a date prior to
the completion date. It is later submitted *infra*, that liquidated damages
obligations are almost invariably expressed to cover one particular class of
damage only, namely that caused by failure to hand over the project for
occupation on the required completion date, and not those quite different
delay damages which in a construction project can easily be incurred by
the owner during the construction period—for example, those liabilities
to other contractors or to adjoining owners or statutory authorities caused
by the contractor's failure to meet any agreed intermediate completion
dates for parts of the work or to comply with a more generalised duty of
due diligence (itself no doubt defined or interpreted by reference to any
intermediate or final completion dates which may have been expressly
agreed).[15]

---

[12] *Lucas* v. *Godwin* (1837) 3 Bing.N.C. 737; *Lowther* v. *Heaver* (1889) 41 Ch.D. 248, both
illustrated *infra*.
[13] See generally for this *infra*, Subsection (4), paras. 9·013–9·021.
[14] See, *e.g.*, *per* Rolfe B. in *Lamprell* v. *Billercay Union* (1849) 3 Exch. 283, 308, cited *infra*,
para. 9·020.
[15] See the analagous case of *Akt. Reidar* v. *Arcos* [1927] 1 K.B. 352 and the discussion *post*,
Chap. 10, para. 10·002.

While there is an apparent absence of authority on this point in England it is submitted in Subsection (7), *infra*, that, despite a relatively recent dictum to the contrary,[16] construction contracts in general are subject to an implied term of due diligence on the part of the contractor which in appropriate cases, and particularly after notice, will entitle an owner to rescind the contract at common law in the absence of an express termination clause.

Finally, it is desirable to be clear as to the precise meaning of "completion" in a time obligation. There is surprisingly little English authority on the point, but it is clear that the requirement will be less rigorous than in other contractual contexts. Usually it will mean bona fide completion free of known or patent defects so as to enable the owner to enter into occupation.[16a] The words "practical" or "substantial" in the English standard forms probably do no more than indicate that trivial defects not affecting beneficial occupancy will not prevent completion (the more so, of course, if the contract provides for a maintenannce or defects liability period).

(2) Where Time Specified For Completion

Most construction contracts expressly specify a date for completion. The **9·006** law in common law countries is uncompromising in insisting that, independent of fault, failure to complete by an unequivocal promised date will expose the contractor to a claim for damages for that failure, which in the absence of a liquidated damages clause (discussed *post*, Chapter 10) will fall to be calculated in accordance with the principles set out in Chapter 8. Events over which the contractor may genuinely have no control, such as weather, strikes, labour or materials shortages, or damage or obstruction by third parties for whom the owner is not responsible, will afford him no excuse or defence, in the absence of express provision, unless they are such as to frustrate the contract entirely, which it has been seen will only rarely occur in a construction context,[17] or unless the promised completion date has ceased to be applicable on one of the recognised grounds discussed *infra* subsection (3). Precisely the same rule applies to commercial contracts in other fields, of course.

On the other hand, in a normal construction contract the contractor's promised completion date will almost never be treated as of the essence, even in cases where express provisions might be said to support such a view, so that an owner will normally never be able to treat the contract as repudiated merely on the ground that the completion date has passed— see *infra*, subsection (4). In such a case, the contractor will be able to recover the full price of the work, subject to any cross-claim for damages for the delay.[18] As a matter of detail, where a date for completion is speci-

---

[16] *Per* Staughton J. in *Greater London Council* v. *Cleveland Bridge and Engineering Co. Ltd.* (1984) 34 BLR 57, 67.

[16a] See *ante*, paras. 4·029–4·030, and paras. 5·048–5·049. See also *post*, paras. 10·058–10·059 and the *Jarvis* case, para. 10·099.

[17] See *ante*, Chap. 4, Section 3(3), paras. 4·245–4·246.

[18] *Lucas* v. *Godwin* (1837) 3 Bing. (N.C.) 737; *Young* v. *Kitchin* (1878) 3 Ex. D. 127.

fied, the contractor will have until the last hour of the day fixed for completion in which to finish the work.[19]

(3) Where Specified Time Inapplicable

9·007   Where a contract is for defined work, so that there will be an express or implied obligation to complete,[20] completion within a reasonable time will be implied if no time or date is specified in the contract. The same result occurs where a contractual completion date has been specified, but has ceased to be applicable. This can happen where there has been agreement to that effect; where there has been waiver of an earlier breach of the completion obligation, or an election by the owner to leave the contract on foot which might otherwise have been cancelled for this reason; or where the owner has in one way or another prevented completion within the contract time without any breach on his part (as for instance, by ordering extra work); or by failing to give possession or by some other breach of contract.

ILLUSTRATIONS[21]

9·008   (1) Contractors undertook to complete the joinery work for a brewery in 4½ months for a price of £17,000, and to pay liquidated damages of £40 per week for late completion. The owners sought to deduct £200 for 5 weeks' delay. At the trial it was agreed that 4 weeks of the delay had been caused by a late start due to delays by other workmen of the owners, but one week was due to the contractor's own workmen. *Held*, by Parke B., there being nothing to show a new contract to perform in 4½ months ending at a later date, neither one week's nor any liquidated damages could be deducted. *Holme* v. *Guppy* (1838).[22]

        (2) A developer owner sought to deduct delay penalties, being a stipulated £1 per week per house for six houses, from the contract sum because the works had not been completed till 12 weeks after the completion date. The contractors replied that, by a subsequent agreement, they had undertaken to carry out certain extra works in a reasonable time, that these were mixed up with the original work, that the owners well knew that the original work could not be completed before the extra works, and that all the work had been completed within a reasonable time. *Held*, by the Court of Common Pleas, on demurrer, that the second agreement amounted to a waiver and also prevented performance of the first by the named date, so that it was a good answer to the claim for the fixed sums: *Thornhill* v. *Neats* (1860).[23]

---

[19] *Startup* v. *McDonald* (1843) 6 M. & G. 593.
[20] For what constitutes completion see *ante*, Chap. 4, paras. 4·006 *et seq*., and for the "practical" or "substantial" completion which usually terminates the liability for delay damages, see *ante*, paras. 4·029–4·030, and paras. 5·048–5·049.
[21] In addition to the cases illustrated, see *Joshua Henshaw & Son* v. *Rochdale Corporation* [1984] K.B. 381 and *Electronic Industries* v. *David Jones* (1954) 1 C.L.R. 288, Australia.
[22] 3 M. & W. 387. This would not prevent a claim for ordinary damages, of course.
[23] 8 C.B.(N.S.) 831; see also, *Courtnay* v. *Waterford & Central Ireland Rly. Co.* (1878) 4 L.R.Ir. 11.

(3) A contractor undertook to complete a railway contract in Ontario by a **9·009** named date. There was a termination clause enabling the engineer to give notice if it appeared that the work would not be completed in the manner and within the time specified in the contract. After the date for completion work continued and payments were made under the contract until the engineer served a notice under the termination clause requiring a resumption of progress, and subsequently terminated the contract. *Held*, by Wilson J., that the continuation of work without agreement on a new date for completion meant that a reasonable time should be allowed for that purpose, and the contract prices must be presumed to continue to apply to the work done after that date: *McDonnell* v. *Canada Southern Rly.* (1873).[24]

(4) A company contracted to supply iron by 12 equal deliveries commencing in January. Between January and November the purchaser requested them to postpone delivery, which they did. In December, he asked them to deliver the whole undelivered balance. The company refused to supply more than the December delivery, and the company sued for non-delivery. *Held*, by the Exchequer Chamber, that the company was now bound to deliver the balance within a reasonable time and, not having asked for such time, had wrongly repudiated the contract: *Tyers* v. *Rosedale Iron Co.* (1875).[25]

(5) Contractors agreed to build a bridge by a named date. Alterations to the **9·010** girders in the structure were ordered later, which the contractors alleged had made completion of the whole bridge by the named date impossible, and they repeated the plea made in *Thornhill* v. *Neats* that completion of the original work could not take place before completion of the altered work. The owners cross-claimed for liquidated damages, but the jury found that the contractors had completed within a reasonable time following the variation, and some delays by the owners in supplying drawings. On appeal from the jury, the owners argued that there had been no evidence of any express agreement to substitute reasonable time for the completion date which had been the assumed basis of the demurrer in the *Thornhill* case. *Held*, by Fitzgerald B., that no doubt there was no express evidence of a term being agreed for completion within a reasonable time, but the jury were justified in concluding that it never would or could have been the intention of the parties that the additional work was to be performed within the stipulated time, so that the obligation had been one to complete in a reasonable time, and the cross-claim must fail. *Courtnay* v. *Waterford & Central Ireland Rly. Co.* (1878).[26]

(6) Joiners undertook work on a building where other tradesmen were being employed by the defendants, in the following terms: "We offer to execute the work ... for the sum of £2,128 and undertake to finish our department of the work by April 15 next." The joiners start of work was delayed by plasterers, from whom the defendants had omitted to obtain an obligation as to time. The defendants argued that time was of the essence, and that since there had been no default or prevention on their own part, they were not liable to pay for the work. *Held*, by the Court of Session, that either there was an implied condition precedent that the joiners be given possession so as to make completion by the contract date possible, or the defendants, by omitting to bind the plasterers to complete by a fixed date, had prevented the joiners from completing in time, and consequently the latter were entitled to the price of the work: *Duncanson* v. *Scottish Investment Co.* (1915).[27]

---

[24] 33 Upp Can. Q.B. 313 Ontario.
[25] L.R. 10 Exch. 195. Compare and distinguish *Kingdom* v. *Cox*, see *infra*, para. 9·020.
[26] 4 L.R. Ir. 11.
[27] 1915 S.C. 1106.

9·011

(7) Car builders undertook to build a body on a Rolls-Royce chassis supplied by them. The car was to be ready by a specified date (which was held to be of the essence of the contract). After that date the buyer continued to press for delivery, and new dates were promised and accepted by him, but delivery still was not effected, and he eventually gave notice that he would not accept if it was not ready by a certain date. *Held*, completion by the original date had been waived, but an obligation to complete within a reasonable time was substituted therefore; the date stipulated in the notice was reasonable, and the buyers were entitled to reject the car: *Charles Rickards Ltd.* v. *Oppenheim* (1950).[28]

(8) The plaintiff contracted to put on a television display in the defendant's shop over a number of agreed days, but due to industrial action in the vicinity agreed at the defendant's request to postpone the display to a date to be mutually agreed in the future. After further postponement the defendant finally decided he did not wish to have the display, and when the plaintiff claimed damages the defendant claimed that there had been a mutual release. *Held*, by the High Court of Australia, that the plaintiff had never intended to waive his ultimate right to do the work, and where mutual co-operation was needed to give effect to a contract the party concerned must comply within a reasonable time after receiving notice, so that the defendant was liable; *Electronic Industries* v. *David Jones* (1954).[29]

9·012   In so far as a case may show that a completion date has ceased to be applicable *for purposes of recission* by reason of agreement or waiver by the owner, it should not be supposed that any such acts of the owner will necessarily or even probably mean that he is thereby abrogating, waiving or reducing his right to damages, liquidated or otherwise. Thus, an owner who treats the contract as subsisting after the completion date may, as a matter of common sense, have every intention of exacting full common law or liquidated damages as from the stipulated completion date and not from some later date in the future.[30] Quite different and most unusual conduct will be needed to show that the owner has accepted a new date for this latter purpose.[31] Apart from an agreement to suspend the works for one reason or another, it is not easy to conceive of a situation in building or engineering contracts where such an agreement or waiver could arise, unless associated with some act of prevention. Accordingly, the circumstances in which some later reasonable date for completion replaces the contract date for purposes of assessing delay damages in building or engineering contracts are likely to be limited to cases of prevention or breach of contract by the owner or his architect or engineer.

---

[28] 1 K.B. 616.

[29] 91 C.L.R. 288.

[30] See, *e.g. Electronic Industries* v. *David Jones* (1954) 91 C.L.R. 288, *supra*, and see also the cases as to liquidated damages, see *post*, Chap. 10, Section 2(4), paras. 10·054–10·055.

[31] In most sophisticated contracts, of course, an express extension of time clause exists for this very purpose—see Chap. 10, *post*, paras. 10·063 *et seq.*

(4) Whether Time of the Essence

One way in which this consequence can arise, of course, will be as a result   **9·013**
of express provision.

ILLUSTRATION

By Clause 2(a) of a leasing agreement for a computer, there were to be
three-monthly instalment payments over a period of five years, "punctual
payment of each of which shall be of the essence of this Lease". Clause 5
provided for termination by notice or by taking possession in the event of
default in punctual payment, and Clause 6(a) that in such a case the lessee was
to pay all arrears of rentals, all further rentals until the end of the lease less a
discount for advance payment, and damages. *Held*, by the Court of Appeal,
that Clause 6(a) was a penalty in failing to take account of the re-sale value of
the property and also in failing to distinguish between trivial and important
breaches and should be struck down for that reason, but that independently
of Clauses 5 and 6(a), Clause 2(a) conferred an entitlement to determine the
contract and recover damages for the loss of the contract whatever the gravity
of the breach: *Lombard North Central PLC* v. *Butterworth* (1986).[32]

Thus it would seem that an express "time of the essence" provision, if   **9·014**
acted on in respect of a breach which would not otherwise justify
rescission, may to that extent enhance the damages recoverable, since
they will include any damages (as, for example, loss of profit) consequential on the termination itself. Thus, it was said in the *Lombard* case:

"It is possible by express provision in the contract to make a term a condition,
even if it would not be so in the absence of such a provision. A stipulation that
time is of the essence, in relation to a particular contractual term, denotes
that timely performance is a condition of the contract. The consequence is
that delay in performance is treated as going to the root of the contract, without regard to the magnitude of the breach. It follows that where a promisor
fails to give timely performance of an obligation in respect of which time is
expressly stated to be of the essence, the injured party may elect to terminate
and recover damages in respect of the promisor's outstanding obligations,
without regard to the magnitude of the breach".[33]

However, it has been a characteristic of poor draftsmanship of recent
years, in nearly all commercial fields, that "of the essence" wording is frequently used to "overegg the pudding" in relation to obviously inappropriate contractual obligations, and should not be accorded the same
weight as when used in a more considered way in more appropriate

---

[32] [1987] 1 Q.B. 527. The entitlement to damages does not seem consistent with Goddard
C.J.'s decision in *Thomas Feather & Co. (Bradford) Ltd.* v. *Keighley Corporation* (1953) 52
L.G.R. 30, illustrated *ante*, Chap. 8, Section 2, para. 8·113.
[33] *Per* Mustill L.J., the *Lombard* case, *supra*, at p. 535. Contrast the *Feather* case, see *ante*,
para. 8·113.

settings, it is submitted. Its extension from the more appropriate setting of completion obligations in conveyancing transactions to the inappropriate setting of construction contractors' performance obligations also reflects the historical origins of construction draftsmanship, and explains a number of the construction contract decisions, it is suggested.

9·015   Time can also be of the essence in the absence of express wording, as a result of interpretation of the contract as a whole together with its commercial background. However, the *Lombard* case did not concern a construction contract, and involved a payment obligation. As already foreshadowed in subsection (1) *supra*, not only have the courts abstained from such interpretations of the completion obligation in construction contracts, but they would appear to have effectively neutralised even express provisions designed to achieve that end by more than one route. These have been listed by a commentator as "looking at the whole agreement" (that is, interpretation of the commercial background and the effect of other clauses), as "the theory of election" (based on the owner's conduct after the date for completion) and, as a third suggestion, the doctrine of substantial performance which could be relied on in the rare case where an owner sought to rescind immediately upon the passing of the completion date, so that an election or waiver finding would not be possible.[34]

9·016   It should be appreciated that the legal consequences in a building contract would be that upon expiry of the stipulated (or reasonable) time the owner might treat the contract as repudiated and dismiss the contractor, and, conversely, that the latter could recover nothing for the work done by him if he had not completed to time.[35] In deciding such matters, the courts have clearly had regard to the practical needs of the transaction as a whole and, if this does not require such a term, have, even in the face of express language, shrunk from bringing about such catastrophic (bearing in mind that, being affixed to the land, building work becomes the property of the owner independently of any act of acceptance by him) and perhaps unintended results. Thus, while the courts have had little difficulty in holding time to be of the essence in some contracts for delivery of goods, or for the exercise of options over interests in land, they have taken a contrary view in respect of most contracts for payment of money, and all contracts for the sale of land. A further consideration in the case of construction contracts (which may also serve to explain the relative lack of authority on this point) is that, even were time to be of the essence, it would afford building owners little practical relief against a recalcitrant builder. In most building contracts the contract period is comparatively lengthy, and long before it has expired the owner or his architect will know that the builder is sufficiently in default for completion by the stipulated time to be for all

---

[34] See Stoljar, "Untimely Performance in Contract", (1955) 71 L.Q.R. 527, 553–556.
[35] See, *e.g. Simpson* v. *Trim Town Commissioners* (1898) 32 I.L.T. Rep. 129, illustrated *post*, Chap. 10, Section 2(3), para. 10·050 and see also *Platt* v. *Parker* (1866) 2 T.L.R. 786, *post*, Chap. 12, Section 1(11), para. 12·053.

practical purposes impossible. Nevertheless, in the absence of an express or implied term no right to terminate can arise under this doctrine until the completion date has passed, while the liability under most building contracts to make interim payments will continue, in spite of the mounting certainty of the owner eventually incurring substantial damage.

It is for this reason that it has been submitted *ante*, Chapter 4,[36] and is submitted *infra*, Subsection (7), that, as a matter of business efficacy, there must be a term implied by law in building and engineering contracts generally that the contractor will proceed with reasonable diligence and expedition. Nearly all sophisticated modern contracts, including the standard forms, in fact contain express terms to this effect, and in addition confer express powers to determine upon the builder failing to proceed with the works with due diligence or reasonable expedition,[37] but it is submitted that proper analysis and the commercial realities require similar (and fundamental) terms to be implied in less formal contracts.

9·017

When, finally, it is remembered that the builder's work on the owners land cannot be refused or returned (as in the case of chattels) it is not surprising that it is only in the most unusual case that the courts will hold time for completion to be of the essence in a genuine building contract. Thus, in *Lucas* v. *Godwin* (1837)[38] Tindal C.J. said:

> "It is not a condition, but a stipulation, for non-observance of which the defendant may be entitled to recover damages; but, even if a condition, it does not go to the essence of the contract, and is no answer to the plaintiff's claim for the work actually done. It never could have been the understanding of the parties, that if the house were not done by the precise day, the plaintiff would have no remuneration; at all events, if so unreasonable an engagement had been entered into, the parties should have expressed their meaning with a precision which could not be mistaken."

Further, the existence of provisions for extension of time or for payment of liquidated damages will generally be regarded (on the "looking at the whole agreement" principle) as incompatible with an intention that time should be of the essence, and it is submitted that the existence of a forfeiture clause conditioned upon reasonable expedition by the builder would similarly be so regarded. Thus, in *Lamprell* v. *Billericay Union* (1849)[39] Rolfe B. said:

9·018

> "Looking to the whole of the deed, we are of opinion that the time of completion was not an essential part of the contract; first, because there is an expressed provision made for a weekly sum to be paid for every week during which the work should be delayed after June 24, 1840; and, secondly, because the deed clearly meant to exempt the plaintiff from the obligation as to the particular day in case he should be prevented by fire or other circumstances

---

[36] See *ante*, Chap. 4, Section 1(3), paras. 4·128–4·129.
[37] See *post*, Chap. 12, Section 1(4)(a). These powers can almost always be exercised at any time, and whether or not the completion date has passed: *Joshua Henshaw & Sons* v. *Rochdale Corporation* [1944] K.B. 381, illustrated *post*, Chap. 12, Section 1(10).
[38] 3 Bing.N.C. at p. 744, illustrated *infra*.
[39] 3 Exch. 283, 305.

satisfactory to the architect; and here, in fact, it is expressly found by the arbitrator that delay was necessarily occasioned by the extra work."

ILLUSTRATIONS

9·019   (1) In a contract to purchase one of a row of houses then being completed by the vendor, the purchaser convenanted to pay an additional sum of £80 provided that the adjoining houses should be completed, i.e. roofed, sashed, paved in front, enclosed with iron railways in front, and occupied by tenants, by April 23rd, 1829. The other requirements were satisfied, but the foot pavements were not all laid down before April 21st due, it was said, to bad weather. *Held*, by Tindal C.J. that the vendor could not recover the £80; *Maryon* v. *Carter* (1830).[40]

(2) A developer owner agreed in 1836 to pay £216 in January 1837 to a builder for work to be done to 6 cottages "*on condition of* the work being done in a proper and workmanlike manner ... and to be completed *by* October 10th, 1836". Some of the cottages were not completed until 5 days late on October 15th, 1836. The owner took them over, but did not pay in January 1987. *Held*, by the Court of Common Pleas, that the delay was no defence to a claim for the price of the work. *Per* Tindal C.J.: "If it be said that the completion by the 10th October is the condition precedent, at least the objection should have been taken in time; in accepting the work done the defendant admits that it is of some benefit to him"; *Lucas* v. *Godwin* (1837).[41]

9·020   (3) Fabricators undertook at the end of November to supply 150 tons of girders, fifty on or before December 31, fifty on or before January 28, fifty on or before March 31, provided drawings for the first fifty tons were supplied by the purchasers within three days, and for the remainder within three weeks. Some drawings were delivered on December 5, and on December 15 an order for fourteen tons only was placed. On March 13, after the suppliers had repudiated the contract, further drawings were sent and a further order for fifty tons. *Held*, that the contract was entire, time was of the essence, the purchasers had failed to supply drawings within a reasonable time, and the suppliers were accordingly not liable in an action for failure to deliver: *Kingdom* v. *Cox* (1848).[42]

(4) A contractor undertook to erect a workhouse, and to complete it by June 24, 1840. There was a power for the architects to order additions, and the work was to be done to their satisfaction. The contractor further undertook to pay liquidated damages of £10 per week if he should fail to complete by June 24, unless hindered by fire or other cause satisfactory to the architects. Final completion was delayed till December 1840 as a consequence of additions ordered by the architects, who were satisfied. *Held*, by the Court of Exchequer Chamber, that the presence of the provision for liquidated damages and the exception for fire or other clauses meant that the time of completion was not an essential part of the contract: *Lamprell* v. *Billericay Union* (1849).[43]

---

[40] 4 C. & P. 295.
[41] 4 Bing.N.C. 737.
[42] 5 C.B. 522. There are in any case a number of conflicting decisions in relation to such instalment contracts, many, no doubt, depending on their particular facts, however—see, *e.g. Tyers* v. *Rosedale and Ferryhill Iron Co.* illustrated *supra*, para. 9·009 and the cases discussed by Stoljar in (1955) 71 L.Q.R. 527, 541–542.
[43] 3 Exch. 283.

(5) A. agreed to make alterations in a house, and to complete the whole work by June 14; B., in consideration of these conditions, agreed to take the house on June 24 for three years, with the option of a lease for seven, fourteen, or twenty-one years. *Held*, by the Court of Common Pleas, that the completion of the whole work by June 14 was a condition precedent to B.'s liability to take the house on the 24th: *Tidey* v. *Mollett* (1864).[44]

It will be seen that none of the above cases lend any support for a "time **9·021** of the essence" interpretation of a contractor's completion obligation in a construction contract, and due to the "bonus" element in *Maryon* v. *Carter* that decision is both understandable and distinguishable. As has been pointed out above, the practical benefit of any such interpretation to the building owner is in any case extremely limited and, for practical purposes, a term requiring due diligence by the builder is more essential for owners in comparatively lengthy contracts for work done such as building contracts, than terms or doctrines almost certainly evolved to suit the requirements of contracts for the sale of land or goods. It is submitted *infra*, Subsection (7) that such a term requires to be implied in construction contracts generally. Indeed the presence of a completion obligation expressed in "time of the essence" terms should be regarded as either indicating a commercial situation differing radically from that in a normal construction project, or else as a sign of inexperienced draftsmanship. In a normal construction setting it would also seem to attract the provisions of legislation such as the English Unfair Contract Terms Act, as an unwarrantable exclusion of the owners liability to pay for completed work under the criteria of that legislation.[45]

(5) Notice Rendering Time of the Essence

The fact that notice can render time of the essence has already been dis- **9·022** cussed.[46] The rules appears to have evolved originally in the case of contracts for the sale of land, where it had been held that, notwithstanding that the stipulated time is not of the essence, time can be rendered of the essence (but only if the other party to the contract has been guilty of unreasonable delay) by service of notice giving a date for completion.[47] The exact basis of this doctrine is not, at first sight, easy to define, since, if time is not of the essence of a contract when it is executed, it is difficult to see how the subsequent unilateral act of one party can alter the position, and indeed this view has been specifically rejected.[48] The practical necessity for such a rule and what is submitted is the correct justification for it,

---

[44] 16 C.B.(N.S.) 298.
[45] See *ante*, Chap. 1, Section 9(7), paras. 1·238 *et seq*.
[46] See *supra*, Section (1).
[47] *Taylor* v. *Brown* (1839) 9 L.J.Ch. 14. (As to the length of the notice, see *Stickney* v. *Keeble* [1915] A.C. 386).
[48] *Per* Fry J. in *Green* v. *Sevin* (1879) 13 Ch.D. 589 at p. 599, and see, *per* Harman J. in *Smith* v. *Hamilton* [1951] 1 Ch. 174 at p. 181.

namely, the evidentiary crystallisation of the defendants' intention no longer to be bound by the contract terms, and the formal withdrawal of any previous waiver of the breach on the part of the plaintiff, has already been suggested.[49] The doctrine has been applied to contracts for the sale of goods[50] and to contracts for sale of goods and work done (to a motor-car),[51] and is now of general application.[52] Those cases were, however, cases where the original stipulated time was of the essence, but performance within this time had been waived earlier, prior to the final breach. In a building contract the remedy might be of some limited value in such circumstances (that is after the completion date), but such a notice can, as already pointed out, be of little practical value to a building owner where the builder is seriously delaying the earlier stages of the work.

9·023   However, in the rare cases where this ground for termination can be relied upon, notice should be given, particularly in a case where the completion date has been waived, although, as previously indicated, there are certainly extreme cases where a failure can be so persistent or flagrant as to evince an intention not to be bound and so justify recission without any notice.[53]

ILLUSTRATION

A demolition contract provided for completion within 42 days, and daily liquidated damages for delay. 4 days after expiry of the period, the owner's solicitor asked the contractor when he would finish, whether in 1, 2, 3 or 4 months. The contractor replied that he could not say. The contractor continued working, but 13 days later the owner forcibly re-possessed the site, completed using another contractor, and forfeited a sum of money deposited as security for due performance. The trial judge had found that the contractor had unreasonably delayed, and that the owner was entitled to damages as well as to forfeit the security. *Held*, by the Court of Appeal, that there was no sufficient evidence of repudiation on the part of the contractor. If the owner was going to act on the contractor's conduct as evidence of not going on, he ought to have told him of it and that he was treating it as a refusal. Allowing him to continue could not justify the re-entry, and the contractor was entitled to the return of his deposit, payment of the price, and loss of profit on the remaining work; *Felton* v. *Wharrie* (1905).[54]

So, too, in *Lowther* v. *Heaver* (1889),[55] Lindley L.J. appears to have doubted, in relation to a forfeiture clause in a building lease entitling the

---

[49] See *supra*, para. 9·002.
[50] See *Hartley* v. *Hymans* [1920] 3 K.B. 475.
[51] See *Rickards (Charles) Ltd.* v. *Oppenhaim* [1950] 1 K.B. 616, illustrated *supra*.
[52] See, *e.g. Carr* v. *J. A. Berriman (Pty.) Ltd.* quoted *supra*, para. 9·001 and Singleton L.J.'s judgment in *Rickards (Charles) Ltd.* v. *Oppenhaim* [1950] 1 K.B. 616 at p. 628, and the passage in Halsbury's *Laws of England* there referred to.
[53] *Carr* v. *J. A. Berriman (Pty.) Ltd.* [1953] A.L.J. 273 (Australia), illustrated *ante*, Chap. 4, para. 4·212, Chap. 7, paras. 7·045–7·048. *Kingdom* v. *Cox* (1848) 5 C.B. 522 illustrated *supra*, para. 9·020.
[54] Hudson, *Building Contracts* (4th ed.), Vol. 2, p. 398 (obviously not an easy case).
[55] 41 Ch.D. 248, illustrated *ante*, Chap. 7, Sect. 4, paras. 7·119–7·122.

lessor to re-enter on undemised plots of the works when not proceeded with for 21 days, whether advantage could have been taken of such a clause without reasonable notice. See further, for the additional need for some unequivocal act, *post*, Chapter 12, Section 1(7).

(6) Reasonable Time

It has been seen that an obligation to complete within a reasonable time sounding in damages arises either because the contract is silent as to time, or because the specified time has ceased to be applicable by reason of some matter for which the owner is responsible. It remains to consider what is a reasonable time. As to this, the House of Lords ruled that where the law implies that a contract shall be performed within a reasonable time, it has

> "invariably been held to mean that the party upon whom it is incumbent duly fulfils his obligations, notwithstanding protracted delay, so long as such delay is attributable to causes beyond his control and he has neither acted negligently nor unreasonably".[56]

It is not, therefore, merely a question of what is an "ordinary time" or what are "ordinary circumstances." Reasonableness will be determined in the light of the circumstances as they actually exist during the period of performance.[57]

> "It was common ground between the parties that the principles I had to apply in this connection were those stated by the House of Lords in *Hick* v. *Raymond & Reid, viz.* that the question what constituted a reasonable time had to be considered in relation to the circumstances which existed at the time when the contractual services were performed, but excluding circumstances which were under the control of the party performing those services. As I understand it, I have first to consider what would, in ordinary circumstances, be a reasonable time for the performance of the relevant services; and I have then to consider to what extent that time for performance ... was in effect extended by extraordinary circumstances outside their control".[58]

Reasonable time is, therefore, primarily a question of fact and must depend on all the circumstances which might be expected to affect the progress of the works. There are few, if any reported cases in England directly involving a typical building or engineering contract, but it is suggested that certain questions require to be answered before a reasonable time can be properly assessed.

9·024

9·025

---

[56] *Per* Lord Watson in *Hick* v. *Raymond and Reid* [1893] A.C. 22 at pp. 32, 33.

[57] *Ibid.* at p. 29 *per* Lord Herschell. See also the discussion on *force majeure* and Act of God, *ante*, Chap. 4, Section 3, paras. 4·265 *et seq*.

[58] *British Steel Corporation* v. *Cleveland Bridge and Engineering Co. Ltd.* [1984] 1 All E.R. 504, 512, *per* Robert Goff J. For the application of this principle in the *Cleveland Bridge* case to a contract for the manufacture and delivery of steel nodes for use in a construction project, see the case reported in (1981) 24 BLR 94, 123–126, and see *ante*, para. 1·268.

In the first place, when arriving at a reasonable time in "ordinary circumstances", the parties may or may not have contracted with the particular resources and capacity of the particular builder in mind. Thus, an owner may have deliberately chosen a small local or jobbing builder, with limited resources of capital, plant and labour, to build his house, in the hope of getting a cheaper or better quality job while sacrificing speedy completion. On the other hand, a builder with limited resources might tender for a large contract in competition with more substantial contractors, and give no indication of his inability to carry out the work as rapidly as them. In the former case the test might well be subjective, and in the latter objective,[59] it is submitted, notwithstanding some of the language in the *Hick* case, because a party may have expressly or impliedly warranted (or discounted) his ability or capacity to maintain progress in a particular situation or at a particular speed.

9·026   Again, while it may be that most factors beyond the builder's control will excuse him, it is possible that expressly or impliedly the parties will have contracted with a particular factor in mind. Thus, whereas there is little doubt that allowance would be made for delay due to an unexpected strike,[60] it would not, it is suggested, follow that a contractor's inability to obtain sufficient labour in competition with other contractors in the district would excuse him. In the case of subcontractors of all kinds, whether nominated or otherwise, it is submitted that the tendency of the courts should be not to excuse the main contractor from meeting his main contract obligation in any case where delay is caused by some act or omission within the subcontractor's control, though for that reason outside the main contractor's direct personal control, since, in such a case, the contractor will or should have his remedy against the subcontractor, who in law is the contractor's agent for the purpose of carrying out the works, whether nominated or not.[61] Any tendency to excuse the main contractor would in effect be an invitation to subcontractors to default on their obligations, and might well result in the owner failing to recover his own loss whereas the contractor might still be able to recover any loss he personally might have suffered at the hands of the sub-contractor.[62]

9·027   Again, it may be a question whether the parties contracted with a builder's other commitments in mind. In approaching this question, it should be borne in mind that with the increasing degree of specialist and sub-contracted work in the building industry, the direct responsibilities of the main contractor have become correspondingly limited to the provision of a site-organisation, a non-specialised labour force, and materials

---

[59] See *Attwood* v. *Emery* and *Hydraulic Engineering Co.* v. *McHaffie*, illustrated *infra*.

[60] Compare the *Cleveland Bridge* case *supra*, as reported in BLR

[61] See, for the analogous case of quality of work, *ante*, paras. 4·072–4·074, and the passages from *Young and Marten* there referred to at pp. 4·057–8, and see paras. 4·121–4·123. See also *post*, Chap. 13, Section 1.

[62] See, however, the difficult House of Lords decision in *Scott Lithgow Ltd.* v. *Secretary of State for Defence* (1989) 45 BLR 6, illustrated *ante*, Chap. 5, para. 5·037, analysed and doubted in the editor's *Beyond the Contractor's Control* in (1991) 7 Const.L.J. 3.

and plant, so that in most cases the builder, by entering into the contract, is, in effect, warranting that he has or will have at least these available in sufficient quantity for due performance of his obligations.[63] All these are matters which will, no doubt, be taken into consideration when making the initial "ordinary circumstances" assessment, before considering the actual post-contract circumstances.

ILLUSTRATIONS

(1) An order for the manufacture of iron hoops specified delivery "*as soon as possible*". The order was placed in November 1855, and delivery was not made until February 1856, due to many other outstanding orders which the suppliers had not yet carried out. The purchasers argued that the suppliers should have given priority to their own order, or should have sub-contracted the work elsewhere. *Held*, by the Court of Common Pleas, that provided the goods were completed within a reasonable time using all means available, the words did not have the meaning alleged and the suppliers had properly performed their contract; *Attwood* v. *Emery* (1856).[64]

(2) Plaintiff manufacturers contracted to make a pile-driving machine for delivery in a month's time, and in turn contracted with the defendants for a part of the machine to be made and delivered to them "*as soon as possible*". The defendants knew of the plaintiff's contract and that the part was needed by the end of the month, but they finished the part a month late, and the ultimate purchaser refused to accept the machine. The defendants' delay was due to the fact that at the time of their contract they did not have a foreman competent to prepare patterns necessary for its manufacture. The trial judge held that the plaintiffs might reasonably assume from the words used that the defendants had at the time all reasonable appliances to enable them to proceed without delay and that the defendants' failure to start the work with reasonable diligence was a circumstances within their own control. *Held*, by the Court of Appeal, affirming the trial judge, that the plaintiffs were entitled to damages. *Per* Bramwell L.J. the words meant an undertaking to do the work within a reasonable time and in the shortest practicable time. Every customer knows at the time of giving an order that a manufacturer or tradesman may have other orders on hand, and *Atwood's* case did not go beyond saying that he is not bound to put all other work on one side to complete an order. It must be taken that the defendants had undertaken to do the work with such appliances as they might reasonably be expected to have. *Per* Brett L.J. the *Atwood* case only held that the delay due to the size of the business and the circumstances of having several orders on hand was to be excused. *Per* Cotton L.J. the words meant that the defendants would make the part as quickly as it could be made in the largest establishment with the best appliances. The surrounding circumstances must be looked at, and these showed that the part was to be supplied as quickly as it could be with all proper appliances available; *Hydraulic Engineering Co. Ltd.* v. *McHaffie Goslett & Co.* (1878).[65]

9·028

(3) A bill of lading did not specify the time for discharge. During unloading a strike occurred which delayed the ship twenty-five days longer than

9·029

---

[63] Under an optional clause in the RIBA form of contract, however, he is entitled to an extension of time even on these grounds—see clause 23(*j*) of the 1963 forms.
[64] 26 L.J. C.P. 73.
[65] 4 Q.B.D. 670.

otherwise would have been the case. *Held*, by the House of Lords, that the obligation on the consignee was to unload within a reasonable time, and that that obligation was discharged if he unloaded in a reasonable time under the circumstances as they obtained at the time of performance, assuming that those circumstances, so far as they caused delay, were not caused or contributed to by him: *Hick* v. *Raymond* (1893).[66]

(4) By a charter a cargo was to be "discharged with all reasonable dispatch as customary." The custom at the port was to discharge into railway wagons. Without any negligence on the part of the charterers, but owing to stress of work, and a consequent deficiency in the number of wagons available, the ship was delayed. *Held*, by the Court of Appeal, that the charterers, having done their best to procure the appliances that were customarily used for discharging such a ship, and having used them with proper dispatch, were not liable for delay: *Lyle Shipping Co.* v. *Cardiff Corporation* (1900).[67]

9·030

(5) Shipbuilders contracted to build and deliver a vessel by a certain date, but the contract provided for an extension of time for delay through certain specified causes "or other circumstances beyond the builders' control." A suitable berth for building the vessel did not become vacant in the shipbuilder's yard until three months before the date named for completion. The vessel was not completed to time. An arbitrator found that the parties contemplated that the vessel would be built as soon as a suitable berth became vacant, and that the vessel until then occupying the berth was delayed in building through causes of the same kinds as those specified as justifying an extension in the later contract. *Held*, by Wright J., that on the findings of the arbitrator, the delays to the earlier vessel must be regarded as covered by the extension of time clause, and allowance must be made for the delay in completing the previous vessel: *Re Lockie and Craggs* (1902).[68]

(6) In a project for the manufacture and supply of 150 steel nodes to be used in the exterior of a building, no terms for price or delivery were ever finally agreed, though the nodes were made and delivered. *Held*, by Robert Goff J., applying the *Hick* v. *Raymond* principle to a reasonable period for manufacture in ordinary circumstances, nothing should be added for delays due to two alterations in the materials specification carried out by the manufacturer on his own initiative, but delay caused by rejection of a first casting due to a new requirement of the purchaser, and delays due to strikes, should be added to the period; *British Steel Corporation* v. *Cleveland Bridge and Engineering Limited* (1981).[69]

9·031   The principles to be applied in assessing reasonable time in a case where no time for completion has been specified in the contract are, therefore, reasonably clear, though a decision as to what will constitute the initial "reasonable time in ordinary circumstances" period may involve, as the cases show and has been submitted *supra*, an examination of the background and of the resources which might reasonably be expected to be provided by the contractor in question at the time of contracting.

Where, however, the reasonable time obligation arises because a stipulated date has ceased to be applicable by reason of prevention or breach, a

---

[66] [1893] A.C. 22; followed in *Sims & Co.* v. *Midland Ry.* [1913] 1 K.B. 103.
[67] [1900] 2 Q.B. 638.
[68] 86 L.T. 388.
[69] 24 BLR 94, 125.

special difficulty can arise. No doubt the original contract completion date will, in the great majority of cases, tend to be accepted by both sides as evidence of what is a "reasonable time in ordinary circumstances", so that the new reasonable time for completion will be arrived at by adding such additional periods of delay as can be shown to have been caused by the prevention or breach (including any further delays beyond the control of the contractor occurring during that additional period). The problem arises, however, if the contractor wishes to assert that the original contract completion date (or extended completion date) was not itself reasonable, either because of delays due to previous events beyond his control but not covered by any available extension of time clause for example, or, because of errors or any other reason, that the original contract period had been under-estimated and was inadequate. There does not seem to be authority on this point in the Commonwealth, no doubt because extension of time clauses of considerable latitude are present in so many contracts at the present day, so that resort to a reasonable completion date is now relatively unusual. In principle, the compensatory principle underlying damages for the breach of contract[70] would suggest that any new reasonable date should be arrived at by extension of the contractual completion date, rather than *de novo*. A fortiori, this would seem to be the case if there has been no breach and merely an act of prevention. The other, perhaps more legalistic or theoretical view would be that once the contract period no longer applied it should have no further legal significance.[70a]

It also seems possible that, in deciding on a reasonable time for completion in such a case, there should be consideration of the circumstances stipulated in any contractual extension of time clause as justifying an extension of time, either as indicating circumstances which should be taken into account, or possibly as excluding any circumstances not mentioned in the clause.

(7) Due Diligence and Expedition Terms

Express liquidated damages clauses for delay in completion, while they might loosely be considered, together with a stipulated or reasonable date for completion, as representing the comprehensive obligation of a construction contractor for due progress, can be seen on closer examination to be targeted at one narrow aspect only of the damage which an owner may incur as a result of delay in progress—namely damage resulting exclusively from *delay in completion*. In other words, the clauses are aimed only at damage which results from a *delayed resumption of possession* by the owner. It is with this particular narrow obligation and class of damage that the present chapter has hitherto been concerned. This damage, in the great majority of cases, will take the form of loss of rents or profits or commercial loss of use of the completed building,[71] though in

9·032

---

[70] See *supra*, Chap. 8, Section 2, para. 8·110.
[70a] Compare the *Lodder* v. *Slowey* principle, see *ante*, para. 4·230.
[71] See *ante*, Chap. 8, paras. 8·162–8·163.

some special cases the start of a later construction contract on the same project may have been made to depend on completion of the earlier contract, so that any liability of the owner to pay damages to the second impeded contractor will, if contemplated by the earlier contract within the rules of remoteness, flow directly from delayed completion of the earlier contract, in the same way as loss of rents, etc., and so be subsumed by any liquidated damages for delay in completion of that contract.[72]

9·033 However, entirely different forms of damage, caused by *delay in progress during construction*, can occur long before the completion date has arrived, and so not qualify for reimbursement under the provisions of any liquidated damages clause (unless, and then only to the extent that, they may have the effect of delaying re-entry by the owner). While no doubt in many cases such earlier "intermediate" delays by the contractor may involve no damage to the owner, unless and until completion itself is delayed, there are also many cases where immediate and serious damage can result. This will usually take the form of liabilities of the owner (or, in a sub-contract, of the main contractor) to third parties, such as other contractors or sub-contractors, or to adjoining owners or public utilities, with whose requirements the work may have had to be co-ordinated by the owner or his advisers, and with whom commitments may have had to be undertaken. Wherever there is an express "due diligence" term (as in almost all English standard forms at the present day), or where there are express intermediate completion dates stipulated in the contract which the contractor has failed to meet, intermediate delays of this kind will of course be a breach of contract for which such damages of the owner will be recoverable. Even more importantly from the owner's point of view, such failures of due diligence during the construction period may be such as to show clearly that the contractor is unable, or in some cases unwilling, to meet his completion obligations (often in real life, in the latter case, due to taking on profitable work elsewhere which, given his resources, is incompatible with a full discharge of his existing obligations).[73] Since express "due diligence" provisions of the kind described will almost invariably be linked to express provisions entitling the owner to terminate the contract, he is thereby provided with an immediate sanction against a recalcitrant or failing contractor, without needing to await a perhaps long distant completion date. The necessity for such express provisions, which is so compelling that it has survived producer pressures to exclude them in even the most producer-influenced standard forms, is compounded by the fact that, as has already been seen in this chapter, a mere stipulated completion date obligation is rarely likely to be held to be of the essence, and even so any right to rescind can easily be lost or unsafe to operate, by reason of election or waiver theories, in the absence of a still further notice.

9·034 As foreshadowed *supra*, Subsection (4), it is submitted that, even in the absence of an express term for due diligence and of any linked express

---

[72] See *post* Chap. 10, paras. 10·002–10·005.
[73] See further *infra*.

termination clause, both such terms require to be implied by law, in construction contracts and subcontracts generally, as a matter of business efficacy. The primary obligation will, it is submitted, sound in damages if within the rules of remoteness, as where the nature of the work undertaken indicates that work by other contractors of the owner, or in a subcontract of the main contractor, or commitments entered into with neighbours or others, are within the contemplation of the contract as being dependent on the maintenance of a reasonable rate of progress. Furthermore, where a contractor persists in a rate of progress bearing no relation either to a contractually promised or reasonable date of completion, and the owner accordingly gives notice requiring a reasonable or improved rate of progress but the contractor then fails to proceed at a reasonable rate, it is submitted that he will be evincing either inability to complete, or an intention no longer to be bound by the contract, in either case justifying rescission by the owner. Otherwise, provided the builder does not by unequivocal refusal openly evince an intention no longer to be bound (thus exposing himself to the assertion of an anticipatory repudiatory breach), the owner will, in the absence of such an implied term, be without remedy until the completion date has passed, and in the usual case where time is not of the essence probably not even then, until a still later notice is served.[74]

This submission can be tested by considering a short and relatively **9·035** informal construction contract with a stipulated contractual completion date, but with no, or a relatively small liquidated damages provision. The contractor has the opportunity of taking on profitable work elsewhere, and with limited resources reduces his efforts so as to accommodate the other contract (all the more likely if he has succeeded in "front-loading" his prices on both contracts).[75] It would be absurd, it is submitted, if the owner was to be without remedy until after a perhaps distant completion date, and then only for the perhaps inadequate damages resulting from late completion *simpliciter* (and by which time, moreover, a failing contractor might well be in liquidation). Equally, if in the same informal contract the owner had to the knowledge of the builder entered into the usual commitments with third parties, on the basis of the contractor proceeding with reasonable diligence in the light of his promised or a reasonable completion date, it would be absurd that he should escape all responsibility for the resulting damage suffered by the owner. Indeed, it is submitted that the universally accepted term unquestionably implied by law for completion within a reasonable time (as previously explained a term well suited to contracts for the sale of land, or the sale or manufacture of goods, but of little or no practical value during the comparatively lengthy period

---

[74] Compare *Felton* v. *Wharrie* (1905) Hudson, *Building Contracts* (4th ed.), Vol. 2, p. 398, illustrated *supra*, para. 9·023.
[75] See the editor's "Contract Policy for Money" in *Construction Contract Policy* (1989) published by the Centre of Construction Law and Management, King's College London, pp. 225–226 for these practices. For "front-loading" see also *ante*, Chap. 8, Section 1, paras. 8·009–8·010.

of performance of construction contracts on the owner's land) can in practice only be given effect, as in the leading case of *Hick* v. *Raymond Reed*,
supra, by analysis of the time required by a contractor of the appropriate
class on the assumption that he does perform with due diligence. The two
concepts are, it is submitted, inextricably linked in any contract involving
the performance of comparatively lengthy services by the contractor
while in occupation of land belonging to the owner, which is the essential
characteristic of a construction contract.

9·036   It is highly significant in this context, it is submitted, that the Codes in a
number of civil law countries (not always perhaps noted for their practicality in more modern commercial contexts) never appear to have had any
doubt on this score. Thus, in 1980 the Codes of the Federal Republic of
Germany, Italy and Switzerland all permitted rescission by the owner
(hirer) for contractor delay before the time fixed for completion, if it
became apparent that work had not begun on time or its progress was
unduly delayed, subject only to the need for a warning notice.[76] In
addition, there is a right to damages and, if fault is present, even without
prior warning.[77]

9·037   Surpisingly, however, some common law courts appear to have felt difficulty in accepting this view.

ILLUSTRATION

Contractors undertook to manufacture, deliver and erect gates and gate
arms for the Thames Basin, with a series of intermediate key dates for completion of different sections of the work. The formula in an index-based fluctuations clause (Clause 51) applicable to the manufacturing costs of the gates
and arms entitled the contractors to payments for labour and materials based
on the difference between a tender base index, and the index at either average
(for labour), or fixed (for materials) dates in the latter part of a defined
"Manufacturing Period". By a proviso to Clause 51, no account was to be
taken of any amount by which any cost incurred by the contractor had been
increased "by the default or negligence of the contractor". While the contractors met all their required key dates, the owners argued that the contractors had unnecessarily prolonged certain later and minor processes at the end
of the manufacturing period long after the vast bulk of their costs had been
incurred, so that the formula produced an unnecessarily high figure bearing
no relation to the prevailing indices during manufacture. There was a liquidated damages clause, but only for late completion of the whole of the works
and not for the intermediate key dates. There was no due diligence clause
simpliciter, but by Clause 19 of the Conditions the owners were empowered
to take the work out of the contractor's hands "if the Contractor shall neglect
to execute the Works with due diligence and expedition". The owners argued
that, once started on manufacture, the contractors should have proceeded
with due diligence, so reducing the sums recoverable under the clause. *Held*,

---

[76] Civil Code Arts. 636, paras. 1 and 634, paras. 1–3; Civil Code Art. 1662, para. 2; and Civil
Code Art. 366, paras. 1 and 2 respectively.
[77] See Lorenz, *International Encyclopedia of Comparative Law*, (1980) Vol. VIII, Chap. 8,
paras. 8–19, p. 23.

by Staughton J., that though the point was very nicely balanced, and though the result in the case did not depend on it, he would answer one of the arbitrator's questions by holding that while neglect to execute works with due diligence and expedition would entitle the owners to dismiss the contractor under Clause 19, it would not itself be a breach of contract on the part of the contractors entitling them to damages. *Per* Staughton J.: "If there had been a term as to due diligence I consider that it would have been, when spelt out in full, an obligation on the contractors to execute the work with such diligence and expedition as was reasonably required in order to meet the key dates." *Held*, by the Court of Appeal, that there was no implied term that, once he had started to manufacture, the contractor was obliged to finish manufacture faster than was necessary to meet his delivery obligations. *Per* Parker L.J.: "You cannot have diligence in the abstract. It must be related to the objective." *Greater London Council* v. *Cleveland Bridge and Engineering Company Ltd.* (1986).[78]

[Note: The core of the owners' argument in the above case was that the **9·038** contractors were entitled to choose any time to start the period for manufacture, but that once they had started they must proceed diligently without regard to the required delivery dates. This was elicited and analysed by the Court of Appeal before being rejected, but not by Staughton J. The argument was obviously untenable, since the implied term would require a duty to proceed at a pace which would obtain the maximum pricing benefit for the owner under the clause,[79] and might even involve a duty to proceed slowly in some circumstances.[80] Both Staughton J. and the Court of Appeal were, however, clearly right to reject arguments based on the proviso to Clause 51, and Staughton J. and Parker L.J. were both also clearly right in holding that a term for due diligence cannot be defined except in terms of any contractual or extended dates for completion. There is no inconsistency whatever, it is submitted between such a term and two *dicta* (cited by Staughton J.) of Wright J. and Vaughan Williams L.J. in *Wells* v. *Army and Navy Co-Operative Society*[81] to the effect that the contractor must, within reasonable limits, be allowed to decide for himself at what time he will need an owner's co-operation with information, etc., in order to do his own work.[82] It is clear from both Parker and Woolf L.JJ.'s judgments in this case that they were not excluding an implied term for due diligence related to the contract completion dates, and the headnote in BLR in regard to this case in the Court of Appeal is wrong in so stating. Staughton J.'s view on this point was not only, as he himself expressly conceded, unnecessary to the result, but it failed to identify the true nature of the term being contended for by the contractor, as later analysed and demolished in the Court of Appeal.]

It may perhaps be inferred that, because in many cases it may be evident **9·039** that damage is unlikely to be incurred by the owner until completion of a construction contract, the Courts (and indeed early draftsmen) in common law countries, accustomed to the use of the concept of a time of completion obligation in conveyancing and sale of goods or manufacturing contracts, too easily assumed that a precisely similar obligation would be a satisfactory solution to the problem of delay in construction contracts,

---

[78] 34 BLR 50.
[79] See Parker L.J., *ibid.* at pp. 76–78.
[80] See, *per* Woolf L.J., *ibid.* at p. 79.
[81] (1902) 86 L.T. 764, Hudson, *Building Contracts*, (4th ed.), Vol. 2, pp. 346, 352, 354.
[82] For these *dicta*, see *ante*, Chap. 4, paras. 4·146 and 4·177.

without appreciating the practical inadequacy of a term aimed only at the time of completion where work is being done on an owner's land over a relatively long period of time. This was compounded by the fact that the owner's own draftsmanship, probably of conveyancing origin as in all the early construction contracts, frequently prescribed a named date for completion, often with express "time of the essence" references still to be found in some old-fashioned contracts at the present day, with liquidated damages provided as the remedy for breach of that particular obligation. As a matter of analysis, it could well be argued that an implied term for due diligence and expedition (which if so expressed would in fact also subsume the remedies available for failure to achieve a promised or reasonable completion date) is in reality and as a matter of business efficacy, and indeed as a matter of law, the primary basis of the contractor's implied obligations as to time in all construction settings.

However, the contract completion date represents an unconditional obligation, not dependent on fault (subject to permitted extensions of time) against, and by which, as Parker L.J. indicated in the *Cleveland Bridge* case *supra*, the due diligence obligation will be measured and governed.

(8) Programmes Supplied by Contractor

9·040 The tenth edition and its 1979 Supplement noted an increasing practice of contractors, whether or not contractually required to do so, of putting forward highly optimistic programmes to the owner or his A/E showing completion a considerable time ahead of the contract date. If approved by the A/E (who in general would not of course wish to discourage the contractor from completing early) these documents might then be used:

(a) to justify allegations of late performance against the owner (for example, for late delivery of information or possession of the site) incompatible with those dates and
(b) to increase the alleged period of delay on which a claim could be calculated, and even in some cases to make a delay claim possible where the contract date had not in the event been exceeded.

Disregarding the fact that it is a common and respectable technique in programming to plan for an earlier completion than that actually expected, thus allowing a "float" for unforeseen contingencies and implying no expectation of earlier completion, it was submitted in the 1979 Supplement that unless the contractual provisions, or some collateral agreement, were much more explicit in substituting the programme dates for the contract dates on a *bilateral* basis (for example, by advancing the completion dates against which damages for delay would become payable by the contractor) there could be little force in such contentions. This view has since been adopted in the English Official Referees' courts.

(1) Bills of Quantities under the 1963 JCT forms required the provision, **9·041**
within one week from the date of possession, of a programme chart of the
whole of the works, including that of nominated sub-contractors and other
direct contractors and public utilities, showing a completion date *no later than
the date of completion* in approved bar-chart form, Clause 21 required the
contractor to begin and proceed diligently with the works completing the
same *on or before* the Date of Completion. *Held*, by Judge Fox-Andrews
Q.C., allowing an appeal from an arbitrator (a) that the contractor was
entitled to complete in advance of the completion date, whether or not he was
contractually bound to supply or as a fact had supplied a programme containing an earlier date but (b) that there was no implied term compelling the
owner or his servants in that event to perform their own obligations so as to
enable the contractor to complete at the earlier date: *Glenlion Construction
Ltd.* v. *The Guinness Trust (1987).*[83]

(2) Special Conditions in the Bills, in a contract for the refurbishment of 34
Council houses with tenants in occupation, indicated that the houses would
be handed over in batches of 4 at weekly intervals for completion in 10 weeks
(which if strictly complied with would have permitted completion of the
whole in 19 weeks), but the start and completion dates for the contract in the
main documentation gave the contract period as 25 weeks. The contractor
was disrupted by the owners, who admitted liability for the additional loss and
expense, but disputed a prolongation calculated by reference to the 19 week
period: *Held*, by Judge Sir William Stabb Q.C., following the *Glenlion* case,
that the Special Conditions in the Bills, though expressed to take precedence
over the General Conditions, were in the nature of programming intentions
and imposed no obligation on the contractor to complete at the earlier 19
week date, so that the prolongation should be calculated from the 25 week
date: *J.F. Finnegan Ltd.* v. *Sheffield City Council* (1988).[84]

The purpose of contractual requirements for a programme to be sup-   **9·042**
plied by the contractor is often misunderstood, and is primarily to enable
the owner, or his A/E, to plan their own arrangements for giving possession, supplying information and working drawings, and co-ordinating
the work of other contractors or nominated sub-contractors, and only secondarily for use in connection with the contractor's extension of time
applications or monetary claims, or to impose additional time obligations
on him. Against this background, in the absence of clear language such
provisions should not be interpreted as altering the substantive rights or
obligations of the parties, though no doubt a programme may be some,
although not conclusive, evidence as to what is a reasonable time for the
discharge of both parties' obligations under the contract.

The ICE Conditions have, since 1973, contained a rather complicated
(and from the owner's point of view ill-advised) code for the supply of a
programme, which appears to confuse in the same provision programmes
of progress with information about methods of working, and which can

[83] 39 BLR 94.
[84] 43 BLR 130.

result in the engineer being obliged to intervene with instructions in matters involving methods of working or temporary works, and expose the owner to financial claims.[85] Following his requesting information on these matters, the Conditions also provide for the submission of later programmes should earlier ones not be complied with.[86] While many standard forms contain provisions that approval of a programme is not to relieve *the contractor* of his responsibilities,[87] they generally lack precision in explaining the purpose of requiring the programme or the precise legal consequences of its submission, approval or disapproval.[88]

(9) Nature of Required Completion

9·043   In the last resort the degree of required completion needed to discharge the contractor's obligation to complete to time will be a matter of interpretation, but can be expected to differ from other aspects of the contractor's obligation to complete. In English standard forms of contract employing liquidated damages clauses for delay, this is often expressly described as "practical" or "substantial" completion, but there is no reason to suppose that these expressions mean anything very different from the word "completion" *simpliciter* when used or implied in the context of completion to time. It is submitted that this will, in the absence of contrary indication, mean when the work reaches a state of readiness for use or occupation by the owner, and free from any known omissions or defects which are not merely trivial. Following his requesting information on these matters, thus defects not known at the relevant time, however important when subsequently discovered, will not prevent the discharge of this particular aspect of the completion obligation, and so terminate a contractor's liability to the owner for damages for delay, whether general or liquidated. This subject has been considered and various judicial observations in this context have been noted *ante*, Chapters 4 and 5,[89] and is further discussed in greater detail *post*, Chapter 10.[90]

---

[85] See particularly sub-clauses 14(3)–14(6), commented on in the editor's "The ICE Conditions of Contract, fifth edition", pp.' 54–59.

[86] Clause 14(2).

[87] See, *e.g.* clause 14(7), ICE Contract.

[88] Contrast the Singapore SIA Private Sector Contract clause 5, reproduced in C.C.P.P., pp. 558–559, which endeavours to explain the precise consequences of both approval and disapproval.

[89] See paras. 4·029 and 4·030, and 5·048–5·049.

[90] See paras. 10·058 and 10·059.

CHAPTER 10

PENALTIES AND LIQUIDATED DAMAGES

SECTION 1. CONSTRUCTION AND EFFECT OF CLAUSES

(1) Generally

Contracts often contain provisions for the payment of sums of money or **10·001** the forfeiture of goods or other property in the event of particular specified breaches of the contract. These provisions vary very considerably, but their main objectives are to act as an inducement to due performance of a particular contractual obligation, or to regulate beforehand in an agreed and certain manner the rights of the parties, rather than leave them to the less predictable remedies otherwise available, and in particular the assessment of damages in the event of breach of the obligation in question.

The simplest provisions of this type are provisions stating in round figures what payments are to be made or what the damages are to be in a certain event. These are classical liquidated damages or penalties provisions, and are most commonly found in building contracts in relation to the contractor's obligation to complete the work within the specified time.

It is with these clauses that the present chapter is concerned. But a forfeiture clause making provision for the payment of money, or for forfeiture of plant or materials as damages in the event of determination by the owner may also fall into the same general category.

All these clauses require to be distinguished from clauses which on their true construction empower a party to do something upon payment of a sum of money. In such cases, the act is a permitted act, and not a forbidden one, and the sum of money is in the nature of the price for being permitted to do it. Thus if in a farming lease a tenant covenanted not to sell or carry away hay without consent, save upon payment of an increased rent of £10 per ton so carried away and sold, he would have the right to do so, and could not be prevented from doing so by injunction.[1] On the other hand, if a bank employee covenants not to enter the employment of any other bank, and promises to pay £1,000 by way of penalty should he do so, he will not be permitted to enter other employment upon payment of the £1,000, and an injunction will issue.[2] Again, demurrage payments under a charterparty are agreed damages for detention of a vessel but do not entitle the charterer to detain the vessel by paying demurrage.[3]

10·002   It will not matter that the contract uses the word "penalty", as some still do, if the sum is in reality an estimate of damage or is intended as a limitation of damage and not *in terrorem*[4]; but in all cases where the act in question is a breach of contract, the law will inquire whether the payment or forfeiture provided for in the contract is a "penalty", in a special more modern sense of the word meaning that it is not in reality an estimate of damage and is excessive. If it is held to be a penalty, in this sense, the party claiming it will not be permitted to recover the full amount, if his damage has in fact been less; but on the other hand; he will remain limited to that amount if his damages have been greater (even if a sum which is less than the likely damages can ever be a penalty at all, not being, *ex hypothesi*, oppressive or *in terrorem*).[5] On the other hand, if it is held to be liquidated damages, the aggrieved party will be entitled to the stipulated sum, whether his real damage be greater, or less, or non-existent.[6]

It is very important in all such cases, however, to analyse carefully and precisely what breach, and sometimes what precise class of damage arising from the breach, is the object of the clause. Other breaches, or other classes of damage, however closely related, may escape its operation. In most construction contracts, for example, it will be damage occurring

---

[1] *Woodward* v. *Gyles* (1690) 2 Vernon 119.
[2] *National Provincial Bank* v. *Marshall* (1888) 40 Ch.D. 112.
[3] *AKT Reidar* v. *Arcos Ltd.* [1927] 1 K.B. 352.
[4] Notwithstanding Lord Atkin leaving the question open in *Cellulose Acetate Silk Co. Ltd.* v. *Widnes Foundry (1929) Ltd.* [1933] A.C. 20, at p. 26, this last point, strongly suggested in the Court of Appeal judgments in the *Widnes* case ([1931] 2 K.B. 393), seems finally and satisfactorily concluded by the Supreme Court of Canada in *Elsley* v. *J.G. Collins Insurance Agencies Ltd.* (1978) 83 D.L.R. (3d) 1, illustrated *infra*, paras. 10–016.
[5] See the Court of Appeal judgments in the *Widnes* case and Dickson J.'s judgment in the *Elsley* case, all of which support or confirm this view.
[6] See the *Widnes* case.

after, and exclusively as a result of, late re-entry by the owner, which will be the objective of the liquidated damages clause, and not, for example, damage resulting from earlier delays or failures of due diligence.

ILLUSTRATIONS

(1) A contractor suspended work, later going bankrupt, and the owners took over the work, completing six weeks late. They claimed for the additional cost of completion under the termination clause, and also liquidated damages for the delay. *Held*, by the Court of Session, that the clause was intended to govern a delay in completion by the contractor himself, and not by other contractors following a termination, and while the owner was entitled to damages for the delay, he was not entitled to liquidated damages. *Per* Lord Johnston, the clause contemplated failure to proceed "in natural course but not to time": *British Glanzstoff Manufacturing Co. Ltd.* v. *General Accident Fire and Life Assurance Corporation Ltd.* (1912).[7]   **10·003**

(2) A charterparty for a number of voyages required the charterers to load a "full and complete cargo" at a stipulated daily rate of loading, and provided that, should the ship be delayed beyond the time stipulated for loading or discharging, demurrage was to be paid at a daily rate. The ship did not load at the stipulated rate of loading while in Archangel, with the result that a date in October was passed after which a ship destined for a British port could only, by virtue of section 10 of the Merchant Shipping Act 1906 and the onset of winter, be loaded with 554 standards of timber rather than the full 850 standards. The shipowner brought an action for the lost freight payable on the reduced cargo, and the charterers contended that they could only be liable for the stipulated demurrage. *Held*, by the Court of Appeal, that the provisions for demurrage quantified the damages not for the complete breach but only for such loss as would normally arise from the longer detention of the vessel, and not the loss of freight caused by the separate breach of loading less than full cargo: *AKT Reidar* v. *Arcos Ltd.* (1927).[8]

(3) Unsuitable equipment used by contractors led to major structural defects in a building, which resulted in a suspension of work and extensive remedial work being required before it could be completed. The owners, in addition to the additional cost of completion, claimed substantial damages for loss of rents and profits and financing charges due to the delay. The contractors contended that the owners were limited to the liquidated damages specified in the contract. *Held*, by the Court of Session, following the *Glanzstoff* case, that the liquidated damages only applied to a contractor being late in completion and the owners could recover the financing charges: *Chanthall Investments Ltd.* v. *F.G. Minter Ltd.* (1976).[9]   **10·004**

[Note: The report of this case is unaccountably vague as to the relevant facts. Apparently the owners' pleadings alleged that the remedial work was done by other contractors, and it may be surmised that the contractors had at the time been disputing liability, but on the other hand the contractors' pleadings alleged that the contract had never been rescinded by the owners. It is not clear at precisely what stage the defects were discovered. Lord Keith's judgment in first instance, when considering the *Glanzstoff* case, appeared to treat

---

[7] 1912 S.C. 591, at p. 599; *aff'd.* [1913] A.C. 143, H.L.
[8] [1927] 1 K.B. 352.
[9] 1976 S.C. 73.

the taking-over of the contract by the owners in that case as not of great significance. It is submitted that delays in completion, however serious, caused by a contractor's defective work later duly repaired by him during the construction period, will be subsumed by the liquidated damages as in the next case illustrated *infra*.]

10·005   (4) A contractor built a new office building for a local authority under the RIBA/JCT design-and-build standard form, with the usual liquidated damages clause and provisions for insurance of the works against fire. The building was seriously damaged before practical completion by a fire caused by the negligence of sub-contractors. The contractor proceeded to re-build and complete the building 67 weeks late, for which he was entitled under the extension of time clause to a full extension of time. The council sued the main contractors in contract and tort for a wide range of heads of damage caused by the fire. *Held*, by Judge Fox-Andrews Q.C., that interest on capital invested, furniture storage costs, certain additional staff costs, loss of income from car-parking charges, and additional repairs and modifications to telephones in the old premises, had all been caused by late completion under the terms of the liquidated damages clause, so that since a full extension of time had been granted not even liquidated damages could be recovered. Damage to certain items of property already installed in the new building and not covered by the contractual insurance, and extra professional costs incurred in the re-building work, provided they too were not covered by the contractual insurance, were not due to late completion and were therefore recoverable: *Surrey Heath Borough Council* v. *Lovell Construction Ltd.* (1988).[10]

(5) A contract in the RIBA/JCT 1977 revised form provided for five "sub-areas", each with a separate and earlier completion date than the final completion date, but the liquidated damages and completion provisions in Clauses 21 and 22 of the conditions only contemplated one date for possession and completion respectively.[11] The official referee granted summary judgment on the basis that the date for completion of the last area regulated the amount of permissible set-off for liquidated damages. *Held*, by the Court of Appeal, that on the footing that Clause 22 regulated liquidated damages by reference to the last stipulated completion date, there was a prima facie case that the clause did not exclude unliquidated damages for breaches of the earlier completion dates, and unconditional leave to defend should be given: *Turner & Sons Ltd.* v. *Mathind* (1986).[12]

(2) Distinction between Penalties and Liquidated Damages

10·006   The actual description of the sum or payment in a contract is of little importance, even if the words "penalty" or "liquidated damages" are used. The distinction between the two, when used in their legal sense, and the tests to be applied, are regarded as authoritatively stated in the following passage from the judgment of Lord Dunedin in *Dunlop Pneumatic Tyre Co. Ltd.* v. *New Garage & Motor Co. Ltd.*[13]:

---

[10] 42 BLR 26.
[11] For some reason an extremely common error of advisers preparing contract documentation for owners.
[12] 5 Const.L.J. 273.
[13] [1915] A.C. 79 at p. 86.

"1. Though the parties to a contract who use the words 'penalty' or 'liquidated damages' may prima facie be supposed to mean what they say, yet the expression used is not conclusive. The court must find out whether the payment stipulated is in truth a penalty or liquidated damages.

2. The essence of a penalty is a payment of money stipulated as *in terrorem* of the offending party; the essence of liquidated damages is a genuine covenanted pre-estimate of damage.[14]

3. The question whether a sum stipulated is penalty or liquidated damages is a question of construction to be decided upon the terms and inherent circumstances of each particular contract, judged of as at the time of making the contract, not as at the time of the breach.[15]

4. To assist this task of construction, various tests have been suggested, which if applicable to the case under consideration may prove helpful, or even conclusive. Such are:

(a) It will be held to be a penalty if the sum stipulated for is extravagant and unconscionable in amount in comparison with the greatest loss that could conceivably be proved to have followed from the breach.[16]

(b) It will be held to be a penalty if the breach consists only in not paying a sum of money, and the sum stipulated is a sum greater than the sum which ought to have been paid.[17] This, though one of the most ancient instances, is truly a corollary to the last test.

(c) There is a presumption (but no more) that it is a penalty when 'a single sum is made payable by way of compensation, on the occurrence of one or more or all of several events, some of which may occasion serious and others but trifling damages'.[18]

(d) It is no obstacle to the sum stipulated being a genuine pre-estimate of damage that the consequences of the breach are such as to make precise pre-estimation almost an impossibility. On the contrary, that is just the situation when it is probable the pre-estimated damage was the true bargain between the parties."[19]

ILLUSTRATIONS

(1) A plaintiff/builder agreed to forfeit and pay £10 per week for every **10·007** week after the expiration of the six weeks limited for the doing of certain repairs to a church, until the said work should be completely finished. The owner claimed to set off four weeks at £10, but the builder argued that the language showed it was a penalty and the owner must prove his real damage. *Held*, by the Court of King's Bench, that the £10 a week was in the nature of liquidated damages, as the amount of damage was difficult of ascertainment by a jury, and was therefore properly fixed by the parties beforehand to prevent any dispute as to *quantum*: *Fletcher* v. *Dyche* (1787).[20]

---

[14] *Clydebank Engineering and Shipbuilding Co.* v. *Don Jose Ramos Yzquierdo-y-Castaneda* [1905] A.C. 6.

[15] *Public Works Commissioner* v. *Hills* [1906] A.C. 368; *Webster* v. *Bosanquet* [1912] A.C. 394.

[16] Illustration given by Lord Halsbury in the *Clydebank* case, *supra*.

[17] *Kemble* v. *Farren* (1829) 6 Bing. 141.

[18] Lord Watson in *Lord Elphinstone* v. *Monkland Iron and Coal Co.* (1886) 11 App.Cas. 332.

[19] *Clydebank* case, *supra*, *per* Lord Halsbury; *Webster* v. *Bosanquet*, *supra*, *per* Lord Mersey. For a modern example, see *Att.-Gen. for British Guiana* v. *Serrao* (1965) 7 W.I.R. 404, West Indies.

[20] 2 T.R. 32.

(2) An agreement contained a provision that if either of the parties should neglect or refuse to fulfil the said agreement, or any part thereof, or any stipulation therein contained, such party should pay to the other the sum of £1,000, to which sum it was thereby agreed that the damages sustained by any such omission, neglect, or refusal should amount; and which sum was thereby declared by the said parties to be liquidated and ascertained damages, and not a penalty or penal sum, or in the nature thereof. *Held*, by Tindal C.J., that notwithstanding its wording, the agreement applied a very large sum to any breach, however minute and unimportant, so that the sum of £1,000 was in the nature of a penalty: *Kemble* v. *Farren* (1829).[21]

J-008   (3) In settlement of an action for breaking up a road, the defendant gave a form of bond to the plaintiff confessing judgment of £200, with a condition of defeasance if the defendant should reinstate the road by an agreed date in accordance with a plan and with the approval of a surveyor. The road was not completely reinstated by that date, and the plaintiff sued out execution and levied £200 and costs. *Held*, by the Court of Common Pleas, that the £200 was a penalty, and the court referred the question of damages sustained. *Per* Tindal C.J., it would be most unjust for the defendant to be liable for the whole sum for a short delay in completion or if a small part of the work was incomplete: *Charrington* v. *Laing* (1829).[22]

(4) R. contracted to construct a railway. The contract provided: (1) That if, after seven days' notice, R. did not proceed regularly with the works the company might proceed and complete the works themselves, paying for the same out of the money then remaining due to R. on account of the contract. Payments then already made to R. were to be taken as full satisfaction for all works then already done by him. All moneys then due, or which would thereafter have become due to him under the contract, and all the tools and materials on the works, were to become the property of the company. And if the moneys, materials, and tools were insufficient to provide for the completion of the work, R. was to supply the deficiency. (2) That specified sums, increasing every week, should be paid as "penalties" in case of delay. *Held*, by the House of Lords, that the first provision imposed a penalty on R. and that the railway company must account for the value of the plant seized and appropriated by them in settling their accounts with R., but that the second provision provided for liquidated damages, although the word "penalties" was used: *Ranger* v. *G.W. Railway* (1854).[23]

10-009   (5) The plaintiff contracted with the defendant to do certain repairs and alterations to a house, to be completed in a specified time, "subject to a penalty of £20 per week that any of the works remain unfinished" after the stipulated periods. *Held*, that the sum of £20 per week was in the nature of liquidated damages, and could be deducted by the defendant without proving the loss he had actually sustained by reason of the delay: *Crux* v. *Aldred* (1866).[24]

(6) A contract provided for the retention of 15 per cent. of the value of the work done, and that in certain events "the unpaid balance of the work shall be forfeited by G. to the use of the said company in the nature of liquidated damages". *Held*, by the Supreme Court of Maryland, that the forfeiture of the

---

[21] 6 Bing. 141.
[22] 3 M. & P. 587.
[23] 5 H.L.C. 72, at pp. 107–110, 104–105.
[24] 14 W.R. 656.

unpaid value was to be considered as a fixed sum for compensation in the nature of liquidated damages: *Geiger* v. *Western Maryland Railway* (1874).[25]

(7) An engineering contract provided for 10 per cent. retention money, which, in case the contractor failed to perform the contract, was to be forfeited to the employers. *Held*, by the Supreme Court of Georgia, that this was a penalty and not liquidated damages: *Savannah Railway Co.* v. *Callahan* (1876).[26]

(8) A contract contained a clause providing for £10 per week to be paid in case of non-completion to time, and also a provision that in case the contract should not be in all things duly performed by the contractors, they should pay to the governors £1,000 as liquidated damages. *Held*, by the Court of Appeal, that the latter sum was in the nature of a penalty: *Re Newman, ex p. Capper* (1876).[27]   **10·010**

(9) Under a mining lease, the lessee covenanted that he would reinstate the lands from time to time, and at the end of the lease as they were before, or, if not, would pay £100 per acre. He failed to reinstate about 30 acres. An arbitrator found that the actual damage done amounted to £1,375. *Held*, by the Queen's Bench Divisional Court, that £100 per acre was an attempt to assess the damages, and not in the nature of a penalty, and that the whole £3,000 must be paid: *Re Earl of Mexborough and Wood* (1883).[28]

(10) A contract provided that sewerage works should be completed in all respects *and cleared of all impediments and rubbish* by a specified date, and that in default of "such completion" the contractor should forfeit and pay the sum of £100, and £5 for every seven days for which the work should be incomplete after the said date as and for liquidated damages. The contractor argued that the sums applied to the two separate obligations, and that the £100 sum at least was a penalty. *Held*, by the Court of Appeal, that on the true interpretation of the clause the sums were both to be paid on the single event of late completion, and the presumption was that they were liquidated damages and not penalties: *Law* v. *British Local Board* (1892).[29]

(11) A. agreed with B. to pull down and re-build a hotel in carcase before December 25, 1896, and to take a lease for 80 years from June 24, 1896, at a peppercorn for the first year, and £1,000 a year afterwards. Clause 2 of the contract provided that in case of failure to complete within the time allowed, the benefit of the agreement and all buildings and materials were to be forfeited. Clause 11 of the agreement gave power of re-entry in case of non-completion to time, or want of proper diligence, etc., and to take possession of building materials and plant without making any allowance or compensation therefor. A. went into possession in June 1896 and pulled down about £200 worth of materials, but did nothing more and B. re-entered in January 1897, and could only re-let from June 1899, at £900 a year. The official referee assessed substantial damages, but considered that B.'s remedy was limited to seizing the plant or materials. *Held*, by Kennedy J., that in the absence of some such express words as "as and for liquidated damages", clauses 2 and 11 could not be construed as depriving B. of the right to recover actual damages for the defendant's failure to perform the contract: *Marshall* v. *Macintosh* (1898).[30]   **10·011**

---

[25] 41 Md. 4. A similar result was reached by the Full Court of Queensland in *Kratzmann Holdings Pty. Ltd.* v. *University of Queensland* [1982] Qd.R. 682, *infra*, para. 10·017.
[26] 56 Ga. 331; U.S.Dig. 1877, at p. 156.
[27] 4 Ch.D. 724, C.A.
[28] 47 L.T. 516.
[29] [1892] 1 Q.B. 127.
[30] 78 L.T. 750.

(12) W. contracted to supply an electric light installation. The contract provided that the whole of the work except the plant was to be completed by a certain day, subject to a "penalty" for each day of delay, and there was a similar provision as to the plant. *Held*, by the King's Bench Divisional Court, that although the word "penalty" was used, the real intention was that the amounts specified should be treated as liquidated damages. *Per* Kennedy J., one of the principal matters to be looked at was whether the sum fixed was for breach of one particular stipulation or for several breaches which, on their face, might give rise to varying degrees of damage: *Re White and Arthur* (1901).[31]

10·012   (13) A contract for the building of four torpedo boats provided that "the penalty for later delivery shall be at the rate of £500 per week, for each vessel". The vessels were delivered after the specified time. *Held* by the House of Lords, that the sum of £500 per week was liquidated damages and not a penalty: *Clydebank Engineering & Shipbuilding Co. Ltd.* v. *Yzquierdo-y-Castaneda* (1905).[32]

(14) P. agreed to buy 10 motor cars from the B. Co. at prices varying from £320 to £590, which were to be delivered at certain dates. P. deposited £300 with the company, which deposit the company "shall be at liberty to declare to be wholly forfeited" if P. refused to accept delivery and pay for any of the said goods. *Held* by Bigham J., that the fact that the sum in question was to be paid on the breach of any one of a variety of stipulations of different degrees of importance was not conclusive as to its being a penalty; nor was the fact that the sum in question had been deposited at the making of the contract conclusive as to its being liquidated damages, although both these facts formed material elements to be taken in ascertaining the intention of the parties; and that in this case the parties had intended the sum in question to be liquidated damages: *Pye* v. *British Automobile Commercial Syndicate* (1906).[33]

(15) A railway construction contract provided that in the event of non-completion by a certain date the contractor should forfeit the retention moneys under the contract and two other contracts, and also certain necessity money lodged with the railway company's agent "as and for liquidated damages sustained by the defendants for the non-completion". *Held*, by the House of Lords, the amount of retention money was indefinite and depended upon the progress of the construction, and could not therefore be a genuine pre-estimate of loss. The company was therefore not entitled to these sums, but only such damage as it might actually have suffered: *Public Works Commissioner* v. *Hills* (1906).[34]

10·013   (16) A firm of timber merchants entered into a contract with a landowner whereby they bought certain standing timber under the condition: "The wood to be cleared away by April 1, 1918, under a penalty of 10s. a day until such is done." In April, 1919, the wood not having been completely cleared away, the landowner brought an action against the timber merchants for payment of one year's "penalty" at the agreed rate. *Held*, by the Court of Session, that the claim could be brought before completion and that although the sum of 10s. was described in the contract as a "penalty", yet as it was *ex facie* a reasonable pre-estimate of loss, and not a mere random figure, and since it was not averred by the timber merchants to be exorbitant, it must be regarded as liqui-

---

[31] 17 T.L.R. 461.
[32] [1905] A.C. 6.
[33] [1906] 1 K.B. 425.
[34] [1906] A.C. 368.

dated damages and not as a penalty: *Cameron-Head* v. *Cameron & Co.* (1919).[35]

(17) By Clause 11 of a road-building contract in Victoria, the council had the right to determine the contract for insufficient progress, failure to remedy defective work when ordered to do so, Sunday working without permission, or wilful breach of contract. On such a determination, any moneys already paid to the contractor should be taken in full payment and satisfaction of all claims by him, and the deposit and retention percentages provided for in the contract and all materials and plant should remain the absolute property of the council to be disposed of as they thought fit. *Held*, by the Full Court, on a case stated, that since the clause might cover anything from complete failure of the contractor to carry out most important work to a failure to rectify a very slight defect, or a very small part of the work being done on a Sunday, and since the amount or value of the money or property forfeited would be quite indefinite, depending largely on the course of construction of the works and the extent of work done and not paid for, the provisions as to moneys paid being taken as full satisfaction, although not expressed as a forfeiture, and those applying to plant or materials which at the time of the determination were still the property of the contractor, were penalties against which equity would grant relief.[35a] Since, however, under clause 24 of the contract the deposit and retention money could not be earned by the contractor until final completion, that part of the clause was not a penalty: *Bysouth* v. *Shire of Blackburn* (1928).[36]

(18) A contract for delivery and erection of an acetone recovery plant con-   **10·014**
tained a provision, inserted at the request of the owners, for payment of a weekly sum of £20 by way of penalty for every week in default. When sued for moneys due, the owners counterclaimed £5,850 as damages in respect of 30 weeks' delay, but the contractors contended that they were limited in any event to the £600 provided by the contract, which the owners, however, said was a penalty. The trial judge held that the sum was too low to be an estimate of damage, and so a penalty, and awarded the damages claimed. *Held*, by the Court of Appeal, and affirmed by the House of Lords, that the provision was one for liquidated damages and bound the parties. *Per* Scrutton L.J.: "I do not decide that a party is always bound by the figure mentioned from recovering a larger sum; it turns upon whether the sum mentioned can be said to be an estimate of the damage to be paid for the breach; but I find great difficulty in saying that an estimate less than the actual loss can ever be a penalty *in terrorem*.": *Cellulose Acetate Silk Co. Ltd.* v. *Widnes Foundry (1925) Ltd.* (1931).[37]

(19) A sub-contract contained the words; "If the sub-contractor fails to comply with any of the conditions of this sub-contract, the contractor reserves the right to suspend or withhold payment of any moneys due or becoming due to the sub-contractor." *Held*, by the House of Lords, that the provision would entitle the contractor to withhold sums far in excess of the value of his claims; and was void and unenforceable as a penalty: *Gilbert-Ash (Northern) Ltd.* v. *Modern Engineering (Bristol) Ltd.* (1974).[38]

(20) The owner under a road construction contract, in the event of default   **10·015**
by the contractor, was empowered to take over and complete the works him-

---

[35] 1919 S.C. 627.
[35a] Lowe J. dissented on the second category.
[36] [1928] V.R. 562.
[37] [1931] 2 K.B. 393. Slessor and Greer L.J.'s judgments made the same point even more strongly.
[38] [1974] A.C. 689.

self by other persons. If he did so, the contract by Clause 43.3 provided that he could take possession of and permit other persons to use materials or plant owned by the contractor and necessary for the purposes of such completion. The contractor was to have no right to any compensation or allowance for this, other than a right to require the owner to maintain the plant in good working order. On completion the plant was to be handed over to the contractor, but without payment or allowance for fair wear and tear sustained in the meantime, unless a deficiency arose on the cost of completion, in which event the owner might retain in his possession the plant, materials, etc., until payment by the contractor. The Supreme Court of New South Wales, having regard to the great value of the plant, a separate clause for liquidated damages for delay of £1,000 per week, and a required provision of substantial security for performance of the contract, accepted the contractor's argument that Clause 43.3, in giving the right to possession and use of the machinery and plant without payment or making allowance for fair wear and tear, constituted a penalty, and that the contractor was accordingly entitled to recover possession of it before the contract was completed by the owner. *Held*, by the High Court of Australia, (Mason J. dissenting), that the clause did not purport to give the owner any rights of property in the machinery and plant, and the provision allowing the owners to complete with the aid of the plant was both reasonable and in the interest of both parties. The existence of the other clauses and the value of the plant were not relevant factors. *Per* Mason J., the clause was a penalty, first, because the power to take possession was not confined exclusively to use of the plant for completion and, secondly, because of the denial to the contractor of any compensation or allowance for the use or deprivation of the plant etc. *Per* Jacobs J., the use of the plant for completion was likely to reduce the damages otherwise payable by the contractor. Only in the unlikely event of completion at less cost than under the contract might it be possible to set aside Clause 43 at a later stage so as to enable the contractor to claim an allowance for use of the plant: *Forestry Commission of New South Wales* v. *Stefanetto* (1975).[39]

10·016   (21) An employee who had sold his company to new owners covenanted not to compete and to pay $1,000 on default, but nevertheless did compete. The new owners claimed an injunction and damages, including a claim for rectification of the contract so that the $1,000 would apply to each and every breach. The rectification claim was rejected by the trial judge, and the owners then withdrew their claim to liquidated damages and instead claimed general damages on the grounds that the $1,000 was a gross under-estimate of damage if it was to be applied to any and all breaches collectively, and therefore a penalty. The employee had originally resisted a claim for an injunction on the grounds that the covenant in question was too wide, and in any event that there had been an election to claim damages so that an injunction did not lie. The lower courts held that an injunction could be granted against future breaches as well as damages for past breaches, and awarded general damages in excess of the $1,000. *Held*, by the Supreme Court of Canada, that the covenant was reasonable and enforceable, but, after consideration of the *Widnes* case and citing Lord Ellenborough in *Wilbeam* v. *Ashton*, "beyond the penalty you shall not go; within it you are to give the party any compensation which he can prove himself entitled to",[40] the damages should be limited to $1,000. The power to strike down a penalty clause had no place where there was no oppression. If the actual loss turned out to exceed the penalty, the normal rules of enforcement of contract should apply to allow recovery of

---

[39] 133 C.L.R. 507.
[40] (1807) 1 Camp. 78; 170 E.R. 883.

only the agreed sum. A penalty should function as a limitation on the damages recoverable, while still being ineffective to increase damages above the actual loss sustained, when actual loss was less than the stipulated amount: *Elsley* v. *J.G. Collins Insurance Agencies Ltd.* (1978).[41]

(22) By clause 30 of a railway contract in South Australia, the owners were empowered upon default in progress on the part of the contractor, and following notice in writing, to determine the contract; and thereupon all sums of money due or unpaid to the contractor, together with all implements which were his property and all materials provided for him which were on the site, and all penalties for late completion, should be forfeited and become payable to the owners, and the implements and materials became their sole and absolute property, and considered as ascertained damages for breach of the contract. *Held*, by Mitchell J., affirmed by the Full Court of South Australia, that ` Clause 30 was not a genuine pre-estimate of damage but a penalty, and that the contractor could maintain a claim for wrongful seizure, detention and conversion of his plant and materials: *Egan* v. *State Transport Authority* (1979).[42]

(23) The owners cancelled a building contract under a termination clause on the contractor going into liquidation. The contract provided in the usual way for progress payments against certificates, with retention of 10 per cent. but not to exceed in the aggregate 5 per cent. of the contract sum, and not payable until completion and the final certificate. The termination clause provided that any sums in the hands of the owner and not then payable to the contractor under any provision of the contract should be forfeited and retained by the owner, and all moneys previously paid should be deemed to be in full satisfaction of all claims of the contractor. At the date of termination, the contract was approximately half complete, retention totalled some $48,000, and the value of work since the last certificate but not yet due was some $34,000, making a total of some $83,000 which the owners claimed to forfeit. In the event, these moneys were adequate to cover the cost of completion by another contractor with some $7,500 in hand. *Held*, by the Full Court of Queensland (not following the statement with regard to clauses forfeiting retention moneys in the tenth edition), that since the retention could never exceed 5 per cent. of the contract sum and since outstanding progress payments could not exceed more than one month's work, the sum involved at any given point of time would be moderate when compared with the contract sum, and could be said to be a genuine pre-estimate of the potential loss to the owner, and the clause did not amount to a penalty: *Kratzmann Holdings Ltd.* v. *University of Queensland* (1982).[43]

10·017

[Note: The judgments in this case are short but well-reasoned and persuasive. As Connolly J. said, the clause in question did little more on analysis than re-state the existing common law, since the result of a rescission *simpliciter* would be that rights accrued at the date of discharge remain enforceable while rights to accrue in the future are lost.[44]]

(24) A leasing agreement for a computer entitled the lessors to repossess the computer in default of punctual payment of quarterly rentals. Clause 6(a) then provided that, in the event of such repossession, the lessee was to pay all arrears of rentals, and all further rentals which would have fallen due (less a

---

[41] 83 D.L.R. (3d) 1, at p. 15.
[42] 24 S.A.S.R. 5, at p. 20.
[43] [1982] Qd.R. 682. See also the decision to the same effect, on the basis that the retention moneys were not yet earned, by the Full Court of Victoria in *Bysouth* v. *Shire of Blackburn* [1928] V.R. 562, *supra*, para. 10·013.
[44] *Ibid.* at p. 683.

discount for early payment), together with damages for breach of the agreement. *Held*, by the Court of Appeal that the clause was a penalty in so far as it purported to oblige the lessee, regardless of the seriousness or triviality of the breach leading to termination, to make a payment in respect of rental instalments not accrued due: *Lombard North Central PLC* v. *Butterworth* (1986).[45]

10·018

(25) Clause 63(1) of a Hong Kong sewerage contract provided that if "the works or any portion thereof" had not been completed by the contract or extended date, liquidated damages should be payable in accordance with the appendix. Clause 63(4) then provided that "the liquidated damages prescribed for delay to the whole of the works" should be reduced proportionately to the value of any part of the work certified as capable of occupation or use relative to the value of the whole. A special condition provided expressly that, notwithstanding Clause 63(4), liquidated damages should not be less than the minimum amount stated in the form of tender, which was $400. The appendix simply stated two figures opposite Clause 63 of "$HK 400 (min) per day" and "$HK 2,700 (max)". *Held*, by the High Court of Hong Kong (Sears J.), that the provision was void and unenforceable as a penalty since, first, there was uncertainty as to what the intermediate figures should be between the maximum and minimum and secondly, the minimum figure could not be a pre-estimate of damage if more than 85 per cent. of the contract by value was certified under Clause 63(4): *Arnhold & Co. Ltd.* v. *A.-G. of Hong Kong* (1989).[46]

[Note: The provisions of this contract, while certainly not elegantly drafted, seem perfectly clear in their commercial intention, namely that the maximum figure represented the damages where the whole of the work was incomplete, while the intermediate figures represented the reductions effected by Clause 63(4) until the minimum figure was reached. Dealing with the second point, the stipulation of a minimum figure could be easily justified as a pre-estimate of damage, it is submitted, since while a contract remains administratively incomplete, professional and other expenses of the owner will continue to run notwithstanding the physical completion of a very high proportion of the work. The invalidation of the clause seems difficult to justify on either of the grounds put forward, therefore. See the *Arnhold* case *infra*.]

(26) A complex and substantial high-rise commercial development in New South Wales was carried out under a contract where both parties' legal advisers had negotiated a formula for liquidated damages for delay based on the owner's "holding costs" (*i.e.* principally financing charges) for the project during the delay period. It was contended that the sums so calculated were a penalty, not being a pre-estimate of the developer's damages due to loss of profit. *Held*, by Cole J., after admitting evidence of the negotiations, that the sums were not excessive, and in any case increased financial charges represented an acceptable measure of damage for a delayed commercial project: *Multiplex Constructions Pty. Ltd.* v. *Abgarus Pty. Ltd.* (1992).[47]

[Note: This judgment contains a valuable review of English and Australian[48] authorities on the principles governing the invalidation of contractual provisions as penalties, and the differing strands emerging from the leading

---

[45] [1987] 1 Q.B. 527. Contrast *Campbell Discount Co. Ltd.* v. *Bridge* [1961] 1 Q.B. 445.
[46] 47 BLR 129.
[47] Unreported, Sup.Ct., N.S.W., 1992 Case No. 55042.
[48] *W.T. Malouf Pty. Ltd.* v. *Brinds Ltd.* (1981) 52 F.L.R. 442; *O'Dea* v. *Allstates Leasing System* (1983) 152 C.L.R. 359; *Amey-UDC Finance Ltd.* v. *Austen* (1986) 162 C.L.R. 170; *Amey Finance Ltd.* v. *Artes Studios* (1989) 15 N.S.W.L.R. 564; *Esanda Finance Corporation* v. *Plessing* (1989) 166 C.L.R. 131.

cases emphasising variously extravagant or excessive amounts, the assessment not representing a pre-estimate, unconscionability, and oppressiveness.]

(27) The Hong Kong government entered into seven separate contracts for   **10·019**
approach roads and tunnels in their New Territories. The contract in dispute identified a number of intermediate key dates needed to conform with the work of the other contractors. By Clause 29, a daily rate of liquidated damages was provided for failure to meet various key dates, and an additional daily rate was quoted for completing the whole of the work. By Clause 29.4, there was also a provision closely comparable to that in the *Arnhold* case, *supra*, whereby if sections of the work were certified as complete and occupied by the government, the liquidated damages for the whole of the works would be reduced, subject to a minimum daily rate. The contractors sought a declaration that Clause 29 was unenforceable as a penalty. They argued, first, that the liquidated damages for failing to meet the key dates and the whole of the works completion date were cumulative and greater than the true loss; secondly, that, following the *Arnhold* case, the minimum daily rate consituted a penalty; and, thirdly, that the daily rates for failure to meet successive key dates would also be cumulative and exceed any likely damage. *Held*, by the Privy Council, affirming the Hong Kong Court of Appeal, (a) that the damage likely to be suffered by failure to meet a key date, namely possible claims by other contractors against the owners, was different in kind from that caused by late completion of the whole works, and unless the sums were oppressive they were enforceable as liquidated damages; (b) that Clause 29.4 was concerned with completion of sections and occupation by the owner, and not with key dates, but that in any event (doubting the *Arnhold* case) a minimum rate of damages notwithstanding occupation of a substantial part of the works would on the facts be a genuine pre-estimate of damage; and (c) that such cumulative rates of damages for failing to meet successive key dates could on the facts represent a genuine pre-estimate of damage since on later key dates additional other contractors might be delayed and present claims. *Per* Lord Woolf: "It will normally be insufficient to establish that a provision is objectionably penal to identify situations where the application of the provision could result in a larger sum being recovered by the injured party than is actually lost ... so long as the sum payable in the event of non-compliance with the contract is not extravagant, having regard to the range of losses that it could reasonably be anticipated it would have to cover at the time the contract was made, it can still be a genuine pre-estimate of a loss ... and so a perfectly valid liquidated damage provision." *Philips (Hong Kong) Ltd.* v. *A.-G. of Hong Kong* (1993).[48a]

The above cases show that the principles of penalty invalidation apply   **10·020**
equally to provisions which involve taking possession of plant,[49] or regulating the state of accounts following a determination.[50] In the tenth edition it was suggested that provisions for forfeiture of retention moneys (which of course increase progressively in amount as the work is carried out) would be offensive, since in principle there should if anything be a

---

[48a] 61 BLR 41.
[49] See the remarks of Mason J., in the *Stefanetto* case in the High Court of Australia, *supra*, at p. 519.
[50] See, *e.g.* the *Egan* and *Kratzmann* cases, illustrated *supra*, and see the discussion *post*, Chap. 12, para. 12–021.

reduction in potential damage as the work nears completion, thus militating against a "genuine pre-estimate of damage." The contrary view that such provisions can be reasonable is, however persuasively argued and explained in the judgments in the *Kratzmann* case in the Full Court of Queensland, noted *supra*.[51] Coupled with an undoubted increasing judicial tendency, most certainly in England, to view with approval any agreed procedures or remedies which offer savings in judicial time and administrative expense, and given the fact that producer pressures, again particularly in England, are resulting in progressively smaller retention percentages and limits on retention, invalidation of these types of clause as penalties seems today much less likely. Indeed, provided the sums stipulated are neither excessive nor oppressive, the modern tendency seems to be not to subject them to too close analysis.

10·021   Regular weekly or monthly figures for delay are even less open to attack on principle, since they correspond to the essentially reasonable concept of a running loss to the owner while out of occupation, and hence are only likely to be invalidated if they are wholly unreasonable in amount relative to the value of the completed project to the owner. Even here, their administrative convenience makes it increasingly difficult to attack successfully on this ground, except in the most obvious cases of excess. They are particularly suitable for projects which are not directly commercial in character, such as private houses, libraries, schools, subsidised housing and other public buildings and engineering works, where it may not be possible to prove any loss in the direct commercial sense if completion is delayed. It may be a consequence of producer influence, but there would appear in fact to be virtually no reported cases in the United Kingdom where periodical liquidated damages for delay in building contracts have been held excessive so as to constitute a penalty. Liquidated damages clauses in general are not looked on with the same disfavour at the present day, and modern disallowances seem to arise almost entirely in the field of hire-purchase, where Lord Dunedin's principle 4(c) above has frequently been violated.[52]

Finally, it is desirable to note again that liquidated damages clauses for delay by definition represent a pre-estimate of *all* (not some of) the owner's damages caused by delay in completion. So that if there is a fluctuations clause in the contract, the contractor will be entitled to increases in price under that clause during the period of delay, it is submitted, notwithstanding that, but for his own breach of contract, the work would have been done at lower prices and so would have cost the owner less. So too with other clauses, such as variation clauses, where the effect may be the

---

[51] See also the reasoning of the Supreme Court of Victoria in the *Bysouth* case, *supra*, and see particularly the passage in Mason and Wilson JJ.'s judgment in the High Court of Australia in *Amey-U.D.C. Finance Ltd.* v. *Austen* (1986) 162 C.L.R. 170, at p. 193, considered with other High Court authorities by Cole J. in *Multiplex Constructions Ltd.* v. *Abgarus Pty. Ltd.*, unreported, Sup.Ct., N.S.W. 1992 Case No. 55042, where liquidated damages for delay to a commercial development calculated on a "holding cost" (financing) basis were unsuccessfully attacked on that ground.
[52] See, *e.g. E.P. Finance Co. Ltd.* v. *Dooley* [1964] 1 All E.R. 527.

same. Where, however, there is no liquidated damages provision, the additional fluctuations clause payments will be recoverable by the owner, under the basic compensatory principle of damages for breach of contract.[53]

(3) Clauses Operating as Limitations on Damages

A clause stipulating a fixed liquidated periodical sum as damages for delay in completion may be intended by the parties, for good commercial reasons, including factors of price or even the unreadiness of a contractor or supplier to contract on other terms, to limit recoverable damage for delay below that likely to be incurred. Such a clause may make this clear expressly, but very often in construction contracts it will, on its face, be indistinguishable from an ordinary liquidated damages clause.   **10·022**

The very important case of *Elsley* v. *Collins Insurance* in the Supreme Court of Canada, illustrated *supra*, resolves a major uncertainty and shows persuasively that, where a clause is not for this reason a pre-estimate of the likely damage, it will nevertheless continue to be enforced as an upper limit on any damages claimed, whether the liquidated damages clause survives or not. Such a clause is, of course, the very reverse of a penalty, whose essential characteristic, which has earned its strict treatment by the courts, is the oppressive imposition of a financial liability in excess of the likely potential damage.

Although itself concerned with an attack on the original clause on the ground of its being a penalty, the *Elsley* case must equally be authority, it is submitted, for enforcing the sum as a limitation on liability in those situations where a liquidated damages clause has been invalidated by reason of owner prevention (typically, in the case of construction contracts, by the ordering of extras) or owner breach of contract (for example, failure to afford possession of the site or interference by other contractors). A substantial body of case law, complicated by interaction with the contractual provisions for extensions of time commonly found in construction contracts, has evolved concerning this latter basis for invalidation since the last century, and is considered in detail in Section 2, *infra*.

Whether a liquidated damages clause is indeed intended as a damage limitation clause may thus, in the absence of express wording, depend on external evidence showing the inadequacy of the stipulated sum as a pre-estimate of damage, although to avoid confusion well-advised parties should endeavour to make the position clear by express language. As has been seen in the *Arnhold* case, illustrated *supra*, and as will be seen in other contexts later in this chapter,[54] the parties' advisers in construction   **10·023**

---

[53] See *ante*, Chap. 8, para. 8–059, and for an example of this the case of *Peak Construction (Liverpool) Ltd.* v. *McKinney Foundations Ltd.* (1970) 69 L.G.R. 1 illustrated *infra*, para. 10–036.

[54] See, *e.g. Bramall & Ogden Ltd.* v. *Sheffield City Council* (1983) 29 BLR 73, *infra*, para. 10–061.

contracts are notoriously careless or incompetent in their drafting of the ad hoc documentation, in appendices or elsewhere, which is usually required to give monetary effect to a liquidated damages provision in a standard form of contract.

ILLUSTRATION

By Clause 24.2.1. of the 1980 RIBA/JCT form of contract, the owner, upon a certificate of failure to complete under Clause 24.1., was entitled to "a sum calculated at the rate stated in the Appendix" as liquidated damages from that date to practical completion. The "rate" under Clause 24.2. was inserted in the Appendix as "£nil", and the period for the payment was left blank. The owner claimed that the words meant that he was entitled to damages at large for delay in completion, from either the contract date or a reasonable date. *Held*, by the Court of Appeal, that the insertion of "£nil" in the Appendix was an exemption from all liability for delay in completion: *Temloc Ltd.* v. *Erril Properties Ltd.* (1987).[55]

[Note: It seems doubtful if this case should be treated as definitive authority where similar wording is used. The wording at best seems ambiguous, given the position of parties faced with a complicated standard form and desiring merely to avoid a fixed liability in all situations.]

SECTION 2. RELEASE OF LIQUIDATED DAMAGES

(1) Release by Prevention

10·024 It has been seen that for the purpose of treating the contract as repudiated, in the rare cases where time is of the essence, a stipulated date for completion may cease to be applicable for a variety of reasons, including the ordering of extras or other interference or prevention by the owner.[56] Similarly, a binding certificate may be avoided or dispensed with for the same reason.[57] In a case of damages for delay, it is equally obvious that, where the reason is some act of the owner (or his A/E) preventing completion by the due date, it cannot normally, as a matter of interpretation, be the intention of the parties[58] that damages, whether general or liquidated, should be calculated from that date even if the act, such as ordering extras, is not a breach of contract. In many cases, causation considerations will produce the same result.

Liquidated damages stipulated for at a rate for each day or week of delay in completing the works must begin to run from some definite contract completion date, whether specifically named in the contract or

---

[55] 39 BLR 30.
[56] See *ante*, Chap. 9, section (1).
[57] See *ante*, Chap. 6, section 5(4), para. 6–112.
[58] Despite the two quite exceptional cases illustrated below.

defined by reference to some event, such as an order to start work. It follows, therefore, that if the date in the contract has for some such reason ceased to be the proper date for the completion of the works, and no contractual provision exists for the substitution of a new date in the events which have happened, there is in such a case no date from which liquidated damages are to run and the right to liquidated damages will have been lost. This, at least as much as solicitude for the contractor, is the reason for the provision usually known as the extension of time clause.

It is essential for the understanding of the cases below to appreciate that the courts in the nineteenth century viewed any liquidated damages clause as probably being *in terrorem* and with the greatest dislike, and were ready to hold that it was invalidated by virtually any event not expressly contemplated by the contract and not within the contractor's sphere of responsibility. Against that background, an extension of time clause, which might prima facie appear to be inserted for the benefit of the contractor, would more properly be regarded as being for the benefit of the owner, since in a case of prevention or breach by the owner it would serve to keep alive a liquidated damages clause which otherwise, under the strict rules developed by the courts, be held to be invalidated, *provided that by its terms it enabled time to be extended for the breach or act of prevention in question.* For this reason, extension of time clauses were themselves most strictly construed, and only if a sufficiently explicit intention could be found for them to be operated in the particular circumstances involving prevention or breach by the owner or his A/E would they be permitted to save the liquidated damages clause where such circumstances had occurred. In particular, generalised grounds for an extension of time such as "any matter beyond the control of the contractor" or "any matter such as fairly to entitle the contractor to an extension of time" were held not to cover acts of prevention or breach by the owner.[59] Paradoxically, therefore, while so construed they appeared to deny the contractor an extension for a matter outside his control, and so to be adverse to his reasonable interest, such interpretations in fact greatly benefited him by striking down the clause in cases of prevention or breach.

Unless there is a sufficiently specific clause, it is not open to the owner or his A/E, where the contract date has ceased to be applicable, to make out a kind of debtor and creditor account allowing so many days or weeks for delay caused by the owner and, after crediting that period to the builder, to seek to charge him with damages at the liquidated rate for the remainder.[60] ("Day" in liquidated damages clauses includes holidays and Sundays, unless "working days" are specifically referred to.[61]) This will be so

10·025

---

[59] It is noteworthy that Clause 44 of the pre-1973 ICE form of contract did not appear to have been drafted with this part of the law in mind, and accordingly, apart from the ordering of extras, which was specifically referred to in the clause, contracts still using that wording were vulnerable. See the *Perini Pacific* case, illustrated *infra*, para. 10·036.

[60] This was unsuccessfully argued in *Dodd* v. *Churton, infra*, and many later cases, such as *Perini Pacific* v. *Greater Vancouver Sewerage* (1966) 57 D.L.R. (2d) 307, *infra*.

[61] *Brown* v. *Johnson* (1842) 10 M. & W. 331.

even if the event in question can be precisely assessed in terms of delay, such as a late start due to owner default, and not confused with contractor-caused delays, which may make separate quantification controversial or difficult.[62]

As will be seen in the following cases, even where the contract contains a clause empowering the A/E or owner to award an extension of time in general terms, the courts have been reluctant to construe such a clause as giving the A/E or owner power to extend the time in circumstances where the delay has in fact been caused by the act of the owner or his agents.[63] In principle, however, there is no objection to this provided the contract is sufficiently explicit.[64]

In considering the cases, which are not all easy to reconcile, it should be realised that many of them were decided on demurrer, and that when the right to liquidated damages disappeared, the right to recover actual damages subject to proof, would remain. This latter right will operate, as from the ending of a reasonable time for completion, the contract date having gone.[65] However, it seems clear that an owner, having invalidated a liquidated damages clause and contract date by his own act of prevention or breach, will not be permitted to recover a larger weekly or other sum as unliquidated damages on establishing failure to complete within a reasonable time, in the same way as where sums are held to be a penalty.[66]

10·026   In conclusion it should perhaps be stated that the prevention principles to be derived from the cases now seem clear, and not difficult for an expert draughtsman to understand, at least in the context of the liquidated damages clauses in construction contracts, and their associated extension of time clauses. No doubt the better reason for the strict traditional view about the effect of prevention is that the most important practical function of liquidated damages clauses is to confer a power to deduct the damages immediately from moneys due to the contractor on interim certificate once the completion date or extended date has passed. Thus the need for certainty as to the date upon which they will become deductible (particularly where, as is often the case, termination for non-payment provisions also exist) is inconsistent with some retrospective informal reduction of the period of delay to take account of the acts of the owner, if the process has not been specifically authorised and regulated by the contract itself.[67]

---

[62] See this particular situation variously commented on in *Holme* v. *Guppy* (1838) 3 M. & W. 387; *McElroy* v. *Tharsis Sulphur Co.* (1877) 5 R. (Ct. of Sess.) 161, and by Lloyd L.J. in *Rapid Building Group Ltd.* v. *Ealing Family Housing Association Ltd.* (1984) 29 BLR 5.

[63] See also, *infra*, Section 3, "Extension of Time", and for prevention more generally see also Chap. 6, Section 5(4), paras. 6–112 *et seq.*

[64] *Cf.* Clause 23(f) (late instructions) and 23(h) (other contractors of the employer) in the 1963 RIBA standard forms. Except in relation to extras, the 1955 ICE form was not sufficiently explicit: see Clause 44 and the use of the expression "other special circumstances of any kind whatsoever", and the note to the *Perini Pacific* case, *infra*, para. 10–036.

[65] See *ante*, Chap. 9.

[66] See *Elsley* v. *Collins Insurance Agencies Ltd.* (1978) 2 S.C.R. 1, *supra*.

[67] See *Peak Construction (Liverpool) Ltd.* v. *McKinney Foundations Ltd.* (1970) 69 L.G.R. 1, illustrated *infra*, which confirms the law as here stated.

ILLUSTRATIONS

(1) Contractors, who were bound to pay liquidated damages for failure to   **10·027**
complete joinery at a brewery within the stipulated time of four and a half
months, were prevented from starting by the defendant's other workmen.
After conclusion of evidence, it was agreed that this caused a delay of four
weeks, while the contractors were in default later to the extent of one week.
Held, by Parke B., there being nothing to show a new contract to perform in
four and a half months ending at a later date, liquidated damages could not be
deducted from the contractor's claim for the price of the work: *Holme* v.
Guppy (1838).[68]

(2) A contractor agreed to build a railway for a lump sum. By a subsequent
contract, on the owners agreeing to pay a further £15,000 and to supply certain rails and chairs, he undertook to complete by a certain date, and to pay
liquidated damages if he failed to do so. The owners sought to deduct liquidated damages, and the contractor alleged that the delay was due to non-
delivery of the promised rails and chairs. *Held*, by the Court of Exchequer,
overruling Pollock C.B., that the covenant to supply rails and chairs was independent of the covenant to complete, as otherwise non-delivery of one rail or
chair would excuse the contractor from performance, and that liquidated
damages could be deducted; but if the contractor had in reality been
prevented from completing to time, his remedy was a separate claim for
damages for breach of the covenant to deliver, which would include the liquidated damages he had been compelled to pay: *Macintosh* v. *Midland Counties
Railway* (1845).[69]

[Note: The "separate claim" would now be an equitable set-off and available as a defence.[70] But it is submitted that in the light of later authorities the
principle as stated is incorrect, and in fact no right to liquidated damages
could arise once prevention was established in the absence of an applicable
extension of the time clause.]

(3) A builder sued for the balance due under a contract which provided for   **10·028**
completion by a fixed date, and for liquidated damages of £1 per day for delay
in completion. There was a power to order extra work, and the builder was
expressly to be allowed "so much extra time beyond the completion date as
might be necessary" to do the additional work. There were 31 days' delay, and
the owners pleaded that nine were due to the extra works, and 22 were the
fault of the builder. The builder argued that, once extras were ordered, the
contract date had gone and that the owner was entitled only to general and
not to liquidated damages. *Held*, by the Court of Queen's Bench, on demurrer, that liquidated damages might be deducted for the 22 days: *Legge* v. *Harlock* (1848).[71]

(4) A building owner sought to deduct penalties from the contract sum in
respect of 12 weeks' delay. The contractors replied that, by a subsequent
agreement, they had undertaken to carry out certain extra works, that these
were mixed up with the original work, and it was thereby impossible to complete the original work to time, and that all the work had been completed

---

[68] 3 M. & W. 387. (No extension of time clause in this case.)
[69] 14 M. & W. 548.
[70] See *ante*, Chap. 6, para. 6–194 *et seq.*, and *post*, Chap. 14, Section 5(5), para. 14·049.
[71] 12 Q.B. 1015.

within a reasonable time. *Held*, by the Court of Common Pleas, on demurrer, this was a good answer to the claim for penalties: *Thornhill* v. *Neats* (1860).[72]

10·029   (5) A ship building contract provided for liquidated damages for failure to deliver complete by a certain day. If the ship was not so delivered *for any cause not under the control of the builders*, to be proved to the satisfaction of the owner's agent and certified by him, the liquidated damages were not to be enforced for the number of days specified in the certificate. There was very considerable delay, a substantial proportion of which (six weeks) was due to interference by the owners. *Held*, by the Court of Common Pleas (Erle C.J. and Keating J.). following *Holme* v. *Guppy, supra,* that no liquidated damages might be deducted: *Russell* v. *Viscount Sa da Bandeira* (1862).[73]

[Note: The extension of time clause for any cause, "not under the control" of the builders seems to have been largely ignored in this case, but the subsequent cases (see *Wells* v. *Army & Navy Co-op. Society, infra* show that this wording would not be construed to include acts of the owner within its ambit, so that it would not have saved the liquidated damages clause.]

(6) A building contract authorised the engineer to order additions and alterations and to ascertain their value and: "if by reason thereof he should consider it necessary to extend the time for completion of the work, such extension of time shall be given in writing under his hand, or otherwise the time of completion shall be deemed to be not extended." Extra work was ordered, rendering, so it was alleged, performance within the stipulated time impossible. *Held*, by the Q.B. Divisional Court (Wightman and Crompton JJ.), on demurrer and following *Holme* v. *Guppy,* that while ascertainment of the variations by the engineer was a condition precedent to recovery, if the additions made it impossible to complete the work to time, liquidated damages could not be deducted: *Westwood* v. *Secretary of State for India* (1863).[74]

[Note: It is submitted that the express wording of the extension of time clause in this case should have been given effect to: see, *e.g. Sattin* v. *Poole, infra* and that this case was for this reason wrongly decided.]

10·030   (7) An engineering contract contained an extension of time clause under which *it was lawful* for the architect to give an extension of time, *inter alia,* for failure to supply drawings or directions to the contractor in time. There was a separate forfeiture clause empowering the owners to terminate the contract if, in the opinion of the architect, the contractor failed to proceed with due diligence. The contractors sued for wrongful termination, and the owners pleaded that the architect had certified that the contractor had not proceeded with due diligence. The contractors replied that the delay was due to failure to supply plans and drawings and to set out the land. *Held*, on demurrer, by a majority of the Court of Exchequer Chamber, that the architect had no jurisdiction to bind the contractor as to these matters *under the forfeiture clause,* and (*per* Blackburn and Mellor JJ.) that the extension of time clause, by reason of its permissive language, on its true construction only enabled the architect to bind the owners, not the contractors, by any extension of time he might give. The latter would only be bound if they applied for and accepted his decison: *Roberts* v. *Bury Commissioners* (1870).[75]

[Note: It should be pointed out that this latter ground was not necessary for the decision and was expressed by only two out of six judges. The basis of the

---

[72] 8 C.B.(N.S.) 831; and see *Courtnay* v. *Waterford Ry.* (1878) 4 L.R.Ir. 11, illustrated, *ante*, Chap. 9, para. 9–010. The *Thornhill* pleading seems to have been used as a precedent or model in many subsequent cases.

[73] 13 C.B.(N.S.) 149.

[74] 7 L.T. 736, 1 New Rep. 262.

[75] L.R. 5 C.P. 310.

decision (which it is submitted was correct) was that the extension of time clause had no connection with the forfeiture clause, and that the architect's opinion under the latter clause could not be binding when prevention by the other party was alleged. The dicta based on the form of wording seem difficult to support, it is submitted.]

(8) A contractor undertook to build and complete a farmhouse and build-   **10·031**
ings by a named date in accordance with specifications and plans, but subject to extras, alterations or additions which might be made, and to pay liquidated damages for failure to complete, the decision of the owner's inspector as to the time within which they should have been executed to be final. The agreement further provided that no extra works should be undertaken without an order signed by the clerk of works, and in the event of any alteration or addition being ordered, the plaintiff should carry out the original works, with such alterations and additions, in the same manner as if they had been originally comprised in the works of the contract, *and the period for completing the entire works should not exceed the contract period unless a written extension of time was given*. Extras were ordered, and no extension of time was given, although it was alleged that the extras rendered completion by the stipulated date impossible. *Held*, by the Court of Queen's Bench (Mellor, Lush and Hannen JJ.) on demurrer, distinguishing *Roberts* v. *Bury Commissioners, supra*, that on the true construction of the contract the contractors had undertaken to complete by the stipulated date, whatever extras might be ordered, unless relieved by the decision of the clerk of works as to extension of time, which was to be binding: *Jones* v. *St. John's College Oxford* (1870).[76]

[Note: Although later cases have sought to distinguish it, this case does no more than hold that an adverse extension of time decision was binding, it is submitted.]

(9) The contract period was 12 months, with liquidated damages of £50 per week. Due to delays by other contractors or sub-contractors, possession could not be given and work could admittedly not start for a period of time which was itself not disputed. *Held*, by the Court of Session, that the contract could not be treated as one to complete the work in 12 months after the date of obtaining possession, since there were specified contract dates for possession and completion which might be of commercial importance to the contractor and, following the English cases, the liquidated damages clause was avoided and the owner must prove his actual damage: *M'Elroy* v. *Tharsis Sulphur Co.* (1877).[77]

(10) A builder undertook to complete the works "with such addition,   **10·032**
enlargement or alteration of, and deviation from the said work, if any" by a certain date. The architect was given power to extend the time for completion in proportion to extras or alterations ordered by him. Extras were ordered which the jury found prevented completion to time, but no extension was made. *Held*, by Smith J., distinguishing *Russell* v. *Viscount Sa da Bandeira, supra*, and following *Jones* v. *St. John's College*, that liquidated damages might be deducted: *Tew* v. *Newbold-on-Avon United District School Board* (1884).[78]

(11) A building contract authorised the ordering of extra work, which was not to vitiate the contract, but contained no extension of time clause. There was a completion date and a provision for liquidated damages. Extras were ordered, which necessarily delayed completion. In an action by the builder for

---

[76] L.R. 6 Q.B. 115.
[77] 5 Rettie (Ct. of Sess.) 161. Compare Parke B.'s reasoning in *Holme* v. *Guppy, supra*.
[78] 1 C. & E. 260. (The same comment applies as to the *Jones* case *supra*.)

the price, the owner claimed to set off liquidated damages for delay, less a fortnight which he claimed was adequate allowance for the extras. *Held*, by the Court of Appeal, following *Westwood* v. *S. of S. for India, Holme* v. *Guppy*, and *Russell* v. *Viscount Sa da Bandeira*, and distinguishing *Jones* v. *St. John's College*, where there was an extension clause, the provision for liquidated damages could no longer be applied: *Dodd* v. *Churton* (1897).[79]

10·033

(12) A New Zealand building contract empowered the architect to award an extension of time *at the time of giving the order* if extras ordered by him caused delay and the architect was to be absolute judge of the time to be allowed. The architect ordered extras, with the knowledge of the owner, but not in writing, and did not grant an extension at that time, although he certified for payment in full at the end of the contract. The owner relied on the absence of a proper extension and sought to deduct liquidated damages. *Held*, by Prendergast C.J., that under the terms of the contract, orders for extras were required to be in writing, without which the contractor could not recover for their value. The extension of time clause, on its true construction, only applied to extras ordered in accordance with the contract, and the architect accordingly had no power to give an extension of time for improperly ordered extras, so that, the contractor having been prevented from completing by acts of the owner outside the extension of time clause, liquidated damages could not be deducted: *Murdoch* v. *Lockie* (1897).[80]

(13) An owner in New Zealand ordered extras personally, but not in writing as required by the contract, and in such number and of such a size that the final work bore no resemblance to the work as planned. *Held*, by Stout C.J., that by their nature the extras were outside the contract and that, as they had prevented completion by the stipulated date, the damages were set at large and liquidated damages could not be deducted: *Meyer* v. *Gilmer* (1899).[81]

10·034

(14) A builder undertook (by clause 23) to complete by a certain date subject to provisions for extension of time contained in the contract. These (clause 24) provided that the architect "shall make a fair and reasonable extension of time" in respect of, *inter alia*, extras or delay in receipt of instructions from the architect. There was considerable delay, and after completion the builders applied for an extension of time. The architect did not reply at once, and the builders issued a writ based on the sum of £681 certified by the architect as due, subject to penalties. After issue of the writ, the architect wrote extending the time, but not for the whole of the delay, and certified that £231 was due as liquidated damages. The builders wished to call evidence to show that the delay was due to the ordering of extras, lack of information, and other matters involving breach of contract by the owner. *Held*, by the King's Bench Division (Bruce and Phillimore JJ.), distinguishing *Roberts* v. *Bury Commissioners* on the ground that the language of the extension of time clause there was permissive and not mandatory, and also that there was no provision in that case whereby the builder undertook to be bound by the architect's decision as in clause 23 of the present contract, that the evidence was rightly excluded and the liquidated damages certified for must be deducted: *Sattin* v. *Poole* (1901).[82]

(15) Builders undertook to erect buildings for a company within a year, unless delayed by alterations, strikes, sub-contractors "*or other causes*

---

[79] [1897] 1 Q.B. 562, and see *Fuller* v. *The Queen* (1878) 3 J.R.N.S.(S.C.) 125.
[80] 15 N.Z.L.R. 296. See also *Parle* v. *Leistikow* (1883) 4 N.S.W.L.R. 84.
[81] 18 N.Z.L.R. 129. See *ante*, Chap. 7, Section 2(2)(d), para. 7·082, where this case is more fully illustrated.
[82] Hudson, *Building Contracts* (4th ed.), Vol. 2, p. 306.

beyond the contractor's control". By clause 16, the decision of the directors of the company in matters of time was to be final, and liquidated damages were payable if the work was not completed within a time considered reasonable by them. There was one year's delay. The principal cause was sub-contractors, for which the directors were prepared to allow three months. The builders contended that this was insufficient, and also that the delay was due to alterations (*i.e.* within the ambit of clause 16) and also to delay in giving possession and providing plans. *Held*, by the Court of Appeal, that on the evidence there was substance in all these complaints, and it was impossible to say to what extent each one contributed to the delay, but the words "or other causes beyond the contractor's control" could not include the breaches of contract or other acts of the owners in not giving possession and failing to supply plans and drawings in due time, and consequently liquidated damages could not be deducted: *Wells* v. *Army and Navy Co-Op. Society Ltd.* (1902).[83]

(16) A contractor undertook to construct a dredge in New Zealand in a **10·035** contract period of eight months with a completion date in November. The owner was to prepare a site and road access for the construction, but in the event did not make the site available until October, although the contractors were not in fact delayed since they themselves lacked timber for the necessary work. However, the site had not been prepared by the owner, so that when the contractors started work they were delayed by a fortnight carrying out the preparation work themselves. Later in December extra work was ordered which caused further delay. The contractors argued that the liquidated damages clause no longer applied, first, because of the delay caused by the owner in October and, secondly, because of the extras ordered after the completion date in December. *Held*, by Williams J. (a) that following *Holme* v. *Guppy, Russell* v. *Viscount Sa da Bandeira* and *Dodd* v. *Churton*, while the failure to provide the site itself caused no delay, the failure to prepare the site had, in the absence of an applicable extension of time clause, invalidated the liquidated damages clause and (b) that even if the liquidated damages had started to run before the variations were ordered in December they would cease to be recoverable thereafter: *Baskett* v. *Bendigo Gold-Dredging Co. Ltd.* (1902).[84]

(17) A bridge construction company contracted with a railway company to complete the superstructure by a named date, with liquidated damages for delay in completion. The railway company in a separate contract with the bridge company had undertaken to complete the substructure by a named date, which they failed to do, although the contractor's main cause of delay was shortage of steel. *Held*, by the Supreme Court of Canada, Nesbitt and Idington JJ. dissenting on the facts, and following *Dodd* v. *Churton*, that, in the absence of proof that the railway company had not delayed the bridge company, the liquidated damages were not recoverable: *Ottawa Northern and Western Railway Co.* v. *Dominion Bridge Co.* (1905).[85]

(18) A contract for the construction of a sewage disposal plant permitted an **10·036** extension of time for "extras or delays occasioned by strikes, lockouts, *force majeure or other cause beyond the control of the contractor*". Liquidated damages were to be $1,000 *per* day. There was a delay of 99 days, and an extension of time for 46 days, and the owner accordingly sued for $53,000. The trial judge found that 45 days' delay had been caused by the owner's delivery of certain machinery in a defective condition requiring considerable repair

---

[83] 86 L.T. 764, followed by the Court of Appeal in *Peak Construction* v. *McKinney Foundations Ltd.* (1970) 69 L.G.R. 1. See also *Gallivan* v. *Killarney Urban District Council* [1912] 2 I.R. 356, illustrated *infra*, Section 3(3), para. 10·074.
[84] 21 N.Z.L.R. 166.
[85] 36 S.C.R. 347.

work, and that this was a breach of contract by the owner. He accordingly awarded $8,000 liquidated damages. *Held*, by the Court of Appeal of British Columbia, applying *Wells* v. *Army & Navy Co-Op. Society Ltd.*, that on these facts no liquidated damages could be recovered: *Perini Pacific Ltd.* v. *Greater Vancouver Sewerage* (1966).[86]

[Note: This case is of considerable importance, because for all practical purposes the extension of time clause is similar to that in the English fourth edition (pre-1973) ICE conditions, since it has been followed in many overseas contracts which will be similarly invalidated if a part of the contractor's total delay can be shown to be due to any act or omission (other than the ordering of extras) of the owner.[87]]

(19) Under a main contract with a local authority there was an extension of time clause for additions to the works, strikes, *force majeure* "or other unavoidable circumstances". Some of a piling sub-contractor's column bases were discovered to be defective when columns were about to be erected, leading to a suspension of work and reconsideration of the design. The sub-contractor put forward remedial measures which he was prepared to carry out at once free of charge, but the authority inordinately delayed approving the remedial measures, although they had been quickly approved and recommended by an independent engineer called in by them. The authority then deducted liquidated damages in the main contract for the entire period of suspension until they authorised recommencement of work. The main contractor in effect passed on all the authority's claims by seeking to recover from the sub-contractor (a) the liquidated damages for the whole period, and also (b) all payments due under a labour fluctuations clause during the entire delay period after the contract completion date, which the authority had refused to pay. *Held*, by the Court of Appeal, following *Holme* v. *Guppy* and *Wells* v. *Army & Navy, etc.* that: (a) since the owner was responsible for a part of the suspension, and since no applicable extension of time clause covering the owner's delay existed, the liquidated damages clause could no longer be invoked, and the owner was left to recover such damages as he could prove over a reasonable period, which could in turn be passed on to the sub-contractor; and (b) on the basis of the owner's claims for delay now being the actual damage suffered by him, the true measure would be the much smaller sum whereby the fluctuations payments under the main contract were increased by the delay caused by the sub-contractor, compared with what would have been payable under the fluctuations clause but for that delay: *Peak Construction (Liverpool) Ltd.* v. *McKinney Foundations Ltd.* (1970).[88]

10·037　　　(20) A builder in Victoria sued for moneys due on three houses, and the defendant owner sought to set off and counterclaim for liquidated damages for delay in completion. The builder replied, first, that prolonged strikes had frustrated the provisions of the contract relating to completion so that liquidated damages were not recoverable or, secondly, that the owner had obstructed and protracted the time for completion by failure to give full possession, the ordering of extra work, and failure to obtain a necessary local authority permit. The owner applied to strike out these contentions. *Held*, by

---

[86] (1966) 57 D.L.R. (2d) 307, Canada. There was no appeal to the Supreme Court of Canada from this part of the decision: see [1967] S.C.R. 189. See note on this case *infra*. In addition to the cases above, see also *A.B.C. Ltd.* v. *Waltham Holy Cross Urban District Council* [1952] 2 All E.R. 452.

[87] See Clause 44, ICE Conditions, (fourth edition).

[88] (1970) 69 L.G.R. 1. Had liquidated damages been applicable, nothing more would have been recoverable for fluctuations.

Menhennitt J., as to strikes, frustration could only apply to the entire contract, and the allegation should be struck out. As to the prevention allegations, completion to time provisions could be rendered inapplicable by the acts of a party only: (1) if a term was to be implied in the contract which produced that result; or (2) if there had been a variation of the contract itself to produce that result; or possibly (3) if there was an estoppel. On the pleadings as they stood, there was no allegation of an implied term or varied agreement or estoppel, and the reply should be struck out, but the plaintiff should be at liberty to re-plead: *Aurel Forras Ltd.* v. *Graham Karp Developments Ltd.* (1974).[89]

[Note: Menhennitt J. made an exhaustive examination of all the cases illustrated at this point in the tenth edition, as well as of a number of other cases, before reaching his conclusion that the prevention principle depends upon the implication of a term. While the precise basis of the principle may be debated, it is submitted that, if based upon an implied term, the term would be one to be *implied by law* in construction contracts, and probably in many other classes of contract generally, rather than made dependent upon the facts of a particular transaction under business efficacy principles.[90] It is a clear inference from the judgment that once an implied term was alleged this part of the plaintiff's pleading would be allowed to stand. However, Menhennitt J.'s views on this point were clearly not shared by Brooking J. in the Full Court of Victoria in the well-researched and persuasive discussion of the juridical basis for prevention invalidating liquidated damages in the *SMK Cabinets* case, illustrated *infra*.]

(21) The extension of time clause in a New Zealand roadworks contract **10·038** provided that: "Extensions of time will be allowed for delays caused by other contractors on the site, delays in installation of services *or exceptional circumstances*. Extensions of time will not be granted for ... inclement weather which would normally be expected during the contract period." The arbitrator found that there had been 41 weeks of delay for which extensions should be granted, and awarded liquidated damages to the owner for five weeks of delay.[91] Of the 41 weeks, he had awarded 23 weeks for delays said to result from failure by the owner to make prompt payment against the engineer's payment certificates on three occasions, as a result of which the contractor had allegedly reduced labour on the site. *Held*, by Roper J., citing *Perini Pacific Ltd.* v. *Greater Vancouver Sewerage and Drainage District*, the question was not whether the engineer should have granted an extension of time for the owner's breach in delaying payment, but whether that breach relieved the contractor of his liability under the liquidated damages clause. The engineer had had no jurisdiction to extend time on the ground of non-payment, and following the *Perini* case the contractor was not liable to pay liquidated damages: *Fernbrook Trading Co. Ltd.* v. *Taggart* (1979).[92]

[Note: The question of causation and the legal justification for "going slow" appear to have been resolved in the contractor's favour without much consideration or objection in this case.[93]]

(22) Under a 1963 RIBA/JCT form of contract to build 101 houses, the contractor was delayed at the start for a period not exceeding 24 days because of a man and his wife and a dog squatting in an old Austin Cambridge car with various packing cases in one corner of the site. The architect extended time, but the contractor finished some 10 months late and the owners sought to

---

[89] [1975] V.R. 202.
[90] See for this distinction *ante*, Chap. 1, para. 1·181.
[91] [1984] V.R. 391, at pp. 394–396.
[92] [1979] 1 N.Z.L.R. 556.
[93] See *Canterbury Pipe Lines* v. *Christchurch Drainage Board* [1979] 2 N.Z.L.R. 347, discussed *ante*, Chap. 4, Section 3(1)(f) para. 4·223, and illustrated *ante*, para. 6·134.

deduct liquidated damages from the sums due under the contract. The Official Referee, following the *Peak* case, rejected the owner's claim for liquidated damages and gave summary judgment with interest. The owners appealed, claiming unconditional leave to defend. *Held*, by the Court of Appeal, while it was common ground that, on the authority of the *Peak* case, liquidated damages were not recoverable on these facts, general damages of sufficient magnitude to extinguish the claim had prima facie been incurred, and there should be leave to defend. *Per* Loyd L.J.: "I was somewhat startled to be told ... that if any part of the delay was caused by the employer, no matter how slight, then the liquidated damages clause in the contract ... becomes inoperative. I can well understand how that must necessarily be so in a case in which the delay is indivisible, and there is a dispute as to the extent of the employer's responsibility for that delay. But where there are, as it were, two separate and distinct periods of delay with two separate causes, then it would seem to me just and convenient that the employer should be able to claim liquidated damages in relation to the other period ... but it was common ground before us that that is not a possible view ... in the light of the decision of the Court of Appeal in *Peak's* case, and therefore I say no more about it": *Rapid Building Group Ltd.* v. *Ealing Family Housing Association Ltd.* (1984).[94]

10·039   (23) A contractor agreed in May 1980 to supply and install cupboards in a dwelling house before July 15, 1980, with an extension of time for weather, for a price of $2,000. A liquidated damages clause provided for $35 liquidated damages per day as from July 22, 1980. There was a variation clause permitting variations by agreement only, but it made no mention of an extension of time. The contractor only started work about the time for completion, and on or shortly after July 22, one variation, and later others, were ordered, and the works were not completed until much later. The arbitrator found that the variations had delayed completion, but rejected the defence of prevention on the ground that the contractor would not have completed to time in any event. *Held*, by the Full Court of Victoria, (a) that in the absence of an extension of time clause, or unless the contractor undertakes to complete notwithstanding extras or variations, liquidated damages cannot be recovered if completion has been delayed by extras or variations; (b) following *Baskett* v. *Bendigo Gold-Dredging Co. Ltd.* and a dictum of Martin J. in *Anderson* v. *Tuapeka*[95] that extras or variations *ordered after the due completion date* which delay ultimate completion will bring the right to recover liquidated damages to an end, but will not affect liquidated damages already accrued prior to the order; and (c) that it is immaterial that at the date of ordering the variations the contractor is as a result of his own delays unable to complete by the due date: *SMK Cabinets* v. *Hili Modern Electrics Pty. Ltd.* (1984).[96]
[Note: The last finding may be somewhat misleading as expressed. The judgment does not mean that variations or other acts *which cause no additional delay beyond that already incurred by the contractor* will invalidate the clause (*i.e.* which are not on the contractor's "critical path"). Some additional delay in ultimate completion beyond that already incurred by the contractor must be caused by the owner if it is to invalidate the clause.[97]]

---

[94] 29 BLR 5.
[95] (1900) 19 N.Z.L.R. 1.
[96] [1984] V.R. 391. This case is commented on and in some respects doubted or qualified *infra*, Subsection (2), para. 10·044, and see the recent *Balfour Beatty* case, illustrated *infra*, para. 10·046.
[97] See the *Bendigo* case.

It is submitted that the effect to the preceding cases is as follows: **10·040**

(a) that acts of prevention by the owner, whether authorised by or breaches of the contract, will set time at large and invalidate any liquidated damages clause, in the absence of an applicable extension of time clause.[98] Variations whether authorised under the original contract or subsequently agreed, will be regarded as acts of prevention (or of waiver) for this purpose;

(b) that where the act of prevention or waiver goes to part of the delay but not of the whole, the entire liquidated damages clause will still be invalidated,[99] unless an applicable extension of time clause exists[1];

(c) that where there is an extension of time clause, this is regarded as being inserted for the benefit of the owner, to the extent that it may operate to keep alive the liquidated damages clause in the event of delay due to waiver, prevention or breach by the owner or his agents.[2] Where it does not cover the acts of waiver, prevention or breach which have in fact occurred, no decision by a certifier under the clause can bind the builder, or preserve the liquidated damages clause[3];

(d) that general or ambiguous words in an extension of time clause, such as "exceptional circumstances", or "any matters beyond the control of the builder", or "other special circumstances of any kind whatsoever which may occur such as fairly to entitle the contractor to an extension of time"[4] will not for this reason, be construed so as to cover waiver, prevention or breach of contract by the owner or his A/E[5];

(e) but that where the extension of time clause sufficiently clearly covers the owner's waiver, prevention or breach, the liquidated damages clause will be unaffected and will apply[6];   **10·041**

---

[98] *Holme* v. *Guppy*; *Thornhill* v. *Neats*; *Dodd* v. *Churton*; *Wells* v. *Army and Navy Co-op. Society*, *supra*.

[99] *Holme* v. *Guppy*; *Russell* v. *Viscount Sa da Bandeira*; *Dodd* v. *Churton*; *Ottawa North and Western Rly.* v. *Dominion Bridge*; *Wells* v. *Army and Navy Co-op.*; *Peak Construction Ltd.* v. *McKinney Foundations Ltd.*; *Fernbrook Trading Co. Ltd.* v. *Taggart*; *Rapid Building Group Ltd.* v. *Ealing Family Housing Association*; all *supra*.

[1] *Legge* v. *Harlock* (1848) 12 Q.B. 1015.

[2] See *post*, Section 3.

[3] *Murdoch* v. *Luckie*; *Meyer* v. *Gilmer*; *Wells* v. *Army and Navy Co-op. Society*; *Peak* v. *McKinney*. See also *Gallivan* v. *Killarney Urban District Council* [1912] 2 I.R. 356, *infra*, Section 3, para. 10·074. The clause will be equally inoperable in the hands of an arbitrator, it is submitted.

[4] See, *e.g.* Clause 44 of the 1954 and 1973 ICE conditions.

[5] *Wells* v. *Army and Navy Co-op. Society*; *Perini Pacific Ltd.* v. *Greater Vancouver Sewerage*; *Peak* v. *McKinney*; *Fernbrook Trading* v. *Taggart*; *Russell* v. *Viscount Sa da Bandeira*. Contrast, however, the different context of compensatory provisions, where similar words have been held to *include* nominated sub-contractors' defaults: see *Scott Lithgow Ltd.* v. *Secretary of State for Defence* (1989) 45 BLR 1, illustrated *ante*, para. 5·037 and discussed and doubted in (1991) 7 Const.L.J. 3.

[6] *Legge* v. *Harlock*, illustrated *supra*.

(f) a contract may seek to make an A/E's extension of time decisions binding, in the same way as any other certificate of the A/E.[7] If so, in the absence of an applicable extension of time provision, prevention or breach by the owner will, it is submitted, avoid the effect of or need for a certificate, since the certifier will have no jurisdiction to decide whether work has been delayed by such matters.[8] However, if an applicable extension of time clause does exist, and the remaining contract provisions warrant it, the decision will be binding.[9] This is subject to the fact that most modern contracts enable the certifier's decision to be reviewed by an arbitrator or, failing that, by the courts.[9a];

(g) there may be a *very* rare class of case where a contractor undertakes to complete by a certain date, whatever extras may be ordered by the owner and notwithstanding the existence of a liquidated damages clause. Apart from the inherent commercial improbability of such an interpretation, it seems doubtful if any modern court would have so construed the contractor's obligation as worded in *Jones* v. *St. John's College, Oxford*, illustrated *supra*, and the true explanation of the case lay in the very specific wording of its variation clause making the owner's inspector's decision on the matter final. The case appears to have been followed once, by Smith J. at *nisi prius* in *Tew's* case, *supra*, and later courts have clearly had some difficulty in explaining it, while invariably distinguishing it.[10] While the later cases frequently do refer to the possibility of an undertaking of this unqualified kind being given by a contractor, this seems primarily to be in an effort to explain and then distinguish the *Jones* case, rather than a serious expectation that such cases are likely to be found.

10·042   Apart altogether from the owner prevention cases, the possibility that a natural event, such as an earthquake or volcanic eruption or tidal wave, may, if sufficiently unforeseeable, operate in law as an "Act of God", so as to absolve a person either wholly or in part from the performance of an obligation, though this doctrine has usually been applied to obligations in tort rather than contract.[11]

It should be repeated, before passing from this highly technical subject, that the failure of the liquidated damages clause will not prevent unliquidated damages being obtained for failure to complete within a reasonable

[7] See *ante*, Chap. 6, Sections 3 and 4.
[8] *Murdoch* v. *Luckie*, and see *ante*, Chap. 6, Section 5, paras. 6·112 *et seq.*, and the case of *Gallivan* v. *Killarney Urban District Council* [1912] 2 I.R. 356, illustrated *infra*.
[9] *Jones* v. *St. John's College, Oxford, Tew* v. *Newbold-on-Avon*.
[9a] See *ante*, Chap. 6, Sections 3 and 4 for binding certificates generally, and see the cases of *Ramac* v. *Lesser* and *Brightside Kilpatrick* v. *Mitchell Construction* illustrated *ante*, paras. 6·075 and 6·087.
[10] See the discussion in *Murdoch* v. *Lockie* (1896) 15 N.Z.L.R. 296, at pp. 307 *et seq.*
[11] See the discussion *ante*, Chap. 4, para. 4·265 and the case of *Ryde* v. *Bushell* [1967] E.A. 817, East African Court of Appeal, there referred to.

or stipulated time, subject, however, to any stipulated damages or penalty being the upper limit of any sums recoverable.[12]

(2) Prevention by Late Variations

During the past few years, a problem has become recognised under the **10·043** traditional drafting of liquidated damages provisions, most of which require, as a necessary part of their machinery, the ascertainment or certification of a date by which the work should have been completed after any proper extensions, and the subsequent deduction of liquidated damages from interim payment as one of the remedies available to the owner. In situations where the owner desires to order variations during the period of what may be described as "culpable delay" (that is, where liquidated damages have already begun to run after the completion or extended completion date), contractors have frequently sought to argue that the owner's power to order variations has lapsed, so that, if variations are then insisted upon, they set time at large in the same way as an act of prevention.[13] Contractors or their advisers then not infrequently seek to negotiate on the basis of a refusal to carry out any further variations unless the owner will agree to forgo liquidated damages. Again, almost invariably, this situation is not expressly dealt with by the standard form draftsman.

It should be appreciated that, the worse the delay on the part of the contractor has been the more incomplete will be the state of the work when the contract or extended completion date arrives, so that it will be all the more likely, and indeed reasonable, for the owner to wish to exercise his right to order such variations as may then seem desirable at this early stage, however long past the date for completion itself.

The owner's difficulty will often be compounded by the fact that the **10·044** liquidated damages provisions in most modern contracts, as previously explained, will contemplate and depend on a certificate or decision recording the date on which the work ought to have been completed, after allowing for any permitted extensions of time, and from which liquidated damages will then start to run, but do not make provision for any further adjustment of the completion date to take account of later events after that certificate, such as variations ordered during the period of culpable delay, nor for the later adjustment of liquidated damages and their deduction in that event. As a result, the position of the contractor refusing to carry out a variation without concessions by the owner during the period of culpable delay will to that extent be encouraged by the weakness of the contract, and his arguments that unliquidated damages should cease to be payable, or even be repaid, may seem at least superficially supported by the earlier case law on release by prevention.

---

[12] Finally established by the valuable decision of the Supreme Court of Canada in *Elsley* v. *Collins Insurance Agencies Ltd.*, illustrated *supra*, para. 10·016.

[13] For an example of the point being raised on appeal from an arbitrator, see *Bramall & Ogden* v. *Sheffield City Council* (1983) 29 BLR 73, though the point was not decided.

As a matter of first principle, there seems to be no good reason why an owner who orders a variation at a normal stage having regard to the contractor's actual rate of progress should find himself disadvantaged or deprived of his power to order necessary or desirable variations simply because the contractor has through culpable delay caused the contract or extended completion date to pass with the work incomplete. As stated, the more exceptional the degree of delay, the more likely this situation will become. It is very important to note that in the one case among those illustrated *supra* which has considered this problem, there was no extension of time clause for variations at all,[14] so that *any* variation ordered, whether before or after the contract or extended completion date, would inevitably have invalidated the liquidated damages clause on prevention grounds.[15] Where an extension of time clause for variations is present, however, it is submitted that there is no valid reason for treating a "late variation" in this special sense as an act of prevention, even if the draftsman's failure to envisage the possibility of such a variation may make it difficult to apply the full range of the extension of time contractual machinery or to know precisely how to adjust the current deductions of liquidated damages.

10·045   Also as a matter of first principle, while it seems to be commonly thought in professional and construction industry circles when first approaching this problem that the correct adjustment in case of such a late variation or other event should be to "arrest" the running of liquidated damages for the necessary period of additional time before allowing the damages to recommence, this is logically quite wrong. A moment's consideration will show that, if there is still a substantial period before completion can be achieved, quite apart from the contemplated variation, at the time of its being ordered, that period should be available to be "used up" by the owner's continued deduction of liquidated damages until such time as, but for the new variation or event, the works would otherwise have been completed. Not till then will it be logical or equitable to require the owner to forgo the continued deduction of liquidated damages, particularly since in such situations a potential owner's termination, or insolvency of the contractor, may often be in the commercial background.

10·046   Here again, there is evidence that the advantage to contractors of leaving this problem unresolved has been well understood by those responsible for the drafting of the RIBA/JCT standard forms. Thus their post-1980 standard form contains an extension of time clause of the greatest complexity, with provision for no less than three successive dates for consideration and subsequent reconsideration by the architect of extension of time decisions and for the fixing of new completion dates on each occasion. The last of these is to be after practical completion, and there-

---

[14] *SMK Cabinets* v. *Hili Modern Electrics Pty. Ltd.* [1984] V.L.R. 39.
[15] See, however, Martin J.'s dictum to the same effect in *Anderson* v. *Tuapeka County Council* (1900) 19 N.Z.L.R. 1, illustrated *infra*, para. 10·081, where there was an applicable extension of time clause.

fore, by definition, after any period of culpable delay has ended.[16] This last reconsideration is expressly required to contemplate fixing an *earlier* completion date (thus in fact increasing any recoverable liquidated damages) where instructions have been issued involving an *omission* of work "where such issue is after the last occasion on which the Architect made an extension of time" (that is, during the period of culpable delay) but makes no reference to variation instructions issued since the previous extension which result in *additions*, thus avoiding any express indication that such an instruction may be given during that period. Whether Clause 25.3.3.1 of the 1980 RIBA/JCT contract confers such a power would be at the heart of the question of interpretation on this point. The interpretation is unclear, but the failure to make the intention expressly clear while discussing variations ordered since the last extension, and by definition after the date of the Clause 24.2.1 certificate, is remarkable given the commercial importance of the problem and its potential destruction of the owner's entitlement to liquidated damages.

Since the foregoing discussion, the possibly deliberate and excessively complicated wording of the 1980 RIBA/JCT extension of time clause, and the predictable contractor's arguments where variations involving additional work need to be ordered after the start of the period of culpable delay, have finally reached the Courts.

ILLUSTRATION

By Clause 25.3.1.2 of the 1980 RIBA/JCT standard forms the Architect was empowered to grant an extension "by fixing such later date as the Completion Date" if completion "is likely to be delayed beyond the Completion Date" by reason of any so-called "relevant event", which included the ordering of variations. It was conceded that this power of extension (as also to fix an earlier Completion Date, although only after a previous extension, by reason of omissions ordered) must, on its wording, be exercised before the Completion Date[16a] or, if applicable, any extended Completion Date had arrived. However, by Clause 25.3.3 there was a *later* duty to make a further extension, exercisable up to 12 weeks after practical completion, having regard to any relevant event "whether upon reviewing a previous decision *or otherwise*". Variations were ordered during the period of culpable delay, and the architect in his later review under Clause 25.3.3 granted an extension of time of 18 weeks on that account, which he added to his previously fixed Completion Date. The contractors contended, first, that the liquidated damages clause had been discharged and set aside by the variation instructions, arguing that the contractual extension of time for variations applied only to variations *ordered before* the Completion Date. Alternatively, they contended that the extension should be calculated from the date of the variation instruction, and not added to the previously fixed Completion Date. Finally, they contended that liquidated damages might be recoverable until the variation instruction, but not thereafter, citing *Baskett* v. *Bendigo* and *SMK Cabinets* v. *Hili Modern Electrics. Held*, by Colman J., that the words "or otherwise" in Clause 25.3.3.1 envisaged relevant events additional to those previously taken into

10·046A

---

[16] See Clause 25.3.
[16a] This concession is doubted *infra*.

account when fixing the Completion Date on earlier occasions, and there were no words limiting those events to events occurring prior to a currently fixed Completion Date. The contractor's contention would mean that the most trivial variation, representing only a day's work, would destroy the whole liquidated damages regime even when very large liquidated damages were already due. It could hardly reflect the common intention and was most improbable in the absence of some express provision. Accordingly there was power to grant the extension. Secondly, the object of fixing a new Completion Date was to make an allowance for the period of delay caused by the relevant event, and that could only be achieved by extension of the previously fixed Date. Thirdly, the *Baskett* and *SMK Cabinets* cases could be distinguished, since in those cases there was no express power to extend time, as here, for the act of prevention which had occurred: *Balfour Beatty Building Ltd.* v. *Chestermount Properties Ltd.* (1993).[17]

[Note: This decision is greatly to be welcomed, and Colman J.'s strictures against, and analysis of the numerous anomalies arising from the unmeritorious and illogical interpretation being advanced by the contractors were clearly fully justified; but it should be noted that Colman J. was only able to achieve a sensible resolution of the problems created by the convoluted draftsmanship of Clause 25 by fastening on the particular wording governing the later review at the time of practical completion which was expressly required by Clause 25.3.3.1. For this reason, while the case will be of the greatest value where extension of time provisions are worded in general terms, this anomalous argument may well be resurrected if extension of time wording is used which contemplates only the extension of a *future* Completion Date, as was apparently conceded by the parties in regard to the initial extension power conferred by Clause 25.3.1 of the 1980 form (this concession may in fact not be justified on the wording of the contract, it is submitted). Nor was Colman J. required to address the very real problem of the method of adjustment of current deductions of liquidated damages by the owner during the culpable delay period should a subsequent event such as the order of variations justify a further extension of time. Given the great value clearly attached to the possibilities of these legalistic arguments by contractors' representatives, it may be predicted that the last of them has not been heard. It will also be interesting to see if Clause 25 is amended by the RIBA/JCT so as to achieve the sensible results indicated by Colman J.'s reasoning and judgment.]

By contrast, it may be mentioned that the Singapore SIA contract has since 1980 contained express provision for extra work ordered during the period of culpable delay (and indeed for other acceptable grounds of extension involving owner responsibility and occurring during that period) together with necessarily detailed provisions for the subsequent adjustment of deductions of liquidated damages in that event.[18]

(3) Effect of Forfeiture

10·047   If the builder, by abandoning the contract or committing a fundamental breach, thereby entitles the owner to treat the contract as repudiated, or if

---

[17] [1993] 62 BLRI.
[18] See Clause 24(3), reproduced and discussed in C.C.P.P., pp. 541, 581.

the owner is otherwise enabled to operate a forfeiture or determination clause in the contract, the effect of such an event upon the liquidated damages provisions in the contract requires to be considered. In the case of forfeiture or determination clauses, the contract may, of course, contain express provisions dealing with the position, and where this is so they will be given effect,[19] but in the case of a common law rescission following repudiation by the contractor the problem can occur without any such assistance.

In the absence of special provision, it is submitted that liquidated damages accrued due prior to the date of rescission, forfeiture or determination will be recoverable, but in respect of any later delay the owner will be required to prove his damage (if any) in the normal way.[20] (It should, of course, be remembered that, in such an event, an owner's damages will probably arise under two main heads, namely damages for delay, and the additional cost, if any, of completion,[21] and it is the first only of these heads which will be affected by a liquidated damages clause conditioned on delay in completion.)[21a] In support of this view, it has been seen that, since a liquidated damages provision usually contemplates completion by the builder without his being dismissed, it will be wrong without express provision to apply the clause to completion by another builder.[22]

Again, it has been seen that the Full Court of Victoria, consistently with this, has held that, in a case of prevention by the ordering of extras where there is no applicable extension of time clause, liquidated damages already accrued due up to the date of the order for the variations will be recoverable, but only general damages for delay thereafter.[23] This accords with the general principle, following rescission of a contract at common law, that previously accrued rights, including rights of payment up to that time if such exist, will be enforced.[24]

Thus in a case where termination had taken place before any liquidated   **10·048**
damages accrued, the court said:

> "If the concluding provisions of the re-entry clause had been omitted; if there had been a power simply to re-enter and terminate the contract and the company had exercised that power, then we are of opinion ... that the council could not afterwards have claimed these liquidated damages as against the contractor ... Having elected to dispossess the contractor and taken the per-

---

[19] *Baylis* v. *Wellington City* (1886) 4 N.Z.L.R. 84, *infra*. The post-1963 RIBA forms have now made express provision which appears to substitute ordinary damages for liquidated damages in this event: see Clause 25(3)(d).

[20] This passage in the tenth edition was cited and followed by Bugold J.A. in the New Brunswick Court of Appeal in *City of Moncton* v. *Aprile* (1980) 29 N.B.R. 631, at p. 683.

[21] See *ante*, Chap. 8, Price and Damages, paras. 8·111, *et seq*.

[21a] See *supra*, paras. 10·002 *et seq*.

[22] *British Glanzstoff Manufacturing Co. Ltd.* v. *General Accident Fire & Life Assurance Corporation Ltd.*, 1912 S.C. 591; [1913] A.C. 143, illustrated *supra*, para. 10·003, as well as *infra*, para. 10·050.

[23] *SMK Cabinets* v. *Hili Modern Electrics Pty. Ltd.* [1984] V.R. 391, illustrated *supra*, para. 10·039.

[24] See the discussion *ante*, Chap. 4, Section 3(1)(h) and (i), paras. 4·227 and 4·228.

formance of the contract out of his hands they must have been taken to abandon their right to these damages."[25]

Conversely, as in many forms of contract liquidated damages become due immediately on the date when completion should have occurred, and provision is made for a right of immediate deduction of liquidated damages from moneys due after that date[26] (for example, on interim certificate) financial rights or obligations may well have accrued by the time of determination or rescission, and it would to say the least, be highly inconvenient to reopen the whole state of accounts between the parties, as would be the case if the liquidated damages provision was held to have been invalidated retrospectively upon forfeiture. However, there have been a number of cases where liquidated damages have been recovered following entry and completion by the owner, and it is submitted that in the last analysis the question is one of interpretation of the termination and liquidated damages provisions, rather than one of election or estoppel.

ILLUSTRATIONS

10-049   (1) A contract for work provided: (1) that liquidated damages should be paid for each day beyond the day fixed for completion; (2) that in case of breach the owner might take the works out of B.'s (the contractor's) hands, and if the balance of the contract price was not sufficient to pay for completion by a second contractor, B. should pay the difference; and that if the works were not completed by the second contractor in time, in consequence of B.s default, the owner should give an extension of time, and that B. should pay liquidated damages for the delay caused by such extension. B., after delaying the work about five months, wrote and said that he had decided to proceed no further. *Held*, by the New Zealand Court of Appeal, that B. was liable to pay: (1) liquidated damages from the date fixed for completion to the date on which he threw up the work; (2) the sum required to make up the price to that of the second contractor; and (3) liquidated damages for the further delay caused by an extension of time given to the second contractor: *Baylis* v. *Wellington City* (1886).[27]

(2) A building contract gave the owners power to deduct liquidated damages from the retention money. The contract also empowered the owners, in case of undue delay by the contractor, "to terminate the contract, so far as respects the performance of the same under the directions and by means of the contractor, *but without thereby affecting in any other respects the liabilities of the said contractor.*" The contract was terminated under this provision, and W., one of the contractor's sureties, took an assignment of the contract, and agreed to complete the works in accordance with the original contract. In consequence of the delay by the original contractor, W. could not complete in the stipulated time. *Held*, by the Divisional Court, that the words "without

---

[25] *Per* Kennedy J. in *Re Yeadon Waterworks Co. and Wright* (1895) 72 L.T. 538, at p. 540, illustrated *infra*.

[26] See, *e.g.* Clause 22 of the post-1963 RIBA forms and Clause 47(1) of the 1955 ICE form.

[27] 4 N.Z.L.R. 84. Extension of time to the second contractor is a form of words for the additional delay.

thereby affecting in any other respects the liabilities of the said contractor" effectually kept alive the owners right to deduct liquidated damages from the retention money, and that W. was subject to the contractual liabilities of the original contractor and to the deduction of liquidated damages until completion: *Re Yeadon Waterworks Co. and Wright* (1895).[28]

(3) A contract to do work for £1140 at a gas works in Ireland provided for liquidated damages of £10 per week, and also empowered the owners, if the contractor failed to proceed properly with the work, to enter and complete at the contractor's cost, or to set off such cost against any sums due or to become due under the contract. The contractor defaulted after the completion date had passed, and the owners took over the work and completed. At the time of re-entry, £600 had been paid and a further sum of £200 was certified but unpaid, and there was also a £200 retention. The trial judge awarded the contractors £540, being the balance of the full price for the completed work, less £150 for the cost of completion and £260, being liquidated damages for delay up to the time of the owner's re-entry. *It was admitted that the contract had not been rescinded. Held*, by the Irish Court of Appeal, that, not having completed, the contractor was only entitled to the certified but unpaid £200, against the £150 and £260 counterclaimed for cost of completion and liquidated damages until re-entry: *Simpson* v. *Trim Town Commissioners* (1898).[29]

[Note: Despite the statement of Fitzgibbon C.J. that "the terms are clear which make (the contractors) liable to liquidated damages for delay", the report does not indicate any special language in the liquidated damages or re-entry clauses comparable to that in the *Yeadon Waterworks* case. The £150 was presumably claimed under the contract and not as damages for failure to complete, since, if so, credit would have had to be given for the retention, it is submitted.[29a]]

10·050

(4) A contract for the construction of works by a specified date provided for liquidated damages for each week of delay beyond that date. It further provided that the owners might, if the contractor should suspend the works, engage others to complete them. The contractor became bankrupt and suspended the works, and the owners had them completed, but completion was delayed until six weeks after the specified date. The owners claimed from the contractor, *inter alia* damages in respect of this delay. *Held* that the owners must prove their damage and could not rely on the liquidated damage clause, which applied only where the contractor himself completed: *British Glanzstoff Manufacturing Co. Ltd.* v. *General Accident Fire & Life Assurance Corporation Ltd.* (1912).[30]

(5) A civil engineering contract in New Brunswick was ultimately terminated by the owners when the contractors refused to proceed. The termination clause gave the owners the right upon such a default "to take the whole work, or any part or parts thereof specified in the said notice out of the hands of the Contractor and the Contractor shall ... vacate possession and give the said work ... to the Engineer who may re-let the same to any other person or may employ workmen and provide materials". The contract then provided that in case the work was taken over in this way "it shall in no way affect the relative obligations of the Corporation and the Contractor in respect of their obligations nor shall it be any excuse for delay in completing the same ...". *Held*,

10·051

---

[28] 72 L.T. 538.
[29] 32 I.L.T. Rep. 129, Ireland.
[29a] See *ante*, Chap. 8, paras. 8·114 and 8·123.
[30] 1912 S.C. 591; [1913] A.C. 143.

by the New Brunswick Court of Appeal, affirming the trial judge and citing the tenth edition, that liquidated damages could not be recovered. *Per* Bugold J.A.: "the general rule is that if by reason of default by the contractor the owner becomes entitled to terminate the contract the owner is entitled only to unliquidated damages in respect of the time period after termination": *City of Moncton* v. *Aprile* (1980).[31]

10·052   It can be seen from the above cases that there developed a traditional form of diffuse wording in some provisions for the owner's re-entry on contractor default which stipulated expressly that the contractor's liabilities under the contract were to continue unaffected following the owner's exercise of his rights of re-entry and of completion of the work. A particularly diffuse form of this draftsmanship is to be found in English-influenced civil engineering standard forms, where the words contemplate either a "termination of employment" or an "enter and expel" power upon contractor default "without thereby avoiding the Contract *or releasing the Contractor from any of his obligations or liabilities under the Contract* or affecting the rights and powers conferred on the Employer or Engineer by the Contract ... ".[32] The Divisional Court in *Re Yeadon* clearly considered that this type of wording would enable liquidated damages to be recovered for the period following the termination until completion, but in the *Aprile* case the New Brunswick Court of Appeal ignored apparently even stronger wording, to the effect that the delay liability should continue after re-entry, when denying the owner liquidated damages. Conversely, in *Simpson* v. *Trim*, the Irish Court of Appeal was content to impose liquidated damages where no such supporting language seems to have been present, but that of course was only up to the time of re-entry, although the report shows that there had been a substantial delay thereafter.

10·053   The cases would thus appear to be in conflict, although the difficulty arises only because of the obscurity of the draftsmanship. It is difficult to conceive of a modern draftsman, instructed to provide for liquidated damages to apply throughout the period of completion by another contractor, adopting such wording to achieve this purpose, rather than provide simply and expressly to that effect. It is not clear, incidentally, in what other areas of the contract this diffuse wording may be thought to have some useful consequence.[33]

Moreover, if the intention is indeed for liquidated damages to continue to apply after re-entry or termination, reasonably competent draftsman-

---

[31] 29 N.B.R. 631 at p. 683.

[32] See also the "termination of employment" power in Clause 63.1 of the FIDIC fourth edition, and the "enter and expel" powers in Clause 63(1) of the fourth and fifth ICE conditions, Clause 44.1 of the FIDIC E. & M.E. second edition (1980) and Clause 63(1) of the FIDIC third edition contracts respectively.

[33] See *E.R. Dyer Ltd.* v. *Simon Build/Peter Lind Partnership* (1982) 23 BLR 23, where Nolan J. appears to have thought that there was a distinction between such "enter, expel and complete" clauses and other clauses expressed to determine the contract itself. See also *post*, Chap. 12, para. 12·008.

ship at the present day could be expected to deal specifically with the problems of delay arising under any completion contract entered into by the owner, though this is rarely, if ever, attempted.[34]

The whole subject of re-entry provisions which expressly accord to the owner the same or sometimes even greater rights than those he would obtain on a common law rescission should he proceed to complete the project, but which at the same time expressly provide that their exercise shall not release the parties from their obligations under the contract, requires reconsideration by the courts, it is submitted. It seems quite possible that the draftsmen who traditionally employed or still employ this formula had or have little or no clear idea of their objective in doing so. Modern case-law has, in any event, now established that a common law rescission does leave certain categories of contractual provision alive so as to continue to regulate the subsequent position of the parties, even in the absence of specific draftsmanship.[35]

(4) Effect of Payment Without Deduction

As a practical matter an owner faced with the problem of a contractor defaulting on progress and who is already in culpable delay under the terms of a liquidated damages clause may find it desirable in some situations to "nurse" the contractor, particularly one who may be in financial difficulties, through to completion, rather than risk precipitating his financial failure by the reduction in the contractor's cash flow which an immediate deduction of liquidated damages might cause. For this reason, liquidated damages deduction provisions will almost invariably be expressed by competent draftsmen in the owner's interest in permissive rather than mandatory terms, and this will in any event be the commercial intention of such provisions in the great majority of cases. A building owner will not, therefore, apart from express provision in the contract, lose the right to liquidated damages by paying the builder moneys otherwise due to him without deduction, or by permitting the continuation of work after the due date for completion. However, in some rare forms of contract the provision for deduction from moneys due may be construed to be mandatory and exclusive, and in such cases failure to make the deduction may disentitle the owner from recovering the damages. The cases which suggest this may well have been inspired by the then strong dislike of the courts for liquidated damages provisions and anxiety to afford an escape from their consequences, and courts should be slow to follow them at the present day, it is submitted.

10·054

---

[34] See, however, Clause 32(8)(g) of the Singapore 1980 SIA contract, reproduced in C.C.P.P., pp. 604–605, which covers this situation expressly.

[35] See *ante*, Chap. 4, para. 4·227.

ILLUSTRATIONS

10·055
(1) A building contract provided that in the event of delay the builder should forfeit and pay to the employer £5 weekly, such penalty to be deducted from the amount which might remain owing on the completion of the work. *Held*, by Parke B., that the owner had a double remedy, to deduct or recover as a payment: *Duckworth* v. *Alison* (1836).[36]

(2) F. contracted with R. to do the masonry work on buildings which R. was erecting. The work was to be done by April 1. F. did not complete it till July 1. R. allowed F. to go on with the work after April 1, and made payments under the contract. *Held*, by the New York Court of Appeals, that there was no release or discharge of the stipulation as to time, and that F. was liable in damages to R.: *Ruff* v. *Rinaldo* (1873).[37]

(3) In the event of delay, a contractor undertook to "forfeit and pay to (the owner) £20 a week, to be paid to and retained by the employer ... for each and every week during which such work shall remain unfinished." Interim payments were made for 14 months after the completion date without retaining any sum for liquidated damages. *Held*, by the Court of Exchequer Chamber, that by this conduct the owners had disentitled themselves from recovering liquidated damages: *Laidlaw* v. *Hastings Pier Co.* (1874).[38]
[Note: The court also found that the architect's unqualified certificates were evidence that he had exercised a power of extension of time in the contractor's favour[39] so the owners were accordingly bound by them. The finding, while unanimous, was therefore not strictly necessary to the decision, and there is no indication in the report that *Duckworth* v. *Alison, supra,* or any cases were referred to in this context. In *Baskett* v. *Bendigo Gold-Dredging Co.*[40] the court rightly felt a difficulty about the words "to be paid to ... the employer" in *Laidlaw's* case, and it is suggested that it is of doubtful authority on this point.]

10·056
(4) A contract to construct a dredge in New Zealand provided that the work should be completed within eight months from the acceptance of the tender, "failing which the sum of £2 for every working day by which such time of eight calendar months shall be exceeded will be deducted from any money due to the contractor by way of liquidated damages, and not in the nature of a penalty." *Held*, by Williams J., following *Laidlaw's* case, *supra*, that if the employers wanted to recover penalties they could only do so by deducting them, and that if moneys were paid without deducting penalties which had accrued, the penalty clause was gone: *Baskett* v. *Bendigo Gold-Dredging Co.* (1902).[41]

(5) A contract for building torpedo boats provided that "the penalty for later delivery shall be at the rate of £500 per week for each vessel." Delivery was delayed, but payment was made in full. *Held*, by the House of Lords, that such payment in full did not bar a claim for the liquidated damages: *Clydebank Engineering & Shipbuilding Co. Ltd.* v. *Yzquierdo y Castaneda* (1905).[42]

---

[36] 1 M. & W. 412.
[37] 55 N.Y. 664.
[38] Hudson, *Building Contracts* (4th ed.), Vol. 2, p. 13, further doubted *infra*, para. 10·073.
[39] See *infra*, paras. 10·073 *et seq.*
[40] (1902) 21 N.Z.L.R. 166, *supra*.
[41] *Ibid.*
[42] [1905] A.C. 6.

(5) Release by Completion, and Partial Re-entry or Occupation

It is self-evident that "completion" will bring the right to liquidated dam-   **10·057**
ages to an end, but it may be difficult to decide what is completion for this
purpose, in particular if the owner enters into possession while the work is
partly incomplete, or only retakes possession of part of the work.

It is submitted that if completion is sufficient to justify the application of
the doctrine of substantial performance of the contract as a whole, but the
owner chooses to re-enter, the right to liquidated damages will usually
cease. However, in some situations notwithstanding re-entry into partial
possession, the owner may continue to suffer damage, in which case it may
be arguable on the facts that the agreed liquidated damages should continue until the contract is completely performed, and that all that can be
inferred from the re-entry is an understandable wish to reduce the loss or
inconvenience of the owner rather than a waiver of the right to liquidated
damages.

ILLUSTRATIONS

(1) H. contracted to repair T.'s house, under liquidated damages of $25 for   **10·058**
each week's delay. There was delay for eight weeks, but T. moved in after
three weeks, when the repairs were substantially completed. *Held*, that T. was
entitled to set off liquidated damages for eight weeks up to entire completion,
as his moving in before the repairs were completed was no waiver of his right
to claim for the whole period: *Horton* v. *Tobin* (1887).[43]

(2) In a contract in Alberta worth $20,000, the owner re-entered at a time
when minor defects worth about $200 were still outstanding, and the architect
was demanding that they be remedied forthwith. *Held*, by Beck J., that the
contract had been substantially performed, and liquidated damages ceased to
run upon the re-entry: *Watts* v. *McLeay* (1911).[44]

Under the scheme of most modern contracts, liquidated damages come   **10·059**
to an end on "practical" or "substantial" completion of the whole of the
project, but a liability to make good defects survives for a limited period.[45]
Probably the most accurate definition to date of the state of completion
contemplated by provisions for completion to time in building and engineering contracts, and whether or not expressly described as "practical" or
"substantial" completion, is that of Lush J. adopted by the Full Court of
Victoria: "the work ... carried out in accordance with the contract ...
except for departures from the contract which were either latent or

---

[43] 20 Nov.Sc. (8 Russ. & Geld.) 169.
[44] 19 W.L.R. 916, Canada.
[45] See *ante*, Chap. 5, paras. 5·039 *et seq*., for this liability, and for the "practical" and "substantial" completion concepts see *ante*, Chap. 4, para. 4·029–4·030, and paras. 5·048–5·049.

undiscovered or merely trivial"[46]—even though that case involved a builder/developer and purchasers and not an ordinary building contract.

This definition may become important when an owner or purchaser enters an apparently satisfactory building on completion, and defects later manifest themselves which, if known at the time, would have justified refusal to enter, or of a certificate of practical or substantial completion by the architect or engineer. In such a case it will usually no longer be possible, it is submitted, for an owner, even where the question of completion is open to dispute on the merits and he is in no way bound by any relevant certificate, to seek to recover liquidated damages retrospectively on the ground that the works were not in fact properly completed at the time of re-entry. The scheme of most sophisticated building contracts for the commencement of the defects liability or maintenance period (together with, for example, the old latent defect exception to the binding effect of the pre-1980 JCT/RIBA final certificate)[47] is inconsistent with any such intention (which if correct, would mean that an owner could add a claim for liquidated damages whenever he claimed damages for defective work, and however long after completion the defects were discovered).[48] Re-entry and occupation of the whole on apparent completion will, therefore, terminate liquidation damages permanently, in the absence of fraud, it is submitted. On the other hand, consequential damages, including, if necessary, the cost of going out of occupation or loss of rents or profits during repairs, will be recoverable if newly discovered defective work needs repair after an owner's re-entry.[48a]

10·060   The foregoing discussion relates to the great majority of construction contracts which prescribe a single date or time for completion, with accompanying liquidated damages for delay in completion of the project as a whole (indeed there is no reason to suppose that contracts without liquidated damages provisions, or where no specific completion date is prescribed, will be interpreted any differently in the context of a claim for damages for delay in completion).[48b]

More substantial or complex projects have often, however, prescribed "sectional" or phased completion, where the essential characteristic will be separate required completion dates for defined different parts of the project. More recently, a second more sophisticated type of provision, originating in the English RIBA/JCT 1963 standard forms, envisages a

---

[46] *Morgan* v. *S. & S. Construction (Property) Ltd.* [1967] V.R. 149, Australia, illustrated *ante*, Chap. 4, para. 4·012 and see also the speeches of Viscount Dilhorne and Lord Wilberforce in *J. Jarvis & Sons Ltd.* v. *Westminster Corporation* [1970] 1 W.L.R. 637, at pp. 646C, 647B, 649H and 650E.

[47] See Clause 30(7) of those contracts and the cases *ante*, Chap. 6, paras. 6·068 *et seq.*, and 6·182.

[48] See the discussion *ante*, Chap. 4, Section 1(1), para. 4·029, and the passage from Viscount Dilhorne's judgment in *J. Jarvis & Sons* v. *Westminster Corporation* [1970] 1 W.L.R. 637, at p. 647 there referred to. See also the case illustrated *infra*, para. 10·099.

[48a] See *ante*, Chap. 8, para. 8·156.

[48b] See also *ante*, Chap. 9, Section (9), para. 9·043.

potential "partial occupation" resulting from entry into a part of the project by the owner *with the ad hoc consent of the contractor* prior to completion of the whole, and then provides, in the context of liquidated damages, that the sums stipulated for completion of the whole project will be rateably reduced in proportion to the relative value of the occupied part to the value of the whole.[49] Partial occupation provisions can, incidentally, represent a very valuable power for owners dealing with reclacitrant contractors at the end of a project, but only, in the last resort, if exercisable *as of right* in the absence of contractor consent. Such provisions are not at present to be found in standard forms apart from the Singapore 1980 SIA contract.[50]

Both sectional completion and partial occupation provisions, although   **10·061**
perfectly simple in principle, frequently prove too much for owners' advisers when preparing the contract documentation.[50a] Thus, in sectional completion cases, the documents routinely omit to provide anything but a simple liquidated damages sum for the whole project,[51] and in partial occupation cases the need to reconcile any inconsistency between that draftsmanship in a standard, or printed, form and the specific requirements the parties may wish to make for phased or sectional completion dates on their project has frequently not been understood by owners' advisers.[52]

ILLUSTRATIONS

(1) A contract for 123 dwellings in the RIBA/JCT standard form provided by Clauses 21 and 22 for a completion date as stated in the appendix, and for payment of a sum calculated at the rate stated in the appendix as liquidated damages. The appendix stated a single date for completion and provided for liquidated damages "at the rate of £20 per week for each uncompleted dwelling". However, by Clause 16(e) of the conditions it was also provided that, in the event of the owner entering into possession of a part of the work with the consent of the contractor, the sum to be paid or allowed under Clause 22 as liquidated damages should be proportionately reduced on the basis of the value of the occupied part relative to the full contract sum. The contractor was in delay, and the arbitrator awarded liquidated damages during the period of delay, reducing them at the rate shown in the appendix as and when the individual houses came to be completed and taken into possession. *Held*, by Judge Hawser Q.C., that in the absence of any provisions in the contract for sectional completion of the houses at different dates, Clause 16 must apply, and liquidated damages could not be claimed and deducted as provided for in the appendix. The owners might consider amending to claim general damages: *Bramall & Ogden v. Sheffield City Council*, (1983).[53]

---

[49] See Clauses 16 and 18 of the 1963 and 1980 JCT/RIBA forms respectively, and see the *Arnhold* and *Philips (Hong Kong)* cases, illustrated *supra*, paras. 10·018 and 10·019.

[50] See the two "with consent" and "without consent" partial occupation provisions in Clause 26(1) and (3) of the Singapore SIA 1980 contract, reproduced in C.C.P.P., pp. 582–584.

[50a] See also *supra*, para. 10·023, and *Arnhold* and *Philips* cases.

[51] See, *e.g. M.J. Gleeson (Contractors) Ltd.* v. *London Borough of Hillingdon* (1970) 215 E.G. 165; *Turner and Sons Ltd.* v. *Mathind Ltd.* (1986) 5 Const.L.J. 273, the latter illustrated *infra*.

[52] See, *e.g. Bramall & Ogden* v. *Sheffield City Council* (1983) 29 BLR 73, illustrated *infra*.

[53] 29 BLR 73.

[Note: This case is illustrated only as indicating the difficulties mentioned. Effect could have been given to the obvious intention of the parties either by giving overriding effect, as a matter of interpretation, to the appendix (which had been completed by the parties with the specific project in mind as against the printed condition of contract Clause 12), or possibly, depending on the facts, by way of rectification.]

10·062   (2) A contract under the RIBA/JCT standard form for flats and garages and associated works provided for phased handover on successive dates of five "sub-areas". The architect gave separate practical completion certificates, and then separate notifications of the dates when the sub-areas should have been completed, and thereafter deductions of liquidated damages were made in each case. The appendix provided for liquidated damages at £1,000 per week, but referred only to one date for possession and one for completion. The official referee, in an action by the contractor for sums due under the contract, granted summary judgment in favour of the contractor on the basis that the liquidated damages could only be deducted after the completion date for the last of the sub-areas. *Held*, by the Court of Appeal, that even though the liquidated damages might only be recoverable from the date for completion of the last sub-area, this did not prevent the owner from proving his damages for failure to meet the phased completion dates for the earlier sub-areas, nor would the liquidated damages operate as a ceiling in the case of these earlier breaches, and, since these might prima facie exceed the balance claimed, there should be unconditional leave to defend. An alternative argument by the contractors that the liquidated damages of £1,000 per week fell to be reduced by the proportion of contract work entered and occupied should be rejected, since Clause 16 applied only to parts occupied with consent and not to parts in respect of which the contractor was contractually obliged to complete by a certain date: *Turner and Son Ltd.* v. *Mathind* (1986).[54]

[Note: For a further example where the extension of time requirements for successive phases of a project defeated not only the draftsman, but also the House of Lords when asked to imply a term which would resolve the difficulty, see *Trollope & Colls Ltd.* v. *N.W. Metropolitan Hospital Board*.][54a]

SECTION 3. EXTENSION OF TIME

(1) Drafting of Extension of Time Clauses

10·063   Provision is frequently made in building contracts for the architect or engineer to grant extensions of time for completion of the work where delay due to certain specified causes has occurred. At first sight such a clause appears to be designed primarily for the benefit of the builder, since its effect, if the clause is operated, will be to reduce or avoid his liability to pay liquidated damages in the event of the delay in question. This is certainly so where the delay is due to causes for which the builder would otherwise be responsible, for example bad weather, or strikes. But as has been seen,[55] such clauses are also of substantial benefit to the owner since, in the absence of an applicable clause of this kind, the liquidated damages

---

[54] 5 Const.L.J. 273.
[54a] [1973] 1 W.L.R. 601, illustrated *infra*, Section 3(7), para. 10·091A.
[55] See *supra*, "Release by Prevention", paras. 10·024 *et seq.*

provisions will cease to have effect in those cases where the delay, or even a small part of it, is due to some prevention or default of the owner or his agents, or any other matter for which he would be responsible.

Although it has been seen that general "beyond the contractor's control" types of wording cannot safeguard a liquidated damages clause from invalidation if acts of prevention or breach occur,[56] there seems no reason to suppose that more explicit, although still general, wording such as "any act of prevention or breach of contract on the part of the owner or his A/E"[57] will fail to achieve this purpose.

One result of the case law on prevention set out in section 2, *supra* is that **10·064** a contractor will be offered a complete escape from a liquidated damages clause, notwithstanding, perhaps, very serious delays on his own part, provided only that he is in a position to show some delay, however minor, caused by what can be shown to be owner prevention or breach. In the absence of, or indeed in addition to, the use of a compendious but specific clause of the kind described above, draftsmen should therefore in the owner's interest be careful to identify and provide expressly for the commoner incidents of construction projects which can cause delays, however relatively unimportant, of this particular kind.

First and foremost, it goes without saying that there must be an express power to extend time for variations and extra work,[58] and nearly all more sophisticated contracts do today make that provision. The other two principal categories of breach which can constitute prevention by an owner will be information delays and failure to give possession. Again, most modern contracts do cover the former, which is perhaps the commonest basis of contractors' claims in practice. So far as possession is concerned, the cases illustrated above are sufficient to show that comparatively minor failures, often at the beginning of the work, can easily occur in practice.

Failures of possession, provided they can be omitted from specific reference in the extension of time clause (with their absence perhaps camouflaged from unsuspecting owners by some generalised "beyond the contractor's control" ground of extension which, as has been seen, will not save the clause even in the case of a very minor infringement) can offer particularly effective opportunities for contractors to invalidate the liquidated damages provisions as a whole, since many other types of breach, such as minor interferences or delays caused by other contractors or public utilities, or failures of the A/E to release definitive final construction drawings for some parts of the work over a short period, can on the facts arguably justify a complaint of failure to afford possession of the site, and so of prevention by the owner.

---

[56] See *supra*, para. 10·040. Contrast the House of Lords' interpretation of this wording as *including* the defaults of nominated sub-contractors in a different compensatory context in *Scott Lithgow Ltd.* v. *Secretary of State for Defence* (1989) 45 BLR 1, doubted in (1991) 7 Const.L.J. 3 and illustrated *ante*, Chap. 5, para. 5·037.

[57] See, *e.g.* Clause 23(1)(o) of the Singapore SIA post-1980 contracts, reproduced in C.C.P.P., p. 580.

[58] *Dodd* v. *Churton, supra.*

10·065   There is every indication that the opportunities to invalidate liquidated damages clauses afforded by the absence of an express extension of time for failure to give possession have been well understood for many years in the English building industry. Thus while in civil engineering contracts an express right to an extension of time for failure to afford possession of a part of the site has been present in the standard forms for nearly a century,[59] the complete absence of any such ground of extension in the RIBA/ JCT, forms never usually averse to affording every possible protection for the contractor, has been a significant and noticeable feature of those contracts.[60] This omission has been pointed out by commentators on a number of occasions, although often treated by them as a matter of inadvertence and without its significance being fully appreciated. Finally in 1980, when a wholly new RIBA/JCT form was being published, it may have been thought that a continued failure to deal with this omission would attract further comment, and in Clause 25.4 of the 1980 contract a decision was apparently taken to conclude a list of approximately 23 different grounds of extension of time with the following "Relevant Event" in Clause 25.4.12:

> "Failure of the Employer to give in due time ingress to or egress from the site of the Works or any part thereof through or over any land, buildings, way or passage adjoining or connected with the Site and in the possession and control of the Employer, in accordance with the Contract Bills and/or the Contract Drawings, after receipt by the Architect/Supervising Officer of such notice, if any, as the Contractor is required to give, or failure of the Employer to give such ingress or egress as otherwise agreed between the Architect/ Supervising Officer and Contractor."

10·066   It will be seen that while this lengthy and convoluted draftsmanship at first sight might appear to give an extension of time for failure to give possession of the site *simpliciter*, on closer analysis it will be seen to deal with only one highly unusual situation *off* the site.[61-62] There seems no conceivable reason for instructing a draftsman to select such an abstruse and limited interference with access as a ground for an express extension of time entitlement, while at the same time excluding from the clause any reference whatever to failure to afford possession of the site or a part of the site itself, other than a deliberate intention to leave failure or obstruction of possession, of however small duration or extent, still available as a ground for invalidation, under the existing case law, of the entire liquidated damages machinery in the contract. There is, for example, almost no major or relatively complex building contract (as, for example, hospital contracts which are not on a "green field" site) where some small temporary interference with possession cannot usually be discovered if the history of the project is sufficiently closely examined. If so that the absence of the

---

[59] See, *e.g.* Clause 42(1) of the 1954 and 1973 ICE contracts.
[60] See, for a typical example of its operation, *Rapid Building Group Ltd.* v. *Ealing Family Housing Association*, illustrated *supra*.
[61-62] See also Clause 13.1.2.1.

ground of extension can effectively emasculate the entire liquidated damages machinery in the RIBA/JCT forms.

Although there is no objection to draftsmanship which merely provides **10·067** for the time to be extended for defined reasons, with the A/E often named as the owner's agent for the purpose of ascertaining and notifying the contractor of the extension while leaving the precise machinery for doing so undefined, in practice successive matters may occur during a construction project which justify an extension, so necessitating a series of such decisions. However, a time must eventually arrive when, having regard to the original contract completion date and the events which have since occurred and any properly granted extensions, the project ought to have been completed. If there is to be a right of deduction by the owner from interim or other moneys currently due, as opposed to a right to sue or deduct after completion of the contract, this will obviously be the date when a right of deduction can first be properly exercised, and many if not most modern contracts accordingly provide expressly for the ascertainment of this final date, often of course the subject of a special reviewing certificate of the A/E, following which the subsequent deduction or recovery of liquidated damages can begin to be made. This is, for example, the Clause 22 certificate referred to in the cases illustrated above under the pre-1980 JCT/RIBA standard forms.

It has been seen that the great majority of construction contracts at the **10·068** present day make no express provision for extensions of time due to later events after the period of culpable delay has commenced, or for the subsequent adjustments to the deduction or recovery of liquidated damages which any such further extensions of time would then require.[63] Where subsequent events occur which are in law the contractor's risk or responsibility, such as weather, strikes, damage to the works or interference by third persons, no further extensions will usually be justified either as a matter of law or of reasonableness, since by definition the contractor will be in breach of the contract and, as a matter of causation, but for his breach the works would have been completed and the events in question would not have delayed construction. On the other hand, later events which are caused by the owner's acts or omissions or breaches of contract, or which are in the owner's areas of contractual responsibility, may either invalidate any further operation of the liquidated damages clause under the prevention principles already discussed in Section 2, *supra*, or, if covered by an applicable extension of time provision, may reduce or modify the liability. In the absence of express provision, however, this may give rise to the problems of adjustment of the damages discussed in Section 2(2), *supra*, where an indication is given of what it is submitted is the correct approach for such adjustments, and reference made to the relevant express provisions which deal with this in the Singapore SIA form of contract.[64]

---

[63] See *supra*, Section 2(2), para. 10·043.
[64] See the 1980 Singapore SIA contract, Clause 24(3), reproduced and discussed in C.C.P.P., pp. 541, 581.

(2) Whether Decision of A/E Binding

10·069   While a person is frequently nominated by the contract to exercise the power to extend time, usually, of course, the owner's A/E, at the present day that function will, it is submitted, be treated as administrative in character and not quasi-arbitral so as to bind either party permanently,[65] although a concept of "temporary finality" (particularly in regard to the owner's deduction power once the contract or extended contract completion date has passed) may in some cases be the objective of the draftsman.[66] In the absence of wording which clearly calls for temporary or permanent finality, extension of time or liquidated damages decisions of the owner or his A/E will, it is submitted, be subject to review by an arbitrator or by the courts.[67]

ILLUSTRATIONS

(1) By Clause 5.02 of the JCCB 1985 Australian standard form the architect was constituted "assessor, valuer or certifier" in respect, *inter alia*, of extensions of time under Clause 9.01 (matters beyond the control of the contractor including defaults of the owner and others) or Clause 9.07 (variations), and by Clause 9.03 he was required to determine what if any extension should be granted. By Clause 5.02.03 either owner or contractor could refer decisions of the architect to arbitration. The arbitration clause, Clause 13, was in general terms, and provided that a notice of dispute was a condition precedent to the commencement of proceedings "whether by way of litigation or arbitration", but contained no express "open up review and revise" powers. The contractor disputed a rejection by the architect of an application to extend time. *Held*, by Cole J., following *Brodie* v. *Cardiff Corporation*,[68] that it was implicit that an arbitrator appointed under Clause 13 had power to review and substitute his decision for that of the architect, and (distinguishing *Northern Regional Health Authority* v. *Derek Crouch Construction Co. Ltd.*,[69] since the contract permitted litigation as well as arbitration), that the courts, in the absence of arbitration, had jurisdiction to determine the question of extension of time: *KBH Construction Ltd.* v. *PSD Development* (1990).[70]
[Note: Cole J. noted that the *Crouch* case has been noted without disapproval in a number of later English cases, but was not asked to consider, apparently, the New South Wales Full Court decision in *Piggott* v. *Townsend* in 1923,[70a] which appears to have escaped attention in the text-books (that fact itself an indication of the novelty of the *Crouch* view).]

10·070   (2) The liquidated damages clause provided that the *architect or arbitrator* might award an extension of time for certain reasons and grant a certificate to

---

[65] See, for an explanation and history of this, C.C.P.P., paras. 17–06 *et seq.*

[66] See Clause 31(11) of the Singapore 1980 SIA contract, reproduced in C.C.P.P., p. 599.

[67] See *ante*, Chap. 6, Section 1(1), para. 6·002 and Section 3(1), paras. 6·031 *et seq.* (and *pace* in the case of the English courts, the *Crouch* case, doubted and criticised *ante*, Chap. 6, paras. 6·063 *et seq.*, and 6·094). See also Subsection (6), *infra*, on the effect of the A/E's extension of time decisions.

[68] [1919] A.C. 337, illustrated *ante*, Chap. 7, para. 7·068.

[69] [1984] Q.B. 644.

[70] 21 N.S.W.L.R. 348.

[70a] See *ante*, Chap. 6, para. 6.063.

that effect. The arbitration clause referred all disputes "except those expressly stipulated to be determined by the architect or employer" to an arbitrator. The final certificate was expressed to be conclusive evidence, subject to the rights of the parties under the arbitration clause, of the value of the works and materials. The owner was entitled to deduct and retain any sums due to him out of moneys due to the contractor. The architect issued a final certificate making no allowance for liquidated damages. The owner claimed to deduct liquidated damages, but the contractors contended that he was bound by the certificates. *Held*, by Lord Kilbrandon, that the extension of time clause was expressly subject to the decision of the arbitrator, and the final certificate itself was subject to review by the arbitrator; but even if it were not, it was conclusive only as to the value of the work, and the owner could accordingly deduct and retain liquidated damages: *Port Glasgow Magistrates* v. *Scottish Construction Co. Ltd.* (1960).[71]

However, in the case of certain English standard form sub-contracts containing apparently unqualified arbitration clauses (although without the express "open up review and revise" formula), one English and one Northern Irish court have held that an architect's extension of time decisions under the clauses in those forms were a condition precedent to the recovery of liquidated damages by the main contractor, and to that extent final and binding on an arbitrator.[72] It has been submitted in Chapter 6[73] that these cases require reconsideration, particularly since the reverse situation (rejected application for extension binding on contractor) was neither considered nor discussed in the judgments.

(3) Effect of Unqualified Certificate

For some decades now in England it has been unusual to find contractual **10·071** provisions which require an A/E's extension of time decisions or the deduction of liquidated damages to be regulated by or recorded in the A/E's payment certificates, or even in the final certificate. There is little doubt that this reflects the important commercial reality already mentioned *supra*, namely that deduction of liquidated damages (as opposed to their ultimate recovery) is intended only as a permissive remedy exercisable at his discretion by the owner in the light of commercial considerations, such as the "nursing" of a contractor in financial difficulties through to completion, although these considerations will not, of course, apply after completion or to the final certificate.

---

[71] 1960 S.L.T. 319, Scotland.
[72] *Brightside Kilpatrick Engineering Services Ltd.* v. *Mitchell Construction* [1975] 2 Lloyd's Rep. 493; *Savage Brothers Ltd.* v. *Shillington Heating Ltd.* (1985) 5 Const.L.J. 275, illustrated and commented on *ante*, Chap. 6, Section 4(3), paras. 6·087 and 6·088. See, however, *Roberts* v. *Bury Improvement Commissioners* (1870) 5 C.P. 310, where some judges at least in the House of Lords considered that an extension of time decision in the contractor's favour under that contract would have bound the owner. However, this was *obiter* and the climate in the industry in regard to the status of A/E's certifying decisions has changed considerably since that time, as explained *ante*, Chap. 6, and in C.C.P.P. paras. 17–06 *et seq*.
[73] Section 4(3), *ante*, para. 6·087.

Most English contracts, therefore, contain an entirely separate certifying machinery outside the payment certificates (or even the final certificate) which govern the recovery and deduction of liquidated damages. In such contracts, the issue by the A/E of apparently unqualified payment certificates will accordingly carry no implication that an extension of time application made previously, for example, has been granted. Clauses 22 and 24 of the pre- and post-1980 RIBA/JCT forms and Clauses 44(3) and (4) and 47(4) of the Fifth ICE conditions, are examples of this type of certifying machinery, and are intended to result in a definitive and if necessary revised and finalised date for completion, following which the owner is expressly permitted to exercise a deduction remedy should he choose to do so, or alternatively to recover the damages by action either then or at a later date.

In modern English construction contracts, therefore, the issue of unqualified payment certificates is irrelevant to the owner's right to deduct or recover liquidated damages, although in some contracts there may be a last date prescribed for doing so, as in the post-1980 RIBA/JCT standard forms.[74] In other contracts, the terms of the final certificate clause itself may prevent any subsequent operation of the liquidated damages machinery,[75] but these latter types of contract are more concerned with the question of the time for exercise of the extension power itself, dealt with separately *infra*, subsection (5). Unqualified certificates will not in general, therefore, prejudice an owner seeking to deduct or recover liquidated damages, but the wording of each contract will require careful consideration. Thus where no particular machinery is prescribed by the contract, time can be extended orally and informally, and an unqualified certificate for payment issued after the contract completion date may at least be evidence of time having been extended by the A/E himself.[76]

ILLUSTRATIONS

10·072　　　(1) After completion, an owner, without mentioning delay, instructed his architect to issue a certificate for what was due, and the architect gave a certificate without deducting liquidated damages. The owner more than once promised to pay on this certificate. The builder tendered evidence of hindrance and waiver by the owner. *Held*, by Crowder J., that the question of liquidated damages was in any event concluded by the architect's certificate: *Arnold* v. *Walker* (1859).[77]

(2) A contract provided for liquidated damages for non-completion to be paid to or deducted by the owner from any money due to the contractor, and that the contract period should not be exceeded unless an extension of time

[74] See Clause 24.2.1.
[75] See the perhaps controversial decision on Clause 30(7) of the 1963 standard forms in *H. Fairweather Ltd.* v. *Asden Securities Ltd.* (1979) 12 BLR 40.
[76] *Laidlaw* v. *Hastings Pier Co.*, *infra*, and see *per* Stout C.J. in *Anderson* v. *Tuapeka County Council* (1900) 19 N.Z.L.R. 1, at p. 8.
[77] 1 F. & F. 671.

was allowed in writing.[78] The inspector certified payment without making any deduction. *Held*, by the Court of Queen's Bench (Mellor, Lush and Hannen J.J.), that a certificate had not been made a condition precedent to recovery of liquidated damages by the owner and the owner could accordingly deduct them from the amount certified: *Jones* v. *St. John's College, Oxford* (1870).[79]

(3) A contract in Ontario provided that in any dispute the architect's decision should be final. The contract also contained provisions for payment and certification of the final balance after completion, "subject to any deduction for the non-fulfilment of the terms of the agreement." No complaint was made, but on presentation of the final certificate the owners sought to deduct liquidated damages for delay. *Held*, by the Court of Queen's Bench (Wilson J.), that on the wording of the contract they were entitled to do so: *Simpson* v. *Kerr* (1873).[80]

(4) A contract provided for £20 per week to be forfeited to the owners by the contractor, and paid to and retained by them as liquidated and ascertained damages for each week during which the work remained unfinished, but that the engineer should have power to grant extensions of time in certain circumstances. All disputes were to be referred to the engineer *whose decision was to be final*. Extras were ordered, but not in writing or countersigned as required by the contract, and for 14 months after the completion date the engineer issued certificates which were paid in full, including his final certificate, and none of which took no account of the penalties. When sued on the certificates, the owners disputed liability for the extras and sought to deduct liquidated damages. *Held*, by the Court of Exchequer Chamber, that by paying without deduction the owners had disentitled themselves from recovering the liquidated damages. In addition, on the facts there was evidence that the engineer, by issuing his certificates without any deduction, including his final certificate which took no account of the penalties, had in fact exercised his power to extend the time, since no particular form for doing so was set out in the contract. *Per* Coleridge C.J., the penalties were to be reserved or retained the moment they accrued from time to time: *Laidlaw* v. *Hastings Pier Co.* (1874).[81]

[Note: Although this was a decision of five judges, who appear to have been unanimous, it is not easy to support on the first ground. The wording of the liquidated damages provision was no different from that in many other contracts, although the contract was silent as to the machinery for carrying it out. The court appears to have been influenced by the engineer's role as an effective arbitrator, there was an element of prevention or default on the part of the owners, and no apparent support for the owners' contentions on the part of the engineer. The second ground seems easier to sustain, and was cited by Stout C.J. in the New Zealand Court of Appeal in *Anderson* v. *Tuapeka County Council*, illustrated *infra*.]

10·073

(5) A contract empowered the architect to award extensions of time, but made no specific provision for him to deal with liquidated damages in his certificates. There was delay, but he certified without any deduction. The contractors took a preliminary point of law, contending that the certificate was conclusive evidence that time had been extended. *Held*, by Phillimore J., that while the certificate was very strong evidence that the architect had extended the time, it was not conclusive, and it was open to the owners to prove that he

10·074

---

[78] See the clause in more detail, *supra*, para. 10·031.
[79] L.R. 6 Q.B. 115. This case is more fully illustrated *supra*, Section 2, para. 10·031.
[80] 33 Upp.Can.Q.B. 345.
[81] Hudson, *Building Contracts* (4th ed.), Vol. 2, p. 13. See also *Anderson* v. *Tuapeka County Council* (1900) 19 N.Z.L.R. 1, illustrated *infra*, Subsection (5), para. 10·081.

had not in fact determined the matter: *British Thomson-Houston Co.* v. *West* (1903).[82]

(6) A contract made the engineer's decision final in the event of any dispute. He also had power to order extras, but his power to order extensions of time was expressed to be referable only to strikes or lock-outs. The final certificate included the value of extras, but contained no deduction for penalties or delays arising from the extras. *Held*, by the Irish King's Bench Division (Gibson and Madden JJ., Boyd J. dissenting), that the engineer had no power to determine the question of liquidated damages in respect of delay due to extras, his certificate did not prevent that issue being raised, and as in fact the delay was due to the extras, the provision for liquidated damages was of no effect: *Gallivan* v. *Killarney Urban District Council* (1912).[83]

(4) Contents of Certificate

10·075   Since early times, architects and engineers appear to have had the greatest difficulty in issuing certificates which sufficiently comply with the requirements of the contracts which they have chosen or been required to administer. In the case of payment certificates, including final certificates, it has been seen that the courts have shown a fairly generous latitude in interpreting letters or other documents issued by the A/E as fulfilling the contractual requirements,[84] but in the case of the extension of time documentation, on which a right of deduction seriously affecting the contractor's cashflow will almost invariably depend, and also no doubt reflecting earlier judicial attitudes of disapproval of liquidated damages provisions generally, the courts have approached the attempts of A/Es to provide the required documentation with much more severity, even in cases where the A/E's intentions have appeared to be tolerably clear. As a result, owners have on a number of occasions found difficulty in enforcing their remedy, particularly at the interlocutory stages of a dispute.

ILLUSTRATIONS

(1) An owner proferred a letter from the architect saying that he was entitled to deduct liquidated damages under Clause 16 (the equivalent of Clause 22 of the priced main contract forms) of the RIBA/JCT prime-cost contract, as justification for set-off of liquidated damages against a contractor's claim for moneys due. The letter gave full details of the date from which damages should run and the actual completion date, together with calculations showing the sums due. *Held*, by the Court of Appeal, that the letter did not make clear what extensions had been granted, nor did it record the architect's opinion that the work ought reasonably to have been completed by the date shown as the start of liquidated damages in the letter, so that it was

---

[82] 19 T.L.R. 493. See also the *Port Glasgow Magistrates* case, *supra*, para. 10·070.
[83] [1912] 2 I.R. 356. Compare *Dodd* v. *Churton* and *Murdoch* v. *Lockie*, illustrated *supra*, paras. 10·032 and 10·033.
[84] See *ante*, Chap. 6, Section 6(1) and (2), paras. 6·153 *et seq.*

not a valid Clause 16 certificate, and the set-off failed: *Token Construction Ltd.* v. *Charlton Estates Ltd.* (1973).[85]

(2) An architect acting under the 1963 RIBA/JCT main contract wrote a **10·076** letter to five named nominated sub-contractors informing them that in his recent extension of time given to the main contractor a stipulated period for their work had been allowed "in accordance with clause 27(D)(ii) of the main contract against the extensions which they had claimed." In another letter to the main contractor, he allowed the stipulated against the longer period of extension which had been requested by the main contractor in respect of that nominated sub-contractor. Clause 27(D)(ii) of the main contract was a clause requiring the architect to certify that a nominated sub-contract ought reasonably to have been completed within the sub-contract or its extended period, as was also required by Clause 8(a) of the relevant sub-contract, so that the architect's intention was, in the light of the two letters, quite clear: in an action by the sub-contractor for moneys due, the main contractor sought to deduct liquidated damages. *Held*, by Higgins J., following the *Token* case, that notwithstanding the reference to clause 27(D)(ii), the language was ambiguous and did not indicate sufficiently clearly that the work ought reasonably to have been completed by the required date: *Savage Brothers Ltd.* v. *Shillington Heating Ltd.* (1985).[86]

(3) An architect in Hong Kong issued a purported certificate under Clause 22 of the main contract that "the works" ought reasonably to have been completed by a named date. A copy was sent to one only of the nominated sub-contractors on the project. Clause 8(a) of the sub-contract required a certificate to be given to the main contractor with a copy to the nominated sub-contractor in writing stating that in the architect's opinion the sub-contract work ought reasonably to have been completed within the specified or extended sub-contract period, as a condition of the main contractor being entitled to damages for delay in completion from the sub-contractor. The main contractor sought to lead evidence by reference to correspondence showing that the architect intended the certificate to refer to the sub-contract work. *Held*, by Godfrey J., following the *Token* case, that, it being admitted that compliance with clause 8(a) was a condition precedent, the sub-contractor was entitled to summary judgment: *Pyrok Industries Ltd.* v. *Chee Tat Engineering Co. Ltd.* (1988).[87]

A word of caution is required as to the ultimate substantive result in the **10·077** above cases, concerned as they are with questions of summary judgment. The absence of a valid certificate of delay or of reasonable completion under provisions like these can have no ultimate consequence, it is submitted, unless on the true construction of the contract the certificate, or its absence, is to be final and conclusive. Even if final and conclusive, the question also arises whether it is a case of "temporary" or permanent finality. For example, Clause 8(a) of the English standard forms of sub-contract involved in the above cases is expressly stated in the sub-contract

---

[85] 1 BLR 48. At this time, the *Dawnay* line of cases entitling a contractor to summary judgment in the absence of an expressly permitted set-off had not been overruled. The case is much more fully illustrated, together with the contents of the architect's letter, *ante*, Chap. 6, Section 6(2), para. 6·158.

[86] 5 Const.L.J. 295, illustrated and doubted *ante*, Chap. 6, para. 6·088.

[87] 41 BLR 124.

to be condition precedent, but the question still remains whether, assuming withholding of a certificate is seen as rejection of an owner's or, in a sub-contract, the main contractor's application by the A/E, it is open to review by an arbitrator or, failing an arbitrator, by the courts, that is, the "finality" may be "temporary" only. It has been suggested in Chapter 6 that, in spite of recent decisions in England, it should not be assumed that the A/E's certificate (or refusal of a certificate) in regard to extension of time under these forms of contract or sub-contract will be *permanently* binding on the parties, and that consideration needs to be given to the reciprocal effect which might result from such an interpretation (for example, the contractor or sub-contractor bound by the architect's refusal of an extension of time, or the owner or main contractor by its allowance).

In addition, the question must arise whether formal defects in attempted certificates can be corrected by using a further fully complying certificate. Again, there is the question of the normal damages for delay which in most contracts with liquidated damages provisions will be an alternative should the liquidated damages clause fail for any reason. It would obviously be quite wrong if such damages were to be recoverable as an alternative to liquidated damages in a case of owner prevention, as has already been seen *supra*, but not in a case where it is only inadequate certification which has taken place. As a further consideration, the particular English sub-contract forms in the above cases do not as a fact usually contain *liquidated damages* provisions as such. While setting up an apparent liquidated damages machinery of certification and extension of time these sub-contracts actually provide for payment of *ordinary damages* due to delay in completion provable by the main contractor in the usual way, with the machinery effectively regulating the period of culpable delay to be used for calculating the damages, but not the quantum of damages.[88] Finally, at the present day many liquidated damages provisions are, due to producer pressures, in reality limitation of damage clauses.

It seems unlikely that either party to modern construction contracts or sub-contracts intends to accord more than, at the very most, a purely temporary administrative jurisdiction on the A/E to deal with matters of delay and immediate deduction of liquidated damages,[89] as was undoubtedly the case in some of the earlier Victorian contracts.

(5) Time for Exercise

10·078   In practice, architects and engineers often delay reaching a decision on questions of extension of time until a very late stage in the work, or even after actual completion. It remains to consider to what extent this may be permitted by the contract. It should be said at once that it has perhaps not

---

[88] See, *e.g.* Clause 8(a) of the FASS "green form" sub-contracts.
[89] See *ante*, Chap. 6, Sections 1(1) and 3(1) for the general question, and Section 4(3) and the *Ramac*, *Brightside* and *Shillington* cases there illustrated and commented on.

been sufficiently appreciated by judiciaries in the past that this practice usually suits the contractor concerned admirably, since for the time being it averts the prospect of any imminent deduction of liquidated damages while giving the contractor more time to assemble and prepare detailed arguments showing why an extension is justified, and with the additional aspect that, in the negotiation of various other claims and counterclaims which usually precede the issue of the final certificate, the owner's claim for damages may be compromised or withdrawn. Whatever the contractual requirements, therefore, there may frequently be present elements of waiver or estoppel which may prevent subsequent complaint as to the lateness of the extension of time decision. On the other hand, an opposing consideration may be that where a perhaps controversial event has occurred which may or may not justify an extension, a contractor, particularly in a contract with potentially very heavy liquidated damages for delay in completion, may understandably wish to have an early indication of the A/E's decision on granting an extension, which will then enable the contractor to balance the cost of incurring uneconomical acceleration expenditure against the advantage of eliminating the liquidated or other damages risk.[89a]

10·079   Thus it has been seen that express refusal or continued failure to deal promptly with an extension of time application on the part of the A/E, as in all matters requiring certification, can absolve the party concerned from the necessity of obtaining the certificate or extension,[90] as well as constituting a breach of contract sounding in damages.[91] However, the more usual situation involved in real life is one of procrastination, or of a "wait and see" attitude, whether in making an application for an extension of time by the builder, or in dealing with it by the A/E. So far as failure by a contractor to give a required notice of a claim for an extension is concerned, it has been held that such a contractual requirement will not usually be interpreted as a condition precedent, although lateness or failure to give the notice in time may entitle the owner, on appropriate facts, to damages.[92]

The present discussion, however, is concerned with the ascertainment, in the absence of express provision, of the time when an extension should be made by the A/E and, the consequences should there be a failure to consider and make the extension within that time. It goes without saying that this discussion is not concerned with a considered rejection of the contractor's claim, so that no grant of an extension is made in the permit-**10·080** ted time for that reason. So far as the legal effect of failure or delay in making the decisions under an extension time clause is concerned, the position was stated since at least the fourth edition of this book to be as follows:

[89a] Compare the *Peru Corporation* case *infra*

[90] See, *e.g. Watts* v. *McLeay* (1911) 19 W.L.R. 916, Alberta, *ante*, Chap. 6, para. 6·120.

[91] See *Perini Corporation* v. *Commonwealth of Australia* [1969] 2 N.S.W.R. 530, *ante*, Chap. 6, para. 6·133.

[92] See *per* Vinelott J. in *London Borough of Merton* v. *Leach* (1985) 32 BLR 51, at p. 90, and see *ante*, Chap. 4, Section 1(5), paras. 4·132 *et seq*. See also *per* Nourse L.J. in *Temloc Ltd.* v. *Errill Properties Ltd.* (1987) 39 BLR 30, at p. 39.

"Where there is power to extend the time for delays caused by the building owner, and such delays have in fact taken place, but the power to extend the time has not been exercised, either at all or within the time expressly or impliedly limited by the contract, it follows (unless the builder has agreed to complete to time notwithstanding such delays) that the building owner has lost the benefit of the clause, as the contract time has in such case ceased to be applicable, there is no date from which penalties can run, and therefore no liquidated damages can be recovered."[93]

It seems that this statement in the fourth edition was derived from the combined effect of two New Zealand cases, namely a dictum of Prendergast C.J. in *Murdoch* v. *Lockie*,[94] where the contract expressly required an extension to be given at the time of ordering a variation, which was cited and applied three years later by the New Zealand Court of Appeal in *Anderson* v. *Tuapeka County Council*,[95] where no express time for making the extension was specified.

ILLUSTRATIONS

10·081
(1) A contract in New Zealand provided that "in the event of any alteration ... being required, the engineer should allow such an extension of time *as he shall think adequate*", and that any sum as liquidated damages should be computed from the expiration of such extended time. Extra works were ordered, but no reference was then made by the architect to extension of time. Some months after the contract completion date, the architect, for the first time, deducted penalties from the sum due in his June interim certificate, which contained the words "Less penalties for May 26 days at £3.00, £78.00", and thereafter continued deducting penalties in later certificates. Later still, he ordered further extra works, again without reference to extension of time. The contractor sued to recover the deducted penalties. *Held*, by the New Zealand Court of Appeal, that while the certificate clearly intended to substitute a new date for completion and grant an extension of time up to that date, it was too late, since the power should have been exercised at the time of ordering the extras, and the contractor could recover in full: *Anderson* v. *Tuapeka County Council* (1990).[96]

[Note: It should be observed that the above case was concerned with the time for granting an extension in respect of variations (extra work) which had been ordered by the architect, but the contract, unlike that in *Murdoch* v. *Lockie*, was silent as to the precise time for granting the extension. Despite Stout C.J.'s view as to the meaning of the emphasised wording, there was no convincing express wording suggesting that it should be at the time when the variation was ordered, unlike the quite specific wording in the *Murdoch* case. Moreover there seems to be no valid reason, it is submitted, why an architect should not in the case of some types of variation, in the absence of express provision, wait until the varied work has at least been partially if not entirely completed before determining the amount of the extension—as *e.g.* where the line of a sewer is altered to what may or may not turn out to be more

---

[93] Hudson, *Building Contracts* (4th ed.), p. 528; *op. cit.* (6th ed.), p. 359.
[94] (1897) 15 N.Z.L.R. 296, illustrated *supra*, para. 10·033.
[95] (1900) 19 N.Z.L.R. 1, illustrated *infra*.
[96] 19 N.Z.L.R. 1.

difficult ground. No argument or discussion of this kind appears to have taken place, and it is submitted that the case would not be so decided at the present day in the light of these now better understood considerations.]

(2) A contract provided that: "it shall be lawful for the engineer ... to grant **10·082** from time to time and at any time or times ... such extension of time for completion ... *and that either prospectively or retrospectively*, and to assign such other time or times, for completion as to him may appear reasonable." The engineer's decision under this clause was to be final. The contract completion date was November 1931. There were many complaints about the contractor's progress during construction, but some extras were also ordered, and the work was not finally completed until late July 1932. The architect in December wrote saying that he was considering deducting liquidated damages and inviting replies. After receiving two letters from the contractor which sought to justify the delay, the architect then wrote giving details of his reasoned decision on extension of time in October, but invited any further comments before he finally reported to the owners. In November he finally issued a certificate granting an extension of time until February 1932 and certifying liquidated damages for the period between February and July 1932. *Held*, by du Parcq J., approving the sixth edition p. 359 of this book, and citing *Anderson* v. *Tuapeka County Council*, the use of the words "retrospectively" and "assign such other time or times for completion" would permit an extension given within a reasonable time of the delay in question coming to an end, but the wording could not be read as allowing an extension to be given after the substituted date for completion, and liquidated damages could not be recovered: *Miller* v. *London City Council* (1934).[97]

[Note: While the facts are not entirely clear from the report, the architect's conduct seems to have been unexceptionable in this case and very much in accordance with the modern practice in England at the present day, and there was no possible prejudice to the contractor. It seems very possible, having regard to the obvious benefit received by the contractor as a result of the delayed decision following the contemporary dispute as to progress, that elements of waiver and acquiescence by the contractor had almost certainly been present, although this was not argued before the Court.]

(3) The then standard form of RIBA/JCT contract provided that: "if in the **10·083** opinion of the architect the works be delayed ... (for a number of causes ...) the architects will make a fair and reasonable extension of time for completion." The contract completion date was February 1949. One month before that, in January 1949, the contractor made two applications for an extension of time of 12 months, based on non-availability of labour and materials, which the architect only formally acknowledged, although the owners later wrote refusing the extension. The work was completed in August 1950, and the architect wrote in December 1950 extending the time until May 1949, and also certified that the work should have been completed then. The owners claimed liquidated damages from May 1949 to August 1950. The contractor took no step to dispute the architect's decision or invoke the arbitration clause, but took a preliminary point of law that the extension was given too late. *Held*, by the Court of Appeal, citing *Sattin* v. *Poole*,[98] and distinguishing *Miller* v. *London City Council* on the ground of the very.special wording "assign such other time or times for completion" in that case, that the power could be exercised at any time: *ABC Ltd.* v. *Waltham Holy Cross Urban District Council*.[99]

---

97 50 T.L.R. 479.
98 (1901) Hudson, *Building Contracts* (4th ed.), 306.
99 [1952] 2 All E.R. 452.

[Note: In this case Denning L.J. expressed the opinion that it would usually be necessary for an architect to wait until actual completion in case further events might occur justifying an extension of time, such as strikes.[1] If that was right, not only would there be no power under these forms of contract to deduct liquidated damages until actual completion by the contractor had been achieved, but the contractor would also be entitled to contractual extensions of time for matters such as strikes or bad weather, occurring during a period of culpable delay, neither of which propositions will usually be correct, it is submitted. Only a matter for which the owner is responsible (*e.g.* prevention by extras or breach of contract) will justify an extension or other adjustment once the certified date when the work should have been completed has passed and liquidated damages have become deductible, it is submitted.[2]

10·084   (4) Clause 35.2 of a West Australian contract in the standard CA 24.1/1964 form required the contractor to give the earliest possible notice of a claim for extension of time *for any cause considered to justify an extension of time*, and if the engineer "considers the causes *such as to justify an extension of time* and that all reasonable action has been or will be taken to prevent such delay the engineer *shall grant* such extension of time as he thinks fit". Clause 40.1 gave a power to order variations, and required a similar early notification by the contractor "if his obligations under the contract would be affected by the variation order", and for a counter-notification "forthwith" that the engineer confirmed or withdrew the order. If confirmed, the contractor's "obligations shall be varied as required by the Engineer". Orders for variations were given, but no confirmation of the orders were apparently requested or given, and the contractor subsequently made prompt applications for extension of time. In November 1969 the contractor wrote summarising his applications but saying that he was not yet in a position to assess a likely completion date and suggesting a meeting for that purpose. In December 1969, two further letters were written asking for an extension of six and a half weeks for one matter and reserving an unspecified claim for other variations. In April 1970, the engineer acknowledged the contractors various outstanding letters and proposed a meeting to discuss them, and after discussions wrote later in April 1970 giving his final decisions on extending the completion date, accompanied by another letter certifying deduction of liquidated damages. The work was in fact completed in late May 1970. The contractor claimed that by failing to nominate a date for completion following the ordering of a variation, the owner's right to claim liquidated damages had been lost. *Held*, by Burt J., although the generalised wording in Clause 35.2 could not cover preventions due to the ordering of variations, Clause 40.1 did empower the engineering to give an extension for variations; but, applying *Miller* v. *London City Council*, and citing the sixth edition, p. 359, the power must be exercised within the time fixed by the contract or a reasonable time. Under Clause 35.2 it would need to be within a reasonable time of the order being given, and under Clause 40.2 at the time of confirming the order (which in this case could be implied), so that liquidated damages were not recoverable: *MacMahon Construction Ltd.* v. *Crestwood Estates Ltd.* (1970).[3]

[Note: This decision seems open to doubt on a number of accounts. Apart from questions of waiver and the contractor's admitted failure to stipulate himself the extension required until the April meeting, the extension was made before the work was finished and *ABC Limited* v. *Waltham Holy Cross*

---

[1] *Ibid.* at pp. 454H–455A.
[2] See the discussion on prevention by late variations *supra*, Subsection (2), paras. 10·043 *et seq.*
[3] [1971] W.A.R. 162.

Urban District Council, with which it seems inconsistent, was apparently not cited. There do not appear to be any express words in either of the two clauses requiring an immediate extension decision at the time (the word "forthwith" in Clause 40.2 applies only to the *confirmation* of the order and not to any subsequent "variation of the obligations of the contractor", *i.e.* extension of time, made by the Engineer under that clause.

(5) Clause 11.4 of a New Zealand Civil Engineering contract provided that **10·085** "should the amount of extra or additional work of any kind whatsoever which may occur be such as fairly to entitle the Contractor to an extension of time for the completion of the work *the Engineer shall determine* the amount of such extension."[4] The engineer postponed dealing with the extension claims until the end of the contract in order to assess the full effect of the delay events. On a review by the court of the engineer's decision on extension of time, the contractor argued that there was no power to extend time after the contract time for completion had expired, so that the right to liquidated damages had been lost. *Held*, by Casey J., following the *ABC* case, that the extension could be given at any time after completion *until the engineer was functus officio*, so that liquidated damages were in principle recoverable: *N.Z. Structures Ltd.* v. *McKenzie* (1979).[5]

(6) The contract completion date, in a New Zealand contract containing the same extension of time clause as in the *N.Z. Structures* case, was December 30, 1975. The contractor applied for extensions of time in November 1975 because of extra delays by other contractors. On March 2, 1976 the engineer gave an extension until March 24, and on April 29 a further extension until June. In the event, the contract was completed 46 weeks after the final extended date allowed by the engineer, but the arbitrator awarded a further 41 weeks extension, leaving the contractor liable for five weeks. The contractor argued that the extensions given after the specified contract completion date were too late, and that liquidated damages were not recoverable. *Held*, by Roper J., after extensively reviewing the *Anderson, Miller, ABC* and *McMahon Construction* cases, that it was reasonable to make the extension of time after the contract completion date, and that liquidated damages could be recovered: *Fernbrook Trading Ltd.* v. *Taggart* (1979).[6]

While most of the above cases are concerned with extensions due to the **10·086** ordering of variations, in principle there must also be a proper time for making an extension on the many other grounds permitted by modern construction contracts, including "neutral" matters such as weather or strikes, or matters of owner responsibility, such as provision of information or affording possession of the site; or delays caused by his other contractors. The tenth edition of this book contained the following passage:

"There are, it is suggested, three possible constructions of extension of time clauses in so far as the time for exercise of the power is concerned. In the first place, the contract may contemplate that the power should be exercised at once upon the occurrence of the event causing delay. This construction may

---

[4] Compare the identical wording of the English fourth edition of the ICE conditions.
[5] [1979] 1 N.Z.L.R. 515, at p. 540. In the event, however, Casey J. held that the contractor was entitled to a full extension of time.
[6] [1979] 1 N.Z.L.R. 556.

be appropriate to non-continuing causes of delay such the ordering of extras. Secondly, the contract may contemplate that the power should be exercised when the full effect upon the contract programme is known. This is appropriate to continuing causes of delay such as strikes, withholding of the site, and so on, or to cases, like some extras, where precise estimation may be difficult or impossible. Or, thirdly, the contract may contemplate exercise of the power at any time before issue of the final certificate. Since the case of *ABC Ltd.* v. *Waltham Holy Cross Urban District Council*, a decision on the then current RIBA form of contract which distinguished *Miller* v. *London City Council* on somewhat slender grounds, it is suggested that this latter interpretation will normally prevail in the absence of clear language to the contrary, particularly as the ambit of most modern extension of time clauses usually comprehends delays due to causes of many different kinds. Even, however, where a contract clause is in the second of the above categories, the extension of time need not necessarily be granted before the contract date for completion. If, for example, a strike were to last beyond the contract date, the extent of the delay could not be known, or the necessary extension of time granted, until after the contract time had expired."[7]

10·087   There seems no need to modify the views expressed in this passage, but before the widest possible interpretation of the time for granting an extension of time is too easily adopted as a result of the *ABC* case, it is important to bear in mind the distinction between those individual applications for extension of time made from time to time during the construction period on which the contractor may request an early decision, and the later more definitive review called for by many contracts with the object of arriving at a finalised completion date, and authorising deduction from current payments. It will be the apparent objective of most liquidated damages clauses to enable the owner to deduct from moneys due on interim certificate, and for this purpose a supplementary "reasonable completion" certificate or decision of this latter kind is a logical necessity. There may also be the consideration that the contractor should be entitled to receive an early indication, if asked for, of the A/E's decision on individual grounds of extension as they arise, so as to enable the contractor to decide whether or not to incur possible substantial acceleration expenditure and avoid the prospect of paying liquidated damages.[8] That might point, perhaps, to decisions on individual grounds of extension within a reasonable time of the effect on overall progress being made known:

10·088   "I think it must be implicit in the normal extension clause that the contractor is to be informed as to his new completion date as soon as it is reasonably practical. If the sole cause is the ordering of extra work then, in the normal course, the extension should be given at the time of ordering so that the contractor has a target for which to aim. Where the cause of delay lies beyond the employer, and particularly where its duration is uncertain, then the extension order may be delayed, although even there it would be a reasonable inference to draw from the ordinary extension clause that the extension should be

---

[7] This passage was mentioned with approval in both the *N.Z. Structures* and *Fernbrook Trading* cases.

[8] See *Perini Corporation* v. *Commonwealth of Australia* [1969] 2 N.S.W.L.R. 530 illustrated *ante* Chap. 6, Section 5(5) para. 6·133, and see Chap. 8, Section 2(3), pp. 8–119.

given a reasonable time after the factors which will govern the exercise of the engineer's discretion has been established. Where there are multiple causes of delay there may be no alternative but to leave the final decision until just before the issue of the final certificate."[9]

So far as the "final review" type of certificate or extension is concerned, this would certainly point to a duty owed by the certifier *to his client* to carry out a final review of all current relevant grounds of extension at or about the time when the work should have been completed, which by definition will be before the works have actually been completed. However, since a delayed decision on this can benefit no-one but the contractor, it by no means follows that the time obligation to be implied in the contract between the owner and the contractor should be the same, and there is no reason at all why such a review should not be made at a considerably later date, limited only, no doubt, and possibly not even then, by the date when the A/E's final payment certificate is given.

However, it is submitted that the earlier cases may have been at fault, **10·089** and the later cases perhaps somewhat less so, in too easily putting forward or acquiescing in the notion that lateness in granting an extension of time (apart from being a breach of contract which will undoubtedly sound, if necessary, in damages, in much the same way as a contractor's failure to give notice or make his application for an extension of time)[10] should be treated in the same way as a case of prevention, or as a condition precedent, so having the effect of invalidating the liquidated damages clause altogether. There is no reason, either in legal principle or on consensual interpretative grounds, for so construing an express or implied obligation in a construction contract to grant an extension within a stipulated or a reasonable time, it is submitted. The strict view seems to have been first put forward, not unreasonably in a very different prevention context, by Prendergast C.J. in *Murdoch* v. *Lockie*, and in the very different judicial climate then obtaining in regard to liquidated damages clauses in general. As has been seen, *Murdoch* v. *Lockie* was rapidly adopted and applied by the New Zealand Court of Appeal in the *Anderson* case in 1900, and was stated as an effective rule of law in the fourth edition of this book in 1914, and in the sixth edition at page 359, which was followed by Burt J. in the *McMahon* case, *supra*. It can be seen that that view was rather more tentatively stated in the tenth edition.[11]

Given the quite different attitudes at the present day to liquidated damages provisions, and bearing in mind that producer pressures have meant that many liquidated damages clauses are effectively damage limitation clauses, and also having regard to the obvious advantages to contractors of deferred decisions on extension of time, thereby postponing any drain on their cashflow by way of deduction, there no longer seems any sufficient

---

[9] *Per* Roper J. in *Fernbrook Trading Ltd.* v. *Taggart* [1979] 1 N.Z.L.R. 556, at p. 568.
[10] See the discussion *supra* and the case of *London Borough of Merton* v. *Leach* (1985) 32 BLR 51 there referred to.
[11] See the tenth edition, p. 644.

reason, it is submitted, for according the contractor any remedy other than a right to damages, if provable, in the event of an extension of time decision being unnecessarily or unreasonably delayed in breach of contract.

10·090   This is not to say that in principle a contract may not contain sufficiently express provisions designed, for whatever reason, to bring the right to liquidated damages to an end if not exercised by a certain time.

ILLUSTRATION

A contract in the 1963 RIBA/JCT form had a completion date of March 1974. By May 1975, while work was still continuing, extensions totalling nine weeks were granted, and in June 1975 the architect certified under Clause 22 that the work ought reasonably to have been completed by May 1975. Practical completion took place in December 1975 and in 1976 the architect granted a further extension until October 1975, but no new Clause 22 certificate was issued. The final certificate was in July 1977, and in March 1978 the architect issued a Clause 22 certificate confirming October 1975 as the "reasonable completion" date. The contractor contended that liquidated damages could not be recovered on the basis of the 1978 Clause 22 certificate, since it was too late. *Held*, by Judge Sir William Stabb Q.C., (a) that the final certificate was under the wording of Clause 30(7) of the contract, conclusive, in the absence of notice of arbitration within the permitted time, that the works had been finished to time, and additionally (b) that even if not, the architect was thereby rendered *functus officio* so that he had no power to issue a later Clause 22 certificate, and liquidated damages were not recoverable: *H. Fairweather Ltd.* v. *Asden Securities Ltd.* (1979).[12]
[Note: It may be inferred that the second Clause 22 certificate was issued to remedy a procedural oversight, since the effective extensions had already been granted in 1976. With respect to this distinguished and experienced judge, neither ground of his decision seems very convincing, on a careful examination of the wording of Clause 30(7). The contract conditions would not in any case, unlike the 1980 forms, seem to have permitted a further Clause 22 certificate after the first had been given, and on the strict legalities, the owner might have chosen to rely on the earlier Clause 22 certificate, giving credit by way of waiver for the longer period of extension later granted, it is submitted. The case, however, illustrates the possibility of express provisions designed to terminate a right to liquidated damages if not exercised in time, and also the distinction between individual extensions and the special review decision leading to a finalised extended completion date.]

It should be noted that in the recent *Balfour Beatty* case it was conceded in the Court of Appeal that the wording of the extension of time clause in Clause 25.3.1 of the RIBA/JCT 1980 contract did not permit an extension of time to be given, and a new date fixed as required by the clause, after the contract or a previously extended date had passed.[12a] This concession seems a doubtful one on the wording; but in any event it should be remembered when construing doubtful wording in an extension of time clause on

---

[12] 12 BLR 40.
[12a] See *supra*, para. 10·046.

this point that nearly all provisions of this kind will of necessity involve a retrospective decision in the above sense in cases where a continuing cause of delay (such as a strike or some legal impediment to progress) commences before, but continues after, the contract or a previously extended date has passed; since until the cause of delay has ceased to operate it will be impossible to fix a new date or determine the length of the extension.

(6) Effect on Damages Claimed by Contractor

Where the cause of delay is due to breach of contract by the owner, and there is also an applicable power to extend the time, the exercise of that power will not, in the absence of the clearest possible language, deprive the contractor of his right to damages for the breach,[13] nor will it conversely establish his right to damage for the breach although it may of course rank as an admission by the owner's agent for evidentiary purposes. Thus, in *Roberts* v. *Bury Commissioners*[14] Kelly C.B. said:

10·091

> "It is provided that it shall be lawful for the architect to grant an extension of time, but it is neither said that the architect must give it ... nor that the contractor must accept whatever extension of time the architect is pleased to give, in full satisfaction of his claim for damages."

Provisions which attempt to achieve this result will be strictly construed against the owner.

ILLUSTRATION

A contract provided by Clause 11 that non-delivery of the site, delay in giving the written order to commence, or delivery of plans, drawings, sections "or any other delay from whatever cause alleged against the council or its officials" should not vitiate the contract or entitle the contractor to any allowance in respect of money, time or otherwise other than such extension of time as might be given. The extension of time clause included, among other things, delay due to extras ordered by the council. *Held, obiter*, by du Parcq J., clause 11 did not include delay during construction due to extras, or interference by other contractors of the employer: *Miller* v. *London City Council* (1934).[15] [Note: The above type of clause, relatively common in the United States, is there known as a 'no damage' clause. These are discussed *ante*, Chap. 8.][16]

---

[13] See, *e.g. Trollope & Colls* v. *Singer* (1913), Hudson, *Building Contracts* (4th ed.), Vol. 1, p. 849, illustrated *ante*, Chap. 4, Section 2, para. 4·181 and *Lawson* v. *Wallasey Local Board* (1883) 11 Q.B.D. 229, illustrated *ante*, Chap. 6, para. 6·015.

[14] (1870) L.R. 5 C.P. 310, at p. 327.

[15] 50 T.L.R. 479.

[16] Section 2(4)(b), para. 8·217.

(7) Phased Completion

10·091A   In addition to provisions for partial re-entry or occupation with a reducing effect on liquidated damages as discussed in Section 2(5) *supra*, phased completion (that is to say provisions for separate completion dates and damages for identified parts of a project) is now contemplated by at least one United Kingdom standard form (the fifth and subsequent ICE Conditions, with their provisions for "Sectional Completion" under Clause 47). In the absence of carefully considered provisions, parties can make use of ordinary unaltered standard forms without realising the complications in regard to extension of time likely to result.

ILLUSTRATION

Phase I of a contract using the RIBA/JCT standard forms was to be completed on April 30th, 1969, subject to extensions of time under Clause 23. Phase III was necessarily dependent on completion of Phase I, and was to start six months after the certificate of practical completion of Phase I, and be completed by April 30th, 1972, subject to extension of time grounds which made no mention of Phase I being completed late as a ground for extension. Phase I was delayed by 59 weeks, for which an extension of time for Phase I of 47 weeks was given. This had the effect of reducing the period of construction for Phase III from 30 months to 16 months (as a result of the 59 weeks delay to Phase I) unless an extension of time could be given for Phase III. The owners (who understandably could not find nominated sub-contractors for Phase III able to quote for such a reduced period) sought a declaration that the contract period for Phase III was subject to the extensions properly due and granted for Phase I. The contractors, who were contending for a longer extension for Phase I than that given, contended that in any case no extension could be granted for Phase III on account of extensions granted for Phase I. A majority of the Court of Appeal held that there was an implied power of extension for Phase III in the terms submitted by the owners, and also (*per* Lord Denning M.R.) that the prevention principle in any event applied to discharge the Phase III completion date. *Held*, by the House of Lords, that there were four possible formulations of the implied term involving an extension of Phase III equivalent to: (a) those extensions for Phase I which had been due to acts of the owners; (b) the extensions actually certified by the architect for Phase I; (c) those extensions properly allowable for Phase I (*e.g.* by an arbitrator); and (d) the total actual period of delay on Phase I; and that, in view of the various quite different alternatives, no term could be implied. *Per* Lord Dilhorne: he was satisfied the real intention had been to allow 30 months from actual completion of Phase I for completion of Phase III: *Trollope & Colls Ltd.* v. *N.W. Metropolitan Hospital Board* (1973).[16a]

[Note: The contractor's contention in this case was clearly a tactical precursor to legal argument that the owners' proposed nominations for Phase III were a breach of Clause 27(a) of the contract, which would invalidate the liquidated damages provisions altogether, and possibly also secure monetary compensation in return for agreeing to the late nominations. Lord Denning seems to have been alone in appreciating that, if there were any delays to Phase I for which the contractor was responsible, that would prevent the contractor from asserting any breach of contract by the owners when nominating

---

[16a] [1973] 1 W.L.R. 601.

sub-contractors for Phase III, so that an implied term as contended for by the owners extending Phase III for those matters where the contractors were entitled to an extension on Phase I would, quite apart from being the most sensible and likely in subjective terms of the parties' intentions, neatly deal with any possible further anomalies arising from the operation of the term itself. This was, of course, a "one-off" contract, and the result not only anomalous but difficult to square with any reasonable consensual or "business" interpretation. The spectacle of contractors contending *against* their being given an extension of time is not, of course, unusual having regard to the somewhat artificial nature of the *Peak* v. *McKinney* doctrine.[16b] The facts of this particular case might well justify an application of good faith principles, were these to become part of English law.][16c]

Section 4. Summary of Preceding Sections

In view of the complication of the earlier case-law in the English courts on liquidated damages and extension of time clauses, itself principally due to an anxiety to avoid the effect of liquidated damages clauses on the assumption that they were likely to be *in terrorem*, and oppressive, although this view is certainly not shared at the present day by judges or court administrators in England—it may be useful if a short summary is attempted of the preceding sections of this chapter and of the present state of the law. This is as follows: **10·092**

(a) While it is undoubted law that fixed sums, whether *in terrorem* by virtue of their excessive amount, or for other reasons not a genuine pre-estimate of the likely damage and oppressive, payable in the event of delay in completion will not be recoverable as penalties, virtually no cases are reported in England or the Commonwealth in which periodical fixed sums stipulated as damages for delay in completion by the contractor have been invalidated as being excessive. Periodical fixed sums are undoubtedly acceptable in principle in construction contracts as a means of pre-estimating this class of damage, and will be enforced whether or not any damage has as a fact been incurred, or, if it has, regardless of its extent.

(b) Acts of prevention or breach of contract by the owner, even if causing a very small part of a total delay, will, however, invalidate a liquidated damages clause, leaving the owner to prove his damages at large, unless a clear and sufficiently specific extension of time clause applies to the prevention or breach in question. A summary of the various refinements of this proposition in regard to the specificity of extension of time clauses has already been given at the end of Section 2(2) *supra*.[17]

[16b] Compare *Westminster C.C.* v. *Jarvis Ltd.* [1970] 1 W.L.R. 637, 645, *per* Viscount Dilhorne, cited and illustrated *infra*, paras. 10·098–10·099, and *Bilton (Percy) Ltd.* v. *G.L.C.* [1982] 1 W.L.R. 794.

[16c] See *ante*, Chap. 1, Section 6(3).

[17] Para. 10·040.

10·093   (c) Theories of owner prevention or breach which serve to invalidate a liquidated damages clause, so that damages become at large, will be of no advantage for those owners whose provable damage at large exceeds the stipulated sums since, quite apart from any other objections, the weekly or other stipulated sums will still operate as a limitation on the owner's recoverable damage for late completion.[18]

(d) The A/E's extension of time decisions under many modern contracts will be in two categories, namely those upon individual applications made during the construction period and based on successive grounds of extension or other events as and when they arise, and those made upon a final review in order to determine when, but for any preceding events qualifying for an extension, the work should have been completed. The latter class of decision will be necessary, in one form or another, if the contract is to give the owner power to deduct liquidated damages from moneys due on interim payment before completion. The latest producer-dominated standard forms of contract in England require more than one revising decision of the A/E in this latter category, providing additionally that the revising decision can only be in favour of the contractor and not of the owner, and also requiring return of any excess liquidated damages previously deducted.[19]

10·094   (e) Nearly all modern standard forms are defective in failing to deal specifically with events for which the owner is responsible, including particularly the ordering of variations, arising during the period of culpable delay after liquidated damages have begun to run. As submitted *supra*, there seems no good reason why there should be any limitation on the power of an owner to order variations during this period, or why the operation of the liquidated damage clause should be invalidated in this situation, which has only arisen due to the contractor's breach, and will be progressively more likely the worse the delay by the contractor.[20] In view of the failure of standard forms to address this problem, and the increasing awareness of contractors and their advisers of the tactical opportunities offered thereby, it seems certain to trouble the courts in the future, unless the *Balfour Beatty* case, illustrated and discussed *supra*, Section 2(2), leads to improved policies and draftsmanship.

(f) In accordance with general principles, an A/E's decisions or certificates on extension of time will not, in the absence of sufficiently clear language, bind either party, and will be open to review by an

[18] *Elsley* v. *Collins Insurance Agencies Ltd.*, illustrated and discussed *supra*, Section 1, paras. 10.016 and 10.022.

[19] Compare Clause 44(4) of the ICE fifth edition, and Clause 25.3 of the 1980 RIBA/JCT contract.

[20] See *supra*, Section 2(2), paras. 10·043 *et seq.*, and the solutions adopted by the Singapore SIA 1980 contract there referred to.

arbitrator or the courts.[21] In this it may be relevant to distinguish between a temporary finality regulating the interlocutory position (and in particular deduction from current payments), pending arbitration or litigation, and permanent conclusive effect, either where a certificate authorising deduction or recovery of liquidated damages has been given, or where no or no valid supporting certificate has been obtained.

(g) While certain earlier cases may have suggested that a liquidated damages provision will be invalidated by extensions of time given at a late stage (variously after the date when the work should have been completed, or after actual completion, or in the case of variations after the time they were ordered) most modern contracts in England are worded so as to permit extensions to be given up to the time of final certificate or when the A/E becomes *functus officio.*[22] Even if earlier dates for the A/E's decisions are expressly or impliedly required by the contract, it has been submitted that these are directory only and, if breached, sounding in damages if provable, but that they should not be interpreted as a condition precedent so as to invalidate the liquidated damages clause.[22a]

10·095

(h) However, certain sub-contract standard forms in England (and now some "management" contracts), do contain wording apparently making the A/E's (or manager's) certificate, or a mere statement of account, either conclusive or a condition precedent to the main contractor's or manager's deduction of liquidated damages and there have been a number of recent cases in England where this draftsmanship has succeeded. It has been submitted in Chapter 6 that the problems raised by this new draftsmanship have not as yet been satisfactorily understood or resolved by the courts, who should in particular consider whether it is only temporary finality which is intended, and also take into account considerations of mutuality before deciding that a certificate or its absence is to have permanent consequences as between the parties.[23]

(i) However, there is in principle, of course, no objection to sufficiently clear language rendering any certificate conclusive, or delay in certifying extensions of time a bar to recovery or deduction of liquidated damages.[24]

---

[21] See *ante*, Chap. 6, Section 1(1), paras. 6·005 *et seq*. and Section 4(4), paras. 6·078 *et seq*., and see *supra*, Section 3(4), para. 10·069.

[22] See Section 3(5), *supra*, paras. 10·078 *et seq*.

[22a] See *supra*, para. 10·089 *et seq*.

[23] See Chap. 6, Section 4(3), paras. 6·068 *et seq*., and Section 6(7), paras. 6·194 *et seq*., and the cases of *Ramac Construction* v. *Lesser; Brightside Kilpatrick* v. *Mitchell Construction; Savage Brothers* v. *Shillington* and the recent management contract cases there illustrated and discussed.

[24] Compare Clause 24.2.1. of the RIBA/JCT 1980 forms (expressly requiring a demand by the owner in writing before the date of the final certificate), and see also the case of *Fairweather Ltd.* v. *Asden Securities* (1979) 12 BLR 40 on the effect of the final certificate under the 1963 forms, *supra*, para. 10·090.

SECTION 5. POLICY OF LIQUIDATED DAMAGES AND EXTENSION OF
TIME CLAUSES

10·096   The advantage of a liquidated damages clause is that it can be operated
with comparative clarity and certainty in the case of a builder not making
satisfactory progress, and that it removes all doubt from what might otherwise be an expensive and complicated enquiry, namely the amount of
damage suffered by the owner as a result of the delay. From this point of
view, it is particularly useful where the owner's loss is difficult to assess in
monetary terms, as for example, a local authority's late receipt of a public
building such as a swimming-pool or school, or of loss-making projects,
like subsidised public housing.

Ḥowever, the practical value to owners of liquidated damages clauses, if
regarded as a sanction designed to secure a proper degree of progress, is
greatly reduced by the perhaps not sufficiently understood practical difficulties which an owner's A/E is likely to encounter when administering an
extension of time clause and endeavouring to fix a new completion date,
the more so in the light of the now steadily lengthening grounds for extension of time found in modern standard forms. While a really detailed programme showing all the more important events and dates (rather than the
uninformative indications in bar chart form of the first and last dates for
various trade or work processes so often proffered as required programmes by contractors) can provide some help to the A/E, the fact
remains that the contractor, with his far more detailed and private knowledge of his original scheduling of his own work and that of his various
sub-contractors and suppliers of materials, is in a much better position to
advance arguments and justifications in favour of an extension as a result
of events occurring during the construction period than the owner's A/E
will be to refute them. This unavoidable disadvantage will be compounded to the extent that any programme information supplied by the
contractor is vague and generalised, and by the absence of the very useful
tool, under the great majority of standard forms, which a required contractual make-up of prices would provide[25] quite apart from the number
and suitability of the grounds of extension permitted by the extension of
time clause.

10·097   It is for this reason that it has been suggested at a number of points in
this book that the uncontroversial and continuous inducements arising
from the use of suitably weighted instalment stage payments, rather than
value-based periodical interim payment, will be far more effective in securing good progress than any sanction represented by the liquidated damages clauses to be found in most English standard forms,[26] and indeed in
such clauses generally.

Apart from these practical difficulties of enforcement, it has already
been pointed out in the present chapter that the liquidated damages pro-

---

[25] See *ante*, Chap. 7, para. 7·109 for this inadequacy in the standard forms.
[26] See *ante*, Chap. 6, Section 6(7), para. 6·186, and Chap. 8, Section 1(7), para. 8·105.

visions of the RIBA/JCT standard forms are liable to be invalidated altogether as a result of two sets of circumstances which commonly occur in many construction projects, namely where possession of any part of the site, however small or unimportant or for however short a period, has not been afforded by the owner at all times[27] and, secondly, where a variation instruction is issued during the period of culpable delay after the properly extended contract completion date has passed.[27a] As there pointed out, these give the appearance of being calculated lapses in the draftsmanship of the clauses.

In addition to these considerations, there are two long-standing grounds of extension of time in the RIBA/JCT forms which do much to reduce the practical value to the owner of the liquidated damages provisions in those forms.

The first important ground is that provided for in Clauses 23(g) and **10·098** 25.4.7 of the 1963 and 1980 RIBA/JCT forms, namely delay on the part of nominated sub-contractors or suppliers which the main contractor has taken all practicable steps to avoid or reduce. This means that, however culpable the delay by such a sub-contractor, and whatever its effect on the progress of the works as a whole, the owner loses any right to recover *his* loss from the main contractor. If it were not for the extension of time clause, the latter could be sued by the owner for liquidated damages and could then pass on the liability to the sub-contractor by suing on the sub-contract. By contrast, most careful provisions are contained in the main contract ensuring that the *main contractor* can recover *his own* damages from nominated sub-contractors and that sums so recovered should be for his benefit and not the owner's.[28] This would be understandable if the extension of time clause was conditioned upon delays by nominated sub-contractors caused by some act or default of the owner, but it is, of course, perfectly general. The clause has been in existence for many years in the United Kingdom, and by reducing their potential liability to the main contractor offers no encouragement to nominated sub-contractors to maintain proper progress in their work. In view of the increasing proportion of building work carried out by such specialists in England,[29] such a clause can only militate strongly against the prospect of building contracts being carried out by the contract completion date, and it is difficult to understand the policy underlying it, which merely prejudices the owner and benefits defaulting sub-contractors.[30] The preceding sentences of this paragraph (then in the ninth edition) have now received powerful judicial support:

> "Paragraph (g) is highly anomalous and would appear to have been included in this form of contract without any regard to the manifest injustice and

[27] See *supra*, Section 3(1), paras. 10·065 and 10·066.
[27a] See *supra*, Section 2(2), paras. 10·043 *et seq.*
[28] See Clauses 27(a)(vi), 27(b), and proviso to Clause 30(5)(c) of the 1963 forms, and the comparable 1980 provisions.
[29] In many cases over 50 per cent. of the work by value.
[30] See also the approval of a passage in the ninth edition criticising the working of this clause by Edmund Davies L.J. in *J. Jarvis & Sons Ltd.* v. *Westminster Corporation* [1969] 1 W.L.R. 1448, 1453, C.A.

indeed absurdity implicit in it. It is in my view unjust and absurd because . . . it leaves the employers to bear the loss caused by a delay for which they are in no way to blame and allows the party at fault . . . to escape from the liability which they would otherwise justly have to bear . . ."[31]

"It is indeed curious that in this form of contract issued by the RIBA and approved by members of many other bodies one should find a provision under which a sub-contractor can benefit from it own default."[32]

"Such an illogical consequence suggests that the condition which creates it has been inserted and drafted without any clear appreciation of its purpose or scope . . . a serious reflection on the clause; indeed I cannot believe that the provisional body, realising how defective this clause is, will allow it to remain in its present form."[33]

Despite the lapse of some 10 years since these remarks, paragraph (g) was included unchanged in the new 1980 forms and remains unchanged at the present day in the later versions of the RIBA/JCT 1980 forms.[34]

10·099   Furthermore, a special difficulty arises from the peculiar wording in Clause 23(g), namely "delay *on the part of* nominated sub-contractors or suppliers" (as opposed to delay *caused by* such sub-contractors). What if the sub-contractor is not guilty of delay himself but his bad work or poor co-operation, for instance, delays the main contractor? In fact it was this particular infelicity of wording which unintentionally provided the House of Lords with the opportunity to find an escape from the anomaly referred to in their above criticisms.

ILLUSTRATION

Nominated sub-contractors were due to complete their piling work by June 20. Towards the end of May a defect became apparent in one pile. No. 43. This was remedied, and the sub-contractors purported to complete on June 20, removing their equipment from the site a few days later. On July 21 a meeting was held to discuss possible shortcomings in the piles, and the sub-contractors were subsequently recalled to the site to examine the piles, a number of which were found to be defective. Replacement piles were then constructed, but the work was not completed till September 29, a delay of three months. The sub-contractors, in proceedings against the owners for a declaration which had been originally commenced by the main contractors, argued on behalf of the main contractors that they (the sub-contractors) had been guilty of "delay on their part", so that the main contractor was entitled to an extension of time from the owners under Clause 23(g), so that they (the sub-contractors) would not accordingly be liable to the main contractors for the owners' damages. The owners contended that, since the sub-contractors had completed their work, their subsequent recall and carrying out of remedial work did not

---

[31] *Per* Salmon L.J. in *Jarvis* v. *Westminster Corporation* [1969] 1 W.L.R. 1448, at p. 1458. See also the criticisms of Edmund Davies L.J. in the Court of Appeal, and the further criticisms in the House of Lords ([1970] 1 W.L.R. 637).

[32] See *per* Viscount Dilhorne in the House of Lords, *supra*, at p. 645.

[33] *Per* Lord Wilberforce *ibid.* at p. 650.

[34] See Clause 25.4.7.

amount to "delay on their part", and that the owners were accordingly entitled to liquidated damages against the main contractor. *Held*, by the Court of Appeal, overruling Donaldson J., that the sub-contractors had on the facts never completed their work to the satisfaction of the architect until September, so that there had been delay by them, and accordingly the main contractor was entitled to an extension of time. *Held*, by the House of Lords, overruling the Court of Appeal, that "delay" within the meaning of the clause did not run after there was such completion of the sub-contract works as would enable the main contractor to take over himself; that there had been apparent completion of the sub-contract works, notwithstanding the latent defects; and that the sub-contractor's return subsequently had been to remedy a breach and not to carry out the sub-contract itself. Accordingly, there had been no "delay on the part of" the sub-contractor, and the owners were entitled to liquidated damages against the main contractors, which they could in turn recover from the sub-contractors: *Westminster Corporation* v. *Jarvis Ltd.* (1969).[35]

[Note: There had of course been delay "caused by" the sub-contractors.]

The above case, while it is primarily concerned with the interpretation   **10·100**
of Clause 23(g) of the post-1963 RIBA forms, is also of the greatest importance in defining precisely what is meant by "practical" or "substantial" completion in building and engineering contracts.[36]

The second ground, optional in the RIBA standard forms,[37] is the inability of the contractor "for reasons beyond his control and which he could not reasonably have foreseen" at the date of the contract, to obtain labour or materials essential for the works. Such a clause is, equally, no encouragement to merchants and suppliers of building materials to honour their obligations as to delivery. With extension of time clauses of this description in common use, it can only be said that the original purpose of the liquidated damages clause has been effectively undermined in the building industry, and the sanctions against sub-contractors' and suppliers' failure to meet their delivery obligations effectively reduced.

As a summary of the foregoing, a properly drafted liquidated damages   **10·101**
clause should:

(a) explicitly confer a power to extend time in general terms for any breach of contract or act of prevention by the owner, and in particular terms by reason of variations of the work or delay in issuing instructions or information, or failure to give possession;

(b) define with precision any other circumstances for which an extension of time is to be granted, and avoid general expressions;

(c) make it clear that the power to extend time is exercisable at any time;

---

[35] [1969] 1 W.L.R. 1448.

[36] See *Morgan* v. *S. & S. Construction Property Ltd.* [1967] V.R. 149, Australia, *ante*, para. 4·012, and the discussion *ante*, Chap. 4, paras. 4·029 *et seq.*, Chap. 5, paras. 5·048–5·049, and *supra*, Section 2, para. 10·059.

[37] Clause 23(j), 1963 edition. Then an optional provision, but now mandatory: see Clause 25.4.10 of the 1980 forms.

(d) empower the owner either to deduct damages from any payment or sum certified as due under the contract, or to recover them from the contractor by way of action or arbitration, at least until the time of the final certificate.

Other contractual provisions should expressly regulate:

10·102   (a) the precise extent to which any further extension should be granted by reason of events or causes (including in particular the ordering of variations) which are the responsibility of the owner and which occur during the period of culpable delay after liquidated damages have already become recoverable, together with the appropriate subsequent adjustments to the deduction or recovery of liquidated damages in such an event[38];
(b) the desired operation of any fluctuations clause during a period of culpable delay[39];
(c) the desired operation of the liquidated damages clause during the period of completion by another contractor following a termination by the owner.[40]

10·103   All these matters have been the subject of express drafting in the Singapore 1980 SIA contract, and reference to its provisions may be of some assistance, although of course different solutions may be preferred.[41]

The extent to which any A/E's decisions as to extension of time or the final reviewed completion date should be final and conclusive, or only temporarily so, or not at all, should also be clearly stated. If any degree of finality is called for, the degree of desired mutuality (that is, the extent to which decisions are to be binding on *both* parties) falls to be considered. In most cases, although this is a matter of pure policy and may depend on the relative bargaining power of the parties, the potential impact, if the liquidated damages are substantial, upon the contractor's cashflow would suggest that no finality should attach to the A/E or other certifier's decision, except in situations where the A/E's status as an independent professional in private practice may warrant its being regarded as a protection for the contractor as well as the owner.

---

[38] See *supra*, Section 2(2), paras. 10·045, and see Clause 24(3) of the Singapore S/A contract reproduced in C.C.P.P., p. 581.
[39] See *ante*, Chap. 8, Section 1(2)(c), para. 8·059.
[40] See *supra*, Section 2(3), para. 10·053.
[41] See SIA 1980 contract, Clauses 23(o) (prevention or breach as ground of extension); Clause 24(2) (deduction at any time until final certificate); Clause 24(3) (later events during delay period); Clause 32(8) (position after termination) and Clause 38(4) (fluctuations), reproduced in C.C.P.P., pp. 580, 581, 604–605 and 616, respectively.

CHAPTER 11

VESTING AND SEIZURE OF MATERIALS AND PLANT

SECTION 1. OWNERSHIP IN THE ABSENCE OF EXPRESS PROVISION

(1) Generally

Most standard form building contracts contain express provisions govern-   **11·001**
ing the ownership, as between owner and contractor, of materials or plant.
The effect of such provisions will be considered in Section 2, Express Provisions, below. In the absence of such provisions, however, questions of
ownership fall to be determined on general principles, the most important
of which is that the intention of the parties to be deduced from the surrounding circumstances will prevail, and that decisions on one contract
will not necessarily be applied rigidly in all situations. In considering problems of this kind, it is important to distinguish between goods, materials or
fittings on the one hand and equipment or plant on the other. Barring
certain hybrid or borderline cases, the former are intended for incorporation into the buildings or other works contemplated, whereas the latter,
even if temporarily attached, will usually require to be removed from the
building or site when the work is completed. Thus, an obviously important, but not conclusive consideration, where a problem of disputed ownership arises, may be whether the materials or plant in question have in
fact been affixed to the land or buildings of the owner, but the purpose or
intention in doing so may override this factor.

1201

A particular example of this will be the case of temporary works.[1] Some of these may be intended for ultimate removal or salvage, such as certain types of coffer-dam, or shuttering or piling. Equally, other types, while no longer serving any structural or other function in relation to the permanent work once in place, may as a matter of either technical impracticality on the one hand, or economic considerations on the other, (as, for example, the cost of extraction balanced against ultimate salvage value) be intended to be left permanently *in situ*. Here again intention will be the deciding factor, it is submitted, rather than the fact or degree of fixing.

11·002   In the seventh edition of this work many illustrations from shipbuilding contracts were cited, but it is obvious that a shipbuilding contract differs from a building contract in a most vital respect, namely, that the work is not being done upon, nor is it affixed to, the land of the owner, and the shipbuilding cases are consequently usually concerned with two main questions, *viz.*: at what point of time does the "general property" in the ship as a whole pass to the owner or purchaser, and, secondly, what is included with the ship when the property does pass. In the present edition, shipbuilding examples will only be referred to where it is thought that a proposition of general application is illustrated, and in considering them this essential difference from construction contracts should not be forgotten. In the present section it is proposed to consider materials and plant or equipment separately, and to deal with cases where no express provision as to the property in them exists. It should be borne in mind that in those cases where the ownership whether of materials or plant is effectively transferred to the building owner, by express provision or otherwise, the transfer is never quite absolute, since it will usually be subject to a right, express or implied, for the builder to remove all the plant, and any excess of materials or goods if they have not been used and fixed, on completion of the work.

(2) Materials, Goods and Fittings

11·003   The well-known rule is that the property in all materials and fittings, once incorporated in or affixed to a building, will pass to the freeholder—*quicquid plantatur solo, solo cedit*. The employer under a building contract may not necessarily be the landowner, but may be a lessee or licensee, or even have no interest in the land at all, as in the case of a main contractor in a sub-contract. But once the contractor, or sub-contractor has affixed materials, the property in them passes from him, and at least as against him they become the absolute property of his employer, whatever the latter's tenure of or title to the land. The contractor has no right to detach them from the soil or building, even though the building owner may himself be entitled to sever them as against some other person—*e.g.* as ten-

---

[1] For these generally, see *ante*, Chap. 1, Section 12(2)(*d*), paras. 1·293 *et seq.*, and 1·311 to 1·314; Chap. 2, Section 6(2)(*d*), paras. 2·138 *et seq.*, Chap. 4, paras. 4·053 to 4·059, and Chap. 7, Section 1(2)(*g*), paras. 7·037 *et seq.* See also *infra*, Section 4, "Old Materials".

ant's fixtures. Nor can the contractor reclaim them if they have been subsequently severed from the soil by the building owner or anyone else. The principle was shortly and clearly stated by Blackburn J. in *Appleby* v. *Myers* (1867)[1a]:

> "Materials worked by one into the property of another become part of that property. This is equally true whether it be fixed or movable property. Bricks built into a wall become part of the house, thread stitched into a coat which is under repair, or planks and nails and pitch worked into a ship under repair, become part of the coat or the ship".

The principle is so firm that, notwithstanding an express provision to the contrary in the contract, the builder will not be able to take advantage of it as against a third party entitled to the land.

ILLUSTRATIONS

(1) Bells were hung in a house by the tenant and left there after the end of his tenancy. *Held*, that the tenant could not maintain trover for them after the landlord had severed them from the freehold, because they remained fixed to the freehold after the expiration of the term, and thereby vested in the landlord as part thereof: *Lyde* v. *Russell* (1830).[2]   **11·004**

[Note: This case is one of landlord and tenant but would, it is suggested, be equally applicable to a case of an unpaid builder and the building owner.]

(2) A burial company sold to the plaintiff a right of burial in a plot of ground for £2 10s., thereby apparently passing the freehold; the plaintiff interred a relative therein, and purchased a monument from the defendant company. The monument was erected, but as it was not paid for, the company removed it. *Held*, by Coleridge C.J. and Mathew J. that once fixed they had no right to remove it, but could only sue for the money: *Sims* v. *London Necropolis Co.* (1885).[3]

(3) Contractors undertook to supply materials for the erection of a factory. Conditions 9(*e*) of the conditions of sale provided that materials erected or otherwise on site remained the contractor's property till paid for. A receiver for debenture holders of the owner sold the freehold to a third party, and the contractors finished their work and rendered their account, but the owner went into liquidation. *Held*, by Plowman J., that since the factory was not a movable building, the materials became annexed to the land as part of the freehold. The contractor was therefore an ordinary unsecured creditor: *Re Yorkshire Joinery Co. Ltd.* (*in liq.*) (1967).[4]

(4) Manufacturers sold diesel engines which it was contemplated by both parties would be incorporated into generating sets for re-sale by the buyer. All goods were to remain the property of the sellers until the full purchase price had been paid. There was also a right to retake possession in the event of non-payment, but no other express rights. On the insolvency of the buyer the unpaid sellers obtained a temporary injunction in respect of three generators   **11·005**

[1a] L.R. 2 C.P. 651 at p. 659.
[2] 1 B. & Ad. 394.
[3] 1 T.L.R. 584.
[4] 111 S.J. 701.

which were on the buyer's premises. This was later lifted on an undertaking by the receiver to segregate the sale proceeds and await the Court's determination. The engines were designed to be fixed to the generators but were removable. In two cases the engines had been in a deliverable state so as to satisfy the Sale of Goods Act requirements, and had been incorporated in the generators and identified to the sub-buyers. In one case the engine had not been incorporated or identified and was not in a deliverable state. *Held*, by Staughton J., that in the latter case, no re-sale had yet taken place, and the sellers had had a right to re-take possession for non-payment at the time of the injunction, but in the other two cases the engines had already been effectively sold to the sub-buyers at the time of the injunction; so that the sellers were only entitled to the sale proceeds in the latter case, and must prove in the liquidation for the remainder: *Hendy Lennox (Industrial Engines) Ltd.* v. *Grahame Puttick Ltd.* (1984).[5]

[Note: It is implicit in the above case that effective sales to the sub-buyers would confer an indefeasible title on them under section 25 of the Sale of Goods Act, leaving the original sellers to prove in the buyer's insolvency. Only the two sales had been effective so that the property had passed to the sub-buyers, but in the other case it had not done so. The original sellers' right to the proceeds of sale, it should be noted, did not arise directly out of any express term in the original supply contract, but as a result of the terms on which the initial temporary injunction had been lifted. It will be seen (see *infra*, Sub-clause (7)) that express retention of title provisions which apply to composite articles into which goods sold are to be mixed or re-worked will fail in their effect under section 395 of the 1985 Companies Act unless registered as a charge under that section, which in practice is rarely if ever likely to be done unless a chattel is of exceptionally high value.][6]

11·006   On the other hand, a contractor is usually bound by his contract to complete the works, or to keep them in good repair till completion, or to remedy defects, and a consequential right, as against his employer, to remove and replace materials for these purposes is clearly necessary to give the contract business efficacy. Thus, in *Appleby* v. *Myers*,[6a] where the contract was for the installation and maintenance of certain machinery, Blackburn J. said:

> "We think that the plaintiffs, who were to complete the whole for a fixed sum, and keep it in repair for two years, would have had a perfect right, if they thought that a portion of the engine which they had put up was too slight, to change it and substitute another in their opinion better calculated to keep in good repair during the two years, and that without consulting or asking the leave of the defendant".

Moreover, as was rightly pointed out in the Full Court of Western Australia, even if the property in materials on site has passed to an owner following an interim payment which includes their value, there will be an implied obligation to leave the goods on site in the possession of the con-

---

[5] [1984] 1 W.L.R. 485. Illustrated further *infra*, para. 11·058.
[6] For other cases of goods worked-up into other goods see *infra*, Sub-section (7), Third Party Rights and Retention of Title, para. 11·051.
[6a] See *supra*.

tractor for the purpose of carrying out and completing the contract.[7] So too in a case where property is made to pass on delivery to the site.[8] The limited nature of this transfer of "property" under the express terms of contracts providing for interim payments which include the value of materials brought onto the site is further illustrated by the language of these clauses in many modern English standard forms, which expressly provide that, notwithstanding the passing of property, the contractor is to remain responsible for any subsequent loss or damage to the materials.[9]

Until, however, materials are actually affixed to land, or incorporated   **11·007**
into the works of a construction project, the property in them, as against the building owner, will in law remain with the contractor or an unpaid seller, notwithstanding that they may have been approved by an owner or contractor or the A/E and brought onto the site, unless the agreement between the parties shows an express intention to the contrary. All the contractual provisions must be carefully considered, however.

ILLUSTRATIONS

(1) A builder contracted to build an hotel for a specified sum, payment to be by instalments at certain dates. In the event of his becoming bankrupt, the owners were empowered to take possession of "work already done" by him, subject to paying a fair proportion of the contract price to be determined by the architect. The builder became bankrupt. Before the bankruptcy, he had delivered certain wooden sash-frames to the site for inspection and approval by the clerk of works. They were then returned to his workshop to be fitted with iron pulleys after approval, and were there when the act of bankruptcy was committed. They were redelivered to the site three days later, before the fiat of bankruptcy was issued. The trustee of the builder sued the owners for the frames or their value. *Held*, by the Court of Exchequer, that despite the owner's approval, at the date of the bankruptcy the property in the frames remained in the builder, as they had not been affixed; further, that as they had not been affixed they were not "work already done" by the builder so as to empower the owners to take possession; and that in any event this power, being expressed to arise upon bankruptcy, was on general principles void. "This is not a contract for the sale and purchase of goods as removable chattels; it is a contract to make up materials, and to fix them; and until they are fixed, by the nature of the contract, the property will not pass": *Tripp* v. *Armitage* (1839).[10]

(2) Under the terms of a shipbuilding contract the ship was to become the   **11·008**
property of the owner upon payment of the first instalment of its price. There was in addition a power for the owner to enter and complete the work in the

---

[7] *Davidson* v. *Claffey Construction Ltd.* (1958) 60 W.A.L.R. 29, see *infra*, para. 11·029.
[8] See, *e.g. Bennett & White (Calgary) Ltd.* v. *Municipal District of Sugar City (No. 5)* [1951] A.C. 786, illustrated *infra*, Section 2, para. 11·029.
[9] See, *e.g.* Clause 14(1) of the main contract in *Archivent Sales & Developments Ltd.* v. *Strathclyde Region Council* (1984) 27 BLR 98 illustrated *infra*, para. 11·057, and a number of the other cases illustrated *infra*, Section 2, paras. 11·022 *et seq.*
[10] 4 M. & W. 687, *per* Lord Abinger C.B. at p. 698. See also *Williams* v. *Fitzmaurice*, *infra*, para. 11·013, and *Sumpter* v. *Hedges* [1898] 1 Q.B. 673, *ante*, para. 4·011.

event of default on the part of the contractor "using such materials of [the shipbuilder] as shall be applicable to the purpose". The shipbuilder defaulted and became insolvent after the property in the ship had passed, following the first instalment, and the owner later entered the yard to complete the vessel. At the time of the bankruptcy there had been a number of materials in the yard which had not yet been incorporated or specifically appropriated by the shipbuilder, but some had been selected by the owner beforehand and others were piled inside the ship or stored in an adjoining shed. None had actually been used. *Held*, by the Court of Common Pleas, that the owner was not entitled to any of the materials under the terms of the agreement, since, not having been used, the property had not passed at the date of the bankruptcy: *Baker* v. *Gray* (1856).[11]

[Note: No reliance appears to have been placed on the above quoted user or seizure clause by the owners in this case.]

(3) A sub-contractor undertook to supply and erect two specified storage tanks, to be paid for after completion. When partly finished, a receiver of the main contractor was appointed. One tank was nearly complete and one just started. The tanks were built resting on, but not fixed to, a level concrete foundation, and when complete it would be practically impossible to remove them without taking them to pieces. *Held*, by Romer J., that the property would not pass until completion, and the sub-contractor was entitled to require payment *in full* from the receiver before agreeing to complete as requested by both building owner and receiver: *Bellamy* v. *Davey* (1891).[12]

11·009   (4) Main contractors for a complete electrical installation costing £1,363 sub-contracted the supply and erection of a storage battery for £286. *Held*, by the Court of Appeal, that although the matter was one of the greatest difficulty, on the true construction of the sub-contract it was a contract of sale of the component parts of the battery with a supplemental contract for erection after delivery of the parts to the owner's premises; that delivery of the goods to the railway station for onward carting by the main contractors to the site prior to erection by the sub-contractors was an unconditional appropriation of goods in a deliverable state, and the property accordinly passed on delivery to the main contractors under section 18 of the Sale of Goods Act 1893, notwithstanding that the work of erecting remained to be done; so that the sub-contractors could only prove in the liquidation: *Pritchett & Gold* v. *Currie* (1916).[13]

[Note: Both the *Bellamy and Pritchett & Gold* cases are, of course, somewhat unusual, but are included in order to illustrate the different views which can be taken as to the passing of property in unfixed materials in construction projects, depending upon the particular facts. In each of the two cases the building owners were involved in the litigation, and their position as against the unpaid supplier depended upon whether the property had or had not passed from the supplier to the main contractor.]

(5) Specialist sub-contractors in Southern Rhodesia undertook to supply, erect, commission and test sewage disposal equipment for a main contractor. The sub-contract was silent as to the ownership of the equipment to be sup-

---

[11] 25 L.J. C.P. 161. For quotations from the judgments in this case explaining the Court's reasoning, see *infra*, Section 2, para. 11·040.

[12] [1891] 3 Ch. 540. The right to payment in advance in such a case depends on the bankruptcy law and does not depend upon the contract—see *post*, Chap. 16, para. 16·028.

[13] [1916] 2 Ch. 515. This case disapproved of the reasoning in *Bellamy* v. *Davey* in so far as it dealt with the position between the sub-contractor and the building owner, see *supra*, but not on the question of the property passing.

plied. The equipment was delivered and taken charge of and stored by the main contractor. The sub-contractors admitted that in the majority of their formal sub-contracts there was an express provision transferring the ownership to the main contractor or owner on delivery to the site. *Held*, by Hathorn J., following *Seath* v. *Moore* and *Reid* v. *Macbeth & Gray*,[14] that, in the absence of express provision, the time when ownership was intended to pass must be determined by having regard to all the terms and circumstances of the particular contract; there was no presumption that ownership should pass either on delivery or on incorporation, but in the present case ownership was to pass when the equipment was incorporated into the main works. Till then the main contractor was merely acting as custodian of such plant and equipment as might have been delivered: *Edward L. Bateman Ltd.* v. *Eric Reed Ltd.* (1960).[15]

(6) Timber merchants supplied timber to main contractors at three sites being developed under separate contracts for one owner. In all the supply sub-contracts there was a retention of title clause, and in two out of the three cases the main building contract provided for monthly payments of 97% of valuations of the work executed, including the value of all materials on site, but that the property in the materials should not pass to the owner until payment of the relevant instalment. However, in the third main contract there was merely a provision for stage payments on account of a percentage of the contract price, although without the stages or percentage being stipulated, and with no mention of materials on site or of property passing. In this third case payments were in fact made by the owner against the value of both work done and materials on site. The main contractor went into liquidation, at a time when there was unfixed timber on the site at all the contracts which had been formally valued, but not yet paid for. The suppliers sued the contractor's liquidator and the owner for the value of timber. *Held*, by Judge Davies Q.C., in regard to the third contract, that, as against the contractor, even if materials had been paid for by the owner they remained the property of the contractor in the absence of express provision transferring the property to the owner, so that the unfixed timber remained the property of the suppliers. "I accept that there was an arrangement whereby interim payments would be made against the worth of work done and materials on site intended for inclusion in the development. It is common practice in the industry for interim payments to be made on that basis against the contract price. However, valuation of work and materials for that purpose does not usually connote the purchase by the employer of site materials so valued. The assessment is merely a convenient means of determining the amount which should, in fairness to the contractor, be advanced to him from time to time against the contract sum." *W. Hanson (Harrow) Limited* v. *Rapid Civil Engineering Ltd.* (1987).[16]

11·010

---

[14] (1886) 11 App.Cas. 350 (H.L.) and [1904] A.C. 223 (H.L.) respectively.

[15] 1960 (4) S.A. 151 (Southern Rhodesia). To avoid any confusion, it should be noted that while the subject-matter of this particular case is commonly referred to in the industry as "plant," it is not "construction plant" or "contractor's plant", or equipment in the sense used in Sub-section (1) *supra*, or Sub-section (3) *infra*, and later in this chapter, being intended for permanent incorporation into the works, and really ranks as "materials" or "goods" for the purpose of the present Sub-section.

[16] 38 BLR 106, 113. (In the remaining two contracts the judge proceeded to hold that the owner did not, by virtue of his failure to pay against the certificates in question, obtain an indefeasible title under section 25 of the Sale of Goods Act 1979—see the case illustrated on this *infra*, para. 11·058.) See also the discussion on the effect of interim payment, *infra*, para. 11·054.

11·011   *Tripp* v. *Armitage (supra)* was approved in *Seath* v. *Moore* (1886)[17] (a ship-building case, but one of the leading cases in this branch of the law), where Lord Watson said:

> "Materials provided by the builder, and portions of the fabric, whether wholly or partially finished, although intended to be used in the execution of the contract, cannot be regarded as appropriated to the contract or as 'sold' unless they have been affixed, or in a reasonable sense made part of the corpus";

and Lord Blackburn said in the same case[18]:

> "But it is competent to parties to agree for valuable consideration that a specific article shall be sold, and become the property of the purchaser as soon as it has attained a certain stage: though if it is part of the bargain that more work shall be done on the article after it has reached that stage, it affords a strong prima facie presumption against it being the intention of the parties that the property should then pass. I do not examine the various English authorities cited during the argument. It is, I think, a question of the construction of the contract, in each case, at what stage the property shall pass; and a question of fact, in each case, whether that stage has been reached".

11·012   Other shipbuilding cases illustrating this principle are *Wood* v. *Bell* (1856),[19] *Baker* v. *Gray* (1856),[20] *Reid* v. *Macbeth & Gray* (1904)[21] and *Re Blyth Shipbuilding and Dry Docks Ltd.* (1926).[22] (These are in fact strong cases, since the decisions to a large extent override express provisions in the contract which might have been intended to pass the property but which were held not to be sufficiently explicit for this purpose. Thus, in *Baker* v. *Gray* where the property in the ship itself had passed under a vesting clause, the owner was unable to claim unfixed materials under that clause when his seizure clause had not been operated in time.[23] And in *Reid* v. *Macbeth & Gray*, it was provided that

> "the vessel, as she is constructed ... and all materials from time to time intended for her, whether in the building-yard, workshop or river or elsewhere shall, immediately as the same proceeds, become the property of the purchaser and shall not be within the ownership, control or disposition of the builders",

yet the property in plates intended for the ship, lying at a railway station, which had been passed by a Lloyd's surveyor at the builder's works and marked with the number of the vessel and the position they were to occupy, was held not to have passed. Again in *Re Blyth Shipbuilding, etc., Ltd.* (1926) it was provided that "all materials and things *appropriated for*"

---

[17] 11 App.Cas. at p. 381.
[18] *Ibid.* at p. 370.
[19] 25 L.J.Q.B. 321.
[20] 25 L.J.C.P. 161.
[21] [1904] A.C. 223.
[22] [1926] Ch. 494.
[23] See *supra*, para. 11·008, and see the quotations from the judgments *infra*, Section 2, para. 11·040.

the vessel should become the purchaser's property, but it was held that worked material approved by the purchaser's surveyor did not pass under this clause. Again, in *Seath* v. *Moore* (1886) itself, a series of contracts for the construction of marine engines, the provision was that "all materials laid down for the purpose of constructing the same shall become, and be held as being, the absolute property of" the purchaser.)

However, it would seem that, depending on the facts, something less **11·013** than actual affixing will sometimes be sufficient to pass the property in construction contracts—*e.g.* actual placing into the corpus of the building, without the final stage of fixing being completed.

ILLUSTRATION

The plaintiff agreed to build a house complete for the defendant, no mention being made of the flooring in the specification. The plaintiff prepared flooring boards, brought them on the premises, and planed and fitted them to certain rooms, but refused to lay them down without extra payment. Other boards were left by him in an adjoining field, not fitted to any particular room. *Held*, by the Court of Exchequer, first that the flooring had been omitted from the specification by inadvertence and it was always intended that the price should include for flooring so that the plaintiff was not entitled to recover for the flooring as an extra; and, secondly, that he could not sue for conversion of the flooring boards left by him in the rooms and subsequently used by the defendant for the completion of the building, but that he could do so for the boards left in the field: *Williams* v. *Fitzmaurice* (1858).[24]

Those shipbuilding cases where the property in unfixed chattels was **11·014** held to pass with the ship have been rather special cases, involving articles such as rudders, cables, cordage, fishing-gear, charts, instruments, etc,[25] and, by virtue of their subject matter, are unlikely to be directly applicable to a building contract, where the essence of the transaction is the completion of work rather than the sale of the subject-matter of the work.

The shipbuilding cases are further discussed in Section 2.[26] As will be seen, they are in general, often understandably, not consistent with the leading decisions in those building cases where express provisions exist regulating the ownership or right to use plant and materials.

While building contracts may or may not contain express provisions regulating the passing of property in materials or goods or fittings, they do very frequently contain provisions for payment *on account* of materials delivered to the site (or even in some English standard forms for materials not yet delivered to the site),[27] or general interim or progress payment

[24] 3 H. & N. 844. See also *Sumpter* v. *Hedges* [1898] 1 Q.B. 673, illustrated *ante*, para. 4·011.
[25] See, *e.g. Woods* v. *Russell* (1822) 5 B. & Ad. 942; *Clarke* v. *Spence* (1836) 4 A. &. E. 448 and *Goss* v. *Quinton* (1842) 12 L.J.C.P. 173.
[26] See *infra*, paras. 11·040–11·041.
[27] See, *e.g.* Clause 30(2a) of the 1963 RIBA/JCT and Clause 54 of the 1973 fifth edition ICE standard forms respectively.

provisions calculated by reference to the value of unfixed materials brought onto the site for use in the works as well as of work carried out. The effect of these express provisions on the passing of the property in the goods or materials concerned, either on delivery or on subsequent certification or payment, is considered *infra*, Section 2(2).[28]

(3) Contractor's or Construction Plant

11·015   Plant may be defined for this purpose as anything required for carrying out the work, but not intended for ultimate incorporation in the land or buildings as part of the permanent work. The case of unfixed plant gives rise to little difficulty, since in the absence of express provision it is not difficult to see that the property will remain throughout in the contractor. In many cases, however, plant will be attached, albeit temporarily, to the land or buildings. Familiar examples are huts, hoarding, scaffolding, form-work, hoists and cranes. In every case the intention of the parties to be deduced from the surrounding circumstances must be considered. There is, of course, little difficulty in implying a term that the builder should be at liberty to take away the plant when no longer required, particularly where removal involves no injury to the land or building. But this does not entirely answer the question, in the absence of express provision, in whom is the property, or does it enjoy any status of "irremovability", while the plant remains attached and still required for completion or construction? So-called "tenants' fixtures" are perhaps an analogous example. There is, however, little direct authority on the subject.

ILLUSTRATIONS

11·016   (1) Forty years previously a fender and hatch had been placed by a miller in a mill stream to prevent the escape of water. The hatch was fixed to the land, but the fender, though it could be removed was essential to it. The banks of the stream and the surrounding land did not belong to the miller. *Held*, by the Court of Queen's Bench, citing *Mant* v. *Collins* (1842) where a door had been lifted off its hinges, that it was a matter of evidence for the jury whether by agreement the hatch did not remain the property of the miller: *Wood* v. *Hewitt* (1846).[29]

          (2) A building owner let the hoarding separating the premises from the street to one advertising company, while his builder let it to another. There was a clause in the building contract "that the hoardings are not to be let for advertising." In an action between the rival advertising companies, *held*, by Kekewich J., that the hoarding belonged to the builder, and that his tenants had acquired a title, although the builder might, under the express provision of the contract, be liable in damages to the owner: *Partington Advertising Co.* v. *Willing & Co.* (1896).[30]

---

[28] Paras. 11·044–11·045.
[29] 15 L.J.Q.B. 247; 8 Q.B. 913.
[30] 12 T.L.R. 176.

(3) Clause 15(b) of a contract for the construction of sprinkler systems on a **11·017** farm in Southern Rhodesia vested ownership of all plant equipment and materials brought onto the site in the owner, and also gave him the right to order their removal and replacement if unsatisfactory. The main contractor sub-contracted much of the work, and when the owner later teminated the contract and a sub-contractor attempted to remove his plant and materials, the owner obtained a temporary injunction preventing the sub-contractor from doing so. The contractor's acceptance of the sub-contractor's quotation had enclosed a copy of the main contract conditions and stated "the conditions as laid down in the [main] contract documents must be adhered to at all times . . . you will be paid on the same basis as [the main contractor]", and the owner relied upon this document to show that the property had passed under the main contract vesting clause. *Held*, by Murray C.J., that the subcontract wording had been insufficient to incorporate the main contract vesting clause; but that even if it had, only the main contractor and not the owner could sue upon or enforce the sub-contract, and the sub-contractor was entitled to recover his plant and materials: *Triangle Ltd.* v. *John Burrows Ltd.* (1958).[31]

[Note: The latter part of this judgment may not be right. If the subcontract had fully incorporated the clause and the owner had been in possession, the sub-contractor would clearly have been in great difficulty in attempting to assert ownership and obtain recovery of the materials, it is submitted.]

It is suggested that, on the principles which seem to emerge from the **11·018** cases on express provisions[32-33] some kind of property, or at least a status of irremovability, may pass to the building owner in *attached* plant—for instance, scaffolding or form-work or cofferdams *in situ*—and that persons claiming the same through the builder might be defeated until at least the time for removal in the normal course of doing the work has arrived. But the question is speculative and there seems to be no clear authority on the point.

Section 2. Express Provisions

(1) Generally

Clauses in building contracts relating to rights over materials and plant are **11·019** commonly of two kinds, namely: what may be termed "seizure" or "user" clauses, often associated with a clause for forfeiture of the contract as a whole, under which the building owner is empowered at his option to take possession or assume ownership of materials and contractor's plant and use them to complete the work in certain specified events (usually some default of the builder), and, on the other hand, "vesting" clauses, including the provisions for interim payment, (commonly based on the value of

---

[31] [1958] (3) S.A. 81. See also *Dawber Williamson Roofing Ltd.* v. *Humberside County Council* (1979) 14 BLR 70, illustrated *infra*, para. 11·030.

[32-33] See the discussion at the end of Section 2(1), *infra*, paras. 11·032 *et seq.*

unfixed materials or goods brought onto site) under which ownership or a right of detention is expressed to pass automatically in certain specified events—often, for instance, upon delivery to the site, or, in the case of materials or goods, upon certification for interim payment or upon payment itself.

Examination of the cases shows, however, that this common distinction between the clauses is not particularly useful. The more important distinctions between the clauses are, it is submitted:

(a) that they may be expressed to operate automatically in a certain event on the one hand, or on the other hand they may be brought into operation at the owner's option in a certain event, and

(b) that they may purport to transfer ownership, on the one hand, or a variety of lesser rights such as possession, user or mere detention, or a simple status of irremovability on the other.

The classical vesting clause operates automatically, and usually purports to transfer ownership. The seizure clause operates at the owner's option, and may often transfer rights less than ownership. But every possible combination of these characteristics can be found in practice. None of these provisions can, of course, affect *pre-existing* rights of third persons in the plant or materials, unlike incorporation of materials which may well do so. Furthermore, it will be seen that, in so far as such clauses are expressed to take effect on bankruptcy or insolvency (as opposed to failure to proceed with due diligence or some substantive breach of contract), and are in fact exercised on that ground, they will be void against the contractor's trustee or liquidator.[34]

11·020   While the clauses may purport to transfer full ownership, or a lesser right, such as the right of possession, or a mere right of detention, even these distinctions are likely to be obscured when the rights concerned are carefully analysed. For instance, a seizure clause may often purport to give a mere right to possession and use of materials and plant for a limited period, *i.e.* until completion of the work. Where materials are concerned, however, it is obvious that once they have been used and incorporated under such a clause, the ownership will pass. On the other hand, despite an apparent transfer of absolute ownership under a vesting clause, it will usually, it has been submitted, be necessary to imply a term, if the contract is silent upon the point, re-transferring the ownership of *plant* (and indeed of any surplus materials) on completion to the builder.[35] Moreover, transfer of ownership to the building owner will be subject to his obligation to leave the plant or materials in the possession of the contractor to enable him to complete the work, subject to any right of the owner to enter and complete himself.[36] As will be seen, the necessarily qualified nature of all

---

[34] See, *e.g. Tripp* v. *Armitage, supra,* para. 11·007, and see also *post,* Chapter 16, Bankruptcy and Insolvency, paras. 16·035 *et seq.*

[35] *Cf.* Clause 33, ICE Conditions.

[36] See *Davidson* v. *Claffey Construction Ltd.* (1958) 60 W.A.L.R. 29 (Full Court), illustrated *infra,* para. 11·012.

the property or other rights which pass under such clauses has frequently been recognised by the courts.

In addition, both seizure and vesting types of clauses are frequently found in the same contract. Where this is so, each may be treated as supplementary to the other, so that one may achieve the owner's object where the other may fail. Furthermore, despite the vital distinction between plant and materials, which is obviously of the greatest importance in construing these clauses, in many older contracts plant and materials were classed together and dealt with by the same provision.

11·021   There would seem to be no general rules and the relevant provisions of every contract must be considered before their exact legal effect can be determined. However, provided the provisions of the contract are clear, the courts will give effect to any expressed intention to transfer the rights of possession or ownership to the building owner (subject to any pre-existing rights of third parties or any overriding statutory provisions).

The cases below are, as one would expect, frequently concerned with the rights of third parties in the materials or plant in question, since, as between the parties themselves, their rights and obligations under the contract do not usually depend upon any very exact analysis of the nature of the ownership or other rights transferred. In considering the cases, the fact that property which the contract purports to pass will often be of the qualified nature referred to above should not be forgotten. This factor may mean that a third party claiming through one of the parties to the contract—*e.g.* an execution creditor or assignee of one of them—can be defeated even though the contract has been effective in transferring the "property" to the party through whom he claims, by virtue of the fact that the opposing party still retains a limited interest until completion of the kind previously described, so that the transfer is not absolute. In the cases set out below, numbers (1) and (2) may be regarded as examples of seizure clauses passing a right less than ownership. Number (3) is not a decision on a contractual provision, and does not apply the English law, but nevertheless illustrates very well the essential differences between rights in plant and materials, and their qualified nature. Numbers (4) to (19) are either vesting cases in classical form, or cases where ownership is expressly purported to be transferred.

ILLUSTRATIONS

11·022   (1) Railway company owners entered into a contract with R., a builder, for the construction of a bridge over their railway. The contract provided that if the owners' architect considered that R. was not proceeding with proper expedition, the owners might, on seven days' notice, use the implements and materials for the time being used by R. in or about the works, and complete themselves, and R. was to pay any additional expenses. It was also expressly provided that the owners were to have a lien on the implements and materials on the site of the bridge as security for completion. On July 31, a fiat of bankruptcy issued against R. On that date the owners took possession of the implements and materials used by R. On August 1, they gave notice under the contract, and, on August 2, they started to complete the bridge, using some of the materials and detaining the remainder as against the trustee in bankruptcy. *Held*, by the Court of Queen's Bench, that the use of the materials prior to expiry of the notice was a conversion, but after expiry the owners were entitled to use them, and also to use and detain both materials and plant being used for the work not only on the site of the bridge but also on adjoining land not belonging to the owners. *Held*, also, that any lien created by the contract would merge in actual ownership in so far as materials were worked up: *Hawthorn* v. *Newcastle-upon-Tyne & North Shields Railway* (1840).[37]

(2) A building contract provided that if the contractor should fail to proceed, or become bankrupt, the architect might, on two days' notice, appoint others to complete, and seize and retain all materials, plant and implements, and also all materials wholly or partially made up or ready for fixing which were still on the contractors' or owners' premises, and might either proceed with the work or sell the materials and apply the proceeds to the completion of the work, provided the builder had received advances under the contract. Further, that if the contract be put an end to in this way, the contractors might not remove either work, materials, implements, scaffolding or plant, which must be appropriated for the use of whoever might finish the work. The contractors received considerable advances under the contract, including the value of materials, plant and implements on the premises. They then filed a petition for liquidation. Three days afterwards they were given notice under the contract for failing to proceed, and on expiry the owners took possession of all materials and plant. *Held*, by Bacon C.J.B., following *Hawthorn* v. *Newcastle Railway*, that they were entitled to detain them as against the trustee: *Re Waugh, ex. p. Dickin* (1876).[38]

11·023

(3) A draft contract in Scotland, which was never executed by the parties and objected to by the builder in other respects, contained a clause declaring that all materials, articles and others which the builder should bring upon the building owners' premises for the purposes of the work should not be thence removed until the full completion of the contract, but be held as pledged to the building owners for due performance of the work. The builder commenced operations and the owners raised no objection to his doing so without signing a contract. The builder eventually became bankrupt, leaving a crane and various materials on the site. The trustee demanded delivery, which was refused, and the building owners used both plant and materials to complete, and maintained their refusal to deliver after completion. *Held*, by the Court of Session, that the building owners were entitled to use both materials and plant for completion, subject to payment for the materials and the use of the crane, but must deliver up the crane on completion: *Kerr* v. *Dundee Gas Light Co.* (1861).[39]

[Note: This Scottish case is not a decision upon the wording of the contract, which was never executed, and turns upon the special rght of retention in Scottish law, but it is useful in illustrating the distinction between plant and materials and in showing the presumed intentions of the parties.[40]]

---

[37] 3 Q.B. 734. The judgment of Denman C.J. in this case proceeds on the basis that there had been a default by the builder. Had the determination been based on the bankruptcy alone it would, it is submitted, have been invalid—see fn. 34, *supra*. For a modern case where premature action in entering and labelling contractor's plant was held not to be repudiation of the contract, see *Earth and General Contracts Ltd.* v. *Manchester Corporation* (1958) 108 L.J. 665, illustrated *ante*, Chap. 4, para. 4·216.

[38] 4 Ch.D. 524.

[39] 23 D.(Ct. of Sess.) 343.

[40] See the judgment quoted *post*, paras. 11·038 *et seq*.

(4) Under a contract with a railway company, materials and plant provided by the contractor became the absolute property of the company when placed on the land, and the contractor was to have no property in them, except the right of using them on the land for the purpose of the works, and, on due completion, the right to the return of unused materials and plant, and in the event of their being used by the company on his default, to compensation for their use. There was also provision for monthly payments of 95 per cent. of work executed and materials supplied. *Held*, by Stuart V.-C. that materials brought onto the site were not so absolutely the property of the company as to be seizable under a judgment against it: *Beeston* v. *Marriott* (1864).[41]

(5) A contract provided by Clause 7 that all materials which should have   **11·024**
been brought on the premises by the builder for the purpose of erecting the buildings *should be considered as immediately attached to and belonging to the premises*, and that no part thereof should be removed without the owner's consent, and by Clause 8, that in case the builder should fail to proceed with the erection and completion of the houses within the time specified, it should be lawful for the owner to enter and take possession of the land and all bricks and other building materials thereon for his own absolute use and benefit. A judgment creditor of the builder sought to seize certain materials before any action had been taken under Clause 8. *Held*, by the Court of Common Pleas, that Clause 7 gave the building owner at the least an equitable interest in the materials so as to disentitle the sheriff from seizing them, and further that Clause 8 did not in any way limit the owner's rights under Clause 7. *Held*, also, that even if Clause 7 transferred the legal title, it did not require registration under the Bills of Sale Act 1854, since it was not "an assignment, transfer or other assurance" or a "licence to take possession" of personal chattels: *Brown* v. *Bateman* (1867).[42]

(6) A building lease agreement contained a provision that the lessee builder should not remove any sand or other materials from the premises, and that all materials brought thereon should become the property of the lessors. A judgment creditor of the builder seized the materials. *Held*, by the Court of Common Pleas, following *Brown* v. *Bateman*, that they could not be taken in execution; further the transfer of property did not require registration as a Bill of Sale under the 1854 Act: *Blake* v. *Izard* (1867).[43]

(7) An engineering contract provided that the plant brought by the con-   **11·025**
tractor onto the works was to be deemed the property of the owners for the time being, and was not to be removed during the progress of the works without the written order of the engineer, and, in the case of suspension of the works due to default of the contractor, was to be subject to be used in and about the completion of the works. The works were suspended, the contractor went into liquidation, and the owners having completed the works themselves, the plant was by agreement sold. *Held*, by Bacon C.J.B., that the effect of the above clause was to give the owners a right of use only, and the trustee could not have removed the plant without being liable in damages. But the ownership of the plant remained in the contractor, and the trustee was accordingly entitled to the proceeds of sale. Nor could the owners set off the value of the plant against sums due to them from the contractor by invoking

---

[41] 8 L.T. 690. Discussed *infra*, para. 11·037. Compare also the closely comparable case of *Banbury, etc., Ry.* v. *Daniel*, later illustrated para. 11·026.
[42] L.R. 2 C.P. 272. On Bills of Sale, see also the Full Court of West Australia's decision in *Davidson* v. *Claffey Constructions Ltd.* (1958) 60 W.A.L.R. 29, illustrated para. 11·029 *infra*, and see *infra*, para. 11·046, and *post*, Chap. 16, para. 16·050.
[43] 16 W.R. 108.

the "mutual dealings" clause in bankruptcy:[44] *Re Winter, ex p. Bolland* (1878).[45]

(8) A building contract contained no vesting clause in the usual sense, but provided that the owner, upon default by the builder for a certain number of days, might re-enter upon the land and expel the builder, and on such re-entry all the materials then in and about the premises should be forfeited to and become the property of the landowner "as and for liquidated damages." The builder became bankrupt, and then defaulted for the requisite number of days, whereupon the owner entered and seized the materials, which were then claimed by the trustee. *Held*, by the Court of Appeal, that the builder's interest in the materials was a defeasible one, and the trustee obtained nothing better than the builder had, and accordingly his claim must fail: *Re Garrud, ex p. Newitt* (1881).[46]

11·026   (9) A clause in a building lease agreement made between an intended lessor and lessee provided that "all building and other materials brought by the intended lessee upon the land shall, whether affixed to the freehold or not, become the property of the intended lessor." An execution creditor of the intended lessee took certain of the materials in execution. On interpleader, the creditor contended that the contract required registration as creating an equitable interest in chattels under the Bills of Sale Act 1878. *Held*, by the Court of Appeal, that even if an equitable interest of this kind required registration[47] which on the authority of *Brown* v. *Bateman* (see *supra*) was doubtful, the moment the materials were brought onto the premises the property in the materials had passed in law to the intended lessor, and on the authority of *Brown* v. *Bateman* and *Blake* v. *Izard* that did not require registration. The builder's agreement was at no time an equitable assignment of anything, but a legal contract that, upon the happening of a particular event, the property in law should pass in certain chattels, which the event itself would identify without the necessity of any further act on the part of anybody, and which could not be identified before: *Reeves* v. *Barlow* (1884).[48]

(10) A railway contract provided for initial *loan* payments at a rate of 75% of the value of materials brought on site, later to be replaced by instalment payments to be certified by the engineer "at a rate of 90% in respect of the value of the works executed and materials delivered", rising to a rate of 100% when £50,000 out of a total contract of £254,000 had been certified. There was no express reference to the property passing. A dispute arose as to the amount which the contractor had been paid following certification by the engineer, and the owner sought an injunction restraining the contractor from removing his materials from the site. *Held*, by Pearson J., following the shipbuilding case of *Woods* v. *Russell*,[49] and not following *Tripp* v. *Armitage*, that the inference was that, as and when materials were certified by the engineer, they became the property of the owners: *Banbury Railway Company* v. *Daniel* (1884).[50]

---

[44] As to which latter see *post*, Chap. 16, para. 16·014.
[45] 8 Ch.D. 225, discussed *infra*, paras. 11·038–9; *cf. Kerr* v. *Dundee Gas Light Co. supra*.
[46] 16 Ch.D. 522. No contention that this provision might be a penalty was advanced by the trustee—as to which see *ante*, Chap. 10, Section 1.
[47] See *infra*, para. 11·046.
[48] 12 Q.B.D. 436, C.A.: *per* Bowen L.J., applying *Brown* v. *Bateman*, see *supra*, and *Blake* v. *Izard*, see *supra*.
[49] (1822) 5 B. & Ad. 942.
[50] (1884) 54 L.J. Ch. 265.

[Note: This case, cited as authority in the Tenth Edition, should clearly now be regarded as wrongly decided—see the powerful analysis and examination of the authorities made by White J. in South Australia in 1982.[51]]

(11) A contract for the construction of a school contained a provision **11·027** (clause 10) that "all plant, work and materials brought to and left upon the ground by the contractor or to his order for the purpose of carrying out the contract, or of forming part of the works, *shall be considered the property of the Board*, and the same shall not on any account be removed or taken away by the contractor without the express licence of the architect." The clause also provided that the Board should not be in any way answerable for any loss or damage which might happen to such plant, work or materials. There was no provision for the revesting of either plant or materials. Finally, by clause 20 it was provided that, if the builder should delay performance, the Board after giving notice might enter and take possession, and in that event the plant and materials should be forfeited to the Board. After the builder became bankrupt, the Board gave the necessary notice and took possession of the plant and materials. The trustee contended that, at the time of the bankruptcy, and before the forfeiture was exercised under clause 20, the goods were the property of the Board as true owners by virtue of clause 10, but that they were in the order and disposition of the builder with their consent, and consequently passed to the trustee under the "order and disposition" (*i.e.* reputed ownership) clause in bankruptcy. *Held*, by Wright and Bigham JJ., that the language of the agreement was wholly different from that in *Reeves* v. *Barlow* (see *supra*). The opening words of clause 10, when read in connection with the remainder of the clause, and with reference to the purpose and scope of the whole contract, made it clear that it was not intended to vest the materials at once in the building owners. All that the Board had was a contractual right to have the goods remain on their land for use by the builders in the construction of the building. Accordingly, the Board were not the true owners at the time of the bankruptcy, the "order and disposition" clause did not apply, and their subsequent forfeiture under clause 20 was valid and defeated the trustee's claim: *Re Keen, ex p. Collins* (1902).[52]

(12) Under a building lease agreement between intending lessor and lessee, the lessor was empowered to take possession of materials in the event of the lessee's default. It was further provided that all materials brought onto the land were to be deemed to be annexed to the freehold. *Held*, by Wright J., that this latter provision passed the property to the lessor, who was the true owner, but they were in the order and disposition of the lessee in such circumstances as to make him the reputed owner, and the trustee of the lessee was accordingly entitled to recover their value from a mortgagee of the lessee who with the consent of the lessor had entered and used the materials to complete some of the houses: *Re Weibking, ex p. Ward* (1902).[53]

(13) A contract for the construction of a harbour contained a provision that **11·028** in case the builder became bankrupt the owners might enter and take possession of the works and complete them, and also provided that: "The whole

---

[51] *Egan* v. *State Transport Authority* [1982] 31 S.A.S.R. 481, illustrated *infra*, para. 11·031, and discussed *infra*. See also the dictum of Judge John Davies Q.C. to the same effect in *W. Hanson (Harrow) Ltd.* v. *Rapid Civil Engineering Ltd.* (1987) 38 B.L.R. 106, 113, illustrated and cited *supra*, para. 11·010.

[52] [1902] 1 K.B. 555, further discussed *infra*, para. 11·036. See *post*, paras. 16·052 *et seq.* for a full discussion of the bankruptcy rules of reputed ownership.

[53] [1902] 1 K.B. 713. With the recent abolition of reputed ownership in England the more likely basis of any claim by a building owner will be under section 25 of the English Sale of Goods Act 1979—see *infra*, para. 11·054, and see *post*, Chap. 16, para. 16·050.

of the plant and materials brought on to the ground by the contractor is to be marked with his initials in legible characters. All such plant and materials shall be considered the property of the company until the engineers shall have certified the completion of the contract". The contractor gave a Bill of Sale on plant and materials to H. Later he became bankrupt, and the owners took possession. H. sued them on his Bill of Sale. *Held*, by Farwell J., applying *Reeves* v. *Barlow* (1884),[54] (and distinguishing *Re Keen, ex p. Collins* (1902),[55] on the ground that the words in that contract rendered it plain that no property, as a matter of construction, ever passed), that the plant and materials were vested in the owners subject to the condition that when completion was certified the property would revert to the contractor; that the clause was intended as a security for completion of the work; and even though the owners had not completed the work or employed another contractor, H. could not recover the materials: *Hart* v. *Porthgain Harbour* (1903).[56]

(14) A building contract provided that "the plant tools and materials provided by the contractor shall from the time at which they respectively may be brought upon the site ... and during the construction and until the completion of the said works become and continue the property of the Board, and the contractor shall not remove the same or any part thereof without the consent in writing of the engineer". By other clauses, the contractors were to make good loss or damage to the works or plant by any accident, and were to be advanced 50 per cent. of the value of plant, the advances to be repaid at 5 per cent. per month by deduction from monthly certificates. The contractors on orders of the Minister of Munitions given under statutory regulations ceased work and sold the plant to other persons, and the Board claimed the proceeds of sale and an injunction. The contractors argued that the contract was at an end. *Held*, by Bray J., that the contract had only been suspended and that, following *Hart* v. *Porthgain Harbour Co.* (1903) and distinguishing *Re Keen, ex p. Collins* (1902), the property had passed to the Board, but that the Minister had power under the regulations to order this sale and the Board were not entitled to the proceeds of sale, *Metropolitan Water Board* v. *Dick Kerr & Co.* (1917).[57]

11·029   (15) Under a contract for the construction of certain tunnels in Canada it was provided that "all machinery, tools, plant, materials, equipment, articles and things whatsoever provided by the contractor ... for the works ... shall from the time of their being so provided become and until the final completion of the said work shall be the property of His Majesty for the purposes of the said works". The contractors provided a large amount of plant at the site. The local authority raised an assessment on the contractors, under an Act imposing liability upon either the owners or persons in legal possession of assessable personal property. The contractors contended that the Crown were the owners of the property, and that the contractors' interest was limited to a licence to use the plant and equipment. *Held*, by the Privy Council, following *Reeves* v. *Barlow* (1884) and *Hart* v. *Porthgain Harbour Co. Ltd.* (1903)[58] that the Crown were the owners of the property, but that while delivery onto a Crown site was a delivery to the Crown and vested the ownership in the Crown, there was a notional or actual bailment or redelivery of possession to the builders for the purpose of carrying out the building contract, and they

---

[54] See *supra*.
[55] See *supra*.
[56] [1903] 1 Ch. 690.
[57] [1917] 2 K.B. 1 at p. 13—Bray J.'s decision on suspension was over-ruled and the contract held to have been frustrated in the Court of Appeal, *ibid*. at p. 19.
[58] See *supra*.

were accordingly in legal possession of the property. (The assessment was then held invalid for other reasons): *Bennett and White (Calgary) Ltd.* v. *Municipal District of Sugar City* (1951).[59]

(16) Section 5 of the Australian Bills of Sale Act 1899 required registration of "any agreement *by way of sale, security, gift or bailment*" which either transferred property or a right to possession of chattels, or which conferred a right or licence to possess or seize chattels. Under a building contract in West Australia there was provision for progress payments which included the value of materials, and an express provision that following certification and payment the materials were to become the property of the owners. By Clause 19 the owners were also empowered to re-enter and seize and use the materials on the contractor's default. When the contractor became bankrupt, an unpaid supplier seized the unfixed materials, but then interpleaded. The trial judge had held that the provisions in the building contract constituted a Bill of Sale requiring registration, and found in favour of the contractor's trustee in bankruptcy. *Held*, by the Full Court, certification and payment under a building contract could not be considered a contract of sale. Even after the title had passed under an express provision, the building owner was constrained to leave the goods on the site for the fulfilment of the undertaking. The purpose of payment was to provide the builder with some remuneration in reduction of the total sum ultimately payable, and it was only by the express terms that the property in materials could vest in the owner. The express provisions for vesting in this contract did not constitute a Bill of Sale under the additional scope of the 1899 Act, since they could not be regarded as a sale, security, gift or bailment: *Davidson* v. *Claffey Constructions Ltd.* (1958).[60]

(17) Sub-contractors for the supply and fixing of a slate roof for a school had **11·030** 16 tonnes of roofing slates on the site when the main contractor went into liquidation. At that time the sub-contractors had not been paid for the slates, but the main contractor had received their value from the owner less retention under the interim payment provisions in clause 30(2) of the 1963 RIBA/ JCT form. The owner prevented the sub-contractor from removing the tiles, and ultimately the subcontractor completed the work for the owner on a "fix only" basis without receiving payment for the tiles. By clause 14(1) of the main contract the property in the unfixed slates passed to the owner upon payment of the certificate which included their value, though the risk of loss or damage was to remain with the contractor. Further by Clause 25(4)(a) of the main contract, unfixed materials on the site became the property of the owner on the automatic termination of the contract for insolvency in that clause. By Clause 1(1) of the standard form sub-contract, the sub-contractors were *deemed to have notice* of the main contract conditions, but there was no express provision for passing the property to the main contractor. The owners relied on this clause in the sub-contract, coupled with Clause 14(1) of the main contract, and at one stage also relied on section 25(2) of the Sale of Goods Act 1983 as passing an indefeasible title to themselves.[61] *Held*, by Mais J., following *Tripp* v. *Armitage* and *Seath* v. *Moore*, that materials brought onto a site under a "supply and fix" sub-contract remained the property of the sub-contractor until fixed, and Clause 1(1) of the sub-contract was not sufficient to pass the property to the main contractor on delivery to site, so that in the absence of privity between the owner and the sub-contractor, the former could not assert ownership against the latter unless the main contractor had

---

[59] [1951] A.C. 786.
[60] 60 W.A.L.R. 29.
[61] I.E. as a purchaser without notice from a buyer left in possession by a seller; see also *infra*, for this section of the Act, Sub-section (7), para. 11·051 *et seq.*

first obtained a good title from the sub-contractor. The "supply and fix" sub-contract was not a contract for the sale of the tiles to the main contractor, so that section 25(2) of the Act of 1893 could not assist the owners, who were liable to the sub-contractor for the value of the slates as damages for their wrongful conversion; *Dawber Williamson Roofing* v. *Humberside City Council* (1979).[62]

[Note: This case, for the reasons stated in the commentary to BLR, should not be regarded as an invariable interpretation of all sub-contracts with a similar clause relating to the main contract, since an intention to pass the property to the main contractor may well be inferred in those cases where payment of the sub-contractor is made dependent upon certification under the main contract, or from other provisions in the sub-contract recognizing the potential rights of the owner of the goods in question.]

11·031   (18) By Clause 30 of a railway contract in South Australia progress payments were calculated by reference to 75 per cent. of the value of materials on site. There was no vesting clause passing the property in the materials to the owner, though there was a clause permitting seizure of both plant and materials following a lawful determination of the countract by the owner. The owner terminated and seized both plant and materials, and used or sold them. Ultimately the owner's determination was held to be unjustified and unlawful, but due to a harsh binding certificate provision the contractor had been unable to obtain damages for breach of contract.[63] The contractor now claimed damages in tort for conversion of the plant and materials, and the owners argued that the damages in the case of materials should be reduced since they had become the owner's property (either as to 75 per cent. or on payment of a further 25 per cent.). *Held*, by White J., following Wolf S.P.J.'s dictum in *Davidson* v. *Claffey Constructions*,[64] and not following *Banbury* v. *Daniel*,[65] which had been wrongly decided, the property had not passed and the contractor was entitled to recover damages for conversion. *Per* White J., part payments made in a construction contract with reference to the value of materials which it is expected will soon be incorporated into the works cannot be accepted as creating a property interest in the paying owner without express provision. The purpose of instalment payments is not to pay for the materials, but as a practical measure to enable the contractor to keep working: *Egan* v. *State Transport Authority* (1982).[66]

(19) A contractor lawfully terminated a building contract in Victoria and was entitled to damages. Certain unfixed doors and door frames had been delivered to the site prior to the termination, but were removed by the contractor at the time of termination. Under the contract, the contractor was entitled to interim payment for unfixed materials if delivered to the site. The contractor assessed the part of his damages relating to the doors on the footing that they had become the property of the owner on delivery, and that accordingly the owner was liable to pay for their full value on their being offered by the contractor. *Held*, by Murray J. following the *Egan* and *Davidson* cases, and not following *Banbury* v. *Daniel* and a statement based on it in the tenth edition, that the mere fact that the contract permitted the builder to claim progress payments for materials delivered to the site was not, in the absence of express provision, sufficient to justify a finding that the property

---

[62] 14 BLR 74. See also *Triangle Ltd.* v. *John Burrows Ltd.* [1958] (3) S.A. 81, illustrated *supra*, para. 11·017.

[63] See the earlier proceedings in the High Court of Australia, *ante*, Chap. 6, para. 6·137.

[64] (1958) 60 W.A.L.R. 29, 34, illustrated *supra*.

[65] Illustrated *supra*.

[66] 31 S.A.S.R. 481, 537. See the like views expressed by Judge John Davies Q.C. in *W. Hanson (Harrow) Ltd.* v. *Rapid Civil Engineering Ltd.* (1987) 37 BLR 106, illustrated and cited *supra*, para. 11·010.

in the materials had passed to the owner before their incorporation into the building: *R. J. Grills Ltd.* v. *Dellios* (1988).[67]

At first sight it may seem difficult to reconcile the earlier of the above **11·032** cases. In *Bennett and White (Calgary) Ltd.* v. *Sugar City* (1951), the Privy Council appears to have thought that the distinction between some of the above cases depended upon the use of words such as "considered" or "deemed" in the vesting clauses, as opposed to clauses where the words used were "be and become",[68] or where the property was stated to pass in straightforward and unqualified terms, and it must be admitted that until its eighth edition the present book lent some support to this view. But in *Hart* v. *Porthgain Harbour* (1903)[69] Farwell J. had said:

> "In my opinion the true construction of the clause 'all such plant and materials shall be considered the property of the company' is that it vests the property in the materials in the company at law subject to a condition that, when the engineer shall have certified the completion of the contract, the contractor shall be at liberty to remove them"

and he felt no difficulty in distinguishing *Re Keen, ex p. Collins* (1902) on the grounds that "there were words in the contract which rendered it plain that no property ever passed". What those words were is shown in the judgment of Bigham J. in *Re Keen, ex p. Collins*, when he said that the vesting clause in this form, if read by itself, was an ambiguous phrase, but "when read in connection with the rest of the same clause and with reference to the whole purpose and scope of the contract" (which included a forfeiture clause as well), "it becomes reasonably clear that it was not intended to vest the materials at once in the building owners".

Quite apart from the cases of *Hart* v. *Porthgain Harbour* and *Brown* v. **11·033** *Bateman*, where the word "considered" was used, it is suggested that a careful examination of the judgments in the remaining cases does not, with the greatest respect, support the Privy Council's view, and that it is in fact a misleading exercise to pose the question between disputing parties as depending on whether or not "the property passes" through the use of particular words in the contract. Part of the difficulty arises because the same clauses in many of the cases govern both plant and materials, when a moment's consideration shows that in most cases the parties cannot intend the same consequences to arise in the case of plant and surplus materials on the one hand and incorporated materials on the other. Indeed it is apparent that only in very rare and unusual cases will the parties intend the property to pass in any absolute sense at all. Where this is so, the courts will, of course, give effect to the parties' intention.[70] But in the great majority of cases the transfer is not absolute, and even where no express provision exists in the contract it is necessary to imply a right to the

---

[67] [1988] V.R. 136.
[68] See, *per* Lord Reid at pp. 813 and 814.
[69] [1903] 1 Ch. 690 at p. 694.
[70] See *e.g. Re Garrud, ex p. Newitt* (1881) 16 Ch.D. 522, *supra*.

revesting at least of equipment, plant and surplus materials; and in *Bennett and White (Calgary) Ltd.* v. *Sugar City*, the Privy Council further held that prior to completion the contractors were entitled to legal possession of plant.

11·034   Until the remarkable analysis and examination of the cases made by White J. in *Egan* v. *State Transport Authority*, one of the most valuable discussions of this point was to be found in the judgments in the Scottish case of *Kerr* v. *Dundee Gas Co.* (1861).[71] There the Lord Justice-Clerk had said:

> "Retention is a right of a varying character, which is always measured according to the title on which that possession is held, which is the ground of the right of retention. Now, what was the nature of the defender's title? It was a title arising *ex contractu*. It is in vain to consider to what extent, or in what sense, delivery of these materials into the possession of the defenders made them the property of the defenders. In one sense it did, and in another sense it did not. But in performance of the contract obligation, these materials were delivered, and in my view the right emerging to the defenders was that they were entitled to retain them for those purposes of the contract for which they were brought there, *viz.*: to be worked up into the work contracted to be executed. And, therefore, I come to the conclusion, without any difficulty, that the defenders were entitled to keep these materials, and to use them in building the tank. But on the other hand, they must allow the pursuer the value of these materials; because although they have paid for all the work done, they have not paid for these materials ...
>
> "But as regards the other portion ... representing the value of the plant and tools brought onto the defender's premises, not to be permanently worked up into the work contracted for, but merely to be used temporarily in the execution of the work, it is obvious that there is, in point of fact and legal principle, a plain distinction between this part of the claim and the other. But here there is no longer the same right of retention on the part of the defenders, but a more limited right than they had over the stores and other materials; and it was more limited just in exact correspondence to the purposes for which the plant and tools were brought on the defenders' ground. Their right of retention ... was necessarily limited to the contract purposes; for the tools were there to be used for the purpose of executing the works contracted for, not to be exhausted in executing the work, as the materials were, but to be used temporarily, and returned (no doubt deteriorated by wear and tear) as soon as the works were executed ... And therefore, while they were entitled to retain the crane and other tools to be used in the execution of the contract, on the completion of the contract there arose in the trustee two rights. In the first place, a right to a reasonable consideration for the use of the tools, that being parallel to his right to payment of the value of the materials. But, secondly, there was a right on the part of the trustee to restoration of the plant and tools as they stood at the completion of the works. ... "

11·035   Once the qualified nature of these interests is understood, the decisions fall, it is submitted, into a logical pattern. Indeed it may be inferred with some confidence that, as in many other areas of construction contracts, the traditional draftsmen simply failed to understand the underlying realities on which the wording would be required to operate in sufficient detail, and

---

[71] 23 D. (Ct. of Sess.) 343 at p. 348.

that the courts found themselves struggling with inept draftsmanship in order to achieve a sensible implementation of the contract intention by whatever means the draftsmanship would allow. Thus, the courts have rightly acted on the basis that the clauses are inserted not merely to enable the contract to be performed, but also to obtain due security for its performance[72]; interim payment clauses to help finance the contractor rather than to purchase materials[72a]; and seizure clauses to enable the work to be completed rather than transfer plant, or goods, or their value to the owner on a permanent basis.[72b] It will be seen that in every single case (except where the now obsolete doctrine of reputed ownership in bankruptcy was successfully invoked in *Re Weibking, ex p. Ward* (1902)[73] the courts have prevented materials or plant from being seized or claimed by creditors, trustees, or other third parties before the completion of the work, thus giving effect to this view of the purpose of the clauses. This protection has not been limited to cases where the claim has been made through the builder, but has even been extended to cases where the claim has been through the building owner, and the important residual rights of the builder in the plant and materials would otherwise have been prejudiced.[74]

On the other hand, once the work is complete, the purpose for which the **11·036** property or interest in plant has passed is satisfied, and the builder's trustee or others will be entitled to recover.[75] The case which has, perhaps, given rise to most difficulty, *Re Keen, ex p. Collins* (1902),[76] was a case where the builder's trustee, in order to avoid the effect of a clear-cut forfeiture provision, had to put forward the somewhat paradoxical contention that, prior to the forfeiture, the goods in question had vested immediately on delivery to the site in the building owners under the vesting clause, so that he would be in a position to invoke the reputed ownership provisions in bankruptcy. The court defeated his claim by pointing out that there were other provisions in the contract inconsistent with immediate vesting, and that in effect an apparent vesting clause only gave a contractual right to have the goods remain on the land for use by the builder.[77] Yet within a week of this decision, one of the judges in the case (Wright J.) held that the property *did* pass to the building owner in a dispute between the builder's trustee and the holder of a bill of sale given by the builder.[78]

---

[72] See, *per* Farwell J. in *Hart* v. *Porthgain Harbour* and *per* Bowen L.J. in *Reeves* v. *Barlow*, *supra*.

[72a] See the *Davidson* and *Egan* cases, *supra*.

[72b] See *Re Winter* and the *Egan* case, both *supra*.

[73] [1902] 1 K.B. 713. For a full discussion of this doctrine, see *post*, Chap. 16.

[74] *Beeston* v. *Marriott* (1864) 8 L.T. 690.

[75] *Re Winter, ex p. Bolland* (1878) 8 Ch.D. 225; *Kerr* v. *Dundee Gas Co.* (1861) 23 D. (Ct. of Sess.) 343.

[76] [1902] 1 K.B. 555.

[77] *Cf. Re Winter, ex p. Bolland*, see *supra*.

[78] *Re Weibking, ex p. Ward* [1902] 1 K.B. 713, distinguished, in so far as the application of the doctrine of reputed ownership to the facts was concerned, in the case of *Re Fox, ex p. Oundle & Thraptson R.D.C.* [1948] Ch. 407, referred to *post*, Chap. 16, para. 16·053.

11·037   It may be doubted whether, in the normal case, much turns upon whether "the property" is held to "pass," (with immediate redelivery of legal possession to the builder[79] and an ultimate implied right to revesting), or whether all that is held to pass is a mere right of user or retention on the site,[80] since it is submitted that the above cases show that only in most exceptional circumstances will the courts permit the later rights of third parties, claiming through a party to the contract, to interfere with due completion. In effect, the courts appear to recognise possessory rights, albeit of a qualified or even temporary character, somewhat akin to a lien, which will be binding *in rem* (that is to say, against all the world claiming subsequently) as coming into existence as a result of these provisions. In the case of *Beeston* v. *Marriott* (1864), for instance, it is suggested than an execution creditor of the *lessee* would have had as short shrift as was in the event received by the execution creditor of the *lessor*, and it may well be that the effect of many of these clauses, whether of the "seizure" or "vesting" type, will be to create differing interests in plant and materials which will defeat persons claiming the goods through *either* contracting party. Thus, in *Beeston* v. *Marriott*,[81] Stuart V.-C. said:

11·038
> "It is true the contract says that ... these chattels shall be the absolute property of the company, and that the plaintiff shall have no property in them, but immediately afterwards follow these exceptions qualifying that absolute right of property ... which the first words of the contract give ... The right of using them, the rights, as to some of them, of becoming absolutely possessed of them, and the right to demand compensation ... if this company shall use them, so qualify the right of the company and give such a right and interest of a legal character to the plaintiff in these chattels, that they cannot be considered the property of the company so as to be taken in execution. They are chattels upon the ground of the company, dedicated to a particular purpose, in which purpose both the plaintiff and defendants are interested as to the use of the chattels, and, as to the surplus, they are ultimately to become the absolute property of the plaintiff. *Chattels in that situation cannot be taken in execution*".[82]

And in *Re Winter, ex p. Bolland* (1878),[83] Bacon C.J.B. said:

> "This plant might have been protected against execution by this agreement—that it was to be deemed property that was to be left in the hands of the Commissioners for the purposes of the contract—but not with respect to the claims of the creditors if he became bankrupt".

11·039   This last remark shows clearly the true *ratio decidendi* of the cases, it is submitted. By virtue of the fact that there must have been an implied right to revesting of the plant concerned in that case, it was clear that the trustee

---

[79] *Bennett and White (Calgary) Ltd.* v. *Sugar City* [1951] A.C. 786, and see *Davidson* v. *Claffey Constructions Ltd. supra.*
[80] *Hawthorn* v. *Newcastle Ry.* (1840) 3 Q.B. 734; *Re Waugh, ex p. Dickin* (1876) 4 Ch.D. 524; *Re Keen, ex p. Collins* [1902] 1 K.B. 555; *Re Winter, ex p. Bolland* (1878) 8 Ch.D. 225.
[81] See *supra.*
[82] Compare the decision on closely comparable facts in *Banbury, etc., Ry.* v. *Daniel*, illustrated *supra*, para. 11·026.
[83] A case where the trustee sued after the work was completed—see *supra*, para. 11·025.

must be entitled to the proceeds of sale of the plant on completion of the work. The court achieved this commercially necessary result by holding that "the property did not pass" to the building owner under the clause in question, and the case is cited as an authority for that proposition. But had the claim been by a judgment creditor *of the builder* during the currency of the contract, Bacon C.J.B.'s statement shows that in the court's view he too would have been defeated, in which event the case would, no doubt, have been cited later as authority for the proposition that the property *did* pass to the owner under the clause in question.

In the foregoing discussion and illustrations, the shipbuilding cases **11·040** have been deliberately omitted. As has been previously pointed out, these cases differ on their facts in important respects, since while on a building site it can safely be assumed that all plant and materials have been brought there for the purpose of the owner's work, in a shipbuilder's yard materials and plant are on the shipbuilder's land, and may well be being used for other work. The shipbuilding cases undoubtedly exhibit a divergent tendency in the interpretation of express terms governing the ownership or possession of unfixed materials, in that the courts have been justifiably reluctant, even in the face of express provisions, to hold that the property in materials will pass to the purchaser until they have been incorporated in the ship. The cases of *Baker* v. *Gray* (1856),[84] *Seath* v. *Moore* (1886),[85] *Reid* v. *Macbeth and Gray* (1904),[86] and *Re Blyth Shipbuilding and Dry Docks Ltd.* (1926),[87] have already been referred to.[88] On the other hand, in *Re Walker, ex p. Barter* (1884),[89] the property in unfixed goods and materials "bought or ordered for" a ship and her engines was held to pass under a vesting clause, where a wider forfeiture clause failed in its effect by reason of its being exercised on the ground of bankruptcy. Again *Woods* v. *Russell*[90] was relied on by Pearson J. when holding that the property passed under an interim payment provision in *Banbury Rly Co.* v. *Daniel*.[91] Of these cases, *Baker* v. *Gray* is the only one to be cited at all frequently in building cases, and it has been frequently distinguished.[92] Examination of the judgments of Jervis C.J. and Cresswell J. in *Baker* v. *Gray* shows that, as a matter of construction, while the contract was interpreted as passing the property *in the ship* at an early stage, it did not intend to pass the property in the unfixed timber until it had been at the least used, if not necessarily actually fastened, in the ship:

> "Perhaps the parties might have intended that the timber which had been provided for the construction of the ship should be the property of the

[84] 25 L.J.C.P. 161.
[85] 11 App.Cas. 350.
[86] [1904] A.C. 223.
[87] [1926] Ch. 494.
[88] See *supra*, para. 11·012.
[89] 26 Ch.D. 510, illustrated on the bankruptcy point *post*, Chap. 16, para. 16·040.
[90] (1822) 5 B. & Add. 942.
[91] (1884) 54 L.J., Ch. 265, illustrated and now doubted *supra*, para. 11·026.
[92] *e.g.* in *Brown* v. *Bateman* (1867) L.R. 2 C.P. 272, see *supra*.

defendant if the shipbuilder should fail in the performance of his contract, but I do not think … the language employed is sufficient to carry out that intention. I think there is only a provision for the ship becoming the defendant's property; but as to the materials, so long as they remain on the premises and the property of the builder, the defendant has the right to use them, and until they are actually used and put into the corpus of his ship, they remain the property of the builder. … It is not necessary to say whether it would be requisite, in order to give the defendant an interest in the materials, that they should be actually *fastened* to the ship".[93]

11·041   The shipbuilding cases are, it is submitted, of doubtful authority in construing express terms in ordinary building and engineering contracts, and the leading cases of *Brown* v. *Bateman, Reeves* v. *Barlow* (1884) and *Hart* v. *Porthgain Harbour Co.* (1903) leave little doubt, as stated in the tenth edition, that the courts will give effect to the prime purpose of vesting and seizure clauses alike, namely, the provision of security for the due completion of the works, which may entail defeating the later claims of third parties, *whether made through the owner or the builder*, at least until completion of the work.[94]

To avoid misunderstanding of the effect of the above cases, it should be pointed out that, in cases involving claims by a contractor's trustee or liquidator, the rights of other parties in plant or materials, whether of ownership, or seizure, or detention, will prevail over any claim advanced on behalf of the insolvent estate, provided that the contract out of which the rights of the other party are derived *was itself entered into* before the bankruptcy or insolvency (that is, applying the ordinary rules of "relation back"), and it will not affect a claimant that his contractual rights did not crystallise (for example, by delivery to site) or were not exercised (for example, by seizure) until after the bankruptcy.[95]

11·042   A powerful analysis and examination of the cases relating to vesting and seizure provisions which seems likely to prove seminal was provided by White J.'s remarkable judgment in 1982 in the Supreme Court of South Australia in the case of *Egan* v. *State Transport Authority*.[96] That analysis showed persuasively that the case of *Banbury* v. *Daniel*[97] had been wrongly decided by Pearson J. in the Chancery Division in 1884 (when he held that a typical interim payment provision calculated by reference to the value of unfixed materials on site, but with no further express provision with regard to passing the property, carried the inference that the property in the materials would pass to the owners immediately upon certification) and that the statement made in the tenth edition under subsec-

---

[93] (1856) 25 L.J.C.P. 161, *per* Jervis C.J.

[94] For a recent case on the passing of the property in an offshore floating facility see *Davy Off-Shore Ltd.* v. *Emerald Field Contracting Ltd.*. (1992) *Financial Times*, January 28 (Hobhouse J.); *affd.* [1992] 2 Lloyd's Rep. 142 C.A.

[95] *Re Waugh, ex p. Dicken* (1876) L.R. 4 Ch.D. 524; *Re Garrud, ex p. Newitt* (1881) 16 Ch.D. 522; *Re Keen, ex p. Collins* [1902] 1 K.B. 555; and see further on this *infra* para. 11·049 and *post*, Chap. 16 para. 16·041.

[96] [1982] 31 S.A.S.R. 481, 433–547. See also the remarkable and valuable analysis of the effect of inflation on damages made by White J. in the same case, *ante*, Chap. 8 para. 8·153.

[97] (1884) 54 L.J. Ch. 265, illustrated *supra*, para. 11·026.

tion (2) *infra* on the strength of the *Banbury* case (to the effect that payment provisions in respect of materials will normally pass the property to the building owner on payment) was not justified.

The cases illustrated above have been primarily concerned with dis-   **11·043** putes over the ownership or possession of materials or plant between the original parties to the construction contract, or with parties claiming through them, such as judgment creditors, or assignees of either party. However, as previously stated, these provisions cannot bind persons with a *prior* title to the goods or materials who are strangers to the later contract. An examination of the subject of vesting and seizure clauses for materials and goods (as opposed to plant where the considerations are different) cannot be concluded, however, without also considering the cases on retention of title, which in the context of construction contracts can be expected to give rise to disputed claims between unpaid sellers or suppliers of the main contractor on the one hand and the building owner on the other (or occasionally with the contractor's trustee or liquidator). In the former case these will depend on the interplay between any retention of title provisions in the sale or supply sub-contract and the vesting or seizure provisions of the main contract. These cases, and relevant legislation in England which can alter the parties' rights in such situations in important respects, are discussed in greater detail in subsection (7) *infra*, and also *post*, Chapter 16, Section 7(4).[97a]

A further ground for invalidating vesting or seizure clauses may be that in legal terms they constitute a penalty, in that they are oppressive and bear no reasonable relationship to the owner's need to complete the project, or as a reasonable pre-estimate of his likely damage or loss on seizure or termination. Cases on this have been illustrated and discussed *ante*, Chapter 10.[98]

(2) Effect of Provisions for Payment

In the absence of explicit statements passing the property in materials or   **11·044** plant to the owner, the provisions commonly found in construction contracts for instalment or other progress payments on account calculated by reference to the value of materials or goods brought on to the site (and usually less a retention or other percentage) will not, by themselves, have the effect of passing any property in the unfixed materials to the owner, whether on delivery to the site or on subsequent certification or payment of their value. Pearson J.'s judgment to that effect in *Banbury* v. *Daniel* in 1984[99] was convincingly disapproved as explained by White J. in *Egan* v. *State Transport Authority*[1] in South Australia nearly a century later in 1982[2]:

[97a] See para. 16·049.   [98] Section 1(2), paras. 10·006 *et seq.*
[99] Illustrated *supra*, para. 11·026.
[1] Illustrated *supra*, para. 11·031.
[2] See the discussion immediately *supra*, para. 11·042.

> "My main reason for not following *Banbury's* case ... is that I am unable to accept the proposition that payments made with reference to the value of materials—materials being the external 'yardstick' used by the parties which, they hope, will soon be incorporated into the works—have the effect of creating any property interest in the paying owner. Payments have long been recognised as being merely agreed instalments in reduction of a lump sum price, made on that account to keep the building contractor on the job. The purpose of instalment payment is not to pay *for* the materials, in the sense that a purchaser of land or of specific goods pays money for, or towards the purchase price. Instalment payments are made in contracts like this as a practical measure to enable the contractor to keep working under the contract; they are made also in reduction of the lump sum contract price. Such payments have been described as the 'lifeblood' of the contract ... ".[3]

The same view, without reference to any authorities, was later succinctly and persuasively expressed by Judge John Davies Q.C. in the English Official Referee's Courts in 1987.[4]

11·045 It may perhaps be added that the practicalities of this type of interim valuation are probably not generally understood outside the industry, and in all but very unusual types of unfixed goods or materials will militate strongly against any possibility of tracing or precise identification of unfixed goods or materials as against any particular payment or certification. The reason is that the periodical valuations of the quantity surveyor will usually make an arbitrary assessment, often based solely on delivery vouchers during the preceding valuation period, rather than a detailed inventory of the as yet unfixed materials stored on site at the time of any one valuation. This stock of unfixed materials will tend to constitute a "rolling fund", and any individual item, if traced, would theoretically be the subject of several successive valuations or certifications as unfixed materials until incorporation in the work, when it would now fall to be revalued on the quite different basis of completed work in place.

Modern contracts (for example, Clause 14 of the 1963 RIBA standard forms) frequently provide expressly that unfixed materials paid for in this way become the property of the owner;[5] and some English Standard Forms also confer discretionary power on the A/E to certify payment for suitably identified materials or goods off the site. These provisions are usually only a part of the machinery of interim payment, however, and, it is submitted, cannot be regarded in either case as outright purchases of the materials, so that surplus materials will ultimately revest in the builder.

(3) Whether Vesting or Seizure Clauses are Bills of Sale

11·046 The Bills of Sale legislation of the 19th Century in both England and the Commonwealth imposed certain formal requirements on defined cate-

---

[3] *Per* White J., (1982) 31 S.A.S.R. 481, 537.
[4] *Hanson (Harrow) Ltd.* v. *Rapid Civil Engineering Ltd.* (1987) 38 BLR 106, 113, illustrated and cited *supra*, para. 11·010.
[5] *Cf.* the case of *Re Fox, ex p. Oundle Thrapston R.D.C.* [1948] Ch. 407, referred to *post*, Chap. 16, para. 16·053.

gories of contracts or documents which could be regarded as bills of sale of identified chattels, and prevented their enforcement unless registered. Due to early doubts as to whether the legislation applied to documents transferring equitable rather than legal interests in chattels, the 1878 Act in England, and the 1899 Act in Australia, for example, somewhat expanded the categories of documents falling within earlier Acts.

The cases, illustrated *supra*, show that the English Courts resolutely refused to apply this legislation, despite the apparent width of its definitions, to the vesting or seizure clauses to be found in construction contracts, which they presumably felt were quite different in substance and intention from the transactions at which the leglisation had been aimed, and in Australia a first attempt to invoke the somewhat wider wording of the 1899 Act against a building owner in a construction contract only appears to have been made (in the event unsuccessfully) nearly 60 years later in the West Australian Courts in 1958.[6] In England, *Brown* v. *Bateman* and *Blake* v. *Izard* under the 1854 Act, and *Reeves* v. *Barlow* under the wider 1878 Act, held the legislation inapplicable by the end of the nineteenth century in the case of vesting and seizure clauses alike.[7]

In terms of principle, vesting clauses, being in effect contracts whereby **11·047**
chattels vest in a qualified manner in the building owner, and attaching as they do to unspecific and unidentified chattels, are clearly dissimilar to the assignments and assurances of identifiable chattels which are the target of the Bills of Sale Acts, while forfeiture clauses, though admittedly licenses to take possession of chattels within section 4 of the English Act of 1878,[8] for example, are not intended as security for a present debt but for damages which may or may not become due from the builder on a determination. On the other hand, an assignment by a builder, as a security for a loan, of his rights under a building agreement, together with all plant and materials on the site, under which the assignee was in certain events entitled to take possession and complete, was held to be a bill of sale of the plant and materials.[9]

Bills of sale should be distinguished from registrable charges on a company's assets under section 95 of the 1948 Companies Act and later legislation, as to which see *infra*, Subsection (7), "retention of title," and *post*, Chapter 16, Section 7(4).

(4) Validity of Seizure or Forfeiture

Ordinary vesting clauses, if operative, usually operate to transfer the **11·048**
property on an easily determined event, such as delivery to the site, or on certification or payment in the case of materials. Provisions for forfeiture

---

[6] *Davidson* v. *Claffey Constructions Ltd.* (1958) 60 W.A.L.R. 29, illustrated *supra*, para. 11·029.

[7] These cases are illustrated *supra*, Sub-section (1) paras. 11·024/5.

[8] See also the Australian 1899 Act.

[9] *Church* v. *Sage* (1892) 67 L.T. 800.

or seizure, however, will depend upon taking possession by the owner, the right to which is usually conditioned on default by the builder. In such cases, a lawful and justified termination will need to be established before the property will be held to pass.

ILLUSTRATION

G. entered into a contract with S. under which there was a power of forfeiture in the event of delay or default by G. with power to take the work out of G.'s hands and use plant and materials, and it was also provided that S. might apply any moneys to which G. would otherwise be entitled in satisfaction of losses or expenses caused to S. by G.'s default; and further, that the plant and materials which at the time of the delay or default should be in or about the site of the works should thereupon become the absolute property of S. and should be valued or sold, and the amount of such valuation or of the proceeds of such sale be credited to G. in reduction of the moneys (if any) recoverable from him by S. S. took the work out of G.'s hands, and G. brought an action for breach of contract, which was referred to arbitration. *Held*, by Lord Romilly M.R., that the plant and materials did not become the absolute property of S. until it had been established that loss or expense had been occasioned to S. and an interlocutory injunction was awarded to restrain S., from removing and selling the materials and plant pending the arbitration: *Garrett* v. *Salisbury Railway* (1866).[10]

Cases where vesting or seizure provisions have been invalidated as penalties have been considered *ante*, Chap. 10.[11]

(5) Time of Vesting or Seizure

11·049   This may be of considerable importance in determining the rights of third persons, and must be gathered from the contract. It may be made to depend on the A/E's opinion or certificate, or upon a default of the contractor after notice given by the owner. As against a trustee or liquidator of the contractor, (unless, perhaps, there has been disclaimer[12]) the time of vesting or seizure relative to the date of the bankruptcy or liquidation is immaterial, since the trustee can obtain no greater interest than the bankrupt, and if it is a defeasible interest, it matters not that the defeasance follows the bankruptcy, provided that the contract conferring the right was entered into without notice of any act of bankruptcy.[13] But where the builder's ownership or possession of the property has come to an end

---

[10] L.R. 2 Eq. 358.
[11] Section 1(2), paras. 10·006 *et seq.*
[12] As to which see *post*, Chap. 16, pp. 16·011 *et seq.*
[13] *Re Waugh, ex p. Dicken* (1876) L.R. 4 Ch.D. 522. *Re Garrud, ex p. Newitt* (1881) 16 Ch.D. 522; *Re Keen, ex p. Collins* [1902] 1 K.B. 555 and *Hawthorn* v. *Newcastle Ry.* (1840) 3 Q.B. 734, and for a full discussion see *post*, Chap. 16, pp. 16·037 *et seq.*

before the vesting or seziure has taken place, this will be fatal to the building owner's rights.

ILLUSTRATION

A building agreement provided that on failure by the builder to proceed with due diligence the owner might give notice in writing, and thereafter the builder should not be at liberty to remove any of his plant from the premises, and the building owner should have a lien upon the plant till the notice was complied with. The sheriff seized the goods on behalf of a creditor of the builder. Subsequently the owner served the notice in writing. On interpleader, *held*, by Bray and Phillimore JJ., that the prior possession obtained by the sheriff prevented the notice taking effect: *Byford* v. *Russell* (1907).[14]

As between the parties, a mistakenly premature seizure will have few practical consequences provided that events validating the seizure occur shortly thereafter.[15]

(6) Reputed Ownership

The statutory rules as to reputed ownership, whereby property belonging to a third person, but voluntarily left by him under the "order and disposition" and in the apparent ownership of a debtor at the time of his bankruptcy, will vest in the trustee, leaving the true owner to prove in the bankruptcy, was always unique to the law of personal bankruptcy, and had no place in the case of a company insolvency. Its abolition in England, as a result of the Insolvency Act 1986, represents one of the few substantive changes in the law of insolvency as it affects third persons in construction projects made by that Act, and a knowledge of its existence is now required only for the better understanding of those older cases concerning vesting and seizure clauses in which the doctrine played a part in the final decision, as in *Re Keen, ex p. Collins* and *Re Weibling, ex p. Ward*,[16] or in any Commonwealth jurisdictions where the doctrine may still be in force.   **11·050**

(7) Third Party Rights and Retention of Title

The foregoing cases have shown that no vesting or seizure clause can operate to prejudice *pre-existing* interests of persons not parties to the contract   **11·051**

---

[14] [1907] 2 K.B. 522.
[15] See, *e.g. Hawthorn* v. *Newcastle Ry.* (1840) 3 Q.B. 734, illustrated *supra*, paras. 11·022, and *Earth and General Contracts Ltd.* v. *Manchester Corporation* (1958) 108 L.J. 665, illustrated *ante*, Chap. 4, para. 4·126.
[16] Illustrated *supra*, para. 11·027. For reputed ownership see further *post*, Chap. 16 para. 16·052.

in the plant or materials. In many cases plant is hired by the builder, or, in the case of large contractors, may be owned by a subsidiary company. This represents a serious practical inroad on the apparent security for due completion which an owner may possess under such clauses. Perhaps the commonest examples of such pre-existing rights are represented by the retention of title clauses in the subcontracts of suppliers to main contractors.

Over the past two decades there has been a spate of draftmanship in commerce generally whereby unpaid sellers or suppliers of goods and materials delivered to their customers before payment, have sought, by express terms in the contract of sale, to safeguard their interest (particularly with buyer insolvency in mind) by retaining ownership in the goods transferred until full payment has been obtained. These "retention of title" clauses have attempted an ever-increasing scope, progressing, for example, from provisions for retention of ownership of the objects sold until payment *simpliciter*, to the imposition of a trust or charge on the proceeds of re-sale in the event of any contemplated onward sale by the buyer; or on any composite goods or articles into which it is contemplated that the original goods sold may be mixed or re-worked by the buyer; or, again, imposing a trust on the proceeds of sale of such composite goods or articles. In addition, the sum secured by these provisions has progressed from the purchase price of the original goods delivered to all or any sums due for any other goods supplied during the course of business under other contracts between the same buyer and seller,[17] and even under contracts between the buyer and any other companies in the same group as the seller.[18]

11·052   While these more exotic examples of retention of title clauses are less likely to occur in construction contracts, problems of disputed title can in any case be confidently expected from straightforward retention clauses after delivery of goods or materials to a construction site by unpaid suppliers of the main contractor. These will arise out of the conflicting claims of the supplier under the terms of the supply sub-contract which retain ownership in the supplier on the one hand, and the express terms of the main contract transferring ownership to the building owner (or following physical attachment or incorporation of the goods or materials into the land or buildings of the owner) on the other, as well as any more direct disputes between the unpaid supplier and the main contractor's liquidator or receiver.

Since it is inescapable that retention of title provisions are primarily designed to secure a privileged status for the unpaid seller's claim over potential unsecured creditors of the buyer in the event of the latter's insolvency, such provisions can expect to be relatively rigorously treated,

---

[17] See, *e.g. Borden (UK) Ltd.* v. *Scottish Timber Products Ltd.* [1981] Ch. 25, illustrated *infra*, para. 11·056.
[18] See, *e.g.* such a clause recently up held in the House of Lords in the Scottish case of *Carron Co. Ltd.* v. *Thyssen Edelstahwerke AG* (H.L.) 15.10.1990.

either as a result of judicial interpretation, or by intervention on the part of the legislature.[19] In the latter case two principal statutory provisions can impose important limitations on the intended operation of a retention of title clause.

First, section 95 of the Companies Act 1948 (now section 395 *et seq.* of **11·053** the Companies Act 1985, as replaced by sections 93 *et seq.* of the Companies Act 1989) renders void any charge on company assets which has not been registered (as charges on unfixed goods and materials or plant of the kind encountered in construction contracts will almost invariably not be in practice). The latest (1989 Act replacement) definition of "charge" is "any form of security interest (fixed or floating) over property".[20] In this context, a contract requiring registration has been defined, under the old wording, as one which, by way of security for payment of a debt, confers an interest in property defeasible on payment of that debt.[21] However, a contract under which a seller merely *retains* ownership in *his own* property, or which reserves other rights to himself in respect of that property until full payment, such as rights of entry and seizure, has been held by the Court of Appeal not to require registration under the Act.[22] By contrast, a contract which seeks to charge *other property* of the buyer into which it is contemplated that the particular goods sold will be mixed or re-worked in favour of the seller will be void if not registered.[23] Also, a contract expressly passing the *legal* title to the buyer at once, but imposing an equitable charge in favour of the seller until full payment, will be registrable under the Act.[24] All the above cases seem consistent with the latest definition of "charge" in the replacement section 395(2) of the 1985 Act, which will not apply to unpaid sellers retaining title.

Secondly, section 25(2) of the Sale of Goods Act 1893, now section 25 of **11·054** the 1979 Act, provides that where a person who has *bought or agreed to buy* goods obtains possession with the consent of the seller and subsequently transfers them *by way of "sale pledge or other disposition"* to another person who receives them in good faith and without notice of any right of the original seller in the goods, he will in that case confer the same (that is, it would seem, an indefeasible) title on that other person as delivery by a mercantile agent in possession with the consent of the owner would do. Thus, in a construction contract the title of a building owner to goods or materials delivered to the site following interim payments on account which have included their value *and which are made under a contract which provides expressly for the property to pass to the owner in that event* will by virtue of this section of the Act defeat that of an unpaid sup-

[19] See the stringent analysis and judgment of Templeton L.J. in *Borden (UK) Ltd.* v. *Scottish Timber* [1981] Ch. 25.
[20] (Replacement) s.395(2) of the 1985 Act.
[21] *Re Bond Worth* (1980) Ch. 228.
[22] *Clough Mill Ltd.* v. *Martin* [1985] 1 W.L.R. 111. The latest (replacement) wording of section 395(2) of the 1985 Act seems entirely consistent with this decision.
[23] *Per* Buckley and Templeton L.JJ. in *Borden (UK) Ltd.* v. *Scottish Timber* [1981] Ch. 25, *Re Peachdart Ltd.* [1984] Ch. 131.
[24] *Re Bond Worth* [1980] Ch. 228.

plier to the main contractor, notwithstanding any retention of title clause in his favour in the supply sub-contract.[25]

However, two important limitations on the operation of section 25 may be encountered in practice in construction contracts. First, in the case of many supply contracts, particularly nominated ones, the owner, or his A/E, will often have prior notice of the unpaid seller's rights under the supply sub-contract. Secondly, a *supply and fix* or *supply and erect* subcontract will not usually satisfy the statutory requirement that the main contractor should have *bought or agreed to buy* the materials or goods in question, since it will not be a contract of sale.[26]

However, so far as judicial interpretation is concerned, provided sufficiently clear language is used, the English Courts have not seemed to be reluctant to give full effect to retention of title clauses. It will be seen that little difficulty will be encountered where the goods or materials remain separate and distinct in their original form, but working into or mixing with other goods or materials may create difficult problems.

ILLUSTRATIONS

11·055   (1) A sale of aluminium foil to fabricators provided that "the ownership of the material to be delivered ... will only be transferred to the purchaser when he has met all that is owing to" [the sellers]. The clause proceeded to deal with articles fabricated from the foil by providing that the ownership of such articles should be given to the sellers as "security" for full payment, and that the buyers would keep the articles as fiduciary owners, but with power to sell such articles to third persons in the normal course of business, and in that event they were to assign any rights against the sub-purchasers to the sellers until payment. There was no express provision relating to the sale of *unused* foil, but it was common ground that there was an implied term that its sale to third parties was also permitted. The fabricators went into liquidation, and a bank account in the receiver's name contained a sum representing the proceeds of sale of *unused* foil which the fabricators had sold *as such* to third parties. The sellers claimed the sums in the account, but the receiver contended that in the absence of an express or constructive trust, the sellers could not trace the proceeds of sale and must prove in the liquidation as creditors. *Held*, by the Court of Appeal, that the obvious purpose of the clause in the contract of sale was to secure the sellers in the event of insolvency against the risk of non-payment after they had parted with possession, but not with the legal title to the foil, whether or not that material retained its identity before payment. In order to give effect to that purpose there had to be an implied term in relation to the *unfabricated* foil compelling the fabricators to account for the proceeds of re-sale in the same way as for the fabricated articles, on the basis of a normal fiduciary relationship of principal and agent, or bailor and bailee; so that the sellers were entitled to recover the proceeds of the sub-sales from the

---

[25] *Archivent Sales and Developments Ltd.* v. *Strathclyde Regional Council* (1984) 27 BLR 98 (Court of Sess. Outer House), illustrated *infra*, para. 11·057.

[26] See, *e.g. W. Hanson (Harrow) Ltd.* v. *Rapid Civil Engineering Ltd.* (1987) 38 BLR 109, illustrated *supra*, para. 11·010; but see the difficult case of *Pritchett & Gold* v. *Currie* [1916] 2 Ch. 515, illustrated *supra*, para. 11·009.

fabricators and their receiver: *Aluminium Industrie Vaassen B.V.* v. *Romalpa Aluminium Ltd.* (1976).[27]

[Note: The facts of this case are not, as pointed out in later cases, likely to arise again, and the nature of the implied terms was, in the circumstances, a very special one implied "in fact", and not by law. Had the *fabricated articles* or their proceeds of sale been in issue, it follows from the next case, illustrated *infra*, that the sellers claim would have been invalidated in the absence of registration under section 95 of the Companies Act 1948. However, the case's principal interest lies in its showing that the manifest intention to secure priority in the event of the insolvency of the buyers was not held to infringe any underlying policy or principle of insolvency law].

(2) A contract for the sale of fibre to carpet manufacturers contained a **11·056** provision that "*equitable and beneficial* ownership shall remain with us until full payment has been received ... or until prior resale, in which case our beneficial entitlement shall attach to the proceeds of resale ... (b) Should the goods become constituents of or converted into other products ... we shall have the equitable and beneficial ownership in such other products ... ". Substantial sums were owing to the sellers when the buyers went into receivership, and the sellers asserted a prior claim to unsold fibre or the proceeds of sale of the fibre. *Held*, by Slade J., that under the terms of the contract the *legal* property in the fibre had passed to the buyers on delivery and they were free to sell or deal with it in the ordinary way, but the clause created a floating equitable charge on the fibre by the buyers in favour of the sellers or on the proceeds of resale and on the products of which it might become a constituent. Since the relevant charge arose by way of grant back by the buyers in favour of the sellers, the charges had been "created" by the buyers within section 95(1) of the Companies Act 1948 and, being unregistered, were void against the other creditors of the buyers: in *Re Bond Worth Ltd.* (1979).[28]

(3) Resin was sold to chipboard manufacturers under a contract providing that the property should pass only when all goods in both this and other contracts between buyer and seller had been paid for in full. It was contemplated by the parties that the resin would be used within a very short time of delivery in the manufacture of chipboard, so that it would no longer be identifiable or separable from the chipboard. In the buyer's liquidation the sellers contended that any chipboard manufactured with the resin or the proceeds of sale of any such chipboard were charged with the outstanding sums due to them. *Held*, by the Court of Appeal, that this was not a contract of bailment, since it was always intended that the resin should be used and would not be returnable in the same form; that once used, the resin ceased to exist, and with it the seller's title to it; that as it had lost its identity it could not be traced into the chipboard, which was a new product; and, distinguishing the *Romalpa* case, that no interest or charge on the chipboard or the proceeds of its sale could be implied from the contract. *Per* Buckley and Templeman L.JJ., even if the sellers had acquired a charge on the chipboard, the charge would have arisen from the parties' agreement and, being unregistered, would be void as against the liquidator and other creditors under section 95 of the Companies Act 1948: *Borden (UK) Ltd.* v. *Scottish Timber Products Ltd.* (1979).[29]

(4) A supply sub-contract of ventilators to a main contractor for incorpor-   **11·057** ation into a school provided that "until payment of the price in full is received

---

[27] [1976] 1 W.L.R. 676.
[28] [1980] Ch. 228. See also *Re Peachdart Ltd.* [1984] Ch. 131.
[29] [1981] Ch. 25.

by the company the property and the goods supplied by the company shall not pass to the customer". The value of the ventilators was included in an interim certificate, and the main contractor was paid the sums which had been so certified. Clause 14(1) of the 1963 RIBA/JCT main contract standard form provided that unfixed materials should not be removed except for use on the works unless the architect had consented to such removal, and that the property in such materials would pass to the building owner on receipt of payment under interim certificates which included the value of the materials. When the suppliers sued the owners for delivery up of the ventilators on the insolvency of the main contractors, the latter argued, first, that the clause operated to establish a hypothec in favour of the seller which the law of Scotland would not recognise,[30] and secondly, that by virtue of section 25(1) of the Sale of Goods Act 1893 the owners had obtained an unimpeachable title from a buyer in possession of the goods, namely the main contractor. *Held*, by Lord Mayfield, that the clause in the sub-contract did not create a hypothec which the Scottish courts would not recognise, but (2), that the main contractor, notwithstanding the inhibition on removal from the site in Clause 14(1) of the main contract, had been in possession of the goods following their delivery by the suppliers to the site, and that when the goods were certified and paid for by the owner there had been a "sale, pledge or other disposition thereof" by the main contractor to the owner, so that the conditions of section 25(1) were satisfied and the owners had obtained an indefeasible title: *Archivent Sales and Developments Ltd.* v. *Strathclyde Regional Council* (1984).[31]

[Note: This case is not, of course, authority for there having been a *sale* to the owners, but a sufficient transfer of property from the main contractor to constitute a "pledge or other disposition" within section 25(1), it is submitted. The court also seems to have felt it necessary to consider whether the circumstances of the delivery conformed to a sale by a mercantile agent, but this is not necessary on a proper interpretation of the section, it is submitted.]

11·058   (5) Three diesel engines were sold to buyers for incorporation by them into generating sets. All property in the goods was to remain in the sellers until the full purchase price had been paid. When the buyers went into receivership, two of the sets had been sufficiently identified and incorporated in a deliverable state into the sets under contracts of sale with sub-purchasers. A temporary injunction preventing sale was lifted on condition that the sale proceeds would be segregated. The sellers brought an action claiming the proceeds of re-sale. *Held*, by Staughton J. considering and distinguishing the *Romalpa* case, that there had been no attempt by the contract to deal with mixed or manufactured objects as in *Romalpa*; there was no obligation to segregate the goods when storing them; there was no mention of any fiduciary or trust obligation and no mention of any proceeds of sale; so that it could not be implied from the terms of the agreement that the buyers occupied a fiduciary position in relation to the proceeds of sale: *Hendy Lennox (Industrial Engines) Ltd.* v. *Grahame Puttick Ltd.* (1983).[32]

(6) The retention clause in a contract for the sale of yarn retained ownership in the seller until full payment, and if payments were overdue, or upon the insolvency of the buyer, the seller was entitled to enter and re-possess. Following receivership, the receiver refused re-entry to the seller, but the trial judge held that the contract had created a charge which was registrable under section 95 of the Companies Act 1948, so that the seller did not have a right to the goods. *Held*, by the Court of Appeal, that the mere retention of rights by

---

[30] This doctrine would seem comparable to section 95 of the Companies Act 1989 in England.
[31] 27 BLR 98. See also the doubts expressed in the Note to the *Hanson* case *infra*.
[32] [1984] 1 W.L.R. 485, 499. Also illustrated *supra*, para. 11·005.

the seller could not be regarded as "conferring an interest in property defeasible upon payment of a debt", adopting Slade J.'s definition in *Re Bond Worth*, and the receiver was liable for damages in conversion for wrongly refusing re-entry to the sellers. *Per* Robert Goff L.J., under the first sentence of the clause, the buyer did not, by way of security, confer on the plaintiff an interest in property defeasible upon the payment of the debt so secured. On the contrary, the plaintiff retained the legal property in the material for the purpose of providing himself with security. *Clough Mill Ltd.* v. *Martin* (1984).[33]

(7) Timber merchants supplied timber on three sites to main contractors on terms of trading which provided that the property should not pass until payment of the price. The main contracts on two of the sites[33a] provided for 97 per cent monthly payments against valuations by the owner's manager of both work and unfixed materials on site, and provided expressly that the property in unfixed materials should not pass until payment. The main contractor went into receivership at a time when there were unfixed materials on the two sites, which had been formally valued by the manager but had not so far been paid for. the suppliers wrote to the owners claiming the materials, but the owners used them, and when sued in tort for conversion relied on section 25 of the Sale of Goods Act 1979. *Held*, by Judge John Davies, that assuming that there had been an agreement to sell under the terms of the two main contracts, until payment there was only an "agreement to sell" by virtue of the definition in section 2(1) of the Act, so that there had been no "*sale*, pledge or other disposition" by the main contractor to the owner which would satisfy the requirements of section 25, and the owners must pay damages for conversion: *W. Hanson (Harrow) Ltd.* v. *Rapid Civil Engineering Ltd.* (1987).[33b]

[Note: It also seems at least arguable, it is submitted, that a building owner does not have "possession" or "receive delivery of" unfixed materials on a building site, having regard to the degree of physical control and rights of use intended to be exercised over them by the builder, in addition to the question whether such an interim payment provision, notwithstanding an express term for transfer of the property," is in reality a sufficient "sale" of unfixed materials within the meaning of the act—compare the Bills of Sale cases. If this is right, the *Archivent* case may need re-consideration.]

SECTION 3. LIEN

(1) Common Law and Equitable Liens

In the cases in the previous sections of this chapter it will probably have been noticed that the right of the building owner or builder over materials and plant is occasionally described, either in the contract or by the courts, as a lien.[34]   **11·059**

In its proper sense, lien means the right of a person *in possession* to retain the property of another until certain claims have been satisfied. A

---

[33] [1985] 1 W.L.R. 111.
[33a] See the case as to the third site illustrated *supra*, paragraph 11·010.
[33b] 38 BLR 106.
[34] See, *e.g. Tripp* v. *Armitage* (1839) 4 M. & W. 687, *supra*, para. 11·007; *Hawthorn* v. *Newcastle Ry.* (1840) 3 Q.B. 734, *supra*, para. 11·022; *Banbury, etc. Ry.* v. *Daniel* (1884) 54 L.J. Ch. 265, see *ante*, para. 11·026.

general lien enables the property to be detained until the general state of accounts between the parties has been satisfied, a particular lien until charges for work done to the property in question have been met. In both cases the lien arises by operation of law, not by contract. In the cases of common law liens, no power of sale exists. In the case of equitable liens (which arise on the sale of land), such a power does exist. No lien in either of these senses can arise from the carrying out of building or engineering work on the land of another.

Equitable liens are in the nature of a charge on property, and do not depend either on contract or upon possession by the party asserting the lien. The right is said to be founded on a principle of equity that if a person obtains possession of property under a contract for payment of its value, he will not be allowed to keep it without payment. It is, therefore, in the nature of a right less than ownership against the party in possession, and perhaps also against persons claiming through him.[35]

(2) Contractual Liens

11·060   Where a right, similar in its characteristics to a lien, is created by a contract, express or implied, the contract itself must be examined in order to determine exactly what rights over the property concerned the parties have intended to create. There is, however, a tendency, where a contractual right less than ownership is intended to pass, to describe it as a lien if it appears to have characteristics analogous to a lien propel.[36] In most cases the term is used to mean a right, in the nature of a pledge or security for due performance.

Whether or not particular powers, such as powers of user or sale, are attached to a contractual lien, must depend on the contract itself. A simple express provision for a lien to arise in favour of a party to the contract in a given situation will presumably give rise only to the rights and entitlement of a common law lien should that party be in possession or in a position to obtain or take possession.[37]

Where the basis of the right is contractual, however, and the contract contemplates a situation in which a lien might otherwise arise independently of contract, the contractual provisions should be regarded as exhaustive, it would seem.

ILLUSTRATION

11·061   Clause 27 of a railway contract in South Australia contained a provision for interim payment based upon 90 per cent of the value of work done and 75 per

---

[35] Compare Halsbury *Laws of England* (4th ed.), Vol. 28, para. 504.
[36] *Re Waugh, ex p. Dicken* (1876) 4 Ch.D. 524, where a seizure clause purporting to transfer ownership was so described. See the discussion by White J. in *Egan* v. *State Transport Authority* (1982) 31 S.A.S.R. 481, 545–546.
[37] For an express term see *Hawthorn* v. *Newcastle Railway*, illustrated *supra*, para. 11·022.

cent of unfixed materials on the site, but there was no provision for the passing of property on certification or payment. Clause 30 was a separate seizure clause arising on contractor default, which provided that plant and unfixed materials on site should become the absolute property of the owner following notice of termination. The owner unlawfully determined the contract, and used or sold the plant and materials, and when sued in tort for conversion argued that even if the property had not passed he had been entitled to a lien on the unfixed materials. *Held*, by White J., that at all material times until seizure the contractor had been in possession to the exclusion of the owner, so that the conditions for both a common law lien and an equity lien had not been satisfied. So far as the contractual lien was concerned, Clause 27 implied a right of the owner to the retention monies as part of his contractual security, and Clause 30 gave still further security in the form of the right to seize plant and materials upon a lawful termination. Where a contractual relationship might involve a lien the parties' rights must be limited by the extent of the contract made, and no additional security could be provided by this means, so that the contractor was entitled to damages; *Egan* v. *State Transport Authority* (1982).[38]

The use of this expression in the context of building contracts is, there- **11·062**
fore, likely to be misleading, since no lien will arise from the performance of a building contract under any principle of law.

Where goods or materials have not yet been incorporated into the work, so that they remain the property of the original seller or supplier, a lien becomes a theoretical possibility. Where such goods are, or have become the property of the main contractor, they will usually be under his physical control, so that no question of a lien, which is a right to detain by a person not the owner, can arise. In *Bellamy* v. *Davey* (1891),[39] however, Romer J. apparently held that an unpaid sub-contractor, whose goods were on the site but were too heavy to move, had a lien on the goods *as against the building owner*, but this part of the case was doubted by the Court of Appeal in *Pritchett & Gold* v. *Currie* (1916)[40] and in principle seems to have been wrongly decided on this point.

(3) Mechanics' Liens

In certain countries with a pioneer tradition it was found that artisans and **11·063**
skilled workmen (the forerunners of present day sub-contractors) were often left unpaid by unscrupulous entrepreneurs who decamped after receiving payment in full for their houses from the early settlers. This led to "mechanic's lien" or similar legislation in countries like New Zealand, The United States and some provinces in Canada, which imposed a charge on completed buildings in favour of unpaid workmen and sub-contractors. This legislation became extremely technical and complicated, and in more recent years such of it as has still survived has not infrequently led

---

[38] 31 S.A.S.R. 481, 543 *et seq.*
[39] [1891] 3 Ch. 540, illustrated *supra*, Section 1, para. 11·008.
[40] [1916] 2 Ch. 515, illustrated *supra*, Section 1, para. 11·009.

to abuse at the instance of the more modern types of relatively powerful sub-contractor, with a view to obtaining payment of exaggerated claims from developers or main contractors at a late stage of the project when sales to first occupiers or purchasers will be imminent, or even already concluded. Registration has often formed a part of the more modern legislation in this field. This subject, which only applies to a limited number of jurisdictions, and which, where it has survived, has given rise to extremely detailed legislation and case law, has had no counterpart in England, and is not considered suitable for detailed treatment in the present book.

SECTION 4. OLD MATERIALS

11·064   In some cases building contracts contain a provision that the contractor shall make use of, or be entitled to, old and other materials belonging to the employer for the purposes of the work. Furthermore it may, even in the absence of express provision, be an inevitable consequence of carrying out the work that surplus materials will result. In some cases the ownership of those materials may be quite valuable, and questions of some difficulty may arise in arriving at the contract intention. Thus, an obligation to excavate foundations would not of itself entitle the builder to appropriate the sand, gravel or other material so won, but an obligation to remove materials without any provision as to their disposal would seem to pass the property therein to the contractor, who would be at liberty to dispose of them as he thought fit. In many demolition contracts, for example, where the salvage value is high, the price may even be a negative one, payable by the contractor to the owner.

Whether or not such provisions involve adjustment of the contract price, and if so in which direction, may not always be clear, therefore.

ILLUSTRATION

H., a builder, sued for £800, the price payable on completion. The architect had certified completion. The contract had contained a clause, "All the old lead to be displaced by new is to become the property of the contractor, who will make a due allowance for the same." The owner pleaded a set-off of £38, being the value of the old lead, but the builder asserted that he had made the allowance when arriving at his price. *Held*, by the Court of Common Pleas, that as H. had not proved that he had informed the owner or the architect that in making his estimate he had allowed for the value of the old lead, the set-off should be allowed: *Harvey* v. *Lawrence* (1867).[41]

---

[41] 15 L.T. 571.

CHAPTER 12

FORFEITURE AND DETERMINATION

Section 1. The General Nature of the Power to Forfeit or Determine

(1) The Owner's Right to Possession

In the absence of express provisions to the contrary, the contractor in ordi-   **12·001**
nary building or engineering contracts for the execution of work upon the

land of another has merely a licence to enter upon the land to carry out the work. Notwithstanding that under the terms of his contract a contractor may be entitled to a considerable degree of exclusive possession of the site for the purpose of carrying out the work,[1] such a licence may be revoked by the owner at any time, and thereafter the contractor's right to enter upon the site of the works will be lost. The revocation, however, if not legally justified under the contract, will render the owner liable to the contractor in damages, but subject to this the contractor has no legally enforceable right to remain in possession of the site against the wishes of the owner.[2]

Doubt was cast on the validity of this last proposition by an unexpected judgment in the Chancery Division in England in 1970. There, after a massive review of the jurisprudence of contractual licences, Megarry J. refused to grant an injunction compelling a contractor to leave the site after the building owner had terminated a construction contract on the certificate of the architect confirming lack of due diligence under the provisions of its termination clause.[3] The *Twickenham Garden* case was noted, in the tenth edition of this book published in the same year as the decision, as being then currently under appeal; but the case later settled and did not proceed to appeal. It was immediately and powerfully criticised by the Editors of the Law Quarterly Review,[4] and some years later both doubted and criticised in the light of subsequently reported cases in the 1979 Supplement to the tenth edition. The case had in fact just been preceded by a well-reasoned decision to precisely opposite effect in Victoria,[5] and shortly after was persuasively analysed and disapproved, apparently independently, in two outstanding judgments by Mahon J. in New Zealand[6] and by Helsham J. in New South Wales.[7] While not openly disapproved, the case has not been followed in the Official Referees' courts in England,[8] and the actual decision, when applied to the practical basis of a construction contract rather than the very different situations of the contractual licence cases considered by Megarry J., seems difficult

---

[1] For the implied term and the nature of the contractor's interest, see *ante*, Chap. 4, paras. 4·144 *et seq.*

[2] This passage, with no material modifications in its ninth edition form, was accepted and approved by Lush J. in *Porter* v. *Hannah Builders Pty. Ltd.* [1969] V.R. 673—see *infra*, Section 3(2), paras. 12·084 *et seq.* where the subject is fully considered.

[3] *Hounslow London Borough Council* v. *Twickenham Garden Developments Ltd.* [1971] Ch. 233.

[4] (1971) 87 L.Q.R. 309–312.

[5] *Porter* v. *Hannah Builders Pty. Ltd.* [1969] V.R. 673, see *infra*, para. 12·089.

[6] *Mayfield Holdings Ltd.* v. *Moana Reef Ltd.* [1973] 1 N.Z.L.R. 309. Illustrated *infra*, para. 12·092.

[7] *Graham H. Roberts Pty. Ltd.* v. *Maurbeth Investments Pty. Ltd.* [1974] 1 N.S.W.L.R. 93, see *infra*, para. 12·093.

[8] See, *e.g. Tara Civil Engineering Ltd.* v. *Moorfield Developments Ltd.* (1989) 46 BLR 72.

to explain or support.[9] It is beyond doubt that at the present day it does not represent the law in Australia.[10]

(2) Determination of the Contract

A very varied terminology has been used both judicially and in commerce   **12·002**
to describe the process by which a party, unilaterally and by his own action, brings a contract to an end before it has been fully performed either by himself or the other party. Thus forfeiture, determination, termination, renunciation, rescission (and even repudiation when applied to the action of the innocent party in ending the contract),[11] have been variously used in the cases and elsewhere. In context the different descriptions should generally be regarded as synonymous, with no significant differences of consequential effect. In the present chapter the words "determination" or "termination" will generally be preferred. A contract may be lawfully terminated by a party in two of the following ways.

(a) Common law determination

This will be by *operation of law*, and will occur where the guilty party has   **12·003**
committed a fundamental (that is, repudiatory) breach (or in some cases what is called an *anticipatory* repudiatory breach) and the innocent party has then by word or action elected to accept the repudiation and terminate (rescind) the contract. This total process, often described in this book and elsewhere to distinguish it from *contractual* determinations as "rescission", does not depend on any express contractual provision, except insofar as the contract may have chosen by its terms to indicate such importance or gravity to a particular contractual obligation that any breach of which will justify a common law determination. The effect of such a common law determination is to release both parties from further performance, and to entitle the innocent (rescinding) party most importantly to damages for breach of contract, (including those resulting from the loss or abandonment of the contract itself), though with certain alternative or supplementary remedies also available. Provided that the determining party acts reasonably within the rules of mitigation of damage, however, there will be no particular course of action required of him, so that a construction owner rescinding the contract at common law, for example, will not, provided he acts reasonably, necessarily be obliged to complete the project, but may abandon it and compute his resulting damages accordingly. While a common law determination will provide a

---

[9] See *infra*, paras. 12·089 *et seq.*, where other contrary and later Commonwealth cases are noted.
[10] See the clear dictum of Latham C.J. in *Cowell* v. *Rosehill Racecourse Ltd.* (1937) 56 C.L.R. 605, 621 followed, and applied by Lush J. in *Porter's* case see *supra*, and by Helsham J. in the *Graham Roberts* case see *supra*, and by Southwell J. in the *Chermar Productions* case, all illustrated and considered *infra*, Section 3(2)(b), paras. 12·089 *et seq.*
[11] As, *e.g.*, by Irvine C.J. in *Bysouth* v. *Shire of Blackburn* [1928] V.L.R. 562, 569.

high degree of freedom and flexibility of remedy to the determining party, therefore, he must assume the burden of establishing that the breach of contract was, either intrinsically or on the particular facts, sufficiently fundamental to justify the determination in law. This subject has been considered *in extenso* in the context of construction contracts see *ante*, Chapter 4.[12] The present chapter is, therefore, primarily concerned with contractual terminations.

(b) Contractual determination

12·004   The second way in which a party may lawfully determine the contract will be by exercising powers to that effect expressly provided for in a contractual termination clause. Such a termination will be different from a common law determination in two vital respects. In the first place, it will not be necessary to establish that the breach or event on which the clause is expressly conditioned is of the fundamental repudiatory character required for a common law determination. It will be sufficient that it has been contractually defined or nominated as a ground for contractual determination. On the other hand, however, a contractual termination will provide no remedies to the rescinding party beyond those expressly conferred by the termination clause itself.[13] As will be seen, the draftsmanship of termination clauses in construction contracts has been traditionally inept, not infrequently stipulating financial consequences or seizures of property which could not be justified on a common law determination or by the ordinary rules governing the measure of damage, so that they may be unenforceable as penalties, while on the other hand unduly circumscribing a determining owner's damages or remedies on the assumption that he will always wish or be in a position to complete the project.

Moreover, exact and meticulous compliance by the determining party with any formal or procedural requirements laid down in the termination clause, for example, as to notices or time limits, will usually be required if a *contractual* termination is to be successful[13a], whereas the formal requirements for a successful common law determination are much more broadly based and require little more than a clear and unequivocal indication of his intentions by the determining party.[14]

12·005   However, common law and contractual determinations can in practice easily overlap, since contractual clauses are, not surprisingly, frequently conditioned on breaches which, either by simple definition, or by their gravity in the events which have actually occurred, will be sufficiently serious to justify a common law determination as well. In such cases, a con-

---

[12] Section 3, Discharge from Further Performance, paras. 4·204 *et seq.*

[13] See, *e.g.*, Thomas Feather & Co. (Bradford) Ltd. v. *Keighley Corporation* (1953) 52 L.G.R. 30, illustrated *ante*, Chap. 8, Section 2, para. 8·113.

[13a] See, *e.g. Hill* v. *London Borough of Camden* illustrated *infra*, para. 12·040.

[14] See *ante*, Chap. 4, paras. 4·213 *et seq.*

tractual determination which may fail by reason of failure to comply exactly with the contractual notice or other requirements or descriptions, may be "rescued" if it can qualify as an effective common law determination on the same facts.[15] It is a further criticism of the draftsmanship of owner's determination clauses that they habitually fail to provide for or envisage this exercise of concurrent or alternative common law rights of determination, or at the very least to make clear, in the owner's interest, that the contractual rights are in addition and without prejudice to the exercise of any available common law rights (although it is clear, it is submitted, that this is prima facie the proper interpretation of a contractual termination clause which is silent on the matter).[16]

The foregoing discussion has primarily been concerned with termination clauses entitling *the owner* to determine. These were the only clauses usually found in construction contracts before the Second World War. Producer pressures, and the spread of international contracting, have led to contractors' termination clauses, primarily based upon failure to pay sums certified without good cause, though in England the grounds for contractors' terminations have been greatly expanded by the RIBA/JCT standard forms of building contract to cover, in what may often be quite inappropriate and anomalous situations,[17] construction delays due to causes which have become quite common at the present day, but which are in no sense the responsibility of the owner or his architect and indeed on established and well-justified case-law under the inclusive price principle[17a] would otherwise be the contractor's responsibility. Further anomalous rights of determination have been permitted, either by deliberate policy or as a result of the lax draftsmanship of the RIBA/JCT forms, in the case of delays caused by nominated sub-contractor defaults. For example, the clauses have enabled main contractors to determine the contract against the owner as a result of delays caused directly or indirectly by defective materials being used,[18] or by bad workmanship or even wrongful abandonment of their work by such sub-contractors.[19]

In contractor terminations the valuable alternative common law right of quantum meruit under the *Lodder* v. *Slowey* rule[20] can be of great advantage, by enabling a contractor who may have underpriced a contract to be paid higher reasonable prices.[21]

---

[15] As in *Bysouth* v. *Shire of Blackburn* [1928] V.L.R. 562, 572, *per* Irvine C.J., illustrated *infra*, para. 12·007.

[16] See *infra*, para. 12·006.

[17] See the detailed criticisms in C.C.P.P., paras. 29–20—23 and 30–24, for example.

[17a] See *ante*, Chap. 4, paras. 4·036 *et seq*.

[18] *Gloucestershire County Council* v. *Richardson (trading as W. J. Richardson & Son)* [1969] 1 A.C. 480, illustrated *ante*, Chap. 4, para. 4·122.

[19] *John Jarvis Ltd.* v. *Rockdale Housing Association Ltd.* (1986) 36 BLR 48 (C.A.), analysed and in part doubted by the editor in (1987) 3 Const.J.L. 274, and illustrated see *ante*, para. 5·036 and *infra*, para. 12·020.

[20] Discussed *ante*, Chap. 4, Section 3(1)(j), paras. 4·230 *et seq.*, and see *infra*, para. 12·083. And see Fitzgerald P.'s valuable judgment in *Iezzi Constructions Ltd.* v. *Currumbin Crest Developments Ltd.* (1994) 13 A.C.L.R. 39, Qd. C.A.

[21] See, *e.g.*, the *Renard Constructions* case illustrated *infra*, para. 12·025, and see *ante*, Chap. 4, para. 4·230, and Chap. 1, para. 1·272.

(3) Contractual Determination not Exclusive

12·006   As pointed out above, the principal objectives of a contractual termination clause are two-fold. The first will be to define those situations in
which a right to terminate will arise, and where difficulties of fact or law
might make it difficult to establish a common law determination—for example failure of the contractor to remove or remedy defective work
within 10 days of being ordered to do so, or failure to proceed generally
with due diligence.[22] In the case of a contractor's determination, the usual
example will be failure to pay certified sums within a stipulated number of
days, but there are also certain construction delays, including those caused
by sub-contractor default, on which the current RIBA/JCT contractor's
determination rights in England have been based since 1963.

The second objective of a contractual determination clause will be to
provide ancillary rights and remedies for the determining party which a
common law determination would not do, such as forfeiture or seizure and
continued use of plant and materials or their value in order to complete
the project, or the assignment to a determining owner of any desired
sub-contracts.

These various factors will mean that, in the absence of express provision, contractual determinations by either party are not intended as a
substitute for, or to exclude, the common law rights to rescind. While
some standard form determination clauses contain express "without
prejudice to other rights or remedies" wording, this is not in fact necessary, and it is submitted that, in the context of construction contracts generally, neither owners' nor contractors' determination clauses should be
treated as impliedly excluding the parties' common law rights.[23]

ILLUSTRATIONS

12·007   (1) Clause 11 of a roadworks contract in Victoria entitled the owners to
determine the contract by giving notice to that effect if in the opinion of the
Engineer there was a failure of due progress, or if defective work was not
remedied within seven days of his requiring it in writing, or if in the judgment
of the Engineer there was a wilful breach of contract by the contractor, or if
any work was done on Sunday without permission. The owners served a
notice that they had absolutely determined the contract, alleging in the notice
that the contractor had wilfully breached the contract by not completing to
time and not carrying out certain work in accordance with the specification,
but there were no references to the opinion or judgment of the Engineer, nor
conformity to the specific grounds as defined in Clause 11. The owners in their
pleadings contended that there had been a valid contractual determination
under Clause 11 of the contract, while the contractor contended that there

---

[22] For submissions as to the implied terms on this last obligation, see *ante*, Chap. 4, Section
1(3), paras. 4·128–4·129, and Chap. 9, Section (4), para. 9·032, and for the difficulties of the
defective work implied term, see *ante*, Chap. 5, Section 2(1), paras. 5·025–5·027.

[23] See for this general principle *Chitty on Contracts* (26th ed.), para. 1614.

had been a repudiation of the contract. On a point of law by case stated, and relying only on the contract, the wording of the notice, and the pleadings in the action, *held*, by the Supreme Court of Victoria, that since none of the four grounds as defined in Clause 11 was to be found in the descriptions of the breaches as alleged in the notice, it could not be regarded as an election by the owners to exercise the power under Clause 11. The notice did, however, amount in law to a renunciation of the contract by the owners outside Clause 11. Whether on the facts as pleaded, or by way of future amendment to the pleadings, the owners would be justified in rescinding outside the clause was not a matter currently before the Court: *Bysouth* v. *Shire of Blackburn* (1928).[24]

[Note: It may be inferred that what was principally at issue in this case was the owners' entitlement to the contractor's plant and certain financial forfeitures expressly permitted by Clause 11 (which later in the event were invalidated by the Court as being penalties).[25]]

(2) Clause 8 of a labour-only sub-contract entitled the main contractor to determine the sub-contract by a notice in writing if the sub-contractor wholly suspended the works or failed to proceed expeditiously *and remained in default for seven days after being given notice in writing* by the main contractor. The contractor wrote a letter in September 1985 requiring the sub-contractors to work a full working day in accordance with the sub-contract conditions. 11 months later in August 1986 the sub-contractors, as pleaded by the main contractor, wholly suspended work and the main contractor then telexed: "By reason of your withdrawal of labour from the above contract without sufficient notice to ourselves we are obliged to give notice of termination of the contract." *Held*, by Judge Bowsher Q.C., on a preliminary issue of law, that accepting the 1985 letter as a "first notice" under Clause 8, due to the lapse of time there was no sufficient connection between it and the 1986 letter of termination for the "two-tier" notice requirement of Clause 8 to be satisfied, and the termination could for that reason not be supported; but, there was no reason to imply a term that Clause 8 was to be the only machinery for terminating the contract, and the clause existed side by side with the common law right of termination of the contract, on the validity of which the substantive trial would have to decide. *Architectural Installation Services Ltd.* v. *James Gibbons Windows Ltd.* (1989).[26]

It has been seen, *ante* Chapter 4, that even on a common law determi-   **12·008**
nation certain types of contractual provision will continue to regulate the rights of the parties after the rescission has taken place, and that it is incorrect to regard the contract as wholly "gone", and so of no further effect, as some earlier judgments had suggested.[27]

It is also self-evident that owners' contractual termination clauses will almost invariably contain provisions designed to regulate the post-termination situation (particularly, for example, the details for completing the project by another contractor following on the termination). Both types of determination, therefore, will have in common this factor of some terms

---

[24] [1928] V.L.R. 562, 570–573.
[25] See the case illustrated on this *ante*, Chap. 10, para. 10·013.
[26] 46 BLR 91. But see the Court of Appeal of Tanzania's decision in *Mvita Construction Co. Ltd.* v. *Tanzania Harbours Authority* (1988) 46 BLR 19, which followed the same reasoning where there was delay in serving the final notice under Clause 63 of the FIDIC second edition conditions in the absence of a continuing breach; but wrongly, it is submitted, ruled that Clause 63 excluded any common law remedy.
[27] See *ante*, Chap. 4, Section 3(1), and the cases there referred to.

surviving the termination, the difference being only one of degree, but the essential feature of both will remain that the determinations release the parties from further performance (and indeed in a construction setting often positively require discontinuance and departure by a contractor in breach). This need for survival of some terms of a contract following a common law rescission was not widely appreciated until the case of *Heyman* v. *Darwins* in 1942,[28] and this may explain the diffuse and, in practical terms, apparently meaningless expressions employed by some earlier English civil engineering draftsmen in their termination clauses, which have survived to the present day. Thus, Clause 63 of the 1973 ICE fifth edition entitled the owner, on notice in writing under that clause, to

> "enter upon the Site and the Works and expel the Contractor therefrom *without thereby avoiding the contract or releasing the Contractor from any of his obligations or liabilities under the Contract or affecting the rights and powers conferred on the Employer or the Engineer by the Contract* and may himself complete the Works ..."

Other standard forms use similarly confusing wording, sometimes making an apparent distinction between "determining the contract" and "determining the employment of the contractor". It would seem that this is simply poor and diffuse draftsmanship of the kind so often encountered in construction contracts at all levels, and that the draftsmen using it have not in fact had any specific practical intention or distinction in mind. The ICE wording in England has recently caused confusion and difficulty.

ILLUSTRATION

12·009   Clause 16(1) of the FCEC standard form of civil engineering sub-contract provided: "If the Main Contract *is determined for any reason whatsoever* ... then the Contractor may at any time thereafter by written notice to the Sub-Contractor forthwith determine the Sub-Contractor's employment under the Sub-Contract." Following this the sub-contractor was to be entitled to payment of the value of work done and all expenses, but not loss of profit. The owners re-entered and expelled the main contractor under the termination clause in the main contract, which was in the ICE fifth edition standard form quoted *supra*, on the ground of failure to proceed with due diligence and persistent or flagrant neglect to carry out the main contractor's obligations, and on the same day the main contractor wrote to the sub-contractors stating that his contract had been determined, and in turn determining the sub-contract under Clause 16. Nevertheless, an arbitrator awarded the sub-contractors loss of profit. *Held*, by Nolan J., that the invocation of the owner's powers under Clause 63 of the main contract, since it expressly was not to release the contractor from any of his obligations under the contract and additionally imposed certain duties on the owner in the exercise of his powers to complete the work, and use and sell plant, and temporary works, and materials, could not be regarded as "determining" the main contract, since the word "determi-

[28] [1942] A.C. 356.

nation" implied releasing a party from further performance. Consequently the sub-contract had in turn not been "determined" under Clause 16 and the sub-contractor was entitled to loss of profit: *E. R. Dyer Ltd.* v. *Simon Build/ Peter Lind Partnership* (1982).[29]

[Note: It may be speculated that the late distinguished draftsman of the form of sub-contract used in this case[29a] would have been astonished by the construction placed on his use of the word "determination" in the sub-contract, which as a simple matter of interpretation must, it is submitted, have contemplated the overwhelmingly most likely situation in which the sub-contract might be brought to an end as a result of the exercise of the owner's powers in the main contract. There was in fact only one other form of contractual "determination" provided for in the main contract (the hardly ever used War Clause 65). The marginal note (admittedly not strictly admissible) to Clause 63 in the main contract was entitled "Forfeiture". The reasoning in the judgment fails to note that contractual obligations continuing to bind the rescinding party (*e.g.* limitation of damage clauses) will be a normal feature even of a common law determination. Moreover, the words "for any reason whatsoever", in a sub-contract provision the principal practical purpose of which is to disallow loss of profit, are designed to emphasise, it is submitted, the inclusion even of cases where the main contractor is at fault, and so normally liable to pay loss of profit damages. Under the main contract, fault of the contractor, or even a confrontation which was disputed, would in real life almost invariably attract a Clause 63 termination as being the simplest available remedy to the owner rather than a less certain common law rescission, and would be the obvious, if not the principal, target of the sub-contract clause, it is submitted. The case affords a classic example of the "literalist" type of judicial interpretation of commercial documents criticised so heavily by Lord Diplock in the *Miramar Maritime* and *Antaios* cases.[30] Unfortunately, the case was followed on this particular point a year later by the Court of Appeal in Tanzania, it is submitted wrongly.[31]

These considerations make it highly desirable for owners' advisers to take account of any possible rights of common law rescission when a contractual determination is in contemplation by their clients, and to consider the advantages and practicability of exercising the common law rights either concurrently, or in the alternative (against which there can be no objection in principle, it is submitted).[32] Additionally, draftsmen of contracts should, in the owner's interest, make express provision for this possibility, and also, in the same interest, for the extension of any of the ancillary remedies available to the owner on a contractual determination to his common law rescissions as well.[33] Ideally, an owner's determination clause should also recognise the common law freedom of the owner to abandon the project and calculate his damages accordingly, where it is reasonable to do so, and extend it to determinations under the clause.[34]   **12-010**

---

[29] 23 BLR 23.   [29a] Keith Goodfellow Q.C.

[30] [1985] A.C. 191, 201, considered *ante*, Chap. 1, Section 9(1), paras. 1·217–1·220.

[31] *Mvita Construction Ltd.* v. *Tanzania Harbours Authority* (1988) 46 BLR 19.

[32] See, *e.g.*, *per* Moffitt J. in *Re an arbitration between Stewardson Stubbs & Collett Ltd. and Bankstown Municipal Council* [1965] N.S.W.R. 1671.

[33] See the Singapore S.I.A. 1980 contract, Clauses 32(2) and (10), reproduced in C.C.P.P., pp. 600 and 606.

[34] *Ibid.*, Clause 32(9), reproduced in C.C.P.P., p. 605.

Although the cases show that the courts are prepared to decide by interpretation whether action or notice terminating a contract is taken or given under the contractual termination clause on the one hand, or to be regarded as an acceptance of the contractor's repudiation at common law on the other,[35] a competent adviser should ensure that any notice given makes its legal basis expressly clear, or, in an appropriate case, that the notice is being given separately from, or as an alternative to, any determination by other means.

(4) Events on which the Express Power Usually Conditioned

(a) Owners' determinations

12·011   There has been a great variety of grounds for determination customarily specified in the contractual termination clauses of construction contracts in the past. However, the practical exigencies of construction contracts, coupled with an understandable reluctance of the law to accord the legal status of a "condition" (that is, a fundamental term justifying rescission at once if broken) to earlier breaches occurring during the construction period, no doubt in the light of the long-term nature and ultimate overriding completion obligation of the contractor in construction projects, has meant that termination clauses became primarily focused, first, on enforcing reasonable progress during the construction period, and, secondly, in securing prompt rectification of defective work. In both cases it has been seen that the evolution of a sufficiently stringent implied term by the courts, or indeed any term at all prior to completion, has not proved easy in these two respects.[36] In the case of unsatisfactory progress, earlier more primitive contracts were simply conditioned on failure to commence work or to complete by the due date. These were soon expressed as a failure to proceed at such rate as would enable the works to be completed by the due date, but it was not long before it was appreciated that even this wording could produce serious difficulties once the completion date had passed.[37] As a result, failure to proceed with due diligence, without reference to any specified or extended date of completion, came to be seen by better informed advisers as an essential contractual ground of termination. Later still, as a sensible protection for the contractor, an earlier warning or notice from the A/E, accompanied by continuation of the default for a specified period thereafter before any definitive notice of determination could be served, became a widely used formula for termination. These latter "two-tier" due diligence clauses have, rightly, become the basis of the more modern domestic standard forms in England.

---

[35] See the *Bysouth* and *Architectural Installations* cases illustrated *supra.*
[36] See *ante*, Chap. 4, Section 1(3), paras. 4·128–4·129, and Chap. 9, Section 1(4), para. 9·032 for due diligence, and Chap. 5, Section 2, paras. 5·025–5·027 for defective work.
[37] See *Walker* v. *London and North Western Rly. Co.* (1876) 1 C.P.D. 518 and *Joshua Henshaw & Sons* v. *Rochdale Corporation* [1944] K.B. 381, illustrated and considered *infra*, paras. 12·047 and 12·049.

In the case of defective work, while some earlier and more primitive clauses simply stipulated failure to comply with the specifications or drawings, the more modern tendency has again been to introduce the greater precision and fairness of a "two-tier" approach, based on failure to rectify or remove defective work continuing over a stipulated period following an earlier notice or instruction from the owner's A/E.

However, many other detailed and perhaps more easily abused grounds **12·012** of owner determination are to be found in the cases, such as removal of materials from the site without permission; not maintaining the works properly; sub-contracting or assignment without consent; and Sunday working without permission; as well as much more generally expressed grounds, again open to abuse, such as not complying with the A/E's orders or directions; *any wilful* breach of contract;[38] or any repudiation of the contract certified by the engineer.[39]

The draftsmanship of many termination clauses is, in fact, typically lacking in precision, if not at times almost whimsical, as evidenced by the FIDIC International Civil Engineering Contracts, where, for example, the third edition lists as grounds for termination suspension of the works, and "not executing the Works in accordance with the Contract or persistently or flagrantly neglecting to carry out his obligations under the contract", without, however, any more specific mention of the really essential ground, from the owner's point of view, of failure to proceed with due diligence. This was followed by the fourth edition in 1987, which now does list, but only by an indirect reference, a failure of due diligence *so as to secure completion by the contract date*, which, as already indicated *supra*, fails to deal with failures of due diligence *after* that date has passed.[40] It is again not untypical of the draftsmanship of these contracts to see new wording introduced into a leading international standard form of contract as late as 1987 which immediately resurrects an anomaly against the owner's interest arising from inappropriate wording noticed more than a century ago in the Court of Common Pleas in *Walker's* case,[40a] with the result that properly advised owners generally, and even the English domestic standard forms, had discarded such wording many decades ago.

Owners' determination clauses, as already noted, frequently confer **12·013** detailed ancillary powers on the owner. Some may be financial or other forfeitures, or physical seizure provisions, primarily intended to give the owner a degree of financial security or protection against the cost of completion in the event of the termination, (though these, if unrealistic or

---

[38] Compare the *Bysouth* case *supra*.

[39] See Clause 61.1(*a*) of the current (1987) FIDIC fourth edition. Whether this new provision in the FIDIC contract is intended to suggest that every rescission at common law by the owner must be certified by the engineer, or that the owner's powers on a common law determination shall be limited to those in the clause, are not matters which the draftsman has seen fit to elucidate, and are typical examples of official institutional civil engineering draftsmanship. See for a further remarkable example, Clause 44.1 of the Australia N.P.W.C. Edition 3 contract, at issue in *Renard Constructions Ltd.* v. *Minister of Public Works* (1992) 26 N.S.W.L.R. 234 illustrated *infra*, para. 12·025.

[40] See Clause 63.1(*b*)(*ii*), and Clause 46.1.   [40a] See *infra*, para. 12·047.

excessive, may risk being avoided and set aside as penalties, if they cannot be regarded as either a reasonable pre-estimate of the likely damage resulting from the termination or as a reasonable security against the likely final cost of completion).[41] Other ancillary powers may be more directly concerned to assist the process of completing the outstanding work using other contractors. Ancillary powers generally are shortly discussed further *infra*, Section 2.

(b) Owners' "convenience" clauses

12·014   Convenience clauses, as they are generally known in the United States, are owners' determination clauses expressly *not* conditioned on any breach or event or default for which the contractor could be regarded as legally responsible, but exercisable simply at the discretion of the owner. In United States Government contracts, where they have been continuously in existence since the Civil War,[42] some such wording as "for the convenience of the Government" or "in the best interest of government" has often been used, but no special importance attaches to this, and in principle it is sufficient if the wording of the contract simply distinguishes the right of termination from one based on contractor default or responsibility. Typically, the clauses co-exist in the same contract as a separate default termination clause, and at the present day the United States courts will not be slow to fasten on and implement any wording of the contract suggesting a requirement of election by the owner between the two remedies.[43] The practical effect and purpose of the clauses is that they usually permit recovery of contract or reasonable value, plus a reasonable profit *on the work done prior to the termination*, as well as settlement of subcontractor accounts and any removal or other expenses, but disallow any claim for loss of profit on the remaining work. Nor do they, of course, confer any of the special ancillary rights on the owner to be found in default termination clauses.

12·015   Despite the fact that in construction contracts damages in respect of loss of profit on the remaining work will often be far more difficult to establish than is commonly thought,[44] this is not so true in the case of manufacturing or other procurement contracts, and over their long history in the United States convenience clauses in these contracts have provoked a huge jurisprudence dating from the 19th century, and stemming from contractor plaintiffs' desire to obtain loss of profit on cancelled work. This has been partly at least either countered or provoked by a "constructive termination for convenience" argument on the part of public owners in those cases where their attempted default determinations have been held to be

---

[41] See the cases on penalties illustrated and considered *ante*, Chap. 10, Section 1(2), paras. 10·007 *et seq.*, and in particular the *Egan* case, *supra*, para. 10·016, and for typical express provisions relating to plant and materials see also Chap. 11, Section 2(1).

[42] *U.S.* v. *Corliss Steam Engineering Corporation* 91 U.S. 321 (1876) and see the history examined in *Troncello* v. *U.S.* 681 F2nd 756, 764–6 (Ct. Cl. 1982).

[43] *Rogerson Aircraft Corporation* v. *Fairchild Industries* 632 F.Supp. 1494 (1986).

[44] See *ante*, Chap. 8, Section 2(3)(b), paras. 8·172 *et seq.*

unjustified and wrongful, in order to limit the owner's liability to that which could have arisen under the convenience clause had it been invoked. Another fertile area of dispute has occurred where the convenience clause was indeed expressly invoked by the owners, but for criticised reasons, such as the obtaining of a more attractive price from another contractor or source. It can be inferred from the cases that after the Second World War the contractors' arguments in both these areas of dispute received considerably increased support from the federal judiciary in the Court of Claims. Thus, in 1961 the "constructive termination for convenience" argument was rejected in a seminal case where the Government, after failing to justify a termination based on default, had sought to limit their liability for wrongful repudiation by retrospectively invoking the convenience clause.[45]

Where the motive for an expressly invoked convenience termination was to secure a more attractive price elsewhere, a decision in 1974 which had upheld such a termination and rejected a loss of profit claim by the contractor was disapproved in a further seminal Court of Claims case in 1982.[46] The later case, however, attached importance to a particular element of the facts, namely that the State had at the time of its original contract known, or had the means of knowing, the source of supply at lower prices which provided the motivation for the later convenience termination.[47]

On the other hand, where a contract was cancelled by government offi-   **12·016**
cers in the bona fide belief that the contractor's bid had been invalid, and in another case where, under a wrong but bona fide interpretation of the contract, the government failed to order as much work from the contractor as it should have done and placed some of its work elsewhere, the presence of a convenience clause, although not expressly invoked, prevented loss of profit being recovered in both cases;[48] and a convenience clause exercised as a result of doubts as to the suitability of the contract specification was upheld even though the inadequacy of the specification had been the fault of the Government.[49]

However, outside the United States there appears to be little or no authority on these points, though "convenience" determination clauses undoubtedly do exist in some public or private contracts in England and the Commonwealth. It is probably preferable to approach the two areas of

---

[45] *Klein* v. *U.S.* 285F 2nd 778 (1961), and see *Goldwasser* v. *U.S.* 325F 2nd 722 (1963), and *Rogerson Aircraft Corporation* v. *Fairchild Industries* 633 F. Supp. 1494 (1986), distinguishing *College Point Boat Corporation* v. *U.S.* 12 (1925) and *John Rainer & Co.* v. *U.S.* 325F 2nd 438 (1963).

[46] *Troncello* v. *U.S.* 681F 2nd 756 (1982), disapproving *Colonial Metals* v. *U.S.* 494F 2nd 1353 (1974).

[47] See this pointed out in a Note highly critical of convenience clauses generally and analysing the *Troncello* case in (1983/4) 52 George Wash. Review 892, and see for earlier criticisms of the clauses Perlman & Goodrich, Termination of Convenience Settlements (1978) 10 Pub. Contract. L.J. 1(6); see also Nash & Cibinic *Federal Procurement Law* paras. 1104–07 3rd ed. (1980).

[48] *John Rainer & Co.* v. *U.S.* 325F 2nd 438 (1963), *Nesbitt* v. *U.S.* 345F 2nd 583 (1965).

[49] *Nolan Bros.* v. *U.S.* 405F 2nd 1250 (Ct. Cl. 1969).

dispute referred to above in terms of first principle, it is submitted, rather than by too close an adherence to the Court of Claims cases, where an element of administrative policy and practice rather than strictly consensual theories has often underlied many Court of Claims doctrines.

Dealing first with the "constructive termination for convenience" theory, while both United States and English law undoubtedly take the view that a determination for default which fails can be rescued if another fact or default justifying determination is present though unknown to the determining party at the time,[50] it seems a very doubtful analogy, it is submitted, to apply that principle to a case where an owner has available to him at all times a convenience remedy which he deliberately chooses not to exercise. Standing by itself, that is not a valid reason for supporting any constructive termination argument, it is submitted.

12·017   In terms of first principle, a convenience clause may be regarded, it is suggested, as primarily designed, in the absence of express indication to the contrary, to give the owner the commercial freedom to abandon the project, or a part of it, either permanently or temporarily at any time. It may also be regarded, it is again suggested, as intended to afford an owner who is dissatisfied with a contractor's progress or work with an alternative and less controversial remedy than that available under an accompanying default-based termination clause, thus avoiding the expense and risks of a contested default determination while sacrificing some of its financial and procedural advantages.

On this view, it is submitted, on the analogy of the authoritative Commonwealth and later English cases similarly restricting the power to order omissions by way of variation, that it will be a breach of contract for an owner to exercise the remedy, in the absence of sufficiently express wording, if his purpose in doing so is to obtain the more attractive prices of another contractor to complete the work.[51] In such a case, incidentally, there seems to be no reason why knowledge of the alternative source or price on the part of the owner at the time of contracting should be a necessary ingredient or of any relevance in establishing his breach, which depends on placing a reasonable as opposed to an exploitative interpretation on the variation power.

If this view of convenience clauses is correct, and the owner exercises the power because he has decided to abandon the project either permanently or for the time being, or because he is bona fide dissatisfied with the contractor's performance but prefers to avoid a default-based confrontation, there will be a legitimate exercise of the power, it is submitted. On the other hand, where the owner has repudiated the contract by some other breach, so that the contractor is entitled to and does rescind at common law, or where the owner has unsuccessfully sought to determine the

---

[50] See the cases referred to in *Chitty on Contracts* (26th ed.), para. 1709, and see *College Point Boat Corporation* v. *U.S.* 267 U.S. 12 (1925) *supra.*

[51] See *Carr* v. *J. A. Berriman Pty. Ltd.* (1953) 27 A.L.J. 273 High Court of Australia, and the cases illustrated *ante*, Chap. 7, Section 2(2), paras. 7·043 *et seq.*

contract at common law or under a default provision in order to obtain the remedies and damages available against the contractor in such a situation, it will follow that a ruling which deprives the contractor of loss of profit or other consequential loss in that event will mean that the convenience clause has in effect been interpreted as a partial "no damage" or exclusionary clause, operating automatically in all situations, and whether or not in fact invoked at the time by the owner. While in principle there is no objection to any such limitation of damage following a wrongful determination by the owner, sufficiently clear wording should be required for such a result to be achieved, it is submitted,[52] and the normal tendency, in the absence of sufficiently clear language, should be to interpret such clauses as affording a useful remedy to an owner in the two principal situations envisaged, but not as providing a shield against wrongful determinations or repudiations of the contract on his own part.

(c) Contractors' determinations

Many if not most private forms of contract will, for obvious reasons, **12·018** contain no express contractor's termination clause. Even in the case of the standard forms, civil engineering forms such as the English ICE Conditions contain no such clause, no doubt reflecting the very high proportion of public owners in the civil engineering industry, where the owner's ultimate solvency will accordingly not be in question. The obvious principal target of such clauses, particularly in an era of financial stringency and high borrowing rates for bank or commercial working capital, will be any sustained failure of the owner to make interim payments when due. Here again, the law had difficulty in implying sufficiently stringent terms or the status of a "condition" to such obligations.[53] Contractor determination clauses based on failure to pay will usually be on a "two-tier" notice basis, requiring a continued non-payment for a stipulated period following an earlier notice to pay. This basis has been largely adopted for standard main and sub-contract building industry forms in England, and has quite understandably also been present in successive editions of the FIDIC international civil engineering forms.

However, almost uniquely in the Western World, the producer orien- **12·019** tation of the English RIBA/JCT forms has produced, even in their local authority versions, elaborately drafted grounds for contractor termination based on a relatively short period of delay caused to the works by any one of a lengthy series of defined instructions or situations. Remarkably, on close analysis many of these situations are not even ones where the owner or his A/E are likely to be at fault and, more remarkably, the wording will even permit determination in situations where the A/E has failed to react sufficiently swiftly to situations caused directly by con-

---

[52] Express "no damage" clauses have indeed operated successfully in termination situations—see *Woollatt Fuel* v. *Matthews Group* (1979) 101 D.L.R. 3d 537, Canada, *ante* Chap. 8, Section 2(4)(b), paras. 8·217 *et seq.* and 8·222.
[53] See *ante*, Chap. 4, Section 1(a)(iii), paras. 4·032 *et seq.*, and Section 3(1), para. 4·221.

tractor or sub-contractor default, or where the contractor would otherwise be legally responsible (as, for example, for strikes or bad weather or
insured risks).[54] More remarkably still, these particular clauses are *not*
drafted on a "two-tier" notice basis, so that the owner can find the contract
suddenly determined without warning against himself, and with no opportunity of rectifying or addressing what may be a highly legalistic and
opportunistic complaint. There seems no conceivable commercial or legal
justification for a legal or other professional adviser to advise or permit an
owner client to enter into a contract containing such a clause,[55] notwithstanding the presence in it of an "unreasonable and vexatious" proviso
such as is found in these English standard forms, but which has singularly
failed to provide satisfactory protection for owners.

ILLUSTRATION

12·020   At the commencement of work for a project in June 1983 nominated piling
sub-contractors arrived on site about two weeks late and completed in early
July about 3½ weeks late. The sub-contractor had not, in breach of their sub-
contract, tested and proved the piles, and the owner had tests carried out on
three piles which were found to be defective. Although called on to remedy
the piles, the sub-contractors refused to do so and left the job. During July and
August the architect at once took steps to obtain competitive tenders in order
to make a second nomination in view of the sub-contractors' repudiation. On
July 15th, in response to a letter from the contractor making enquiries, he
wrote "You should cease work on this element of the contract". Neither the
architect, nor the contractor interpreted this instruction as one to postpone
work on the contract as a whole, but in September the contractor was advised
by counsel that the letter had constituted on the facts which had occurred an
instruction to postpone work under Clause 23.2 of the 1980 contract, and the
contractor immediately terminated without warning under Clause 28.1.3.4 of
the contract, as one month had expired since the letter of July 15th, and further work on the project had been effectively suspended for that period.
Clause 28.1.3.4, however, contained a specific proviso "unless caused by the
negligence or default of the Contractor". The clause also contained a general
proviso that the termination should not be "unreasonable or vexatious".
Held, by the Court of Appeal, that though the piling sub-contractors' work
had been defective and they had wrongly abandoned and repudiated their
sub-contract, the words "negligible or default of the Contractor" in Clause 28
did not include the negligence or default of a *nominated* sub-contractor
(although they did include other sub-contractors), and that although neither
the architect nor the contractor had interpreted his letter in July as an instruction to postpone work, and the contractor had terminated without warning,
while the architect had taken all steps open to him promptly to secure a second nomination and was "astonished and stunned" to receive the termination

---

[54] *Gloucestershire County Council* v. *Richardson* [1969] 1 A.C. 480, illustrated and critically
discussed *ante*, Chap. 4, para. 4·122; *John Jarvis Ltd.* v. *Rockdale Housing Association Ltd.*
(1986) 36 BLR 48 (C.A.), illustrated together with the *Gloucestershire* case, see *ante*, para.
5·037, and critically examined by the editor in *The Bickerton Albatross Once More* (1987) 3
Const.L.J. 274.
[55] The RIBA/JCT clause is considered and analysed in detail in C.C.P.P. paras. 29–20—23
and 30–24.

letter, and although the contractor would have been entitled under the contract to all loss and expense arising as a result of the postponement instruction, the contract had been converted into a contract with two winters and the contractor might not succeed in establishing all his claims to additional loss successfully, so that it was not "unreasonable or vexatious" to exercise his contractual right to determine: *John Jarvis Ltd.* v. *Rockdale Housing Association Ltd.* (1986).[56]

[Note: Counsel in this case had apparently conceded that the letter in question was a "postponement instruction" under the terms of the contract. This seems wrong. Bingham L.J.'s judgment has been fairly freely paraphrased *supra*, in regard to the "unreasonable and vexatious" proviso. While this question must inevitably be a matter of degree, that on a close analysis of the factual background of this case it would be hard to conceive of a more favourable situation for the invocation of the proviso. As to the exclusionary wording for "contractor negligence or default", this was clearly the result of inept draftsmanship of Clause 28.1.3.4, as had been specifically pointed out in C.C.P.P. prior to the *Jarvis* case.[57] There are also judicial comments by Bingham L.J. on the history of the wording and of the reasonableness of the construction, which seem to have been at least as to the former, *per incuriam*, and the case has been analysed in considerable detail and the court's interpretation of Clause 28.1.3.4 in part doubted and criticised.[58]]

(5) Relief against Forfeiture

It has been seen *ante*, Chapter 10 that contractual compensatory provisions conditioned on a breach of contract which are not a genuine pre-estimate of damage will, on principles originally evolved by the Courts of Equity, be unenforceable as penalties, and that these principles have been extended in construction contracts to the ancillary financial provisions associated with contractual determination clauses, including financial forfeitures of moneys already due and forfeitures of property such as materials and plant, as well as to liquidated damages clauses as such. In such cases equity, and later the common law, would only permit recovery of proven actual loss or damage, subject to the stipulated sums acting as a "cap" should the damages prove to be greater.[58a]

12·021

A closely related principle of equity, generally described as relief against forfeiture, may also theoretically be available (although so far it would seem in only a limited class of cases) to prevent a party from enforcing contractual provisions which, while not directly concerned with providing compensation for breaches of contract, render it unconscionable for a party to retain the benefits arising from such provisions, for example, on a forfeiture of the contract. This principle differs somewhat from those governing the avoidance of penalties,[59] and requires to be applied in the light of the circumstances prevailing at the time of exercising the forfeiture, rather than, as in the case of the law relating to penalties, in the light of

---

[56] 36 BLR 48.
[57] In C.C.P.P., para. 30–24.
[58] See *The Bickerton Albatross Once More* (1987) 3 Const.L.J. 24.
[58a] See *ante*, Chap. 10, paras. 10·020/021:
[59] *Stockloser* v. *Johnson* [1954] 1 Q.B. 476, 488, *per* Denning L.J.

the contractual provisions and of the facts as known at the time of contracting.[60]

12·022   The principle will be applied, it seems, to a contract of sale which provides for sums to be paid in advance or as part payment but which subsequently become irrecoverable at law by reason of a rescission on the part of the seller if the buyer is unable to complete, when, subject to payment of any damages suffered, the instalments may be ordered to be repaid by the seller where it would be unconscionable for him to retain them;[61] or again where a defaulting buyer who is now able to offer the full price may be relieved of a forfeiture of this kind.[62]

The principle is most commonly seen in the equitable relief against forfeiture by a landlord for breach of covenant, but it has a potentially wider application. At one time it was thought that it was confined to two principal heads, namely where the object of the transaction, and of the right to forfeit, was essentially to secure payment of money and, secondly, cases of fraud, accident, mistake or surprise (which latter would exclude mere inadvertence as well as, *a fortiori*, wilful defaults).[63]

However, the modern position appears to be that inadvertent breaches, but only in very exceptional cases wilful breaches, may nevertheless qualify for relief:

> "Established and, in my opinion, sound principle requires that wilful breaches should not, or at least should only in exceptional cases, be relieved against, if only for the reason that [the determining party] should not be compelled to remain in the relation of neighbourhood with a person in deliberate breach of his obligations".[64]

The broad principle as stated by Lord Wilberforce in the *Shiloh Spinners* case would appear to be:

> "it remains true today that equity expects men to carry out their bargains and will not let them buy their way out by uncovenanted payment. But it is consistent with these principles that we should re-affirm the right of Courts of Equity in appropriate and limited cases to relieve against forfeiture for breach of covenant or condition where the primary object of the bargain is to secure a stated result which can be effectively attained when the matter comes before the Court, and where the forfeiture provision is added by way of security for the production of that result. The word "appropriate" involves consideration of the conduct of the applicant for relief, in particular whether his default was wilful, of the gravity of the breaches, and of the disparity between the value of the property of which forfeiture is claimed as compared with the damage

---

[60] *Campbell Discount Co. Ltd.* v. *Bridge* [1961] 1 Q.B. 445, 456–7, *per* Holroyd Pearce L.J.

[61] *Dies* v. *Bank of International Mining & Finance Corporation* [1939] 1 K.B. 724, cited by Denning L.J. in the *Stockloser* case *supra*, but explained, however, as based on a total failure of consideration in the House of Lords in *Hyundai Heavy Industries Co.* v. *Papadopoulos* [1980] 2 A.E.R. 29, illustrated and discussed *ante*, Chap. 4, Section 3(1)(h), paras. 4·228 *et seq.*, and so not usually applicable in construction contracts.

[62] *Stockloser* v. *Johnson* [1961] 1 Q.B. 476, 488–491, *per* Denning L.J.

[63] See *Shiloh Spinners Ltd.* v. *Harding* [1973] A.C. 691, 722, *per* Lord Wilberforce, citing *Hill* v. *Berkley* (1811) 18 Ves. Jun. 56.

[64] *Ibid.*, at p. 725F, *per* Lord Wilberforce.

caused by the breach. Both as a matter of history and by the nature of things, different considerations apply to different covenants . . ."[65]

It has been seen from the discussion *supra*, that determination clauses in **12·023** construction contracts, particularly in the past, have not infrequently been conditioned on relatively minor breaches by contractors (as, for example, Sunday working without permission, sub-contracting without consent, or a failure to rectify possibly very minor defective work). Alternatively they may be expressed in general terms which could also cover very minor breaches ("any wilful breach", for example). Equally, contractors' determinations can easily be exercised on purely inadvertent breaches which are easily repaired, such as an accidental failure of posting or transmission of interim payment by a substantial owner with an otherwise impeccable payment record, or very minor delays during construction caused directly by contractor or sub-contractor breach and fully compensatable under the contract terms or by damages, as in the *Jarvis* case illustrated *supra*.[66] All of these might qualify, it is submitted, for relief within the principles stated in the *Shiloh Spinners* case cited *supra* but, as the facts of that case itself show, the English courts have been and remain extraordinarily reluctant to grant relief, particularly, it would seem, in commercial contracts, (though it should be noted that one specific ground for refusing relief, namely the impossibility of the courts' supervising the doing of work, has now been expressly disavowed by Lord Wilberforce.)[67]

In fact there appear to be no reported cases of equitable relief being granted against the determination of a construction contract, and it appears to be taken for granted in the industry and indeed amongst legal advisers in England that provided a ground of termination can be established which complies with the letter of a termination clause, however legalistic or obviously opportunistic the termination may be, it will be upheld and the opposing party exposed to the full rigours (subject to avoidance of penalties) of the remedies provided by the clause. Conversely, and perhaps by way of an unconscious counterweight, the slightest failure to comply with the letter, as, for example, by a mistaken re-entry one day early in a "two-tier" notice case, will cause the termination to fail, however serious or indeed irreparable the guilty party's earlier breach, unless it can be "rescued" as a common law rescission.

One or two apparent exceptions may be noted. Thus, where a contrac- **12·024** tual termination for failure of due diligence depended upon the engineer's

---

[65] *Ibid.*, pp. 723G–724. Compare Cardozo J.'s very similar statement of principle in the closely analogous situation of substantial performance in *Jacob & Youngs* v. *Kent* 129 N.E. 889 (1921), cited *ante*, Chap. 4, Section 1(1)(a), para. 4·022. Despite this relatively liberal declaration of principle in the House of Lords, the Court of Appeal, who had granted relief against forfeiture by an assignor for failures to fence off the assigned property properly, were reversed by the House of Lords on the ground of the wilful and continuing nature of the breaches.

[66] See para. 12·020.

[67] *Shiloh Spinners* case *supra*, at p. 724CD.

certification, the Court of Appeal of New Zealand over-turned a determination on the ground of an *objective* lack of fairness by the certifier, who had previously honestly but mistakenly under-certified interim payments, thereby provoking the contractor into wrongly suspending work. In that case, the Court declined, however, to hold the owners in breach of contract, allowing the contractor remuneration for work done only, a modification of remedies not easy to reconcile with common law contractual principles.[68] In another case in New Zealand, Smellie J. held a termination to be unfair and invalidated because the engineer had failed to give a sufficiently clear up-date of his present intention to determine after repeated earlier complaints at meetings followed by acquiescence in continued work by the contractor.[69]

The above two cases, which are not easy to rationalise, depend in the last resort, however, upon the Court's interpretation of the termination clause and of its associated procedures rather than on any over-riding principle, it is submitted. Although usually it will be sufficient to show compliance with the defined requirements of a termination clause, which may themselves require to be assessed objectively (as, for example, failure to proceed with due diligence), it remains that the commercial reasonableness, or otherwise, of an owner's decision to determine (or indeed a contractor's) will not generally be questioned, however opportunistic it may be seen to be. However, in the following Australian case involving unusual and apparently old-fashioned draftsmanship lacking in any commercial precision, but clearly designed to confer the widest of discretions on the owner both to suspend payment or determine the contract, the implication of a reasonableness limitation in arriving at the decision to determine was imposed by the Court which, given the width of the grounds stipulated for determination, is easily understandable.

ILLUSTRATION

12·025   By clause 44.1 of a government sewerage contract in New South Wales under the N.P.W.C. (3 ed.) (1981) form of contract, if the contractor defaulted in the performance of *any* stipulation, etc., in the contract or refused or neglected to comply with *any* direction of the Principal or Superintendent given in writing, the Principal might suspend payment under the contract, and by notice in writing call on the contractor to show cause why the work should not be taken over and the contractor expelled from the site, or the contract be cancelled. The "Show Cause" notice was required to specify the default refusal or neglect on which it was based, and if within the period specified in the notice the contractor failed to show cause "to the satisfaction of the Principal" the latter might exercise the power to take over the work or cancel the contract. The contractor conceded that there had been a delay for which he

---

[68] *Canterbury Pipelines Ltd.* v. *Christchurch Drainage Board* [1979] 2 N.Z.L.R. 347, illustrated *ante*, Chap. 6, Section 5(5), para. 6·134.
[69] *Brown & Docherty* v. *Whangarei County* [1988] 1 N.Z.L.R. 33, illustrated *ante*, Chap. 4, Section 3(1)(c), para. 4·215.

was responsible, but the most difficult and unprofitable part of the work had been completed when, some three months before its likely completion by the contractor, the Principal determined under the clause. The arbitrator held that the determination had been unreasonable, and that consequently the contract had been wrongly determined, and awarded reasonable remuneration to the contractor in excess of the contract price for the whole work. He found as facts that the Superintendent, who through a subordinate was primarily responsible for the decision by the Principal, had not been informed of the full facts by his own subordinates, and in particular, due to a mistake in dates, he had been given an inaccurate picture of recent progress; he was unaware that delays in the supply of materials by the owners had not been taken into account in a recent extension of time decision; he was told that there had been defective work, but not that all criticisms of workmanship contained in site instructions had been promptly rectified; he had not been told that since the "show cause" notice the number of men had been increased and a new and experienced foreman appointed; and he was not informed that any new contractors appointed would be unable to finish any earlier than the present contractor. On an appeal by the government, the appeal was allowed by Cole J. on the ground that it was sufficient for the Principal to act honestly in good faith, which he had done, and Clause 44 did not require him to act reasonably in exercising the powers it conferred, so that the contract had been rightly determined. *Held*, by the New South Wales Court of Appeal, (Priestley and Handley JJ.A., Meagher J.A. dissenting on one point) that both the Principal's consideration of the contractor's case and the subsequent determination under Clause 44.1 must each be exercised reasonably, so that the termination had been wrongful. (*Per* Meagher J.A., since the Principal's decision had been grounded on misleading, incomplete and prejudicial information, he could not be "satisfied" as required by the clause and the determination was wrongful on that ground). *Held*, also, that the arbitrator under a generally worded arbitration clause had jurisdiction to review the reasonableness of the decision, and, following *Lodder* v. *Slowey*, that the arbitrator had properly allowed the contractor larger sums by way of *quantum meruit* on the wrongful determination than would have been due under the contract. *Renard Constructions Ltd.* v. *Minister of Public Works* (1992).[70]

The termination provision in Clause 44.1 of the *Renard* contract illustrated above seems to have been designed to confer a maximum of discretionary power to terminate on the officials of the Ministry, and on its wording the procedure could obviously be activated following quite trivial defaults. In this respect it was comparable to many older forms of nineteenth-century contract. Faced with such wording, it is not at all surprising that the majority of the New South Wales Court of Appeal imposed a reasonableness requirement extending to the exercise of the determining power itself, and not merely in relation to the ascertainment of the underlying facts by the certifying officer.   **12·026**

Two views are possible of this potentially very important case. On the narrower view, the combination of harsh wording, on its face stipulating quite trivial or minor breaches as possible grounds for termination, together with its stipulation of the subsequent "show cause" procedure, would require an implication of reasonableness to give effect to its pre-

---

[70] 26 N.S.W.L.R. 234, discussed further *infra*, para. 12·028. See also in the *quantum merut* point, Fitzgerald P. in *Iezzi Constructions Ltd.* v. *Currumbin Crest Developments Ltd.* (1994) 13 A.C.L.R. 39.

sumed intention and avoid an opportunistic termination on obviously trivial grounds. In Handley J.A.'s view this interpretation was supported even more strongly by the arbitration clause expressed in general terms, which would otherwise be of little or no value in the event of a dispute under the clause (that is, the principle in *Brodie* v. *Cardiff Corporation*).[70a]

12·027   On a wider view, which was undoubtedly taken by Priestley J.A., who was prepared to find a term implied *by law* into this class of contract generally, as well as an implied term "ad hoc" or "in fact" based on the wording of the specific contract, there will be such an implied term of reasonableness in *construction contracts generally* wherever there are termination clauses expressly conditioned on contractor default. However, Priestley J.A.'s very full judgment on this point, and the examples which he gives, make it plain, it is submitted, that the implied term will be such as to invalidate only an obviously and wholly unreasonable determination which no reasonable owner could be expected to enforce,[70b] but not so as to permit doubt over a termination where finely balanced considerations might lead some owners only, but not others, to choose to "nurse" the contractor rather than to dismiss him. On the other hand, Meagher J.A., it should be noted, dissented strongly on any implication of reasonableness in the exercise of the power to terminate, though the expressed ground of his otherwise concurring judgment (that is, the Principal having acted on incorrect or insufficient information during the "show cause" procedure) does not seem a logical basis for invalidating a termination unless it leads in turn to an objectively unreasonable exercise of the power.

It will be of great interest to see how this case is subsequently applied and interpreted. Much of Priestley J.A.'s reasoning, it should be noted, can be equally applied to *contractors'* determinations for non-payment, which can also be of an opportunistic nature, as where an owner's failure to pay by the stipulated date is accidental or in respect of a very small sum, for example, both of which can easily happen, and where there is an otherwise good record of regular payment.

(6) Good Faith, *Ex Aequo et Bono* or other Limitations

12·028   Under modern recessionary and financial pressures opportunistic contractual terminations, bearing no relationship to genuine hardship or unreasonable, actual or potential damage suffered by the rescinding party, and whether by owners or contractors, have become an increasingly common feature of construction contracts, as indeed in many other areas of commerce. The preceding subsection has served to show, it is submitted, that the long established doctrine of equitable relief against forfeiture in England, while readily applicable in terms of judicially stated principle to opportunistic terminations,[71] have in fact been so sparingly applied by the English Courts that there appears to be no example of their appli-

---

[70a] See *ante*, para. 7·068.
[70b] See (1992) 26 N.S.W.L.R. 234, 256–63.
[71] See Lord Wilberforce's dictum in the *Shiloh Spinners* case *supra*, para. 12·022.

cation in a construction case. It has also been seen that this extreme, and in modern conditions perhaps unrealistic, conservatism is unlikely to represent commercial parties' concensual intentions, and has even extended to the application of contractual provisions which positively invite the intervention of the law in such situations, such as the "unreasonable and vexatious" provision in the RIBA/JCT standard form contractors' determination clauses, which proved of so little value to the Housing Association owners in the *Jarvis* case.[72]

The remarkable *Renard Constructions* case in the New South Wales Court of Appeal illustrated *supra*, is clearly explicable by the unusual "show cause" express wording and machinery of its termination clause, calling for an implication of reasonableness in order to avoid an interpretation which would effectively place one party at the mercy of the other. Quite different considerations, however, will apply, it is submitted, if a clearly defined ground of termination, however minor or unimportant, is established beyond doubt and the termination clause, as many do, simply permits termination in such an event without indulging in "show cause" or other qualifying wording. Much more than this relatively conservative view of the *Renard* case is required if termination clauses without the *Renard* special "show cause" wording are to be restrained by concepts of fairness, reasonableness or good faith. In fact Priestley J.A.'s judgment expressly states, firstly, that on the clause before him reasonableness was to be implied both at the stage of considering the contractor's submissions showing cause, and at the next stage when deciding whether or not to exercise the right of re-entry or cancellation; and, secondly, Priestley J.A. was careful to hold expressly that in addition to an ad hoc implied term (based no doubt on the specific "show cause" wording), there was also a similar implied term *in law*,[72a] applying to construction contract termination clauses generally, where conditioned on slow or unsatisfactory work or on the insolvency of the contractor.[73] If Priestley J.A.'s view is accepted, therefore, the case represents a highly important change in the attitude hitherto adopted by the courts in regard to the validity of determination clauses in construction contracts.

In other jurisdictions, however, considerable restraints already exist **12·029** against what may be described as the opportunistic use of determination clauses, whether by the owner or the contractor. In United States jurisdictions this seems likely under the developing tendencies of good faith doctrines, now expressly recognised or accepted, in general if not detailed terms, by the Uniform Commercial Code and in the Second Restatement of the Law of Contract in 1981, but not as yet in England.[74] Internationally,

---

[72] Illustrated *supra*, para. 12·020, where the refusal to give effect to this express wording is noted and doubted.

[72a] See *supra*, para. 12·027.

[73] See, *per* Priestley J.A. (1992) 2 N.S.W.L.R. 234.

[74] See *ante*, Chap. 1, Section 6(3), paras. 1·197, 1·199, where the theory of the implied covenant of good faith and fair dealing is discussed. See also Priestley J.A.'s examination of the authorities.

also, the trend to encourage the introduction of the concept into commercial and other contracts is obvious,[75] though there is a pressing contemporary need for these authorities and others to define more precisely and in positive terms what are the practical constituents of the good faith concept which it is proposed to incorporate into the contracts in question or adopt as part of contract law generally.

In civil law countries, the scope for unreasonable or opportunistic determination of contracts is constrained not only by good faith concepts but, in many such countries, by *"abus de droit"* doctrines, as well as by procedural requirements that rescission of a contract cannot be effective without the approval of the Court, though this latter requirement does not apply to determinations in exact compliance with express *"de plein droit"* contractual provisions (*"resiliation de plein droit"*). There is no reason to doubt from the practice of the Courts in these countries that where, for example, the criteria for equitable relief against forfeiture enunciated by Lord Wilberforce in *Shiloh Spinners* v. *Harding*[76] have been satisfied, and certainly where an opportunistic determination has been motivated by desire to escape from an unsatisfactory transaction, or deprive the other party of its benefit, rather than by the unsatisfactory performance of the other party, approval of such actions can be withheld and their exercise held wrongful in such jurisdictions.[77]

12·030   Additionally, in countries with Codes similar to the French Civil Code, there are commonly found *"mise en demeure"* provisions requiring what is in effect a minimum reasonable period of notice of intention to rescind before a court's approval of a rescission will be obtained; but again these will not over-ride compliance with express *"de plein droit"* contractual notice provisions, and so may be of limited importance in the many construction contracts which contain express termination clauses.[78]

English law in particular would seem to have been slower to provide relief to parties with no record of persistent or serious default who are bona fide willing and able to perform their existing and future contractual obligations, but find their contracts liable to be determined on unreasonable or opportunistic grounds. The implication of a term of reasonableness restricting the exercise of the remedy in such situations, as suggested by Priestley J.A. in the *Renard Constructions* case, offers a possible basis for mitigating this harshness if the rules of relief against forfeiture cannot be more widely applied. Good faith theories might also, if, and when accepted into English law, play a useful role in this field of contract law.

---

[75] See Article 7(1) of the United Nations Convention on Contracts for the International Sale of Goods, and the UNCITRAL Model Law of Arbitration provisions which encourage parties to arbitration agreements to stipulate expressly to that effect.

[76] [1973] A.C. 691, 723 G.H., cited *supra*, para. 12·022.

[77] For rescission and *abus de droit* in France, see C. C. Article 1382, and the following Cours de Cassation decisions: April 8th, 1987, Civ. 3e Bull Civ. III No. 88, p. 53; Cass.Com. 21st February 1978; Cas.Com. 17th January 1978; Cas.Civ. 13th December 1972; Cas.Civ. 22nd February 1968; Cas.Com. January 19th, 1959, and Cas.Com. February 6th, 1957.

[78] For *mise en demeure*, see C.C. Article 1146, but see also C.C. Article 1139. This would seem unlikely to affect more substantial construction contracts in France, where express notice provisions using the necessary *"de plein droit"* formula can be expected.

(7) Necessity for Unequivocal Act

A power to determine, whether arising under the general law or express **12·031** condition of the contract, must be exercised in an unqualified manner by some act sufficient to show that the power actually has been exercised, although neither writing nor any other formality is necessary, unless expressly provided for by the contract, see also the discussion *ante*, Chapter 4, Section 3(1)(c).[79] If, as is often the case, the sense of the contract is to confer a discretionary remedy upon one or other of the parties, it will make no difference that the wording may require the contract to terminate automatically in a certain event. In such cases, some act invoking the provision by the party entitled to do so must take place.

ILLUSTRATIONS

(1) A licence by deed to mine, etc., contained a condition that if the licensee neglected to work the mines for a certain time, the indenture and the liberties and licences thereby granted should "cease, determine, and be utterly void and of no effect". *Held*, that the word, "void" in the proviso meant *voidable* by the grantor, and that in an action against the licensee for trespass it was necessary to show that the grantor, or some person claiming under him, had by some act evinced his intention to avoid the licence: *Roberts* v. *Davey* (1833).[80]

(2) A building contract empowered the building owner to forfeit the contract in case of the builder's bankruptcy. The builder became bankrupt and his trustee completed the work. *Held* by the Court of Appeal, that the trustee must be held to have completed under the original contract, and not a new contract, as the building owner had taken no active steps to forfeit: *Drew* v. *Josolyne* (1887).[81]

[Note: In this case, distinguishing *Tooth* v. *Hallett* (1869),[82] it was held by the court that, although it is not necessary that writing or any particular formality should be used in order to exercise the power, yet it must appear that as a matter of fact the power has been actually exercised.]

Thus, many construction contracts, while containing provisions for **12·032** determination on contractor default which are evidently discretionary, accompany them with separate determination provisions nominally expressed to operate automatically in certain defined events which will normally be a prelude to insolvency, as well as upon formal winding-up orders being made. In the case of the English RIBA/JCT forms there is a provision for a determination of the contract, expressed to be "automatic" in a number of events connected with the contractor's bankruptcy or liqui-

---

[79] *Drew* v. *Josolyne* (1887) 18 Q.B.D. 590, C.A.; *Roberts* v. *Davey* (1883) 4 B. & Ad. 664, *infra.*
[80] 4 B. & Ad. 664. See also *Marsden* v. *Sambell* (1880) 28 W.R. 952; 43 L.T. 120, illustrated *infra*, para. 12·052.
[81] 18 Q.B.D. 590, C.A. See also *post*, para. 14·043.
[82] L.R. 4 Ch.App. 242. See *post*, Chap. 14, Assignment, para. 14·050.

dation, but with provision for "reinstatement" of the contract thereafter by agreement.[83] Apart from doubt as to the substantive validity of any clauses abrogating contractual rights which are conditioned expressly on insolvency,[84] it is submitted that the above principles will apply and that notice or some other overt action will be necessary before such a clause can be relied on to show that the contract has been determined.

(8) Contractual Notice Requirements

(a) Generally

12·033   Nearly all modern contractual determination clauses require written notice in one form or another at the time of final determination, though not all earlier contracts did so. As has been seen, however, the notice requirements may be in "two-tier" form, with or without a requirement of continuation of the breach for a specified period of time after a "first" notice or instruction before a "second" definitive notice of actual determination can be given. In every case the clause must be carefully considered and closely followed in all respects, both as to the contents and timing of the notices, but the courts will usually regard the notices as commercial documents, and provided they make clear reference to the substance of what is required by the determination clause (and ideally, of course, by express reference to the applicable clause of the contract and special grounds in respect of which they are given) the form of words used will usually not be important. Applying this principle, notices referring the reader to the applicable clause of the contract and identifying the default are generally likely to be sufficient.[85] On the other hand, time limits or requirements must be meticulously complied with, particularly those requiring a continuation of default for a specified period.[86]

(b) Contents of notice

12·034   Particularly where a determination clause is conditioned on a number of different eventualities or defaults of the contractor, it is evident that any required preliminary notice should sufficiently identify the particular ground relied upon, if that is called for by the contract (and particularly where continuation of the default is made a condition of any second notice), but further detail, particularly in regard to a generalised ground like lack of due diligence, will not usually be called for.

---

[83] Clauses 25(2) and 27(2) of the 1963 and 1980 forms.
[84] See *post*, Chap. 16, paras. 16·056 *et seq.*
[85] *Re Stewardson Stubbs & Collett Ltd.* [1965] N.S.W.R. 1671.
[86] See *Eriksson* v. *Whalley* [1971] 1 N.S.W.L.R. 397, and the cases *infra*, para. 12·035.

Thus, in *Pauling* v. *Dover Corporation* (1855),[87] Parke B. said:

> "If the engineer had desired the plaintiff to do some particular act, for exam-
> ple, to pull down some of his work, he ought to give him a notice to that effect,
> specifying to what extent he wished to have the work pulled down; but here
> the engineer's objection is that the work is generally performed negligently,
> and that being so, the engineer is entitled to give a general notice."

ILLUSTRATIONS

(1) A building contract provided that, in case it appeared to the owner or   **12·035**
his engineer that the contractor was not proceeding to execute the work properly or with due expedition, they should be at liberty to give notice in writing
to the contractor to remedy defects or supply sufficient materials and labour,
and that on his failure to comply with such notice within seven days, they
might take the work out of his hands. The notice sent to him was: "I give
notice to you to supply all proper materials and labour for the due prosecution of the works, and to proceed therewith with due expedition, and further, that if you shall for seven days after giving this notice fail or neglect to
comply therewith, I shall, as engineer, and on behalf of the Corporation, take
the works wholly out of your hands." *Held* by the Court of Exchequer, that
this general notice was enough, and that a forfeiture for non-compliance with
it was valid: *Pauling* v. *Dover Corporation* (1855).[88]

(2) A building contract provided that in case the works were not carried on
with such expedition and with such materials and workmanship as the architect might deem proper, he should be at liberty, with the consent of the owner,
to dismiss the contractor after notice. *Held* by the Ontario Court of Common
Pleas, that such notice must intimate to the contractor in what respect the
architect was dissatisfied with the conduct of the works, and what he required
to be done as regarded expedition, material and workmanship, so that during
the time mentioned in the notice the contractor might have the opportunity of
removing the architect's objections; failing which, and after the expiration of
the time mentioned in the notice and not before, the architect might dismiss
him: *Smith* v. *Gordon* (1880).[89]
[Note: The tenth edition stated that insofar as the clause in the above case
contemplated two quite different classes of breach, the decision was easily
explicable, but that it was difficult to see how a notice requiring expedition
could be more specific, and it was submitted that a notice based on defective
work need do no more than identify the defect and need not specify cause or
remedy. The subsequent cases see *infra*, confirm this, it is submitted.

(3) Clause 25(1) of the 1963 RIBA/JCT form of contract provided that if   **12·036**
the Contractor should make default in a number of respects including "(b) If
he fails to proceed regularly and diligently with the works", then the architect
might give notice specifying the default and if the contractor should continue
such default for 14 days after receipt of that notice the owner might within ten
days after such continuance by notice determine the employment of the contractor. After many strikes and delays, the architect finally wrote "I hereby
give you notice under Clause 25(1) of the contract that in my opinion you have

---

[87] 24 L.J.Ex. 128, at p. 129.
[88] 10 Ex. 753.
[89] 30 Up.Can.C.P. 553.

failed to proceed regularly and diligently with the works and unless within 14 days after receipt of this letter there is an appreciable improvement in the progress of the works the Council will be entitled to determine your employment in accordance with Clause 25(1)". The Contractor, who had also argued unsuccessfully that the principles of natural justice applied to the determination as a whole, so that the architect was obliged to give him a hearing and receive representations,[90] additionally contended that the architect's "first" notice was invalid (a) because it did not give details or reasons why there had been failure to proceed diligently; (b) because it referred to the architect's opinion, whereas the clause made no reference to that; and (c) because the reference to an improvement in progress amounted to a representation which might have misled the contractor into thinking that the contract would not be determined provided there was an "appreciable" improvement in progress even though insufficient to constitute "regular and diligent" progress; and finally (d) because although the notice was signed by the senior partner of the firm of architects and on their headed notepaper, it did not purport to be signed on behalf of the partnership, who were the named architects in the contract. *Held*, by Megarry J., that none of these objections to the notice were justified. *Hounslow London Borough Council* v. *Twickenham Garden Developments Ltd.* (1970).[91]

12·037   (4) Under the standard E5b Australian building contract an owner in New South Wales, in the event of (*inter alia*) the contractor's failure to proceed with due diligence and in a competent manner, was entitled to determine his employment if the default was continued for seven days after a "first" notice in writing specifying the default and stating the owner's intention to determine his employment. The owner's "first" notice stated: "Pursuant to Clause 22(*a*) of the conditions ... notice is hereby given that within the terms of item (ii) of the above-mentioned clause the Proprietor intends to determine the employment of the Builder within 14 days after receipt of this Notice if the Builder fails to proceed with the Works with reasonable diligence or in a competent manner." The Contractor contended that the notice did not sufficiently specify the default and should have identified the respects in which the builder had failed to proceed with due diligence or in a competent manner. *Held*, by the Court of Appeal of N.S.W., that the defaults the subject of the clause were directed to the builder's general approach to his work and to a state of lack of diligence or incompetence rather than detailed manifestations of it, and that the notice was valid. *Brenmar Building Co. Ltd.* v. *University of Newcastle* (1977).[92]

(5) Clause 13 of the Australian Standard Domestic Building Contract BC3 provided that if the Contractor (*inter alia*) failed to proceed with due diligence and in a competent manner, and if such default was capable of remedy, and should continue for seven days after notice in writing specifying the same and stating the owner's intention to determine the contractor's employment, then the owner might do so. The owner's solicitor's "first" notice to a contractor in New South Wales stated: "We have been instructed to notify you of our client's intention to serve, not less than 7 days from the date of receipt hereof, a Notice on your company pursuant to the provisions of Clause 13, which Notice shall determine your employment as Master Builder under the said Contract on the grounds set out in sub-clause (b) of Clause 13 *viz*.: Failure to proceed with the Works with due diligence and in a competent manner." The contractor submitted that the notice did not

---

[90] See the case illustrated on this *ante*, Chap. 6, Section 5(4), para. 6·123.
[91] [1971] Ch. 233, 258–61, 264–6.
[92] December 12th, 1977, unrep.

sufficiently specify the default and that it should have identified the respects in which he had failed to proceed with due diligence and in a competent manner. He also contended that as the notice did not by its terms require the contractor to remedy the defaults, it was defective, submitting that the purpose of the notice was to give him an opportunity to remedy his default, and that the notice must make clear that the contractor was being given such opportunity. *Held*, by Smart J., following the *Brenmar* case, that the first objection was invalid. As to the second, a contractor receiving a notice in this form would be sufficiently seized of the default and the proprietor's intended course of action. Clause 13 informed him of the consequences of continued default and it was up to the contractor whether he wished to take action to avoid or nullify any notice of determination, so that the second ground of challenge also failed: *George Bevan Enterprises Ltd.* v. *Robert Patrick Ltd.* (1987).[93]

(c) Time requirements of notices

12·038

Exact compliance with time limits for notices will usually be required, and will be treated as a condition precedent to a valid determination of a construction contract. This is particularly so where continuation of a default or a state of affairs is required for a stipulated number of days before a "second" or definitive notice of determination may be served. Under most systems of law such references to a number of days are, incidentally, to "clear" days, so that any subsequent notice or action indicating determination must occur on the day following the expiry of the stipulated period. There appears to be a conflict of view between the English Court of Appeal (though in that case strictly *obiter*) and decisions in the Australian Courts, however, as to whether the final determination in a "two-tier" clause may itself be *posted* before the clear days have expired, provided it arrives thereafter, or stipulates a particular future date for the determination which is after the expiry of the stipulated period.

ILLUSTRATIONS

(1) Clause 17 of the RAIA/MBFA contract provided that if the contractor   **12·039** failed to proceed with due diligence and continued the default for 14 days after receipt of notice in writing specifying the default and stating the intention to determine the owner might thereafter determine the contract by registered mail. *Held*, by Moffit J., that a notice posted on the last day of the period and purporting to terminate the contract forthwith but which was received after the expiry of the period was not effective to determine the contractor's employment: *Re Stewardson, Stubbs & Collett Ltd.* (1965).[94]

(2) Clause 19 of the RAIA/MBFA contract provided for an initial default notice by registered post, and that the contractor's employment might be similarly terminated if the default continued for 14 days. The "second" notice was posted on the fourteenth day after delivery of the "first" notice. *Held*, by

---

[93] (1988) 7 A.C.L.R. 34.
[94] [1965] N.S.W.R. 1671.

Collins J., (*Re Stewardson* not being cited to him), the default must continue for 14 days after service of the first notice before the second notice could be posted, so that though it in fact arrived on the fifteenth day it was invalid: *Eriksson* v. *Whalley* (1971).[95]

12·040   (3) Clause 26 of the RIBA/JCT standard form entitled the contractor to determine the contract by notice by registered post or recorded delivery if the amount due on any certificate was not paid within 14 days and the default continued thereafter for seven days after receipt of a notice from the Contractor stating that notice of termination "will be *served* if payment is not made within 7 days". On April 2, 1979, a "first" notice was delivered under the clause by hand, duplicated in a recorded delivery letter posted on the same day and received by the Council on April 3, 1979. On April 10, 1979, the contractors sent a recorded delivery letter determining their employment, which was received on April 11. In an action by the contractors suing for moneys due on the certificate the council argued for the first time during an interlocutory appeal to the Court of Appeal that the determination of April 10, 1979, had been invalid. While refusing to exercise their discretion and permit the point to be raised, the Court of Appeal after argument nevertheless *held*, that even on the assumption that the delivery by hand on April 2 could not be relied on, a "second" notice of determination of a construction contract would not take effect until its receipt, and that this was confirmed by the use of the word "served" in Clause 26; that this argument had not been put to Collins J. in *Eriksson* v. *Whalley*; and that since the notice of determination was received or "served" on April 11, the notice had in fact been valid: *Hill* v. *London Borough of Camden* (1980).[96]

(4) By Clause 13 of the Australian BC3 domestic standard form the owner was entitled to determine the contractor's employment by registered mail if he failed to proceed with due diligence and continued the default for seven days after notice in writing specifying the default. The owner's solicitors gave a "first" notice in writing to the contractor on July 1, 1986, and on July 9, gave notice by registered mail determining his employment *as from* July 11 (which, allowing for the exclusion of Saturdays and Sundays under the terms of the contract, was the first day on which their employment could properly have been determined following the earlier notice). *Held*, by Smart J., that, notwithstanding that the notice, unlike the notices in the *Stewardson* and *Eriksson* cases, did not purport to take effect at once but from a future named date, the notice determining employment could not be put in the post by registered mail until after the default period had expired so that the notice was premature and ineffective: *George Bevan Enterprises Ltd.* v. *Robert Patrick Ltd.* (1987).[97]

12·041   Smart J.'s judgment in the *George Bevan* case shows that the *Stewardson* and *Erikkson* judgments in New South Wales had apparently been arrived at independently. The reasons given by Smart J. for his own ruling seem persuasive and preferable to the English Court of Appeal's construction in *Hill* v. *Camden*, which made no reference to the underlying commercial background. On their construction, an owner posting a notice before expiry of the period could not be sure that at the last minute the

---

[95] [1971] 1 N.S.W.L.R. 897.
[96] 18 BLR 31.
[97] (1988) 7 A.C.L.R. 34. Illustrated more fully *supra*, para. 12·037.

contractor might not bring his default to an end (and indeed this would be even more obviously the case in a contractor's determination based on non-payment, as in the *Hill* case, which could take place literally in the last seconds of the last day). Moreover, as Smart J. pointed out, a contractor in an owner's determination who was endeavouring to make arrangements to end the default would on this interpretation be placed in a quandary following receipt of a premature, or advance notice of termination. These practical commercial considerations point strongly, it is submitted, to the parties' consensual intentions, apart from considerations of preferring the more reasonable interpretation, as far more likely to accord with the Australian judgments in clauses where stipulated periods are required to elapse before a notice of determination, whether by the owner or by the contractor, and where either the possibility of the other party ending his breach or a minimum period of continuous breach is contemplated.

(d) Formalities of notice

It is a common feature of construction contracts at the present day that   **12·042**
they contain provisions that notices under the contract generally may be given in writing and posted to a particular address, whether of the contractor or the owner. The object of these clauses is clearly to avoid any allegation of non-receipt by higher management, for example, provided that delivery in the course of post to the stipulated address and/or recipient is proved. Additionally, it is common to find provisions that important notices, such as determination notices, and sometimes the earlier "first" notices before determination, should be given by registered mail or by recorded delivery. Given the large sums at stake on a determination of construction contracts, parties have not been slow to argue that, notwithstanding proof of actual receipt or delivery, the requirement for a particular form, such as registered mail or recorded delivery, is mandatory, so that a notice delivered by another method (as, for example, delivery by hand or by ordinary post) will for that reason alone be invalid.

It may be that in some cases at least the contractual purpose, particularly in regard to any final or "second" determination notice (where, effectively, nothing more can be done on either side and the notice must, accordingly, either by good or bad depending on its substantive justification) is that the owner can thereupon safely treat the contract as determined and begin to take any requisite action himself (as, for example, by safeguarding the site and unfixed materials) as from the time of *posting* by the stipulated means. The contractor's right to seize materials which have already been paid for at the time of a contractor's determination under the RIBA/JCT contracts, for example may be similarly safeguarded. However, there is no specific authority in point on this, and the general tendency has been to treat such notices of determination as operating from the time of *receipt* or *service* rather than of posting.[98] On any view as to that

---

[98] *Hill* v. *London Borough of Camden* (1980) 18 BLR 31.

point, however, *delivery* at a stipulated address by the stipulated means will terminate the contract at that moment without any further need for proof of actual receipt by higher management or by a fully authorised representative within the contracting party's organisation.

12·043   The object of these provisions in construction contracts would, usually, appear to be to protect the interest of *the determining party*, and not to convey some special protection or advantage on the defaulting party. In the RIBA/JCT contracts the same provisions are present in the contractor's determination clause as in the case of the owners. On the other hand, a contractor might perhaps argue, in the case of an owner's determination, that he had made his own internal arrangements for immediate action at an appropriate level on delivery of notices by the specified means of delivery to the required address, so that proven delivery by some other means might not activate his own internal arrangements and reach higher management immediately. Obviously, this argument, if it is valid at all, will apply more strongly to an earlier "first" notice, where action on the contractor's part might avert a subsequent termination, than to the "second" definitive determination notice itself.

These considerations are relevant because the governing principle in such cases appears to be that enunciated by Buckley J., in a case where a party inviting an offer stipulated a means of acceptance by himself which was not stated to be the only method which would be binding, namely that acceptance could be communicated in any other mode provided it was not less advantageous to the other party.[99] There, actual receipt of the acceptance by the defendant's surveyor was seen as more advantageous than the stipulated acceptance *by posting* to the defendant himself. Buckley J.'s statement of principle was adopted and applied by Lord Denning in the Court of Appeal, in a case where an option was to be exercisable by a stipulated date in successive years by notice sent by registered post or recorded delivery to the grantor's solicitor's registered address, but it was an unregistered letter which was received by them in time at those premises.[1] An opposing view, however, was taken by Collins J. in New South Wales in 1971, in a case where a construction contract required the "first" default notice to be by registered post, but it was in fact delivered by hand to the foreman on the site, though there were also separate timing reasons for invalidating the notice.[2] This strict view was followed in another construction contract by the Singapore Court of Appeal in 1981, where *Yates Building Co. Ltd.* v. *Pulleyn* was considered but distinguished on the ground that there were advantages to a contractor arising from such a requirement in an owner's determination clause, (although these were not

---

[99] *Manchester Diocesan Council for Education* v. *Commercial & General Investments Ltd.* [1970] 1 W.L.R. 241, 246.
[1] *Yates Building Co. Ltd.* v. *Pulleyn & Sons (York) Ltd.* (1976) 237 E.G. 183, *per* Denning L.J., applying the old American case of *Elias* v. *Henshaw* (1819) 1 Wheaton 225. See also *Goodwin & Sons* v. *Fawcett* (1965) 175 E.G. 27. This view was also supported *obiter* and tentatively by Ormrod L.J. in *Hill* v. *London Borough of Camden* (1980) 18 B.L.R. 35, 48.
[2] *Eriksson* v. *Whalley* [1971] 1 N.S.W.L.R. 397.

satisfactorily explained in the judgment), and the determination was invalidated on that ground.[3]

However, in 1991 in New South Wales, where an Australian standard form by Clauses 13 and 25 permitted notice by ordinary post for the "first" default notice, but stipulated registered mail for the "second" determination notice, Cole J., after reviewing a number of authorities in other contexts, distinguished *Eriksson* v. *Whalley* on somewhat slender grounds and held that a "second" determination notice which had unquestionably been received was fully effective in the absence of evidence of service by registered mail.[3a]

12·044

The trend at the present day certainly seems to be to accept proved service by any means, and, in the absence of express provision, requirements of form of this kind are regarded as "directory" or "facultative" as opposed to "mandatory" or "obligatory". It seems just possible, however, that different considerations might apply to "first" notices, where actual receipt by effective management is obviously likely to be critical from the substantive point of view, and the "second" definitive notices which may be little more than a communication of a decision to determine amply evidenced in any event by other actions. Proof of actual service, if relied on, will need to be made either to a stipulated address, even if by other than the stipulated means, or to a sufficiently responsible and duly authorised representative, it is submitted, and it goes without saying that the contents of the notice must show the invocation of the contractual remedy with no possibility of doubt, so as to distinguish the notice from the complaints of default or warnings of possible future determination which can be a commonplace in the correspondence between parties in construction contracts in situations where they have become at arm's length over substantive matters.

(9) Who is to Ascertain Events?

Unless the provisions of the contract are such, within the principles considered in Chapter 6 *ante*, as to make the A/E's or other certifier's opinion or decision final and binding as to the occurrence of the event on which a power to determine may be exercised,[4] this must be ascertained, as any other fact is ascertained, by a court or arbitrator. It has been seen that, *where the contract so requires*, this may extend to the reasonableness of any contractually required consideration by the owner or A/E of "show cause" representations by the contractor as to why the contract should not

12·045

---

[3] *Central Provident Fund Board* v. *Ho Bock Kee* (1981) 17 BLR 21, 35.
[3a] *Kennedy* v. *Collings Construction* (1991) 7 B. & C.L. 25, applying *Spectra Ltd.* v. *Pindari Ltd.* [1974] 2 N.S.W.L.R. 617.
[4] See for an early example in regard to a determination clause, *Stadhard* v. *Lee* (1863) 32 L.J.Q.B. 75, illustrated *ante*, Chap. 6, para. 6·025.

be determined, as also of the reasonableness of any subsequent decision by the owner to determine under the clause.[5]

The only qualification to this arises from the *Crouch* interpretation in the English Court of Appeal of those arbitration clauses in the traditional English form which confer the well-known express "open up, review and revise" power on the arbitrator.[6] If the *Crouch* view is correct, there may be a class of contracts where the A/E's certificate, or decision, or opinion under the determination clause will be binding on the courts should they become seised of the dispute, though not on an arbitrator appointed under the contract. The *Crouch* dicta has been criticised and doubted, see *ante* Chapter 6, as both contrary to principle and also, apparently *per incuriam*, to clear binding authority in England, expressly followed both in New Zealand and by the Full Court of New South Wales.[7]

(10) Interpretation of Clauses

12·046   It has occasionally been stated judicially that determination clauses will receive a strict construction, that is to say in the same sense as exclusion clauses, in an endeavour to restrain their operation.[8] There is in fact little evidence of this, probably because in construction contracts, it is suggested, the practical necessity for sanctions against delay or defective work during a long term period of occupation of the owner's land by the contractor has been recognised as reasonable, as well as, in more producer-sensitive times, the need for contractor protection against chronic non-payment. Thus, it has been seen that the courts have adopted a practical and liberal attitude to the contents of determination clauses,[9] and have shown a marked reluctance to restrain legalistic or opportunistic contractual determinations by either party by applying relief against forfeiture or good faith doctrines,[10] or by applying "unreasonable and vexatious" provisos.[11] The one respect where meticulous compliance with the letter of the clauses can be said to have been insisted upon has been in the enforcement of contractual time limits.[12]

However, one area where signs of an initial strictness of interpretation by the courts can be detected has resulted from earlier inexperienced draftsmanship conditioning owners' determination clauses on progress being insufficient to enable completion to time (begging the question, no

---

[5] *Renard Constructions Ltd.* v. *Minister for Public Works* (1992) 26 N.S.W.L.R. 234, illustrated *supra*, para. 12·025.

[6] *North Regional Health Authority* v. *Crouch Construction* [1984] Q.B. 644.

[7] See *ante*, Chap. 6, Sections 4(2) and (4), para. 6·063 and para. 6·094; and see also the author's extensive and critical analysis of the case and of the history of these clauses in construction contracts and the relevant jurisprudence, in C.C.P.P., Chap. 17. See additionally *Piggott* v. *Townsend* [1926] 27 S.R., N.S.W. 25, not mentioned in C.C.P.P.

[8] As to these see *ante*, Chap. 1, Section 9(4), paras. 1·231 *et seq.*

[9] See *supra*, paras. 12·034 *et seq.*

[10] See *supra*, paras. 12·021 *et seq.*

[11] *Jarvis* v. *Rockdale Housing Association* illustrated *supra*, para. 12·020.

[12] See *supra*, para. 12·038.

doubt inadvertently, of the perhaps more serious consequences for the owner of later delays when the contract completion date has passed). As will be seen, a more pragmatic approach by the courts later supervened when interpreting such wording.

ILLUSTRATIONS

(1) A clause in the formal agreement for the construction of a dock **12·047** provided that if the contractor should fail to complete the works within the contract period or (*inter alia*) be delayed in proceeding with the completion of the works according to the specification, it should be lawful for the owners to take the works entirely, or in part, out of his hands, and in that event the contractor was to be entitled only to sums actually accrued due at that time less the owner's expenses. The agreement was to be construed with, and to be in confirmation and enlargement of, any stipulations in the specification. The specification itself contained a separate provision that, should the contractor fail to proceed in the manner and at the rate of progress required by the engineer, his contract should be considered void so far as related to the remaining work, and all sums of money due to the contractor, together with materials in his possession, and all named penalties should be forfeited to the owners. There was no provision for extension of the completion date, but by mutual consent the contractors continued with work thereafter until the owners finally gave a lengthy notice reciting the provisions in the contract, and stating their intention to take the works out of the contractor's hands and employ others as provided in the agreement. Also in the same document, a separate notice was given that the contract should be considered void in regard to remaining work, and that the sums of money materials and penalties were thereby forfeited to the owners. On the single question whether the avoidance of the contract and forfeitures of materials and money had been valid, *held*, by the Court of Common Pleas, that the owners had not been justified in law in taking possession of the contractor's materials. *Per* Archibald J. "The clause in our opinion can only be acted upon and enforced within the time fixed for the completion of the works, for time is clearly of the essence of the contract, and it is only with reference to the time so agreed that the rate of progress can be determined. If, as has happened, the time has been exceeded, there may be a new contract to complete in a reasonable time; but to give the clause in question any application to a reasonable time after the time originally fixed has expired would be, without any express provision, to make the company judge in their own case what was a reasonable time, and to enable them in their own favour to avail themselves of a most stringent and penal clause.": *Walker* v. *London and North Western Railway Co.* (1876).[13]

[Note: It is clear from the report that the provision on which the Court had been asked to rule was the later one in the specification. The reasoning seemed to be that the "rate of progress required by the engineer" in the specification provision should be regarded as controlled by the reference to completion of the works within the period limited by the contract to be found in the preceding part of the agreement itself, although that in turn refers to the

---

[13] 1 C.P.D. 518, 531–2 (apparently followed by the Divisional Court in *Wood* v. *Tendring Rural Sanitary Authority* (1886) 3 T.L.R. 272.

contractor being "delayed or prevented in the completion of the works according to the specification."]

12·048   (2) By Clause 11 of a construction contract in Victoria, if the contractor failed to make such progress as the engineer deemed sufficient to ensure completion of the work *within the specified time*, or to execute any work in an imperfect manner and should fail to rectify any such cause or complaint for seven days after being required to do so in writing, then in either case it would be lawful for the Council absolutely to determine the contract and to seize materials belonging to the contractor. An extension of time was granted to the contractor, but the extended date then passed and no further application was made. A dispute arose with the engineer as to the way in which the contractor was carrying out the work, and the engineer gave him notice to do so properly in accordance with the contract, and subsequently the Council determined the contract. *Held*, by the Full Court, following *Walker* v. *LNWR*, that a determination after the extended contract completion date was invalid, and that materials in dispute were the property of the contractor and not of the Council: *Essendon & Flemington Corporation* v. *Ninnis* (1879).[14]

[Note: This seems a sweeping application of the *Walker* interpretation, since the dispute was over quality of work and had nothing to do with any concept of due diligence related to the completion date. It would probably be otherwise decided at the present day, it is submitted.]

12·049   (3) Clause 28 of a contract for the erection of a sewage plant provided that the contractor should carry out the work with due diligence and as much expedition as the surveyor should require and in case the contractor should fail to do so, *or* if the works were not being carried out with such progress as would enable them to be efficiently completed at the time specified, then the corporation might take the work out of the contractor's hands and take possession of his plant tools and materials as their absolute property. The completion date passed without any extension of time being applied for or granted, and work continued to be carried out until, some six months later, the corporation's surveyor gave notice requiring the contractors to complete their work satisfactorily and expeditiously, and subsequently the corporation gave notice taking the work out of their hands. *Held*, by the Court of Appeal, that a statement in Hudson's *Building Contracts* (6th edition), page 412 based on the *Walker* case was too wide; that the Official Referee had been right in holding that after the contract date had passed without any extension the duty was to complete the contract within a reasonable time; and that Clause 28 could be applied without difficulty to the situation after the completion date had passed: *Joshua Henshaw & Son* v. *Rochdale Corporation* (1944).[15]

[Note: *Walker's* case was distinguished, without any expressed disapproval, on the ground that the forfeiture clause in that case was different and did justify its result. Clearly what influenced the court was the *alternative* "due diligence" obligation in the determination clause before them, which was not in terms related to the contract date for completion. On the cases, therefore, a determination clause ineptly conditioned only upon a rate of progress related to a contract or extended contract completion date will still not be exercisable after that date. In principle this seems correct, since to hold otherwise would be, in effect, to re-draft the contract, however obvious the need for an additional contractual forfeiture ground in that situation might seem to be.]

---

[14] 5 V.L.R. 236, and see *Mohan* v. *Dundalk Newry & Greenore Railway Co.* (1880) 6 L.R. Ir 477.
[15] [1944] K.B. 381.

(11) Effect of Waiver and Estoppel

Although the circumstances may have occurred under which the right to **12·050** determine arises by the terms of the contract, an owner may find himself precluded from enforcing the forfeiture, either because he has waived his right, or because he has, by his own actions, rendered it inequitable that he should so so, and is therefore estopped;[16] just as at common law he must accept a repudiation promptly, and may lose the right to rescind by a failure to do so.[17] This subject has already been considered *supra*, subsection (7), necessity for unequivocal act.

Subject to the express wording of the clause, a contractual power of forfeiture must be exercised within a reasonable time after the occurrence of the breach on which the power is conditioned to arise.[18] Otherwise, the breach, unless it is a continuing one, will be deemed to have been waived.[19] (In principle it is clear, it is submitted, that this means within a reasonable time after the innocent party has learned of the breach, since no waiver can be imputed if in fact there is no knowledge of what is being waived, and there can be no duty owed by an innocent party to detect the breaches of the guilty party.) Further, failure to complete to time is not, generally, to be regarded as a continuing breach.[20] On the other hand, failure to use due diligence clearly is a continuing breach, and it has been suggested that as a matter of business efficacy there must be an implied term to this effect in most contracts for work and labour,[21] and that whether or not such a term is fundamental, notice will serve to crystallise the position and, if there is no improvement, establish the necessary intention no longer to be bound,[21a] thereby entitling the owner to treat the contract as repudiated.[22]

If the building owner positively treats the contract as subsisting after the **12·051** date when the right to forfeit occurs, he will be regarded, *a fortiori*, as having waived his right.[23] However, if the breach is a continuing one, the making of payments to the contractor after the breach does not amount to a waiver.[24] The extent to which mere delay in exercising a right to forfeit

---

[16] See for an analogous case, *Canterbury Pipe Lines Ltd.* v. *Christchurch Drainage Board* [1979] 2 N.Z.L.R. 347.

[17] See *ante*, Chap. 4, paras. 4·213 *et seq.*, a closely allied subject with cases highly relevant to the present discussion.

[18] Compare the cases where a "second" notice of determination is not sufficiently connected in content and time with the "first" notice, see *supra*, para. 12·007, and the *Architectural Installation Services* and *Mvita Construction* cases there illustrated or referred to.

[19] *Marsden* v. *Sambell* (1880) 28 W.R. 952, illustrated *infra*.

[20] *Platt* v. *Parker* (1886) 2 T.L.R. 786, C.A.

[21] See *ante*, Chap. 4, paras. 4·128, and Chap. 9, para. 9·032.

[21a] See *ante*, Chap. 9, Section (5), paras. 9·022 *et seq.*

[22] Only, however, if he makes his election clear—see, *e.g. Pigott Construction Ltd.* v. *W. J. Crowe Ltd.* (1961) 27 D.L.R. (2d) 258, illustrated *ante*, para. 4·158, and *infra*, para. 12·080.

[23] *Walker* v. *North Western Rly.* (1876) 1 C.P.D. 518, *Ex p. Newitt, re Garrud* (1881) 16 Ch.D. 522, C.A., *cf. Joshua Henshaw* v. *Rochdale Corporation* [1944] K.B. 381.

[24] *Cooper* v. *Uttoxeter Burial Board* (1864) 11 L.T. 565, (defective work) illustrated *ante*, Chap. 5, para. 5·010. See also *ante*, Chap. 10, Section 2, paras. 10·054 (liquidated damages).

will operate as a waiver of that right is a question of fact.[25] A waiver operates once and for all in respect of that particular right of forfeiture to which it relates.[26] Where, however, a fresh right arises, or the breach is a continuing[27] one, the new or continuing right is unaffected by a previous waiver. The following cases further illustrate the difficulties, already referred to, arising out of the older termination conveyancing habit of conditioning clauses in construction contracts upon, or by reference to completion by a stipulated date, as opposed to a requirement of due diligence or expedition.

ILLUSTRATIONS

12·052   (1) A clause in a building agreement (not amounting to a demise) provided that in case of default in not completing the buildings on successive dates the owner should be at liberty to re-enter and seize the materials. Successive defaults had been made and several periods of indulgence granted, but there had been no waiver of the last default. *Held*, by Wightman J., that the owner was entitled to re-enter and seize the materials: *Stevens* v. *Taylor* (1860).[28]

(2) Under a building agreement a builder agreed to complete by June 24. The builder was not to remove any materials delivered on the site, unless he had a written licence. There was also a forfeiture clause in the event of the work not being duly proceeded with. Part of the work was not completed by June 24. The building owner sent an agent on July 15 to prevent the removal of materials, and "to keep an eye" on the houses. The builder removed materials on July 31, under protest from the building owner. The building owner brought an action to restrain the builder from trespassing, alleging that by non-completion on June 24, and possession by the building owner's agent on July 5, the premises and materials had become forfeited. *Held*, by the Court of Appeal, Fry L.J., (1) that the intervention of the building owner's agent had not been an unqualified election to avoid the agreement; (2) that the election must be exercised within a reasonable time, or at all events not after the party against whom it was claimed had been allowed to alter his position on the faith of the continuance of the contract; but (3) that the removal of the materials on July 31 was a fresh breach of the contract, for which the building owner was entitled to forfeiture. as there had been no countervailing rescission by the builder, even assuming that the building owner had earlier refused to recognise the contract as subsisting and thereby given the builder a right to rescind: *Marsden* v. *Sambell* (1880).[29]

12·053   (3) An owner went on making advances after the failure of the contractor to complete on a particular day. *Semble*, that this amounted to a waiver of the right of forfeiture: *Re Garrud, ex p. Newitt* (1881).[30]

(4) A builder, under a building agreement, agreed to build certain houses by a certain day, and if they were then not completed, that the building owner

[25] *Morrison* v. *Universal Marine Insurance Co.* (1873) L.R. 8 Ex. 197; *Marsden* v. *Sambell* (1880) 28 W.R. 952; 43 L.T. 120.
[26] *Platt* v. *Parker, Marsden* v. *Sambell, infra.*
[27] See also for this whole subject *ante*, Chap. 4, paras. 4·213 *et seq.*
[28] 2 F. & F. 419.
[29] 43 L.T. 120, C.A.
[30] 16 Ch.D. 522, illustrated *ante*, Chap. 11, para. 11·025.

might re-enter and take possession. The building owner agreed to make advances, and the builder having failed to complete, the building owner went on making advances after the date for completion. *Held*, by the Court of Appeal, that this amounted to a waiver of the right to forfeit: *Platt* v. *Parker* (1886).[31]

There have, of course, been numerous more modern cases where, due **12·054** to the absence of a clear election by the rescinding party, whether on a contractual or common law determination, the determination has failed. If then acted upon irretrievably by one side or the other, as will usually be unavoidable given the factual matrix of any contract for work carried out on the land of another, this can easily involve a repudiatory breach by the party who is essentially in the right and, ironically, a successful rescission by the party in the wrong. These cases are referred to shortly *supra*, sub-section (7), "Necessity for Unequivocal Act", and in greater detail *ante*, Chapter 4.[32] It has been seen that these difficulties have even led to special legislation in British Columbia designed to enable a party subjected to excessive demands in the name of the contract to comply under protest without taking an ultimate stand and prejudicing his position,[33] although this type of legislation will only assist in one special type of confrontation which may produce a construction contract determination.

(12) Set-off and Contractors' Determinations for Non-payment

A special problem can often arise in the case of contractor determinations **12·055** conditioned on non-payment of sums due or certified for interim payment. These are usually, as already explained, based on continued non-payment for a stipulated period after a "first" notice requiring payment in a "two-tier" type clause. The difficulty concerns the validity of the contractor's determination in cases where the owner can put forward a cross-claim by way of set-off as justification for his non-payment of the sum certified or due.

It is evident that a contractor's determination clause can be intended, and so worded, that the right to determine is unaffected by any set-off or cross-claim not already taken into account by the certifier—in other words the interim certificate, for the purposes of the determination clause, is to be conclusive, leaving the owner with no option but to pay, and pursue his cross-claim later by arbitration or in the courts. However, it has been seen that under the traditional interim certification wording of the English RIBA/JCT standard forms (copied widely in many other contracts at home and overseas) the certificate of the architect does *not* prevent the

---

[31] 2 T.L.R. 786, C.A. See also *Felton* v. *Wharrie* (1906) Hudson, *Building Contracts* (4th ed.), Vol. 2, p. 398, illustrated *ante*, Chap. 4, Section 3(1)(c), para. 4·214 and see *post*, Chap. 9, para. 9·023.

[32] Section 3(1)(c) and (d), paras. 4·213 *et seq*.

[33] See *ante*, Chap. 4, para. 4·220.

owner raising any cross-claim *by way of defence to an action on the certificate*,[34] and indeed there is no reason to suppose that this will not also be the case under the payment provisions of the ICE standard forms. Clearly, it would be absurd if the owner was free to raise a cross-claim by way of set-off when sued for interim payment, but could find the contract successfully determined against him in such a case for non-payment of the full sum certified, and in fact there is nothing in the wording of the RIBA/JCT contractor's determination clauses, which are conditioned on failure to pay "the amount due on any certificate",[35] or "the amount properly due on any certificate",[36] which will have this effect, it is submitted.[37]

12·056   In cases where permissible set-offs exist, therefore, a contractual determination under these forms can be expected to be invalid if the owner can subsequently justify the extent to which he has failed to pay by showing a then valid cross-claim. Some owners have sought to argue, however, that should subsequent research disclose cross-claims unknown at the time of the purported determination (as, for example, defective work not yet detected at that time, or earlier accidental over-certifications in favour of the contractor for any reason), then these could be retrospectively relied upon to justify the previous non-payment of a certificate, though unknown at that time. While naturally everything must yield in such a case to the wording of the particular contract, it has been submitted earlier in this book that in the absence of any other indication expressions such as "due on any certificate" in a contractor's determination clause should be interpreted as at most permitting valid bona fide cross-claims known to the owner at that time.[38]

Even on this interpretation there can, however, remain a further, more refined problem arising from the fact that most interim certification provisions require the work to be valued up to a certain date, usually the end of the calendar month in English contracts, with certificate and payment due at intervals of a number of days thereafter, and that a cross-claim occurring or becoming known after the payment is certified, or even after it becomes due, such as a major uninsured fire, or a structural accident due to contractor default, or the discovery of a major defect, can strictly only justify a set-off against the next, but not the current, certificate. The following, although not a termination case, illustrates the point.

---

[34] See generally *ante*, Chap. 6, Section 1(1), and Section 3(3), and more particularly Section 6(7), paras. 6·194 *et seq.*, and the seminal House of Lords decision in *Gilbert-Ash (Northern) Ltd.* v. *Modern Engineering Bristol Ltd.* [1974] A.C. 689.
[35] Clause 26(1)(*a*) of the 1963 Forms.
[36] Clause 28.1.1 of the 1980 Forms.
[37] See on this "Interim Certificates: Another Heresy" [1987] 3 Const.L.J. 172 commenting on *Lubenham Fidelities and Investments Co. Ltd.* v. *South Pembrokeshire District Council* (1986) 33 BLR 39, illustrated *ante*, Chap. 6, paras. 6·042 and 6·193, where a contractor's sureties sought unsuccessfully to determine under the RIBA/JCT Forms on the basis of sums which *should have been*, but were not in fact, included in an architect's certificate.
[38] See *ante*, Chap. 4, Section 3(1)(e), paras. 4·221–4·222.

ILLUSTRATION

Contractors sued on five successive interim certificates, none of which had   **12·057**
been paid, in one action, and the owners pleaded a set-off alleging in somewhat general terms defective and delayed performance of the work as a
whole. Each certificate was required to be paid within 21 days of its issue. The
owners argued that their set-off should be assessed as at the date of the contractor's bringing the action. The contractors argued that any set-off must be
considered as at the dates when payment fell due. *Held*, by the Court of Session Inner House, that whether there was a set-off depended on a *contempo-*
rary cross-claim at the date when payment became due, and must be
considered and applied separately in regard to each successive certificate:
Redpath Dorman Long Limited v. *Cummins Engineering Limited* (1982).[39]

There appears to be an absence of authority on this difficult point as it
affects the operation of a contractor's determination clause for non-
payment. However, it has been held that contingent *future* damage which
has not as yet arisen will not invalidate a determination for non-payment.

ILLUSTRATION

A local authority failed to honour an interim certificate issued by their   **12·058**
architect, and in response the contractors wrongly reduced their labour and
plant at the site, although they maintained supervisory staff and did not
encourage nominated sub-contractors to leave. The authority asserted that
the contractors were repudiating their contract, and wrote alleging failure to
proceed regularly and diligently with the works. Five days later the contractors gave a "first" notice under Clause 26(1)(*a*) of the RIBA/JCT 1963 forms,
and subsequently a "second" notice determining their employment under the
contract. The owners responded purporting to rescind the contract at common law unless work resumed within two days. The contractors then brought
proceedings for the sums which had been certified, and the authority alleged
repudiation by the contractors' "going slow", and a set-off of damages for
delay against the certified sum, although the contract completion date had not
yet been reached. *Held*, by the Court of Appeal, that the contractors had not
repudiated the contract, since they did not purport to leave the site and their
conduct indicated they intended to treat the contract as subsisting: at most the
owners might have had some small claim if there was ultimately an undue
delay in completion of the contract as a result of the partial cessation of operations which had taken place; and the contractor's notice of determination
had been valid: *Hill* v. *London Borough of Camden* (1980).[40]

The great majority of contractor determination claims for non-payment
suffer from a drafting lacuna of this kind which can greatly reduce the
effectiveness of the clause and make its operation uncertain of success.

---

[39] 1982 S.L.T. 489, Court of Sess.
[40] 18 BLR 31.

SECTION 2. EFFECT OF EXERCISING A FORFEITURE CLAUSE

(1) Generally

12·059   A party rescinding a contract at common law will be entitled to damages, including those resulting from the forfeiture itself.[41] In the case of a contractual determination, however, the nature and extent of the rights of a party properly exercising such a power will depend on the express terms of the relevant clause. So a valid termination for sub-contracting without consent in circumstances which would not have justified a common law rescission will not entitle an owner to recover the additional cost of completion by another contractor in the absence of express provision.[42]

The legal consequence may be expressed to be either to determine the contract itself, or (even in the case of contractors' determinations under the English Standard forms) to "determine the employment of the contractor". There would appear to be no significant or practical distinction between these two expressions. Indeed in some owners' determination clauses the power is expessed as being simply one to re-enter, or to take the work out of the hands of the contractor and engage others, without reference either to determination of the contract, or of the contractor's employment. Again there would appear to be no significant meaning or distinction intended by this "re-entry" or "take-over" wording. Many such clauses are additionally accompanied by positive statements to the effect that the contract will nevertheless continue in being, or that the contractor's obligations under the contract are to remain unaffected. It has been pointed out *supra*,[43] that in most cases it is not possible to give any intelligible practical meaning even to this latter wording, and that it is in any case a feature of nearly all rescissions or forfeitures effected by one party, whether at common law or under a contractual determination clause, that there will be at least some provisions of the contract which will continue to govern the parties' rights and obligations thereafter.[44]

12·060   One general principle governing any type of determination of a contract is that, in the absence of express wording, any sums accrued due and payable *prior* to the determination will still be recoverable *whether by the innocent party or the party in breach* (subject in the latter case, of course, to any cross-claim by the rescinding party for damages).[45] Thus, following a contractor's determination for non-payment, unpaid instalments previously due (even if, for example, representing elements of advance pay-

---

[41] See *ante*, Chap. 8, Section 2(2)(d), para. 8·168 for owners' determinations and Section 2(3)(a) and (b), paras. 8·172–8·173 for contractors' determinations.

[42] *Thomas Feather & Co. (Bradford) Ltd.* v. *Keighley Corporation* (1853) 52 L.G.R. 30, illustrated *ante*, Chap. 8, Section 2, para. 8·113.

[43] See para. 12·008–12·009.

[44] *Heyman* v. *Darwins Ltd.* [1942] A.C. 356, discussed in this context with other cases *ante*, Chap. 4, Section 3(1)(h), paras. 4·227–4·229, and see also *supra*, para. 12·008.

[45] See *ante*, Chap. 4, Section 3(1)(h) and (i), paras. 4·227–4·229.

ment in substantial excess of the value of work done) will, nevertheless be recoverable in full by the party entitled unless there has been (as in construction contracts can only rarely happen) a total failure of consideration for the payments.[46] Again, in an owner's determination, any liquidated damages for delay *already accrued due* to him at the time of termination will be separately recoverable if so desired.[47] By virtue of the same principle, even a contractor who has repudiated the contract or whose contract has been validly determined by the owner will, in the absence of express provision, be entitled to recover any sums if accrued due and payable to him under the terms of the contract prior to the determination, (as opposed to the value of unpaid work carried out if not yet due).

However, owner's contractual determination clauses frequently con-   **12·061** tain an express provision that after the determination the owner will not be liable to pay any further money on account of the contract until the expiry of the maintenance period of any completion contract,[48] or until "completion" of that contract.[49] Depending on their wording, therefore, these clauses may even prevent sums already certified and due, but still unpaid at the time of the determination from being recoverable (which is quite likely to be the commercial intention of such clauses, having regard to the heavy damages liable to be incurred by any owner as a consequence of determining a construction contract) and not (as might otherwise be the case) limited in their operation to work done since the last certificate but not yet ranking for certification at the time of determination.

(2) The Rights Conferred

Modern owner's determination clauses are relatively simple, generally   **12·062** giving the owner a discretionary right to re-enter and use all materials and plant, and providing for the ascertainment of all loss and expense occasioned thereby in considerable detail, but in terms generally consistent with the rules for ascertaining the measure of damage on a rescission under the general law (which would itself entitle the owner to complete using another contractor as a recoverable head of damage for breach of contract). The earlier cases reveal a considerable variety in the nature of the rights given by building and engineering contracts to the owner under the forfeiture clause, some of which might, on principles already

---

[46] *Hyundai Heavy Industries Ltd.* v. *Papadopoulous* [1980] 1 W.L.R. 1129, H.L., distinguishing *Dies* v. *British and International Mining* [1939] 1 K.B. 724.
[47] See *ante*, Chap. 10, Section 2(3), paras. 10·047 *et seq.*
[48] Compare Clause 63 of the ICE and related contracts.
[49] Compare Clause 27.4.1 of the 1980 RIBA/JCT Forms, construed as meaning "practical completion" under those contracts in *Emson Eastern Ltd.* v. *EME Developments Ltd.* (1991) 55 B.L.R. 114.

discussed,[50] be held to be inapplicable as penalties at the present day. The following are typical examples:

(a) To seize materials

12·063
(1) To seize the materials and take possession of the whole or part of the work already done.[51]

(2) To seize the materials and use them.[52]

(3) To use up the materials and use the plant on the site to complete the works or to have them completed, without making payment for the same.[53]

(4) To use and sell the surplus materials and the plant, after completion of the works, to recoup loss.[54]

(5) To become possessed of the materials absolutely (leaving open the question of damages against the contractor);[55] or of the materials and plant.[56]

(6) To become possessed of the materials and things on the site absolutely as and for liquidated damages.[57]

(7) To become possessed absolutely of the materials and plant, paying for them the amount fixed by the architect.[58]

(b) To seize money in hand

12·064
(1) To keep or forfeit the money due or accruing due to the builder,[59] either by a condition that "the amount already paid to the builder by the employers shall be considered to be the full value of the works executed by the builder up to the time when such notice shall have expired",[60] or by a condition that "the builders shall not be entitled to claim from the employers any payments whatsoever for any work done or labour or materials provided or used since the accrual of any then preceding instalment".[61]

(2) To forfeit for breach of contract named sums of money as ascertained damages for the non-fulfilment of the contract.[62]

---

[50] See *ante*, Chap. 10, Section 1(1) and (2).
[51] *Tripp* v. *Armitage* (1893) 4 M. & W. 687.
[52] *Baker* v. *Gray* (1856) 25 L.J.C.P. 161.
[53] *Mohan* v. *Dundalk Rly.* (1880) 6 L.R.Ir. 477.
[54] *Garrett* v. *Salisbury & Dorset Rly.* (1866) L.R. 2 Eq. 358.
[55] *Davies* v. *Swansea Corporation* (1853) 22 L.J.Ex. 297.
[56] *Roach* v. *Great Western Rly.* (1841) 10 L.J.Q.B. 89.
[57] *Ex p. Newitt, re Garrud* (1881) 16 Ch.D. 522, C.A.
[58] *Roberts* v. *Bury Commissioners* (1870) L.R. 5 C.P. 310, Ex.Ch.
[59] *Roach* v. *Great Western Rly.* (1841) 10 L.J.Q.B. 89.
[60] *Davies* v. *Swansea Corporation* (1853) 22 L.J.Ex. 297.
[61] *Mohan* v. *Dundalk Rly.* (1880) 6 L.R.Ir. 477.
[62] *Walker* v. *London and North Western Rly.* (1876) 1 C.P.D. 518.

(c) To complete the works

(1) To complete the works or to employ some other person so to do, **12·065**
paying the same out of any money due to the builder on account of
the contract.[63]
(2) To take possession of the works and to pay whatever number of
men may be left unpaid by the builder, and to set on more hands
and deduct the cost from the contract price.
(3) To procure and pay for all labour and materials out of the money
that may then be due or that may become due to the contractor,[64]
and if the cost to the employers shall exceed the balance in their
hands, to recover the excess from the builder.[65]

(d) Agreement void or voidable on re-entry

The agreement upon re-entry to be: **12·066**

(*a*) Void absolutely;[66]
(*b*) Void at the option of the employers, without prejudice to any right
of action by the employers against the builder;[67]
(*c*) Void at the option of the employers as far as relates to the works or
maintenance remaining to be done.[68]

[Note: The cases cited above do not necessarily turn upon the application of the form of words with which they appear, but are, in each case,
examples of contracts in which that form of words was used.]

(3) What Sums are Included in Forfeiture

It has been seen that older determination clauses often contain provisions   **12·067**
forfeiting any moneys due to the contractor at the time of determination.
Such clauses may be held to be penalties, depending upon their exact
interpretation, and consequently of no effect without proof of actual damage.[69] But where valid, it will be necessary to ascertain precisely the moneys which are to be forfeited under the terms of the clause. A power to
forfeit retention money as such will usually not include money due and
payable under certificates already given but not yet paid, and conversely

---

[63] *Mohan* v. *Dundalk Rly.* (1880) 6 L.R.Ir. 477; *Re Walker, ex p. Barter* (1884) 26 Ch.D. 510,
C.A.
[64] *Stadhard* v. *Lee* (1863) 3 B. & S. 364.
[65] *Walker* v. *London and North Western Rly.* (1876) 1 C.P.D. 518; *Re Walker, ex p. Barter*
(1884) 26 Ch.D. 510, C.A.
[66] *Tripp* v. *Armitage* (1839) 4 M. & W. 687; *Re Garrud, ex p. Newitt* (1881) 16 Ch.D. 522, C.A.
Even where the word "void" is used, this usually means no more than "voidable". See
supra, para. 12·031.
[67] *Davies* v. *Swansea Corporation* (1853) 22 L.J.Ex. 297.
[68] *Walker* v. *London and North Western Rly.* (1876) 1 C.P.D. 518, see *supra*, para. 12·047.
[69] See generally *ante*, Chap. 10, Section 1(2) for cases including the *Egan* case, see para.
10·016.

forfeiture of certified sums may carry no implication as to sums retained. There may also be cases on the chronological borderline where work has been certified but payment is not yet due at the time of determination (many contracts prescribe a number of days, and in some "one-off" cases quite long periods, after the certificate before the sums certified become due). The commercial purpose of such forfeiture provisions is likely to be the same as in the case of those provisions which state that no further sums are to be payable after the determination prior to completion by other contractors,[70] but the wording of each contract must be closely considered.

In the case of retention, the contract may make it clear that this will not in any event become due until practical or other completion has been achieved by the original contractor. If so, the contractor will never become entitled to the money following a valid determination, so that a forfeiture provision will not strictly be particularly relevant.[71] The following early American cases illustrate the differences of interpretation which can arise in cases where an owner or his draftsman have preferred the advantages of financial forfeiture provisions of this kind rather than to seek damages for breach of contract. They are not cited as being authoritative, but should be considered together with the more modern penalties cases involving forfeiture of retention money discussed in Chapter 10.[72]

ILLUSTRATIONS

12·068   (1) An engineering contract provided for 15 per cent. retention money. The owners had power to terminate the contract if they were dissatisfied with the rate of progress, etc. *Held*, that the retention was by way of indemnity and not of forfeiture, and that the contractor was entitled to it subject to any damage sustained by the owners by reason of the default, negligence, or misconduct of the contractor: *Philadelphia, etc. Railway* v. *Howard* (1851).[73]

(2) An engineering contract provided for payment at the rate of 90 per cent. of the value of the estimated work done, and empowered the engineer, in case the contractor did not observe his contract, to declare the contract at an end, and provided that any sum due to the contractor was then to be forfeited to the owner. *Held*, by the Maine Supreme Court, that this clause only applied to the 10 per cent. retention money, and not to instalments which had been certified for: *Ricker* v. *Fairbanks* (1855).[74]

12·069   (3) In a contract for the construction of a railroad there was a condition that upon forfeiture "the unpaid part of the value of the work done" should be "forfeited by the said contractors to the use of the employers" in the nature of liquidated damages at the time of the forfeiture; the owner had in hand the 15

---

[70] See *supra*, para. 12·064.

[71] See *ante*, Chap. 10, Section 1(2), para. 10·020, and the view that for this reason forfeiture of retention would not be a penalty expressed by the Victoria Full Court in *Bysouth* v. *Shire of Blackburn* [1928] V.R. 562 there illustrated, as also *Kratzmann Holdings Ltd.* v. *University of Queensland* [1982] Qd. R 682 there illustrated.

[72] See Sections 1(2), paras. 10·006 *et seq.*

[73] 13 How, U.S. 307.

[74] 40 M. 43.

per cent. retention money, and in addition was indebted to the contractors in a certain amount on account of the monthly estimates. *Held*, by the Maine Supreme Court, that the latter amount was not intended to be included in the forfeiture, but only the 15 per cent.: *Geiger* v. *Western Maryland Railway* (1874).[75]

(4) A. agreed to do certain work for B., 10 per cent. of the payments to be retained and forfeited in case of A's breach of contract. C. contracted with A. to do the work on the terms stipulated between A. and B. C. failed to do the work and A. completed it. *Held*, by the Supreme Court of Florida, that C. could not claim the retention money: *Lara* v. *Greely* (1885).[76]

(5) H. contracted to construct a canal for the Government. The contract provided that a percentage was to be retained as security for the performance of the contract. H. abandoned the contract. *Held*, that H. could not maintain an action for any of the retained money, if the Government had been damnified to a greater extent: *Hennegan* v. *United States* (1883).[77]

However, modern forms of owner determination clause do not usually rely on financial forfeiture provisions of the kind described, with their risk of attracting invalidation as penalties, although they still survive in some Australian forms. Certainly the English standard forms proceed on the assumption that the owner will invariably wish to complete the works by another contractor, and so, with certain ancillary powers directed to that end, effectively purport, when examined in detail, to do little more than entitle the owner to the additional costs of such a completion over and above what would have been payable under the contract had the contract not been determined—in other words the same measure of damage as that permitted by the ordinary law for a contractor's breach resulting from his failure to complete.[78] This latter type of clause is considered in Subsection (4) immediately *infra*.   **12·070**

(4) Position of Owner Completing after Determination

An owner completing the contract after a determination, whether at common law or under a contractual clause, is not in the position of a mortgagee in possession whose actions are jealously scrutinised. Subject to the principles of mitigation of damage, whereby only obviously unreasonable conduct will serve to reduce the damages otherwise recoverable by an innocent party for breach of contract,[79] the owner, though naturally bound to account to the contractor and those claiming under him (as, for example, assignees of the sums due under the contract) in computing the cost of   **12·071**

---

[75] 41 Md. 4. This and the preceding cases are probably in line with modern English law in holding retention money not to be a penalty in these circumstances—see *ante*, Chap. 10, para. 10·020.

[76] 20 Fla. 926; U.S.Dig. (1885), p. 119.

[77] 17 Ct. of Cl. 273; U.S.Dig. (1883), p. 159.

[78] See this considered *ante*, Chap. 8, Section 2(2)(a) and (d), paras. 8·123 and 8·168.

[79] See *ante*, Chap. 8, Section 2(2), paras. 8·115 in the case of contractors' breaches.

completion and also in making any necessary allowances for differences between the final work and the originally contemplated contract work, will be allowed a reasonable discretion in the way in which he completes, whether this determination results from a rescission at common law or under a contractual determination clause conditioned on default:

12·072

"Now when a contractor gets into difficulties ... and the employer is in consequence put to the extreme inconvenience and annoyance of having himself to complete the work I think the employer should be allowed a large discretion in the way in which he completes it, and that the contractor, in the absence of fraud or extreme negligence, cannot complain if the work be carried out in an uneconomical manner."[80]

"The contractor cannot, in the absence of fraud or extreme negligence, complain if the work be carried on in an uneconomical manner ... every allowance should be made in considering the conduct of the employer for the position in which the default of the contractor has placed him."[81]

"It would be wholly inconsistent with the whole spirit and scope of the contract to suppose that contractors might file a bill in this court to have the whole accounts of the contract taken, because through their own default the company were obliged to take possession of the plant, the value of which was not to be ascertained by the engineer."[82]

12·073   This general duty to account for the cost of completion, relevant where an owner is claiming damages following a common law rescission, or under a contractual determination clause conditioned on default and permitting recovery either in general terms or more specifically in the form of the cost of completion itself, will not, however, exist or be relevant, it should perhaps be emphasised, if the contractual determination clause is of the financial forfeiture type discussed in Subsection (3) *supra*.[83] Provisions of that type are, in effect, liquidated damages provisions and, if not set aside as being penalties, will apply as the agreed measure of the owner's entitlement upon his exercise of the determination powers, and any profit arising to the owner as a result of an unexpectedly economic completion cost, or any loss resulting from an unexpectedly costly completion, will be legally irrelevant.[84]

12·074   Where the clause provides that the owner shall complete the works after taking possession, it would seem that completion means completion under and subject to the terms of the contract, in so far as they are then applicable, and that the owner would be at liberty to add to, alter or omit parts of the works only if and so far as there was power reserved by the contract to add to, or alter or omit. Such a clause may not be apt, therefore, to cover the owners position where he wishes to complete radically different works, and in such a case the owner may need to rely on ordinary damages rather than upon the specific remedies conferred by the clause. It

---

[80] *Per* Williams J., in *Fulton* v. *Dornwell* (1885) 4 N.Z.L.R. (SC) 207; followed in *Dillon* v. *Jack* (1903) 23 N.Z.L.R. 547.

[81] *Per* Williams J. in *Fulton* v. *Dornwell* (1885) 4 N.Z.L.R. 207.

[82] *Per* James L.J. in *Sharpe* v. *San Paulo Ry.* (1873) L.R. 8, Ch.App. 597, 610.

[83] See also the cases *ante*, Chap. 10, Section 2(1), paras. 10·027 *et seq.*

[84] See *ante*, Chap. 10, Section 1.

has already been suggested that the modern standard forms are to be criticised in that they do not make provision for this possibility by enabling the owner to sue for damages immediately upon determination should he decide to abandon the project. Many contracts also postpone any accounting until the end of any completion contract, whereas the owner's damages can in fact often be computed with considerable accuracy as soon as a priced completion contract has been agreed with a completion contractor, and the risk to the owner arising from possible contractor insolvency where the owner's rights are postponed in this way may not be sufficiently covered by this type of provision.

It should not be forgotten that, in the absence of express provision, the **12·075** owner on a contractual forfeiture will be entitled to damages assessed under the general law, if the forfeiture can also be justified under the general law. This will include the additional cost of completion and damage due to delay in completion, and indeed any other consequential losses within the rules of measure of damage,[85] and no difficulty will arise in taking account of omissions or additions in the work actually done. Nor would there be any need to await completion of the work by a second contractor.

Similarly, other heads of damage assessed in this way may be recoverable, despite the omission of the forfeiture clause to provide specifically for them. Thus, the pre-1963 RIBA forms of contract did not, while providing for the recovery of the cost of completion from the contractor on an owner's determination, make any express provision for the recovery of damages for delay in completion. If the determination was based on facts justifying rescission under the general law, it seems clear in, the absence of any expressed intention to exclude such damages, that damages for delay would be recoverable in addition to the other damages specifically provided for in the determination clause. The 1963 forms[86] were amended in the owner's interest in this respect. Whether liquidated damages are recoverable on determination under a forfeiture clause has already been considered.[87]

SECTION 3.   WRONGFUL FORFEITURE

(1) When Forfeiture is Wrongful

A contractual power of determination will be wrongly exercised if the **12·076** events upon which it is conditioned are not established (unless the contract provides for that question to be concluded by a binding opinion or certificate). In the great majority of modern contracts the question will be subject to review by an arbitrator or the courts, however; and it has also been seen that the courts have, under some clauses, been prepared to

---

[85] See *ante*, Chap. 8, Section 2(2), paras. 8·156 *et seq*., and Chap. 10, Section 2(3), para. 10·047.
[86] Clause 25(3)(*d*).
[87] See *supra*. Chap. 10, Section 2(3), paras. 10·047.

imply a term that the exercise of the power itself should be reasonable.[88] Contractual determinations will also be wrongful if exercised prematurely in breach of a contractual time limit, however marginally.[89] Even where the failed contractual determination can be "rescued" if the facts show an acceptance of a repudiation justifying a common law rescission, that may still not entirely rescue an improperly exercised contractual forfeiture, to the extent that any rights outside the general law specifically provided for in the determination clause will now not be enforceable, although the common law consequences, sometimes outside and in excess of the express remedies provided by the clause, will now be available.

12·077   Thus, premature action under a forfeiture clause conditioned on progress may not automatically involve a common law repudiation. However, some other basis justifying a common law rescission must be established.

> "It was argued that B. and D. can justify the conversion under the 'user' clause as arising on the cesser for working for fourteen days, on the ground that the receiver had in fact refused to go on, and that, although the fourteen days had not run out, there was every reason to believe the work would never be recommenced, ... but B. and D. commenced working on the ship within the fourteen days allowed, and thereby, in our opinion, prevented a resumption of work by the builders or those claiming under them. It was indeed suggested that the receiver had declared his intention of not further prosecuting the work. *But even if he had authority so to do, there is no satisfactory evidence of his having communicated to the [employers] any fixed intention on his part not to complete the ship.*"[90]

Again, although the common law right to damages confers substantial protection on the innocent party, the most important respect in which it will differ from the usual specific remedies in building and engineering contracts is that it confers no right to seize or use plant or materials not the owner's property at the time of the determination, nor any rights to assignment of the benefit of any important sub-contracts, both of which are common features of owners' determination clauses.

12·078   It is an unavoidable feature of construction contracts that an owner's purported determination will in nearly all cases constitute a repudiatory breach if, whatever the general merits, it later transpires that the determination was invalid. In such a case, if the contractor has accepted the repudiation by leaving the site, (which he must almost invariably do[91], although he may choose to allow the owner some time for reflection, since the nature of his interest in the land does not entitle him to remain on the site against the will of the owner)[92] the owner will be liable for the possibly heavy damages attendant upon repudiation and cannot, if he discovers his

---

[88] *Renard Construction* v. *Minister of Public Works* (1992) 26 N.S.W.L.R. 234, illustrated and discussed *supra*, para. 12·025.

[89] See *supra*, paras. 12·038–12·039.

[90] *Per* Fry L.J., in *Re Walker, ex p. Barter* (1994) 26 Ch.D. 510, at p. 520, C.A.; and see *Frost* v. *Knight* (1872) L.R. 7 Ex. 111.

[91] See *ante*, Chap. 4, Section 3, paras. 4·145.

[92] See however, the doubts created in England by the *Twickenham Gardens* case discussed *supra*, para. 12·001, and it and the other cases illustrated *infra*, paras. 12·084 *et seq.*

mistake, restore the contract *status quo ante* without the agreement of the contractor. On the other hand, acts short of expelling the contractor from the site, giving rise to perhaps small or nominal damage, may, though wrongful, not amount to repudiation by the owner.[93]

Thus, the purported exercise of a power to forfeit may be invalidated either by reason of the fact that the events upon which it is conditioned have not occurred; or, although such an event has happened, that under the prevention principle it was caused by the act of the party seeking to exercise it, or his agents,[94] or that a correct notice has not been given;[95] or that a sufficiently clear election to exercise the right has not been made;[96] or that there has been delay or other conduct recognising the continued existence of the contract after knowledge of the breach, if the breach is not a continuing one. Nor can a wrongful forfeiture be justified by reference to a *subsequent* event which would have justified it.[97] On the analogy of the cases relating to the dismissal of a servant,[98] however, a forfeiture purportedly made in respect of a breach which has not in fact occurred may be justified by proof of another breach *existing at the date of forfeiture*.[99]

ILLUSTRATIONS

(1) Owners determined a contract under a forfeiture clause conditioned **12·079** upon failure to proceed with the works with due diligence. The contractor pleaded that the delay was due to failure by the architect to set out the works and issue drawings in time. *Held*, by the Court of Exchequer Chamber, on demurrer, that despite an architect's certificate in the owner's favour, this was a good plea in support of the contractor's claim for damages; *Roberts* v. *Bury Commissioners* (1870).[1]

(2) A building lease agreement provided for the granting of leases of individual houses as they were completed. There was a proviso for re-entry on the unleased plots should the rent be in arrear, or if at any time the works were not proceeded with for 21 days. *Held, per* Lindley L.J., that it was doubtful if any

---

[93] *Cf.* the wrongful interference with plant in *Earth & General Contracts Ltd.* v. *Manchester Corporation* (1958) 108 L.J. 665, and the refusal to enter into a lease in *Sweet & Maxwell Ltd.* v. *Universal News Services* [1964] 2 Q.B. 699, both illustrated *ante*, para. 4·216. See also the fuller discussion *ante*, Chap. 4, paras. 4·209 *et seq.*

[94] See, *e.g. Roberts* v. *Bury Commissioners* (1879) L.R. 5 C.P. 310, illustrated *ante*, Chap. 6, para. 6·013, and Chap. 10, para. 10·030 and for the principle itself see *ante* Chap. 1, Section 6(2), and Chap. 6, Section 5(4).

[95] See, *e.g. Lowther* v. *Heaver* (1889) 41 Ch.D. 248, *infra*, and see the cases on invalid contractual notices *supra*, paras. 12·033 *et seq.*

[96] See *supra*, para. 10·031, and see *ante*, Chap. 4, Section 3(1)(c).

[97] *Re Walker, ex p. Barter, ex p. Black* (1884) 26 Ch.D. 510. Except, it would seem, in cases of bribery and fraud. See *ante*, Chap. 3, para. 3·079, and the case of *Panama, etc., Telegraph Co.* v. *India Rubber, etc., Co.* (1875) L.R. 10 Ch. 515, illustrated *ante*, Chap. 6, para. 6·109.

[98] See, *e.g. Boston Deep Sea Fishing Co.* v. *Ansell* (1888) 39 Ch.D. 339.

[99] In *Heyman Construction Ltd.* v. *Algrephy Ltd.* (February 1966, unrep.) Sir Percy Lamb O.R. did so decide.

[1] 5 C.P. 310, illustrated more fully *ante*, paras. 6·013 and 10·030. This became a favourite 19th century plea to avoid binding certificates, see *ante*, Chap. 6, Sections 3 and 6.

advantage could be taken of the clause without giving reasonable notice: *Lowther* v. *Heaver* (1889).[2]

(3) An architect fraudulently refused to give a certificate of completion, and the owners then took possession of the site and certain plant. *Held*, that their entry was wrongful; and the owners were liable in damages for the value of the works despite the absence of a certificate, on the ground that they had prevented the builder from completing the works: *Smith* v. *Howden Union* (1890).[3]

[Note: It does not appear from the report of this case whether there was a forfeiture clause or not.]

12·080   (4) F. contracted to pull down some houses for W. by a certain time, and was to pay so much a working day by way of liquidated damages for delay. F. delayed beyond the fixed time, and on being asked if he could complete in four months said that he could not say. There was no other evidence of renunciation or abandonment of the work by the builder. W. entered after 13 days and refused to let F. complete. *Held*, by the Court of Appeal, that the termination was wrongful. If W. wished to treat F.'s reply as an abandonment of the contract, he should so have informed him at once and not waited 13 days and then acted without warning: *Felton* v. *Wharrie* (1906).[4]

(5) Plastering sub-contractors were told in September, 1956 that their work would soon be required. The main contractor later neglected to provide temporary heating (as required by the main contract) which slowed down progress considerably, and later in the year told the sub-contractors that they would not now be required till the following spring. They visited the site in March, 1957, for an inspection, and made no protest till April, 1957, when they were required to start work, but refused to do so unless a new price was agreed. *Held*, by the Ontario Court of Appeal, that the failure to provide heating and consequential delay under the main contract, although it might have been a breach of an implied term in that contract to proceed expeditiously, did not go to the root of the sub-contract or constitute repudiation. Even if it did amount to a repudiation, the sub-contractors had not elected to treat it as such, but had continued to treat the contract as on foot thereafter, and they were accordingly in breach of contract: *Pigott Construction Ltd.* v. *W. J. Crowe Ltd.* (1961).[5]

12·081   In the last of the above cases, it will be seen that, had the sub-contractors continued to work under protest, they might have recovered the equivalent of their new prices by way of damages against the main contractors. The case underlines the importance in doubtful cases of minimising the risk of a wrongful rescission or termination by relying on the right to damages.[6]

---

[2] 41 Ch.D. 248 at p. 258, more fully illustrated *ante*, Chap. 7, para. 7·122. Compare the cases on "void" and "voidable" in determination clauses, see *supra*, paras. 12·031 and 12·066.

[3] Hudson, *Building Contracts* (4th ed.), Vol. 2, p. 156, more fully illustrated *ante*, paras. 6·118.

[4] Hudson, *Building Contracts* (4th ed.), Vol. 2, p. 398. This was a 42-day contract—see the case illustrated *ante*, Chap. 4, Section 3(1)(c), para. 4·214, and *ante*, Chap. 9, Section (5), para. 9·023. Compare the *Brown & Docherty* case *ante*, para. 4·215.

[5] 27 D.L.R. (2d) 258 (Canada), more fully illustrated *ante*, Chap. 4, para. 4·158. See also *Tannenbaum Meadows Ltd.* v. *Wright-Winston Ltd.* (1965) 49 D.L.R. (2d) 386, *ante*, Chap. 4, Section 1(1)(1) pp. 4·017.

[6] See this subject more fully discussed *ante*, Chap. 4, Section 3(1) para. 4·218, and the recent British Columbia legislation there referred to.

As stated, the courts have in the absence of sufficiently clear wording been reluctant to construe a provision in a determination clause requiring supporting certification by the owner's A/E or some third party as binding on either the courts or an arbitrator.[7] In the great majority of cases where this is so, a finding by either tribunal that the determination was factually unjustified must inevitably mean that the owner, by exercising the right of re-entry, however bona fide his grounds for doing so, will have committed a repudiatory breach which will have been adequately accepted by the contractor quitting the site, so that restoration of the parties to their previous position will almost invariably be impractical, leaving the courts with no option but to find that one of the parties will be liable to the other for all the consequences of a repudiatory breach.[8]

(2) Remedies for Wrongful Forfeiture

(a) Damages

Generally, the measure of damages in the case of a wrongful forfeiture   **12·082**
falls to be determined by the ordinary common law rules.[9]

> "The right of the appellant (the contractor) would be to recover such amount of damages as would put him in as nearly as possible the same position as if no such wrong had been committed—that is, not as if there had been no contract, but as if he had been allowed to complete the contract without interruption."[10]

This subject is dealt with in greater detail *ante* Chapter 8.[11]

ILLUSTRATIONS

(1) P. agreed to build a ship for R., to be paid for by four instalments of £750. P. became bankrupt, and when the ship was nearly finished and all the instalments except the last were paid, R. wrongfully took possession of the ship and prevented completion. *Held*, that the assignees of the bankrupt P. were entitled to the £750 less the cost of what was still required to be done when the defendant took possession: *Woods* v. *Russell* (1822).[12]

(2) The plaintiff had nearly completed a sewerage contract and the engineer fraudulently refused to certify. The defendants took possession of the

---

[7] See *Roberts* v. *Bury Commissioners* (1870) L.R. 5 C.P. 310; *ante*, Chap. 6, para. 6·013, Chap. 10, para. 10·030, as distinguished in *Sattin* v. *Poole* (1901) Hudson, *Building Contracts* (4th ed.), Vol. 2, p. 306, illustrated *ante*, Chap. 10, Section 2(1), para. 10·034.
[8] See the compromise attempted by the Court of Appeal of New Zealand in the *Canterbury Pipelines* case, discussed *ante*, Chap. 4, Section 3(1)(f), para. 4·223, and illustrated *ante*, Chap. 6, para. 6·134, and the other cases and the recent British Columbia legislation on this point considered in Chap. 4, Section 3(1)(c) and (d), paras. 4·218–4·220.
[9] See *ante*, Chap. 8, paras. 8·109 *et seq.*
[10] *Per* Lord Cranworth in *Ranger* v. *G.W. Ry.* (1854) 5 H.L.C. at p. 72.
[11] Section 2(2)(a) and (d), paras. 8·119 and 8·168 (contractor in breach) and 8·172 (owner in breach).
[12] 5 B. & Ald. 942.

works and certain plant. *Held*, that the plaintiff was entitled to damages for prevention of completion, such damages being what he would have been entitled to if he had completed and the engineer had certified; and judgment was given for the unpaid balance of the contract price, extras properly ordered, extras previously certified, and the value of the plant seized: *Smith* v. *Howden Union* (1890).[13]

(b) *Quantum meruit* alternative

12·083   But a contractor who has accepted the wrongful repudiation of his contract is not restricted to suing for damages for breach on contract. He may, as an alternative, where he has elected to treat the contract as rescinded, sue upon a *quantum meruit*. This will be of advantage if the contract rates have been low or uneconomical. The potential importance and value to contractors of this rule, which has its counterpart in United States jurisprudence, and its juridical basis is discussed *ante*, Chapter 4.[14-15]

ILLUSTRATION

L. guaranteed the due carrying out by M. of a contract to construct certain works for a borough council. M. made default and the council called upon L. under his guarantee. L. agreed with S. for the completion of the works by S. by a contract which provided that S. should be bound by the conditions of M.'s contract. L. left the supervision of the contract to the council, who prevented S. from proceeding with the expedition contracted for, and wrongfully seized the works. *Held*, by the Privy Council, that, as against S., L. had made the council his agent, and that, as the delay was caused by their acts, the re-entry could not be justified, so that S. was entitled to treat the contract as determined and sue for a *quantum meruit*, the measure of which was the actual value of the work, labour and materials, instead of bringing an action for damages for breach of contract: *Lodder* v. *Slowey* (1904).[16]

Forfeiture under express provisions in the contract frequently involves seizure or use of plant. Where the forfeiture turns out to be wrongful, the builder will naturally be entitled to damages for any plant seized by the owner, in detinue and conversionas.[17]

---

[13] Hudson, (4th ed), Vol. 2, p. 156. (*Cf. Smith* v. *Gordon* (1880) 30 Up.Can.C.P. 552.). Some credit would in principle be due for work not completed, if not merely trivial.

[14-15] Section 3(2)(i), para. 4·230.

[16] [1904] A.C. 442. Followed in the *Renard Construction* case in the N.S.W. C.A. and see Fitzgerald P.'s important judgment in *Iezzi Constructions Ltd.* v. *Currumbin Crest Developments Ltd.* (1994) 13 A.C.L.R. 39, Qd. C.A.

[17] See the cases collected *ante*, Chap. 11, Section 2(1), paras. 11·022 *et seq.*, and in particular the seminal judgment of White J., in *Egan* v. *South Australia Ry. Authority* (1982) 31 S.A.S.R. 481 there illustrated and discussed.

(c) Right to possession of owner

This subject has been previously discussed *ante*, Chapter 4, Section   **12·084**
4(2)[17a] and mentioned *supra*, Section 1(1).[17b] Prior to the *Twickenham
Garden* case in England in 1971,[18] English law seemed clear that no injunction will ordinarily be granted to restrain the exercise of the powers given
by a forfeiture clause, for the contractor can be amply compensated in
damages if the forfeiture is wrongful, whereas if the contractor were
allowed to continue the work, the court could not specifically enforce the
contract, nor compel the due completion of his obligations.[19] There are
many other compelling practical reasons for this view, which apply equally
where there is no forfeiture clause as such but the owner, whether or not in
breach, simply wishes to re-enter.

> "To suppose, in a case like this, where, if the company are wrong, ample
> compensation in damages may be obtained by the contractor, that the com-
> pany are to have a person forced on them to perform these works whom they
> reasonably or unreasonably object to (whereas there would be no reciprocity
> if the wrong were on the other side) for the purpose of compelling the per-
> formance of the works, is more than I am able to do."[20]
> "The court cannot enforce specific performance of the works; it cannot
> look after the acts and conduct of the plaintiff, nor say how far he does or does
> not depart from what is right in executing the works or professing to execute
> them. If he is, or shall be wronged by his exclusion from the works, and by the
> act of the company in executing the works themselves, that will be a case for
> damages to be assessed and given, either in this court or in a court of law; but it
> is not a case for specific performance, or relief analogous to specific perform-
> ance, which to proceed to grant an injunction on this part of the prayer of the
> bill would necessarily amount to."[21]

In the case of a ship-repairing contract, which provided that if the   **12·085**
repairers failed to do the work the owners should be at liberty to enter the
shipbuilder's yard and do the work, it was held by Lord Romilly M.R. that
the court could not decree specific performance of the contract, and would
therefore not restrain the builder's trustee in bankruptcy from selling the
dock in which the ship lay.[22]

But in a case where the court considered that a forfeiture clause and
arbitration clause should be read together, an interim injunction was
granted restraining the owners pending the arbitration.

[17a] See paras. 4·305 *et seq*.
[17b] See para. 12·001.
[18] *Hounslow LBC* v. *Twickenham Garden Developments Ltd.* [1971] Ch. 233.
[19] See *ante*, Chap. 4, Section 4, paras. 4·297 *et seq*.
[20] *Per* Knight Bruce L.J. in *Garrett* v. *Banstead and Epsom Downs Ry.* (1864) 12 L.T. 654. See
     also *Jennings* v. *Brighton Sewers Board* (1872) 4 De G.J. & S. 735n.
[21] *Per* Knight Bruce L.J. in *Munro* v. *Wyvenhoe, etc., Ry.* (1865) 12 L.T. 655.
[22] *Merchants Trading Co.* v. *Banner* (1871) L.R. 12 Eq. 18.

F. contracted with the corporation of H. to sink wells. By Clause 2 of the contract it was provided that if any difficulty or dispute should arise between the council or the engineer and the contractor as to the mode of carrying out the work or the interpretation of the contract or otherwise in relation thereto, the same should be referred to arbitration. Clause 10 empowered the corporation to dismiss F. from the works, if in the judgment of the engineer the work was improperly conducted, or sufficient dispatch was not used. Under this latter clause the corporation dismissed F. from the works. F. moved for an injunction to restrain the corporation from doing so. *Held*, by Farwell J., that the dispute was within the arbitration clause and there was an implied term that the owner would not act on the clause once the matter had been properly referred to arbitration until the decision of the arbitrator had been given. An injunction was granted until judgment or further order, or until the arbitrators should have held the judgment of the engineer correct: *Foster and Dicksee* v. *Hastings Corporation* (1903).[23]

[Note: This case was decided on an interlocutory application as a matter of urgency and, in so far as it related to the granting of an injunction, may not be of general application. Farwell J. clearly doubted the bona fides of the engineer, and was influenced by the fact that the owners had purported to act without any previous complaint.]

12·086　　　In certain cases a building owner would be restrained from using or selling materials or plant seized by him, where the loss sustained by him upon a forfeiture had not been ascertained, but this was of course, an entirely different situation involving the contractor's and not the owner's property.

Owners took the works out of a contractor's hands and completed them. By the terms of the contract the owners might sell the contractor's plant and apply the money in or towards the satisfaction of losses and expenses. *Held* by Lord Romilly M.R., that they could not do so until it was proved that losses and expenses had been sustained. An injunction was granted to restrain the owners from removing and selling the plant pending an arbitration: *Garrett* v. *Salisbury and Dorset Railway* (1866).[24]

12·087　　　But as a general rule the builder could not restrain the owner from forfeiting the contract, while the owner could restrain the builder from inter-

---

[23] 87 L.T. 736.
[24] L.R. 2 Eq. 358. See also *ante*, Chap. 11, para. 11·048.

fering with his taking the works out of the builder's hands, subject to an undertaking in damages if the court required it.

ILLUSTRATION

R. contracted to construct a bridge for the C. corporation. The contract contained a condition that if, in the opinion of the engineer, R. was not making due progress, the corporation might enter and complete. Under this condition the corporation gave notice to R. of their intention to enter. R. refused to give up the works. The corporation brought an action against R. and applied for an interlocutory injunction to restrain R. from preventing the corporation from taking up and completing the works. *Held*, by Chatterton V.-C. that the injunction should be granted on the corporation's undertaking in damages: *Cork Corporation* v. *Rooney* (1881).[25]

The whole of the foregoing discussion and cases on this subject, with no   **12·088**
modifications of substance, represented the law as it appeared and was stated in the tenth edition of this book. However, one additional and very important confirmatory dictum had been given by Latham C.J. in a racecourse "ticket" case in the High Court of Australia as long ago as 1937, which was not noticed in the tenth edition:

"... an ordinary building contract enables the building contractor to go upon the land for the purpose of conducting building operations so that he can perform his contract and earn his expected profit. His right continues to exist even if the building owner wrongfully repudiates the contract. But the only remedy of the building contractor for infringement of the right is in damages. If he goes on the land against the will of the owner he may be treated as the trespasser."[26]

As will be seen, there seems no doubt that at the present day this is a correct statement of the law in Australia, whatever the state of the law in England. It also accords with the underlying commercial and consensual realities of construction contracts generally.

ILLUSTRATIONS

(1) Clause 41 of an Australian building contract was a "two tier" owner's   **12·089**
determination clause conditioned on failure to maintain a satisfactory rate of progress, and both notices under the clause were duly served by the public owners of a school, who subsequently brought proceedings for an injunction to prevent the contractor from continuing in possession of the building site. There was an arbitration clause in the contract in general terms covering all

---

[25] 7 L.R.Ir. 191.
[26] *Cowell* v. *Rosehill Racecourse Ltd.* (1937) 56 C.L.R. 605, 621, [1937] A.L.R. 273, 278, *per* Latham C.J.

disputes, and the contractor applied for a stay for arbitration. *Held*, by Lush J., that the claim for an injunction could be put in two ways; firstly that the contract had been properly determined under Clause 41, or secondly that, even if the notice was in breach of the clause, the notice had served to determine the builder's licence to be upon the land, so that the action, not being founded upon the contract would not be within the terms of the arbitration clause; and that, following *Cowell* v. *Rosehill Racecourse* and *Wood* v. *Leadbitter*,[27] the builder had merely a licence to enter the land and carry out the work, which could be determined at any time and the licensee transformed into a trespasser. On the question of relief by interlocutory injunction, to refuse the injunction would mean that the owners would be compelled to accept performance from the contractor, or that nothing could be done in performance of the contract for a considerable time. The first would be against the general policy of the law, and the second obviously undesirable. Moreover, damages would not be an adequate remedy for the owners if possession was withheld, and the injunction would be granted: *Porter* v. *Hannah Builders Ltd.* (1968).[28]

[Note: In all respects this judgment might be regarded as a model of the law as then understood in England, with a careful examination of all relevant authorities. It was not cited to Megarry J. in the next following case, but Lush J.'s reliance on the *Cowell* case in the High Court of Australia, which had expressly not followed *Hirst* v. *Picture Theatres Ltd.*[29] (on which latter Megarry J. particularly relied) and the fact that the *Cowell* case was cited in the *Hounslow* case, suggests that Megarry J. would not have been persuaded to a different view.]

12·090   (2) Progress on a major public housing project became increasingly delayed, the principal cause being strikes over the implementation of the contractor's bonus scheme. At first the architect granted extensions, but ultimately came to the conclusion, following a resumption of work, that the contractors, who were demanding increased contract prices as a condition of continuing work, were not making serious or competent efforts to control the labour force or obtain proper productivity, and accordingly served notice under Clause 25 of the RIBA contract for failure to proceed regularly and diligently with the work. There being no improvement, the council owners by a further notice determined the contractors' employment. The contractors refused to leave the site, alleging that the determination was unjustified, and the Council brought proceedings for possession, damages and an interim injunction, conceding that the issue of the determination's validity would have to be litigated or arbitrated. *Held*, by Megarry J., that although the contractors had no right to insist on the owners continuing to perform the contract, the contract was for the execution of specified works on the site during a specified period; although the contractors did not have a licence coupled with an interest, the contract was at least subject to *an implied negative obligation not to revoke the licence except in accordance with the contract* during that period, so that without compelling evidence of a valid determination by notice the Court would not grant an injunction compelling the contractors to leave. Since it was not possible to come to a view on conflicting affidavit evidence whether the notices were justified, the status quo would be maintained and no injunction would be ordered: *Hounslow LBC* v. *Twickenham Garden Developments Ltd.* (1971).[30]

---

[27] 13 M&W 838.
[28] [1969] V.R. 673.
[29] [1915] 1 K.B. 1, C.A.
[30] [1971] Ch. 233.

[Note: Some of the facts in the first two sentences of this illustration do not **12·091** appear from the report, and are *ex rel* the editor. Apart from the overwhelming practical objection that the decision avowedly produces a position of legal stalemate, with a contractor in possession unable to insist on being paid and an owner out of possession unable to make arrangements for completion of the project, and apart from the objection of first principle that such a situation could not possibly have represented the contract intention, since it deprives any clause for re-entry based on controversial facts of any practical value, while presenting the contractor with what is in effect a lien on uncompleted work, the decision is open to the legal criticism that Megarry J. relied heavily on the "ticket" and "theatre license" cases in support of his "implied negative term"[31]—but these cases were different from building contracts in the most fundamental sense, since the whole object of the transaction in a "ticket" case is the occupancy of the seat by the ticket-holder for the relevant performance or period, and similarly in a "theatre" case the occupancy of the theatre by the theatre company for the period of their run; whereas the occupancy of the land in a building case is purely secondary to the primary object, which is the construction of a building for the owner by the contractor. Once that object has been effectively terminated, whether rightly or wrongly, (and specific performance cannot be granted of such a contract so as to revive it) the object of the occupancy has, it is submitted, disappeared. See the editorial criticism of the case in (1971) 87 L.Q.R. 309–12, and the exemplary discussion of these points by Lush J. in Victoria in the *Porter* case *supra*.]

(3) A building owner in New Zealand, on the basis that there had been **12·092** overpayments and defective work, refused any further payments until the defects were remedied. The contractor slowed work to a near standstill, and the owner called in new contractors, but they were denied access. The owner then applied for an interim injunction for the removal of the contractor from the site. *Held*, by Mahon J., that the licence granted by the building owner was not a licence coupled with an interest; and (not following the *Twickenham Garden* case) that there was no implied covenant not to revoke the licence in breach of contract; even if there was such a negative covenant, it was of no materiality, since the contractor would indirectly thereby obtain specific performance of the building contract, whereas the building owner could not, so there would be no mutuality. There were two principal objections—the implied licence was not necessary for business efficacy, and a contract of this kind could not be specifically enforced. The implication of a term would bring about an impasse, in which the delay before the contractor could get any further payment would be insurmountable; he would not be able to pay sub-contractors; and the architect's authority to co-operate with the builder would be withdrawn; so that the contractor could gain no benefit from staying on the job. From his point of view it would be better to claim for unpaid work to date and loss of profit, since his only object in any case was completion at a profit, while the owner's was to secure completion in accordance with the plans and specification. Both these objects could be achieved, even if the owner was in breach, if he was free to complete by another builder. Furthermore, a determination might be based on defective work. If so the *Twickenham Garden* case would compel the building owner, in a disputed case, to stand by and watch his building completed in a defective manner. No contractor or owner would ever agree to such express terms: *Mayfield Holdings Ltd. v. Moana Reef Ltd.* (1973).[32]

---

[31] *Hurst's* case see *supra*, and *Winter Garden Theatre (London) Ltd.* v. *Millenium Productions Ltd.* [1946] 1 All E.R. 678, C.A., [1948] A.C. 173, H.L.
[32] [1973] 1 N.Z.L.R. 309.

[Note: The examination, at pages 318–319 of this outstanding judgment, of the practical reasons why no terms should be implied is masterly and convincing. It also contains a clear and thorough examination of the case law as to contractual licences (at pages 316 *et seq.*), and as to the availability of specific performance (at page 321) and of the concept of mutality (at page 323). The case does not, for some reason, appear to have been cited to Helsham J. in New South Wales in the next following case.]

12·093

(4) A warehouse building in New South Wales was near completion for an investment company when disputes arose as to how much was due, and the contractor changed locks on the property to prevent the owner's agent from showing round prospective tenants. After various manoeuvres by the parties attempting to dispossess each other, the owner ultimately secured physical possession, and wrote to the contractor that the contract was at an end and that he was revoking his licence to enter or remain upon the premises. The owner no longer wished to employ the contractor for the purpose of finishing the work. Both parties had given notice of arbitration. The contractor sought a declaration that the owner was not entitled to revoke his licence, that it had not been revoked, and consequential relief. *Held*, by Helsham J. (a) that while the contractor had a contractual licence subject to an implied negative covenant not to revoke it while the contract was still on foot, the licence was revocable at will, subject only to interference by equity; (b) that equity would not order specific performance of an ordinary building contract, as opposed to building-lease type contracts; and (c) that on the assumption that the revocation was wrongful, which would have to be determined in the arbitration, no sufficient reason existed for an injunction, since damages would be a sufficient remedy, and to grant an injunction would be to force the defendant to pay a disputed claim in advance of the arbitration, or to have the building completed by a builder with whom he was in dispute: *Graham H. Roberts Pty. Ltd.* v. *Maurbeth Investments Pty. Ltd.* (1974).[33]

12·094

(5) Disputes arose as to whether there was compliance with the specification under a roadworks contract incorporating the ICE fifth edition standard form, and following a notice condemning certain work the Engineer issued a certificate pursuant to Clause 63(1)(*c*) that the contractor had failed to remove and replace the defective work after being required to do so, and the owners thereafter gave notice in writing of intention to expel the contractor from the site. The contractor disputed the validity of the notices, and obtained an *ex parte* injunction restraining the owners from removing him from the site. *Held*, by Judge Bowsher Q.C., discharging the *ex parte* injunction, that if the *Twickenham Garden* case decided that it was wrong to assist a party to break the contract and prevent the other party from performing the contract, that disregarded the agreement of the parties as to what should be done between a dispute arising and determination of the dispute by an arbitrator. Here the parties had agreed by the determination clause that the question should be put in the hands of the Engineer for the time being and the balance of convenience was strongly in favour of the Court supporting the Engineer's decision until the dispute was finally resolved: *Tara Civil Engineering Ltd.* v. *Moorfield Developments Ltd.* (1989).[34]

12·095

(6) Under a "cost-plus" building contract in Victoria the contractor's application for an extension of time was refused by the architect, and when the owner made deductions of liquidated damages the contractor suspended work. The owner then gave notice to the contractor purporting to terminate

---

[33] [1974] 1 N.S.W.L.R. 93.
[34] 46 BLR 72.

his licence to remain in possession of the site, and by further notice purported to determine the building contract. The contractor refused to give up possession, and each party applied to the Court for injunctions. *Held*, by Southwell J. following *Cowell's* case and *Porter's* case, that while it was not possible to reach any view as to the merits of the dispute between the parties, the contractor's licence to remain on the site had been revoked, whether rightly or wrongly, by the owner's notice, so that the contractor had become a trespasser, and in the circumstances an injunction should be granted to the owner restraining the contractor from continuing in possession of the site. *Per* Southwell J.: Lush J.'s statement in *Porter's* case that "The essence of the principle applied in *Cowell's* case is that the licence may be determined and the licensee transformed into a trespasser even if the determination involves a breach of contract" should be adopted as a correct analysis of the law: *Chermar Productions Pty. Ltd.* v. *Prestest Pty. Ltd.* (1989).[35]

The *Twickenham Garden* case has also not been followed, and Mahon J.'s judgment in the *Moana Reef* case preferred, in Malaysia.[36] As a statement of general principle, as well as in its application to construction contracts it is submitted that the *Twickenham Garden* case cannot be supported, although clearly there may be unusual cases where the balance of convenience may involve an owner being restrained from determining a construction contract (though even then only in a case, it is submitted, where there is an intention to complete the project on the part of the owner).　　**12·096**

ILLUSTRATION

Under the terms of a construction contract in Victoria a termination by the owner would automatically have the effect of calling in the contractor's performance bond. After receipt of a "first" notice alleging delay in progress, the contractor brought proceedings before the "second" notice to restrain the determination and the calling of the bond. The evidence showed that there had been an increase in the labour force recently, and that completion would take place in three months time; and there was no evidence before the Court of bad work being carried out, and no counter-affidavit on behalf of the owners contradicting the contractor's evidence that progress was satisfactory. *Held*, by Smith J., that on the balance of convenience an injunction should be granted: *Robert Salzer Constructions Ltd.* v. *Elmbee Ltd.* (1990)[37]
[Note: It seems a reasonable inference that a prospective calling of the bond by the owner which was not bona fide was the principal issue in this case, and the absence of evidence of a genuine need of the owner to recover possession makes the decision understandable.]

It seems clear that the *Cowell* and *Porter* cases in Australia represent the correct application, both in terms of principle and of the underlying　　**12·097**

[35] 7 B.C.L. 46 Australia, (1992) 8 Const.L.J. 44.
[36] *Kong Wah Housing Development Sdn. Bhd.* v. *Desplan Construction Trading Sdn. Bhd.* [1991] 2 M.L.J. 117, *per* Abdul Malek J.; noted in (1992) 9 I.C.L.R. 91.
[37] (1991) 10 A.C.L.R. 64.

practicalities of construction contracts, and the consensual intention indicated by the wording of contractual determination clauses, of the law of contractual licences in this field. The nature of the possession of a site transferred by an owner to a contractor is clearly limited to and governed by the carrying out of work on the site, it is submitted. If, to take an extreme example, the owner changes his mind about the desirability of the project for commercial reasons, and wishes to discontinue it altogether, there can be no doubt, it is submitted, of his right to expel the contractor, and any claim by the latter to remain and be permitted to continue the contract would be absurd. This factor alone is sufficient to negate any implied negative covenant against revocation of the license, it is submitted. If this is so, it is difficult to see how any distinction can be made in a case where, rightly or wrongly, an owner has lost confidence in the contractor's ability to complete the project satisfactorily. On these aspects of the problem the judgment of Mahon J. in the *Moana Reef* case seems wholly convincing.

It may finally be pointed out that in confrontational situations it is not unusual for each side in a construction contract to attempt contractual or common law determinations against the other at or about the same time. In such situations it is submitted that the correct approach, independent of where the merits lie, must be to safeguard the owner's ultimate right to re-possession of the site. The same considerations do not, of course apply to disputed forfeitures of the contractor's plant or materials, where, for example, a contractor's notice may well be held to prevail over an owner's seizure.[38]

---

[38] See *e.g. A.G. of Hong Kong* v. *Ko Hon Mau (t/a Koz Construction Co.)* (1988) 44 BLR 144.

CHAPTER 13

SUB-CONTRACTS

Section 1.　Generally

(1) Ordinary or "Domestic" Sub-contracts

13·001　While there may be some doubt in the case of a construction contractor's general obligations, for example, to control and supervise the site and labour-force, on the ground that these may be personal in character,[1] there is usually no objection to vicarious performance of much of the work itself, in the absence of contractual provisions to the contrary.[2] Such vicarious performance will in practice be secured by the contractor entering into what in a substantial project is likely to be a very considerable network of sub-contracts. Disregarding the contracts of employment of the contractor's own employees, these will include sub-purchases of materials, fittings or goods from merchants and others, some of which may in reality be for work, but for work carried on off the site in factory or workshop conditions by a supplier/sub-contractor, such as precast concrete units or carpentry or joinery items. Others may be for the doing of work only (that is to say, on the site), or for the supply of labour only, or for mixed sub-contracts of a "supply-and-fix" character, such as the work of erection or installation on the site of goods and fittings supplied by the sub-contractor; while others may be sub-contracts for more conventional construction work, not differing in character from the main contractor's own work. Furthermore, the growth of specialisation and technology in the construction industry has led to the widespread use of substantial sub-contracts involving not only the supply of materials and the doing of work, but also responsibility for design by the sub-contractor—examples are the structural steel or reinforced or precast concrete frame of a large modern building, specialist piling and foundation work, heating and ventilation, specialist roofing and floors, metal windows, electrical work, and so on.

13·002　Many of these latter sub-contracts, therefore, may be of a "design-and-build" character,[3] or, where no actual work but delivery only is involved, of a sale of goods character, in each case with terms likely to be implied by law, in the absence of express provision or reliance by the owner upon some other person such as the A/E, warranting the suitability of the work or materials for their required purpose.[4]

Where sub-contracting has been left to the commercial discretion of the main contractor, there will be little difficulty imposing full and unreduced express or implied obligations as to the design suitability or quality of such "domestic" sub-contracted work on the main contractor in favour of the owner, since in such cases full reliance on the main contractor, and on the

---

[1] See *post*, Chap. 14, Section 2(4), paras. 14·019 *et seq*.
[2] See *post*, Chap. 14, Section 1(2), paras. 14·003 *et seq*.
[3] See *ante*, Chap. 3, Section 1(4), para. 3·026.
[4] See *ante*, Chap. 4, Section 1(2), paras. 4·063 *et seq*., and in the context of nominated sub-contractors particularly, Section 1(2)(a)(i) and (iv), paras. 4·075 and 4·108.

main contractor alone, is apparent and easily established. Where, however, it is known from the outset that the work in question will in reality be carried out by sub-contractors or suppliers by reason of its specialist character, *a fortiori* if the sub-contractors are to be selected by or agreed with the owner under "sourcing" or nomination arrangements in the main contract itself, main contractors have constantly sought to deny reliance on themselves personally, and consequently to seek a reduction in their own liability for defective or unsatisfactory sub-contract work or materials or goods, or indeed for any other failures of sub-contract performance. These arguments will be superficially at their most attractive in cases where the sub-contractor is known to have undertaken design responsibilities.

These arguments, which are basically pleas *ad misericordiam*, have led to a substantial and not always consistent jurisprudence in all jurisdictions, due to their occasional success in persuading some courts to disregard the important and wider advantages of the chain of liability principle, first clearly enunciated in England, perhaps, in the case of *Young & Marten Ltd.* v. *McManus Childs*.[5] This subject has been discussed *ante*, Chapter 2 in the context of the delegation of design duties by the owner's A/E, and at a number of points in Chapter 4 in the context of the main contractor's contractual responsibility to the owner for the design, suitability and quality of such sub-contracted work.[5a]

(2) Nominated Sub-contracts

It is very common in English or English-influenced construction contracts   **13·003** of any degree of sophistication to find that those more important or specialised sub-contracts which contain a design element will be the subject of nomination provisions in the main contract, whereby the owner reserves the power to nominate or select a sub-contractor or supplier for identified work or materials, with whom the main contractor is then required to enter into an appropriate sub-contract. However, the English nomination system is equally available for any sub-contract deemed sufficiently important by the owner's advisers, usually from the point of view of quality or price, where no design duty is involved. Indeed, depending on the availability to the owner of a class of professional adviser in the specialized field in question, it may simply be a matter of choice or convenience whether or not such an adviser, as, for example, a heating or structural engineer or electrical consultant, will be engaged by the owner to design and supervise the sub-contract work, or whether on the other hand its design will be left to the nominated sub-contractors, who in that

---

[5] See *ante*, Chap. 2, paras. 2·114 to 2·123, and Chap. 4, paras. 4·075 *et seq.*, paras. 4·079, 4·108, and the cases illustrated *ante*, paras. 4·082 to 4·099, particularly 4·092 *et seq.* (Design); paras. 4·119 to 4·123 (Materials); and paras. 4·124–4·125 (Workmanship).
[5a] See *ante*, Chap. 4, paras. 4·060, 4·073 *et seq.*, 4·091 *et seq.*, and 4·108–4·110.

case will in their sub-contract, expressly or impliedly assume the design responsibilities themselves in their sub-contract.[6] In either of these design situations identical main contract nomination procedures are in practice likely to be used. In some cases, of course, no class of design professional may be available to the owner, as with many manufactured installations, such as high speed lifts, or electrical switch gear, or waste disposal plants, so that, as in the case of some turnkey main contracts, there will often be no practical alternative for the owner but to rely on the specialist manufacturer or supplier of the goods or work processes in question for their design and suitability.[7] A number of such cases are illustrated *ante*, Chapter 4, Section 1(2)(a)(iv).

13·004   In the United States the relatively primitive solution often adopted by owners and their advisers has been to stipulate a restricted list of named sub-contract "sources" for identified parts of the work or materials in the original tender contract documents, from which the tendering contractor is left free to choose and price his own tender, and this practice or method also, of course, obtains in many English specifications, sometimes in more general terms, which do not actually name sub-contractors or suppliers, but require the work to be of an "approved" quality or from an "approved" source.[8]

In the United States, a common type of arrangement in Government contracts, not involving owner nomination as such but giving a substantial degree of negative control, is to require a tendering main contractor to name in his tender the sub-contractors he proposes to use for certain identified parts of the Works, and to bind himself, if awarded the contract, not to use any other sub-contractor for the work in question without the consent or approval of the owner. The Court of Claims has been ready, however, to imply that such approvals should not be unreasonably withheld, and has held the owner liable to the contractor in damages for breach of contract where consent was capriciously withheld and the sub-contract later had to be terminated with consequential loss to the main contractor.

ILLUSTRATION

13·005   Clause 24 of a Government contract provided that there should be no substitution for a named sub-contractor for the clearing and footings work on a 57 mile transmission line, unless there was an "unusual situation after the award" and the contractor was to submit a complete justification for the change in writing and obtain the approval of the Contracting Officer. The contractor found out on the day following the award of the main contract that there were doubts as to his proposed sub-contractor's financial standing and supplied the information he had about this to the Contracting Officer, but the latter did not examine the evidence he supplied; received representations

---

[6] For the complications of, and effect on the design responsibility of any professional advisers to which these arrangements can give rise, see *ante*, Chap. 2, Section 6(2)(a), paras. 2·114–2·123.

[7] See *ante*, Chap. 3, paras. 3·026 *et seq.*, and paras. 4·108 *et seq.*, and see C.C.P.P., paras. 24–06 *et seq.*

[8] See, *e.g.* the cases illustrated *ante*, Chap. 5, Section 1(5), paras. 5·017–5·019.

from the sub-contractor alleging "bid-shopping" by the main contractor which he did not pass on to the latter for his comments; and considered himself bound by the contract wording to refuse to allow another sub-contractor or the main contractor to do the work. Later the sub-contractor was in serious delay due to financial difficulties, and the main contractor finally had to complete the work himself. *Held*, by the Court of Claims, that the discretion in Clause 24 was not absolute and the Contracting Officer had acted arbitrarily and capriciously in refusing consent, so that the contractor was entitled to damages for breach of contract. *Meva Corporation* v. *United States* (1975).[9]

However, the system for nomination of sub-contractors which eventually evolved in England by the end of the Second World War was considerably more sophisticated, and detailed. The system, and the owner's and his A/E's duties under it, has been described in considerable detail *ante*, Chapter 4, Section 2(5),[9a] to which reference should also be made. Its principal characteristics (until the evolution of still more complicated systems in the 1973 ICE and 1980 RIBA/JCT forms) have been as follows:

13·006

    (i)   The owner, not the contractor, is given a wide power to select sub-contractors *at any appropriate time after the main contract has been entered into.*

   (ii)   While the work or materials to be sub-contracted in this way could, in theory be described in detail in the original main contract documents, a system involving use of some convenient symbol, such as a P.C., or Provisional Sum inserted in the bills of quantities or specification, with only a bare minimum of description amounting perhaps to one sentence of a few words, is used to identify the parts of the work in respect of which the power to nominate may be exercised. In a great number of cases under this system detailed drawings or specifications of the sub-contracted work will only be received by the main contractor at the time of the nomination instruction.

  (iii)   To eliminate the impractical pricing uncertainty which such a system would otherwise inevitably induce, the main contractor is entitled to a risk-free price and profit on the nominated work, in the shape of whatever may turn out to be the "prime cost" (that is, the final net cost to the main contractor) of the sub-contracted work—in other words, whatever may be finally due to the sub-contractor under the terms of his sub-contract—plus a stipulated profit additional to this prime cost.

  (iv)   The English standard methods of measurement and standard forms of contract in combination produce, in both industries, rates of profit for nominated work very greatly in excess of any obtainable by a contractor pricing for his own work even in the

13·007

---

[9] 511 F 2nd 548.
[9a] See *ante*, Chap. 4, paras. 4·184–4·191.

most favourable market conditions. This is achieved partly by inviting contractors to tender a percentage or other *profit* against items for that purpose in the bills of quantities or specification (with a recommended 10 per cent. often to be found in the standard methods as an acceptable figure), together with additional items for *attendance* to be priced by the contractor, and finally, and even more importantly, by deceptively worded provisions for a "cash discount" in the standard forms. In any other industry, these latter might have been expected to justify a charge of misdescription, since the "small print" of the English standard forms, in both industries, discloses that in fact no financing element justifying a "cash discount" description is involved, and the items in question are in reality pure profit in the main contractor's hands entitling him to a further 2½ per cent. or 5 per cent. of pure profit on turnover for work and materials-only sub-contracts respectively. This is because the main contractor, under the detailed payment provisions of the standard forms of main and sub-contract (in both industries) will be entitled as against the owner to receipt of main contract interim payments, which will be inclusive of sub-contractor's accounts, a stipulated number of days *before* he himself will become liable to pay the sub-contractor for the work or goods in question.

(v) As a further safeguard for contractors, the English standard forms usually give the contractor the right to object to a nomination on a number of stipulated grounds. These provisions are usually poorly conceived and rarely, if ever, avoid a difficult and impractical impasse in the event of factual disagreement as to the ground of objection.[10]

13·008   The profitability combined with the risk free element of the pricing of nominated sub-contract work under the English standard forms, which in some projects in the United Kingdom can reach a proportion as high as 50 or 60 per cent. of the total contract price, and which by reason of the gearing element in construction work can represent a huge return on the capital employed, is such that in times of recession it is in practice used to subsidise loss-making prices quoted by competing main contractors in respect of their own work. Moreover, the flexibility of the system in postponing the necessity for full pre-planning at the tender stage, while at the same time committing the client or the contractor to the project by permitting it to go out to tender nevertheless, has also made it attractive for both good, but frequently bad, reasons in professional quarters. Both these factors, and particularly the element of risk free profitability, tend to be

---

[10] See, however, the "owner over-ride" solution, which protects both parties, devised in Clause 22(3) of the Singapore S.I.A. Contract Conditions, reproduced in C.C.P.P., paras. 591–2.

firmly concealed or suppressed in discussion of the nomination system in the industry, where persistent but ingenuous criticism of the alleged unfairness of the system is advanced in order to justify and achieve reductions in the main contractor's responsibility for nominated sub-contractor default. There has seemed to be insufficient understanding of this background by the English judiciary in more recent years since the *Jarvis* case in 1969, with the result that, in a number of cases where the draftsmanship has been obscure, they have allowed themselves to be persuaded into interpretations having the effect of breaking the "chain of liability" between owner and defaulting sub-contractor by absolving the main contractor (and so inevitably the sub-contractor) from responsibility for nominated sub-contractor default, in contrast to earlier relatively robust judicial decisions.[11]

Ordinary or domestic sub-contracts create few if any problems for owners. The owner will have selected his main or "prime" contractor for normal commercial reasons, and insofar as his own advisers may wish to secure or impose rights and obligations in respect of the work to be carried out, these can be effected in the main contract, and nothing agreed between the main contractor and his sub-contractors can serve to reduce the contractor's eventual responsibility to the owner, or the latter's rights against the main contractor as stipulated by the main contract. Insofar as, for practical purposes, it may be necessary for other contractors with different skills to take part in the project, their ideal status from the owner's point of view will be as sub-contractors to the main contractor, leaving all problems of co-ordination and control with the main contractor. On the other hand, should the owner decide for any reason to enter into any direct contractual arrangements giving him rights against such other contractors, the owner may well find himself under potentially serious implied liabilities to the main or prime contractor, or indeed to any other direct contractors, for any loss or disturbance caused by the other contractor.[12]

13·009

---

[11] See, *e.g.* for this latter trend *Gloucestershire County Council* v. *Richardson* [1969] 1 A.C. 480, illustrated *ante*, Chap. 4, Section 1(2)(b), para. 4·122; T.A. *Bickerton & Sons Ltd.* v. *North West Metropolitan Regional Hospital Board* [1970] 1 W.L.R. 607 (H.L.), discussed and analysed *ante*, Chap. 4, Section 2(5), paras. 4·193–4·194, and extensively considered *infra*, Section 3(2); *Norta Wallpapers (Ireland) Ltd.* v. *Sisk & Sons (Dublin) Ltd.* [1978] I.R. 114, illustrated *ante*, Chap. 4, Section 1(2)(a), para. 4·092; *John Jarvis Ltd.* v. *Rockdale Housing Association Ltd.* (1987) 36 BLR 48 C.A., illustrated *ante*, Chap. 5, para. 5·036, and Chap. 12, Section 1(4)(b), para. 12·020, discussed and criticised in detail (1987) 3 Const. 274; and *Scott Lithgow Ltd.* v. *Secretary of State for Defence* (1989) 45 BLR 1, H.L., illustrated *ante*, para. 5·037, and discussed and criticised (1991) 7 Const. L.J. 3. Contrast *Young & Marten Ltd.* v. *McManus Childs Ltd.* [1969] 1 A.C. 454, illustrated *ante*, Chap. 4, Section 1(2)(b), para. 4·121; *J. Jarvis & Sons Ltd.* v. *Westminster Corporation* [1970] 1 W.L.R. 637, illustrated *ante*, Chap. 10, Section 5, para. 10·099, and see particularly the judicial criticisms in that case; and *Independent Broadcasting Authority* v. *E.M.I. Electronics Ltd.* (1979) 11 BLR 29 (C.A.) ((1980) 14 BLR 1, H.L.), illustrated *ante*, Chap. 4, Section 1(2)(a), para. 4·094. For this subject generally, and for a discussion of the latest RIBA/JCT cases in England up to 1986, see C.C.P.P., Chap. 21, and see the cases *ante*, paras. 4·108 *et seq.*

[12] For the owners responsibility for other contractors see *ante*, Chap. 4, Section 2(3)(c), paras. 4·151 *et seq.*, and see this developed, from the point of view of an owner's choice of contracting arrangements for a project in C.C.P.P., paras. 23–36—38 and 24–10—12.

It will be seen that the crucial nature of the advantage and indeed objective sought by owners in arranging for sub-contracting, and so distancing themselves from responsibilities to or for such other contractors on the project, was early recognised and given effect to in the English courts even in those earlier construction contracts where the intention in regard to such other selected contractors had not been spelt out in very clear terms.[13]

13·010   As a matter of simple analysis, it is evident that any deliberate reduction of main contractor responsibility, or any assumption of owner responsibility to compensate a main contractor for sub-contractor default, must be potentially disastrous for the owner, since in the absence of his entering into some sort of separate contractual relations with the defaulting sub-contractor, thus defeating his principal objective, the owner will have no available remedy against anyone. Moreover, and since by definition the owner's remedy against the main contractor will have been reduced or eliminated, the latter's contractual rights as against the sub-contractor, at least in regard to the owner's losses or would-be claims, will to that same extent have been emasculated as a result of the main contractor's own contractual protection in that regard. This will reduce both the incentive and available sanctions for full enforcement of the sub-contract by the main contractor. By contrast, the "chain of liability" principle, whereby the main contractor remains fully liable to the owner for sub-contractor default, whether or not personally at fault, will enable the main contractor in turn to bring home full responsibility for the owner's loss as well as the main contractors "personal" damages against the defaulting sub-contractor, acting as a healthy inducement to proper performance by the sub-contractor.

Nor should it be assumed that "direct warranty" or other contractual relationships between owner and sub-contractor provide easy or satisfactory solutions. On the contrary, such arrangements, if known to all at the time of entering into the various contracts, will be calculated to introduce bewildering complications into the interpretation of the express or implied responsibilities of the various parties for defaults of the other parties in what will have become essentially triangular relationships. For example, it would become arguable by main contractors that the known existence of owner "direct warranty" remedies against a sub-contractor made unnecessary the implication of any terms in the main contract as to the suitability, quality or timely progress of such a sub-contractor, and even that the owner was now impliedly responsible to the main contractor for any defaults of the sub-contractor, and that ambiguous main contract provisions should be interpreted in that light. Precisely similar anomalies will also arise from any compensatory pro-

---

[13] See *infra*, Section 2, and in particular the *Leslie*, *Mitchell* and *Hampton* cases there illustrated.

visions in the main contract if interpreted as extending to sub-contractor default.[14]

The case law showing the application, and on occasions rejection, of this **13·011** fundamental principle of main contractor responsibility for sub-contractors, nominated or otherwise, and in the particular context of the design or suitability and quality of work for materials, has been reviewed in considerable detail in Chapter 4.[15]

Those concerned with drafting main contracts should therefore be particularly careful to fix the main contractor with the fullest responsibility in every respect for the work of nominated or selected sub-contractors. There is no hardship in this, since the main contractor, who under most modern forms of contract has, as already stated, wide express powers to reject selected sub-contractors who will not enter into a suitable sub-contract (and who, it has been submitted, has an implied right in any event to refuse such nominations[16]), or indeed for any more general reason, such as incompetence or inadequate financial resources will be entitled, when sued or suffering deduction at the hands of the owner, to recover damages to an equivalent amount under the sub-contract. The draftsman should also bear in mind that any provision or interpretation of a main contract absolving the main contractor from responsibility for acts or defaults of a nominated sub-contractor is open to the serious objection that it will prevent the owner from recovering his loss from either party.

Draftsmen have traditionally sought to assert the undiminished **13·012** responsibility of the main contractor for the nominated sub-contractor's work by the use of some such expression as "such persons are hereby declared to be sub-contractors employed by the contractor"[17] or "shall be deemed to be sub-contractors of the contractor."[18] This phrasing was adopted because certain decisions of the courts prior to the First World War had held that the contractor was entering into these sub-contracts as agent or trustee for the owner, and the draftsman clearly considered that such wording would be sufficient to indicate a no privity, and therefore no responsibility, objective.[19]

These expressions had been entirely successful in this aim for at least 70 years prior to 1970, and it was regarded as axiomatic, for example, that in the event of an abandonment or repudiatory breach by a nominated sub-

---

[14] See *Scott Lithgow Ltd.* v. *Secretary of State for Defence* (1989) 45 BLR 1 H.L. illustrated *ante*, para. 5·037, which graphically illustrates the anomalies arising from the extension of an ambiguous compensatory provision to include sub-contractor default. See the case analysed and criticised in "Beyond the Contractor's Control", (1991) 7 Const. L.J. 3. For the similar anomalies arising from the interpretation of an extension of time provision as applying to sub-contractor delays, see *J. Jarvis & Sons Ltd.* v. *Westminster Corporation* [1970] 1 W.L.R. 637 and the outspoken comments of the House of Lords in that case, cited *ante*, Chap. 10, Section 5, paras. 10·098 *et seq.*

[15] See *ante*, Chap. 4, Section 1(2)(a), (b) and (c). See also *infra*, Section 3.

[16] See *ante*, Chap. 4, paras. 4·060 and 4·185.

[17] *Cf.* Clause 27(*a*) of the RIBA/JCT 1963 conditions.

[18] *Cf.* Clause 59(1) of the ICE 1955 (4th edn.) conditions.

[19] See, however, *infra* para. 13·087, where the House of Lords disregarded the wording in the *Bickerton* case.

contractor, the main contractor would himself be in breach of contract, entitling the owner to damages, though the position in regard to selection of another sub-contractor remained unclear. The history on this point has been reviewed in detail earlier in Chapter 4, in the context of a possible obligation of the owner to renominate a second sub-contractor in this situation.[20]

Apart from this form of express wording in the two principal private sector contracts, the English government contract CCC/Wks/1 and its successor GC/Wks/1 had made the position even clearer by simpler and more direct wording:

> "The Contractor shall make good any loss suffered or expense incurred by the Authority by reason of any default or failure, *whether total or partial*, on the part of any [nominated] sub-contractor."[21]

Moreover, in the later GC/Wks/1 contract any duty of the owner to renominate is expressly rejected.[22]

13·013   However, in the case of the RIBA/JCT contracts, this principle (and indeed the already quoted express "declaratory" wording of those contracts) was ignored by the House of Lords in 1970 in the case of *Bickerton* v. *North West Metropolitan Regional Hospital Board*,[23] when holding that, on a disclaimer of a nominated sub-contractor's sub-contract by the sub-contractor's liquidator, the owner was under a duty to the main contractor to renominate a successor sub-contractor in such a situation, and also to meet the additional costs of the replacement sub-contractor's higher price. It would seem to follow that on this view (if accepted) the main contractor was not himself to be regarded as in breach of contract. Whether or not this was so, the tenth edition, published in the same year as the case, stated that the *Bickerton* interpretation "can confidently be predicted to occupy the time of the English courts for many years in an effort to control and regulate the difficulties and anomalies to which it must inevitably give rise."[24] *Bickerton*, and the subsequent cases in which the courts have endeavoured in similar situations to grapple with the difficulties it has created in the interpretation and application of the RIBA/JCT main contract forms (prior to the new explicit policies of the 1980 forms), as well as of the many English and Commonwealth forms which have continued to use the pre-1980 RIBA wording,[25] are extensively considered and illustrated *infra*.[26]

---

[20] See *ante*, Chap. 4, Section 2(5)(b), paras. 4·191 *et seq.*
[21] GC/Wks/1, 1973 (2nd ed.), clause 31(3). ("Total" connotes a repudiatory breach, "partial" non-repudiatory.)
[22] *Ibid.*, clause 38(5), clearly *post* Bickerton drafting.
[23] [1970] 1 W.L.R. 607, extensively considered *infra*, Section 3(2). See also *ante*, paras. 4·193 *et seq.*
[24] Tenth edition, p. 742.
[25] See, *e.g.*, *City of Adelaide* v. *Jennings Industries* (1985) 57 A.L.R. 455 High Court of Australia, the subject of C.C.P.P., Chap. 22.
[26] See Section 3(2), paras. 13·066 *et seq.*

(3) Express Prohibitions on Sub-contracting

These usually take the form of prohibitions on sub-contracting any part of **13·014**
the work (that is, in making arrangements for its vicarious performance)
without the approval or consent of the owner. They are to be found in
almost all English standard forms, with or without savings that the owner's
consent should not be unreasonably withheld, and often in association
with prohibitions against "assignment of the contract".[27] The sanction for
enforcment is usually to be found in the owner's termination clause.

Even where there is no express provision that consent should not be
unreasonably withheld, it is submitted that in many cases, depending on
the nature of the project, such a limitation may need to be implied, though
there is little authority on this in the Commonwealth.[27a] If so, the contractor, if able to show loss, could recover damages for the breach. Thus, it
has been seen that an arbitrary and unjustified refusal to permit the substitution of a new sub-contractor for one whose financial resources were in
doubt has been held by the United States Court of Claims to be a breach of
an implied term of the contract.[28]

SECTION 2.　BUILDING OWNER AND SUB-CONTRACTOR

(1) Generally

There are three principal ways in which an owner, notwithstanding the
existence of a sub-contract made between his main contractor and a third
party, may nevertheless exercise rights or remedies, or be subject to liabil- **13·015**
ities, as between himself and the sub-contractor. These will be, first,
through a liability in tort; secondly, through the procedural mechanism
provided by what have recently become known as the "name borrowing"
provisions to be found in modern English main or sub-contract forms of
contract, particularly the RIBA/JCT forms, whereby the owner is empowered by the main contract to sue the sub-contractor in the name of the
main contractor, or conversely where the sub-contractor is empowered by
the sub-contract to sue the owner in the name of the main contractor; and
thirdly by reason of a "direct warranty" or contract entered into between
the owner and sub-contractor in addition to that between the sub-contractor and main contractor. These three relatively special situations are
separately considered in subsections (3), (4) and (5) *infra*.

---

[27] See *ante*, Chap. 14, Section 6, paras. 14·055 *et seq.*, and the *Linden Gardens* case, para. 14·057.
[27a] See *ante*, Chap. 12, Sections 1(5) and (6) for the possibility of equitable relief or an implied term of reasonableness.
[28] *Meva Corporation* v. *U.S.* 511 F 2nd 548 (1975), illustrated *supra*, para. 13·005.

(2) No Privity of Contract

13·016   It cannot be over-emphasised that no privity of contract between an
owner and another contractor can arise out of a sub-contract concluded
between the owner's main contractor and the other contractor. Where the
sub-contractor has been selected by the owner, as in the case of nominated
sub-contracts, early attempts were made to argue that the main contractor
or the A/E had on the facts contracted as an agent or trustee of the owner,
and at one time this view appears to have prevailed in the courts, at least in
relation to nominated or selected sub-contractors.[29] However, the later
cases made it clear that only the most special and unusual facts, showing
that the owner expressly or by some unusual conduct authorised the main
contractor or the A/E so to contract, would justify such a finding, which is
contrary to the purpose of the usual main contract and the practice and
expectation when negotiating contracts informally between the various
parties in the construction industry.[30]

The history of the courts finally (and rightly) rejecting the notion of
privity between a building owner and his selected sub-contractor is shown
in the cases illustrated at the end of the present subsection,[30a] but under the
present system of nomination, which is widely used and understood in the
industry, it can often happen that architects need to obtain quotations
from and negotiate with tendering sub-contractors (particularly those
whose work or products are subject to long delivery dates) during the
planning stage of a project at a time when the identity of the ultimately
successful tendering main contractor may still be unknown. In such cases
it is generally well understood by the parties that the sub-contractor will in
due course be required to enter into a sub-contract with the successful
main contractor when appointed. Sub-contractors, however, even after
accepting an order from the main contractor, sometimes seek to rebut the
usual inference of privity with the main contractor if the main contractor
becomes financially embarrassed, in an endeavour to charge the building
owner for their work; and it is easier to advance such an argument in cases
where the original sub-contract negotiations have taken place with the
architect. The two modern cases now illustrated are examples of this type
of situation.

ILLUSTRATIONS

13·017   (1) An architect, prior to letting the main contract, which was in the 1948
RIBA form, arranged with a nominated supplier of facing bricks for stocks to
be held available for delivery by certain dates. In due course the main contractor placed his order, having been informed by the architect of the delivery

---

[29] See *Crittall Manufacturing Co.* v. *London County Council* (1910) 75 J.P. 203 and other
cases illustrated *infra*.
[30] See, *e.g. Hampton* v. *Glamorgan C.C.* [1917] A.C. 13, *infra*.
[30a] See *infra*, paras. 13·031 *et seq*.

arrangements which he had made with the supplier. The supplier defaulted on his promised dates, and the architect authorised certain changes in the work to assist the contractors in the resultant shortage of bricks. The main contractors claimed extra payment under additional loss and expense provisions for compliance with architects instructions on the ground that the arrangements for delivery and subsequent later changes in the work amounted to architect's instructions on behalf of the owner involving a variation. *Held*, by Sellers J., following *Leslie* v. *Metropolitan Asylums District* and *Mitchell* v. *Guildford Union*,[31] that the delivery arrangements were part of the nomination; that the supply contract was a separate one between contractor and supplier and that the main contractor was bound to provide the bricks by the stipulated dates; and the change in the work being authorised to assist him in a matter which was primarily his liability, no variation was involved: *Kirk & Kirk Ltd.* v. *Croydon Corporation* (1956).[32]

(2) A contract in South Africa contained a clause for the nomination of suppliers for all practical purposes identical with that in the RIBA standard forms. Reinforcement steel was to be obtained from a nominated supplier under a P.C. item.[33] At an interview at which was present a representative of the owner, the architect, the main contractor and the supplier, the latter was asked by the architect to reduce his prices but refused to do so. The supplier stated he would require a deposit of £3,000 and complained about the main contractor being a slow payer, but was reassured by the owner's representative, who said that a substantial loan had been arranged and that the supplier would be paid monthly on the certificates issued to the main contractor by the architect. Later that day the architect wrote a letter to the supplier as follows: "*On behalf of our clients* [the owners] *we accept your tender*. ... The sum of £3,000 to be paid by S. Keidan & Co. (the builders) on acceptance of this order by you ...," to which the supplier replied by letter making various stipulations including "the sum of £3,000 to be paid as mentioned above" and ending "Our acceptance of your order is hereby confirmed." The main contractor the same day wrote to the owners authorising them to pay the £3,000 and debit the main contractor's account. It was not clear whether the architect had sent the main contractor copies of his letter to the supplier and their reply, but the main contractor was at all times aware of the arrangements being made. *Held*, by the South African Court of Appeal, following *Hampton* v. *Glamorgan C.C.*[34] and *Leslie* v. *Metropolitan Asylums District*,[35] that the language of the main contract effectively permitted the architect, notwithstanding that he was the agent of the building owner, to conclude a contract between the contractor and the sub-contractor, and that bearing this in mind the correct inference on the facts, in spite of the wording used in the correspondence, was that the contract had been made between the main contractor and the supplier and not with the owners: *Concrete Construction Ltd.* v. *Keidan & Co. Ltd.* (1955).[36]

The South African Court of Appeal in the above case is to be congratulated on drawing the correct conclusions from the practice of the industry   **13·018**

---

[31] Both illustrated *infra*, paras. 13·032 and 13·034. For the changes in the work, see the case illustrated *ante*, Chap. 7, para. 7·028.

[32] [1956] J.P.L. 585. Unfortunately the report is very short.

[33] *I.e.* it was to be supplied by a nominated sub-contractor—see *infra*, Section 3.

[34] See *infra*, para. 13·037.

[35] See *infra*, paras. 13·032.

[36] (4) S.A. 315 South Africa.

and giving effect to the true intention of the parties in the face of very inaccurate descriptions of their arrangements made by the parties themselves. The reference by the court to the architect contracting as agent for the contractor is not, as the court itself made clear, to be taken literally; the case decides that where an A/E in negotiation with sub-contractors is known to be acting under the nomination procedures of the main contract he will be regarded as negotiating on behalf of the main contractor rather than the owner, since it is with the main contractor that the sub-contractor is expected to contract, although the A/E will have neither implied, nor ostensible authority to contract for either party in the full sense.[37]

ILLUSTRATION

An architect informed a sub-contractor that his tender was accepted and that in due course an order would be placed by the main contractor. The main contractor's order introduced a new term that the main contractor would be under no liability for interim payment until approved and paid for by the owner. The sub-contractor started work, which was certified but not paid for by the owner, and the sub-contractor sued the main contractor, arguing that the architect's letter had concluded the sub-contract terms. *Held*, by Blain J., no contract had been concluded with the architect, and the sub-contractor had accepted the main contractor's additional term by starting work without protest, so that his claim failed. *Davies Shopfitters Ltd.* v. *William Old* (1969).[38]

13·019   In cases where work has to be put in hand and an order of some kind placed before the main contractor has been selected, however, there may be a contingent liability of the owner to the sub-contractor, in the event that no main contractor materialises ready and willing to place the necessary order.[39] The nature of this liability will depend on the exact terms of any negotiations between the owner or his A/E and the sub-contractor. It should be remembered that a private A/E cannot, without express authority, bind his client in contract,[40] so that it is not impossible that if unauthorised negotiations have taken place between the A/E and the sub-contractor on the faith of which the latter has commenced work, the A/E may find himself personally liable for breach of warranty of authority.[41]

Another situation in which, despite the general rule of lack of privity, the owner and sub-contractor may establish a direct legal relationship may arise if during the course of negotiations warranties are given or representations made by a supplier or sub-contractor on the faith of which the

---

[37] As to the latter, see *ante*, Chap. 2, paras. 2·061 *et seq.*
[38] 67 L.G.R. 395; 113 S.J. 262.
[39] Compare the analogous contingent liability of the owner for quantity surveyor's fees under the old practice, *ante*, Chap. 2, para. 2·287.
[40] See *supra*, n.37. For local authority architects see *ante*, paras. 2·065–2·066.
[41] See *ante*, Chap. 2, Section 5, para. 2·080.

owner or his A/E instructs the main contractor to place his order with the sub-contractor.

ILLUSTRATIONS

(1) The director of a paint firm interviewed the managing director of pier-owners and later their architect, and made representations as to the suitability of his company's products for the protection of the pier from corrosion, as a result of which the main contractors were required to order the firm's paint. On the paint proving defective, the pier owners sued the paint manufacturers, alleging that the representations were contractual warranties as to the suitability of the paint given in consideration of the pier-owners causing their contractors to order the paint. *Held*, by McNair J., that the contention was correct and the manufacturers were liable to the pier-owners in damages: *Shanklin Pier Co. Ltd.* v. *Detel Products* (1951).[42]

13·020

(2) The nursery manager of the plaintiffs, who were chrysanthemum growers, visited the defendants, who were sand suppliers, looking for a fine sand suitable for propagating the plants. The defendants suggested a particular sand, and produced an analysis of it showing a very low iron content. An assurance was also given that deliveries would conform to the sample. The defendants quoted a price "*ex pit*" but said it might be cheaper for the growers to provide their own transport. Apart from one delivery, the plaintiffs did not buy the sand directly from the defendants, but placed orders for it with a firm specialising in the transport of building materials, which itself obtained the sand from the defendants' pits. The plaintiffs were in fact induced to buy the sand by the defendants' representations, which were incorrect but innocent, as the iron content was far higher than that indicated, so that the plants were damaged. *Held*, by Edmund Davies J. the statements were not mere representations, but were warranties forming part of a collateral contract, and were enforceable notwithstanding that no specific main contract was discussed at the time they were given. Two ingredients only were needed, (1) a promise or assertion as to the nature, quality or quantity of the goods which might reasonably be regarded as made with an intention to create legal relations and (2) acquisition of the goods in reliance on the promise or assertion: *Wells* v. *Buckland Sand Ltd.* (1964).[43]

Where an owner receives a representation of this kind from a sub-contractor *after* all contracts have been concluded, so that consideration from the owner in deciding to order the placing of the sub-contract will not be

13·021

---

[42] [1951] 2 K.B. 854.
[43] [1965] 2 Q.B. 170. See for another similar representation by a supplier who appears to have become directly liable in contract to the owner, *Sealand of the Pacific* v. *McHaffie* (1974) 51 D.L.R. 3d 702 (B.C.C.A.), illustrated *ante*, Chap. 2, para. 2·117. See also for another type of collateral warranty in early negotiations *Welsh Health Technical Services Organisation* v. *Haden Young*, illustrated *infra*., para. 13·054.

present, owners today may be able to frame an action against a sub-contractor representor in tort, under the *Hedley Byrne* principle.

ILLUSTRATION

Owners of a television mast in the course of erection wrote to the sub-contractors, whom they had designated in the main contract as its designers, informing them of violent oscillations which had occurred in another similar mast owned by them at another site, and suggesting fuller investigations in order to confirm the original data used for the design calculations of the mast currently under construction. The sub-contractors, by letter dated November 11, 1969, replied to the owner's letter stating that while the oscillations of the other mast might well exceed their permitted limits, in regard to the present mast, "we are well satisfied that the structures will not oscillate dangerously". Following receipt of this letter the owners took no further action. Subsequently, following completion of the mast, it collapsed in conditions of icing and high winds, and the owners then sued the sub-contractors in both contract and tort. *Held*, by the House of Lords, (a) over-ruling the trial judge and Court of Appeal, and applying *Heilbut Symonds & Co.* v. *Buckleton*,[44] that neither side had any contractual intention in their exchange of letters, so that no collateral warranty as to the stability of the mast had been given in contract, but (b) that the sub-contractors had owed a duty of care to the owners when replying to their letter, and that since their design had as a fact been negligent and the owners had relied on the letter when deciding to take no further action, which could well have resulted in the design error being corrected, the sub-contractors were liable in tort to the owners for a negligent misrepresentation under the principle of *Hedley Byrne* v. *Heller: Independent Broadcasting Authority* v. *E.M.I. Electronics Ltd.* (1980).[45]

13·022   It has been explained *supra* that the principal reason why, even in the case of sub-contractors selected by the owner, a contractual relationship with the owner will not easily be inferred (for instance, by holding that the main contractor or architect contracted with the sub-contractor as agent for the owner), is that an informed owner wishing to have construction work carried out usually sees overriding advantages in dealing with one contractor for the performance of the whole work. By this means he obtains one price for the whole work, avoids a multiplicity of contracts and liabilities, and the complicated problems of delay and interference which would certainly arise if the works were to be carried out by various contractors and their workmen, each separately employed by him to perform various parts of the work on the same site, though dependent on each other for speedy and economical progress. In such a situation the ultimate financial responsibility for co-ordinating the work of the various sub-

---

[44] [1913] A.C. 30.
[45] 14 BLR 1.

contractors would fall on the owner, who would become, in effect, his own main contractor.

There is also the consideration, particularly for owners without the commercial advantage of having further work in their gift for the future, that direct contractors will be far more likely to advance and press disturbance and co-ordination claims against a building owner than they would do on the same facts as sub-contractors against a main contractor, on whom they would be likely to be dependent for future work on other contracts. This is particularly true, of course, of domestic sub-contractors, but much less true of nominated sub-contractors, particularly in those cases where, as under the producer-dominated English standard forms, the main contract terms expressly enable the main contractor to pass on sub-contract claims to the owner, as must occur wherever terms are included in a main contract reducing or eliminating the main contractor's responsibilities or providing him with compensation for nominated sub-contractor default, or where claims against the owner are effectively encouraged by offering name-borrowing procedures to the sub-contractor in the sub-contract documentation.

13·023

This intention is not negatived by the fact that in well-drafted contracts the owner expressly retains the *right* (subject to compensation) to employ other contractors on the site himself,[46] since without such a right the main contractor could object that he was not being given free and unfettered possession of the site[47] even though the other work was not connected with his own either in point of time or location, and it is as a defence against such claims that these provisions are primarily directed.

In re-stating the general inference that privity of contract between owner and sub-contractor does not exist, it is quite irrelevant that the sub-contract may in its terms follow closely those of the main contract; for instance, by provisions making the sub-contractor's payment dependent upon the certificates or satisfaction of the architect under the main contract, or empowering the architect under the main contract to order extras or variations in the sub-contract work.[48] Usually such provisions only have the effect, as between the main contractor and the sub-contractor, of constituting the architect the main contractor's administrative agent in the same sense that he is the owner's agent under the main contract.[49] Nor is it relevant that the sub-contractor will normally be conferring a benefit upon the owner by doing the work, which he cannot retrieve, as he could in the case of a chattel, by virtue of the work being attached to the owner's

13·024

---

[46] Clause 29, 1963 RIBA forms; Clause 31, 1955 ICE form.
[47] As to which right see *ante*, Chap. 4, paras. 4·150 *et seq.*
[48] Where there is no such power, the architect, by ordering variations from a sub-contractor, may render the owner liable for them. See illustrations, *infra*.
[49] See, *e.g. Geary, Walker & Co. Ltd.* v. *Lawrence* (1906) Hudson *Building Contracts* (4th ed.), Vol. 2, p. 382, illustrated *infra*, para. 13·101. (The interpretation of sub-contracts which purport to incorporate all or some provisions of the main contract, often in informal terms, frequently gives rise to difficulties due to lack of precision or forethought when providing for the incorporation in vague and general terms. See Section 4, *infra*.)

land,[50] unless the sub-contractor can bring himself within the principles of unjust enrichment and quasi-contract.[51]

13·025   An important consequence of this lack of privity between owner and sub-contractor is that, in the event of default by the sub-contractor, while the main contractor can of course sue for breach of contract, in such a case he can only recover to the extent of his own damage, not the owner's, and the two types of damage will usually differ very considerably. Thus, the main contractor's damage caused by sub-contractor breaches will be in the form of the reduced profitability of his own contract, due, for example, to the loss of productivity and extended site overhead costs of his own work, or meeting claims by other sub-contractors, or the cost of making good or repairing the sub-contractor's defective work. Only to the extent that the main contract exposes the main contractor to claims by the owner resulting from the sub-contractor's breaches will there be any similarity between the owner's and main contractor's damage. It is this factor which usually makes complicated "name-borrowing" procedures, and those contemplated by the English RIBA/JCT standard forms in particular, of reduced practical value in dispute situations. These procedures are discussed *infra*, Sub-section (4).[51a]

13·026   It has already been pointed out that the RIBA standard forms in effect confer immunity on defaulting sub-contractors against meeting *the owner's* losses on a delayed contract by expressly giving the main contractor a right to an extension of time for nominated sub-contractor's delays,[52] and a remarkable result of this is seen in the *J. Jarvis* v. *Westminster Corporation* case,[53] where a sub-contractor operating an informal "name-borrowing" procedure (with a "neutral" and indemnified main contractor not taking part in the argument though a party to the proceedings) was actually (though in the end unsuccessfully) asking the court to accept that delay to the works *had been caused by his own default* on a true interpretation of Clause 23(g),[53a] in order to avoid his own liability to pay the owner's liquidated damages to the main contractor for onward transmission to the owner.

In what clearly seems to have been a similar but informal "name-borrowing" exercise, a defaulting sub-contractor, admittedly fully liable in contract to the main contractor for the delays and damage caused by

---

[50] See *ante*, Chap. 5, paras. 5·003 *et seq.*
[51] See *ante*, Chap. 1, Section 11.   [51a] See paras. 13·046 *et seq.*
[52] (While at the same time taking explicit pains to see that any damages recovered from a sub-contractor shall be the property of the contractor and not the employer—Clause 30(5) (c) proviso—and while attempting to make specific provision to assist in the recovery of liquidated damages *for the contractor* from the sub-contractor—Clause 27(a)(vi), 1963 forms.) See Chap. 10, Section 5, para. 10·098 and the outspoken criticisms of this provision by Viscount Dilhorne and Lord Wilberforce in the House of Lords, and by Salmon L.J. in the Court of Appeal in *J. Jarvis Ltd.* v. *Westminster Corporation* [1969] 1 W.L.R. 1448, C.A., [1970] 1 W.L.R. 637, H.L., there quoted. See also *infra*, para. 13·061 where this provision is further criticised in a passage cited and approved (in its ninth edition form) by Edmund Davies L.J. in the same case, [1969] 1 W.L.R. 1448, 1453.
[53] [1970] 1 W.L.R. 637 (H.L.), illustrated *ante*, Chap. 10, para. 10·099.
[53a] See, *per* Viscount Dilhorne in the *Jarvis* case, [1970] 1 W.L.R. 637, 645.

replacing defective cables supplied by him in a submarine under construction, succeeded in enforcing an unwisely worded compensatory provision in the main contract against the owner in respect of loss incurred by the main contractor as a result of the sub-contractor's admitted breach.[54]

Nor can difficulties of this kind be overcome by an assignment of the main contractor's rights under the sub-contract to the owner, even if the assignment were not to be invalidated as being an assignment of a bare right to sue.[55] Such an assignment could only pass the same rights as those enjoyed by the main contractor.[56]

The only certain way to overcome such difficulties is to ensure by   **13·027**
express provision in the main contract that the work of selected sub-contractors is described in sufficient detail, that any desired warranties as to the quality, design or suitability of the sub-contracted work are set out in the main contract as well as in the sub-contract, and that express provisions absolving the main contractor from responsibility for selected sub-contractor's work are rigorously avoided.

With regard to the latter point, no professional adviser of an owner will discharge his responsibilities competently at the time of preparing contract documentation it is submitted, if he does not at the very least draw his client's attention to the anomalous and potentially damaging consequences of any such provisions.

However, it must be said that in England producer pressures have, since   **13·028**
1973 in the case of the civil engineering standard forms[57] and since 1980 in the case of the RIBA/JCT Building Standard Forms,[58] introduced elaborate nomination schemes (in the latter case of extreme if not impractical complication). These involve a total reversal of the principle of unqualified main contractor responsibility for nominated sub-contractor fault which has hitherto been the essential feature of English nomination systems: the broad effect of both schemes is to make the owner ultimately responsible to the main contractor for all consequential losses arising from nominated sub-contractor default, including repudiated and terminated sub-contracts, together with greatly strengthened (and easily abused) powers of main contractor objection to a nomination. The ICE provisions are perhaps less objectionable from an owner's point of view in at least endeavouring to fix a *solvent* sub-contractor in default with initial primary responsibility, while ensuring ultimate owner responsibility to the main contractor should the sub-contractor become insolvent. Further consideration of these schemes (which are, of course, in marked contrast

---

[54] *Scott-Lithgow Ltd.* v. *Secretary of State for Defence* (1989) 45 BLR 1, H.L., illustrated *ante*, Chap. 5, para. 5·037, the subject of, and criticised in, *Beyond the Contractor's Control*, (1991) 7 Const. L.J. 3.
[55] See *post*, Chap. 14, "Assignment", paras. 14·025 *et seq.*, but see *Constant* v. *Kincaid* (1902) 4 F. (Ct. of Sess.) 901 there referred to, where a bankrupt shipbuilder was permitted to assign to the owner a right to damages for defective work against a sub-contractor.
[56] For a full discussion of the difficulties, see Section 3, *infra*, Building Owner and Contractor.
[57] Clauses 59A(6), 59B and 60(7), commented on and explained in the editor's *The ICE Conditions of Contract* (5th ed.) pp. 196–202, *et seq.*
[58] Clauses 35 and 36, 1980 Edition, in combination with NSC4 sub-contract.

to the provisions of the English GC/Wks/1 government contract,[59]) and the willingness of the English government and public authorities to permit the use of these two standard forms of contract on public projects without protest is, for this apart from more fundamental reasons, surprising.

13·029   At this point in the tenth edition, it was submitted that any express or implied warranties given by a sub-contractor in a nominated sub-contract would not only enure for the benefit of the main contractor under the sub-contract but, by virtue of the "chain of liability" principle enunciated most clearly in the House of Lords in *Young & Marten Ltd.* v. *McManus Childs Ltd.*,[60] would become part of *the main contractor's obligations* to the owner, even if not expressly repeated in the main contract documents, as a result partly of that principle, and partly of the correct interpretation of the post-war English standard form nomination wording in both industries. There is now authority supporting this view,[61] and it is submitted that these cases are clearly right, but there have also been some relatively recent cases which appear to be inconsistent with it.[62]

The subject of main contractor responsibility for nominated sub-contractor default is discussed *infra*, Section 3, and has already been reviewed in some detail, in the context of the main contractor's design and workmanship responsibilities, in Chapter 4.[63]

13·030   The following cases illustrate the somewhat difficult stages by which the courts came to recognise the underlying realities of the various contractual relationships surrounding the sub-contracting of building and civil engineering work, together with the later and rather more sophisticated contracts under which owners expressly came to retain the right to nominate or select sub-contractors and suppliers. These cases remain fully relevant in the interpretation of the very many construction contracts which, both domestically and internationally, have continued to follow the pre-1973 and pre-1980 nomination schemes of the English civil engineering and building standard forms.

---

[59] See the provisions of clauses 31(2) and (3) and 38(5) of that contract cited *supra*, para. 13·012 (the latest edition has, however, made a retreat in insolvency cases, reflecting producer influence even on central government procurement).

[60] [1969] 1 A.C. 454, illustrated and discussed *ante*, Chap. 4, Section 1(2)(b), paras. 4·121, and see paras. 4·072 *et seq.*

[61] See particularly *Comyn Ching & Co. Ltd.* v. *Oriental Tube Co. Ltd.* (1979) 17 BLR 49, 77, *per* Robert G. Goff L.J.; *I.B.A.* v. *E.M.I.* (1980) 14 BLR 1 (H.L.); and *H. Fairweather & Co. Ltd.* v. *London Borough of Wandsworth* (1987) 39 BLR 106 (Judge Fox Andrews Q.C.). See also the discussion *ante*, Chap. 4, paras. 4·108–4·110.

[62] *Norta Wallpapers (Ireland) Ltd.* v. *John Sisk & Sons (Dublin) Ltd.* [1978] I.R. 114 (Irish C.A.); *Holland Hannen & Cubitts (Northern) Ltd.* v. *Welsh Health Technical Services Organisation* (1981) 18 BLR 80 (Judge Newey Q.C.); and *University of Warrick* v. *McAlpine* (1988) 42 BLR 1 (Garland J.), and the other cases *ante*, Chap. 4, paras. 4·082 *et seq.*

[63] See *ante*, Chap. 4, Section 1(2)(a)(b) and (c), paras. 4·079 *et seq.*, 4·108–4·110, and 4·117–4·124.

ILLUSTRATIONS

(1) A. contracted with B. for certain works on A.'s house. C. supplied goods   **13·031**
to B. for use in such works. *Held*, that A. was not liable to C. for their price:
Bramah v. *Abingdon* (Lord) cited in *Paterson* v. *Gandasequi* (1812).[64]

(2) S. employed T. to do certain work. E., who it emerged, after an action by
him against S. had commenced, might be a sub-contractor under T., did certain work, which E. alleged was outside T.'s contract, and he sued S. for the
price of it. *Held*, by Channell B., that E. must prove a distinct contract
between S. and himself: *Eccles* v. *Southern* (1861).[65]

(3) During the progress of building works, the architect, *in the presence of
the building owner*, requested a plastering sub-contractor to gauge the plas-
terwork, which was a more expensive process than that specified, and told him
he would be paid extra. The sub-contractor sued the owner for the extra cost.
Held, there was evidence to go to a jury that the architect had to this extent
been authorised to contract on behalf of the building owner: *Wallis* v. *Robinson* (1862).[66]

(4) A building contract made with the plaintiffs as main contractors pro-   **13·032**
vided that the owners "reserved to themselves the right to employ other parties to execute the works for which provisions are made, and to deduct the full
provided amount (*i.e.* the prime cost plus 10 per cent.) thereon from the contract sum. In such cases the contractors are to allow such parties every facility
for the execution of their several works simultaneously with their own. The
managers are to be at liberty to omit any provisional sums or quantities. *The
contractors are to pay the sub-contractors* the amount provided in the contract
for such purpose, or less or more, as may be certified, and the payments thus
made will be considered as work done by the contractors, and will be included
in the certificate to the contractors next following such payment. No payment
is to be made to such sub-contractors except upon the architect's certificate.
The contractors are to pay such amount as may be certified from time to time
within seven days from the date of the certificate, and should the contractors
neglect or refuse to make such payment within the said period, the managers
shall be at liberty to pay the amount thereof to such sub-contractors, and to
deduct from the contract sum the gross amount which the contractors have
included in their estimate in respect of such work and their profit thereon, the
amount so to be deducted not being less in any case than such amount so
certified." Under the contract, chimney stacks and heating apparatus were
designated as work and materials to be provided by specialists. Specialists
were appointed to execute this work by the architect, who made terms with
them. The plaintiffs were then instructed by the architect to give the orders
and did so, and the work was executed. The main contractors sued the owners
for damages for delay caused by the specialists. *Held*, by the Court of Appeal,
that although the contract would have empowered the owners to contract
direct with the specialists, the specialists had in fact been employed by the
contractors, and the architect's negotiations had in fact been on behalf of the
contractors,[67] who consequently could not recover damages from the owners:
Leslie & Co. Ltd. v. *The Managers of the Metropolitan Asylums District*
(1901).[68]

---

[64] 15 East 66.
[65] 3 F. & F. 142.
[66] 3 F. & F. 307.
[67] Compare *Concrete Construction Ltd.* v. *Keidan*, see *supra*, para. 13·017.
[68] 68 J.P.R. 86.

[Note: This early application of the "chain of liability" principle was expressly approved by Bankes L.J. in the Court of Appeal in *Hampton* v. *Glamorgan County Council*[69] and it and that case in the Court of Appeal (rather than in the House of Lords where the judgments are somewhat generalised) represent, it is submitted, the two early cases of greatest value and authority in this field.]

13·033
(5) Clause 28 of the current RIBA form of contract provided that the provisional sums mentioned in the specification for materials to be supplied or work to be performed by special artists or tradesmen should be paid and expended at such times and in such amounts and in favour of such persons as the architect should direct and the sums so payable should be payable by the contractor without discount or deduction *or by the employer* to the said artists or tradesmen. At the settlement of accounts the amount paid by the contractor to the said artists or tradesmen should be set off against all such provisional sums and the balance added to or deducted from the contract sum. The architect selected a sub-contractor under a provisional sum to supply iron balcony railings, which were delivered, invoiced and debited to the contractor, who wrote back that the architect would certify the amount direct to the owner. Later the architect sent the supplier a certificate *addressed to the owner*, and the sub-contractor sued the building owner *on the certificate*. *Held* by the Court of Appeal, that Clause 28 contemplated payment either by the main contractor or the owner. The proper inference on the facts was that the contractor was acting as agent for the owner, in such circumstances that while the contractor might himself be liable to the sub-contractor, he nevertheless also rendered his principal liable: *Hobbs* v. *Turner* (1902).[70]

[Note: In *Milestone & Sons* v. *Yates Brewery* (1938)[71] Singleton J., in a case where the same form of contract was used, doubted if Clause 28 by itself could effect privity between the owner and sub-contractor and clearly regarded the case as turning upon the later correspondence and on the fact of the certificate being issued to the owner. See also the comments of Lord Haldane L.C. in *Hampton's* case. This form of contract was probably designed to permit the owner the accounting alternative of paying direct, as between owner and contractor, without affecting questions of liability, it is suggested.]

13·034
(6) The plaintiff contracted to do certain works for the defendant owners for a lump sum. The contract provided that the engineering and other specialist work was to be done by named firms, who were to be paid by the plaintiff. The plaintiff *was not to be liable for delay caused by the specialists* or for defective plant supplied by them unless he was guilty of contributory negligence. The specialists caused delay in the execution of the works which caused damage to the plaintiff. The plaintiff sued the owners for this damage alleging that there was an implied promise by them that the delivery of the machinery should not be unreasonably delayed or that the delivery and fixing should be made and done at such reasonable times during the erection of the buildings as would enable the plaintiff to complete the same within the time fixed by the contract or within a reasonable time thereafter. *Held*, by Phillimore J. following *Leslie's* case, that there was no such implied promise and, there being no contract between the defendants and the specialists, that the owners were not liable for the delay: *Mitchell* v. *Guildford Union* (1903).[72]

13·035
(7) The L.C.C. employed L. & Co. as main contractors to erect a building. The contract provided that casements should be ordered from specialists. The

[69] (1915) 84 L.J.K.B. 1306.
[70] 18 T.L.R. 235.
[71] [1938] 2 All E.R. 439, illustrated *infra*, para. 13·124.
[72] 68 J.P. 84.

architect to the council invited the plaintiffs to quote for these casements, saying that the accepted quotation would be inserted in L. & Co.'s contract as a P.C. item; that the plaintiffs should enter into an agreement with L. & Co. to complete the casements to time under a penalty; that the council's architect should have power to vary the work, and that payment should only be made upon the certificate of the council's architect. The plaintiffs quoted a price, and the council requested L. & Co. to order the work, and L. & Co. informed the plaintiffs that they were requested by the council to accept the quotation. The plaintiffs sued the council for the price of the work. *Held*, by Channell J. that while the contract for the casements was prima facie between L. & Co. and the plaintiffs, it was also a contract by L. & Co. as agents for the council, because it was to procure something for their benefit, and because in contracts made to procure work which is the subject of a provisional sum or prime cost item, the building owner is the real principal, and because the price was quoted to the building owner and not to the contractors: *Crittall Manufacturing Co.* v. *London County Council* (1910).[73]

[Note: The reasoning of Channell J. summarised in the above case was expressly disapproved by all three judges in the Court of Appeal[74] in *Hampton* v. *Glamorgan County Council, infra* (see [1917] A.C. at pp. 16 and 17) and by Lord Shaw of Dunfermline, *ibid.* at p. 22, and it is clear that this case, and the case of *Young & Co.* v. *White* (1912) 28 T.L.R. 87, *infra*, was wrongly decided and must be regarded as overruled.]

(8) W. engaged N. to carry out the work of erecting a building. The contract with N. provided that "all specialists executing any work or supplying any goods for which prime cost prices or provisional sums are included in the specification who may at any time be nominated, selected or approved by the architect are hereby declared to be sub-contractors employed by the contractor."[75] The specification referred to in the contract with N. said that "the architects reserve the right in all items of P.C. and provisional amounts to employ the contractor or such other person as they may think fit to execute them." The plaintiffs were specialists in steelwork, and the architects sent to the plaintiffs drawings, inviting a tender for the steelwork contained in the contract as the subject of a provisional sum. The plaintiffs did not then know who the builder was, nor what the terms of the building contract were. They sent a tender to the architects at the request of the architects, and the architects wrote saying that N. was the builder and that they had instructed him to order the work. The plaintiffs wrote to N. asking for the order accordingly. N. tried to extract terms as to discounts, and the plaintiffs wrote to the architects asking them to instruct N. to give them the order as agreed. The order was then given on the terms of the estimate. The architects certified payment to N. of an amount which they stated included a sum for the plaintiffs. N. went bankrupt without having paid the plaintiffs, who sued W. *Held*, by Coleridge J., citing the *Hobbs* and *Crittall* cases, and not following the *Leslie* case, that the contract with the plaintiffs had been made by the architects as agents on W.'s behalf: *Young & Co.* v. *White* (1912).[76]

[Note: This case was expressly disapproved by the Court of Appeal in *Hampton's* case—see *e.g., per* Buckley L.J.]

13·036

(9) Builders contracted to erect a picture theatre for its owners. The contract was in the RIBA form, and provided that "all specialists, merchants,

13·037

---

[73] 75 J.P.R. 203; approving *Hobbs* v. *Turner* (1990) 18 T.L.R. 235.
[74] (1915) 84 L.J.K.B. 1306.
[75] (The formula used in the present-day pre-1980 RIBA forms, including the *Bickerton* and subsequent cases, see *post*, paras. 13·072 and 13·087.)
[76] 28 T.L.R. 87.

tradesmen or others executing any work or supplying any goods, for which prime cost prices or provisional sums are included in the specification, who may at any time be nominated, selected or approved by the architect are hereby declared to be sub-contractors employed by the contractor." Door furniture was the subject of a prime cost item, and manufacturers of door furniture were instructed by the architect as to the fittings required, and before delivery of the fittings. He informed the builders that these fittings would be supplied by the manufacturers. The builders used the fittings in carrying out their contract. *Held*, by the House of Lords, that on these facts the delivery of the goods at the theatre and their use by the builders implied a contract by the builders to pay the manufacturers for them: *Ramsden and Carr* v. *Chessum & Sons* (1913).[77]

(10) A builder contracted with the defendant council to build a school in accordance with the specifications and directions of the Council's architect for a lump sum. The specification contained the following provisional item: "Provide the sum of £450 for a low pressure heating apparatus." There was no provision expressly referring to the carrying out of such work by sub-contractors, nominated or otherwise. The plaintiff, a water engineer, submitted a scheme to the architect for the heating apparatus for £391, and upon the instructions of the architect this offer was accepted by the builder. During the progress of the work the builder paid to the plaintiff £200 on account, but was unable to pay the balance. The plaintiff sued the defendants for the balance. *Held*, by the House of Lords, that the builder's overall obligation to complete the school included the obligation to provide the heating apparatus referred to in the provisional sum, and that the builder, in employing the plaintiff to install the heating apparatus, was acting as a principal and not as the agent of the defendants, and the plaintiff's action failed: *Hampton* v. *Glamorgan County Council* (1917)[78]

13·038   (11) Under the 1931 RIBA form of contract there was power to pay sub-contractors direct on default by the builder. Sub-contractors tendered for the work of flooring, and the tender was accepted in June 1938. Early in June the contractors went into liquidation, and on June 9 the architect, with the acquiescence of the building owner, arranged with a director of the contractors that the latter should take over the contract. The architect sent to the owner, for signature by her, a mandate to the bank from which she had borrowed money on the security of the building advising them of the director's substitution for the company, and authorising payment to him or such nominated sub-contractors as might appear in future certificates. This was sent to the bank. Subsequently, the architect gave the flooring sub-contractors instructions to lay the floors and purported to pledge the owner's credit for that purpose. *Held*, by Asquith J., that the intention of the main contract was that there should be no privity between the owner and sub-contractors. The architect had no authority to contract on behalf of the building owner under the original contract, nor under the substituted contract. The reference in the mandate to the bank to payment of sub-contractors was referable only to the contractual right to pay direct, and the owner had done nothing to ratify the pledging of her credit, and was accordingly not liable to the sub-contractors: *Vigers Sons & Co. Ltd.* v. *Swindell* (1939).[79]

---

[77] 78 J.P.R. 49 (H.L.). No other cases are referred to in the report.
[78] [1917] A.C. 13. See also the judgments in the Court of Appeal (1915) 84 L.J.K.B. 1306.
[79] [1939] 3 All E.R. 590. Compare *Pritchett & Gold* v. *Currie* [1916] 2 CH. 615, illustrated *ante*, Chap. 11 para. 11·009.

It may be noted that the words "are hereby declared to be sub-contrac-   **13·039**
tors ..." (compare "shall be deemed to be sub-contractors" in the ICE
Conditions[80]) seem to have come into use shortly after 1900. Prior to that it
was quite common (as, for example, in *Hampton's* case) to have no special
provision about the exact status of the specialist, and merely to have provisional (or rather *provided*[81]) sums for the work in question. The judgments show that it was often the sub-contract fact or intention which
weighed as heavily with the courts as the exact wording used.

The cases also show that proof of an irretrievable benefit being conferred on the owner will not assist an unpaid sub-contractor to establish
liability against the owner for the value of work done.[82]

Coleridge J.'s judgment in the *Young* v. *White* case clearly reveals an
earlier judicial conflict, perhaps arising originally from the somewhat
imprecise alternative wording of the contract in *Hobbs* v. *Turner*, subsequently taken too far by Channell J. and later still by Coleridge J. in the
Crittall and *Young* cases respectively.[83] That conflict can be regarded as
resolved, as indicated in the Note to the *Crittall* case *supra*, in favour of the
Leslie and *Hampton* reasoning, and the *Ramsden* and *Vigers* cases clearly
represent the correct view of provisions of this kind.

In addition to the cases cited above, reference should also be made to   **13·040**
the two more modern cases of *Kirk and Kirk Ltd.* v. *Croydon Corporation*
(1956) and *Concrete Construction Ltd.* v. *Keidan & Co. Ltd.* (1955), see
supra.[84] The latter decision of the South African Court of Appeal is an
example of the correct principle applied to rescue an inappropriate contemporary documentation of a type very frequently encountered in practice, but *Kirk and Kirk*, in which Sellers J. followed *Leslie's* case, also faced
difficult and complicated facts in which it might easily have been possible
to lose sight of the no-privity principle.

Even where, however, an owner is in direct contractual relations with a
supplier or sub-contractor, it does not always follow that, *ipso facto*, he
will be liable to the main contractor for default by the supplier, although
usually this will be the case. This will depend on the circumstances in
which the direct contract was made, or upon the interpretation of the main
contract, which may sometimes contemplate such a direct relationship
without imposing any liability on the owner to the main contractor.

ILLUSTRATION

A main contract for the construction of two lodges and a back entrance   **13·041**
provided that the owners should pay the stone supplier direct and deduct

---

[80] See *infra*, Section 3(1) for the two current provisions.
[81] See *infra*, Section 3(3).
[82] See the *Hampton* and *Vigers* cases, and the *Pritchett & Gold* case *supra*, and illustrated
ante, Chap. 11, para. 11·009.
[83] See, *per* Lord Shaw in *Hampton* v. *Glamorgan County Council* [1917] A.C. 13, 22.
[84] Both illustrated *supra*, para. 13·017.

the sum from the contract price. With the consent of the main contractor, the owners negotiated with the suppliers and fixed the quantity and price of the stone to be supplied. The suppliers delayed delivery of the stone, and in consequence the contractors sued the owners for the additional cost occasioned by the delay. *Held*, by Tomlin J., that there was no implied obligation on the employers to supply the stone in time. At the highest, they were only obliged to hold the benefit of the contract with the suppliers for the contractors, and accordingly were not liable to the contractors: *Gaze (W. H.) & Sons Ltd.* v. *Port Talbot Corpn.* (1929).[85]

(3) Liability in Tort

(a) Generally

13·042   Liability in tort has been dealt with comprehensively in Chapter 1. The three heads of a possible liability in tort which may be of relevance as between owner and sub-contractor could until recently have been said to be, first, the straightforward liability for physical damage caused to other property, or for personal injury, under the *Donoghue* v. *Stevenson* principle;[86] secondly, the liability for a special category of economic loss, representing the cost of repairing defective work where a health or safety factor is present, under what became known as the *Anns* principle;[87] and, thirdly, a liability for economic loss caused by a negligent misrepresentation under the *Hedley Byrne* principle.[88]

(b) *Donoghue* v. *Stevenson* physical damage

13·043   Though this head of liability could in theory support a claim by a nominated sub-contractor against an owner, as for example for damage done to the sub-contractor's plant, in construction projects this is more likely to involve claims by owners against negligent sub-contractors for physical damage to the owner's property,[89] or to the property of other persons for which the owner is liable.[90]

However, the presence of clauses in the main contract exempting the main contractor from liability, or of provisions for insurance in that contract, may be inconsistent with any duty of the sub-contractor in tort, and so serve to defeat a claim in tort by the owner against him, not because the sub-contractor is entitled to the benefit of such provisions in any contractual sense,[91] but because to impose such a duty of care in tort would be inconsistent with the "contract structure" or "contract setting" in which

---

[85] 93 J.P.R. 89.
[86] See *ante*, Chap. 1, Section 12(3), paras. 1·308 *et seq.*
[87] See *ante*, Chap. 1, Section 12(6), paras. 1·345 *et seq.*
[88] See *ante*, Chap. 1, Section 12(2), paras. 1·290–1·291.
[89] See, *e.g. Rumbelows Ltd.* v. *A.M.K.* (*a firm*) (1980) 19 BLR 25, and *Surrey Heath B.C.* v. *Lovell Construction Ltd.* (1988) 42 BLR 25.
[90] See, *e.g. Greater Nottingham Co-operative Society Ltd.* v. *Cementation Piling and Foundations Ltd.* [1989] Q.B. 71 (C.A.).
[91] See *Southern Water Authority* v. *Carey* [1985] 2 A.E.R. 1077, *per* Judge Smout Q.C., *ante*, para. 1·326.

the sub-contractor had tendered and carried out his work.[92] Thus, an owner's claims in tort against a negligent sub-contractor have been defeated as a result of the express tests on completion and other provisions exempting the main contractor from liability to the owner after completion in the E. & M.E. Model contract;[93] and on a number of occasions by reason of main contract provisions imposing an insurance responsibility for the damage in question on the owner or main contractor.[94]

Furthermore, the terms of direct warranties given by the sub-contractor to the owner have on occasions been perhaps too easily interpreted as excluding any wider liability in tort than that expressly warranted, as where a direct warranty as to the design given by a sub-contractor was held to preclude an owner's action in tort against the sub-contractor for physical damage caused by negligent workmanship.[95]

(c) Economic loss under the *Anns* principle

This liability (for the repair of defects discovered in a building before any accident or physical damage has occurred, and possibly for consequential losses), which had enabled numerous claims to be successfully brought by owners against negligent sub-contractors for more than a decade, was overturned by a major *volte face* of the House of Lords in 1988 in the *D. & F. Estates* case, which distinguished and refused to follow its own earlier *Anns* decision in the case of all private defendants (such as sub-contractors would be)[96] and was finally confirmed by the abolition of the remaining *Anns* liability in the case of public housing authority defendants in the *Murphy* case in 1991.[97]

From the point of view of nominated sub-contractors perhaps the furthest extension of the *Anns* principle, if it was properly to be so regarded, was the case of *Junior Books Ltd.* v. *Veitchi Co. Ltd.* in 1983,[98] where the House of Lords had held a nominated flooring sub-contractor liable for, apparently, negligent workmanship (or perhaps design) in providing the topping of a factory floor, producing an excessive tendency of the floor to become dusty when in use, and necessitating increased maintenance costs over its life. As the case has since been attributed in the House of Lords to

13·044

---

[92] For the cases on this, see the discussions *ante*, Chap. 1, Section 12(3)(d) and 12(10)(c)(ii), paras. 1·325–1·326 and 1·386.

[93] *Southern Water Authority* v. *Carey ibid.*; compare the defeat of an owner's claim in tort against the main contractor by reason of a RIBA/JCT-style main contract final certificate provision in *William Hill Organisation* v. *Bernard Sunley & Sons Ltd.* (1982) 22 BLR 1.

[94] *Welsh Health Technical Services Organisation* v. *Haden Young (IDC, third party)* (1987) 37 BLR 130 (Macpherson J.); *Surrey Health B.C.* v. *Lovell* (1988) 42 BLR 25; *Norwich City Council* v. *Harvey* [1989] 1 W.L.R. 828 (C.A.), see *ante*, Chap. 1, Section 12(3)(d), paras. 1·325 *et seq.*

[95] *Greater Nottingham Co-operative Society Ltd.* v. *Cementation Piling and Foundations Ltd.* [1989] Q.B. 71 (C.A.).

[96] *D. & F. Estates Ltd.* v. *Church Commissioners for England* [1989] A.C. 177.

[97] *Murphy* v. *Brentwood D.C.* [1991] 1 A.C. 398. For the *Anns* doctrine, see *ante*, Chap. 1, Section 12(6), paras. 1·345 *et seq.* and for the *D&F* and *Murphy* cases, *ante*, paras. 1·353 *et seq.*

[98] [1983] 1 A.C. 520.

the *Hedley Byrne* principle, (though there is no indication in the *Junior Books* report of any positive conduct or representation on the part of the nominated sub-contractor of the kind usually required to support that head of liability), it will be discussed in paragraph (*d*) below.

(d) Economic loss under the *Hedley Byrne* doctrine

13·045   Liability under this principle is discussed in Chapter 1.[99] Sub-contractors in practice frequently do make representations, mostly in regard to suitability, with a view to their product or work being ordered for the project, and it has already been seen that such representations may create collateral *contractual* liabilities,[1] or give rise to the remedies available for innocent misrepresentation, as well as to the relatively new liability in tort under the *Hedley Byrne* doctrine.[1a]

In the absence of any such positive conduct or representations on the part of the sub-contractor, it is now evident, it is submitted, that while in the case of much sub-contractor's work it is eminently foreseeable that the owner will inevitably suffer economic loss if that work is negligently performed, no duty of care to prevent simple economic loss as opposed to physical damage will be held to arise out of the owner/sub-contractor or owner/nominated sub-contractor relationship, in the absence of sufficient explicit contractual warranties given to the owner. The House of Lords' decision in the *Junior Books* case, although applied, or at least accepted as of authority in some early cases,[2] can no longer and to that extent be regarded as good law, and has now been distinguished or disregarded in a number of authoritative cases in sub-contract situations.[3]

(4) Name-borrowing Provisions

13·046   These provisions appear to have emerged for the first time in England in 1963 in the FASS "Green Form" of nominated sub-contract, designed, although with different sponsoring bodies, for use with the new RIBA/JCT main contract forms which had been published earlier in the same

---

[99] Section 12(2), paras. 1·280 *et seq.*

[1] See *supra*, Section 1, paras. 13·019–13·020.

[1a] See, *e.g.* the *I.B.A.* v. *EMI* case, *supra*, para. 13·021.

[2] *Twins Transport Ltd.* v. *Patrick and Brocklehurst (trading as H.V. & C. Patrick Estates Developers)* (1983) 25 BLR 65, Judge Hawser Q.C.), *Welsh Health Technical Services* v. *Haden Young* (1987) 37 BLR 130 (Macpherson J.).

[3] See the discussion and cases *ante*, Chap. 1, Section 12(2)(c), paras. 1·291–1·292, and see *Muirhead* v. *Industrial Tank* [1986] Q.B. 507 (C.A.); *Simaan General Contracting Ltd.* v. *Pilkington Glass Ltd.* [1988] Q.B. 758; *Greater Nottingham Co-operative Society Ltd.* v. *Cementation Piling and Foundations Ltd.* [1989] Q.B. 71 (C.A.); and see also *Ernst & Whinney* v. *Willard Engineering (Dagenham) Ltd.* (1987) 40 BLR 67 (Judge Davies Q.C.).

year. The "Green Form" name-borrowing provisions may be regarded not only as prototypes but as typical examples for the discussion of this type of provision.

It should perhaps be noticed initially that the 1963 RIBA/JCT main contract forms, prepared by a differently constituted body, but indicating a clear foreknowledge of the contents of the new FASS form, and implicitly giving approval to many of its provisions (through the carefully defined rights of main contractor objection in Clause 27(a)(i)–(ix) of the RIBA/JCT form to the individual terms of a prospective nominated sub-contract), in fact exhibit no such implicit recognition or approval of the name-borrowing provisions.

In the FASS "Green Form" the provisions are found at three points in the sub-contract. Thus, a proviso to Clause 7 (concerned with the extent of the architect's power to give instructions in regard to the sub-contract work, including variations) provides that if the sub-contractor requests the main contractor to give notice of arbitration under the main contract disputing the basis for his instructions stated by the architect, then subject to the sub-contractor giving a reasonable indemnity or security the main contractor is to "allow the sub-contractor to use the contractor's name and, if necessary, will join the sub-contractor in arbitration proceedings by the sub-contractor to decide the matter." Similar provisos are to be found in Clause 8(b) of the sub-contract in regard to the architect's refusal of an extension of time for the sub-contract works under that clause, and under Clause 11 of the sub-contract in a case of dissatisfaction with the architect's certificates for interim payment under that clause (with the slight additional modification in this case that the contractor "will, if necessary, join the sub-contractor *as claimant* in the proceedings."

In addition to these three provisos, clause 12 of the FASS "Green **13·047** Form" also provided in general terms:

"The contractor will so far as he lawfully can at the request and cost of the sub-contractor obtain for him any rights or benefits of the Main Contract so far as the same are applicable to the sub-contract works but not further or otherwise."

This draftsmanship shows a typical *insouciance*, as in the case of other drafting of the RIBA/JCT standard forms,[4] in regard to the obvious difficulties and potential anomalies of its interpretation and application in practice—for example, where disputes or set-offs relating to other matters are quite likely to exist between the owner and main contractor, or where there may be differences between the various parties as to the choice of litigation rather than arbitration of their disputes, or where main contrac-

---

[4] Compare the prohibitions on "assignment" discussed *post*, Chap. 14, Section 6, para. 14·055, the "delay of on the part of" wording of Clause 23(g), and the nomination wording itself, commented on *ante*, Chap. 4, Section 2(5)(b), para. 4·194, and also *infra*, Section 3, paras. 13·072–13·073 and 13·086.

tor insolvency may be involved—which have been ignored by the drafts-man and left for resolution by others. It has been suggested that an explanation for this procedure may be due to the presence of "open up, review and revise" wording in the main contract arbitration clause, and its absence in the sub-contract arbitration clause.[5] This seems too charitable, since nothing would have been easier than to include that wording in the sub-contract arbitration clause itself, or to provide for a finality of the architect's certificates in the sub-contract only to the extent of their finality in the main contract,[6] and it seems much more likely that this dif-ference between the main contract and sub-contract arbitration clauses, of far longer standing than the name-borrowing procedures, results sim-ply from the combination of lack of attention and aversion to change on the part of the draftsman so often found in commercial documents.

13·048   The difficulties of application of these clauses have not gone unrecog-nised by the judiciary. Thus, it has been said, when endeavouring to ana-lyse and give effect to name-borrowing procedures:

> "Since, for some reason, the parties have chosen to cloak the reality of their commercial relationship in a particular legal guise, the court can only give effect to the legal relationship they have, to my mind unwisely, chosen to adopt, i.e. that the [sub-contractor's] 'rights' against the [owner] can only be established through [the main contractor].[7]
>
> "Undoubtedly the 'name-borrowing' provisions are very difficult to con-strue and any interpretation does give rise to 'grave difficulties' ... quite what is the nature of the relationship between 'the real' main contractor and the sub-contractor using the main contractor's name, I hesitate to say.[8]
>
> "[Counsel] have pointed out very clearly the problems and perhaps illogi-calities which flow from any interpretation and the difficulties which arise whatever view one takes. In the circumstances it is perhaps unnecessary for me to follow all the possible ramifications ... The clauses are not easy to con-strue. Any interpretation gives rise to great difficulties."[9]

Illustrated below are examples of some of the difficulties which can arise. It may be noted that in the first of the cases the "name-borrowing" relationship arose from a later ad hoc agreement between the parties and not from an original contract term.

ILLUSTRATIONS

13·049   (1) Earthworks sub-contractors brought an action against roadworks main contractors claiming additional payment for the quantities of unsuitable

---

[5] *Gordon Durham & Co. Ltd.* v. *Hayden Young Ltd.* (1990) 52 BLR 61, 80–81, *per* Judge Forbes, Q.C.

[6] The technique adopted by the Singapore 1980 S.I.A. standard form of sub-contract, Clause 14(2) (not reproduced in C.C.P.P.).

[7] *Northern Regional Health Authority* v. *Derek Crouch Construction Co. Ltd.* [1984] Q.B. 644, 665 F, *per* Browne-Wilkinson L.J.

[8] *Gordon Durhman Co.* v. *Haden Young Ltd.* (1990) 52 BLR 61, 89–90, *per* Judge Forbes Q.C.

[9] *Lorne Stewart* v. *William Sindall plc* (1986) 35 BLR 109, 125, 128, *per* Judge Hawser Q.C.

material to be removed. The main contractors in turn joined the County Council owners. In their defence against the sub-contractors, the main contractors' principal contention was the alleged inefficiency of the sub-contractors. Later the sub-contractors settled their claim against the main contractors on the basis that the main contractors would vest in them "the right to conduct and control in arbitration proceedings instituted by the main contractors against the Council." When the sub-contractors took over the proceedings, the Council sought a declaration that the sub-contractors were bound by the allegations of inefficiency made against them in the main contractors' pleadings. *Held*, by the Court of Appeal, affirming the trial judge, that the Council were free to amend their own pleadings to allege the matters previously pleaded against the sub-contractors, but there was no reason why the sub-contractors should not exercise all the main contractor's rights, whatever they might be, against the Council: *A. Monk & Co. Ltd. v. Devon County Council* (1978).[10]

(2) Main contractors brought High Court proceedings against sub-contractors under the 1978 revised FASS "Green Form" sub-contract claiming damages for delay in carrying out the sub-contract work and were supported by an architect's certificate under Clause 8(*a*) of the sub-contract. After the commencement of those proceedings, the sub-contractor unilaterally operated the procedure under the Proviso to Clause 8(*b*) of the sub-contract, and initiated an arbitration in the name of the main contractor against the Council claiming an extension of time, direct loss and expense, and damages for delay caused by the Council and the main contractors. Later the Council decided to settle the sub-contractor's arbitration claim on receipt of an adverse expert report, and though the main contractors at one stage had considered a stay of their own High Court proceedings so as to join in the arbitration, this was decided against and the main contractors then took no further part in the arbitration proceedings, which soon after resulted in a *consent* award, whereby the architect's certificate was revised and the sub-contractor awarded an extension of time on the basis of the delay having been caused by the main contractor. The sub-contractors then amended their defence in the High Court proceedings brought by the main contractor, contending that the arbitrator by his award had revised the architect's certificate; that time had now been extended; and that as a result they could not be liable for delay to the main contractors. *Held*, by Judge Forbes Q.C., that while the name-borrowing provisions of the contract authorised arbitration in the name of the main contractor, this authority was limited to specific matters of dispute between the sub-contractor and the Council which did not involve any conflict with the main contractor, so that the compromise resulting in the consent award did not bind the main contractor in his dispute with the sub-contractor: *Gordon Durham & Co. Ltd. v. Haden Young Ltd.* (1990).[11]

13·050

[Note: Judge Forbes' decision and indeed reasoning in this case is eminently sensible, and obviously reflects the presumed intentions of any reasonable party, while avoiding the insuperable difficulties of issue estoppel likely to arise. While the case graphically justifies the prescient wording of Lord Donaldson M.R. that "every conceivable complication will arise if [the main contractor] disagrees with the case which the nominated sub-contracted wishes to submit in their name",[12] the decision involves a fairly considerable gloss on the contract wording, and emphasises the inadequacy of the name-borrowing concept and of its draftsmanship.]

---

[10] 10 BLR 9.
[11] 52 BLR 61.
[12] *Northern Regional Health Authority* v. *Derek Crouch Construction Co. Ltd.* [1984] Q.B. 644, 674.

13·051   "Name-borrowing" provisions are, of course, likely to be involved with another very difficult procedural aspect of many construction disputes, namely tripartite disputes as affected by the unavoidable absence of third party remedies (unless permitted by legislation[12a] or express contractual provision) in cases where it is desired to arbitrate such disputes. Here, too, serious procedural complications are frequently encountered.

ILLUSTRATION

A main contractor under the RIBA/JCT standard form commenced High Court proceedings against a hospital authority, claiming an extension of time and loss and expense, and then successfully resisted their application for a stay for arbitration. Later the main contractor himself started an arbitration in relation to the boilerhouse which was a part of the project, and which was said not to overlap with the other delays claimed in the action. Later still, a nominated sub-contractor for work at the boilerhouse commenced an arbitration against the authority using the FASS "Green Form" sub-contract name-borrowing procedures, and the same arbitrator was in the event appointed in each case. The authority then applied for an injunction to restrain continuation of the arbitrations and effectively bring the whole dispute under one roof in the High Court. *Held*, by the Court of Appeal, it would with care be possible for the arbitrator and the Court to avoid deciding on overlapping matters, and since the sub-contractor's claim might otherwise be delayed, and the Court, as opposed to an arbitrator, would in any case not have power to review the architect's decisions on extensions of time, the injunctions should be refused. *Northern Regional Health Authority* v. *Derek Crouch Construction Ltd.* (1984).[13]

[Note: This was, of course, a highly controversial decision in so far as the Court of Appeal took a restricted view of the courts' jurisdiction to review certificates,[14] and the procedural decision itself seems a strange one in the light of the main contractor's tactical changes of front, but it serves to show the extremely complicated backgrounds in which the name-borrowing procedure is likely to be invoked.]

13·052   Quite apart from purely procedural complications, the major substantive difficulty with these provisions, namely that there is no necessary relationship between the damage suffered or prices in the main and sub-contracts, has already been pointed out *supra*. While heroic attempts to define the precise status of a name-borrowing plaintiff or claimant under these provisions were made both by Judge Hawser Q.C. and Judge Forbes in the two cases illustrated above, it seems doubtful whether the draftsman himself had any clear idea of what was being aimed at, or how it was to be applied or operate in practical situations, and it is, on analysis, difficult to see any advantages, for any party, which outweigh the difficulties and disadvantages of these ill-considered procedures.

[12a] As in the Hong Kong Arbitration Acts.
[13] [1984] Q.B. 644. See for a further complicated case the *City Centre* case, *post*, para. 18·113.
[14] See *ante*, Chap. 6, Section 4(2), paras. 6·063 *et seq.*, and see C.C.P.P. Chap. 17 for a detailed historical examination of the authorities and criticism of this aspect of the case.

(5) Direct or Collateral Warranties

(a) Collateral warranties

It has been seen *supra* in Subsection (2) that during the preliminary   **13·053**
stages of discussion or negotiation between sub-contractors on the one
hand, and owners or their architects on the other, express or implied collateral warranties or undertakings having contractual force can easily
come into existence, for example in the not uncommon situation where a
sub-contractor makes representations as to the suitability of his work or
product in order that it should be ordered for the project. These negotiations, in the case of work or items on long delivery, may often need to take
place at a time when the main contractor has not yet been selected. Usually it will be the intention that any preliminary direct contractual
relationship which comes into existence in this way will be subsumed and
replaced by any subsequent contract between main and sub-contractor.[15]
However, this will not necessarily always be so.

ILLUSTRATION

Mechanical engineers were invited to tender by a hospital board's agents as   **13·054**
nominated sub-contractors for the heating and plumbing work in new resi-
dential accommodation, at a time when the main contractors had not yet been
appointed. Clause 10 of the conditions of the sub-contract tender stated that
the main contractor or the building owner would bear the sole risk of fire as
defined in Clause 20 of the RIBA/JCT main contract; and by Clause 11.5 of
the tender conditions the applicable insurance clause in the main contract was
to be Clause 20*b* or Clause 20*c* (under which insurance was to be taken out by
the owner and the works were to be at his sole risk against fire and the other
insured risks). The sub-contractor's tender was accepted by the Board's
agents prior to execution of the main contract, and the main contractor later
when appointed accepted the sub-contractor's tender and placed the order.
Later the roof was damaged by a fire caused by the negligence of the sub-
contractor's workmen, and the owner sued the sub-contractors in tort. *Held*,
by Macpherson J., that at the outset there had been a contract between the
owner and the sub-contractor. The sub-contract tender form constituted an
offer to enter into the sub-contract at the tendered price on condition that the
owner would bear the sole risk of fire. Looked at in reverse, if the sub-contractors had not entered into the sub-contract with the main contractor on the
tendered terms the owner could have sued them for damages for the higher
cost of another sub-contract. Alternatively, there was a collateral warranty
given by the owner to bear the sole risk in consideration of the sub-contract-
or's entry into the sub-contract with the main contractor. In addition, following *Southern Water Authority* v. *Carey*[16] and distinguishing *Junior Books* v.
Veitchi,[17] this "contract setting" was a "consideration negativing or limiting

---

[15] Compare the *Davies Shopfitters* and other cases illustrated *supra*, paras. 13·017–13·019.
[16] [1985] 2 A.E.R. 1077; see this and the other cases discussed *ante*, Chap. 1, Section 12(3)(d),
    para. 1·325, and see Section 12(10)(c)(ii), para. 1·386.
[17] [1983] A.C. 520.

the scope of any duty of care" within the second part of Lord Wilberforce's statement in the *Anns* case, so that on that ground also the claim failed: *Welsh-Health Technical Services Organisation* v. *Haden Young (FDC, third party)* (1987).[18]

(b) Direct sub-contractor warranties

13·055   Apart from the collateral contracts or warranties arising either expressly or impliedly and often informally during early negotiations between owner and sub-contractor, specific forms of express direct warranty to be given by nominated sub-contractors to owners have been recommended in England by the RIBA/JCT, as part of the industry pressures to secure reductions in main contractor responsibility to the owner for nominated sub-contractor default which had been encouraged by the *Bickerton* interpretation of the nomination wording of the 1963 RIBA/JCT forms,[19] and as a palliative or justification for the decrease in owner protection now afforded by the main contract provisions themselves.

While such direct warranties might seem to offer a superficial advantage to owners, and while competent advisers to owners may well, in certain special situations, advocate obtaining such a direct warranty, particularly where the relative financial standing of main contractor and prospective sub-contractor, or the importance or great cost of the sub-contract might make it desirable, the use of such warranties on a wide scale as recommended by the RIBA/JCT, so that their presence will form a part of the background known to both parties at the time of entry into the main contract, carries a serious danger that the owner's protection, previously enjoyed through implied terms *in the main contract* as to the quality or suitability of the sub-contract work or as to diligent progress by the sub-contractor, may be still further reduced, and that the owner may even be exposed to implied obligations *owed to the main contractor* warranting the proper performance of the nominated sub-contract work, thus entirely subverting the entire no-privity sub-contract objective of the English nomination system.[20]

13·056   Quite apart from these considerations, the wording of the direct warranties as drafted and recommended by the RIBA appear, while offering apparent protection, to be ingeniously calculated to reduce still further the owner's right as against the sub-contractor below the level he might himself have enjoyed against the main contractor without the express warranty. These RIBA/JCT warranties fall into two parts. The first part, in regard to design and suitability of the sub-contract work, offers a warranty of *due care only*, rather than the unqualified warranty of suitability for its required purpose, independent of fault, which the law rightly implies in

---

[18] 37 BLR 135. See also the other collateral warranty cases referred to *supra*, Subsection (1).

[19] For the *Bickerton* case, see further *infra*, Section 3.

[20] Explained *supra*, Section 1, paras. 13·016 *et seq.*

contracts of sale and other arms length commercial contracts where the purchaser or consumer is obliged to rely on the skill and judgment of the seller, or contractor. The crucial disadvantages for a purchaser or construction owner of a warranty qualified by the need to prove negligence rather than simple unsuitability have been explained at some length earlier in this book in the context of turnkey contracts, or those other contracts, where, in regard at least to some part of the works, there is reliance on the contractor for the design, rather than on the owner's A/E.[21]

The second part of the recommended RIBA/JCT direct warranties **13·057** relates to due progress. With perhaps ingenuous but unnecessary complication, this warranty is related to the main contract extension of time provisions, crucially compounded by the difficulties of application and interpretation of the critical "delay on the part of"[22] wording of that clause,[23] which notwithstanding its condemnations in the House of Lords in 1969, still remains unchanged. This method of drafting the sub-contract warranty in relation to progress can be confidently expected, in the light of the well known case law, to produce anomalous and unjust results reducing still further the practical value of the warranty to the owner, and it is difficult to avoid the conclusion that this is no accident.[24] There is yet a third pitfall awaiting the owner whose advisers have permitted him to use the RIBA/JCT recommended warranty, since other breaches of contract such as defective work are not mentioned. All three deficiencies were relevant in the following case.

ILLUSTRATION

An owner obtained a direct warranty from a piling nominated sub-con-   **13·058** tractor in the recommended RIBA/JCT form, which by Clause A(1) gave a due care warranty as to the design of the sub-contract work, and by Clause A(2) gave a due progress warranty in terms that the sub-contractor would not expose the owner to an extension of time claim under the main contract. In the event, the sub-contractors drove their piles negligently, so that adjoining property was damaged and, apart from his liability to the adjoining owners, the owner suffered damage caused by the delay to the main contract. Liability for the damage to the adjoining property was not resisted, but due to the deficiencies in the warranty, the owner was obliged to sue the sub-contractor *in tort* for his consequential delay and other losses. *Held*, by the Court of Appeal, that since the direct warranty applied only to design and to slow progress by the sub-contractor, but was significantly silent as to defective or negligent working, this was a consideration negativing any duty in tort to avoid economic loss resulting from that cause: *Greater Nottingham Co-operative Society Ltd.* v. *Cementation* (1988).[25]

---

[21] See *ante*, Chap. 3, Section 1(4)(*a*), paras. 13·028–13·029; Chap. 4, Section 2(a)(i), paras. 4·075 *et seq*.
[22] See *ante*, Chap. 10, Section 5, para. 10·099, and the case of *J. Jarvis & Sons Ltd.* v. *Westminster Corporation* [1970] 1 W.L.R. 637 (H.L.) there illustrated.
[23] RIBA/JCT 1980 forms, Clause 25.4.7.
[24] See C.C.P.P., paras. 29–18, 30–26.
[25] [1988] Q.B. 71.

13·059   The *Greater Nottingham* case was decided while the case of *Junior Books* v. *Veitchi*,[26] which had permitted recovery of economic loss in tort by an owner against a nominated sub-contractor, was still a major subject of discussion and accepted as of potential authority; but the Court of Appeal's reasoning affords an illuminating insight into the deviousness and complication of the RIBA/JCT draftsmanship, which had clearly entirely escaped the owner's advisers at the time of contracting.[27] All that would be necessary, of course, to afford an owner proper protection (subject to any wider considerations arguing against the generalised use of direct warranties as previously explained) would be a short undertaking duly to perform all the obligations express or implied undertaken by the nominated sub-contractor in his sub-contract in consideration of the sub-contractor being nominated, and indemnifying the owner against any breach of or failure to perform the sub-contract. Owners' advisers in England appear consistently to fail in their duty to note and point out the defects of these particular recommended direct warranties to their clients.

On the question of the enforcement by owners of direct warranties in general, it has been held, in what may not be the last word on the subject, that sums due to an owner for breach of a direct warranty by a sub-contractor may not be set off by the owner against summary proceedings brought by the main contractor for payment of sums certified by the architect in interim certificates under the RIBA/JCT forms of contract which include sums due to the nominated sub-contractor in question for work done by him.[28]

(6) Express Trust and Pay Direct Provisions

13·060   The former but not the latter types of express provision in the sub-contract can give sub-contractors rights against moneys still in the hands of the owner, though these are usually only likely to be exercised in the event of the insolvency of the main contractor. These provisions are discussed *infra*, Section 5, and also in considerable detail *ante*, Chapter 8, Section 1(3)(b).[28a]

Section 3.   Building Owner and Contractor

(1) Main Contractor Responsibility for Nominated Sub-contractor

13·061   It has been shown *supra*[29] that the cardinal feature of the English nomination system which grew up during the first half of the nineteenth century

---

[26] [1983] A.C. 520.

[27] The deficiencies of the "on the part of" wording had been pointed out as early as 1969, even before the *Jarvis* case had reached the House of Lords—see the editor's "Building and Civil Engineering Standard Forms", page 110.

[28] *George & Taylor & Co. Ltd.* v. *G. Percy Trentham Ltd.* (1980) 16 BLR 15.

[28a] See paras. 8·087–8·088.

[29] Section 2(2), para. 13·016.

was its "no privity" objective, with the result that the main contractor must accept unqualified legal responsibility to the owner for all aspects of the nominated sub-contractor's work, in the same way as for a "domestic" sub-contractor, in the absence of wording to the contrary. Apart from the use of ill-considered express terms, such as the express ground of extension of time for delays on the part of nominated sub-contractors in Clause 23(*g*) of the RIBA/JCT standard forms, (excoriated for its anomalous results in the strongest possible terms in 1970 by the House of Lord's judgment in *Westminster Corporation* v. *J. Jarvis & Sons Ltd.*[30]) this position can be seen to be firmly established, even in cases where the wording was unclear, in the case law, illustrated and discussed in Section 1 *supra*.

Thus in the ninth and tenth editions of this book it was stated of these main contract exculpatory clauses:

> "The effect of such clauses does not appear to have been properly considered, since they merely have the effect of reducing the liability of defaulting sub-contractors to the advantage of no-one else, since in the event of the Employer being entitled, for instance, to liquidated damages for such delays, the main contractor would otherwise recover the amount as damages from the sub-contractor and not be out of pocket himself".[30a]

However, two developments after 1970 brought about breaches of the no privity objective. First, a major (although limited) breach resulted from the unexpected interpretation by the House of Lords in the *Bickerton* case of the particular wording of the nomination provisions in the then current RIBA/JCT standard forms. The *Bickerton* interpretation placed the owner under a duty to re-nominate a successor sub-contractor if the sub-contract had been terminated as a result of its repudiation by the owner's original nominee, and to pay any additional account of the second nominee.[31]

Secondly, the two principal English standard forms introduced complicated nomination schemes which unmistakably abandoned the objective altogether, in 1973 and 1980 respectively.[32] These two standard form schemes are shortly noted *supra*,[33] and are not further discussed in this book, though their extreme complication may well produce problems in the future. Their policies are in stark contrast to the policy of the English GC/Wks/1 government contract, which has continued to maintain the no privity objective in wording of unusual brevity and clarity,[34] and which expressly excludes any *Bickerton* type re-nomination duty on the part of the owner.[35]

13·062

---

[30] [1970] 1 W.L.R. 637, quoted and illustrated *ante*, Chap. 10, Section 5, paras. 10·098–10·099.

[30a] (Tenth edition, p. 766). Cited with approval by Davies L.J. in *Westminster Corporation* v. *Jarvis* [1969] 1 W.L.R. 1448, 1453.

[31] *Bickerton* v. *North West Metropolitan Regional Hospital Board* [1970] 1 W.L.R. 607, see *infra*, para. 13·066.

[32] *i.e.*, the ICE fifth edition and the 1980 RIBA/JCT standard forms.

[33] (Para. 13·028).

[34] See clauses 31(2), and (3), and 38(5).

[35] The latest 1990 version of this form does, however, now make a partial retreat in the event of nominated sub-contractor insolvency. See Edition 3 Clause 63(9).

However, the basic no privity objective remains of the greatest importance in the interpretation of main contracts for a number of reasons. First,
there are many forms of contract in use both in England, and the Commonwealth which either follow the older standard forms, or which for
good reason have chosen not to adopt the later ICE/RIBA/JCT schemes,
or which, in less formal cases, simply provide for nomination with no
express discussion or definition of the main contractor's responsibility at
all. All such contracts should continue to be interpreted in the light of an
underlying no privity business objective, it is submitted.

13·063   Main contractor responsibility for sub-contractor default has in fact already been considered in detail at a number of points earlier in this book
in different contexts. Thus, the main contractor's implied responsibilities
for nominated sub-contractor *design* have been exhaustively considered
in Chapter 4,[36] and also for *quality of materials*,[37] and for *workmanship*.[38]
Additionally, responsibility for a nominated sub-contractor's *due progress*, in the light of the express terms of the RIBA/JCT extension of time
clause, has been considered in Chapter 10.[39] Main contractor responsibility has also been discussed in the present Chapter *supra*, Section 1(1),
Section 1(2) and Section 2(1).

13·064   One result of the use of the P.C. and Provisional Sum procedure[40] to
denote the work or materials which are to be the subject of owner selection or nomination is that in many cases the main contract documents will
not contain the detailed description of this work which would be expected
in the case of the main contractor's own work. All that may be seen in the
contract documents in such cases may be some such item as "structural
steel work. P.C. Sum £40,000". The detailed description of the work to be
carried out will only be found in the sub-contract documentation, including the quotations and correspondence which often pass between the sub-
contractor and the A/E in the first place, and any subsequent correspondence with the main contractor prior to his placing of the order. Even
where a formal sub-contract in the FASS "Green Form" is used, it is quite
usual for the sub-contract schedule or specification describing the work to
consist merely of attached copies of the original quotations and acceptance. In all these cases it is submitted, in the absence of contrary provision,
that the drawings, specification or descriptions of the sub-contract work
forming part of the sub-contract, in whatever form they may be, must
also be regarded as constituting the work undertaken by the main contractor as his own obligation to the owner arising under the nomination

---

[36] See *ante*, Chap. 4, Section 1(2)(a)(i) and (iv), paras. 4·075 *et seq.* and 4·108.
[37] See *ante*, Chap. 4, Section 1(2)(b), paras. 4·117 *et seq.*
[38] See *ante*, Chap. 4, Section 1(2)(c), paras. 4·124–4·125. And see particularly *Young and
Marten Ltd.* v. *McManus Childs Ltd.* [1969] 1 A.C. 454, and the difficult cases of *Gloucestershire County Council* v. *Richardson* [1969] 1 A.C. 480; *Norta Wallpaper* v. *Sisk* [1978]
I.R. 114; and *University of Warrick* v. *McAlpine* (1988) 42 BLR 1 there referred to, paras.
4·092 *et seq.*
[39] Chap. 10, Section 5, paras. 10·098–10·100.
[40] See further as to this *infra*, Subsection (3), para. 13·089.

provisions of the main contract, and to that extent will have become part of the main contract itself:

> "[It was] argued that that would not be so because … the specification was a document related only to the sub-contract and not the main. So it was in the first instance, but the work required to be done by it was clearly brought within the ambit of the main contract by the contract bills and by Clause 11(3) of the main contract, which directed the architects to issue instructions in regard to the expenditure of prime cost. The instructions which he in fact gave to [the main contractor] to employ the plaintiffs as nominated sub-contractors are the provisions with regard to nominated sub-contractors contained in Clause 27, so in my view the specification is relevant for all purposes as well under the main contract as under the sub-contract."[41]

13·065

This statement of Robert Goff L.J., as he then was, represents a vitally important (not least because never previously so clearly stated in the Courts) and entirely correct analysis, it is submitted. It is further submitted that the same principle should normally apply to *applied obligations* of the sub-contractor (for example, of good workmanship, or of unconditional suitability independent of fault where reliance is placed on the sub-contractor in regard to design), and that, by the same contractual process and for the same reasons, these will become part of the main contractor's obligations in the main contact, whether separately stated there or not.

(2) *Bickerton* and the Duty to Nominate

Under the traditional nomination systems in English construction contracts little difficulty was to be anticipated in the case of everyday "partial" breaches of contract by nominated sub-contractors during the construction period not leading to rescission, such as defective work or delay in progress. In such cases the owner or his A/E would exercise the normal sanctions under the main contract, withholding payment, or deducting the cost of repair in the case of defective work, or recovering or deducting by way of set-off or cross-claim liquidated or general damages for delay (unless there was an applicable extension of time clause). However, in the case of a "total" breach (for example, abandonment by the sub-contractor, or an accepted repudiation and termination of the sub-contract by the main contractor) the question then remained as to how, and with what consequences for the main contract, the nominated sub-contract work should be completed.

13·066

On a traditional "no privity" interpretation of the nomination provisions, the main contractor would in such a situation be in breach of contract in failing to complete using the nominated sub-contractor, as he had undertaken to do; but it would be in his own interest to reduce or eliminate

---

[41] A valuable and entirely correct analysis by Robert Goff L.J. in *Comyn Ching* v. *Oriental Tube Co.* (1979) 17 BLR 47, 77, C.A. (the clause numbers cited relate to the clauses of the pre-1980 RIBA/JCT standard forms).

to nominal proportions any damages payable by himself to the owner, and to recover the full sums due from the owner, by offering substantial performance in the form of making arrangements for completion of the work by himself or by another sub-contractor.[41a]

13·067   On an intermediate interpretation of the contract, the owner might perhaps retain the right, which he might or might not choose to exercise, to nominate the person to complete the sub-contract work, but be liable to pay no more for it than would have been payable under the original nominee's sub-contract, and without prejudice to any set-off, or right to damages, since the contractor would still be at least nominally in breach.[41b]

On a quite different interpretation, the owner might be regarded as under a duty to appoint a new sub-contractor (so being in breach of contract and failing to mitigate its damage if he did not do so, or delayed unreasonably in giving the necessary instructions) and might even be liable for the new sub-contractor's account whether or not he was himself in breach, and notwithstanding that the situation had arisen solely because of the first sub-contractor's breach.[41c]

13·068   Additionally, under very strongly producer-orientated, or carelessly drafted forms like the RIBA/JCT contracts, there might be a possibility that the owner would be *financially liable to the main contractor* under compensatory contractual provisions (based on compliance with architect's instructions, for example), or on delay by the architect in giving instructions—compare Clauses 11(6) and 24 of the 1963 RIBA/JCT standard forms). There would also be the question whether the contractor would be entitled to an extension of time, either for delay in giving the renomination instruction itself or for the inevitable delays caused to the programme as a result of the instruction and the earliest completion dates which could be offered by the second "mid-stream" nominees. These last and more extreme interpretations in fact represent the overall effect of the later schemes expressly adopted by the 1973 and 1980 ICE and RIBA/JCT contracts respectively.

13·069   It is important to note in this context that it is not in practice possible, in the absence of really specific draftsmanship, to distinguish in a main contract between voluntary repudiations by solvent nominated sub-contractors on the one hand, and the decisions of the trustees or liquidators of insolvent sub-contractors to exercise their (in fact and law voluntary) right to disclaim the sub-contract on the other. As a result, on analysis, there can be no interpretation of more generally worded nomination provisions which differs in its results according to whether a sub-contractor's repudiation on "dropping out" of the sub-contract has been "voluntary," or "involuntary" as "the result of" insolvency, since these expressions in any case usually imply basically false distinctions. An interpretation of generalised wording which imposes liabilities on the owner in the case of a sub-

---

[41a] See for a classic U.S. example of the mitigation principle Cardozo J. in *Jacob & Youngs* v. *Kent* 129 N.E. 889 (1921), see *ante*, paras. 4·020–4·022.
[41b] See GC/Wks/1, Clause 38(5).   [41c] The *Bickerton* interpretation.

contractor's insolvency, like the *Bickerton* interpretation, cannot, therefore, avoid doing so in a case of deliberate repudiation by a solvent sub-contractor as well, unless the contract itself has made that distinction very expressly.[42] Moreover, the presence of such an express provision might well persuade a contractor's trustee or liquidator, who would not otherwise have done so in order to avoid a major proof in the insolvency, to disclaim the sub-contract now that this could be done with relative impunity.

In the *Bickerton* case the House of Lords held that under the RIBA/   **13·070**
JCT nomination provisions the owner was under a duty to make a second nomination following a repudiation by a nominated sub-contractor's liquidator (as it happened, in a voluntary liquidation) and to pay any additional sums due under the account of the second nominee to the main contractor. The *Bickerton* case was decided very shortly before the tenth edition of this book was published, but was, nevertheless, there analysed and criticised in considerable detail,[43] and in the present edition the law resulting from *Bickerton* and a number of subsequent cases has already been reviewed at some length in Chapter 4.[44]

Consideration of the subsequent cases seeking to apply and interpret   **13·071**
Bickerton has shown clearly that, despite the efforts of contractors to establish such claims, none of the relevant provisions of the (pre-1980) RIBA/JCT contracts—for example, in relation to extension of time under Clause 23, or to compensation for additional loss and expense for architect's instructions or late instructions under Clauses 11(6) or 24 (and despite the long and detailed lists of qualifying events categorised in those clauses)—have been found to be applicable to the performance by the owner of this alleged duty, or of architect's instructions relating to it. This affords powerful support for the view that the original *Bickerton* interpretation was mistaken, and certainly not one ever contemplated by the draftsman, it is submitted. The later cases show the courts becoming entangled in increasingly convoluted analyses and explanations in their attempts to justify and implement the original interpretation in entirely predictable, but more obviously damaging situations.

ILLUSTRATIONS

(1) Clauses 27 and 28 of a post-1963 RIBA/JCT form of main contract pro-   **13·072**
vided in relation to sub-contractors and supplier respectively: "Where prime cost sums are included in the contract bills or arise as a result of . . . provisional sums in respect of persons to be nominated by the architect to . . . execute work [or in respect of material or goods to be fixed by the contractor], *such sums shall be expended in favour of such persons as the architect shall instruct,*

---

[42] See for an example *City of Adelaide* v. *Jennings Industries* (1985) 57 A.L.R. 455, illustrated *infra*, paras. 13·083–13·085.
[43] Tenth edition, see Chap. 4, pages 333–337.
[44] See *ante*, Chap. 4, Section 2(5)(b), paras. 4·191 *et seq*.

and specialists ... or others who are nominated by the architect ... are hereby declared to be [sub-contractors employed by the contractor ... referred to as "nominated sub-contractors"] [suppliers to the contractor ... referred to as "nominated suppliers]".[45] Clause 27 also provided that nothing in the conditions should render the owner in any way liable to a nominated sub-contractor, and Clause 30(5)(c) provided that in the settlement of accounts any sums paid or allowed to the contractor by the sub-contractor were to be the property of the contractor, not of the owner.

13·073   Nominated heating sub-contractors appointed under this contract went into voluntary liquidation before starting work, and the liquidator refused to carry on with the sub-contract. The main contractor did the work by his own heating division on a without prejudice basis, contending that the owner was bound to nominate a second sub-contractor and pay the main contractor the greater amount of the second sub-contractor's account, while the owner contended that there was no duty to renominate, or to pay more for the work than the amount of the original sub-contractor's account suitably adjusted, if necessary, for variations. *Held*, by the House of Lords (overruling Sir Walker Carter in *K. Cross (Doncaster) Ltd.* v. *Yorkshire (East Riding) County Council* (1966)[46] and the Court of Appeal of Northern Ireland in *J. M. Reilly Ltd.* v. *Belfast Corporation* (1968)),[47] that the words "such [P.C.] sums shall be expended in favour of such person as the architect shall instruct" in Clause 27(a) of the contract must be interpreted as referring to the sums due under the relevant sub-contracts, and not the P.C. sums themselves,[48] and by virtue of these words there was a duty on the owner to make a second nomination when the first sub-contractor repudiated at a time when the relevant "sum" would not have been wholly expended. *Per* Lord Reid: "The principal contractor has no right or duty to do the [prime cost work] himself when the nominated sub-contractor drops out any more than he had before the sub-contractor was nominated ..." *Per* Lord Hodson, Clause 27(a) should be construed as "requiring 'nomination when necessary.'" *Per* Lord Dilhorne "[The purpose of Clause 27] ... is to provide that prime cost work can only and shall only be carried out by persons nominated by the architect": *Bickerton* v. *North West Metropolitan Regional Hospital Board* (1970).[49]

13·074   (2) A heating nominated sub-contractor under the RIBA/JCT form of main contract went into liquidation during the course of the sub-contract. The architect made a second nomination, but had been guilty of some delay in doing so, so that there was an initial delay for that reason. In addition, it was impossible to find a second sub-contractor able to offer the completion dates of the first sub-contractor, so that there was an unavoidable and greater delay due to that cause. The architect granted a single extension of time for both elements of delay and, when the main contractor eventually failed to complete by the extended completion date, liquidated damages were deducted by the owner in respect of other delays for which the main contractor was responsible. The contractor contended that under the extension of time

---

[45] See the powerful criticism of the obscurity of this RIBA wording by Danckwerts L.J. in this case in the Court of Appeal, [1969] 1 All E.R. 977, 996. The emphasised words had been present in the RIBA forms since at least 1902—see *Hobbs* v. *Turner*, illustrated *supra*, para. 13·033—and the latter words since at least 1912—see *Young* v. *White supra*, para. 13·036.

[46] October 12, 1966, unrep., Sir Walker Carter Q.C.

[47] June 28, 1968, unrep.

[48] See this further explained C.C.P.P., para. 21–15. The concept seems quite erroneous, but is clearly the source of the House of Lords' interpretation. The words had been used in RIBA contracts since at least 1902, see *supra*.

[49] [1970] 1 W.L.R. 607, 613, 617, 623.

Clause 23 there was no applicable power to extend time for the element of delay caused by the impossibility of finding a sub-contractor able to meet the first sub-contractor's completion date (it was conceded that Clause 23(*g*) of the contract only covered delay "on the part of" nominated sub-contractors and so did not apply). As there was delay caused by the owners but no applicable extension of time, the contractor contended that, on well-known principles, the liquidated damages clause had been invalidated,[50] and the damages could not be recovered. *Held*, by the House of Lords, that as to the earlier element of delay caused by the late instructions, there was an applicable ground of extension under Clause 23(*f*) of the contract (late instructions). As to the more important and later delay, there had been no duty on the owner to nominate a second sub-contractor who could complete by the first sub-contractor's date, but only to obtain the best possible dates, so that there had been no fault by the owner in regard to that delay, which had been caused by the first sub-contractor's repudiation. Strictly, though he had in fact been given an extension of time, the main contractor had been liable in liquidated damages for that element of delay: *Percy Bilton Ltd.* v. *Greater London Council* (1982).[51]

[Note: This case, while emphasising that an owner re-nominating promptly   **13·075**
will not be in breach of contract, shows that no ground of extension had been provided in the main contract to cover the delays which might follow from a re-nomination instruction, and so supports the view that its draftsman had never contemplated such an instruction. However, Lord Frazer in addition expressed the view *obiter* that the main contractor could have refused to accept the second nomination (which he had not in fact done) under Clause 27(*a*)(*ii*) of the conditions, by virtue of its incompatible completion date,[52] and that if so, this would produce a contractual stalemate, since while the owner would not be in breach when unable to find a sub-contractor offering a compatible date, he could only in that case omit the work in question unless he was prepared to negotiate and obtain the contractor's agreement to the later date offered by the prospective sub-contractor. This extraordinary practical consequence, if correct, is a further indication of the insuperable difficulties created by the original *Bickerton* interpretation, it is submitted.]

(3) A nominated sub-contractor appointed under a RIBA/JCT main con-   **13·076**
tract had his sub-contract lawfully terminated by the main contractor when the work was about half done. At that time £60,000 had been paid to the main contractor and then to the sub-contractor, but it was later discovered that the work had been done so badly that wholesale demolition, removal and replacement was required at an ultimate cost of £240,000. The architect gave a second nomination instruction within a reasonable time, while giving a separate instruction under Clause 6(4) of the main contract requiring the main contractor to remove and make proposals for remedying the defective work already done and paid for.[53] The main contractor objected to the re-nomination on the ground that it did not cover the remedial work, and also because of its late completion date. *Held*, by the Court of Appeal, applying *Bickerton*, that the contractor was neither obliged nor entitled to do the remedial work, which must be done by nominated sub-contractors, so that the nomination was rightly objected to on that ground; and also because of the incompatibility

---

[50] See *ante*, Chap. 10, Section 2(1), paras. 10·024 *et seq.*, for this well-established aspect of the prevention principle.

[51] [1982] 1 W.L.R. 794, analysed in detail in C.C.P.P. paras. 21–20—22 ((1984) 3 A.C.L.R. (No. 4) p. 2).

[52] The correctness of this latter view is doubted for the detailed reasons explained in C.C.P.P., para. 21–22.

[53] A perfectly logical position, it is submitted. See also the *Jennings Industries* case, *infra*, para. 13·084.

of its completion date. Following a valid re-nomination, the owner would be obliged to pay the full cost of the remedial work. It was no objection to a re-nomination that there appeared to be a lacuna in the extension of time clause in that it contained no applicable ground for an extension, since there could be an implied term that if the re-nomination were accepted an appropriate extension would be granted: *Fairclough Building Ltd.* v. *Rhuddlan Borough Council* (1985).[54]

13·077   [Note: The judgments also indicate agreement with Lord Frazer's view in *Bilton* that a nomination instruction with an incompatible later date would constitute a postponement instruction under Clause 21(2) of the RIBA/JCT conditions, thus justifying an extension of time on that stated ground in Clause 23 of the RIBA/JCT conditions,[55] (and also additional payment under Clause 24). This misunderstands that provision, it is submitted. A Clause 21(2) postponement instruction is clearly differentiated in the contract from other instructions, such as a variation instruction, which only incidentally have the effect of delaying completion of the work, and it seems obvious that it is intended to apply to instructions in cases where the owner's primary or sole purpose is to secure postponement of some or all of the work for reasons of his own, it is submitted.]

13·078   The above cases were all concerned with the owner's duties following on assumed *justified* terminations of a nominated sub-contract, and it remains unclear whether the *Bickerton* interpretation and duty would apply where the main contractor had *wrongfully* determined the sub-contract. The attractions of the prospective compensation available to the main contractor under one of the numerous provisions for additional loss and expense to be found in the RIBA/JCT forms were such as to make it certain that attempts would be made by main contractors, following the *Bickerton* case, to involve the owner in the termination process itself. These have so far proved unsuccessful.

ILLUSTRATION

13·079   A heating sub-contractor nominated under the provisions of the RIBA/ JCT 1963 standard forms progressively delayed his part of the work, and the main contractors eventually wrote to the architect requesting permission to determine the sub-contract. He replied that he did not himself agree to this, but pointed out that all sub-contractors were the responsibility of the main contractors. Later he issued a certificate under Clause 27(*d*)(*ii*) of the main contract entitling the main contractor to receive damages from the nominated sub-contractor for delay in completion under the terms of the sub-contract, and some two months later the sub-contractors ceased work altogether. The main contractors then gave a preliminary notice to the sub-contractor prior to terminating the sub-contract, and on the same day wrote to the architect requesting instructions to determine the sub-contract, and also for a second nomination. The architect replied that the determination of the sub-contract did not require his authority; that if the sub-contract was later determined a

---

[54] 30 BLR 26. Analysed in detail in C.C.P.P., para. 21·34 *et seq.*
[55] See also *M. Harrison & Co. (Leeds) Ltd.* v. *Leeds City Council* (1980) 14 BLR 118. See the argument to the contrary in C.C.P.P., para. 21·21.

successor would be selected and nominated; but that the determination must be by the main contractors. The contractors then determined the sub-contract and a new sub-contractor was nominated, but the contractors brought proceedings against the owner claiming the expenses caused by the first sub-contractor's delay. On a preliminary issue the contractors contended that on the true construction of the main contract the architect was, by virtue of its various provisions for the issue of instructions by the architect, obliged to instruct the main contractor whether or not to determine the nominated sub-contractor's employment. *Held*, by the Court of Appeal, that while the *Bickerton* case required a substitute nomination even though there was no specific provision in the main contract to that effect, that had been necessary to enable the work to be done by a sub-contractor as contemplated by the contract. None of the seventeen examples of main RIBA/JCT contract clauses dealing with instructions to be given by the architect indicated that he should intervene with instructions where a sub-contract was to be determined, and since there was no problem of making the contract workable following a termination if the owner were to re-nominate a successor, there was no obligation for the contractor to obtain consent before determining, or any power for the architect to interfere by instructing the dismissal of the sub-contractor: *James Longley & Co. Ltd.* v. *Borough of Reigate and Banstead* (1982).[56]

It will be seen that the English courts have consistently endeavoured to resist a predictable series of attempts by contractors to extend the *Bickerton* interpretation by arguing that an owner who re-nominates a second sub-contractor following the first nominee's repudiation should be treated as being in breach of contract, or at least contractually responsible to the main contractor for all loss and expense resulting from the re-nomination instruction (and not merely payment of the second nominee's account as in *Bickerton*). It was even suggested that the owner should compensate the contractor for the consequences of any earlier breaches by the first nominee prior to the termination. This last contention would be the equivalent of a warranty by the owner of due performance on the part of the nominated sub-contractor, and was expressly rejected by Lord Frazer in the *Bilton* case.[57] In that case the House held, on the contrary, as has been seen, that the owner was entitled to liquidated damages against the main contractor for the pre-termination nominated sub-contract delays. The latest attempts to achieve contractual compensation for the re-nomination itself have centred on the many compensatory provisions to be found in the RIBA/JCT forms, particularly those relating to a postponement instruction under Clause 21(2) (wrongly, it is submitted, for the reasons stated in the Note to the *Bilton* case *supra*) and in C.C.P.P.[57a]   **13·080**

It is important to appreciate that the *Bickerton* interpretation, even if correct, is, on a really careful analysis of its judgments, dependent on the *express* wording of the pre-1980 RIBA/JCT nomination provision in Clause 27 of those forms, it is submitted,[57b] and not, as seems to have been   **13·081**

[56] 22 BLR 36.
[57] [1982] 1 W.L.R. 794, 800.
[57a] See C.C.P.P., paras. 21–34 *et seq.*
[57b] See, also on this, *infra*, para. 13·086 and *ante*, para. 4·194.

implicitly agreed in the judgment in the *Longley* case, on any "business efficacy" implied term of more general application. The case has no relevance to contracts using a different wording, or to the many construction contracts where the nomination power is not defined in any detail.[58]

13·082   The *Bickerton* case is also discussed at some length, together with the history of the other cases, earlier in this book in Chapter 4.[59] It is also, together with the *Bilton* and *Fairclough* cases in England, and the important *Jennings Industries* case in the High Court of Australia, the subject of two chapters in C.C.P.P.,[60] where both the legal reasoning and view of the practical background indicated by the *Bickerton* judgments is similarly questioned. As there pointed out, the finding of a *justified* right to object under Clause 27(*a*)(*ii*) of the main contract on the ground of the incompatibility of the second nominee's offered completion date, as suggested in *Bilton* and. confirmed in the *Fairclough* case, depended upon there being no applicable extension of time clause covering that particular delay (as in the *Fairclough* case, by reason of an amended standard form, there was not) in Clause 23 of the main contract. Had the usual unaltered "delay on the part of nominated sub-contractors" standard form ground of extension in that clause been present in the *Fairclough* contract, those words would have been apt to include, it is submitted, delays caused by a second nominee's late offered completion date in combination with any earlier delays of the first nominee, and if so this would remove the reasons for the valid objection under Clause 27(*a*)(*ii*) which had been the basis of the *Fairclough* case.[61] It should be reiterated, however, that these more detailed arguments only apply, of course, like the *Bickerton* interpretation itself, to contracts which use or follow closely the wording and related clauses of the English 1963 RIBA/JCT forms, and have no application to construction contracts generally.

13·083   Nevertheless, *Bickerton* was followed, despite some additional and apparently contrary wording in a contract, in Queensland in 1981.[62] However, in 1985 the High Court of Australia, while noting and distinguishing, but not openly disapproving *Bickerton*, in fact drew practical conclusions from the facts of the case before it (it is submitted entirely correctly) which, it may not have been appreciated, essentially demolished the expressed basis of the *Bickerton* judgments.

---

[58] See the contrary suggestion made by White J. in the Full Court of South Australia in the *Jennings Industries* case, illustrated *infra*, paras. 13·083–13·084, and disagreed with on this particular point in C.C.P.P., para. 21–27 *et seq.*, and effectively rejected by the High Court of Australia in the same case, as discussed *infra*.

[59] See Chap. 4, Section 2(5)(b), paras. 14·191 *et seq.*

[60] C.C.P.P., Chaps. 21 and 22.

[61] For this, see C.C.P.P., 21–36.

[62] *Re Townsville Hospital Board, Ex p. Jennings Industries* [1981] 2 Q.R. 592. See C.C.P.P., para. 21–30.

ILLUSTRATION

A South Australian main contract was in the Ed. 5a form. An extremely complicated nomination scheme under that form[63] entitled the main contractor by Clause 15(f) to receive instructions whenever a nominated sub-contractor's default might justify termination of the main contract if committed by the main contractor. These were to include instructions whether or not to terminate the sub-contract, as well as re-nomination instructions, and the owner was obliged to pay the main contractor full compensation for compliance with them, subject to the owner being entitled to retain any damages obtained by him using the name of the main contractor against the sub-contractor.[64] By Clause 15(g), however, Clause 15(f) was *not* to apply to a "special" class of nominated sub-contractor who had either been designated in the original main contract documents or appointed by agreement with the main contractor after the contract. However, by Clause 15(g) the main contractor was still to have the advantage of Clause 15(f) "in the case of the bankruptcy or liquidation" of even such a "special" sub-contractor. The remaining nomination provisions were similar to the RIBA/JCT pre-1980 forms, except that by Clause 13(c) of Ed. 5a it was provided in general terms that the contractor was not to be relieved of responsibility for the parts of the works sub-let to nominated sub-contractors.

13·084   By the time of practical completion a "special" nominated heating sub-contractor had left behind $80,000 worth of defective or unfinished work out of a total of $580,000 work in his sub-contract. Before the time for remedying defects had arrived the main contractor wrote to the architect stating *incorrectly* that the sub-contractor was in liquidation, and asking for instructions under Clause 15(f) to cover the making good of defects. The architect rightly pointed out that there had not been a liquidation, so that Clause 15(g) did not apply, and advised employment of other sub-contractors for making good defects. The main contractor then wrote to the sub-contractor stating that others would do the work, and that the sub-contractor's account would be debited. At a later stage the architect instructed the main contractor to deal with a list of the nominated sub-contract defects, but subsequently, following a notice to the main contractor from the architect (under a contractual power for the owner to use other contractors on failure of the main contractor to comply with such an instruction and notice) the owner carried out the remedial work itself, for which it ultimately debited the main contractor's account. Meanwhile, seven months later, and before the remedial work was completed, the nominated sub-contractor did go into liquidation. The main contractor then sought compensation, invoking Clause 15(f), and relying on the later liquidation of the nominated sub-contractor. The Full Court of South Australia held, citing Lord Reid's judgment in *Bickerton*, that the owner had been under a duty to nominate another sub-contractor, and that it had been a breach of contract on the part of the owner to do the remedial work itself, so that the owner could not recover the cost of the remedial work.[65] *Held*, by the High Court of Australia, overruling the Full Court, that the owner had been entitled to complete the work himself on expiry of his notice. The architect's letter had been a valid instruction under the defects

---

[63] For the scheme in detail and for some criticism of its draftsmanship, see C.C.P.P., para. 21–24.

[64] For the doubts about the effectiveness of such a provision in recovering the owner's damage see *post*, Chap. 14, Section 4(1)(c), para. 14·032, and see C.C.P.P., paras. 21–22 and 22–05.

[65] A further example of the lengths to which the *Bickerton* interpretation can lead.

liability clause. Under the contract, the contractor was obliged to carry out and complete *the whole* of the works, and by the defects liability clause he was obliged to make good *all* defects. *If the nominated sub-contractor dropped out, the contractor had a choice of engaging another sub-contractor with consent or doing the work himself.* There had been nothing at the relevant time when the original instructions were given entitling the main contractor to call for instructions under Clause 15(*f*): *City of Adelaide* v. *Jennings Industries* (1985).[66]

13·085   [Note: Apart from the obvious difference involved in the very strong contractor protection afforded by Clause 15(*f*) in "non-special" cases, this Australian contract was closely comparable to the RIBA/JCT forms, though there were some minor differences, and a more important one in Clause 13(*c*), between the contract and those used in the *Bickerton* and *Bilton* cases. Nevertheless, it is clear that the High Court found no difficulty whatever (consonant with the commercial and construction realities, it is submitted), in the idea of a main contractor either doing specialist work himself or arranging for it to be done by others in order to discharge his own responsibilities once in breach.[66a] Except in the case of a sub-contractor's liquidation and a successful invocation by the main contractor of Clause 15(*g*), the main contractor under this form of contract would have been bound to do this in the case of a "special" nominated sub-contractor whose sub-contract had been terminated or who had "dropped out." If so, it is difficult to see how, in the admitted absence of any express language in the RIBA/JCT forms to the contrary, a main contractor under those forms should not also be obliged to act in the same way upon the "dropping out" of a sub-contractor in breach of his own and the main contractor's contract, but the contrary view lay at the heart of the *Bickerton* judgments noted *supra*, with which the *Jennings* case is therefore fundamentally inconsistent.]

13·086   *Bickerton* remains a highly unsatisfactory case, but one, in view of the widespread use of the "such sums shall be expended in favour of such persons as the architect may instruct" wording still found in many contracts in England and overseas, which is likely to continue to come before the courts and produce anomalies, heightened by the difficulties of applying the remaining provisions, certainly in the RIBA/JCT contracts, in regard to extension of time and monetary compensation for the architect's instructions which the *Bickerton* interpretation envisages. The interpretation of these words arrived at by the House of Lords involves converting what was undoubtedly intended by the draftsman as a power *to be exercised once and for all* in relation to a P.C Sum at the time of giving his final nomination instruction into a continuing duty, and involves, without any express provision to that effect, providing compensation to main contractors who are in breach of a term of the main contract (the obligation to complete using the nominated sub-contractor). It also involves reducing or eliminating the liability of even solvent sub-contractors for repudiatory breaches of their sub-contracts. The fact that the two principal English standard forms have since produced expressly worded schemes having a

---

[66] 57 A.L.R. 456. The case in the Full Court and High Court is analysed in great detail in C.C.P.P., paras. 21–24—28, and Chap. 22.
[66a] The *Jacob & Youngs* v. *Kent* principle, see *supra*, n.41a.

similar effect, to the great disadvantage of owners, should not encourage jurisdictions which are not bound by the *Bickerton* case to arrive at similar interpretations without sufficiently explicit wording, it is submitted.

To summarise, the *Bickerton* interpretation is essentially open to criti- **13·087** cism on two main grounds of principle, and one on the wording, quite apart from the practical anomalies and difficulties in giving effect to it and to the remainder of the contact. These criticisms are:

(a) It does not pay regard to the clear "no privity" and "main con- tractor responsibility" objectives of the draftsman expressed by the words "are hereby declared to be sub-contractors employed by the contractor", and "nothing in the conditions shall render the employer in any way liable to a nominated sub-contractor."

(b) Its declared basis (that nominated sub-contract work shall only be **13·088** carried out by a nominee, so that even when in breach of that obli- gation, the contractor is prevented from offering substantial per- formance by any other means, and the owner becomes placed under a contractual duty to intervene in a situation created solely by the contractor's failure to perform) is wrong in principle. Many involuntary breaches of contract in regard to the quality and description of the work to be done can and do occur in construction contracts, as where, for example, stipulated goods or materials of the prescribed quality are not available in the market when required for the project. By analogy with the *Bickerton* and *Bilton* reasoning, the contractor in that situation will no longer be bound to perform (a sort of partial frustration of the contract) until the owner has issued instructions for a different material. This has never been the law,[67] and would be subversive of contracting if it was. The notion that central heating work (as has been seen featur- ing strongly in nearly all the re-nomination cases) is so esoteric and of such essential importance that a construction contract can be intended by the parties to reach a state of impasse or frustration, to be resolved only by the owner, in a situation caused by the contract- or's inability to meet his obligations, involves an act of judicial imagination taking over from reality, and it has been seen that the contrary view (that the contractor could make his own arrange- ments for completion, whether by himself or another sub-contract- or) presented no difficulties for the High Court of Australia in the *Jennings* case (nor indeed for the New York Court of Appeals in *Jacobs and Young* v. *Kent*).

(c) The "expending of the P.C. Sum" expression was merely "drafts- man's jargon", almost certainly used as early as 1900 [see *Hobbs* v. *Turner* (1902) illustrated *supra*, paragraph 13–033] for *a finally per- fected nomination* (that is, owner's or A/E's instruction followed by

---

[67] See Cardozo J.'s classical statements in *Jacob and Youngs Inc.* v. *Kent* 121 N.E. 889 (1921), cited *ante*, Chap. 4, Section 1(1)(a)(ii), para. 4·022, and see *supra*, n.41a.

concluded sub-contract), and did not contemplate some continuing
process thereafter during the sub-contract construction period.

(3) Provisional and P-C Sum Items

13·089   One of the peculiar characteristics of the traditional English nomination
draftsmanship (which as has been seen actually preceded in point of time
provisions spelling out the nomination procedure in detail)[67a] is the procedural technique, as can be seen from the wording of the above clauses,
whereby nearly all work intended to be sub-contracted by selected
specialists is designated in specifications or bills of quantities either as a
prime cost or provisional sum or item.[68] Although these terms are in virtually universal use in the building industry, no clear and authoritative
definition of their meaning has emerged from the cases dealing with sub-
contracts,[69] but it is not difficult to see how the terms came into use.

The explanation of the words "provisional sum" emerges clearly from
the judgment of Romer L.J. in *Leslie's* case[70] which points out that these
items in Victorian specifications usually commenced with the words "Provide the sum of £—", and were frequently referred to as "provisions."[70a] It
may be speculated that the word "provisional" was a corruption, meaning
no more than "provided", and did not connote "provisional" in its correct
sense of "contingent". It may be speculated that the expression "P-C"
(standing for prime cost) was an alternative method of describing such
work, since it indicated to the contractor that the work so described would
be paid for on the basis of the actual cost to himself (that is to say, the
actual amount of the sub-contractor's account) as opposed to his being
required to tender a price for it.

13·090   Over the years, however, the origin of "provision" appears to have
become forgotten, and a tendency for the "provisional sum" expression to
be applied to *contingent* work seems to have developed. The expressions
were undoubtedly, however, freely interchangeable for a long period of
time, and certainly lack any real precision and can easily be misleading at
the present day in the absence of a clear-cut definition in the contract
documents, which is almost always lacking.

In the ninth edition of this book it was suggested that the term "provisional sum" was apt to describe work the extent of which had not been
finally determined at the time of letting the contract, while the term "P-C"
was usually applied to items which were determinable, but whose price

---

[67a] See *Hampton* v. *Glamorgan County Council* (1917), illustrated *supra*, para. 13·037.
[68] See, in addition to the present discussion, *ante*, Chap. 3, paras. 3·020–3·021.
[69] The definitions boldly hazarded by Channell J. in *Crittall Manufacturing Co.* v. *L.C.C.*
(1910) 75 J.P. 203 and by Coleridge J. in *Young & Co.* v. *White* (1912) 28 T.L.R. 87 were
expressly disapproved by the Court of Appeal in *Hampton* v. *Glamorgan C.C.* [1917] A.C.
13.
[70] *Leslie* v. *Metropolitan Asylums District* (1901) 68 J.P. 86. See also in *Hampton's* case, *per*
Lord Haldane. Compare the wording in *Leslie's* case, see *supra*, para. 13·032.
[70a] See the *Hampton* case, *supra*, para. 13·037.

was uncertain, usually by reason of an element of choice on the part of the building owner. Thus it was suggested that normally provisional sums would apply to work alone or work and materials, while P-C items would usually apply to materials or fittings which would need to be purchased by the contractor once they had been selected, though there was no hard-and-fast rule.

Since the ninth edition of this book, however, the Standard Methods of Measurement in both industries have put forward somewhat varying definitions of the "P-C" and "Provisional Sum" terms. The expressions, though commonly found in building bills of quantities or specifications, have traditionally not been mentioned expressly in the contract conditions in the RIBA/JCT forms of building contract in the past, and have had contractual significance, if at all, only through any terms of those contracts which have successfully incorporated the building industry Standard Methods of Measurement. On the other hand in the case of the ICE civil engineering standard forms, Clauses 58 of the 1955 and 1973 fourth and fifth editions respectively expressly provided different, though not very precise, contractual definitions of the terms. These perhaps suggest that P.C. items must be carried out or supplied by selected sub-contractors whereas Provisional Sum items may, *at the owner's option*, be carried out or supplied by the main contractor himself or by a selected sub-contractor. The lack of uniformity and precision in all these various definitions, therefore, largely destroys their value in drafting or construing a contract unless they are further defined in more detail by the contract, either expressly or by reference. Persons concerned to interpret particular construction contracts in regard to work described in this way will principally require to ascertain: **13·091**

(a) whether the contractor (and so by implication any domestic sub-contractor he may, subject to any contractual restrictions, choose to employ for the purpose) is permitted to do the work himself. **13·092**

(b) whether the owner, on the contrary, has the power to decide whether the contractor or a sub-contractor or supplier should do the work or supply the material.

(c) whether the work is contingent and provisional, in the sense that it may never be ordered at all.[71]

(d) whether, on the contrary, it is intended that the work will indeed be carried out, but only by a contractor or sub-contractor selected by the owner.

(e) how the work is to be paid for in the settlement of accounts, including the pricing of attendance or ancillary plant or supervisory expenditure, and the calculation of profit or "cash discount" allowances.[72] Precision in these latter matters is often lacking, although

---

[71] Compare Clause 58(1) of the ICE fifth edition.

[72] For the misleading nature of the "cash discount" description and its function as pure profit under the English standard forms, see the discussion *supra*, paras. 13·007–13·008, and *infra*, paras. 13·094 and 13·118.

highly desirable and now somewhat more closely regulated albeit in difficult and obscure language, in the English standard forms.

Particular precision is required in regard to the sums to be paid to the main contractor.

ILLUSTRATIONS

13·093   (1) Where auctioneers were to be paid a lump sum as "commission and out-of-pocket expenses". *Held*, by the Divisional Court, that they were not entitled to retain trade discounts in respect of printing and advertising, although no such discount would have been allowed to their client if he had dealt direct: *Hippisley* v. *Knee Brothers* (1905).[73]

(2) A main contract in lump sum form expressly excluded any fluctuation adjustments to the price. Part of the main contract specification stated "Claims by sub-contractors will not be considered relative to rise and fall. The Builder will pay all such claims and allow for this in his tender". The main contract also provided for the substitution in its accounts of any additional amounts "properly expended in respect of prime cost or provisional sums". The architect nominated a sub-contractor whose quotation included a fluctuations clause. *Held*, by the High Court of Australia, that the specification was probably an old document, and that the builder was entitled to recover the fluctuations payable to the nominated sub-contractor. *Per* Stephen J., "I would require a most clearly expressed provision to overcome the inference that when a proprietor requires a builder to accept his estimate of the cost of an item by including P.C. sums as a mandatory part of the tender, those P.C. amounts, which are only estimates made for the purpose of convenience, are inherently subject to adjustment when the true cost … emerges in due course": *Tuta Products* v. *Hutcherson Bros.* (1972).[74]
[Note: This case is clearly correct in its assessment of the P.C. sum meaning and intention, it is submitted.]

(4) Cash Discount

13·094   The English standard forms, reinforced by the standard methods of measurement in both industries, contemplate that the main contractor will be paid by the owner the full amount of nominated sub-contractors' or suppliers' verified accounts for their work, before a "cash discount" of 5 per cent. in the case of supply-only sub-contracts or 2½ per cent. on work or work and materials sub-contracts. Comparison of the detailed payment provisions in the related sub-contract standard forms and those of the main contract requiring onward payment to nominated sub-contractors by the main contractor, almost invariably shows that, in fact, as between owner and main contractor, no financing element on the part of the main contractor is involved, since his obligation to pay the sub-contractor does

---

[73] [1905] 1 K.B. 1.
[74] 46 A.L.J.R. 119.

not arise until *after* his own entitlement to be paid for the sub-contract work on the certificate under the main contract (in fact, payment under most English standard form sub-contracts has traditionally been made dependent upon main contract *certification*, though there is a current movement in favour of "pay-when-paid" provisions).[74a]

These permitted "discounts" in the main contract therefore represent a **13·095** pure profit on nominated sub-contract turnover in the hands of the main contractor. Coupled with the absence of pricing risk resulting from his entitlement to the full amount of the nominated sub-contractor's account, (whatever that may be, including any claims permitted by the sub-contract) this explains why nominated sub-contract work is so exceptionally attractive and profitable for main contractors, even if no additional sums for profit or attendance are priced in the Bills or Specification, as the Standard Methods expressly contemplate.

The policy of the standard forms is to prohibit any other or greater "discounts", so that these, if obtained, will accrue for the owner's benefit by reducing the sums payable to the main contractor. As between main contractor and sub-contractor, regard must be had to the terms of the sub-contract to decide the main contractor's entitlement to the cash or other discounts—see *infra*, Section 4, Subsection (7).

SECTION 4. MAIN CONTRACTOR AND SUB-CONTRACTOR

(1) Generally

There are obvious and important differences between the background of **13·096** main and sub-contracts in the construction field. Perhaps most importantly, the degree of undisturbed possession of the site to be afforded to the sub-contractor will be almost infinitely variable, by contrast with that usually given to main contractors by the owner.[75]

While RIBA/JCT main contracts and their attendant FASS nominated sub-contract forms set up an architect's certifying machinery for delay which appears to contemplate a single "completion date" for nominated sub-contract work, as for a main contractor's work,[76] in very many cases this is in fact quite unrealistic, and the main contractor is more likely to suffer damage from earlier failures of the sub-contractor to conform to programme, or to the work of others, or with earlier intermediate completion dates, than from any delay in the sub-contractor's final date of departure from the site on completion of his work. Consequently liquidated or general damages conditioned on late completion will usually be an inappropriate and awkward sanction for recovery of the main con-

---

[74a] As to these see *infra*, Section 4(5).
[75] For this and for sub-contractors' possession see *ante*, Chap. 4, Section 2(3)(c), paras. 4·157 *et seq.*
[76] See Clauses 27(d) and 8(a) of the two (pre-1980) forms respectively.

tractor's own delay and disturbance damage due to sub-contractor delay, and may not even reflect accurately that element of main contractor damage resulting from his liability to the owner for late completion of the main contract work, since a relatively small delay in final sub-contract completion may conceal a far greater delay and expense inflicted on a main contractor, and hence deserving of extension of time in the main contract (assuming that any extension of time at all should be allowed for this reason). Disregarding these refinements, questions of delay in the performance of sub-contracts and their impact on the main contractor's responsibilities have also been considered in Chapter 10.[77]

(2) Documentation

13·097 While important sub-contracts may have a final documentation not dissimilar from that in main contracts, with separate sub-contract specifications, drawings, and conditions of contract, it is usual, even in the case of important sub-contracts (many of which under the English standard form procedures will be nominated sub-contracts) to find a much more informal documentation, often not prepared for exchange and execution on a particular date, but instead coming into existence at different times as a result of exchanges of correspondence, quotations, orders, and acceptances of orders, and of meetings or negotiations between the owner or his A/E and the representatives of the main contractor and sub-contractor.

Thus, a main contract may describe the work which is to be performed in a subordinate nominated sub-contract in detail, with its own drawings and specifications, which will then be incorporated by reference and repeated in the later resulting sub-contract. Alternatively and more commonly, however, the use of P-C, and Provisional Sum machinery can mean that detailed descriptions of the work will not exist in the main contract at all at the time it is entered into, and that the detailed sub-contract descriptions will either be prepared and forwarded by the A/E when inviting quotations from tendering sub-contractors, or be prepared by the sub-contractors themselves as part of their quotations.

13·098 In these types of situation, the sub-contract will often only be finally concluded by the sub-contractor's acceptance of the main contractor's order, itself placed with the sub-contractor as a result of an earlier instruction from the architect which had identified and required a still earlier sub-contractor's quotation to be accepted. That original quotation may in turn have identified other documents containing the detailed technical descriptions of the sub-contract work, including any original architect's invitation to tender and its accompanying documents. At any stage up to the final stage of binding acceptance, therefore (whether this is achieved by the main contractor's order, if it contains no counter-offer and if the sub-contractor's quotation has been one capable of binding acceptance,

---

[77] Sections (6) and (7).

or by the final sub-contractor's acknowledgement of the order, sometimes only by conduct in commencing work) either party may seek to introduce its own terms of trading by "Conditions on the Back" or other devices, or to introduce qualifications of a previous document or some new term, so constituting in law a counter-offer. One or other of the documents, from the A/E's invitation to tender onwards, may also incorporate by reference a standard or other form of sub-contract conditions. Highly complicated questions of offer and acceptance, including so-called "battles of the forms", are therefore quite likely to arise in sub-contracts,[78] but much less likely in main contracts.

(3) Incorporation of Terms

As in other areas of commerce, the exchange of documents which lead up to the conclusion of a sub-contract frequently contain references, often in vague terms lacking precision, showing that some other identifiable document or set of contract terms are to apply to the sub-contract. In construction sub-contracts these usually take two principal forms, namely references to a part or all of the main contract itself (or to the main contractor's obligations under it which, by implication if not expressly, the sub-contractor undertakes to perform), on the one hand, and secondly references, often garbled and inaccurate, to some known and publicly available set of documents or standard form which it is intended should constitute the formal sub-contract conditions.   **13·099**

(a) Incorporation of main contract terms

This can give rise to considerable difficulties, since the incorporation is often loosely expressed in the most general words and without any precise or careful consideration of the consequences. Each case must be separately considered to determine the precise purpose and extent to which it is desired to incorporate the term or terms of the main contract. It follows from the absence of privity between the owner and the sub-contractor that, without incorporation, the terms of the main contract, even though well known to both parties, cannot bind the sub-contractor.[79] This will be very much a question of interpretation on a case-by-case basis of often informal documentation in an endeavour to ascertain the parties' objective intentions to be derived from the language used.   **13·100**

---

[78] See for this *ante*, Chap. 1, Section 2(5), paras. 1·023 *et seq.*, and 1·032 *et seq.* and Chap. 3, Section 3(2), paras. 3·066–3·067 and for incorporation of documents generally, see Chap. 3, Section 2, paras. 3·048 *et seq.*

[79] See also as to this *supra*, Section 2, para. 13·016. They may, however, have an important effect *in tort*, as part of the "contract structure" or "setting", see *supra*, para. 13·043, and *ante*, paras. 1·325–1·326.

ILLUSTRATIONS

(1) A sub-contractor undertook to carry out work in accordance with certain specifications in the main contract. One of these provided for disputes to be settled by arbitration. The sub-contractor sued for the price of his work, and the contractor applied for the action to be stayed under the terms of the arbitration clause. *Held*, by the Court of Session, that the arbitration clause was incorporated only to the extent of making the arbitrator's decisions binding on matters of dispute between the main contractor and the owner, but was not incorporated so as to govern disputes between the contractor and sub-contractor: *Goodwins, Jardine & Co.* v. *Brand* (1905).[80]

13·101

(2) A sub-contract provided "the terms of payment shall be exactly the same as ... clause 30" of the main contract. Clause 30 provided for interim payments on certificates of the architect at the rate of 80 per cent. of work done, and for the usual balances on completion as certified by the architect. The architect refused to certify for certain of the sub-contractor's work on the ground that it was defective. *Held*, by the Court of Appeal, that the contractor had a good defence to the sub-contractor's claim: *Geary Walker & Co. Ltd.* v. *Lawrence & Son* (1906).[81]

(3) A sub-contract contained many provisions in similar terms to those in the head contract, but none referring to or incorporating a power of the engineers in the main contract to require the removal of a sub-contractor with whom they were dissatisfied. The sub-contractor was delayed by lack of funds, and the engineers served a notice under the main contract. *Held*, by the Court of Appeal, that (a) the parties had the main contract before them when the sub-contract was concluded, and must be taken to have contemplated this possibility, so that no term could be implied in the sub-contract giving the main contractor power to determine the sub-contract simply upon the engineer's notice being given, and (b) a recital that the sub-contractor had agreed to carry out the work in accordance with the terms of the main contract did not, where other clauses of the main contract were expressly brought into the sub-contract have the effect of incorporating the clause in question: *Chandler Bros. Ltd.* v. *Boswell* (1936).[82]

13·102

(4) Tunnelling sub-contractors in Ontario undertook "the execution of the work ... according to the dimensions and specifications as set forth in the contract between (the main contractors and the owners)." Clause 318 of the general specifications provided "The City also reserves the right for the engineer to stop the excavation or any other portion of the work and to require the contractor to complete the sewer and backfilling up to such point as the engineer may direct before proceeding further with the excavation, and the contractor shall not thereby become entitled to demand or recover any allowance or compensation other than an extension of the contract time." This power was exercised, and the sub-contractor sued the main contractor for damages. *Held*, by Schroeder J., that, following *Chandler* v. *Boswell*, Clause 318 was not incorporated into the sub-contract: *Smith & Montgomery* v. *Johnson Bros.* (1954).[83]

---

[80] 7 F. (Ct. of Sess.) 995. See also *The Portsmouth* [1912] A.C. 1.
[81] Hudson, *Building Contracts* (4th ed.) Vol. 2, p. 382.
[82] [1936] 3 All E.R. 179. (*Cf. Osborn* v. *Leggett* (1930) S.A.S.R. 346 Australia.)
[83] [1954] D.L.R. 392, Ontario H.C. See also the case of *Croft Construction Co.* v. *Terminal Construction Co.* (1960) 20 D.L.R. (2d) 247, illustrated *ante*, Chap. 6, para. 6·042. (Not, perhaps, strictly a case of incorporation.)

(5) The main contractor's order to a nominated sub-contractor contained two provisions: first "The party to whom this order is given shall observe and perform the conditions contained in the contract held by (the main contractor), which can be inspected at their office, and this order shall be deemed to be supplemental thereto"; and secondly—"Payment for this order is to be made (a) as to the amount if any provided . . . in (the main contractor's) said contract for the works in this order . . . in accordance with the certificates and the terms provided in the said contract." The main contract (in the then RIBA form) provided by Clause 21(3)(a) that payment in respect of any work comprised in a nominated sub-contract would not be due until receipt by the main contractor of the architect's certificate relating to the work. *Held*, by the Court of Appeal, that the second provision (but not the first) had the effect of incorporating, as between the main contractor and the sub-contractor, the provisions of Clause 21(3)(a): *Dunlop & Ranken Ltd.* v. *Hendall Steel Structures* (1957).[84]

(6) A main contractor's order to a sub-contractor enclosed a copy of the main contract stating "It must be drawn to your attention that the conditions as laid down in the contract documents must be adhered to at all times . . . You will be paid on the same basis as [the main contractor]." There was a clause in the main contract vesting plant in the owner on being brought to the site, with attendant powers of control over it. Under powers in the main contract the engineer ordered the exclusion of the sub-contractor from the site, being dissatisfied with his work, and the owner brought proceedings to prevent removal of the sub-contractor's plant. *Held*, by the High Court of Southern Rhodesia, that the vesting clause had not been incorporated into the subcontract by the wording used, and in any event only the main contractor could enforce the main contract provision: *Triangle Ltd.* v. *John Burrows Ltd.* (1958).[85]

13·103

(7) Control mechanism sub-contractors gave a quotation to main contractors who were constructing a boiler plant, which was expressed to be subject to the sub-contractors' standard conditions of sale, of which they enclosed a copy. By those conditions the risk of damage to the goods passed on delivery to the main contractor, but the title remained in the sub-contractors until payment (*i.e.* a "Romalpa" clause). The quotation was accepted by the main contractors with the specification and price confirmed, but their order then provided: "Terms and conditions in accordance with Main Contract GC/Works/1, Edition 2 plus Amendment 4 (See Form of Contract attached)." The "Form of Contract attached" was not actually the main contract document, but a further identification of it in the same terms as in the order. By Clause 30(2) of the main contract, every case of sub-letting in connection with the contract was to include a provision that all goods brought onto the site should vest in the contractor. *Held*, by Mervyn Davies J., that the main contractor's acceptance had the effect of incorporating Clause 30(2), and was in fact a counter-offer destroying the effect of the sub-contract "Romalpa" clause, and the main contractor's liquidator was not liable to deliver up the equipment or to hand over the proceeds of its sale to the sub-contractors. *Sauter Automation Ltd.* v. *Goodman (Mechanical Services) Ltd.* (1986).[86]

As a matter of first principle and in the light of the usual real-life intentions of sub-contracting parties, doubtful or ambiguous references to main contract documents or terms are much more likely to be aimed at the

---

[84] [1957] 1 W.L.R. 1102.
[85] [1958] (3) S.A. 811.
[86] 34 BLR 84.

technical descriptions of the sub-contract work to be found in the drawings, specifications or bills of quantities of the main contract rather than at
the contractual or legal provisions in the main contract documentation, it
is submitted.

13·104   One very common form of wording referring to the contents of the main
contract provides that the sub-contractor "shall be deemed to have notice
of all the provisions of the main contract". Though very imprecise, these
evidently have a more limited effect that full-scale incorporation. So in a
case where the main contract contained important rights to compensation
for compliance with architects instructions, and also for loss or expense
claims on a number of grounds, neither provision being present in the
sub-contract, the wording was held not to confer similar rights on the sub-
contractor in those events.[87]

A further provision commonly found in standard forms of sub-contract
will be an indemnity given to the main contractor against any act or omission of the sub-contractor involving the main contractor in liability to the
owner under the terms of the main contract;[87a] or, more simply, "against
and from any breach of contract by the sub-contractor", which latter
would seem to be little more than a re-affirmation of the sub-contractor's
obligations in indemnity form.[87b] Whichever type of indemnity is involved,
it would seem that limitation will not start to run against the indemnitee
(i.e. the main contractor) until the loss has been incurred as, for example, a
claim being made against the main contractor by the owner or by some
third person.[87c]

(b) Incorporation of sub-contract conditions

13·105   As stated, incorporation references to other forms of contract or sub-
contract in sub-contract documentation are common, but frequently garbled and inaccurate. However, the courts will not usually be discouraged
by inaccuracies of nomenclature, and may even positively assist in regard
to uncompleted parts of the documentation, if satisfied by evidence that
the intended document and the precise purpose of its incorporation can be
sufficiently clearly ascertained.[88]

ILLUSTRATIONS

(1) A main contractor's order was in the following terms: "To supply ...
labour, plant and machinery, in full accordance with the appropriate form for

---

[87] *Jardine Engineering Corporation* v. *Shimizu Corporation* (1992) 63 B.L.R. 96, Hong Kong
H.C., Kaplan J.
[87a] See, *e.g.* the FASS 1963 "Green Form" sub-contract, Clause 3(b)(ii).
[87b] See, *e.g.* Clause 3(b)(i) of the "Green Form" *supra*.
[87a] See the discussion and cases referred to *ante*, Chap. 4, paras. 4·289–4·290, and for indemnities generally see *post*, Chap. 15, Section 2.
[88] See, for the subject of incorporation generally *ante*, Chap. 3, Section 2, paras. 3·048 *et seq*.

nominated sub-contractors RIBA 1965 Edition." *Held*, by the Court of Appeal, that evidence could be received that the RIBA was not connected with any form of nominated sub-contract, but had published a 1963 Edition of a main contract; that the NFBTE and the FASS had issued in 1963 a form of nominated sub-contract (commonly known as "the Green Form") headed "for use where the sub-contractor is nominated under the 1963 Edition of the RIBA form of main contract"; that in the light of the evidence the words in the sub-contract would be understood in the trade as referring to "the Green Form"; that the words "RIBA 1965 Edition" were an added description not intended to restrict the preceding expression and could be ignored as a false and inaccurate description; and that the words were sufficient to incorporate the arbitration clause of the "Green Form" into the sub-contract: *Modern Buildings Wales Ltd.* v. *Limmer and Trinidad Co. Ltd.* (1975).[89]

(2) A main contractor's order stipulated that the sub-contract documents **13·106** should comprise (*inter alia*) a Standard Form of Tender and Conditions of Contract. After identifying the main (RIBA) form of contract, it then stated: "The Conditions applicable in the sub-contract with you shall be those embodied in the RIBA as above agreement." The Standard Form of Tender stipulated that a sub-contract should be executed, and that it should be in terms equivalent to those of the NFBTE and FASS "Green Form", but no such sub-contract was in the event ever executed. The work was completed and a dispute arose over damages for delay. *Held*, by the Court of Appeal, (a) that the reference to the RIBA form was only to those clauses in the form relating to nominated sub-contractors; Clause 27 of that form made certain stipulations not inconsistent with the "Green Form"; and that the sub-contract should be interpreted in the light of what the parties would have agreed in a formal sub-contract using that form, had they executed it; and further (b) that a completion date for the sub-contract subsequently agreed by the parties but never formally entered by them into the Appendix of the Green Form (since it had never been finally completed by the parties) could be treated as though inserted in the Appendix: *Brightside Kilpatrick Engineering Services* v. *Mitchell Construction* (1975).[90]

It would seem that more distinct and specific words may be needed if the objective is the arbitration clause rather than the other provisions of another contract or sub-contract,[91] and the special requirement of writing under the English Arbitration Acts may also prevent effective incorporation of such a clause.[92]

(4) Quotations to Tendering Main Contractors

Domestic sub-contractors are often requested to give quotations to pro-   **13·107** spective main contractors in order to enable them to price their main contract tenders and in the knowledge that they are required for that purpose.

---

[89] [1975] 1 W.L.R. 1281.
[90] [1975] 2 Lloyds Rep. 493.
[91] *Aughton Ltd. (formerly Aughton Group Ltd.)* v. *M. F. Kent Services Ltd.* (1991) 57 B.L.R. 1, 32, and see *T. W. Thomas & Co. Ltd.* v. *Portsea Steamship Co. Ltd.* [1912] A.C. 1 there cited and followed.
[92] *Ibid.*

By contrast, in a situation where a main contractor has already been appointed at the time of requesting a quotation, there is clearly no reason why the quotation, like any other offer, cannot be withdrawn at any time before its acceptance. However, where the main contractor to the knowledge of the parties will be tendering on the faith of the sub-contractor's quotation, the question arises whether the sub-contractor will be permitted to withdraw his tender, so perhaps inflicting a loss on the main contractor if his price cannot be matched, should the latter subsequently be awarded the main contract.

In such a case where the main contractor can be seen to have accepted an obligation to place the sub-contract with the sub-contractor in the event of his own tender being successful, consideration for an implied promise to keep the offer open is clearly present, so that the quotation cannot be withdrawn and no difficulty arises.[93] Where, however, the background known to the parties is the quite common one that the main contractor is seeking quotations from a number of sub-contractors themselves tendering in competition, it will clearly not be possible without more to imply an undertaking by the main contractor to place the order with any particular sub-contractor, even if his tender is the lowest, and consideration in any usual sense in return for an obligation of the sub-contractor to keep his own offer open would not seem to be present. A leading case in California, based on the doctrine of promissory estoppel, has nevertheless held a sub-contractor bound in these circumstances, and this position, which seems realistic, has been adopted in the Second United States Re-Statement of Contracts.[94]

(5) "Pay when Paid" Provisions

(a) Generally

13·108 Traditionally the liability of the main contractor to make payments to sub-contractors, in regard to both interim and final payment, has been conditioned in the English standard forms of sub-contract upon the *certification* of the sums in question by the owner's A/E under terms of the main contract, usually with stipulation for payment within a specified number of days thereafter. In the United States, and in the various standard forms of sub-contract to be found in Malaysia, Singapore and Hong Kong (and now increasingly in England itself), however, "pay when paid" provisions, usually requiring *payment by the owner* in addition to main contract certification as a condition of sub-contractor entitlement, have become increasingly common. Again, it will occasion small surprise that the standard form draftsmanship has shown little interest in, or understanding of

---

[93] See the recent Canadian cases referred to *ante*, Chap. 1, Section 2(3), para. 1·026.
[94] Section 89(2), and see *Drennan* v. *Star Paving Co.*, 333 P.2nd 757 (1958), *ante*, Chap. 1, Section 2(3), para. 1·027. See, however, the criticisms of this view by Sweet, *Legal Aspects of Architecture, etc.*, 3d Edition, Section 32–02.

the practical working details required for satisfactory implementation of such provisions (in particular dealing with cases where owner cross-claims, or set-offs unrelated to the sub-contract work, are the reason for the owner's non-payment of the main contractor). In addition in a number of sub-contract forms in Hong Kong, Malaysia and Singapore there has been drafting carelessness in failing to apply the "pay when paid" formula throughout the sub-contract (for example, by omitting reference to it in provisions for payment of retention, or of the final balance or, even where present in those cases, for regulating the payments to be made to the contractor following a determination of the sub-contract by either party).

The principal problems arising under these provisions are, therefore, first the more general question whether the provisions are intended as administrative only, and so limited to regulating the timing of payments under the contract while not preventing ultimate recovery, or whether on the other hand, they are to operate as a binding condition of liability permanently preventing recovery by the sub-contractor (in the event, for example, of the owner's insolvency), and, notwithstanding satisfactory completion in all respects of the sub-contract work. In such cases it may be necessary in interpreting the sub-contract to decide whether the omission to make "pay-when-paid" provision comprehensively at all points of the sub-contract is an indication of a limited administrative intention only, (so making ultimate payment not dependent on owner payment of the main contractor) or whether it represents no more than drafting carelessness, with owner payment remaining a condition. **13·109**

The second question is whether the sub-contractor subject to a "pay-when-paid" provision is entitled to be paid where the non-payment of the main contractor is the result of some extraneous complaint by the owner against the main contractor unrelated to the sub-contract—in any such dispute between owner and main contractor the owner must, as a matter of law, be giving credit to the main contractor for the work satisfactorily completed by the sub-contractor against any claim the owner may have against the main contractor arising out of other matters. In this context there is in fact a third problem, with which the sub-contract draftsman again unsurprisingly invariably fails to deal, namely the effect of a *partial* payment by the owner, and its distribution between the main contractor and any other sub-contractors who may be subject to "pay-when-paid" restrictions.[95] This subject is also discussed in C.C.P.P.[95a]

(b) Whether a condition of liability

A "pay-when-paid" sub-contract, if intended as a permanent and binding condition of main contractor liability, has many of the features of a joint venture between main and sub-contractor, and may reflect substantial main contractor bargaining power in insisting that the sub-contractor must be content to rely on the credit of the owner for ultimate payment in **13·110**

---

[95] See *infra* (c), para. 13·115.   [95a] See para. 20–03.

the same way as the main contractor has to do himself. There can be no objection in principle to this, despite attempts in some official sub-contractor quarters to invoke concepts of economic duress, or unconscionability, or unfairness when discussing such provisions. The commercial purpose of such a provision will be to protect the main contractor from excessive loss in an owner insolvency, through the requirement that the sub-contractor should effectively share a due proportion of that loss. However, it can be readily conceded that it is certainly not an attractive proposition for sub-contractors commercially, since they will be effectively at risk twice over, that is, in regard to the main contractor's insolvency as well as that of the owner.[96] Thus, it has been seen that since the earliest times in a main contractor's insolvency there will be no right of the sub-contractor against a solvent owner, in the absence of some contractual relationship with him,[97] or perhaps in rare cases some right in tort based on a negligent representation as to the main contractor's solvency.[98] Nor will quasi-contract based on principles of unjust enrichment afford an unpaid sub-contractor a remedy against the owner. If it were so, the owner would not only be liable twice over for the same work in the event of a main contractor insolvency, but in such a case payment by him of the sub-contractor in full would be void against the liquidator as a preferential payment of a creditor in breach of the *pari passu* distribution rules.[99]

13·111   In the United States, however, there have undoubtedly been a number of cases where the courts have held "pay-when-paid" provisions to be no bar to sub-contractor recovery once the sub-contract has been properly completed.

ILLUSTRATIONS

(1) A sub-contract provided that "final payment shall be made within 30 days after completion of the work included in their sub-contract, written acceptance by the Architect, *and full payment therefor by the Owner*". Held, by the Court of Appeals of Georgia, both the acceptance of the Architect and payment by the owner were conditions precedent to payment. "It is open to the construction that the possibility of the owner's non-payment on account of plaintiff's work is the sub-contractor's risk rather than of the prime contractor". *Peacock Construction Co.* v. *West* (1965).[1]

(2) A sub-contract stipulated the total price "no part of which shall be due until five days after Owner shall have paid Contractor therefor, provided however that no more than 90 per cent. thereof shall be due until 35 days after the entire work shall have been completed ... nothing herein to be construed

---

[96] See Fitzgerald P. in *Trade Indemnity Australia Ltd.* v. *Parkinson Air Conditioning* (1994) 13 A.C.L.R. 19, Qd. C.A., and see C.C.P.P., para. 20–03.
[97] *Paterson* v. *Gandasequi, Hampton* v. *Glamorgan C.C., supra,* paras. 13·031 and 13·037.
[98] Compare the architect's liability to a sub-contractor in such a situation in *Day* v. *Ost* [1973] 2 N.Z.L.R. 385, see *ante,* para. 1·284, and for the *Hedley Byrne* principle generally, see *ante,* Chap. 1, paras. 1·280 *et seq.*
[99] See *e.g. Re Holt, ex. p. Gray* (1988) 58 L.J.Q.B. 5, illustrated *infra,* para. 13·121.
[1] 142 S.E.2nd 332.

as preventing Contractor from paying to the sub-contractor all or any part of the said price at any time thereafter as an advance or otherwise". *Held*, by the U.S. 6th Circuit Court of Appeal, that the provision was designed to postpone payment for a reasonable period after work had been completed so as to afford the general contractor an opportunity to procure the funds necessary to pay the sub-contractor, and not to require the sub-contractor to wait an indefinite period of time until the general contractor was paid by the owner: *Thomas Dyer & Co.* v. *Bishop International Engineering Co.* (1968).[2]

(3) A sub-contract was in identical terms to that in the *Peacock* v. *West* case **13-112** *supra. Held*, by the Supreme Court of Florida, following the *Thomas Dyer* case, that the view of the majority of jurisdictions in the U.S. was that this type of wording in small sub-contracts did not indicate the transfer of the risk of owner non-payment to the sub-contractor: *Peacock Construction Co.* v. *Modern Air Conditioning* (1977).[3]

(4) A sub-contract provided that "final payment consisting of the unpaid balance of the Price shall be made within 45 days after the last of the following to occur: (a) full completion of the work by the sub-contractor; (b) final acceptance of the work by the architect and owner; (c) final payment by Owner to Contractor", (together with a number of other conditions). *Held*, by the Louisiana District Court, that the clause should be interpreted to mean 45 days after the listed events would normally have occurred: *Aesco Steel Inc.* v. *Jones Construction Company* (1985).[4]

The *Thomas Dyer* case, however, appears to have relied upon legal **13-113** authorities outside the construction field relating to suspensive conditions. While there seems little doubt, however, that the majority view referred to in the second *Peacock Construction* case *supra*, has established itself in construction contracts in the United States jurisdictions, as reflected in the 1981 Restatement (Second) of Contracts,[5] those United States judgments which have followed this trend have paid insufficient regard, it is submitted, to the commercial background underlying sub-contracting in the construction industry, and in particular to the factor of potential owner insolvency (not likely, of course, to be a factor in government contracts). Moreover, in regard to risks other than insolvency (for example, administrative severity by government or supervisory officers) it might also be intended that the risk should be similarly shared. In all such cases (except only insolvency) the sub-contractor under such a strict interpretation, will, however, be protected in the last resort by implied terms if the main contractor proves unwilling or unable to prosecute the claim for payment against the owner, or to assign his rights of action against the owner to the sub-contractor, it is submitted.

For these reasons, it seems unlikely that English courts would afford assistance to an unpaid sub-contractor under the Unfair Contract Terms Act 1976, for example, or would dispense with the condition imposed by a

---

[2] 303 F.2nd 655.
[3] 353 So. 2nd 840.
[4] 621 F. Supp. 1576 (1985). See also *Seal Tite Cap* v. *Ehret* 589 S. Supp. 701 (1984) New Jersey D.C.
[5] See The Restatements Illustration 1, Comment (b), para. 227.

"pay-when-paid" provision for any other reason, it is submitted, provided they considered that the intention of the language was clear.[6]

13·114   The usual question to be asked when interpreting a "pay-when-paid" sub-contract provision from this point of view is whether (like the interim certification provisions in the RIBA/JCT main contract forms themselves) it is concerned only with the timing of interim payments, or whether it shows a "joint venture" intention to condition all payment of the sub-contractor, and in particular the payment of the final balance, on the owner's prior payment to the main contractor of the moneys due in respect of the sub-contract work. The presence of "pay-when-paid" wording in relation to retention instalments, and particularly the second retention instalment, will obviously support a "joint venture" interpretation where there is no separate provision in the sub-contract regulating the timing and payment of any final balance (as is often the case in less sophisticated construction contracts). The presence of such a provision specifically relating to a final balance is naturally still more likely, subject to any contrary indication expressed (for example, in the arbitration clause) to be conclusive in favour of a "joint venture" interpretation. The judgments in the United States cases *supra*, are to be faulted for not adopting a more textual approach of this kind, and for inadequate consideration of a common commercial background which will frequently support a full "joint venture" consensually-based interpretation, it is submitted. See also a recent Queensland case, where the clause ceased to apply following repudiation by the main contractor.[7]

(c) Owner cross-claim or set-off

13·115   If the only reason for non-payment of the main contractor is a cross-claim or set-off of the owner unconnected with the sub-contract work, it is submitted that the sub-contractor should, under ordinary "pay-when-paid" wording, be entitled to recover the sums otherwise due under the sub-contract for a number of independent reasons, namely,

(a) The giving of credit by the owner to the main contractor for the full value of the sub-contract work, implicit in any cross-claim or set-off of the kind described should, as a matter of analysis, rank as value received by the main contractor which is in all respects indistinguishable, apart from the actual receipt of cash, from a normal payment.

---

[6] See for an analogous but different case, the interpretation placed by the House of Lords on "pay and be paid" club insurance provisions in *Firma C-Trade S.A.* v. *Newcastle Protection and Indemnity Association* [1991] 2 A.C. 1.

[7] *Iezzi Constructions Ltd.* v. *Currumbin Crest Developments Ltd.* (1994) 13 A.C.L.R. 39, Qd. C.A., shows a doubtful majority view limiting a "pay when paid" Clause 10(d) of an Australian sub-contract to interim payment only, but Fitzgerald P.'s "joint venture" minority view seems more persuasive on the wording used—see also his judgment in the *Trade Indemnity* case, *supra*, n.96, where the same clause was considered.

(b) Even if this were wrong, but for the same reasons, a term that such a set-off or cross-claim should rank as payment should, applying both the "officious bystander" and "business efficacy" tests,[8] be implied in the sub-contract.

(c) Under the "prevention principle" a party cannot complain of a breach of contract brought about by his own wrong.[9]

However, while refraining from deciding the point, three Common-wealth courts have all expressed a contrary view in interlocutory proceedings, while giving leave to defend for the point to be argued,[10] although one judge in the first instance did decide the point definitively in accordance with the views presently expressed.[11]   **13·116**

Dealing with an ancillary problem, it is obviously possible for the situation envisaged by a "pay-when-paid" provision (if it is to be interpreted in the full "joint venture" sense), namely owner insolvency, to produce at least some dividend in the liquidation for the creditors—that is, a *partial* payment to the main contractor for his own and the sub-contract work. Additionally, the owner may have himself made part payment before becoming insolvent. A properly drafted clause, therefore, should make provision for this eventuality, the obvious equitable solution being the rateable sharing of sums received before or in the liquidation between the main contractor in respect of his own work (including that of sub-contractors not restricted by "pay-when-paid" provisions) and each "pay-when-paid" sub-contractor engaged on the project (of whom, of course, there might well be more than one).

Provisions for this rateable sharing of any such partial owner payment, as well as the express treatment of owner cross-claims or set-offs as the equivalent of payment, are both to be found, probably alone among standard forms, in the Singapore S.I.A. 1980 forms (where, as in Hong Kong and Malaysia, "pay-when-paid" provisions are widely used in local sub-contracts, including the local standard forms of sub-contract).[12-13]

(6) Payment and Set-off

The same general principles in regard to payment apply to sub-contracts as in the case of main contracts. This applies also to certification, since many if not most forms of nominated sub-contract make interim payment   **13·117**

---

[8] For the principles, see *ante*, Chap. 1, Section 6(1), paras. 1·179 *et seq.*
[9] See *ante*, Chap. 1, Section 6(2), paras. 1·186 *et seq.*
[10] *Hong Kong Teakwood Works Ltd.* v. *Shui On Construction Co. Ltd.* [1984] H.K.L.R. 235 (Hunter J.); *Schindler Lifts (Hong Kong) Ltd.* v. *Shui On Construction Co. Ltd.* [1984] H.K.L.R. 340 (CA. over-ruling Power J.); and *Brightside Mechanical & Engineering Services Group Ltd.* v. *Hyundai Engineering & Construction Co. Ltd.* (1988) 41 BLR 110 (Singapore. Thean J.).
[11] Power J., in Hong Kong.
[12-13] See the S.I.A. main contract form, Clause 30(2)(*a*) and (*b*), reproduced and commented on in C.C.P.P., pp. 593–594.

dependent upon main contract certification or other similar procedures by representatives of the main contractor. Thus, the recent bout of case-law in England, apparently establishing a binding effect on interim certificates under the RIBA/JCT forms of contract and preventing the raising of any set-offs or cross-claims against the sums certified, originally arose as a result of disputed cross-claims by main contractors against sub-contractors' payment claims for summary judgment based on the architect's main contract certificates. There, of the six Court of Appeal decisions on the finality of interim certificates eventually reviewed and in the event reversed by the House of Lords in the *Gilbert-Ash* case in 1973, only one related to an owner's cross-claim against a main contractor under a main contract, and the remainder related to sub-contracts.[14] It has also been seen that very recently there has been a virtual explosion of sub-contract express draftsmanship in England designed to achieve at least a temporary finality for an A/E's or adjudicator's decisions (or even a sub-contractor's or main or management contractor's own decisions in their own cause) on both sums due and main contractors' cross-claims at the sub-contract interim payment stage.[15]

Further special provisions affecting payment of sub-contractors are, first, those in the sub-contract imposing a trust in favour of the sub-contractor on moneys due from the owner to the main contractor; and, secondly, provisions in the main contract empowering the owner in certain events to pay sums owed by the main contractor to the sub-contractor directly and subsequently deduct the equivalent from sums due to the main contractor under the main contract. These two types of provision are considered in Section (5) *infra*, and in some detail *ante*, Chapter 8, Section 1(3)(b).[15a]

(7) Cash Discount

13·118   It has been seen supra Section 3, Sub-section (4), that so-called "cash discounts" are expressly retainable by main contractors in respect of nominated sub-contract work under the nomination schemes in the main contract standard forms in both industries, and that these in reality represent no financing obligation on the part of the main contractor, whom it is contemplated will be paid under the provisions of the main contract in respect of nominated sub-contract work prior to the main contractor's obligation to pay the sub-contractor for that work (although ultimately this must be found in the terms of the nominated sub-contract itself).

In the past it has always been assumed that the entitlement of the main contractor to a cash discount as against the sub-contractor must be dependent upon prompt payment of the sub-contractor in accordance with the requirements of the sub-contract, and many standard forms sub-contract have expressly so provided. The English Court of Appeal appears to

---

[14] For this subject, see *ante*, Chap. 6, Sections 1(1) and 6(7), paras. 6·004 and 6·204 *et seq.*, and see also Chap. 8, Section 1(7), paras. 8·105 *et seq.*

[15] See *ante*, Chap. 6, Section 6(7)(c), paras. 6·198–6·204.   [15a] *Ante*, paras. 8·078 *et seq.*

have effectively held that failure so to provide may in effect convert the so-called "discount" into a straight forward reduction in price not dependent upon prompt payment.

ILLUSTRATION

Clause 16 of a sub-contract was a non-traditional "pay-when-paid" provision, which required payment by the main contractor "within seven days of the receipt of payment" by him under the main contract, "less retention money and amounts previously paid" and less "a cash discount of 2½ per cent. on the difference between the said total value and the said retention money". A considerable number of interim payments having been made between one and eight days late, the sub-contractors disputed the contractor's right to deduct these discounts *in toto*. *Held*, by the Court of Appeal, (Hoffman L.J. dissenting), and over-ruling the trial judge, that the words "if payment is made within 14 days" after the words "cash discount" in the otherwise identical Clause 11 in the standard "Green Form" sub-contract not being present in this sub-contract, the discount was not dependent upon payment within a specific time: *Team Services Limited* v. *Kier Management and Design Limited* (1993).[16]

[Note: Apart from the doubtful propriety of comparison with another admittedly standard form of contract, it is hard not to agree with Hoffman L.J. that a "cash discount" not conditional upon performance of a payment obligation would not be a discount at all, but a straight forward reduction in price. The delays in this case were extremely small, and it may be an example of hard cases making bad law. It is submitted that Hoffman L.J.'s view is to be preferred.]

13·119

SECTION 5.   PAYMENT DIRECT AND EXPRESS TRUST PROVISIONS

(1) Generally

An account of the early emergence of payment direct powers in main contracts, and their later supplementation by sub-contract provisions imposing express trusts in favour of the sub-contractor on any retention or other sums in the hands of the owner and due to the main contractor in respect of the sub-contract work, has been given in Chapter 8, together with a review of the more recent case law on these related types of provision.[17] It has there been submitted that, despite earlier acceptance by the courts of both types of provision, the recent decision of the House of Lords in the *British Eagle* case[18] casts a serious doubt on their validity as against a trustee or liquidator of the main contractor, if sought to be exercised after the insolvency has commenced.

13·120

---

[16] 63 BLR 76.
[17] See *ante*, Chap. 8, Section 1(3), paras. 8·078–8·086.
[18] *British Eagle International Airlines Ltd.* v. *Cie Nationale Air France* [1975] 1 W.L.R. 758, see *ante*, para. 8·083.

(2) Payment of Sub-contractor Direct

13·121   Even in informal contracts architects frequently indicate in their certificates for interim payment to the main contractor what proportion of the sums so certified is referable to nominated suppliers or sub-contractors. This is done with a view to assisting them to obtain payment from the contractor and to prevent the latter from contending, as an excuse for delay in payment, that he has not been paid for the work. This practice also occurs informally where there is no power in the main contract so to certify, and arises from the natural anxiety of the architect on behalf of the owner to avoid disturbance of the contract programme by the departure of dissatisfied unpaid and perhaps important sub-contractors.

Unless, however, there is an express power in the main contract for the owner to pay a sub-contractor directly and to deduct the sums so paid from moneys due to the main contractor, an owner who pays a sub-contractor directly places himself in peril, since he will nevertheless remain liable to pay the main contractor for the same work.

ILLUSTRATION

H., a builder, undertook to do certain work for S. By the contract H. was to pay M., a supplier, £95 net for certain fittings. The architect later increased this sum to £137. H. ordered the goods from M. in his own name, but H. became bankrupt. The architect deducted £95 from the sum payable to H., and S. paid the £95 to M. under an indemnity. H.'s trustee applied to the county court judge for an order directing the architect to certify that £137 was due from S. to H.'s estate, notwithstanding S.'s payment to M. *Held*, by the Divisional Court, that the trustee was entitled to require M. to come into H.'s estate as a creditor, and the order should be made. *Per* Coleridge C.J., S.'s action had been an attempt to interfere with the bankrupt's estate and with the bankruptcy laws: *Re Holt, ex p. Gray* (1888).[19]

13·122   Although there is no authority on the point, it seems possible that in such a case an owner, where there was no contractual power to do so, but acting under the necessity to get the goods delivered and the work completed, might have a right to cross-claim against the builder in quasi-contract for money paid to the defendants' use,[20] or for damages for breach of contract, and if a payment of this kind took place before the bankruptcy or liquidation and without notice of any act of insolvency, it might be a set-off or defence to a claim by the liquidator or trustee under the mutual credit and dealing clause,[21] or as a "contra item."[21a] However, if the payment was made (as usually it would be in practice) with notice or after commencement of a bankruptcy or liquidation, the transaction

---

[19] 58 L.J.Q.B. 5. See *post*, para. 16·010, where this case is more fully illustrated.
[20] See Halsbury *Laws of England*, Vol. 8, pp. 227–229.
[21] See *post*, Chap. 16, para. 16·014.
[21a] See *ante*, Chap. 8, para. 8·087.

would be a preference and in any case void as an unprotected transact-tion,[22] with the result that the owner would be liable to the estate in full and obliged to prove in the bankruptcy or liquidation. But *Re Holt* is clear authority, it is submitted, that if the payment is gratuitous and not made under any compulsion,[23] there could be no relief of any kind against the main contractor and the owner will find himself liable to pay twice for the same work, possibly without even a right to prove in the contractor's liqui-dation or bankruptcy, in the absence of an express contractual right to make the payment.

However, it has been held that where an *express* power to pay direct does exist, the owner may pay direct, provided the conditions stipulated for the exercise of the power have been strictly observed, and such pay-ment, even if made after a bankruptcy will be valid against the builder's trustee or liquidator. It should be noted that if, as is almost invariably the case, the power to pay direct is conditioned upon a failure of the main contractor to pay sums previously certified in favour of the sub-contractor in question, the practical effect of this owner's power is that he pays twice over for the work in question, but subsequently recoups one of the payments.

ILLUSTRATIONS

(1) W. contracted to construct certain sewerage works for an urban district council. The contract provided (Clause 54) that "if the engineer shall have reasonable cause to believe that the contractor is unduly delaying proper pay-ment to the firms supplying the machinery, he shall have power if he thinks fit to order direct payment to them". Another Clause (129) provided for the supply of machinery and plant by seven specified firms. Clause 7 provided for the retention of 10 per cent. of the value of the work executed for six months after completion. On October 12, 1904, W. was adjudicated bankrupt. At this date W. was owed £1,349 as retention on the whole contract, and £224 for the seven firms was payable on the next certificate of the engineer. On February 7, 1905, the engineer, after stating that he had reasonable cause to believe that W. was unduly delaying payment to the specialists, ordered direct payment to them of sums proportionate to the £224. On April 5, he made a similar order bringing the total paid to the specialists to £611, the final balance of their accounts. On April 24, the engineer gave his final certificate that W. was entitled to be paid a further £738, which, together with the £611 paid to the specialists, made up the retention money. *Held*, by Bigham J., that W. had "unduly delayed proper payment of the specialists." The contractor had, by filing his petition, prevented himself from making proper and due payment, and it would have been competent to the engineer to have given his certificate then instead of long after the bankruptcy. *Held*, also, that the power conferred by Clause 54 on the engineer was not annulled or revoked by the bankruptcy of W., and that the specialists were entitled to be paid the two sums of £224 and £611 according to the orders of the engineer in priority to W.'s trustee in bankruptcy; and the £738 remaining retention was also due to the contractor's

13·123

---

[22] See *post*, Chap 16, paras. 16·004–16·007.
[23] See Halsbury, *Laws of England*, Vol. 8, p. 231.

bank as prior assignees of the retention money. *Re Wilkinson, ex p. Fowler* (1905).[24]

[Note: In view of later doubts about this case, *Re Holt* and the strong language of that case disapproving of the pay direct arrangement, does not seem to have been cited to the court.]

13·124   (2) The 1909 edition of the RIBA form of contract, identical to that set out in *Hobbs* v. *Turner* (1902),[25] provided by Clause 28 that provisional sums should be paid to such persons as the architect might direct, and the sums so expended should be payable by the contractor without discount or deduction *or by the employer* to the tradesmen. The architect certified in favour of the contractor for certain sub-contracted work, which he set out in the certificate. The contractors went into liquidation, and the owners claimed as against the liquidator to be entitled to pay the sub-contractors upon certain certificates issued subsequently by the architect in favour of the sub-contractors. *Held*, by Singleton J., that Clause 28 did empower the architect to certify direct payment. But, following Maugham J. in the unreported case of *British S.S. Investment Trust Ltd.* v. *Foundation Co. Ltd.* [26] that the power to pay direct must be strictly construed, and under this form of contract the architect had no power to issue a certificate in favour of sub-contractors once he had issued a certificate in favour of the main contractor in respect of the same work: *Milestone & Sons Ltd.* v. *Yates Brewery* (1938).[27]

(3) Under clause 21(*c*) of the then current RIBA form of contract, the owner was given power to pay a nominated sub-contractor direct if, before "any certificate" was issued to the contractor, the latter could not prove that the nominated sub-contractor's accounts *included in previous certificates* had been duly discharged. Two months after practical completion the contractor went into liquidation, and the architect withheld his final certificate until the court's decision whether unpaid sums in a previous certificate could be deducted. *Held*, by Wynn-Parry J., that the power under clause 21(*c*) could be exercised prior to the final certificate after the work was complete, and was not limited to occasions when an interim certificate was due: *Re Tout & Finch Ltd.* (1954).[28]

13·125   (4) Clause 55 of a main contract in Ireland provided that if the main contractor failed to discharge nominated sub-contractors' accounts included in previous certificates the owner might himself pay such accounts and deduct the amounts so paid from sums otherwise payable. The sub-contract also contained provisions imposing trusts on moneys received by the main contractor for sub-contract work, and also on retention moneys held by the owner. The main contractor went into liquidation, and the liquidator completed the main contract work. A sum of £6,617 had been certified and paid to the main contractor prior to liquidation but not passed on to the relevant sub-contractor. The nominated sub-contractor sought a declaration that the owner might pay him direct the sum of £6,617 and deduct an equivalent amount from the retention moneys due to the main contractor for the contract as a whole, in addition to the retention moneys on the sub-contract work itself, where the liquidator had conceded that there was a trust in favour of the sub-contractor binding on him. The liquidator, however, contended that the provision for direct payment and deduction had the effect of reducing the property of the estate of the main contractor to the detriment of the general body of creditors in contra-

---

[24] [1905] 2 K.B. 713.
[25] See *supra*, para. 13·033.
[26] (1930) December 15.
[27] [1938] 2 All E.R. 439.
[28] [1954] 1 W.L.R. 178.

vention of section 275 of the 1963 Companies Act. *Held*, by Costello J., distinguishing the *British Eagle* case,[29] that the provision for payment direct could not properly be regarded as a contract for the disposal of an asset of the main contractor, and the liquidator took the remaining retention moneys subject to the liabilities affecting them in the main contractor's hands, including their liability to be reduced following the direct payment: *Glow Heating Ltd.* v. *Eastern Health Board* [1988].[30]

(5) A main contractor in Singapore went into liquidation with all current **13·126** interim certificates in his favour fully paid by the owners, but he had himself failed to pay sums certified in two of the latest certificates in favour of four nominated sub-contractors. The government as owners proposed to pay the nominated sub-contractors directly, and to deduct the payment from sums due to the main contractor. The liquidators of the main contractor took out an application to determine whether the payments would contravene the 1985 Singapore Companies Act by making preferential payments to creditors and preventing a *pari passu* settlement of the main contractor's liabilities under the Act. The payment direct power in Clause 20(*e*) of the contract was conditioned on, first, failure to pay sums certified in favour of sub-contractors in previous certificates and, secondly, the event of a winding-up of the main contractor. *Held*, by Thean J., following the *British Eagle* case and not following *Re Wilkinson ex p. Fowler* and *Re Tout and Finch Ltd.*, and applying the general principles of insolvency law in regard to provisions conferring priority in *Re Jeavons* and *Re Johns*,[31] a payment under the first part of Clause 20(*e*), *a fortiori* under the second part, would contravene Sections 280(1) and 327(2) of the Companies Act, and any payment to sub-contractors thereunder would be void as against the liquidators. *Joo Yee Construction (Pte.) Ltd.* v. *Diethelm Industries (Pte.) Ltd.* (1990).[32]

The *British Eagle* case is illustrated and considered *ante*, Chapter 8.[33]   **13·127** The position there taken supports Thean J.'s view in the *Joo Yee* case, insofar as the right to pay direct is sought to be exercised *after* the insolvency, but the question must be regarded as both difficult and open. As pointed out by Costello J. in the *Glow Heating* case, "Romalpa" style retention of title clauses, for example, are clearly designed for a very similar purpose, but are accepted as valid. Moreover, it could be added that "Romalpa" clauses are initiated for the benefit of an immediate party to the contract containing them, namely the seller, whereas the right to pay direct in main construction contracts, which benefits a third party if exercised, owes its origins to owner initiatives designed to safeguard the progress of the project, rather than to sub-contractor initiatives to take their right to payment under the sub-contract outside the normal distribution rules in a main contractor insolvency. They are to be distinguished in this

---

[29] *British Eagle International Airlines Ltd.* v. *Cie Nationale Air France* [1975] 1 W.L.R. 758, illustrated *ante*, Chap. 8, Section 1(3)(ii), para. 8·803.

[30] (1988) 6 I.L.T. 237.

[31] *Re Jeavons, ex p. Mackay* (1873) L.R. 8, Ch. App. 643; *Re Johns, Worrell* v. *Johns* [1928] Ch. 737.

[32] [1990] 2 M.L.J. 66. Compare in South Africa *Administrator of Natal* v. *Magill Grant & Nell (Pty) Ltd.* [1969] 1 S.A.L.R. 660, but contrast in New South Wales *Re: C.G. Monkhouse Pty. Ltd.* (1968) 69 S.R.N.S.W. 429. See further *post*, Chap. 16, Sections 6(5) and (7), and Sections 7(5), (6) and (7).

[33] See Section 1(3)(b)(ii), paras. 8·078 *et seq.* See also *post*, Chap. 16, Sections 6 and 7.

respect from the provisions imposing trusts in favour of the sub-contract-
or, which clearly are due to sub-contractor initiatives and which do have as
their only objective the securing of a preferential status in the main contractor's insolvency, and do arise in favour of a contracting party. For
these reasons, it may be that direct payment provisions in main contracts
are less inherently objectionable in principle, from the point of view of
their interference with *pari passu* distribution among creditors, (a principle, incidentally, accepted in very similar terms in the insolvency legislation in most Commonwealth jurisdictions) than the trust provisions in
sub-contracts, which are akin to the "Romalpa" type retention of title
provisions, essentially designed to give a contracting party, as against another contracting party, protection, in the event of the latter's insolvency,
against the claims of other creditors (and in many countries, in the case of
unpaid sellers of goods, requiring registration in order to be legally effective). These are essentially matters of public policy rather than of contract
interpretation, however.

13·128   A word of caution should perhaps be inserted here drawing attention to
the conditions which have to be satisfied under the provisions for payment
direct in the pre-1980 RIBA and the 1955 ICE forms of contract.[34] There is
an important distinction between the two, because whereas under RIBA
forms the power can be exercised at any time when some further certificate to the main contractor is due, the ICE power could only be exercised
when *a further certificate* was due to the main contractor *in respect of the
sub-contractor's work.* This meant that under the ICE conditions the
engineer, if he suspected that he might wish to certify payment direct in
respect of current work of a sub-contractor, had to ensure that there
would be at least some further sum remaining to be certified in a later
certificate if he was to be able to do so. It also meant that under the ICE
conditions a sub-contractor whose work was completed during one month
could never be paid direct if the engineer certified the whole sum in that
month. However, this lapse of draftsmanship was rectified in the 1973
(fifth) ICE conditions.[35]

Apart from any such contractual complications, the owner must in all
cases and as a practical matter ensure that the ultimate state of accounts
between the main contractor and himself will be in his own favour

(a) as a matter of commercial prudence, since otherwise he will only be
     able to prove in the bankruptcy or liquidation of the main contrac-
     tor for the amount of the sum paid direct, and

(b) because most provisions of this nature only give a right to deduct,
     not to sue, following the direct payment.

13·129   In any event, an owner should *never* pay direct, again as a matter of
commercial prudence, without obtaining an indemnity from the sub-con-

---

[34] Compare clause 27(*c*), 1963 forms and clause 59(2), 1955 ICE forms.
[35] Clause 59(*c*).

tractor to cover the eventuality of the payment being successfully challenged.

In addition to a power to pay nominated sub-contractors directly conditioned on failure of the main contractor to pay the sub-contractor, the owner's determination clause in the RIBA standard forms of contract, and indeed any well-drafted determination clause, will contain a wide power to take an assignment of the benefit of any sub-contract and an unconditional power to pay direct any sub-contractor, whether nominated or otherwise, once a determination has been effected.[36]

In so far as such a determination may be based exclusively on the bankruptcy or liquidation of the contractor, without any other default, however, these powers are likely to be invalid as offending against the policy of the insolvency laws.[37]

(3) Express Trust Provisions

These have already been considered in some detail in the context of trusts imposed on retention sums in Chapter 8.[38] Reflecting an increasing negotiating power of sub-contractors' organisations as against those of main contractors at about the time of the Second World War, and the comparative weakness, from the sub-contractor's point of view, of the existing payment direct remedies, since these required owner initiatives and consent (which the sub-contractor could not compel, and which would only be forthcoming if in the owner's perceived interest), express provisions were inserted into sub-contract standard forms purporting to impose a trust in favour of unpaid sub-contractors. Initially these were on retention sums in the hands of the owner, no doubt because the main contract provisions for retention created the appearance (although not the actual existence) of an ascertainable fund to which the trust could theoretically attach; but later they were imposed on all sums in the hands of the owner, whether retention or not, which might be owing by him to the main contractor in relation to sub-contract work.[39] The validity of these trusts, and their alternative basis of enforceability as equitable assignments of the main contractor's rights against the owner, was upheld against a main contractor's liquidator in 1954,[40] and as binding on the owner as well in more recent cases,[41] and a somewhat complicated case law on the enforcement of such trusts has since developed, much of it concerned with comparable express trusts

13·130

---

[36] Clause 25(3)(*b*), 1963 forms.
[37] See *post*, Chap. 16, paras. 16·029 and 16·035 *et seq.*
[38] See *ante*, Chap. 8, Section 1(3), paras. 8·078 *et seq.* See also *post*, Chap. 16, paras. 16·055–16·056, and in the case of main contracts 16·031.
[39] Compare the *Glow Heating* case in Ireland, illustrated *supra*.
[40] *Re Tout and Finch Ltd.* [1954] 1 W.L.R. 178, illustrated and discussed *post*, Chap. 14, paras. 14·044–14·045.
[41] See *Re Arthur Sanders Ltd.* (1981) 17 BLR 125, *post*, para. 16·018.

imposed by the main contract on retention sums *in favour of the main contractor.*[42]

13·131 Again, the possible invalidity of these provisions on policy grounds as infringing the *pari passu* distribution rules in an insolvency would appear to be open in the House of Lords, particularly following that House's judgment in the *British Eagle* case.[43]

SECTION 6. SUB-CONTRACTOR'S LIEN AND PROPERTY

13·132 In the absence of any provision to the contrary in the sub-contract, a sub-contractor retains the property in materials until they are built into the contract works.[44] However, retention of title clauses in sub-contracts of ever increasing elaboration have become a common feature, particularly of supply only sub-contracts, and pose obvious problems where these conflict with main contract provisions vesting title in the owner upon delivery to the site.[45]

Normally, if the contractor becomes insolvent, the sub-contractor cannot claim any lien or charge on money due to the contractor in respect of the sub-contract work.[46]

SECTION 7. PERFORMANCE OF SUB-CONTRACTS

13·133 In Chapter 4 of this book an attempt has been made to set out the basic general obligations and rights of the parties to a building or engineering contract. It was possible to do this, notwithstanding that under the law of contract everything must naturally yield to the expressed intention of the parties, because the main requirements of such contracts are generally similar in character, and are frequently either left for implication, even in the most sophisticated contracts, or at best expressed in generalised terms lacking in precision. It was thus possible to deal in a general way with questions such as the right of the contractor to possession, the time for giving information to him, his duty to proceed with due diligence and many other more detailed matters.

13·134 As previously discussed *supra*, Section 4(1), such generalisations are neither possible nor useful in relation to sub-contracts. Thus, one type of

---

[42] For this latter, see *ante*, Chap. 8, Section 1(3)(b)(ii), paras. 8·078 *et seq.*, and for the enforceability of these provisions generally, see the submissions *ante*, Chap. 8, Section 1(3), paras. 8·081 *et seq.*

[43] See the discussion *supra*, in regard to payment direct provisions, para. 13·127, and see *ante*, Chap. 8, Sections 1(3), paras. 8·078 *et seq.* and the conclusions there suggested. See finally *post*, Chap. 16, paras. 16·056–16·058.

[44] See the discussion and cases, *ante*, Chap. 11, paras. 11·003 *et seq.*

[45] See *ante*, Chap. 11, Section 2(7), para. 11·057.

[46] *Pritchett and Gold and Electric Power Storage Co.* v. *Currie* [1916] 2 Ch. 515 (see *ante*, para. 11·009. See further for the position in the main contractor's liquidation, *post*, Chap. 16, paras. 16·048–16·057.

sub-contract may require a series of visits to the site, often after relatively short notice (as by a plasterer where a number of buildings or a large number of rooms are involved in one contract), whereas another may require a single unbroken period of working (as in the cse of a sub-contractor for the structural steel frame of a building). Again, one type of sub-contractor may require physically undisturbed possession of the site as a whole (as, for instance, an excavation-only or structural steel sub-contractor) whereas another must of necessity work with, and in dependence upon others (as, for instance, in the case of concreting, shuttering and steel-fixing or in the case, very often, of plasterers and painters) and other finishing trades. Every such contract must turn on its special factual background, and in many cases it would be an almost superhuman task for the draftsman of a single standard form to express with any precision the obligations and rights of the parties as to time for performance and possession of the site in sub-contracted work of this kind. In addition, as already explained *supra*, this kind of work is very often the subject of condensed and loosely phrased documents such as quotations and orders, even though very large sums of money may be involved, and if disputes arise in such cases it may be principally by the implication of terms that the rights of the parties will have to be established. The terms to be implied will be largely governed by the nature of the work carried out by both the employing contractor and the sub-contractor, the contract programme of the former, and the known size and capacity of the sub-contractor's organisation. For the same reasons the obligations with regard to progress are likely to differ in the case of sub-contracts.[47]

Typical examples of the difficult problems of fact likely to arise in such cases are to be found in the Canadian cases illustrated in Chapter 4 of *Smith & Montgomery* v. *Johnson Bros.* (1954),[48] *Pigott Construction Ltd.* v. *W. J. Crowe Ltd.* (1961),[49] and *Swanson Construction* v. *Government of Manitoba* (1963),[50] and for a typical modern example of sub-contractors expecting to work on a congested site, see *Kitsons Sheet Metal Ltd.* v. *Matthew Hall* (1989).[51]

---

[47] See *supra*, Section 4(1), para. 13·096 and more particularly *ante*, Chap. 4, paras. 4·157 *et seq.* See also generally Chap. 9, Sections (6), (7) and (8).
[48] 1 D.L.R. (2d) 392, illustrated *ante*, para. 4·157.
[49] 27 D.L.R. (2d) 258, illustrated *ante*, para. 4·158.
[50] 40 D.L.R. (2d) 162, illustrated *ante*, para. 4·158.
[51] 29 B.L.R. 31, illustrated *ante*, para. 4·160.

CHAPTER 14

ASSIGNMENT

SECTION 1.   ASSIGNMENT OF CONTRACTUAL LIABILITIES

(1) Generally

14·001   Assignment, in its strict sense, means the transfer of one or more, or all of a party's rights arising under a contract to a stranger to the original contract, whether by operation of law or by the act of the person originally entitled to those rights, so as to enable the transferee or assignee to sue upon the contract himself in respect of the assigned rights. In considering this subject, it is essential to distinguish between contractual *rights* on the one hand, and contractual *liabilities* on the other, or, in other language which has been traditionally used, between the benefit and burden of the contract.

In a construction contract, speaking generally, the liability of the contractor is to do work and supply materials, and of the owner (or the main contractor in a sub-contract) to make due payment for them. The correlative rights of the parties are, on the part of the contractor, to receive payment, and, on the part of the owner or main contractor, to have the work done in accordance with the contract. Part of the difficulties which arise in the law of assignment in the case of construction contracts are due to the fact that the rules governing assignment have been evolved from comparatively simple contracts, such as money debts and contracts of sale, while the convenient dichotomy of benefit and burden and rights and liabilities is not so easy to identify in the case of more complicated contracts, of which not the least are building contracts. Thus, in a recent important case in the Court of Appeal, a distinction was made between an owner's *rights arising under the contract*, such as damages for its breach or rights to payment, which in that case could be assigned, and the *right to have the contract performed*, which, by virtue of an ineptly worded standard form prohibition of "assignment of the contract," could not.[1]

It is fundamental that English law, as indeed most legal systems, does **14·002** not recognise or permit the assignment of contractual liabilities *so as to extinguish the liability of the assignor* without the agreement of the other contractee. Thus in *Tolhurst* v. *Associated Portland Cement Manufacturers*[2] Collins M.R. said:

> "It is, I think, quite clear that neither at law nor in equity could the burden of a contract be shifted off the shoulders of a contractor onto those of another without the consent of the contractee. A debtor cannot relieve himself of his liability to his creditor by assigning the burden of the obligation to somebody else; this can only be brought about by the consent of all three, and involves the release of the original debtor."[3]

Moreover, even the benefit of a contract can only be assigned "where it can make no difference to the person on whom the obligation lies to which of two persons he is to discharge it."[4]

So, in construction contracts the owner will be unable to divest himself of the liability to pay for the work, or the builder of his responsibility for duly completing it, in the absence of a novation (that is to say, an agreement supported by consideration to which the other party to the original contract is also a party), or where by some act or conduct the other party acquiesces in the new arrangement.[5]

---

[1] *Linden Gardens Trust Ltd.* v. *Lenesta Sludge Disposals Ltd.* (1992) 57 BLR 57, C.A., *per* Sir Michael Kerr and Nourse L.J.
[2] [1903] 2 K.B. 660.
[3] At p. 668.
[4] *Ibid.* at p. 668.
[5] See, *e.g. Jaegers, etc., Ltd.* v. *Walker* (1897) 77 L.T. 180.

This is well illustrated by the leading case of *Young* v. *Kitchin*,[6] where a builder validly assigned his right to payment under the contract, and his assignee sued upon the contract. The building owner was permitted to set off damages due to delay by the builder to the extent of the assignee's claim as an equitable set-off (or defence), but not to recover any excess, for which the builder-assignor remained liable. Perhaps the most lucid judicial exposition of the law of assignment and its relationship to novation, sub-contracting and vicarious performance is to be found in Staughton L.J.'s recent lapidary judgment in the Court of Appeal in the *Linden Gardens* case.[7]

Contracts of novation[8] (under which the rights and liabilities of one of the original contracting parties are extinguished altogether) require to be distinguished from contracts of guarantee or indemnity, where the original parties remain bound. Contracts of guarantee are dealt with *post*, Chapter 17.

14·002A   In the past, assignment problems likely to arise in connection with construction projects were relatively simple; the great majority being concerned with assignment of rights to receive payment by the contractor, and a very small minority with the owner's right to have the contract performed, as, for example, where a developer might sell a project with the benefit of any previously concluded building contracts to another developer. More recently the increasingly widespread prevalence of defective work in newly completed buildings[8a] rarely raised assignment problems, since the emergence of the *Anns'* liability in tort[8b] had meant that later owners or occupiers could proceed directly in tort against any of the parties concerned with the original construction of the building, including the developer, or his A/E or other consultant, as well as main contractors and sub-contractors, without any need to use assigned rights for the purpose.

However, with the rcent abolition of the *Anns'* liability effected by the House of Lords' decision in the *D & F Estates* and *Murphy* v. *Brentwood B.C.* cases,[8c] the advisers of later owners and occupiers of new buildings discovering defects have, failing a remedy under the Defective Premises Act 1992, been obliged to re-direct their attention to the remedies available by way of assignment at the time of purchase of the property of such contractual rights as their clients' developer vendors or lessors might have possessed against the contractors or A/Es or consultants involved in the original building (such rights would normally be claims for damages for breaches of contract as yet undetected and unknown at the time of the assignment). In fact for some time past purchasers' or lessees' advisers had

---

[6] (1878) 3 Ex.D. 127, *infra*, Section 2.
[7] *Linden Gardens Trust Ltd.* v. *Lenesta Sludge Disposals Ltd.* (1992) 57 BLR 57, 76–81, C.A. The House of Lords, however, reached a different interpretation of the provision—see *infra*, para. 14·057.
[8] Shortly mentioned *infra*, Section 3.
[8a] As to which, see (1990) 6 Const. L.J. 87.
[8b] See *ante*, Chap. 1, Section 12(6).
[8c] [1989] A.C. 177, [1991] A.C. 398.

already been routinely demanding assignment of such rights at the time of the transfer of the property to later owners or lessees, although until the *D & F Estates* case in 1989[8d] it had been unnecessary to seek to pursue these assignment remedies.

It will be seen that the invocation of such assignment remedies is now raising a series of extremely difficult problems never previously experienced in the construction field and indeed only very rarely in the law of assignment generally. These problems are no longer concerned with the principally procedural questions which arose in the past, such as the necessity for joinder of assignors in the case of equitable assignments, or with the more substantive questions such as assignees taking subject to equities, but can now involve very difficult questions of causation and of measure of damage, advanced by defendants admittedly in breach of their contracts, if in a position to show that either the assignor (for example, by selling without knowledge of defects at full market price) or the assignee (for example, by purchasing with knowledge of defects at less than the market value for that reason) have not in the event suffered financial damage thereby, and so, it is contended, conferring an uncovenanted immunity on the defendant contract-breaker. These new and difficult problems following the later disposal by developers or others of newly constructed buildings have been compounded by the (as it happens quite fortuitous) presence in some standard forms of building contract in England of prohibitions against "assignment of the contract" by the owner, whose purpose had been regarded in the past as obscure and which had evidently been ineptly drafted.

A number of these problems were present in two separate construction projects, involving different parties, where the properties were subsequently transferred to new owners together with assignments of the vendors' rights against the contractors under their respective building contracts, and which reached the House of Lords in the form of two appeals heard together in the *Linden Gardens* case in 1993.[8e] As will be seen, important questions which are certain to reach the Appellate Courts in the near future having regard to the frequency with which such situations are likely to recur, still remain unanswered.[8f]

(2) Vicarious Performance of Contractual Liabilities

The rules preventing assignment of liabilities without the contractee's or debtor's agreement do not, however, prevent *vicarious performance* of a party's contractual liabilities without consent in most cases, so that a party to a contract can frequently adequately discharge his obligations by   **14·003**

[8d] [1989] A.C. 187.
[8e] *Linden Gardens Trust Ltd.* v. *Lenesta Sludge Disposals* [1994] 1 A.C. 85 illustrated *infra*, paras. 14·027–14·029 and 14·057.
[8f] See the analysis of the case in the Court of Appeal by the editor in (1993) 109 L.Q.R. 82, and in the House of Lords in (1994) 110 L.Q.R. 42.

arranging for performance by a third person. This is what happens every time a main contractor arranges, by way of a "private" or "domestic" sub-contract, for any part of the work to be sub-contracted. This is not a case of assignment, even if it arises as an incident of a purported assignment of the contract, since the third person vicariously performing the contract cannot sue or be sued, except in tort, by the contractee owner, and the contractor's rights as well as his liabilities remain unaffected. Thus in *Nokes* v. *Doncaster Amalgamated Collieries Ltd.*[9] Viscount Simon said:[10]

> "The rules of law restricting the assignability of contracts are, however, by no means limited to contracts of personal service. In the case of contracts for the sale of goods, for example (unless the contract expressly or by implication covers the purchaser and his assigns), the seller is entitled to rely on the credit of the purchaser and to refuse to recognise any substitute. Similarly, the purchaser is entitled to rely upon the seller and to hold him responsible for due performance. I may add that a possible confusion may arise from the use of the word 'assignability' in discussing some of the cases usually cited on this subject. Thus in *British Waggon Co.* v. *Lea*, the real point of the decision was that the contract which the company had made with Lea for the repair of certain wagons did not call for the repairs being necessarily effected by the company itself, but could be adequately performed by the company arranging with the British Waggon Co. that the latter should execute the repairs. Such a result does not depend on assignment of contract at all. It depends on the view that the contract of repair was duly discharged by the Parkgate company by getting the repairs satisfactorily effected by a third party. In other words, the contract bound the Parkgate company to produce a result, not necessarily by its own efforts, but, if it preferred, by vicarious performance through a sub-contractor or otherwise."

14·004   In general, the law permits the vicarious performance of contractual liabilities except in the case of so-called "personal" contracts where the personal skill, financial credit, or other characteristics of the contracting party, are regarded as of the essence of the contract. Thus in *British Waggon Co.* v. *Lea*[11] Cockburn C.J. said:

> "Where a person contracts with another to do work or perform service, and it can be inferred that the person employed has been selected with reference to his individual skill, competency, or other personal qualification, the inability or unwillingness of the party so employed to execute the work or perform the service is a sufficient answer to any demand by a stranger to the original contract for the performance of it by the other party, and entitles the latter to treat the contract as at an end, notwithstanding that the person tendered to take the place of the contracting party may be equally well qualified to do the service."

In the context of construction contracts, it could in one sense be said that the personality of the owner for whom a construction contractor works may in reality make a substantial difference (for example, in apply-

---

[9] [1940] A.C. 1014·
[10] At p. 1019.
[11] (1880) 5 Q.B.D. 149, at p. 153.

ing the provisions and remedies of the contract in regard to the quality or value of the work, where one owner may be relatively indulgent and another relatively strict); but it would seem that considerations of this kind will not generally be taken into account by the courts in order to prevent an assignment of the contract by an owner or his arranging for vicarious performance by another person of his managerial or administrative functions.[12] However, this same consideration was later relied on in the same case in the House of Lords as justifying the validity on policy grounds of express prohibitions against assignment of the benefit of the owner's contract.[12a]

Most modern forms of building contract, however, contain explicit pro-   **14·005**
visions prohibiting assignment or sub-contracting without consent, in earlier times by the contractor but in some modern English building contracts by the owner as well as the contractor,[13] and also providing for the selection or nomination of sub-contractors by the owner.[14] But in the absence of express provision, the principle is that vicarious performance will not be permitted if the result will be to alter or prejudice the obligations or rights of the other party to the contract. Judged by this test, it is obvious that vicarious performance of the owner's liability to pay in building contracts cannot be objected to. On the other hand, although there is not a great deal of authority upon the point, it is suggested that a builder's general obligations of co-ordination and control of the project will be personal in this sense, and any attempt to transfer performance of these particular obligations would be a breach of contract. A distinction ought, it is suggested, to be made between these general obligations, for example, to control and supervise the site organisation and labour force, and co-ordinate the works generally, and the obligation to carry out and complete the whole of the work in detail. In normal building work certain parts of the work, such as plumbing and plastering, will frequently be carried out by sub-contractors, and in these cases it is clear that vicarious performance of these parts of the works will not be objectionable. Similarly, there are a number of processes in civil engineering work which can be expected to be sub-contracted to specialists or, by contrast, to "labour only" sub-contractors. Thus, in *British Waggon Co.* v. *Lea* the court said:[15]

> "Much work is contracted for, which it is known can only be executed by means of sub-contracts; much is contracted for as to which it is indifferent to the party for whom it is to be done, whether it is done by the immediate party to the contract, or by someone on his behalf."

While, therefore, a considerable degree of sub-contracting is per-   **14·006**
missible, and this will include parts of the work billed to be carried out by

---

[12] See, *per* Staughton L.J., in the *Linden Gardens* case, *supra*, 57 BLR 57, at p. 78, and see Chitty, *op. cit.* at para. 1416.
[12a] See *infra*, para. 14·057.
[13] See *infra*, Section 6.
[14] See *ante*, Chap. 13, "Sub-contracts", paras. 13·003 *et seq.*
[15] See also *supra*, para. 14·004.

the builder, for example, concreting, bricklaying or plastering, there may well be duties of supervision and co-ordination and selection of sub-contractors which a builder cannot transfer, depending on the circumstances surrounding the owner's selection of the builder and the particular contract in question. If this view is correct, then a main contractor's trustee in bankruptcy or liquidator, or a sub-contractor for the whole of the work, will not be able to complete a contract of this kind without the consent of the building owner.[16] This question, however, which has received relatively little consideration by the English courts. The problem is unlikely to arise in cases of bankruptcy or insolvency and is unlikely to arise in practice in other cases, partly because of the standard form express prohibitions on "assigning" or "sub-letting" without consent which, while not very precisely worded in legal terms, appear to be aimed at preventing vicarious performance rather than true assignment,[17] and partly because of the availability of the important and discretionary remedy of rescission obtainable by the solvent contracting party an application to the court in insolvency cases.[18] A further reason why there is a dearth of authority in cases of insolvency is probably that the financial consequences for an owner of a construction contract abandoned in "mid-stream", with only an insolvent debtor to look to for reparation, are so serious that an election by a trustee or liquidator to continue with the contract is usually so attractive that it is unlikely to be resisted (provided that the trustee or liquidator is willing to give security or accept responsibility on the continued contract).

ILLUSTRATIONS

14·007   (1) R., a coachmaker, contracted to let D. a carriage for five years and keep it in repair, and to paint it once during that term. At the time S. was an undisclosed partner with R., but D. only knew of and contracted with R. Three years afterwards D. was informed that R. had retired from business, and that S., his successor, would do the repairs in future. D. refused to deal with anyone but R., and returned the carriage. *Held*, by the King's Bench Division, that he was entitled to do so: *Robson* v. *Drummond* (1831).[19]

(2) A contractor commenced and partially completed a chapel which he had undertaken to build. The contract contained a power of determination in the event of his default. The contractor became financially embarrassed, and discharged his workmen, and, two days after notice had been given under the determination clause, assigned all his assets to trustees for the benefit of his creditors. The trustees corresponded with the owners, who eventually insisted on the forfeiture. The trustees asked for a declaration that they were

---

[16] See *post*, Chap. 16, "Bankruptcy and Insolvency", para. 16·004, and see *Knight* v. *Burgess*, illustrated *infra*.
[17] See Clause 17, 1963 RIBA forms; Clause 3, 1955 ICE forms; Clauses 3 and 4, 1973 ICE forms. See *infra*, Section 6, paras. 14·055 *et seq*.
[18] s.54(4) of the Bankruptcy Act 1914; s.323(5) of the Act of 1948; and see ss.186 and 345(2) of the Insolvency Act 1986. See also *infra*, para. 16·032.
[19] 2 B. & Ad. 303.

entitled to the benefit of the contract and to complete the work themselves, and for an injunction against the owners. *Held*, by Stuart V.-C., that the contract was personal to the contractor and the trustees could not be substituted for him by any assignment, voluntary or otherwise. "What is to be considered here is the right of those who are called 'the contractors' and who have now wholly disappeared from the scene to appoint . . . any other person to set out the work and perform all those personal obligations which they have undertaken.": *Knight* v. *Burgess* (1864).[20]

(3) The plaintiff and another were joint sub-contractors under the defendant to "clean up" certain timber land, *i.e.* remove trees. The other joint sub-contractor assigned to the plaintiff, who completed the work, and sued the defendant for the price. The defendant pleaded that he had not assented to the assignment. *Held*, that there was no reason making it necessary that he should assent, and that he was liable whether he had assented or not: *Smith* v. *Mayberry* (1878).[21]

(4) A wagon company leased to the defendant a number of railway wagons **14·008** for a term of years, and agreed to keep them in repair in return for rents. The company was in the process of going into liquidation, and the liquidators assigned the contract to another wagon company, who were ready and willing to repair the wagons. The repairs were, *per* Cockburn C.J., "a rough description of work, which ordinary workmen conversant with the business would be perfectly able to execute", and the defendant, in entering into the contract, could not be supposed to have "attached any importance as to whether the works were done by the company or by anyone with whom the company might enter into a sub-contract to do the works". In an action by the company and the assignees for rent due, the defendant contended that by making arrangements for performance by another company the contract had been repudiated and that they were not obliged to accept performance by the assigness. *Held*, by the Queen's Bench Division, distinguishing *Robson* v. *Drummond*, that the repair of the wagons by the assignee company was a sufficient performance of the assignor company's agreement to repair and the defendants were liable for rent. It was not necessary to decide what the position might be after the liquidation: *British Wagon Co.* v. *Lea*.[22]

(5) J. contracted to supply to R. iron plates of a certain quality. J. was a manufacturer of, and not a dealer in, the iron plates. J. closed his works and tendered to R. iron plates of the specified quality, but made by another maker. R. rejected them, on which J. brought an action for breach of contract. *Held*, by the Court of Appeal, (1) that evidence was admissible of a custom that where a customer ordered iron plates from a manufacturer, he was entitled to reject plates not of the manufacturer's own make; (2) that even without such evidence the contract implied that the plates supplied should be of J.'s own make: *Johnson* v. *Raylton* (1881).[23]

(6) A contractor undertook to pave certain streets and maintain the surface in good condition for ten years. *Held*, by the Court of Session, that the contract was not personal and the benefit could be assigned: *Asphaltic Limestone Co.* v. *Glasgow Corporation* (1907).[24]

(7) The defendants contracted to supply a coal merchant with 10,000 tons of coal extending over a period of two years. The coal merchant's business,

---

[20] 33 L.J.Ch. 727.
[21] 13 Nev. 427.
[22] 5 Q.B.D. 149.
[23] 7 Q.B.D. 438, C.A.
[24] 1907 S.C. 463.

which he had been carrying on for some years, consisted in carting coals from the defendants' depots and selling it in small quantities to the working classes in the district. The coal merchant assigned the contract to the plaintiff, who had no experience of the coal trade. *Held*, by Hamilton J., that there was that degree of difference between the coal merchant's and the plaintiff's knowledge of the business which constituted an element of confidence personal to the coal merchant, and which rendered the contract unassignable: *Cooper* v. *Micklefield Coal and Lime Co.* (1912).[25]

14·009

(8) A company, whose principal shareholder was an experienced developer, acquired a warehouse from its owners and then entered into a contract for its re-sale, under which the company undertook to have the property refurbished prior to completion of the re-sale in accordance with an outline specification. The company found itself in financial difficulty in meeting its obligations to the first owners, and assigned "the benefit of the re-sale contract" by way of security to them, but expressly subject to its own obligations to its purchasers under the re-sale contract, and the owners in turn covenanted with the company to perform and keep it indemnified against those obligations. The company also assigned to the owners a debt owed to it by its re-sale purchasers which had been agreed in place of a deposit due from them under the re-sale contract. On the company failing to complete its own purchase, the owners informed the re-sale purchasers of the assignment to themselves, and of their intention to carry out the refurbishment works, of which they submitted plans which differed from earlier plans supplied on behalf of the assignor company; and when the purchasers rejected them the owners sought a declaration that, as assignees of the re-sale contract, they were entitled to the deposit and purchase price under that contract on carrying out the refurbishment proposed by them. The specification for the refurbishment in the re-sale contract, although for a fixed price, had in fact been extremely flexible, leaving for subsequent decision the number of windows, the locations of staircase and entrance, and the internal subdivision of walls, and with only bare descriptions of the heating, electric and fire-alarm systems. There was evidence that in these matters the purchasers had been relying on the expertise of the principal shareholder of the assignor company. *Held*, by the Court of Appeal, that, notwithstanding that, had the principal shareholder died or been replaced, the company would still have remained bound, and while there was no expectation that the company would itself carry out the refurbishment, the contract was personal in the sense that it could not be vicariously performed, and the purchasers were entitled to treat the contract as repudiated and to object to the assignment: *Southway Group Ltd.* v. *Wolff* (1991).[26]

14·010

In the last of the above cases Parker L.J., after referring to *Knight* v. *Burgess*, said:

"In that case much turned upon the wording of the contract, but in my judgment a building contract is one which of itself suggests that there is at least some inference of selection, the more particularly when the works to be carried out are extensive and ill-defined. One would not expect, for example, that anyone would contract with a builder to build at a fixed price a four bedroomed house of brick construction and with wooden windows unless that person had trust and confidence in that builder either from general reputation

---

[25] 107 L.T. 457.
[26] 57 BLR 33.

or recommendation or personal experience and had, in addition, confidence that the builder would co-operate in arriving at the details."[27]

The *Southway* case therefore shows that, in many construction situations, the personality *of the contractor* in regard to the control and co-ordination of a construction project, although not necessarily other parts of the work, will be essential to performance of his contract, and also makes it clear that evidence of the surrounding circumstances may be received in order to establish the personal character of the transaction in question where this is not clear from the contract documents. Thus Bingham L.J. said:

> "Whether a given contract requires personal performance by A., or whether (and if so, to what extent) A. may perform his contractual obligations vicariously, is in my opinion a question of contractual construction. That does not mean that the court is confined to semantic analysis of the written record of the parties' contract, if there is one . . . Where A. and B., perhaps with legal advice, have entered into a long and ambitious written contract, the terms of that contract may well be conclusive or almost so. Where a written contract is short and summary, or the contract is made orally, surrounding circumstances are likely to be of much greater significance: a reliable objective assessment of what the parties intended may well require account to be taken of such matters as the type of contract in question, the state of the market, the commercial position of the respective contracting parties, personal relationships between the main protagonists on each side, and matters of that kind".[28]

The *Southway* case is also of interest in indicating the possible import- **14·011** ance of the distinction between *particular rights* under a contract which may be assigned, since they will not offend either against any general principle of personal contracts or against any contractual term prohibiting assignment, and *the general right to enforce the contract as a whole*, which may so offend for either reason. Thus, had the assignment in the *Southway* case been solely of the assignor's entitlement to repayment of the loan of the deposit money and to the balance of the purchase price which would be due on completion, and had the corresponding performance tendered by the assignee been a refurbishment under the supervision and in accordance with the plans of the assignor's principal shareholder on whom the purchasers had relied, there could have been no objection by the purchasers to the assignee's claim, it is submitted.[29]

In general, it is submitted that the personality of the contractor will be essential in most construction contracts, *a fortiori* where there is no A/E acting for the owner. If this is correct, a trustee or liquidator of the contractor will be unable to complete a construction contract without the owner's consent, particularly if unable to provide the same supervisory and managerial staff for the purpose, and the owner will not have to rely

---

[27] *Ibid.* pp. 45–46.
[28] *Per* Bingham L.J., *ibid.* at p. 53.
[29] See, for a similar distinction made in the interpretation of an express provision against assignment, the majority view in the Court of Appeal in the *Linden Gardens* case, illustrated on this point *infra*, Section 6, paras. 14·057.

only on the discretionary right of the court to permit rescission under section 186 of the Insolvency Act 1986.[29a]

SECTION 2. ASSIGNMENT OF CONTRACTUAL RIGHTS

(1) Generally

14·012   English law at first refused to permit the assignment of contractual rights, but in the case of *equitable* rights or causes of action the courts of equity had made major inroads on this restriction, and by 1875 the assignees of such rights were permitted to sue in their own names without joining their assignors, provided that the assignment was "absolute" (that is, that there was no qualification or limitation on the extent of the debt or chose in action being transferred, and it was not an assignment "by way of charge") and provided also that notice had been given to the debtor. In all other cases, equity permitted recovery but required the assignor to be joined as a co-plaintiff or, on refusal to be joined, as a co-defendant.

These major relaxations were then effectively extended to *legal* rights or choses in action by statute, namely by section 25(6) of the Supreme Court of Judicature Act 1873, as subsequently replaced by section 136 of the Law Property Act 1925. While, however, assignments of *equitable* rights had been and could still be oral, assignments of *legal* rights were required by the statutes to be in writing. In practice, of course, some sort of writing is almost always employed in commerce by parties wishing to assign their rights, and of whatever kind; indeed even assignments of equitable interests will frequently be void if not in writing, if they are equitable interests in property falling within the provisions of section 53(1)(c) of the Law of Property Act 1925.[30]

14·013   Contractual rights under ordinary transactions, including construction contracts, are legal, as opposed to equitable, in character. To obtain the statutory procedural right for the assignee to sue in his own name, an assignment of these (legal) rights must be "absolute", that is to say, the assignor must have transferred *all* the rights in the contract without qualification. However, an assignment will be treated as absolute for this purpose, and not by way of charge, notwithstanding that there is an express or implied proviso for reassignment to the assignor upon repayment by the assignor of a loan, or upon some other event.[31] On the other hand, the assignment will be "conditional", and so not qualify as an assignment under the statute, if the assignment is expressed to come to an end (or, indeed, to come into existence) automatically upon some future event

---

[29a] See *infra*, Chap. 16, para. 16·637.
[30] For a full history and analysis of the present law, see Cheshire, Fifoot and Furmston, *Law of Contract* (12th ed., 1991), Chap. 16; Treitel, *Law of Contract* (8th ed., 1991), Chap. 16.
[31] *Tancred* v. *Delagoa Bay & East Africa Ry.* (1889) 23 Q.B.D. 239; *Hughes* v. *Pump House Hotel Co.* [1902] 2 K.B. 190, *infra*.

without any further act of assignment or reassignment by the parties. The procedural significance of this distinction is explained *infra*, Subsection (2), and its substantive importance is demonstrated by the *Durham Brothers* case, illustrated *infra*. The policy underlying these distinctions is obviously sensible, being to secure the presence of all interested parties in a doubtful case so that they will be bound by any final decision of an assignee's claim.

ILLUSTRATIONS

(1) T. was a creditor of the defendants for work done and plant and **14·014** materials supplied to an amount which was, subsequent to the assignment but previous to the action, ascertained under an award as £31,109. By an indenture between G. and T., reciting the contract with the defendants, a previous advance by G. to T., an agreement to advance £5,000 more, and a still further sum not exceeding £10,000, T., after covenanting to repay with interest such advances, assigned to G. all sums of money due, or to become due to him, T., from the defendants, subject to a proviso for redemption on repayment of all moneys due. *Held*, by the Queen's Bench Division, that G. was held entitled to sue the defendants on this assignment in its own name as "an absolute assignment (not purporting to be by way of charge only)" under section 25(6) of the Judicature Act 1873: *Tancred* v. *Delagoa Bay etc. Railway* (1889).[32]

(2) A firm of builders delivered a document to the plaintiffs as follows: "In consideration of money advanced from time to time we hereby charge the sum of £1,086, which will become due to us from . . . Robertson on the completion of the above buildings as security for the advances, and we hereby assign our interest in the above-mentioned sum *until the money with added interest be repaid to you*." The plaintiffs gave notice to Robertson and sued for the sums due. *Held*, by the Court of Appeal, after considering *Tancred* v. *Delagoa etc. Railway*,[33] that while an assignment under a mortgage with an express proviso for reassignment on redemption was an absolute assignment, as the mortgagor-assignor would have to give notice on the reassignment to the original debtor and the latter would know with certainty in whom the legal right was vested, and while that principle ought not to be confined to cases where there was an express provision for reassignment, the present assignment was nevertheless conditional because of the use of the words "until the money . . . be repaid", which limited the assurance to Robertson, and consequently the plaintiffs, having sued alone, could not succeed: *Durham Brothers* v. *Robertson* (1898).[34]

(3) A building contractor, in consideration of an overdraft from his **14·015** bankers, executed an instrument by way of continuing security to them for all money due or falling due or to become due under his building contracts, and empowering them to settle all accounts in connection with the works and to give receipts for the moneys assigned, and to sue for and take any steps necessary to enforce payment. Notice in writing was given to the building owners. *Held*, by the Court of Appeal, and following the reasoning in *Durham Brothers* v. *Robertson*,[35] that the principle relating to mortgages was not confined to cases where there was an express proviso for reassignment, and the assignment was absolute: *Hughes* v. *Pump House Hotel Co.* (1902).[36]

---

[32] 23 Q.B.D. 239.
[33] See *supra*.
[34] [1898] 1 Q.B. 765.
[35] See *supra*.
[36] [1902] 2 K.B. 190.

An assignment may also be by way of charge only, in which case the right or fund in question is never actually transferred, but the chargee is given a right to payment out of that right or fund. An assignment may also be of a part only of the rights or sum due under the contract, which will not qualify as a statutory assignment.[37] And, finally, an assignment may relate only to a future contractual right, for example, a builder may assign rights under any contracts to be undertaken by him in the future, which, however expressed, can only operate as an agreement to assign. On the other hand, an assignment of rights not yet accrued under an existing contract is valid,[38] including the right to damages for a breach not yet committed at the time of the assignment.[39]

(2) Statutory Assignments

14·016 As explained, the practical importance of identifying absolute assignments is that only these can qualify as *statutory* assignments today under section 136 of the Law of Property Act 1925, replacing section 26(3) of the Supreme Court of Judicature Act 1873. This section provides that *absolute* assignments in writing of any debt or other *legal* thing in action *of which express notice in writing* is given to the debtor, or other person from whom the assignor would have been entitled to claim, are effective to transfer the legal right as from the date of the notice. The effect of this section is procedural, and means that, as from the date of *receipt* of the notice,[40] an assignee under a valid assignment may sue upon the contract *in his own name*, without joining the assignor in the proceedings, and may give a good discharge for the contractual obligation involved without the consent of the debtor. No consideration is necessary to support such an assignment.[41] But the notice must be accurate in all substantial respects, so that if, for instance, it mis-states the date of the assignment, it will be invalid as a *statutory* assignment,[42] although it may be valid as an equitable assignment.

In building contracts it is normal to find that a builder requiring working capital or who finds himself in financial difficulties will assign all moneys due or to become due under a contract to a bank or other creditor.[43] An assignment of the retention moneys alone is also not uncommon in practice. An assignment of this latter kind was held to qualify as a valid statutory assignment in *G. & T. Earle Ltd.* v. *Hemsworth Rural District*

---

[37] *Williams* v. *Atlantic Assurances* [1933] 1 K.B. 81. But see for the case of retention moneys only, *infra*, para. 14·016.

[38] See Section 5(2), *infra*.

[39] See *per* Staughton L.J. in *Linden Gardens Trust Ltd.* v. *Lenesta Sludge Disposals Ltd.* (1992) 57 BLR 57, 93, C.A. See also [1993] 109 L.Q.R. 82, 90–91, illustrated *infra*, Section 4, paras. 14·027–14·029, and not dissented from on this point in the House of Lords.

[40] *Holt* v. *Heatherfield Trust Ltd.* [1942] 2 K.B. 1.

[41] *Re Westerton* [1919] 2 Ch. 104.

[42] *W. F. Harrison & Co. Ltd.* v. *Burke* [1956] 1 W.L.R. 419 (or if the amount of the debt is wrongly stated, *per* Denning L.J., *ibid.*).

[43] See Section 5, *infra*.

Council,[44] by a strong Court of Appeal affirming Wright J., and a number of earlier cases to the same effect.

(3) Equitable Assignments

Even if an assignment cannot take effect as a *statutory* assignment, either   **14·017**
because it is not in writing, or because notice is not given, or because it is
conditional, or by way of charge only, or of part only of the debt, it may
nevertheless be a valid *equitable* assignment. An equitable assignment
may be perfectly effective despite its being by word of mouth only, and
equally need not be supported by consideration,[45] although the completed
transfer of the right in question must be plainly evinced. Nor need notice
to the debtor be given, although this is highly desirable from the assignee's
point of view, since by doing so priority against any other assignee will be
obtained, and any subsequent equities by the debtor contractee against
the debt will be avoided, as also the risk of the debtor's obligation being
discharged by payment to the assignor. While an absolute assignee of any
equitable right can also sue in his own name, this is not the case if the right
is a legal one,[45a] and equity will require the assignor to be joined. Only if
the statute is complied with, in all respects, can the assignee of a legal right
sue in his own name.

   The practical effect of an assignment which does not qualify under the
statute, therefore, is that the assignee cannot sue in his own name alone, if
the debt is a legal one, but must join the assignor as co-plaintiff or, if he will
not agree, as co-defendant.[46] The necessity for this in all cases of non-
absolute assignment is due to the fact that both the court and the debtor
will need to know the exact current state of accounts or of mutual obligations as between assignor and assignee.[47] For the same reason, an
assignor under an equitable or non-statutory assignment may not sue
alone, at any rate once notice of the assignment has been given.[48]

ILLUSTRATION

   Plastering sub-contractors claimed that £1,808 was due to them by the main   **14·018**
contractors. The sub-contractors had entered into an arrangement with their
own suppliers and with the main contractors whereby the latter were given an
irrevocable authority to pay £1,558 to the suppliers as a good and sufficient
discharge of the money due for the plastering work to the extent of the sum so
paid. *Held*, by the Court of Appeal, that the arrangement amounted to an

---

[44] (1928) 44 T.L.R. 758. The case is illustrated *infra*, para. 14·044.
[45] *Holt* v. *Heatherfield Trust Ltd.* [1942] 2 K.B. 1.
[45a] See, *e.g.* an ordinary contractual right.
[46] *Bowden's Patent Syndicate Ltd.* v. *Herbert Smith & Co.* [1904] 2 Ch. 86.
[47] See the *Durham Brothers* case, *supra*.
[48] See, *e.g. Re Steel Wing Co. Ltd.* [1921] 1 Ch. 349 (assignment of part of the debt). Compare
   Cottage Club Estates Ltd. v. *Woodside Estates Co. (Amersham) Ltd.* [1928] 2 K.B. 463,
   discussed in another context *infra*, para. 14·038.

assignment to the suppliers by way of charge of part of the alleged debt due to the plastering sub-contractors, who could not sue for the work done without joining the suppliers: *Walter & Sullivan Ltd.* v. *J. Murphy & Sons Ltd.* (1955).[49]

(4) Assignment of Personal Contracts

14·019 It has already been pointed out, in relation to the vicarious performance of contractual liabilities, that vicarious performance will not be permitted in so-called "personal contracts" where this would prejudice the position of the other party to the contract. This principle is in fact of wider application—for instance, it will prevent an undisclosed principal from suing on such a contract where the agent has expressly described himself as principal,[50] and it will also prevent the assignment of contractual rights in such a case. However, it has been seen that vicarious performance of parts of the work by the contractor, particularly by using sub-contractors, is a common and indeed expected feature of construction contracts.

By the nature of building contracts, it is not likely that an assignment of the parties' *rights*, whether of the builder to receive the price or of the owner to have the work done according to the contract, can prejudice the other party to the contract. In certain special cases it is conceivable that an assignment by an owner in a contract where the work is not very clearly defined, or to a large extent provisional, and where wide powers to order variations are available, might prejudice the builder, depending upon the requirements or standing of the proposed assignee.[51] Moreover, some owners or their A/Es may well be regarded as more strict in their administration of their contracts and in the enforcement of remedies than others, but it would seem that arguments that the owner's rôle in a construction contract is for that reason personal, and so preventing assignment of the benefit of the contract without consent, has not been accepted by the Courts.[52]

ILLUSTRATIONS

14·020 (1) Owners of chalk pits contracted to supply all the chalk requirements for 50 years of a company operating a cement works. The cement manufacturers assigned their whole undertaking, including the benefit of their various contracts. *Held*, by the House of Lords, the chalk pit owners were bound to continue to supply the requirements of the works for the new company: *Tolhurst* v. *Associated Portland Cement* (1903).[53]

---

[49] [1955] 2 Q.B. 584.
[50] See *Humble* v. *Hunter* (1848) 12 Q.B. 310.
[51] See the rather similar position of a vendor undertaking pre-completion building works in *Southway Group Ltd.* v. *Wolff* (1991) 57 BLR 33, illustrated *supra*, para. 14·009.
[52] See Staughton L.J.'s dicta to this effect in the *Linden Gardens* case, (1992) 57 BLR 57, 93, discussed *supra*, para. 14·004.
[53] [1903] A.C. 414·

> (2) A provision merchant agreed to supply a cake manufacturer with all the eggs he should require for his business for one year, the manufacturer undertaking not to purchase eggs elsewhere during that period provided the merchant was able to supply them. During the year the manufacturer transferred his business to a bakery company with branches all over the country, whereas the manufacturer had only three places of business. *Held*, by the Court of Appeal, distinguishing *Tolhurst's* case, *supra*, on the ground that the contract there was to supply the needs of a particular place (the cement works), that the contract was personal and could not be assigned: *Kemp* v. *Baerselman* (1906).[54]

Cases on this subject, depending on their facts and surrounding circumstances, are likely to be found falling on each side of a difficult borderline. It is because of these uncertainties that construction contracts frequently contain express prohibitions against assignment, although often characteristically ill drafted.[55]

(5) Notice

As already stated, notice of an assignment to the debtor or party liable is procedurally essential for a statutory assignment, and while not essential in the case of equitable assignments, is highly desirable from the point of view of the assignee, both in preventing the obligation being discharged by payment or performance of the obligation by the other party to the contract in favour of the assignor; by reducing the risk of any further equities accruing against the assignee; and in securing priority as against other possible assignees.[55a] Only the statutory notice needs to be in writing (except in the case of *equitable* interests in land or personalty, where writing is required under section 137(3) of the Law of Property Act 1925, but this is not likely to arise in building contracts). No particular form is required, but the notice must be clear and unambiguous. The fact of assignment should be stated, and the debtor informed that the assignee is by virtue of the assignment entitled to payment or performance of the obligation in question. A mere indication that payment may be made to a third party as agent for the creditor is insufficient.[56]   **14·021**

(6) Assignee Takes Subject to Equities

Assignees, whether under statutory or equitable assignments, take subject to all defences available against the assignor, including equitable set-offs (that is, cross-claims for damages arising out of the same contract or transaction which rank as a defence up to but not exceeding the amount of   **14·022**

---

[54] [1906] 2 K.B. 604.
[55] See *infra*, Section 6.   [55a] See *supra*, para. 14·017.
[56] See *Percival* v. *Dunn* (1885) 29 Ch.D. 128, *infra*, Section 5(4), para. 14·048.

the claim.[57] The excess thereafter represents a true counter-claim and not a set-off).

ILLUSTRATION

A builder assigned to the plaintiff money due from the defendant building owner on completion of the building. *Held*, by Cleasby B., that the defendant might set off any damages caused by delay of the builder to the extent of the claim, but might not recover damages in excess of the claim against the assignee: *Young* v. *Kitchin* (1878).[58]

This subject and the cases are considered in greater detail in the context of the assignment of moneys due, *infra*, Section 5(5).[58a]

SECTION 3. NEW CONTRACT WITH THIRD PERSON

14·023 This may either take the form of a novation, in which, under a tripartite agreement, an original contracting party is released from, and the third party assumes, his obligations under that contract; or alternatively a simpler bilateral agreement between a third party and one of the original contracting parties, for example, where an owner undertakes to pay the third party, usually in consideration of the third party assuming the responsibilities of the original contractor. Here the terms on which the other contractor drops out or is released form no part of the new agreement.

These are not cases of assignment at all, but bring a new contract into existence on which either party can sue. The substitution may be by express agreement, or it may be implied from the conduct of the parties, though such an implication will be comparatively rare.[59]

In arrangements of this kind, it is important for the parties to define clearly the responsibilities or liabilities of the original contractor to be assumed by his substitute—for instance, any current liability for liquidated damages for delay.[60]

SECTION 4. UNASSIGNABLE RIGHTS

14·024 Certain rights are by reason of their nature not permitted to be assigned. Apart from some perhaps doubtful extensions of the previously discussed

---

[57] For set-off in construction contracts, see *ante*, Chap. 6, Section 1(1), paras. 6·006 *et seq.*, and Section 4(4), paras. 6·068 *et seq.*, and 6·194 *et seq.*
[58] 3 Ex.D. 127.
[58a] Paras. 14·049 *et seq.*
[59] See *Re European Assurance Association, Conquest's Case* (1875) 1 Ch.D. 334; *Scarf* v. *Jardine* (1882) 7 App.Cas. 345; *Head* v. *Head* [1894] 2 Ch. 236.
[60] See *Re Yeadon Waterworks Co. & Wright* (1895) 72 L.T. 832, *ante*, Chap. 10, para. 10·049.

category of rights under "personal" contracts, under which contractual rights of seizure or forfeiture, or under an arbitration clause, have been held not to pass upon an assignment of the benefit of the contract,[61] the principal exception to assignability will be found where what is assigned is a "bare" right to sue for damages of breach of contract.[62]

(1) Bare Right of Litigation

An assignment of a bare right of litigation which is unattached to a lawful **14·025** transfer of other property to the assignee (such as the assignment of a dilapidations claim upon the transfer of a lease,[63] or a ship-builder's assignment on delivery of a ship to a ship-owner of a right of damages against a sub-contractor[64]) offends against the principles of the tort of maintenance, and is unassignable as being a mere "trafficking in litigation", unless the assignee can show what has been described as "a genuine and substantial commercial interest in taking the assignment and enforcing it for his own benefit".[65] In such a case there must be no element of profit as the objective of the transaction, which "would savour of champerty".[66]

(a) As a compromise of litigation

It not infrequently occurs that, in the course of multi-partite litigation, **14·026** one party may compromise a claim against him by another party on the basis of assigning to that party his own rights against yet another party to the litigation. Such assignments have been upheld in appropriate circumstances, notwithstanding objection that they were void as assignments of a bare right to sue.

ILLUSTRATION

Owners of a hospital, where certain stacks had collapsed, sued variously in contract or tort the main contractors, the sub-contractor suppliers of certain concrete rings used in constructing the stacks, and the architects, structural engineers and heating engineers. All parties, except the heating engineers, agreed to contribute and meet the owners' claim in an agreed sum. The structural engineers then agreed with the owners and the remaining defendants that they would meet the heating engineers' proposed share of the total sum in return for an assignment of the owners' claims and of the other defendants' various third party claims against the heating engineers, together with

---

[61] See *infra*, Subsections (2) and (3) respectively.
[62] *Prosser* v. *Edmonds* (1835) 1 Y. & C. (Exch.) 48; *Gregg* v. *Bromley* [1912] 2 K.B. 474.
[63] See *Ellis* v. *Torrington* [1920] 1 K.B. 399.
[64] *Constant* v. *Kincaid* (1902) 4 F. (Ct. of Ses.) 901.
[65] *Trendtex Trading Corporation* v. *Credit Suisse* [1982] A.C. 679, at p. 703F.
[66] *Ibid.* at p. 694G, *per* Lord Wilberforce.

arrangements for reducing contributions if sums were recovered in their names from the heating engineers. No notice was given of the assignments, and the heating engineers objected to them as being void for maintenance and champerty. *Held,* by Judge Newey Q.C., that in the absence of notice the assignment took effect as an equitable assignment of the various claims; and that the structural engineers had a genuine commercial interest in the assignments and in enforcing the claims, so that they were valid and effective, notwithstanding a theoretical possibility of profit from the agreement: *South East Thames Regional Health Authority* v. *Y. J. Lovell* (1985).[67]

(b) On transfer of property

14·027   Not only will an assignment, for example, of a right to damages for breach of contract or for negligence in tort, be effective if made as an incident of a transfer of property, but it now seems established, contrary perhaps to what may have recently been thought, that such an assignment will be effective notwithstanding that, at the date of the assignment, there was no cause of action then known to the assignor, or indeed that, at the date of the assignment, no breach of contract or other cause of action had as yet even occurred.

ILLUSTRATION

(a) In the first (*"Linden Gardens"*) of two cases reaching the Court of Appeal on preliminary issues of law, practical completion of a contract, which had required the removal of all asbestos from a building, took place in 1980. In 1985, however, more asbestos was found, and the owners entered into a contract with new contractors for its removal, and that contract was completed in August, 1985. By December, 1986 the original owners had transferred the entire building to new owners for its full market value, and in January, 1987 they formally assigned to the new owners their claim for damages against the first contractors, which they had already commenced by writ in 1985, *together with all other claims which they might have in respect of the property.* Subsequently, still further asbestos was found, and the later contractors were added to the action as second defendants, while the second assignee owners, who had incurred the very substantial costs of finally removing the remaining asbestos, were *substituted* as assignee plaintiffs *in place of the original assignor owners.* Both of the contractors objected to the assignments. *Held,* by the Court of Appeal, that the second owners, as assignees suing alone, were entitled in law to recover (i) from the first contractors the cost of the second contractors' work which had been incurred by the first assignor owners; and (ii) against the second contractors, the final costs incurred by the second assignee owners in making good the second contractors' work, notwithstanding that at the date of the assignment to them no breach on the part of the second contractors had yet been discovered, and also that the first assignor owners, having secured the full market price for a sound building when selling

---

[67] 32 BLR 127. See also *Constant* v. *Kincaid* (1902) 4 Ct. of Sess. 901; *Hydrocarbons Great Britain Ltd.* v. *Cammell Laird Shipbuilders Ltd.* (1991) 53 BLR 84, both illustrated *infra,* para. 14·033 and 14·036.

to the second assignee owners, had themselves suffered no damage as a result of any breach by second contractor.

(b) In the second ("*St. Martin's*") of the two cases reaching the Court of **14·028** Appeal, owners of a major development in the course of construction transferred it for group tax reasons to an associated investment company in the same group at its full market price, together with an assignment of the full benefit of the building contract. After completion it was found that the podium deck of the main building leaked as a result of alleged defective work by the contractors, which it was conceded must have taken place after the transfer of the property and assignment of the contract, and the assignee investment company met the cost of the necessary repairs. The assignor and assignee companies as *co-plaintiffs* then *jointly* sued the contractors, who argued that no damage had been suffered by the assignors, since they had sold at full market value, and consequently that the assignees could be in no better position and only entitled to nominal damages. *Held*, by the Court of Appeal, upholding the claim (*per* Staughton L.J.), that the assignees could recover in the name of the assignor and that the transfer at full value could be disregarded as *res inter alios acta*, (*per* Nourse L.J. and Sir Michael Kerr) that *the assignees* were prevented from recovering by the terms of an express prohibition of assignment in the building contract, but that *the assignors* had suffered damage and could recover, since under the terms of the assignment agreement they would be liable to indemnify the assignees against the cost of repairs.

Held, by the House of Lords, (a) that in both the *Linden Gardens* and *St.* **14·029** *Martin's* cases express prohibitions against "assignment of the contract" by the owners in all the relevant building contracts were effective to prevent *the assignees* from suing or recovering in both cases. Since the assignors were no longer a party in the *Linden Gardens* action, the contractors' appeal in that case must be allowed; (b) overruling the majority of the Court of Appeal, that in the *St. Martin's* case, the assignor company was not liable to the assignee company for the cost of repairs, on the true construction of the assignment agreement, so that that basis for recovery by the assignor company in the Court of Appeal could not be supported; but (c) that, following the principle in certain bailee cases, the assignor company in the *St. Martin's* case could nevertheless recover the cost of repair which the assignee company had incurred on their behalf, since it was in the contemplation of the building contract as part of a building development project that ownership of the building would pass from the original developers to other parties, on whose behalf the assignor company would need to sue: *Linden Gardens Trust Ltd.* v. *Lenesta Sludge Disposals Ltd.* (1993).[68]

This very important and complex case was followed by the Court of Appeal in *Darlington B.C.* v. *Wiltshier Southern Ltd.*,[68a] but leaves a number of important practical questions unanswered in cases where property has been transferred and contracts assigned but the loss has not, on the facts, been incurred by the party now entitled to sue.[69]

The practical effect of the *Lenesta* case at the time of writing seems to be **14·030** as follows:

---

[68] (1992) 57 BLR 57, C.A.; [1994] 1 A.C. 85, H.L.
[68a] Illustrated *ante*, Chap. 8, para. 8·228A.
[69] See the editor's analysis of the case in the Court of Appeal in (1993) 109 L.Q.R. 82, and in the House of Lords, (1994) 110 L.Q.R. 42.

(a) In the absence of express prohibitions on assignment in a developer's contracts with his contractor or architect, an assignment of his contractual rights against them will be effective to enable the assignee to sue for cost of repair of defects or other damages, notwithstanding that at the time of the assignment no existing breach of contract has yet been discovered or even, as in the *St. Martin's* case, that no breach has as yet been committed. (Staughton L.J. suggested in the Court of Appeal that in such a case the assignor might have to be joined, however.)[69a]

14·031 (b) Where the assignee cannot sue himself for any reason, such as a prohibition against assignment, *the assignor* can sue on the assignee's behalf, accounting to him for the proceeds of the action, if it is the assignee and not the assignor who has suffered the loss. This may, however, be limited to cases where it is in the contemplation of the original contracts, such as those in a development project, that the original contracting party will be passing the property on to other owners or lessees. The House of Lords speeches, however, expressly leave open the question whether this is not an unduly narrow restriction, and that the rule may also apply to all contracts of services carried out on property, such as construction contracts, as an objective measure of damage where work is defective, whether or not transfer of the property to other persons is contemplated by the original contract.

Nevertheless, this case raises a number of difficult and unresolved questions where property has been transferred and assignment has taken place but, on the particular facts, the loss has not been suffered by the party able to sue under the rules relating to assignment of contracts. Very importantly also, the available remedies to an assignee unable to sue for any reason, and whose assignor is unwilling to proceed on his behalf, seem uncertain.[70] The *Darlington* case held that the assignor there was also a constructive trustee.[70a]

(c) Damages recoverable on assignment

14·032 Whether assignments of a right to sue for damages are permitted because of the existence of a genuine commercial interest of the assignee in taking the assignment, or because of a disposal of related property by the assignor, difficult questions of causation can arise where defendants are able to argue either that in the particular circumstances the assignor has suffered only nominal damage, so that the assignee can be in no better position, or conversely that in the circumstances, while the assignor may have suffered damage, the assignee has not.[71] In other words, does the

---

[69a] See 57 BLR 57, 93. See, however, now *Darlington B.C.* v. *Wiltshier Northern Ltd.* (1994), C.A., *ante*, para. 8·228A.
[70] See (1994) 110 L.Q.R. 42. See also *infra*, para. (c), for further cases.
[70a] *Ante*, para. 8·228A.
[71] The former argument was rejected in principle by Staughton L.J. in the *Lenesta* case, *supra*, as has been seen, but was avoided by Sir Michael Kerr's and Nourse L.J.'s findings on the facts. See now the *Darlington* case.

accident of transfer and assignment create, in Lord Keith of Kinkel's phrase, a "legal black hole"[71a] into which the right to damages disappears, leaving the contract-breaker defendant with an uncovenanted immunity?

ILLUSTRATIONS

(1) Ship-builders of two steam tugs sub-contracted the manufacture of the **14·033** engines and boilers. The vessels were delivered to the owners and full payment made both by the ship-owners and the ship-builders, but the engines were later found to be defective, and had to be replaced at a time when the ship-builders were in bankruptcy. The ship-owners thereupon negotiated a settlement with the trustee whereby, in return for an assignment to them of the ship-builder's right of action against the engine-makers, the trustee would be relieved of all further claims by the ship-owners. When sued by the ship-owners as assignees, the engine-makers contended that, since the assignor ship-builders had paid nothing to the ship-owners and had been released from all liability, the assignors had suffered no damage at all; or alternatively that the damages should be limited to the four shillings in the pound which the ship-owners would have recovered from the ship-builders' trustee in the bankruptcy. *Held*, by the Court of Session, that but for the assignment the trustee would have been able to claim in full. Instead he had received, in return for the assignment, a full discharge from the ship-owners, who as assignees were accordingly entitled to recover in full: *Constant* v. *Kincaid* (1902).[72]

(2) The walls of a concrete reservoir collapsed during construction, due to **14·034** the contractor's disregard of orders given by the resident engineer as to the sequence of back-filling behind the walls. When the contractors refused to repair at their own cost and complete, the owners terminated the contract and made a claim for damages against the contractor. The latter's sureties then settled the owner's claim in full for a sum in excess of the amount of their bond, being recouped for this in full by the contractors under their indemnity obligation to the sureties, as part of an overall arrangement whereby the owners agreed to transfer the benefit of their contract of employment of their engineers and permit the sureties to use the owners' name in proceedings against them. The engineers, when sued for negligence in the name of the owners for failing to ensure that their orders had been carried out by the contractor, contended that the owners, having been reimbursed in full, had suffered no loss. *Held*, by the Supreme Court of Canada (Cartwright C.J.C. and Spence J. dissenting), that the sureties, using the name of the owners, were entitled to recover the cost of repairing and completing the reservoir, since the owners would be bound to hand over the proceeds of the action to the sureties if successful, and as a result there would not be double recovery: *City of Prince Albert* v. *McLellan* (1969).[73]
[Note: It is difficult to approve of the majority reasoning in this case. As pointed out by Cartwright C.J.C., the surety had not himself paid the owners under the bond, but simply used the contractor's money to pay the claim in full, so that no question of subrogation arose. Moreover, there is no reason

---

[71a] *Per* Lord Keith of Kinkel in the *G.U.S Property Management* case illustrated *infra*.
[72] 4 Ct. of Sess. 901.
[73] 3 D.L.R. (3d) 385. The case is illustrated and criticised in more detail on the supervision point *ante*, Chap. 2, para. 2·139.

apparent in the report of the case why the owner would be obliged to hand back the surety's payment if the action failed, as the majority judgments in the case apparently thought.]

14·035   (3) In 1970 and 1971 a building, then owned by the assignor company, was damaged by building operations on an adjoining property. In 1975, ownership of the building was transferred by the assignors under company policy to a second company in the same group at book value, and in 1976 the first company assigned all its claims arising out of the adjoining building operations to the second company, which carried out the necessary repairs and, as assignees, sued the defendants in tort for the reduced value of the building or, alternatively, for its cost of repair. The defendants argued that the assignors could have pursued their claim at the date of the assignment; that the only relevant loss for which the plaintiffs could sue was that of the assignors; and that since it was the assignees who had incurred the costs, while the assignors had transferred the building at book value without any deduction for the damage, the assignors had suffered no loss and so there was no claim to assign. *Held*, by the House of Lords reversing the Scottish First Division, that while a sale of the land at a price reflecting its damaged state might, in such a case, be the best evidence of the loss suffered by an assignor, this particular transaction was effected under company policy at book cost regardless of the state of the building, and should therefore be disregarded in considering the assignor's damage, in the same way as if the building had been the subject of a later gift by the assignor. The cost of repair by the assignees was relevant in assessing the damage which the assignors would have suffered if they had continued to own the building. Whether the cost of repair rather than diminution of value was the appropriate measure of damage could await evidence, but it had been wrong to treat the price of the transfer as showing that there had been no damage suffered by the assignors: *G.U.S. Property Management Ltd.* v. *Littlewoods Mail Order Stores Ltd.* (1982).[74]

14·036   (4) Main contractors C. for the construction of an off-shore accommodation vessel sub-contracted the design and supply of a number of hydraulic jacking units to A., who sub-sub-contracted the manufacture and supply of 24 hydraulic cylinders to R.B., who in turn sub-sub-sub-contracted the supply of 48 parts for these cylinders, called cast steel clevises, to B.C. R.B. were financially in some difficulties, and the party likely to be ultimately responsible for later discovered defects in the work were the clevis suppliers B.C. The owners brought an action against C., which was settled; and C. brought proceedings against his sub-contractor A. In these circumstances A. entered into an agreement with his sub-sub-contractor R.B. under which, in the event of A. being held liable to C., R.B. admitted liability to A. and assigned its own right of action against B.C. to A., but on terms that R.B.'s liability to A. should be limited to whatever sum of money might be recovered by A. when proceeding in R.B.'s name against B.C. Shortly after this, A. settled C.'s claim against him for £5,000,000. In proceedings by A. in R.B.'s name against B.C. to recover the £5,000,000, the latter took the preliminary point that, as a result of R.B.'s agreement with A., the possibility of R.B. incurring any loss at all had now been effectively removed, so that A. as assignee of R.B.'s cause of action could recover no more than nominal damages. *Held*, by the Court of Appeal, that the effect of the agreement between A. and R.B. was not to extinguish R.B.'s liability to A., but merely to limit it to such amount as might be recovered in the action against B.C., so that B.C. were in principle liable to

---

[74] 1982 S.L.T. 533. See this case discussed by Staughton L.J. in the *Lenesta* case, *supra*, at pp. 88–90.

indemnify R.B. in full in respect of A.'s liability to C.: *Hydrocarbons Great Britain Ltd.* v. *Cammell Laird Shipbuilders Ltd.* (1991).[75]

A number of other authorities in England where a benefit having the effect of reducing or eliminating the plaintiff's loss, and deriving from some other incidental source, has been disregarded when computing a plaintiff's damages for breach of contract or in tort are discussed by Staughton L.J. in the *Lenesta* case.[76]

(2) Rights of Seizure and Forfeiture

Certain individual rights under a contract otherwise assignable may also **14·037** be so personal in nature as not to pass upon an assignment of the benefit of the contract. Thus in hire-purchase agreements, the right of the owner to enter and seize in default of payment has been held to be a right personal to the original owner, and hence not to pass on an assignment of the benefit of the agreement.[77] It is submitted, however, that, despite any apparent similarity an owner's rights of determination and re-entry onto his own land when faced with a recalcitrant builder under the provisions of a construction contract (which are usually conditioned on breach or other conduct of the contractor requiring to be objectively assessed, and often further subject to an A/E's certification), and conversely a contractor's right to determine for non-payment and to seize and use goods and materials on site, as in the RIBA/JCT forms, can easily be distinguished from the personal nature of a hire-purchase owner's right to enter another person's dwelling-house and seize his chattels. It would be impractical, it is submitted, so to emasculate the owner's control of a construction project upon an otherwise acceptable transfer of property, for example, upon the transfer of a development during construction with an assignment of the benefit of the current construction contract. This view of the nature of the forfeiture power in a construction contract receives support, it is submitted, from the cases which have refused injunctions against construction owners restraining them from wrongful re-entry and expulsion of the contractor from the site.[78] Moreover, it has been seen that the law will not generally take account of the possibility that one person may be relatively more or less indulgent than another in the enforcement of contractual rights and remedies when deciding whether a contract is of such a personal nature that it cannot be assigned or vicariously performed.[79]

---

[75] 53 BLR 84.

[76] (1992) 57 BLR 57, at pp. 84–91. This difficult and rarely discussed subject has also been the subject of an article by Professor John G. Fleming, "The Collateral Source Rule and Contract Damages" (1983) 71 *California Law Review* 56. See the subject further discussed *ante*, Chap. 8, Section 2(6), paras. 8·225 *et seq*. See also the editor in (1993) 109 L.Q.R. 82, 89

[77] *Ex p. Rawlings, re Davis* (1888) 22 Q.B.D. 193, applying *Brown* v. *Metropolitan Counties Life Assurance Society* (1859) 28 L.J.Q.B. 236.

[78] See *ante*, Chap. 12, Section 3(2), paras. 12·084 *et seq*. and the cases there illustrated.

[79] See *supra*, Section 2(4), para. 14·019.

(3) Arbitration Clauses

14·038 It seems to have been thought in the past that a right to arbitration could not pass on an assignment of the moneys due under a contract, although it might pass on an assignment of the benefit of the contract generally.[80] The authority for this proposition appears to have been statements to that effect expressed by Wright J. in a judgment in 1928,[81] where a builder *assignor* of moneys due under a building contract had obtained an award from an arbitrator, but on case stated the award was set aside on the ground that *the assignee* had not been joined. However, Wright J.'s view was openly disapproved, although in a different context, by Lord Greene M.R. and by Morton L.J. in the Court of Appeal in 1946,[82] and distinguished, and not followed by Bingham J. in 1984, when he held that under section 1 of the Arbitration Act 1975 charterers, but for having taken a step in the action, would have been entitled to a stay for arbitration of an action for demurrage brought by the assignee.[83]

It is submitted that Wright J.'s reasoning cannot really be upheld on principle. An assignment confers a right to sue. The contract may have provided that a method of suing available to the parties is to be arbitration. The debtor has and cannot lose the benefit of the clause, and it seems anomalous that the other party can lose the right to go to arbitration merely because there has been an assignment by him of the benefit of the contract. Nor is it clear how an assignee being given the right to arbitrate (as opposed to suing in the courts) can prejudice a debtor who has signed a contract referring disputes to arbitration. Other considerations might well apply to the submission of a specific dispute to arbitration (as opposed to the general submission of a defined class of future disputes which is the essential feature of an arbitration clause in a construction contract), but it is submitted that the decision cannot be supported in regard to an ordinary arbitration clause of this kind.

14·039 However, it would seem that an involuntary statutory assignment, of which no notice was given to the opposing party or to an appointed arbitrator, will deprive an arbitrator already appointed and seised of a dispute of any further jurisdiction, notwithstanding that he proceeds to an award in ignorance of the assignment, unless notice of the assignment and of a continued submission to arbitration has been communicated to him by the parties,[84] as also in the case of a normal assignment by a contracting

---

[80] See *Russell on Arbitration* (20th ed., 1982), p. 169.
[81] *Cottage Estates Ltd.* v. *Woodside Estates Ltd.* [1928] 2 K.B. 453.
[82] *Shayler* v. *Woolf* [1946] Ch. 320, at p. 323.
[83] *Rumput (Panama) S.A.* v. *Islamic Republic of Iran Shipping Lines, The Leage* [1984] 2 Lloyd's Rep. 259. See also *Montepida S.p.A.* v. *JTP-RO Jugotanker, The Jordan Nicolov* [1990] 2 Lloyd's Rep. 11, *per* Hobhouse J.
[84] *Baytur* v. *Finagro Holding S.A.* [1992] 1 Q.B. 610.

party.[85] Moreover, it would seem that failure to give such notice within a reasonable time may lose the right to arbitration.[86]

To transfer the right to arbitrate an assignment must, however, be a legal one (that is, absolute) so as to satisfy section 136 of the Law of Property Act 1925. Apparently an equitable assignment under English law will not enable the assignee to arbitrate.[87] The subjects of succession and of assignment of arbitration agreements are further considered *post*, Chapter 18, Section 3(3).[87a]

SECTION 5.   ASSIGNMENT OF MONEYS DUE

(1) Generally

The foregoing sections of this chapter have dealt with the more general aspects of the law of assignment, including assignments of the entire benefit of a contract, but in practice the commonest examples of assignment in connection with building contracts are the more limited assignments by the contractor of moneys due or to become due under the contract, usually in consideration of the provision of credit facilities or other financial accommodation by the assignee, or as security for an existing debt.[88] It is proposed in this section to examine the practical consequences of the foregoing rules on transactions of this kind.

14·040

(2) Moneys not yet Due

It is no objection to an assignment that the moneys assigned are not yet due, or have not yet been earned at all, and when an expectancy falls into possession the assignment will operate effectively and bind the defined subject-matter of the agreement to assign. A future debt of this kind is within the requirements of section 136 of the Law of Property Act 1925.[89]

14·041

The same principle has already been seen to be applicable in the case of valid assignments of the right to sue for damages for future breaches of contract.[89a]

---

[85] *London Steamship Owners Mutual Insurance Association Ltd.* v. *Bombay Trading Co. Ltd., The Felicie* [1990] 2 Lloyd's Rep. 21; *The Jordan Nicolov* [1990] 2 Lloyd's Rep. 11.

[86] *N.B.P. Developments Ltd.* v. *Buildko & Sons Ltd. (formerly William Townson & Sons Ltd.) (in licq)* (1992) 8 Const. L.J. 377.

[87] See *Herkules Piling Ltd.* v. *Tilbury Construction Ltd.* (1992) 61 BLR 107, *per* Hirst J.

[87a] Paras. 18·124 and 18·125.

[88] Examples of such assignments have already been seen in the illustrations in Section 2, *supra*.

[89] *Holroyd* v. *Marshall* (1862) 10 H.L.C. 191; *G. & T. Earle Ltd.* v. *Hemsworth Rural District Council* (1928) 44 T.L.R. 758.

[89a] See the *Linden Gardens* case, see *supra*, para. 14·027.

ILLUSTRATIONS

(1) A bill of sale assigned to the mortgagee all book debts due and owing *or which might during the continuance of the security become due and owing* to the mortgagor. *Held*, by the House of Lords, a subsequent assignee of the mortgagee received a good title to a debt accruing due after the bill of sale, and notice having been served on the debtor prior to the mortgagor's bankruptcy, his title defeated the trustee in bankruptcy: *Tailby* v. *Official Receiver* (1888).[90]

14·042 (2) G. contracted to build a ship for the defendant for £1,375, £900 to be paid in various instalments according as the work progressed, and the residue on the certificate of completion. G. being in difficulties, the defendant, in order that the ship might be finished, advanced him from time to time sums amounting on October 27, 1876 to £1,015, which was in excess of the amount then due, or, it would seem, earned, since the last of the £900 instalments did not become due till November 23, 1876, and the residue not till February 11, 1877. On October 27, G. borrowed £100 from a third person, and assigned to him £100 out of moneys "to become due" from the defendant. The defendant had due notice of this, but, notwithstanding, subsequently advanced money to an amount greatly exceeding £100 to G. *Held*, by Bramwell L.J. and Cotton L.J. (Brett L.J. dissenting), that the defendant was liable to pay the £100 to the plaintiff assignee, the assignment being a good and equitable one, and that the right of the assignee could not be defeated by a voluntary payment by the defendant to G. or by any subsequent equity: *Brice* v. *Bannister* (1878).[91]

14·043 (3) Interim payment under a building contract was to be at the rate of 80 per cent. of the contract value of the work done, the remaining 20 per cent. to be retained until completion. The contractors, in order to secure a debt of £550 and delivery of further goods by unpaid suppliers, assigned to them "a sum of £1,000 due and owing . . . or which thereafter might become due and owing . . . being part of the retention money mentioned in the . . . specification". After making a further assignment of £600 in similar terms to the same assignees, and giving notice of both assignments, the contractors later went into liquidation after completing sufficient work to earn £1,600 retention, and a trustee appointed by the creditors then completed the work at the creditors' expense, to pay for which only the retention moneys owed by the owners were still available, but which the trustee and the supplier assignees both claimed were due to them. *Held*, by the Court of Appeal, distinguishing *Tooth* v. *Hallet*,[91a] that since the trustee must be regarded as having elected to complete under the original contract, in the absence of anything to show that the owners had exercised a power to terminate, the owners owed no more to the trustee than was due under that contract; that the assignment of the retention moneys held good as against the trustee; and that the supplier assignees were therefore entitled to them as against the trustee: *Drew* v. *Josolyne* (1887).[92]

14·044 (4) A building contract provided for interim payment and for 10 per cent. retention, to be paid into a bank account, although it was not in fact so paid but remained notionally due. The builders assigned to certain suppliers "all moneys now or thereafter to become due to us . . . for retention moneys".

---

[90] 13 App.Cas. 523.
[91] 3 Q.B.D. 569, C.A. (And see *May* v. *Lane* (1894) 64 L.J.Q.B. 236; *Western Waggon and Property Co.* v. *West* [1892] 1 Ch. 271.)
[91a] Illustrated *infra*, para. 14·050.
[92] 18 Q.B.D. 590.

Notice in writing was given at once to the owners. Later the owners paid the retention moneys to the receiver for debenture-holders of the builders. The suppliers brought an action against the owners, who raised no question of priorities, but pleaded that the builders as assignors should have been joined. *Held*, by Wright J., affirmed by the Court of Appeal, and following *Ex p. Moss, re Toward*[93] and *Drew* v. *Josolyne*,[94] the retention money, although not becoming payable till after the assignment, was a debt or legal thing in action which could be assigned within the terms of the Supreme Court of Judicature Act 1873,[94a] and could be sued for without joining the assignors as parties: *G. & T. Earle Ltd.* v. *Hemsworth Rural District Council* (1928).[95]

[Note: Where a conflict arises between the interest of an assignee and a trustee or liquidator, an assignment of moneys to become due will be valid against the trustee provided the moneys have been earned at the date of the bankruptcy, even if not actually due or payable at that date.[96]] Under the involvency legislation in most countries, however, the assignment itself must take place before the date of the bankruptcy, even if the work has already been done and the debt already incurred at that date.[97]]

(5) Clause 11(h) of the standard FASS form of sub-contract provided that, to the extent that the amount retained by the owner under the main contract included any retention money under the sub-contract, the main contractor's interest in the money was fiduciary as trustee for the sub-contractor. The main contractor went into voluntary liquidation after completion of the work but before the expiry of the maintenance period. *Held*, by Wynn-Parry J., that the provision effected a valid equitable assignment of the relevant part of the retention moneys in favour of the sub-contractor, who was accordingly entitled to them whether in the hands of the owner or of the main contractor's liquidator: *Re Tout and Finch* (1954).[98]

The last of the above decisions, which was soon followed by the drafts-   **14·045**
men of the English main contract building standard forms seeking to impose a similar trust on the *main contract* retention moneys *in favour of the main contractor*,[99] together with a decision by Vinelott J. in 1979 compelling the owner to place the retention moneys in a separate bank account, notwithstanding the absence of any express provision to that effect,[1] has since provoked a substantial case law in regard to both main and sub-contract retention moneys as against owners' or main contractors' liquidators respectively. Doubts as to the validity of such pro-

---

[93] (1884) 14 Q.B.D. 310.

[94] (1887) 18 Q.B.D. 590.

[94a] Now s.136 of The Law of Property Act 1925, see *supra*, para. 14·012.

[95] 44 T.L.R. 758. (But see *Williams* v. *Atlantic Assurance* [1933] 1 K.B. 81, where the Court of Appeal held that an assignment of part of a debt could not qualify as a statutory assignment.)

[96] *Re Jones, ex p. Nichols* (1883) 22 Ch.D. 782, see *post*, para. 16·061, as explained in *re Toward, ex p. Moss* (1884) 14 Q.B.D. 310, illustrated *post*, Chap. 16, "Bankruptcy and Insolvency", Section 9, paras. 16·061 *et seq.*

[97] *Farley* v. *Housing and Commercial Developments Ltd.* (1984) 26 BLR 66, *per* Neill J.

[98] [1954] 1 W.L.R. 178.

[99] See Clause 30(4) of the 1963 RIBA/JCT standard forms, and see Clause 30.5.1 of the 1980 forms.

[1] *Rayack Construction Ltd.* v. *Lampeter Meat Co. Ltd.* (1979) 12 BLR 30, doubted *ante*, Chap 8, Section 1(3), paras. 8·084 *et seq.*, but approved by later cases in the Court of Appeal as there stated.

visions in purporting to create trusts as against future trustees or liquidators of the other contracting party and as to the resulting case law,
having regard to an overriding principle of *pari passu* distribution of assets
among creditors inherent in the insolvency law of most Commonwealth
countries, were expressed in the tenth edition, and have been reinforced,
it is submitted, by an important House of Lords decision in another commercial field, which did apply the *pari passu* principle and which seems
inconsistent with the construction cases.[2] As a result it has been submitted
that while the position in the English Court of Appeal in regard to retention moneys in construction cases would seem closed, it nevertheless
remains open and merits re-examination in the House of Lords.[3]

(3) Notice to Building Owner

14·046 This is strongly advisable from the assignee's point of view for a number of
reasons. First, provided the assignment is in writing and not conditional,
or by way of charge only, or of part of the debt only (for this purpose
retention moneys can be treated as a single debt, separate from any
remaining balances due[3a]) the fact of notice will enable it to rank as a statutory assignment, and hence enable the assignee of such a legal right or
debt to sue in his own name, in the same way as an absolute assignee of an
equitable right or debt, without the expense of joining the assignor in the
proceedings.

Secondly, the building owner who disregards the notice and pays the
contractor and not the assignee will do so at his peril, and be liable to pay
twice over.[4]

Thirdly, the assignee will thereby gain priority over any other assignees
there may be who have not already given notice.[5]

Fourthly, the assignee may avoid the creation of any later new equities
against the debt (as, for example, by an owner making further *voluntary*
advances, as opposed to equities subsequently arising under the contract
itself). Even if no notice is given, however, an assignee for value takes
priority over a subsequent garnishee, since the latter can only take under
his order what could properly and without violation of the rights of others
be dealt with by the judgment debtor.[6]

---

[2] *British Eagle International Airlines* v. *Air France* [1975] 1 W.L.R. 758, illustrated *ante*,
Chap. 8, Section 1(3)(b)(ii), para. 8·083, and see also *Administrator, Natal* v. *Magill Grant
and Nell* 1967 (1) S.A. 660, South Africa and *Joo Yee Construction (Pte.) Ltd.* v. *Diethelm
Industries (Pte.) Ltd.* [1990] 2 M.L.J. 66, Singapore, illustrated *ante*, para. 13·126.
[3] See the review of the cases *ante*, Chap. 8, Section 1(3), paras. 8·081 *et seq.*, and see also *ante*,
paras. 13·127 *et seq.*, and *post*, paras. 16·054–16·058.
[3a] See *supra*, para. 14·016.
[4] *Brice* v. *Bannister* (1878) 3 Q.B.D. 569 illustrated *supra*, para. 14·022.
[5] *Ward* v. *Duncombe* [1893] A.C. 369.
[6] *Pickering* v. *Ilfracombe Ry.* (1868) L.R. 3 C.P. 235; *Badely* v. *Consolidated Bank* (1888) 38
Ch.D. 238; *Davis* v. *Freethy* (1890) 24 Q.B.D. 519; *Evans Coleman & Co.* v. *Nelson Construction* (1958) 16 D.L.R. (2d) 123 and see *post*, Section 7, paras. 14·063 *et seq.*

(4) Form of Assignment

The assignment (which often may only be clearly evidenced by the terms   **14·047**
of the notice to the debtor) must be intended to operate as an actual transfer of the right, and must specify the right or fund in question. For example, a mere authority to the owner to pay someone as the agent of the
builder will not operate as an assignment or a notice of the assignment.

ILLUSTRATIONS

(1) A railway contractor gave his bankers a letter directing the railway company to pass the cheques which might become due to him "to his account to
the bank". *Held*, by Sir John Romilly M.R., that this was not an equitable
assignment, as it would have been if it had directed that the cheques should be
passed to the credit of the bank: *Bell* v. *London & North Western Ry.* (1852).[7]

(2) The defendant, Dunn, being the agent for the owner of the Park Estate   **14·048**
at Tottenham, let part of the estate to Davis under a building agreement, and
agreed to make him advances from time to time as the buildings were erected.
Davis being indebted to Percival, the plaintiff, a builder and brickmaker, for
goods supplied for building, handed Dunn the following order: "Dear Sir,
please pay Percival the amount of his account and oblige, £42 14s. 6d. for
goods delivered at Park. W. Davis. To J. Dunn." Money was then and subsequently due from Dunn to Davis, and notice was given of the above order.
Held, by Bacon V.-C., that the defendant was not liable on this, as it was not an
equitable assignment, but a mere polite note by one person asking some other
person to pay his debt, and that it imposed no obligation upon that other
person to pay the debt: *Percival* v. *Dunn* (1885).[8]

Provided, however, that the intention is clear, the language used
is not important. Thus, speaking of an equitable assignment, Lord
Macnaghten said: "It may be addressed to the debtor. It may be couched
in the language of command. It may be a courteous request. It may assume
the form of mere permission. The language is immaterial if the meaning is
plain."[9]

There is no special requirement as to the person who should give the
notice, and it would not seem to matter by whom it is given. Nor is there
any limit of time for giving it (subject to the risk of other assignees acquir-
ing priority).

While statutory assignments must be in writing under section 146 of the
Law of Property Act 1925, this does not apply to *equitable* assignments,
which can be oral. However, assignments of *equitable* rights, if they
involve property rights within section 53(1)(c) of the 1925 Act, are also
required to be in writing. As previously explained, equitable assignments

---

[7] 15 Beav. 548.
[8] 29 Ch.D. 128.
[9] *Brandt's Sons & Co.* v. *Dunlop Rubber Co.* [1905] A.C. 454, at p. 462.

of *legal* rights will not be effective to enable the assignee to sue without joining the assignor. Rights under construction contracts will almost invariably be legal rights (except perhaps rights under express trust provisions) so that the assignor will almost always need to be joined unless a statutory assignment can be relied on.[9a]

(5) Equities

14·049   It has already been stated that the assignee, whether statutory or equitable, takes subject to equities, and that this will include cross-claims for damages arising out of the same contract up to, but not exceeding, the amount of the assignee's claim.[10] The effect of this upon an assignee's right to moneys due under a building contract may well be catastrophic, since despite the fact that substantial sums may have been earned and retained at the time of the assignment, the right to these may disappear upon some subsequent default of the builder, either by reason of a set-off by the owner (as, for example, damages for delay or for subsequently discovered defective work), or because of the exercise of a power of forfeiture by the owner (which latter may, depending on the terms of the contract, prevent the retention moneys, or indeed any other sums, from becoming payable until completion).

ILLUSTRATION

14·050   A contract provided for 25 per cent. retention. There was a power for the owner to employ another builder in the event of non-completion by a certain date. During the course of the work, the builder assigned to a third person £200 out of moneys to accrue due under the contract. The builder went bankrupt after the completion date when the work was still unfinished. The owner wrote to the builder's trustee indicating his intention to forfeit the contract. Later the trustee by agreement with the owner completed the work. *Held*, by the Court of Appeal in Chancery, that on the facts the trustee had not completed under the original contract, but under a new agreement, and consequently the assignee could not claim the £200 as against the trustee: *Tooth* v. *Hallett* (1869).[11]

[Note: In so far as this case might suggest that an assignment of future payments is invalid against the trustee, it has been distinguished and explained in *Drew* v. *Josolyne*,[12] with which it should be compared. As between a prior assignee of moneys to become due and the trustee in bankruptcy, the test is whether, *at the date of the bankruptcy*, the money had been *earned* by the work being done.[13] Normally, however, completion of the work by a trustee in

---

[9a] See *supra*, paras. 14·013 and 14·016.
[10] *Young* v. *Kitchin* (1878) 3 Ex.D. 127, *supra*. See also *Hanak* v. *Green* [1958] 2 Q.B. 9. For a discussion of set-off against sums due for interim payment on the A/E's certificate, see *ante*, Chap 6, Section 6.
[11] L.R. 4 Ch.App. 242. (And see *Young* v. *Kitchin*, *supra*, para. 14·002.)
[12] (1887) 18 Q.B.D. 590, illustrated, *supra*, para. 14·043 and *post*, Chap. 16, Section 7, para. 16·062.
[13] See *post*, Chap. 16, "Bankruptcy and Insolvency", para. 16·061.

bankruptcy will be treated as an election by him to complete under the original contract, and as showing that no power of forfeiture has in fact been exercised by the owner.[14]]

In the case of *Young* v. *Kitchin*,[15] the right to the set-off in question existed at the date of the assignment, but there is no doubt that equities subsequently arising under the assigned contract are equally valid against the assignee.[16]

ILLUSTRATION

A company agreed in 1881 with the Government of Newfoundland to con- **14·051**
struct 340 miles of railway from S. to H. by 1886, in consideration of grants of
land and an annual subsidy, "to attach in proportionate parts . . . as and when
each five mile section is completed and operated". In 1882 the company
assigned a portion of its property and the subsidy to trustees for the bond-
holders. In 1886 only 85 miles were completed, and there was no probability
of anything more being constructed. *Held*, that a proportionate part of the
subsidies was payable for the specified term on the completion of each section. It was further held by the Judicial Committee that as against the assignee
trustees the government had a right to set off, against such proportionate payment of the subsidies for the 85 miles, their claim of damages for non-completion of the whole of the railway: *Newfoundland Government* v.
Newfoundland Railway (1888).[17]

But set-offs arising from matters unconnected with the debt or contract assigned, or purely personal to the assignor, such as the making of further voluntary advances by an owner after the date of notice of the assignment, may not be raised against the assignee by the debtor. This class of case is not always easy to define.

ILLUSTRATION

One Price induced the defendant by fraudulent misrepresentations to pur- **14·052**
chase a newspaper, and assigned the unpaid balance of the purchase money to
the plaintiff. Notice of the assignment was given, and the plaintiff sued the
defendant for the money. The defendant took no steps to have the contract of

---

[14] See *Drew* v. *Josolyne* (1887) 18 Q.B.D. 590, illustrated on this point *supra*, para. 14·043, but see *Re Asphaltic Wood Pavement Co.* (1885) 30 Ch.D. 216, Chap. 17, *post*, para. 16·008 (right to damages not affected).

[15] See *supra*, para. 14·022.

[16] For an analogous case, but not of set-off, see the *Linden Gardens* case, illustrated *supra*, paras. 14·028–14·029, where in one of the two cases before the Court no breach of contract had as yet occurred at the time of an owner's assignment of the benefit of a building contract, but the assignment of the right to damages was nevertheless upheld.

[17] 13 App.Cas. 199.

sale rescinded, but brought in Price as a defendant to his counterclaim, and obtained judgment against him for damages for fraudulent misrepresentations. *Held*, by the Court of Appeal, that he could not set off those damages against the assignees: *Stoddard* v. *Union Trusts Ltd.* (1912).[18]

On the other hand, the fact that a certificate of an architect has been given fraudulently and in collusion with the builder, in order to give him a title to receive money, may be set up by the owner as a defence to an action by the assignee of the builder. This is, of course, a breach of a term of the contract by the builder,[19] and not a mere representation inducing the contract as in *Stoddard's* case.

ILLUSTRATION

14-053   T. agreed, in 1874, to construct a reservoir for a local board for £3,983, to be paid for on certificates of an engineer, L., the last of which was given on February 15, 1876. This certificate was not paid because the reservoir would not hold water, and T. sued the board for £1,067 11s. 6d. as the balance certified to be due. This action was compromised by an agreement dated February 13, 1877, whereby the local board consented to pay T. £800 on August 12, 1877, and to take over the works. On February 24, 1877, T. assigned this £800 to the plaintiffs, who gave notice of the assignment to the board. The board had the reservoir examined in February, 1878, and it was proved in evidence that it was not merely improperly, but fraudulently, constructed, and that L. and T. had conspired together to defraud the board by false certificates given by L. and presented by T. The board did not inform the plaintiffs of the fraud, although they had been in correspondence, till 1879. *Held*, by the Court of Appeal, that this defence being good as against the assignor, the assignees could get no better title; that the board were not bound by acquiescence and delay, and that the plaintiffs could not recover: *Wakefield and Barnsley Banking Co.* v. *Normanton Local Board* (1881).[20]

14-054   An equity does not cease to be an equity for this purpose if it is or has been prosecuted to judgment. So an assignee of a contract under which the debtor has already obtained judgment for damages against the creditor will be held bound to allow the amount of the judgment to be set off against his claim.[21] On the other hand, it goes without saying that the assignee will be bound by all the conditions as to payment binding the assignor, for example, the necessity of obtaining a certificate, notwithstanding his completion of the actual work itself.[22]

---

[18] [1912] 1 K.B. 181. (See also *Re Pinto Leite & Nephews, ex p. Visconde Des Olivaes* [1929] 1 Ch. 221.)

[19] (Of an implied term not to interfere with the certifier, see *ante*, Chap. 6, Section 5(4), para. 6·112 *et seq.*)

[20] 44 L.T. 697, C.A.; strictly, the fraud in this case was a defence to the action on the compromise, it would seem. *Cf.* the case of a surety for due performance of a contract where there has been fraud in obtaining the certificate, *ante*, Chap. 6, para. 6·109, *post*, Chap. 17, para. 17·067.

[21] *Lawrence* v. *Hayes* [1927] 2 K.B. 111.

[22] See, *e.g. per* Lord Blackburn in *Lewis* v. *Hoare* (1881) 44 L.T. 66.

The building owner who has been notified of an assignment must be careful to avoid any mitigation of the terms of the contract in favour of the builder which may prejudice the position of the assignee, for example by making advances to the builder, or he may find himself effectively paying twice over.[23]

SECTION 6.   PROVISIONS AGAINST ASSIGNMENT

(1) Interpretation of Provisions

It is very common in construction contracts to find express provisions pro-   **14·055**
hibiting what is variously described as "assignment" either of the contract itself, or of particular rights or benefits under the contract (such as the right to moneys due), or against sub-contracting or "sub-letting" either the whole or a part of the works. Some of these provisions are drafted as unconditional prohibitions, while others permit the proscribed action if consent is obtained. Most of the provisions restrained assignment or sub-contracting *by the contractor* only, but in England in 1971 producer influences in the RIBA/JCT standard forms inserted a prohibition against assignments *by the owner* as well. Thus, Clause 17(1) now provided that: " 'the Employer shall not without the written consent of the Contractor *assign this contract*'; while in the opposite case Clause 17(2) provided that: 'the Contractor' (1) shall not, without the written consent of the Employer assign this contract, and (2) shall not, without the written consent of the architect (which consent shall not be unreasonably withheld to the prejudice of the contractor) sub-let any portion of the works." In the case of the ICE forms, the prohibition extended only to assignments by the contractor, in terms that (by Clause 3 of the fifth 1973 edition, for example) "the Contractor shall not, without the written consent of the employer, assign this contract", and by Clause 4 that "the Contractor shall not sub-let the whole of the Works. Except where otherwise provided by the Contract the Contractor shall not sub-let any part of the Works without the written consent of the Engineer . . .".

The draftsmanship of these provisions is characteristically inept, showing little understanding of the law of assignment, or of the distinctions between the assignability of benefits and liabilities on the one hand, or between assignment and vicarious performance on the other.

Bearing in mind that: **14·056**

(i) the unilateral assignment of contractual liabilities without consent is impossible, so that the assignor always remains fully liable to the other contracting party for any failures by the assignee;

---

[23] *Brice* v. *Bannister* (1878) 3 Q.B.D. 569, *supra*.

(ii) an assignee takes subject to equities available to the debtor under the contract;

(iii) neither assignment nor vicarious performance of a "personal" contract so as to prejudice the debtor will be permitted in any event,

express provisions against assignment would appear in most cases and for practical purposes to be aimed at prohibiting *vicarious performance* of the liabilities in question (which the courts would in most cases otherwise permit) rather than the assignment of contractual benefits. However, the House of Lords has suggested that in the case of assignment *by the owner*, the draftsman may well intend to prohibit the benefit *of the right to enforce* the contract being transferred to an assignee.

ILLUSTRATION

14·057   In the first of two cases before the Court of Appeal, owners transferred their interest in a building and assigned the benefit of two successive building contracts for the removal of asbestos from the building. The first contract was in the RIBA/JCT standard form, which provided by Clause 17(1) that the owner "should not without the written consent of the Contractor assign the contract". The second contract provided by Clause 3.1 that "neither the Employer nor the Contractor shall without the written consent of the other assign this contract", followed by a provision that the contractor "should not sub-contract the works or any part thereof" without the architect's written consent. In the second case before the Court of Appeal, the prohibition in an assigned building contract was also in the RIBA/JCT Clause 17 form. In the first case, the first owners had assigned a current action for damages already started by them against the first building contractors, and also "all other rights of action currently vested in the assignors which are or were incidental to the leasehold interest in the premises", which it was held included the contract with the second building contractors. In the second case, the first owners had assigned "the full benefit of all contracts . . . whatsoever entered into by the assignor . . . for the construction and completion of the development" to the later owners. All the building contractors in both cases disputed liability to the later assignees on the ground that without consent, which had not been asked for or given, the assignments were prohibited and ineffective. *Held*, by the Court of Appeal, that on the true construction of all the building contracts the assignments in question were not prohibited and were effective to transfer the right to damages for breach of contract to the assignees. *Per* Sir Michael Kerr and Nourse L.J.: all three building contracts when prohibiting "assignment of the contract" *by the contractor* without consent, were only prohibiting *vicarious performance and not assignment of the benefit of the contract*; however, in the case of assignment of the contract *by the owner*, while the contracts on their true interpretation were effective to prohibit the owner's transfer *of the right to have the contract performed*, they did not prohibit assignment *of rights or benefits arising "under the contract", such as the right to damages for a past breach.*[23a] *Per* Staughton L.J., on their true interpretation all three building contracts were only prohibiting *vicarious performance*,

---

[23a] For the significance of this on the facts see the case illustrated *supra*, paras. 14·027–14·029.

whether by owner or contractor, and in neither case were they prohibiting assignment of the benefit of the contracts. *Held*, by the House of Lords, (a) that there was no principle of public policy which, as between an assignee and another contracting party, would invalidate a prohibition against assignment of the benefit of a chose in action, whether of remedies for its enforcement or for breach of contract; but (b) that the wording of the prohibitions against "assignment of the contract" in all three building contracts was effective to prevent assignment by the owner to the assignee *whether of the right to enforce the contracts or to recover damages for their breach*. *Per* Lord Browne-Wilkinson, there were good reasons for a contractor to ensure that he dealt only with his original employer, since some employers in building contracts were more reasonable than others in dealing with disputes, and the parties had not intended to distinguish between the right to performance and the "fruits of the contract", as had been held by the majority in the Court of Appeal: *Linden Gardens Trust Ltd.* v. *Lenesta Sludge Disposals Ltd.* (1992).[24]

[Note: In so far as this case relates to the interpretation of assignment prohibition clauses, much seems to have turned on an analysis of the wording of clause 17 as a whole, including that part of the clause which also prohibited assignment of the contract by the contractor. The wording is an example of the poor draftsmanship of standard form construction contracts generally, and the case should not necessarily be regarded as of conclusive application when interpreting restrictions on "assignment" in other construction contracts. In most standard form contracts it seems unlikely that any really precise intention was in the mind of the draftsman or of those instructing him.[25]

(2) Whether Prohibitions of Assignment Valid

The tenth edition expressed doubt as to whether contractual provisions against assignment were in any case valid at all. Not only did such provisions appear to impose a restraint on alienation of commercial rights which it was in society's interest to encourage, and which had almost certainly been the basis of equity's early intervention to permit assignment in an increasingly industrial society, as also of the later statutory extension from equitable rights to legal choses in action, but there had already been a number of earlier cases or dicta supporting this view in other fields. Thus, in the case of a lease with a covenant against assignment, the Court of Appeal held in 1979 that while such an assignment might be a breach of contract sounding in damages, it would be effective to transfer the lease.[26] Again, where there was a provision in a life insurance policy that "it should not be assignable in any case whatever", the Court of Appeal suggested that while the policy itself might not be assignable, the benefit of the money once received could be the subject of a declaration of trust.[27] Again, the words "not transferable" on a banker's deposit receipt were held not to preclude, as between donor and donee, an equitable assign-

14·058

---

[24] (1992) 57 BLR 57, C.A.; [1993] 3 W.L.R. 408, [1994] 1 A.C. 85, H.L. A.C. 85, H.L.
[25] Contrast the precise statement of intention in Clause 15 of the 1980 Singapore S.I.A. contract, reproduced in C.C.P.P., p. 571.
[26] *Old Grovebury Manor Farm Ltd.* v. *W. Seymour Plant Sales and Hire Ltd.* [1979] 1 W.L.R. 1397.
[27] *Re Turcan* (1888) 40 Ch.D. 5.

ment in favour of the donee.[28] Again, in a case in 1910 involving a prohibition against assignment of earnings in a contract of employment, Darling J. clearly had no doubt that such a provision was completely ineffective.[29]

14·059   However, in 1978 Croom Johnson J. upheld a claim by an assignee of moneys due under a roadworks contract, which had provided that the contractor "shall not assign the contract or any part thereof or any benefit or interest therein or thereunder" without the consent of the owner.[29a] The point was finally raised squarely for decision in the Court of Appeal in 1992 in the *Linden Gardens* case.[30] There Staughton L.J., after considering a number of authorities and sources, stated that, approaching the matter on principle and having regard to the desirability of a piece of property such as a chose in action being transferable, he would himself have decided against permitting prohibition,[31] but for the fact that he regarded the Court of Appeal as bound by an earlier unreported case of its own in 1983, where an amendment to add successor reversioners of a building lease, who were also assignees of the building contract, as second plaintiffs in an action brought by the assignors was rejected, first, because on the facts it would raise a new cause of action after the limitation period had expired and, secondly, because the assignment of the benefit of the building contract had been prohibited by its terms.[32]

14·060   This question, while seemingly closed in the Court of Appeal, appeared to be still open in the House of Lords. However, as has been seen, the position was finally settled, so far as English law is concerned, by the House of Lords' affirmation in 1993 of the Court of Appeal's position on this point in the *Linden Gardens* case itself.[32a]

14·061   In the United States, the Uniform Commercial Code (U.C.C.) has since 1972 provided that:

> "a term in any contract between an account debtor and an assignor is ineffective if it prohibits assignment of an account or prohibits creation of a security interest in a general intangible for money due or to become due, or requires the account debtor's consent to such consignment or security interest."[33]

The authoritative official comment to that section, after noting that cases were "legion" in the United States courts which had held assignments good in face of prohibitory or restrictive terms, and that this shift in legal

---

[28] *Re Griffin* (1898) 79 L.T. 442, *per* Byrne J.
[29] *Tom Shaw & Co.* v. *Moss Empires Ltd.* (1908) 25 T.L.R. 190, and see the other sources and authorities referred to by Staughton L.J. in *Linden Gardens Trust Ltd.* v. *Lenesta Sludge Disposals Ltd.* (1992) 57 BLR 57, at pp. 78–79.
[29a] *Helston Securities Ltd.* v. *Hertfordshire C.C.* [1978] 3 All E.R. 262.
[30] The House of Lords has allowed the appeal from the Court of Appeal decision (see [1993] 3 W.L.R. 408).
[31] (1992) 57 BLR 57, at p. 78.
[32] *Reed Publishing Holdings* v. *King's Reach Investments Ltd.*, unreported, Court of Appeal, May 25, 1983.
[32a] See *supra*, para. 14·057.
[33] U.C.C., art. 9–138(4).

doctrine had taken place in response to economic need, concluded that section 318(4) of article 9 of the Code

> "thus states a rule of law which is widely recognized in the cases and which corresponds to current business practices. It can be regarded as a revolutionary departure only by those who still cherish the hope that we may yet return to the views entertained some two hundred years ago by the Court of King's Bench".

The official comment was equally clear that the provision applied to the assignment of sums due and to become due under "contracts of sale, construction contracts and the like".

Thus, in the construction field, effect has been given to the Code by invalidating prohibitions against assignment without consent in a case of the assignment of the proceeds of a plumbing sub-contract,[34] and in a case where the right to payment under a services sub-contract had been assigned to a bank.[35]   **14·062**

These considerations suggest that in Commonwealth jurisdictions other than England the position, particularly in the light of the cursory nature of the reasoning in the *King's Reach* case, and notwithstanding Croom Johnson J.'s clearly contrary decision in the *Helstan Securities* case, may justify further review. The question depends, of course, on considerations of public policy rather than of legal principle, and is now foreclosed in England by the *Linden Gardens* case.

SECTION 7.   ATTACHMENT OF MONEYS DUE

Attachment is a form of execution available to a judgment creditor who, in his search for assets of the debtor against which to execute, discovers that some third person owes money to the judgment debtor. Such a debt can be attached by what is known to lawyers as a garnishee order, and once the order has been made absolute, the third party debtor (or garnishee) must discharge his liability by payment to the judgment creditor (or garnishor) and not to his original creditor (the judgment debtor). The whole transaction therefore has many similarities to an assignment of the third person's debt by the judgment debtor to the judgment creditor, but there are some important differences. Thus while it has been seen that debts arising in the future may be validly assigned, the power of attachment of debts is more limited, and an order of the court attaching a debt will only be valid if *at the date of the order* the debt was an existing debt.   **14·063**

However, provided there is an existing debt, the fact that it is not yet payable, or not yet ascertainable as to its exact amount, will not prevent it   **14·064**

---

[34] *Aetna Surety Co.* v. *Bedford-Stuyvesant Restoration Corporation* 455 N.Y. Supp. 265 (1982), App. Div., N.Y.
[35] *Mississippi Bank* v. *Nickles & Wells Construction Co.* 421 So. (2d) 1056 (1982), Sup. Ct. of Miss.

being attachable. This arises from the original wording of section 61 of the English Common Law Procedure Act 1854, copied widely in the Commonwealth, which permitted attachment of "debts owing *or accruing*". In an early leading case, this wording was held by Blackburn J. to permit attachment of an entire debt payable by monthly instalments of £10, at a time when only one instalment had become due.[36] Subsequently, the Court of Appeal permitted attachment of a panel doctor's entire remuneration for the year 1913 and for the first quarter of 1914 at a time when, although under his contract of employment payments on account had been made or were due, final detailed ascertainment of the full sums due for the periods in question had not yet been determined.[37]

14·065　　Attachment, therefore, differs from assignment in that debts arising or likely to arise in the future are not attachable under the wording of the English legislation. Applying these principles to construction contracts, it seems clear that sums anticipated to become due for future work not yet carried out at the time of the application for a garnishee order will not be attachable. Similarly, where a debt has not been perfected, as, for example, where attachment is sought before a period of service which will qualify for payment has been completed, there will be no attachable debt.[38] Nor can a right to unliquidated damages for breach of contract be garnished before judgment has been obtained by the contracting party, since it is not a debt.[39]

In the case of construction contracts, however, this concept of a garnishable *"debitum in praesenti solvendum in futuro"* can present special problems where work has been done but not yet paid for at the time of attachment.

ILLUSTRATIONS

14·066　　(1) Judgment creditors of a nominated sub-contractor sought to garnish the moneys owing to him by the main contractor after the sub-contract work was complete but before any certificate relating to it had been issued under the main contract. This was in the pre-1963 RIBA form, which by Clause 24 provided that payments to nominated sub-contractors for their work should not be due from the main contractor until issue of the relevant architect's certificate. The sub-contract itself also provided that payment was to be made "in accordance with the certificates and the times provided in the said [main] contract". The main contractors had obtained all certificates except the final certificate, for which they had applied, and they admitted that when the final

---

[36] *Tapp* v. *Jones* (1875) L.R. 10 Q.B. 591.
[37] *O'Driscoll* v. *Manchester Insurance Committee* [1915] 3 K.B. 499. See also, for sums earned on a daily basis, although only payable twice monthly, *Garner* v. *Strickland* [1955] 4 D.L.R. 329 Ct. of App., B.C.
[38] *Quercetti* v. *Tranquilli* [1941] 4 D.L.R. 63.
[39] *Per* Swinfen Eady L.J. in the *O'Driscoll* case, *supra*, at p. 512.

certificate was issued there would be a sum included in it sufficient to meet the judgment debt, but denied any liability to the sub-contractors until the certificate was issued. *Held*, by the Court of Appeal, that although there had never been a precise decision to this effect, there could be no right to receive payment on account under the contract until the architect had given his certificate, so that there was no debt capable of being garnished by the judgment creditors: *Dunlop and Ranken Ltd.* v. *Hendall Steel Structures* (1957).[40]

[Note: This case has been doubted *ante*, Chapter 6, in regard to its interpretation (arrived at by adopting an opinion expressed in the then *Annual Practice* under Order 45, rule 1) that the certificate was a condition precedent (although as previously stated a view to the same effect was later expressed in the Court of Appeal in *Lubenham Fidelity Investment* v. *South Pembrokeshire Council*[41]). It is submitted that under the wording of these particular forms of contract, as was later laid down unequivocally by the House of Lords in the *Gilbert-Ash* case[42] in the converse situation of an owner's right of set-off against an architect's certificate, no certificate of the architect can bar a contractor from exercising his right to arbitrate or litigate for the sums due to him under the contract. If this is correct, the basis for the garnishee aspect of the decision disappears.]

(2) A sub-contract order form provided: "The amount certified by the Architect to be due in respect to the sub-contract work and any authorized variation thereof shall not become payable until fourteen days after the receipt by the contractor of the appropriate Architect's certificate and remittance from the employer." The sub-contract also permitted the main contractor to take over the work himself, or alternatively terminate the sub-contract, in the event of certain defaults by the sub-contractor. A judgment creditor of the sub-contractor garnished the main contractor's debt at a time when the work was complete and the sub-contractor had submitted his final account, and when it was admitted by the main contractor that some moneys would be due after certain contra-accounts and claims, but before any architect's certificate or remittance from the owner had been received. *Held*, by the Alberta Appellate Division, following *O'Driscoll* v. *Manchester Insurance Committee*[43] and not following *Dunlop and Ranken Ltd.* v. *Hendell Steel Structures* or the statement under Order 45, rule 1 in the *Annual Practice*, that the contract provided for interim payments, with only the final payment retained until completion, and was not therefore an entire contract; that certification by the architect was not a condition precedent to payment; that on the facts existing when the garnishee summons was served the work had been completed, so that a termination was no longer a possibility; accordingly there was a debt, although not yet payable, which could be garnished by the judgment creditor: *Sandy* v. *Yukon Construction Co. Ltd.* (1961).[44]   **14·067**

(3) Local authority owners terminated a contract under Clause 19 of the pre-1963 RIBA form of contract, which provided that on such a termination "the employer shall not be bound by any other provisions to make any payment to the contractor". At the time there was some £1,700 of retention money in the council's hands. On the following day sub-contractors who were   **14·068**

---

[40] [1957] 1 W.L.R. 1102.
[41] (1986) 33 BLR 39, discussed and illustrated *ante*, Chap. 6, Section 6(7), paras. 6·192.
[42] *Modern Engineering (Bristol) Ltd.* v. *Gilbert-Ash (Northern) Ltd.* [1974] A.C. 689, discussed *ante*, Chap. 6, paras. 6·005 and 6·195 *et seq.* See also the clear view expressed by Lord Blackburn in *Lewis* v. *Hoare* (1881) 44 L.T. 66, at p. 67.
[43] [1915] 3 K.B. 499.
[44] 26 D.L.R. (2d) 254.

judgment creditors of the main contractor issued a garnishee summons against the council. *Held*, by the Court of Appeal, that since by Clause 19 no further moneys were to be payable until completion of the work by the council and certification by the architect of their expenses in order to see if any balance would then be due to the contractor, there was no debt capable of being garnished: *Grant Plant Hire* v. *Trickey* (1961).[45]

14·069 In assessing the effect of the above cases in a construction context, it is submitted that, where all the work is complete at the time of the garnishee summons, no serious problem will arise and garnishee orders will be effective, save only in the very rare cases at the present day where a contractor will be *permanently* precluded from suing or arbitrating for moneys due if no A/E's certificate should be given. Where, however, the work is not yet fully complete, but, for example, sums have been provisionally "earned" by way of retention moneys on work already performed at the time of the garnishee summons, there is always the theoretical possibility under a construction contract of set-offs by the owner subsequently arising, or of the exercise of termination or other remedies by the owner against the contractor which may reduce or eliminate the debt altogether—in other words, the debt will be contingent only in such a case, although already provisionally earned. In the *O'Driscoll* case, Swinfen Eady L.J. was at pains to point out that on the facts of that case there was no contingency which could happen to deprive the judgment debtor of his right to remuneration from the garnishee.[46] In the ordinary case before completion, therefore, the position seems uncertain, and more precise language than the traditional "debt due or accruing due" wording[47] indicating the original legislative intention seems desirable, since the situation envisaged is a very common one in construction contracts.

It has already been pointed out *supra*, Subsection (3), that, as between a garnishee and a prior assignee for value, the assignee's claim will prevail even if notice of the assignment has not been given.[47a]

SECTION 8. ASSIGNMENT BY OPERATION OF LAW

(1) Generally

14·070 Transfers of contractual rights can often arise by statute, for example, a statute setting up a statutory corporation to take over the rights and liabilities of other persons. But the commonest examples in practice arise upon bankruptcy or liquidation, or upon the death of a contracting party.[48]

---

[45] 105 S.J. 255.
[46] [1915] 3 K.B. 499, at pp. 511, 513.
[47] See today R.S.C., Ord. 49, r. 1.
[47a] See the cases referred to *supra*, para. 14·046.
[48] The subject of bankruptcy and liquidation is dealt with *post*, Chap. 16.

(2) Death

This subject is also dealt with *ante*, Chapter 4, Section 3(5).[49]   **14·071**
Upon the death of a contracting party, his rights *and liabilities* on *non-personal* contracts vest in his executors or administrators, and, to this extent, the liability of his estate is an exception to the general rule of law which prevents the assignment of contractual liabilities. But the distinction between "personal" and other contracts remains of vital importance, since the former become void upon death and have no future effect thereafter, although rights accrued at the date of death will be enforced.

ILLUSTRATION

S. was appointed on December 5, 1865 as consulting engineer for the construction of works on a railway line, to be completed in 15 months, and his fee was £500 in five equal payments. He commenced, and received £100 in March 1866. He continued two quarters more, and soon after the end of the third quarter and before any payment beyond the £100 had been made, died intestate. Less than three-fifths of the whole work had been performed, but no default of the deceased was proved. *Held*, by the Court of Exchequer, that notwithstanding that the contract was one of personal confidence, and therefore dissolved by death and null for the future, the administrator might recover for the money due for work actually done, *i.e.* the £200 for the two quarters, and was not thrown back on *quantum meruit*: *Stubbs* v. *Holywell Railway* (1867).[50]

In such cases, the estate will not be liable for any damage arising from the death itself.[51]
On the other hand, where there is no personal element, both the burden   **14·072**
and the benefit of the contract pass on the death, and the same result will occur in a personal contract if the death is that of the party whose personality is not material.

ILLUSTRATIONS

(1) The defendant employed the testator to erect a temporary gallery and other woodwork for the purpose of a public dinner, and shortly after the order was given, and before it was begun, the testator died, and the plaintiffs, as executors, performed the work, using the materials of the testator. *Held*, by the Court of Exchequer of Pleas, that the executors might recover for work done and materials supplied: *Marshall* v. *Broadhurst* (1831).[52]

---

[49] See also the discussion of death and illness of a contracting party, *ante*, paras. 4·270 *et seq.*
[50] L.R. 2 Ex. 311.
[51] See, *e.g. per* Pollock C.B. in *Hall* v. *Wright* (1859) E.B. & E., at p. 793.
[52] 1 Cr. & J. 403.

(2) W. engaged D. as a civil engineer in connection with certain harbour works. W. covenanted for himself and his executors to employ D. at a fixed salary for six years. W. raised D.'s salary, and subsequently died. W.'s executors again raised D.'s salary but dismissed him before the expiration of the term. *Held*, by Denman J., that the agreement bound W.'s executors: *Davison v. Reeves* (1892).[53]

(3) The plaintiffs, a troupe of music-hall performers, contracted with a partnership, consisting of the defendants and another person, to give certain performances at a music-hall. The other member of the partnership died before the contract was performed. The plaintiffs had no knowledge of who composed the partnership. *Held*, by the Divisional Court, that the contract was not of such a personal character on the part of the partnership as to be put an end to by the death of the deceased partner: *Phillips v. Alhambra Palace Company* (1901).[54]

---

[53] 8 T.L.R. 391.
[54] [1901] 1 K.B. 59.

CHAPTER 15

INSURANCE AND INDEMNITIES

SECTION 1. INSURANCE

(1) Generally

(a) Purpose of contractually required insurance

Other than professional insurance of the owner's A/E, discussed *infra*,   **15·001**
Subsection (5), which is not usually specifically called for in an A/E's contract of employment though almost invariably taken out in practice, the
insurance sections of the present Chapter are principally concerned with
contractually required insurance of what are almost always *the contractor's*
obligations arising under the construction contract between owner and
contractor. (The provisions for this are not infrequently incorporated into
or otherwise reflected in sub-contracts). Contractors, sub-contractors or
owners may, of course, voluntarily choose to take out insurance against
any risk they wish, but if so this will not in principle affect the

interpretation or administration of their contracts, or of the contractual rights *inter se* of the parties to them. However, an important commercial factor, where contractors or sub-contractors take out *voluntary* insurance, will be the consideration that they will be incurring an additional premium cost which will place them at a pricing disadvantage against competitors who choose not to do so.

On the other hand, *contractually required* insurance may not only, depending on the express wording of the contract, affect the substantive contractual rights of the parties *inter se*, but it will inevitably have the commercial effect, from the owner's point of view, of increasing the contract price by the amount of the premiums involved, either through express contractual provisions, such as provisional sums or other priced items for payment of the premium cost by the owner, or by an unitemised increase in all tendering contractors' price or prices to cover the cost to the contractor of the required premiums.

(b) Two main types of contractor insurance

15·002   The elements of risk traditionally covered by required contractor insurance in construction contracts lie in two areas, namely the risk of damage occurring to the works themselves during construction ("property" or "works" insurance in insurance terminology), and the risk of claims by third parties for personal injuries or damage to their property resulting from the carrying out of the work in the contract ("liability" insurance policies). It is of crucial importance to appreciate that required insurance is almost invariably defined, in both areas, to cover those situations where the contractor would otherwise be contractually responsible to the owner by virtue of express or implied terms of the contract if no insurance was present. In regard to damage to the works, this will arise from the contractor's express or implied completion obligations, independent of fault, under the "inclusive price principle."[1] In regard to third party liability, in nearly all contracts the contractor's *contractual* liability to the owner under express contractual indemnity clauses is expressly conditioned on his own negligence or default, and if so it is only this express liability against which the contractor is usually required to insure.[2] In other words, the objective of the insurance in both cases is to cover economic loss which would otherwise be incurred *by the contractor* as a consequence of *his contractual liabilities to the owner* should the risk concerned eventuate. The only commercial or practical reason for an owner's readiness to pay for such insurance is, therefore, to safeguard himself against the heavy losses the owner would be likely to incur if the contractor's financial resources were to prove inadequate to meet his contractual liabilities in the event of a major loss arising, with the consequential delays and often serious additional cost to the owner if a new contractor had to be

---

[1] See *ante*, Chap. 4, paras. 4·036 *et seq.*, and particularly 4·043 *et seq.*
[2] See, however, for an unqualified indemnity the *Dorset C.C.* case, illustrated *infra*, para. 15·020. For indemnities generally see *infra*, Section 2.

appointed for the project in mid-stream. This is the crucial factor to be borne in mind in drafting and interpreting insurance clauses in construction projects.

(c) Distinction between insurance and bonds

This same factor also serves to emphasise the essential distinction **15·003** between the cover provided by insurance on the one hand as against a due performance bond on the other.[3] In the case of insurance of a contractor against what would otherwise be his own contractual risk, the insurance will pay for the cost resulting from that particular risk eventuating (and so be of direct and substantial benefit to the contractor, while only of indirect benefit to the owner, in the sense explained above). In the case of a typical due performance bond or guarantee, on the other hand, what is being secured to the owner is the financial ability of the contractor to meet his contractual obligations generally. Since it is an essential characteristic of a bond or guarantee that the bondsman is expressly or impliedly entitled to an indemnity from the debtor (contractor) if called on to meet the latter's obligation to the creditor (owner), a bond is, therefore, obviously far cheaper than insurance, since it is simply a secondary obligation, and the bondsman or guarantor will incur no liability under the bond if an anticipated risk or expenditure occurs, provided the contractor has sufficient financial resources to meet his contractual obligations to the owner in that event. Moreover, in England and other Commonwealth countries the liability under a commercial bond is almost invariably expressed to be subject to a fairly restrictive financial limit, and in addition the presence of required insurance of the contractor's liabilities under the contract concerned will also serve to reduce very substantially the possibility of any eventual liability of the bondsman arising under the bond, and so the cost of the bond. Although owners would be well advised to reduce the cost of insurance by providing for substantial insurance "excesses" within the reasonable means of a prospective contractor, and by limiting works insurance only to potentially catastrophic risks,[4] provisions for such excesses or so limiting the insured risks are not commonly found in English contracts, which suggests a lack of understanding or of concern for their clients' interests on the part of owners' advisers and is a tribute to the sales expertise of the insurance industry, as well as indirectly benefiting the bondsman by reducing the latter's area of ultimate risk.

The only reason why owners in construction contracts will be justified in **15·004** insuring against matters which are the contractor's contractual responsibility will accordingly be to avoid the delay and dislocation to the project which might arise if a very substantial loss were to occur, such as a fire or earthquake destroying the entire works at a late stage of construction, or a major accident involving such substantial property or personal injury

---

[3] Bonds and Guarantees are the subject of Chap. 17, *post.*
[4] See *infra* (d), and see C.C.P.P., paras. 23–32—33, and in the case of the English RIBA/JCT Forms, paras. 29–16 and 30–22.

claims by third persons, as to strain the contractor's financial resources beyond their limit. Insurance, as opposed to a bond, will have the advantage of maintaining the continuity of the project under the original contractor's control, which must certainly be lost, with a consequential need to make new arrangements for completion, if the owner's protection is only in the form of a performance bond which needs to be activated, even if that bond is (as in the United Kingdom bonds very often are not) of sufficient amount to cover a large, near total loss works claim or a major accident during construction giving rise to very large third party claims.

(d) Over-insurance common in U.K. standard forms

15·005   It must be said that few owners' advisers in the United Kingdom, and in particular those responsible for the United Kingdom standard forms, appear to have analysed or understood this basic rationale for requiring contractor insurance. By contrast, contractor and insurance industry interests have not been slow to appreciate the advantages of securing a high degree of over-insurance, notably in the progressive extension over the years of a large number of risks for inclusion in the damage to the works "property" cover. Many of these, (such as storm or burst water pipes) are unlikely to produce anything but minor claims well within a normal contractor's means to absorb. Moreover, as stated, owners' advisers rarely make use of reasonable insurance "excesses" within the contractor's means which, together with a reduction in the list of insured risks, would greatly reduce the cost of both works and third party liability cover,[5] as well as act as an inducement to good site management and give a deserved tendering advantage to those contractors already practising it, as against those habitually maximising profit or competing on price by cutting corners on site organisation and protective measures in the knowledge of available owner-paid insurance should losses result.

(e) Ingenuities of wording

15·006   While considering the subject of insurance generally, it should be borne in mind by non-legal readers that insurers, like commercial bondsmen, expend considerable ingenuity in drafting and designing policies which on the surface appear to offer, but on informed and close analysis do not, the full protection expected and required by the assured, and also in employing every device of subrogation, or of settlement of claims in return for assignment of rights, in order to transfer, reduce or eliminate their own liability. Examples of the first tendency are numerous—the virtually valueless "adjoining property insurance" offered, as will be seen, in conjunction with the RIBA/JCT standard forms; a new "indemnity" wording

---

[5] See this developed and explained in C.C.P.P., paras. 23–31—33, 27–52, and for particular criticism of the RIBA/JCT provisions *ibid.* at paras. 29–16 and 30–22. See also the SIA 1980 contract, Clauses 20(1) and 39, C.C.P.P., pp.576–577 and 616–617.

in fire and damage policies which permits the unexpected argument, when a claim is made, that insurance payments for damaged older buildings should be below replacement cost to take account of the higher by-law construction standards now compulsory for a replacement building; the artificial use of the expression "accident" in the policy to assist in avoiding liability if the claim arises from a condition of affairs rather than a sudden event[6]; the "claims made" basis progressively introduced both in England and overseas (with no alteration of premiums) for professional insurance generally, very substantially reducing the effective protection offered by such policies and concealing greatly increased real premium cost if full protection is to be obtained[7]; and, in a field outside construction contracts, perhaps, household contents insurance issued in a form requiring premiums to be related to the value of the entire contents (not of the value of stolen or damaged contents), so enabling apparently attractive low percentage premiums to be charged while also enabling claims to be reduced on well-known "under-insured" arguments.

(f) Subrogation and assignment

Examples of the exploitation of these devices in other fields have been attempts by insurers, in defiance of recognised employment practice and against the wishes of insured employers, to enforce by subrogation claims for an indemnity against the assured's negligent employees, necessitating informal Government intervention[8-9]; the retreat of insurers behind the unsatisfactory client/broker/insurer relationship in order to defeat a claim where disclosure had been made by the client to his broker but not passed on to the insurer; and the device (in the case of a commercial bondsman) of paying in full an owner's claim for damages against a contractor who had been dismissed after a structural collapse, in return for an assignment of the owner's claim against the supervising engineer.[10] Undoubtedly the device of subrogation (whereby an insurer pays a claim in full, and thereupon becomes entitled to sue third persons in the name of the assured in respect of the insured loss) has been constantly used in the construction field, particularly in an attempt to shift the burden of meeting a claim under a contractor's policy onto the shoulders of sub-contractors in particular.

15·007

It is for this reason why construction contracts, wherever there is a possibility of one party being contractually liable to the other in respect of an insured risk, must require the insurance to be in joint names, thus preventing subrogation against the other party by the insurers, which would defeat the whole purpose of the insurance. An example of such joint

---

[6] See *infra*, para. 15·010.

[7] See *infra*, Subsection 5, Professional Insurance, paras. 15·031 *et seq.*

[8-9] See *Lister* v. *Romford Ice & Cold Storage* [1957] A.C. 555, discussed by Lord Denning M.R., in *Morris* v. *Ford Motor Co. Ltd.* [1973] Q.B. 792, 798–9.

[10] *City of Prince Albert* v. *Underwood & McLellan* (1969) 3 D.L.R. 3d 385, illustrated, and doubted *ante*, Chap. 2, para. 2·139.

insurance is to be found in the case of insurance of the works, *infra*, Subsection (2)(a).

(g) Comprehensive project cover

15·008   The industry has of recent years marketed a new type of "Contractor's All-Risk" ("CAR") policy purporting to offer comprehensive insurance in one policy to all the various parties to a construction project, in some cases including even the owner's A/E and as well as other contractors and sub-contractors. It may be surmised that these policies were dictated more by enthusiasm for new insurance business than any real understanding by insurers of the very wide areas of liability without recourse which would inevitably result from such a concept, and early attempts to evade it were to be expected.

ILLUSTRATIONS

15·009   (1) A "CAR" policy had been issued in favour of an owner "and/or Contractors, and/or Sub-Contractors" covering not only the works themselves, but "temporary works or constructional plant belonging to the insured or for which they are responsible." A major item of plant provided and used by an important sub-sub-contractor collapsed in an accident while being dismantled, causing considerable damage to other work and plant. The insurers, by way of subrogation in the name of the owner, sued the sub-sub-contractor in tort, arguing that the policy did not apply to sub-sub-contractors, and in any event did not extend beyond the sub-sub-contractor's plant itself to any other property. *Held*, by Lloyd J., that the policy applied to sub-sub-contractors and, although this was a property and not a liability policy, the sub-sub-contractor had an insurable interest in all the property on the project and not merely in its own property. *Petrofina* v. *Magnaload* (1984).[11]

(2) An insurance policy was expressed to cover the main contractor and "all its subsidiary associated or related companies, all contractors, all sub-contractors or suppliers." A personal injuries claim was brought against a sub-contractor who had not yet been engaged by the main contractor at the time that the policy was taken out, so that the name of the relevant sub-contractor had not been registered or attached to the policy. *Held*, by the High Court of Australia, that the sub-contractors concerned were covered by the policy. *Trident General Insurance Co. Ltd.* v. *McNiece Bros. Ltd.* (1988).[12]

15·009A   Many so-called "CAR" policies nevertheless often seek to exclude, more understandably, claims involving the repair of contractors' defective

---

[11] [1984] Q.B. 127. Contrast Kerr J.'s differing interpretation of an indemnity clause with similar wording in *City of Manchester* v. *Fram Gerrard*, illustrated and doubted *infra*, Section 2, para. 15·059.

[12] 80 A.L.J.R. 574. This case presented the High Court of Australia with considerable difficulties in order to achieve a just result, and the reasons given by the members of the Court differ, and in one case include allowing the claim in quasi-contract. See also the note on this case in (1989) 105 L.Q.R. pages 1–3.

work, or resulting from its design. Having regard to the complexity of the responsibilities for design and workmanship as between the various parties to a construction project, such exclusions need very careful drafting, and can easily cause considerable difficulties of interpretation.

ILLUSTRATION

A quay structure in a dock was to be built within continuous diaphragm walls designed to retain surrounding imported sand reclaimed from the sea. Due to defects of both design and workmanship there were gaps and voids between adjacent concrete panels which had been intended to provide a tight fit at the joints of the sections of the wall, with the result that after completion, when the dock was fitted with seawater, sand was able to escape into and damage it. Sub-contractors, who had been required to remove the sand and to grout and fill the voids created by the escaping sand outside the diaphragm wall, had also been required to rectify the gaps or voids in the walls, and claimed under a Contractors' All Risks policy applicable to the project. The policy provided (a) that the insurers would be liable for physical damage to the insured property howsoever caused, except (b) the cost of replacing or rectifying "defects in design materials or workmanship", unless (c) the property insured had suffered actual loss destruction or damage as a result of such defect, but (d) that additional costs of "introducing improvements betterment or corrections in the rectification of the design materials or workmanship" causing such loss or damage should always be excluded. The insurers agreed to pay for the removal of sand and the grouting and filling of voids outside the walls, but contended that the cost of rectification of the gaps of voids between panels was excluded by the terms of the policy. *Held*, by the Deputy High Court Judge, that the physical damage to the dock could not be regarded as repaired if the gaps were left unrectified, so that more sand would enter and further damage would be inevitable, and since there had been actual loss and damage within (c) the cost of rectifying the design or workmanship defects which had caused the damage was recoverable under the policy, it being admitted that the rectification had not produced a structure better than that originally designed and intended. *Per* Sir Godfray Le Quesne Q.C.: "Policies all bearing the title 'Contractors' All Risks Insurance' vary considerably in their terms": *Cementation Piling Foundations Ltd.* v. *Aegon Ltd.* (1993).[12a]

(h) "Accident" wording

Another deceptive device in the wording of insurance policies is to be found in the not infrequent and artificial use of the words "accident" or "accidental loss" in place of the simpler wording "damage" or "loss". This has provoked a substantial jurisprudence by insurers seeking to avoid liability.   **15·010**

[12a] [1993] 1 Lloyd's Rep. 526. See also the "CAR" cases illustrated in Subsection (5), Professional Insurance, *infra* paras. 15·031–15·033.

ILLUSTRATION

A local authority obtained insurance "against liability arising from accidents giving rise to accidental loss of or damage to property" in the exercise of its by-law and associated supervisory activities. There was also an express exclusion for "error ... in advice ... given" by the authority. Repairs to a building were needed as a result of the negligent issue of a building permit, and failure on inspection to modify a developer's foundation plans to take account of filled ground, with the result that there was movement and subsidence requiring repair, for which the authority was liable to the owners in negligence. The insurers contended that there had been no "accident" or sudden event, and also that the express exclusion applied. *Held*, by the New Zealand Court of Appeal, that the damage arose from an "accident" in the normal meaning of the words in the policy, that there had been negligent omissions, not negligent advice, so that the cost of repairing the inadequate foundations was covered by the policy. *Mount Albert City Council* v. *New Zealand Municipalities Insurance Co-op* (1983).[13]

(i) Sub-contractor insurance

15·011   In considering the cases discussed in this Chapter regard should be had to two matters in particular. In the first place, the owner's prime object in taking out contract insurance will be just as much defeated if important sub-contractors' operations are not also effectively protected by the required insurance, since adverse effects on the progress of the project (the reason for the owner requiring insurance in the first place) may as easily be caused by financial failure of a major sub-contractor which in turn precipitates failure of the main contractor. In the second place, it will assist in an understanding of the reported cases if it is remembered that the device of subrogation is always likely to be used by insurers of owners or contractors in an attempt to recover their loss from sub-contractors, either in the shoes of an insured owner suing the sub-contractor in tort, for example,[14] or of an insured contractor suing in contract. It may only occasionally appear from a report that subrogation has taken place, and that the dispute is not in reality between the apparent parties, but on one side at least is being conducted by and for the benefit of a party's insurers. Subrogation or control of the proceedings by insurers may not even be known to the court, though it may be suspected. This helps to explain the true background to some of the "contract setting" cases, for example, where owners' claims against sub-contractors in tort have been defeated as a result

---

[13] [1983] N.Z.L.R. 190. The typically well researched judgment of this Court examines the authorities in England and the Commonwealth on the use of "accident" wording. See in particular Lord Loreburn in *Trim Joint District School Board* v. *Kelly* [1914] A.C. 667, 691, and compare *Fenton* v. *Thorley* [1903] A.C. 443; *Gray* v. *Burr* [1971] 2 Q.B. 554, 566, 579; *Canadian Indemnity* v. *Walkem Machinery* [1975] 53 D.L.R. (3d) 1, and *Mutual of Omaha Insurance* v. *STATS* (1978) 87 D.L.R. (3d) 169, 183. Contrast *Candler* v. *London & Lancashire* (1963) 40 D.L.R. (2d) 408, and *Robinson* v. *Evans Bros.* [1969] V.R. 885.

[14] See, *e.g. Norwich City Council* v. *Harvey* (1988) 45 BLR 14, C.A., and see further *ante*, Chap. 1, Section 12(3)(d), paras. 1·326–1·327.

of main contract insurance provisions being treated as incompatible with any duty owned by the sub-contractor to the owner.[15]

(j) Summary of insurance discussed in this Chapter

The commercial needs of construction owners are not likely to differ in different jurisdictions, and the insurance industry itself is more international than most. Disregarding the unnecessary degrees of over-insurance already referred to, in particular in the United Kingdom standard forms, the following categories of insurance are likely to be found in association with nearly all substantial construction contracts, namely: **15·012**

(a) *insurance of the works themselves* (usually in joint names to avoid subrogation)[16];

(b) a relatively rare class of *adjoining property insurance*, primarily for the owner's benefit and in joint names for that reason, with some of the characteristics of works (property) insurance, and third party (liability) insurance[17];

(c) a near universal contractor's *third party liability insurance*[18]; and finally

(d) *professional insurance.*[19]

Some of the "CAR" policies previously referred to appear to offer an amalgam of all or some of the above various policies within one document, but the premium levels of these earlier policies seem unlikely to survive for very long, insurers' experience of the claims which such policies are likely to provoke.

(2) Insurance of works

(a) Joint insurance

Clauses requiring insurance of the works during construction are in insurance parlance of the "property" type.[19a] Classically the clauses stipulate a list of those risks—fire, earthquake, and possibly further risks such as flood, storm, etc.—against which it is desired to insure the works under construction, and possibly also the contractor's plant or unfixed materials on site. In most countries fire or earthquake are likely to be the only risks likely to cause damage of such magnitude, particularly at a late stage of construction, for it to be beyond the financial resources of the contractor   **15·013**

---

[15] See *ante*, Chap. 1, Sections 12(3)(d) and 12(10)(c)(ii), paras. 1·325 *et seq* and 1·1386.
[16] See *infra*, Subsection 2.
[17] See *infra*, Subsection 3.
[18] See *infra*, Subsection 4.
[19] See *infra*, Subsection 5.
[19a] See, for example, per Lloyd J. in the *Magnaload* case *supra*, para. 15·009.

to replace or repair the work or plant at his own cost, although there may be sites in some countries where other risks, such as tides, flooding or tropical storms, are capable of causing major damage to the particular project, and so from the owner's point of view may justify cover by contractually required insurance. However, contractor and insurance industry pressures have progressively combined, at least in the United Kingdom, to obtain the inclusion in the list of more and more described risks which, even if they did eventuate, could usually only cause minor damage, as well as to extend the required insurance to contractor's plant or materials on site, the reinstatement or replacement of which should in either case be well within the resources of any contractor of reasonable standing.[20]

15·014 In the case of new construction this type of insurance is almost invariably effected by joint insurance taken out in the names of both contractor and owner.[21] The insurance is usually obtained by the contractor rather than the owner, sometimes with a special policy for the project, or sometimes using a contractor's running policy on which the owner's name is endorsed as a co-assured. If the insurance were to be of the owner alone, the principal purpose of the policy would be defeated, since the insurer would be in a position to subrogate in the name of the owner against the contractor, even in those cases where the cause was not the contractor's or a sub-contractor's fault, by reason of the contractor's breach of his unqualified obligation to complete if he failed to reinstate free of charge,[22] and obviously, in cases of fault, for breach of workmanship or other contractual obligations. This would subvert the overriding object of the insurance, namely to safeguard the contractor from crippling liabilities.

In recent years, however, this has not prevented insurers, defeated by joint insurance as against the contractor himself, from endeavouring to subrogate against negligent sub-contractors in tort. This has been almost uniformly without success wherever the sub-contractor can be shown to have contracted against a background of expected owner or main contractor insurance, even in the absence of explicit provisions to that effect in the sub-contract.[23] A subrogating insurer pursuing a sub-contractor in the name of the owner in tort may also be defeated, on the same principles,

---

[20] See this referred to *supra*, para. 15·005, and, in the case of the English standard forms, the more detailed discussion in C.C.P.P., paras. 29–16 and 30–22, and more generally in paras. 23–32 *et seq.*

[21] See Clause 23 of the ICE Conditions, and Clauses 20A and 22A of the 1963 and 1980 RIBA/JCT contracts respectively.

[22] See *ante*, Chap. 4, paras. 4·003 and 4·043 *et seq.*

[23] *Surrey Heath B.C.* v. *Lovell Construction and Hayden Young* (1988) 42 BLR 30, Judge Fox-Andrews Q.C.; *Norwich City Council* v. *Paul Clark Harvey* [1989] 1 W.L.R. 828, C.A.; (the latter a case of owner insurance under Clause 20C of the pre-1980 RIBA/JCT forms). See further the "contract structure" cases in tort where claims by owners against sub-contractors have failed, see *ante*, Chap. 1, Section 12(3) and (10), paras. 1·325 *et seq.* and 1·386 *et seq.* See also the *Trident General Insurance* case illustrated *supra*, para. 15·009.

by an exemption clause or certificate conferring immunity for defective work *on the main contractor* under the main contract itself.[24]

(b) Owner insurance

Particularly in the case of conversions or additions to *existing premises,*   **15·015**
a fire or other damage policy in the owner's name will almost invariably already exist in relation to the existing premises, and for this reason (and possibly for other reasons in some cases of new buildings) it may sometimes be more convenient for the contract to provide for the owner to make the insurance arrangements himself. While it would be sufficient for the construction contract to require the insurance to be joint insurance, in order to satisfy the basic purpose of requiring the insurance in the first place, the RIBA/JCT contracts have understandably assumed that the insurance in question might sometimes be in the name of the owner only. Presumably to make certain that the objective of contractor protection is achieved without any danger of insurer subrogation, these forms of contract (and those contracts of the many professional institutions in the Commonwealth which have followed the English forms) have for many years provided an alternative version for owner insurance of the works,[24a] in which the insurance clause additionally *provides expressly for the works* (and also in some cases the already existing building) *to be "at the sole risk" of the owner* during the construction period.

It is not easy to see how any competent adviser, whether legal or technical, could recommend this last provision to an owner client, except in regard to specific insured risks, such as fire. Even so, this latter wording may not give full protection from subrogation against the contractor in cases where the contractor has been negligent (as would joint insurance), since express wording of this kind will be interpreted strictly, being in reality an exception clause and, therefore, on a well-known principle of construction[25] limited to cases where contractor negligence is not present, unless there are no areas of strict liability independent of negligence on which the provision could operate. As already stated, such areas of contractor liability independent of fault do, of course, exist in all construction contracts by virtue of the contractor's unqualified obligation to complete, so that it will be to these situations only that such an owner's "sole risk" provision will, in the absence of sufficiently clear wording, be held to apply, it is submitted.

---

[24] *Southern Water Authority* v. *Carey* [1985] 2 All E.R. 1077, (Judge Smout Q.C.).

[24a] See Clauses 20(b) and 20(c) of the post-1963 RIBA/JCT standard forms.

[25] Usually known as the *Alderslade* principle, see *Travers* v. *Cooper* (1915) 1 K.B. 73; *Alderslade* v. *Hendon Laundry* [1945] K.B. 189; *Canada S.S.* v. *R.* [1952] A.C. 192, discussed more fully *infra*, Section 2, paras. 15·040 *et seq.*, in the context of the interpretation of indemnity clauses.

ILLUSTRATION

15·016   By Clause 18 of a painting and repairing contract the contractors indemnified the owner against damage to the works "provided always that such damage is caused by the negligence of the contractor, his servants ... or any
circumstances within the contractor's control," and were also to insure
accordingly. By Clause 19 the works were to be at the sole risk of the owner as
regards loss or damage by fire, and the owner was to pay the contractor for
any materials lost or damaged by the fire. (The report does not indicate
whether the owner undertook to insure.) The works were damaged by fire
found to be caused by the negligence of the contractor's workmen. The contractor (or his insurers) denied that they were liable in the case of fire. *Held*,
by Sellers J., since the requirements of the *Alderslade* principle were not satisfied, namely that there must be no other basis of liability but negligence on
which the clause could operate, Clause 19 did not override Clause 18, and
accordingly the contractor was liable. *Buckinghamshire County Council* v. *Y.
James Lovell & Sons Limited* (1956).[26]

15·017   Quite logically, therefore, in order to preserve the basic rationale for
requiring contractor insurance, the RIBA/JCT forms of contract proceeded to make further provision so as to include cases of contractor negligence in the insurance cover to be provided by the owner. However, this
was not achieved directly by so providing in the works insurance clause,
but instead obliquely, as a result of the quite accidental fact that the
indemnity clause in the RIBA/JCT contracts (very similar to Clause 18 in
the *Lovell* case above, and which should properly have confined itself to
true third party claims for damage to third party property caused by the
contractor's negligence)[26a] contained an indemnity in favour of the owner
in respect of claims for damage to property which was, on its wording and
(quite possibly unintentionally) wide enough to include property damage
claims *by the owner* as well as by third parties, and, moreover, including
damage to the works themselves as well as third party property.
    The RIBA draftsman, however, instead of dealing with the matter in
positive and clear terms in the works insurance clause, for some reason
preferred to make use of this existing wording in the third party indemnity
clause, and merely provided that the wide contractual indemnity obligation as so expressed in regard to property damage claims was to be "subject to the provisions of" the insurance of the works clause. The use of
such typically confusing RIBA draftsmanship to achieve an important
new substantive objective, coupled with the enthusiasm of insurers in pursuing any possible subrogation remedies (possibly compounded by a failure of the Courts or counsel to appreciate the basic rationale for requiring
contractor insurance) have combined to provoke a rich if unnecessary jurisprudence on this draftsmanship wherever the RIBA drafting approach

---

[26] [1956] J.P.L. 196. The very short report of this case in J.P.L. is somewhat misleading in its
description of Sellers J.'s reasoning, which was as stated above, it is submitted.
[26a] For the Insurance against these claims see *infra*, Subsection (4), paras 15·023 *et seq*.

has been followed, including a number of appeals from experienced courts which have had to be allowed.

ILLUSTRATIONS

(1) The indemnity Clause 14(*b*) of the 1952 RIBA Contract provided that **15·018** the contractor should be liable for, and indemnify the owner against damage to property arising out of the works provided it was due to the negligence of the contractor and *subject also as regards loss or damage by fire to the provisions of Clause 15.* The insurance Clause 15 provided that the works should be at the sole risk of the owner as regards loss or damage by fire, and that the owner should maintain a policy of insurance against that risk. Fire broke out due to the negligence of the contractors, and the owner sued for the cost of repair under the indemnity Clause. *Held*, by the Court of Appeal, affirming the trial judge, that on its true construction the indemnity clause must be read subject to the insurance clause, and consequently the risk of damage by fire due to the contractor's negligence was that of the owner and of his insurers. *Archdale James & Co. Limited* v. *Comservices Limited* (1954).[27]

(2) The insurance clause 15(*b*) of an Australian Standard Form provided that "the existing structures" as well as the works should be at the sole risk of the owner as regards loss and damage by fire. The contractor was to work on existing premises, part of which belonged to the owner while the remainder was leased by him from the owner of adjoining land. Under the indemnity Clause 14(*c*) the contractor indemnified the owner from claims for injury and damage to property provided they were due to the contractor's negligence "subject as regards loss or damage by fire to Clause 15(*b*)." A fire caused by the contractor's negligence damaged both parts of the property, and the owner (or his insurers) sued the contractor. *Held*, by the High Court of Australia, that the owner could not recover for his own loss as lessee of the adjoining property, since that was part of "the existing structures" covered by Clause 15(*b*), but that the contractor, who had also been sued by the adjoining freeholder, had no claim against the owner in respect of that liability, since the object of Clause 15(*b*) was to safeguard the contractor from claims for damage to *the owner's* property or interest in the works, and not against property claims by third parties. *K.D. Morris & Sons* v. *G.J. Coles* (1972).[28]

[Note: Here again the Court correctly noted the distinction between "property" and "liability" insurance.]

(3) Under the indemnity Clause 18 of the 1963 RIBA/JCT Standard Form, **15·019** the contractor indemnified the owner against any expense or claim in respect of damage to any property real or personal provided that the same was due to any negligence omission or default of the contractor, "except for such loss or damage as is at the risk of the owner under Clause 20(*c*)". By Clause 20(*c*) "the existing structures ... and the works ... shall be at the sole risk of the [owner] as regards loss or damage by fire ...". The Scottish Court of Session held that a fire caused by the contractor's negligence rendered the contractors liable to the owner under the indemnity clause. *Held*, by the House of Lords, following the *Archdale* case and allowing the appeal, that on the true construction of the two clauses it was intended that the owner should bear the risk of damage by fire including fire caused by the negligence of the contractor.

---

[27] [1954] 1 W.L.R. 459.
[28] 46 A.L.J.R. 464. Compare the *Aberdeen Harbour Board* case illustrated *infra*, para. 15·022.

Scottish Special Housing Association v. *Wimpey Construction U.K. Limited* (1986).[29]

[Note: It seems apparent from Lord Keith's judgment that the strongest argument in favour of the (clearly correct) interpretation arrived at by the House of Lords, namely the owner's commercial interest in securing insurance, whether of the owner or contractor, in a subrogation-proof form so as to protect the contractor from a claim which he would otherwise be unable to meet, and which would have explained and have reinforced the House's decision, did not appear to have been appreciated.]

15·020   (4) Clause 1.7 of a Council's own Conditions required the contractor to indemnify the Council against any "liability, loss, claim or proceedings in respect of … damage to property" and to insure against that risk. Unlike most standard forms, the contractor's negligence was *not* a condition of the indemnity. Clause 2.1 required the Council to "bear the risk of loss or damage in respect of the Works and (where appropriate) the existing structure and contents thereof by fire" and a number of other risks. The contract was for the repair and renewal of a roof of an existing building, which was severely damaged by fire which the Court was asked to assume was caused by the negligence of the contractor. *Held*, by the Court of Appeal, (a) over-ruling the trial judge, that Clause 1.7 on its wording applied only to third party claims and third party property, and not to damage to the Works or to the existing structure, so that the Council could not recover under that clause, but (b) affirming the trial judge, that Clause 2.1, (applying the *Alderslade* principle that the existence of a possible head of damage other than that of negligence is fatal to the effective operation of an exception clause, notwithstanding that the words used may be prima facie wide enough to cover negligence) did not absolve the contractor from liability to the Council for the cost of repairing the damage caused by the fire. *Dorset County Council* v. *Southern Felt Roofing Co. Limited* (1989).[30]

[Note: This case clearly followed the same reasoning as that of Sellers J. in the *James Lovell* case[31] despite the brevity of the report in that case, and is entirely correct in principle, it is submitted. Clause 1.7 on its wording was quite different from the RIBA/JCT wording. The contractor's obligation to the Council to complete might be independent of fault under the inclusive price principle see *ante*, Chapter 4, Section 1(1)(b), and that liability was removed by Clause 2.1, but not his liability for negligence, which needed to be expressly stated in such a case under the *Alderslade* principle.]

15·021   There can be no doubt it is submitted, of the correctness of the above decisions, nor of the logic of a policy of providing for both contractor and sub-contractor immunity for their own negligence, which is not only necessary to satisfy the essential motive of the owner in requiring contractor insurance in a construction contract, but also accords with the broader view taken by the Courts of fire insurance policies for buildings in cases where no construction contract element is present—namely that the real commercial intention is to provide cover against the negligence of the assured even if not specifically spelt out in the policy.[32]

---

[29] [1986] 1 W.L.R. 995.
[30] 6 Const.L.J. 37.
[31] See *supra*, para. 15·022.
[32] *Rowlands Limited* v. *Berni Inns* [1986] Q.B. 211, 225.

On the other hand, the cases show that these considerations will not avail a negligent contractor or sub-contractor where the plaintiff is not one of the contracting parties. Moreover, even where the owner accepts the risk, or an obligation to insure the works himself, this will usually only extend to damage to the works themselves (that is, a "property" liability in insurance terms) and not to third party claims arising from a fire.

ILLUSTRATION

The occupier of a part of premises engaged main contractors to carry out certain work in the premises, who in turn engaged plumbing sub-contractors for part of that work. The sub-contractors' workmen negligently started a fire which damaged the whole building. The sub-contract provided that the sub-contractors should be deemed to have knowledge of all the provisions of the main contract, and their conditions of tender also stated that the main contractor or the building owner should bear the risk of loss or damage by fire as defined under Clause 20(c) of the 1963 RIBA/JCT Standard Form of Main Contract, which required the owner to insure against damage to the existing structure and the works caused by fire. The owners of the whole building sued the sub-contractors in tort, who in turn joined the occupier of the part and the main contractor under the building contract, alleging an implied obligation of the occupier to indemnify the contractor and sub-contractor in respect of their liability to the owner of the whole building. *Held*, by the Court of Session, Outer House, that Clause 20(c) of the contract did not require the owner to insure against liabilities of the contractor or sub-contractor *to third parties* caused by their negligence, so that there was no implied obligation on him to indemnify the contractor or sub-contractor in respect of such liabilities. *Aberdeen Harbour Board* v. *Heating Enterprises* (1988).[33]

15·022

It should perhaps be noted at this point that the presence of works insurance provisions in a main contract may preclude actions in tort by the owner against negligent sub-contractors under "contract structure" or "contract setting" theories.[34]

(3) Adjoining Property Insurance

This is a hybrid, and in practice unusual and difficult type of insurance to obtain contemplated only by the English RIBA/JCT forms of contract, with some of the characteristics of both "property" insurance and "liability" insurance. It is clear that construction contracts, particularly in built-up areas, may carry with them a very substantial risk of at least partial damage to closely adjoining land or buildings, even if carried out carefully. In some cases, under legislation like that in the old London Buildings Acts or their modern successors, for example, such work may be permit-

15·023

---

[33] [1988] 4 Const.L.J. 195. Compare *Morris* v. *Coles*, illustrated *supra*, para. 15·018.
[34] See *ante*, Chap. 1, Sections 12(3)(d) and 12(10)(c)(ii), paras. 1·325 *et seq.* and 1·386 *et seq.*

ted only on terms of an unconditional indemnity, independent of fault, given by the prospective developer to the adjoining owner. There may also be strict liability to the adjoining occupier in tort in such cases.[35] Such an insurance policy to be effective would need to be like a works (property) policy in covering both fault and no-fault situations, as opposed to the readily available contractors' "Public Liability" policies, which give cover against negligence or fault only. On the other hand, it would have to be like a liability policy, since the plaintiff in any proceedings would be the third party adjoining owner, unless he was named as a beneficiary under the policy. Furthermore, to be effective and avoid subrogation between owner and contractor, it would need to be a joint policy.

ILLUSTRATION

15·024   By Clause 14 of the then current RIBA form of contract, the contractor undertook to indemnify the owner against claims in respect of damage to property arising out of the works, provided it was due to the negligence or default of the contractor or his sub-contractors. By Clause 15 he was required, without prejudice to this liability, to effect or cause any sub-contractor to effect such insurances as might be specifically required by the Bills of Quantity. The bills contained a provision as follows: "The Contractor *is to insure or make payment in connection with* the following: ... (b) Insurance of adjoining properties against subsidence or collapse." Without negligence on the part of the contractor or his sub-contractors, bored piles sunk by specialist sub-contractors damaged the adjoining property. The contractor, under a liability policy, had insured *himself* against this risk, but the adjoining owners not surprisingly preferred to sue the building owner, under the unqualified indemnity terms of party-wall awards previously made in their favour, and not the contractor. In an action against the contractor, the building owner contended that he had been in breach in failing to take out the insurance policy for the owner's benefit which would have covered the claim. *Held*, by the Court of Appeal, overruling Gorman J., that the contractor's obligation, on a proper interpretation of the provision in the bills, was only to insure himself, and not the building owner. *Gold* v. *Patman and Fotheringham* (1958).[36]

15·025   It emerged in evidence in the *Gold* case that insurance of adjoining property of this particular kind could only be obtained on a "one-off" basis; that surveys would be required before it could be given; and, if obtainable at all, that premiums would be very expensive. Nevertheless, the RIBA/JCT forms, in a probably unique provision,[37] currently still provide expressly for the taking out of a policy of this kind against damage to adjoining property if required by the Bills or Specification. It is clear from the RIBA/JCT's own literature that this suggested insurance has been

---

[35] See *ante*, Chap. 1, Section 12(5), paras. 1·337 *et seq.*, and Section 12(11), paras. 1·387 *et seq*, and see the case of *Alcock* v. *Wraith* [1991] 59 BLR 16, C.A., there illustrated.

[36] [1958] 1 W.L.R. 97.

[37] Clause 19(2)(*a*) of the 1971 Revision, and Clause 21.2 of the post-1980 forms respectively.

made available in collaboration with insurance interests.[38] This suggested cover, however, appears to be not only misleading, but for all practical purposes valueless, since the expressly described *exceptions* to the required cover in Clauses 19 and 22 of the two contracts respectively (damage due to negligence of the contractor; negligence in the design, or the inevitable consequence of carrying out the work, or in other words non-negligent design) appear to eliminate virtually all conceivable real life eventualities, and any premiums so paid can be fairly regarded as little more than gifts to the insurance industry.[39]

(4) Third Party Liability Insurance

Most sophisticated construction contracts contain a clause which defines those categories of third party claim for which the owner is prepared to accept ultimate contractual responsibility, as between himself and the contractor, and those where, on the contrary, the ultimate responsibility is to be that of the contractor. As yet few if any construction contracts provide expressly for shared, or proportionate, responsibilities,[40] for understandable reasons of administrative and insurance practicality. These clauses are for convenience described, in this section only, as "indemnity clauses", since the contractor's liability under them is expressed in the form of an indemnity given to the owner in respect of those defined categories of claim where the contractor is to be ultimately liable (but for insurance) to the owner. The present policy in the United Kingdom standard forms, as in most of the rest of the world, is to allocate ultimate responsibility for all *personal injuries claims* to the contractor, unless positively caused by the owner or his agents' acts or omissions (recognising the contractor's overriding control over site operations), while claims for *damage to the property of third persons* will be the responsibility of the contractor only if caused by his, or his sub-contractor's "negligence omission or default."[41]

15·026

Consistently with the basic rationale of all required contractor insurance, the policy of the great majority of contracts is to require liability insurance only against the contractor's area of ultimate contractual responsibility under the indemnity clause. *Ex hypothesi*, therefore, where the contractor's liability insurance is defined only by express reference to his liabilities under the indemnity clause, there need not be joint

15·027

---

[38] See C.C.P.P., para. 30–23, and the reference there made to the significant statement about this insurance in the RIBA/JCT Guide to the 1980 contract.

[39] See C.C.P.P., para. 29–27, p. 115, and para. 30–23 where this is explained in more detail.

[40] An exception is in Clause 22(1)(*a*) of the ICE fifth edition.

[41] See Clauses 18 and 20 of the 1963 and 1980 RIBA/JCT Forms respectively. The ICE fifth edition is broadly to the same effect—see Clause 22 (a more complicated clause in some areas) and Clause 24 of that form. See, however, the indemnity clause in the "one-off" *Dorset C.C.* case, *supra*, Subsection (2), para. 15·020. For the meaning of "default" see the *obiter* discussion by Kerr J. in *City of Manchester* v. *Fram Gerrard* (1974) 6 BLR 70, 90, illustrated *infra*, para. 15·059.

insurance, since there can in this case be little or no possibility of subrogation by the insurer against the owner if the insured risk materialises. In fact, the English standard forms, and indeed many insurance policies, normally define this insurance cover by simple reference to the contractor's liability under the indemnity clause in question.[42] In passing it may be noted that in many standard forms there is no express counter-indemnity given by the owner to the contractor in the owner's area of ultimate contractual responsibility, under the terms of the clause, though it seems very possible that this would be implied.

15·028 However, in order to meet the owner's desired objectives it is essential that the contractor's liability insurance should extend to cover all direct or indirect sub-contractors, and most main contract forms require the contractor either to insure, or procure that his sub-contractors should be similarly insured, in respect of third party personal injuries and property claims caused by any of these sub-contractors' negligence or breach of contract. Indeed in the English building industry under many sub-contract forms the main contractor, for practical reasons of convenience, assumes express contractual responsibility in his sub-contracts for taking out the necessary insurance to cover the sub-contractors, and this may often be the implied understanding under which sub-contractors price their quotations in less formal sub-contracts. As a result, actions in tort brought against sub-contractors by owners or main contractors (or more usually their subrogating insurers) have been defeated on a number of occasions on express or implied "contract structure" theories.[43]

15·029 As has been seen, in English contracts the categories of third party claims described in indemnity clauses usually tend to be divided into personal injuries liabilities and damage to property liabilities (that is to say, third parties' and not the owner's, property damage claims), with a very slight difference of responsibility for the two categories in the underlying contractors' indemnity clauses, and so in the related required insurance clauses.

It should, however, be repeated that the particular English RIBA/JCT and some other indemnity clauses do, however contain wording sufficiently wide to cover property claims *by the owner* for damage *to the works themselves*, as opposed to third party claims for damage to their property (and possibily other property of the owner on or near the site but which is not a part of the works being constructed) which are likely to be the real target of the clauses. As stated earlier, this is a drafting anomaly and indeed almost always unnecessary in view of the contractor's other express or implied contractual obligations in regard to damage to the works, but it is of long standing in these particular standard forms of contract, and is probably the unintended and accidental result of earlier con-

---

[42] See Clauses 19 and 21 of the 1963 and 1980 RIBA/JCT form, and Clause 23(1) of the ICE Conditions.
[43] See *ante*, Chap. 1, Sections 12(3) and 12(10), paras. 1·325 *et seq.* and 1·386 *et seq.*, and the cases mentioned *supra*, Subsection 1, para. 15·008.

fused draftsmanship. The words "damage to property" in the contractor's liability insurance policies themselves, on the other hand, may well not have that wider meaning, it is submitted, unless liability under the policy has been defined directly by reference to the liability under the indemnity clause, since, if not, the policies themselves may often be described in "third party" or "liability" terms which would serve to exclude claims by owner. In other respects, however, the words "damage to property" will be given a reasonably extended meaning to cover related economic loss.

ILLUSTRATION

A contractor in error constructed a building which encroached on the   **15·030**
adjoining owner's land. To compromise the latter's claim the contractor
bought the relevant land, and sued the insurers for his loss. The insurers disputed that this was damage to property under the liability clause. *Held*, by the
New South Wales Court of Appeal, that the price paid for the land was covered by the words "damage to property" in the contractor's policy, and were
not to be excluded as "correcting work undertaken by the insured" in a separate express exception clause in the policy. *Tokyo Marine & Fire Insurance* v.
Costain (Australia) (1988).[44]
[Note: The exception referred to in the above policy represents an understandable attitude taken by the insurance industry that their liability policies
should generally not be extended to include the simple cost of repairing contractors' defective work, in contrast to damage done to third parties by defective work, which is obviously a far smaller and less easily abused area of risk.]

In this class of insurance, as in the case of professional liability insurance discussed in Subsection (5) *infra*, the word "design", whether used to describe risks to be included in or excluded from the policy, has led to difficulties of interpretation and to liability under the policy being disputed.

ILLUSTRATION

A contractor's third party liability policy in New Zealand excluded liability
for "defect error or omission in design, plan, specification or formula." Foundations failed due to failure to make provision for reinforcement in the floor
slab, but there was no actual specification or detailed design of the floor slab,
which had proved unsuitable for a house built on filled ground. In the absence
of some such document it was contended that the exclusion did not apply.
Held, by Greig J., that had a claim in tort against the contractors (which in
fact failed for discoverability and limitation reasons) succeeded, it would
have been successfully excluded from the risks insured: *Lester* v. *White*
(1992).[44a]

---

[44] 5 Aust. & N.Z. Insurance Cases 75680 N.S.W., C.A.
[44a] [1992] 2 N.Z.L.R. 483.

(5) Professional Insurance

15·031 Professional insurance of the owner's A/E is in England is not usually made a term of his contract of employment with the owner, although under modern pressures the practice may be changing. An A/E's insurance is, of course, essentially of a liability kind, and designed to cover claims brought against him by the professional's clients in contract, as well as by third parties in tort, for negligence in any of his capacities of design, supervision or administration of the project. Although he may also incur liabilities while supervising the work, the principal objective of this insurance will normally be that of negligence in design. Prima facie such insurance will not include failures of the design which are not caused by professional negligence, as in "state of the art" cases, or in cases of justified non-negligent innovation. On the other hand, depending on the context, other types of policy may be intended to cover (or exclude) design deficiencies where fault is not present.

ILLUSTRATIONS

(1) A contractor's CAR policy contained an exclusion of damage due to "*faulty* design and liabilities arising therefrom." *Held*, by the High Court of Australia, even if damage was caused by non-negligent failure of the design it was excluded from the policy. *Queensland Government Railways* v. *Manufacturers' Mutual Insurance* (1968).[45]

15·032 (2) A turnkey/design-and-build contractor took out a Lloyds' professional indemnity policy covering him in respect of any "omission error or negligent act in connection with the design." The policy, which was a liability policy for claims, was extended by providing that, where the contractors were also acting as designers or project owners, if loss was incurred by them in one of these capacities they should be entitled to recover as if the claim could be made against them in their other capacity. During construction of a quay there was movement and damage which the contractors repaired before completion. The insurers admitted liability for a part of the damage on the basis that there had been negligence in its design, but as to a second part of the damage, while admitting that the design was responsible since it had failed to take account of certain factors, denied liability on the ground that in the circumstances it had not been negligent. *Held*, by Webster J., that the design of the relevant part had not been negligent, and that the contractors had failed to establish any administrative or other failures as between their design and construction departments, so that the insurers were not liable within the wording of the policy for the repairs to the relevant part which the construction department had carried out. *Wimpey Construction (UK) Ltd.* v. *Poole* (1984).[46]

[Note: An important distinction between these two cases lies in the different classes of insurance involved—the former a contractor's policy, the latter a professional indemnity policy. In context the differing interpretations of the wording are understandable.]

---

[45] 118 C.L.R. 314.
[46] [1984] 2 Lloyd's Rep. 499. Contrast the High Court of Australia's decision in *Queensland Government Rys* v. *Manufacturers' Mutual Insurance Ltd.*, illustrated *supra*, para. 15·031.

(3) Developer design-and-build contractors were insured under a "Contractor's Combined Policy" for damage to the Works or temporary works "arising out of any fault defect error or omission in design ... ", subject to a proviso excluding increased costs due to redesigning any "property ... *which is defectively designed*." The insurers paid for certain damage incurred but contended they were not liable for cost of additional works due to redesign. *Held*, by the Court of Appeal, "defectively designed" in the proviso was not the same as "defect in design", and implied blame or fault on the part of the designer, so that the cost of additional works due to redesign where there was a defect but no negligence in the original design, was covered by the insurance policy; alternatively there was an ambiguity to be resolved *contra proferentem* against the insurers. *Hitchens* v. *Prudential Assurance* (1991).[47]

15·033

Shortly after the tenth edition of this book it emerged that the industry, unsurprisingly without any reduction of premiums, had for some time been introducing policies in a new "Claims Made" form—that is to say the premiums only covered so-called "claims made" during the year to which an annual premium related and not, like motor insurance and previous professional insurance policies, liabilities, whenever arising, as a result of *acts or omissions during the relevant premium year*.[47a] Since the great majority of cases of negligence in all professional fields, not excluding that of an A/E, are only likely to be made at a considerably later date, often after investigations have taken place, or after the consequences of the negligence have first become apparent, very little, if any, true cover can be provided by such policies, unless the policy in question has been maintained into future years with the same insurance company until the date when the claim is eventually made—effectively, among other things, a huge if concealed premium increase. But more importantly, if by chance an A/E were to change his insurance company, he could also be defeated because, notwithstanding that the later policy was also on a "claims made" basis, it might not be expressed to cover claims arising from a previous period of professional practice under another policy.

15·034

This highly unsatisfactory situation did not appear to have been understood by the professions for some years, and was compounded by the universal requirement or practice with all such policies that, on every renewal date, insurers require to be informed whether any facts or events have occurred in a previous premium year which may lead to a claim in the future. This might necessitate an A/E informing the insurers, for example, that major defects had been discovered in a building, which were currently under investigation in order to ascertain the cause, albeit with a strong likelihood of contractor fault; or that a contractor had commenced proceedings against the A/E's owner client alleging late information or some other cause of action which might conceivably result in the A/E being joined or proceeded against in the future; or that the A/E's client had

15·035

---

[47] 60 BLR 51. For a further disputed meaning of the word "design" see *supra*, para. 15·030, and the *Lester* v. *White* case there illustrated.

[47a] See the emergence of this recounted in C.C.P.P., para. 5–06, and in 1984–1985 Const. L.J. 4.

brought proceedings against a contractor for defective work which might result later in allegations being made about the design by the contractor, or in a claim for negligent supervision by the owner should the contractor prove unable to meet his liabilities. It is hardly necessary to add that failure to disclose any such facts, even if the likelihood of a claim was remote, could well result, in the present extraordinarily protective state of the law in favour of insurers in regard to disclosure, in the policy being avoided on that ground alone should an attempt be made to enforce it at a later date.

15·036 What had been introduced as an unsatisfactory new type of insurance became near scandalous when some insurers, on receiving information at the renewal date indicating the possibility of a major claim, actually refused to renew the policies, thus retrospectively depriving the assured of cover altogether, notwithstanding his having made payment of the necessary premiums for the year in which the liability had been incurred, and possibly for several years thereafter. When this became more widely known, the London insurance market agreed to a proviso that the policy would be deemed to cover subsequent claims in later years provided notice of events likely to give rise to a future claim had been given during the currency of the policy, but even this concession might not cover a case where no claim had been suspected during the policy period. In any case, at the present day this proviso is simply not present in many policies including particularly those in overseas markets. This state of affairs was justifiably described in the following terms in an appellate division of the New York courts, when finding in favour of the insurers under a legal professional liability policy on non-disclosure grounds:

> "We so hold with a caveat to the Bar, in as much as it would appear that if an attorney were covered by successive 'claims made' policies with different insurers, each containing the particular provisions in *The Home's* policy, the attorney might be unprotected in many commonly arising situations. For instance, if the attorney defaulted in answering a complaint in 1984, but a claim was not made against him until 1985, the 1984 insurer could disclaim coverage because the claim was not 'first made against the insured during the policy period' (authority cited). And the 1985 insurer could disclaim coverage because the policy only indemnifies for acts errors or omissions prior to the policy period if, prior to the effective date of the policy, the insured had no basis to believe that the insured had breached a professional duty. The coverage afforded under 'claims made' policies may thus be in many cases largely illusory."[48]

15·037 These strictures apply equally, of course, to all the insurance policies of other professionals, such as architects and engineers, issued on a "claims made" basis. At the time of writing, professional policies in the United Kingdom do appear to extend cover to future claims in cases where notice of an "occurrence" (a wider expression than receipt of a claim or of notice

---

[48] *Per* the First Judicial Department Supreme Court New York, in *Fogelson* v. *Home Insurance* (1987), New York Law Journal, April 23rd, 1987.

of intention to make a claim) which is likely to give rise to a claim is given to the insurers during the currency of the policy. However, some present policies do also cover unsuspected claims made as a result of professional practice before the policy is taken out. Arrangements of this kind will mean that on a change of insurers the later insurer will be on risk for unsuspected negligence claims arising from earlier practice, while the earlier insurer will remain liable for future claims where an "occurrence" of this kind has been notified before the end of the earlier policy.[49] It would also seem that, on their wording, the cover provided under these policies applies exclusively to meeting the consequences of a judgment or award, so that a claim compromised by agreement would not qualify for insurance in the absence of special agreement with the insurers.[50]

SECTION 2. INDEMNITIES

(1) Generally

In Section 1 *supra*, the "indemnity" clauses governing or re-allocating ulti-   **15·038**
mate contractual responsibility for third party claims as between owner and contractor have been discussed in the particular context of the insurance commonly required in construction contracts to secure the contractor's ability to meet liabilities under those clauses.

It should, however, be appreciated that a draftsman is free to express any contractual obligation, whether of owner or contractor, and whether or not concerned with third party claims or liabilities, in indemnity terms. Thus, a contractor's obligation to carry out the work properly in accordance with the drawings and specification, or the owner's obligation to pay money due on interim certificates within a certain period, can both be expressed simply in those terms, but each obligation can also (very often additionally) be expressed so as to "indemnify" the other party against the breach *simpliciter* or more particularly any claim, damage, loss or expense, etc., arising as a result of the breach in question. This may carry extremely important advantages for the indemnitee both in regard to limitation and quantum of damage—for example, in the above two cases it may entitle the contractor to financing costs and interest for late payment which would not otherwise be obtainable for simple breach of contract,[51] and it may substantially increase the limitation period in favour of an owner indemnitee, in a case of work not done in accordance with the contract, by postponing the date of accrual of the cause of action, and so the starting date for the limitation period, until the occurrence of the damage claim

---

[49] *Patricia Thorman* v. *New Hampshire Insurance Co. (U.K.) Ltd.* (1987) 39 BLR 41, C.A., a
   dispute between earlier and later insurers as to which was on risk (and where, incidentally,
   one of the insurers was the same as in the *Fogelson* case *supra*).
[50] *Ibid*, at p. 49, *per* Sir John Donaldson M.R.
[51] See *ante*, Chap. 8, Section 1(5).

loss or expense.[52] The precise legal characteristics of an indemnity obligation and the date of accrual of the cause of action has already been considered in the context of limitation *ante*, Chapter 4.[53] Since the same rules of strict interpretation applicable to exemption clauses are understandably also applicable to indemnity clauses (and particularly in so far as the latter purport to cover indemnitee negligence), exemption clauses and their interpretation, as opposed to indemnity clauses, will also be incidentally noticed, but not comprehensively treated, in the present Section.

15·039   The express use of the word "indemnity" or "indemnify" in a contractual provision is not essential. The sense and context of the provision may sufficiently indicate the contractual intention to indemnify, so that, for example, an express so-called a "guarantee" by a specialist sub-contractor given to a main contractor that the work using his product will be satisfactory may be treated as an indemnity in the event that the work should fail.[54] Indeed, there may be some circumstances in which an indemnity will be implied even in the absence of any contractual provision at all.[55] It is also important to note that unqualified indemnities can frequently, and perfectly reasonably, be provided by contracting parties in respect of matters which would not otherwise be their contractual responsibility, or which are not within their control. However, in more modern construction contracts in England it has been seen in Section 1 *supra*, in the context of insurance, that this has not usually been the policy in relation to third party liability indemnities (and so any accompanying contractor insurance) in traditional A/E designed English construction contracts, which will usually be conditioned on contractor default, although this is not invariably the case.[56] However, in the case of damage to the works during construction and its associated insurance, it has been seen that this will in any event be the contractor's express or implied responsibility, as a result of the inclusive price principle and the contractors unqualified obligation to complete, whether or not contractor negligence is present.[56a]

(2) Interpretation of Clauses

15·040   It has already been seen in Section 1 *supra* in the particular context of insurance that it is a rule of construction when interpreting indemnity

---

[52] See *ante*, Chap. 4, Section 3(7)(c), paras. 4·289–4·291.
[53] See *ante*, para. 4·289. Most recently analysed and discussed by Lord Goff of Chievely in *Firma C. Trade S.A.* v. *Newcastle Protection and Indemnity* [1990] 3 W.L.R. 78, 93.
[54] *Comyn Ching* v. *Oriental Tube Ltd.* (1979) 17 BLR 47, illustrated *infra*.
[55] As in the case of bona fide requests to company registrars to register invalid or fraudulent transfers of shares—see *Sheffield Corporation* v. *Barclay* [1905] A.C. 392 and *Yeung* v. *Hong Kong & Shanghai Banking Corporation* [1980] 2 All E.R. 599, P.C., the former applied perhaps controversially in a construction case by the High Court of Australia in *The Crown* v. *Henrickson & Knutson* (1911) 13 C.L.R. 473, illustrated *ante*, Chap. 4, para. 4·171, and see *infra*, para. 15·061.
[56] See for an exceptional example, *Dorset County Council* v. *Southern Felt Roofing* (1989) 6 Const.L.J. 37 illustrated *supra*, Section 1, para. 15·020.
[56a] See *ante*, Chap. 4, paras. 4·036 *et seq*.

clauses (as indeed of exemption clauses and even of contractual provisions for payment by one party to the other)[57] that they will be strictly
construed if an indemnitee beneficiary of such a clause seeks to argue that
it is to apply in his favour even in a situation caused by his own negligence
or breach of contract. In the case of indemnity clauses, therefore, while
there will be no difficulty in applying them to cases where *the indemnitor* is
not at fault, they will be very strictly construed if *the indemnitee* seeks to
enforce the clause in spite of his own negligence or fault. It should be
appreciated that the logical case for such a strict interpretation is even
more strong in the case of indemnity clauses, since in a case of indemnitee
negligence such clauses will not only operate, as would an exemption
clause, as a shield against liability, but in addition they will actually entitle
the indemnitee to be paid compensation for any such loss.

> "While an indemnity clause may be regarded as the obverse of an exempting
> clause, when considering the meaning of such a clause one must, I think,
> regard it as even more inherently improbable that one party should agree to
> discharge the liability of the other for acts for which he is responsible".[58]

For this reason and as a general statement, indemnity clauses will nor-   **15·041**
mally only be interpreted so as to be enforceable by a negligent indemnitee if, in the absence of clear wording, there is on examination no other
basis but indemnitee negligence on which the clause can reasonably be
expected to operate. This latter part of the rule is usually known eponymously to lawyers as the *Alderslade* principle.[59]

However, a clause may give a sufficient immediate indication on its
face, and in the context of the particular contract, that it is intended to
cover indemnitee negligence, even though the word "negligence" is not
itself actually used.[60] If so, this will avoid any need to apply the latter part
of the *Alderslade* principle. Where, however, the language, while wide
enough on its face to include indemnitee negligence, is not sufficiently
clear that that is indeed the intention, the *Alderslade* presumption will
defeat it. More precisely stated, the principle requires that there should be
no reasonably likely (although not simply fanciful) other basis for the contemplated loss than indemnitee negligence for the claim to succeed.

Until recently it was considered in a number of cases that the use of the
word "whatsoever" in some such expression as "all claims or demands
whatsoever", or "loss or damage arising from any cause whatsoever", was
by itself a sufficiently express indication of an intention to include indemnitee negligence within the ambit of the clause,[61] and so avoid application

---

[57] See for the latter *Sonat Offshore S.A.* v. *Amerada Hess Development Ltd.* [1988] 1 Lloyd's
Rep. 175, illustrated *infra*, para. 15·046. See also *Farr* v. *The Admiralty infra*.
[58] *Per* Viscount Dilhorne in *Smith* v. *South Wales Switchgear Ltd.* [1978] 1 W.L.R. 165, 168D.
[59] *Alderslade* v. *Hendon Laundry* [1945] K.B. 189. The rule is now usually cited as re-stated by
Lord Morton of Henryton in *Canada S.S.* v. *R.* [1952] A.C. 192, 208, subsequently cited and
approved by Lord Fraser in *Smith* v. *South Wales Switchgear Ltd.*, *supra*, at page 172D, F.
[60] See *White* v. *Tarmac Civil Engineering Ltd.* [1967] 1 W.L.R. 1508, and *Comyn Ching Ltd.* v.
Oriental Tube Ltd. (1979) 17 BLR 47, illustrated *infra*.
[61] *Travers* v. *Cooper* [1915] 1 K.B. 73, *Farr* v. *The Admiralty* [1953] 1 W.L.R. 865, *Gillespie* v.
Bowles Transport [1973] 1 Q.B. 400, C.A.

of the *Alderslade* test. However, it is now clear that this is not so, and that no such immediate presumption from the use of that form of wording will arise.[62]

It may, perhaps, be a question whether the *Alderslade* principle is not today being too rigidly applied by the English commercial judiciary in cases where the context suggests a contrary probable intention but, as so often in commercial contracts, the draftsmanship, unaware of the niceties of legal principle, has failed the parties.

ILLUSTRATIONS

15·042   (1) By Clause 26(2) of the General Conditions of a contract with the Admiralty for the construction of a destroyer wharf, it was provided that the works and all materials on site should stand at the risk and be in the sole charge of the contractor, and that "the contractor shall be responsible for ... and make good any loss or damage thereto *arising from any cause whatsoever other than the accepted risks* ...". During construction an Admiralty vessel negligently collided with the piles of the jetty, and the contractors were instructed by the Superintending Officer to repair the damage. They claimed the cost of compliance with the instructions under the terms of the contract or as damages for breach. *Held*, applying *Travers* v. *Cooper*,[63] the words "any cause whatsoever" were as wide as could be, and should be read as including negligent navigation of a ship by an Admiralty servant, and the contractor was accordingly liable to make good the damage and could not claim extra for doing so: *A.E. Farr Ltd.* v. *The Admiralty* (1953).[64]

(2) A sub-contract contained the following indemnity clause in favour of the main contractor: "the sub-contractor shall indemnify [the main contractor] and the employer and adequately insure *against all employers' liability and third party risks* arising out of the work." A sub-sub-contractor's workman was injured in an accident caused by the main contractor negligently leaving a hole on the site uncovered. The main contractor sued on the indemnity. The sub-contractor argued that the words could apply to a case where, without the personal negligence of the main contractor indemnitee, he might be vicariously liable for the sub-contractor's negligence, so that on the *Alderslade* principle the clause did not extend to negligence by the main contractor. *Held*, by the Court of Appeal (Harman L.J. dissenting), that the indemnity included all third party risks, not merely those caused by the sub-contractor, and the main contractor was accordingly entitled to an indemnity from the sub-contractor: *Westcott* v. *J.H. Jenner (Plasterers) Ltd.* (1962).[65]

15·043   (3) A clause in a contract for the hire of a crane provided that the crane-owner's driver was to be regarded as the servant of the hirer, who was "*alone* to be responsible for *all claims*" arising "in connection with the operation of the plant." An accident occurred due partly to the driver's negligence in oper-

---

[62] *Smith* v. *South Wales Switchgear Ltd.* [1978] 1 W.L.R. 165, 169 (Viscount Dilhorne), 172, 173 (Lord Fraser); and see, *per* Purchas L.J. in *Sonat Offshore S.A.* v. *Amerada Hess Ltd.* [1988] 1 Lloyd's Rep. 145, 155–156.
[63] [1915] 1 K.B. 73.
[64] [1953] 1 W.L.R. 965. This case would now appear to be implicitly over-ruled by *Smith* v. *South Wales Switchgear Ltd.*, see *infra*.
[65] 106 S.J. 281.

ating the crane, and partly to poor maintenance of the crane by the owner, for which latter the Court of Appeal held the owner 40 per cent. liable to the injured plaintiff. *Held*, by the House of Lords, that the wording was sufficiently clear, so that the *Alderslade* principle did not apply to this clause, and it could be enforced by the owner of the crane, notwithstanding his own liability to the third party: *White* v. *Tarmac Civil Engineering* (1967).[66]

(4) A carrier's customer undertook to "keep the carrier indemnified against *all claims or demands whatsoever* by whomsoever made in excess of the liability of the carrier under these conditions." *Held*, by the Court of Appeal, that the words "all claims or demands", "fortified by" the addition of the word "whatsoever", constituted an agreement in express terms that the customer would indemnify the carrier against all claims without exception, including claims arising from the negligence of the carrier: *Gillespie Bros.* v. *Roy Bowles Transport Ltd.* (1973).[67]

(5) The hirers of a crane which was to be driven by the owner's driver **15·044** undertook by Condition 6 to be responsible for recovery of the crane from soft ground, and by Condition 8 to indemnify the owner "against all expenses in connection with or arising out of the use of the plant." The crane became bogged down due to the driver ignoring instructions of the hirer's site agent. *Held*, by the Court of Appeal, neither clause was wide enough to include the negligence of the owner's driver: *British Crane Hire* v. *Ipswich Plant Hire* (1975).[68]

(6) An electrical contractor undertook maintenance work to be carried out at a factory. By Clause 23 of the contract the contractor undertook to keep the factory owner indemnified against "*any liability, loss, claim or proceeding whatsoever under statute or common law* (i) in respect of personal injury to any person whomsoever." An employee of the contractor was injured by an accident caused by the factory owner's negligence and breach of statutory duty. The owner claimed to be indemnified under the clause. *Held*, by the House of Lords, not following *Gillespie* v. *Bowles*, there was no express provision, as required by the first test in *Canada Steamship Co. Ltd.* v. *The King*, for an indemnity in respect of the acts or omissions of the owner's servants as opposed to those of the contractor, and since a liability at common law for personal injuries might be based on some ground other than the owner's own negligence, the third test in the *Canada Steamship* case was not satisfied, and the owner indemnitee was not entitled to enforce the indemnity: *Smith* v. *South Wales Switchgear Ltd.* (1978).[69]

(7) Nominated sub-contractors experienced difficulties on pressure testing **15·045** a type of plastic coated pipe called Gecal, and before proceeding further using this type of tubing, of which they had no experience, demanded guarantees from prospective sub-suppliers. As a result, the suppliers gave a written guarantee that the tubing should "be satisfactory in respect of its suitability for use in closed circuit, central heating systems ... provided that each circuit is tested to a water pressure of 150 lbs per square inch ... This guarantee is extended to cover not only the cost of replacing the heating circuit but also any ancillary damage that may result from any subsequent breakdown ...".

---

[66] [1967] 1 W.L.R. 1508, illustrated further *infra*, para. 15·049. See also *Hadley* v. *Droitwich Construction Co.* [1968] 1 W.L.R. 37, but contrast *British Crane Hire* v. *Ipswich Plant Hire* illustration (5) *infra*. See also *contra McConkey* v. *AMEC* (1990) *The Times*, February 28, C.A.

[67] [1973] 1 Q.B. 400. However, see now *Smith's* case illustrated *infra*.

[68] [1975] Q.B. 303.

[69] [1978] 1 W.L.R. 165.

The nominated sub-contractors replied "In order *to positively cover any eventuality* we would be pleased if you would confirm to us that in the event of a leak occurring after a satisfactory test ... you will indemnify us for any claims." The suppliers replied that the points had already been covered and that "We ... have provided your company with a guarantee that is extremely extensive in the sense that we are prepared to accept responsibility *for your company's future liabilities in every sense of the word.*" The sub-contractors compromised claims against them by the owners and main contractors with a partial payment in settlement, for which they sued the suppliers on the guarantee letters. The trial judge held that the sub-contractors had not in fact been guilty of negligence or bad workmanship, and that since they would not have been liable to the owners their claim against the suppliers failed. *Held*, by the Court of Appeal, that the words "cover any eventuality" and "we are prepared to accept responsibility for your company's liabilities in every sense of the word" in the correspondence would cover the sub-contractors' own negligence. The true construction of the letters was that any claim made against the plaintiffs, whatever its basis, should be the suppliers' responsibility. Further, it was reasonable to compromise the owners' claim having regard to undertakings in the Specification and the possibility of a finding of negligence, and the plaintiffs were entitled to recover under the indemnity all sums including costs paid and their own costs. *Comyn Ching* v. *Oriental Tube* (1979).[70]

15·046

(8) A contractor agreed to supply a drilling rig with personnel and equipment, and to carry out drilling operations for an oil company. Under the terms of the contract the owner was obliged to pay a certain daily rate if operations were shut down by reason of "breakage or failure of equipment" (the Equipment Breakdown Rate). By another provision it was provided that "in the event of *any damage whatsoever* to the Rig ... preventing the Rig from performing its normal intended function" a "Rig Repair Rate" should be payable. An explosion and fire occurred due to the negligence of the contractors, who claimed to be paid at the Equipment Breakdown Rate or Rig Repair Rate. *Held*, by the Court of Appeal, that there was ample scope for the operation of the contract provisions in eventualities not involving negligence on the part of the contractors and the agreement as a whole reinforced the conclusion that the provisions were not intended to apply if the eventualities which would otherwise bring them into force were due to the contractors' negligence: *Sonat Offshore S.A.* v. *Amerada Hess Ltd.* (1987).[71]

[Note: Although this case is concerned with the interpretation of a contractual provision for payment in a situation of payee negligence rather than an indemnity or exemption clause expressed as such, the *Alderslade* and *Canada Steamship* and subsequent cases form an important part of Purchas L.J.'s reasoning in the leading judgment in the Court of Appeal.]

(9) A contract between owners and contractors for the carrying out of work to an existing oil drilling platform in the North Sea provided that each party should indemnify the other against "any claim ... or liability *arising by reason of the injury or death of any employee* ... or damage, loss ... *of the indemnifying party resulting from* ... *or connected with this order* ...". The owners settled a claim by the estate of an employee of the contractors on the basis that the owners' own employees (and not those of the contractors) had been negligent, and claimed an indemnity from the contractors. *Held*, by Hobhouse J, that the effect of the mutual indemnities in the clause was that the liability for the death or injury of either party's employees, or the loss of either party's

---

[70] 17 BLR 47. See also the unsuccessful third party claims cases *infra*, paras. 15·055–15·057.
[71] [1988] 1 Lloyd's Rep. 145.

property, should be borne by the owner of the property or the employer of the employee in question. However, in the light of the strict statutory regime on an offshore platform, in a case of personal injuries or death either of the two parties could be under a civil liability to their employees, which would be by no means fanciful, without there being any negligence by themselves or their servants. Since there was no express language showing that the indemnity was to apply to the parties' own negligence, the principle in *Canada Steamship Limited* v. *R* and *Smith* v. *South Wales Switchgear Limited*[71a] applied, with the result that the owners could not recover on the indemnity. *Held*, further, that even if it could be shown that there had been a breach of statutory duty by the owners, the principle applied to exclude the indemnity, provided that negligence, as was admitted, had been a cause of the damage: *Caledonia Ltd* v. *Orbit Valve Co.* [1994].[71b]

[Note: In this case Hobhouse J. said: "Commercial contracts are drafted by parties with access to legal advice and in the context of established legal principles as reflected in the decisions of the Court ... In the present case there would have been no problem in drafting the contract so as to produce the result contended for". It is difficult to believe that this decision, concerned with a mutual indemnity exchanged between the parties and not an indemnity in favour of one party, could have accorded with the parties' true intentions had they been asked them at the time of contracting. It is perhaps noteworthy that there seems to have been no serious likelihood of a strict liability for the other limb of the indemnity with regard to damage to the parties' property which would not be either wilful or negligent, and Hobhouse J.'s comments with regard to drafting seem to expect a standard of expertise in drafting commercial contracts which, however regrettably, is neither exhibited nor available at the present day, even in the case of legal advisers and certainly in the field of construction contracts. However, the draftsmanship was clearly lamentable.]

It should be noted that a large number of the above cases were decided on appeal overruling lower courts, indicating both the difficulties of interpreting indemnity clauses under the foregoing rules, as well as the very indifferent standards of draftsmanship of many indemnity provisions in commercial documents, since the *Alderslade* rules of interpretation have been known to lawyers for many years. One possible explanation of the prevalence of such ineffective draftsmanship is the reluctance of many negotiating parties in commerce to spell out their requirements too explicitly for fear of prejudicing their bargain. Another may be the tendency of many draftsmen to use outdated or inappropriate precedents without familiarising themselves or properly understanding the current state of the case-law.

(3) "Secondary" Indemnitee Negligence

In the particular context of construction contracts and of the traditional **15·047** third party liability indemnities frequently given by contractors to owner/indemnitees in those contracts, there is every possibility that, even in cases

---

[71a] [1952] A.C. 192; [1978] 1 W.L.R. 165.
[71b] [1994] 1 W.L.R. 221.

where the third party claim which is the subject of the indemnity arises as the direct result of some "primary" default on the part of the contractor indemnitor, the owner/indemnitee or his A/E may also be liable to the third party plaintiff for what may legitimately be regarded as a secondary form of negligence, such as a failure to supervise, or detect, or prevent the contractor's primary default. Similarly in the case of sub-contractor indemnities, the primary default of the sub-contractor indemnitor may often be accompanied by a secondary default of the main contractor indemnitee in failing to supervise or, very often in this context, to maintain or provide a safe place of working, for example. Third party plaintiffs can often be expected in such cases to bring proceedings against both of the contracting parties, and the question will then arise whether the contractual indemnity, although arising in the exactly contemplated circumstances of indemnitor negligence, will be enforceable if a secondary or incidental negligence can also be shown on the part of the indemnitee (assuming that the clause, on the *Alderslade* principle, will usually not sufficiently expressly include such indemnitee negligence).

ILLUSTRATIONS

15·048   (1) Oil company owners by their agent left an oil drum with dangerous vapour on the site of their refinery in the vicinity of the workings of a contractor, who was constructing a tank for them there. As a result, one of his workmen was killed because an earthing fault on his welding machine, which normally would have had no serious consequences, caused an explosion. In an action by his widow, the oil company sought to rely on an indemnity given by the contractor to "indemnify and hold [the owners] safe and harmless against all claims arising out of the operations being undertaken in pursuance of this contract ... in respect of (a) personal injury, including death ... sustained by any employee of [the contractor]." The trial judge found both parties negligent, as to four-fifths the oil company and as to one-fifth the contractor. The oil company relied on the indemnity as against the contractor. *Held*, by the Court of Appeal, that, applying the *Alderslade* principle, the indemnity was not apt to include indemnitee negligence, and could not be enforced. *Per* Slade J.: It was possible that the oil company might require an indemnity against unrecovered costs even in the case of an unsuccessful claim brought by a plaintiff without means. If so, this would be an additional reason for a possible operation of the clause in the absence of negligence, so that the indemnity would not, under the *Alderslade* principle, include the negligence of the indemnitee. *Walters* v. *Whessoe Ltd. & Shell Ltd.* (1960).[72]

15·049   (2) A main contractor A.'s employee was killed by faulty staging provided by a sub-sub-contractor C., and his widow sued C. and the main contractor A. under the Fatal Accidents Acts for breach of the Building Regulations. It was held that the main contractor A. should have inspected C.'s staging and was responsible as to 25 per cent., and C. as to 75 per cent. A. then joined the sub-contractor B. who was responsible to A. for the supply of the scaffolding on the basis of, firstly, an implied term in the sub-contract to provide sound

---

[72] 6 BLR 23.

scaffolding, and, secondly, on the basis of an express indemnity against third party claims. The trial judge found against A. on both grounds. On appeal by the main contractor the claim on the indemnity was not, for unspecified reasons, pursued. *Held*, by the Court of Appeal, applying *Mowbray* v. *Merry-weather*[73] and allowing the appeal, that there was an implied term of the sub-contract as alleged, and the contractual right to damages against the sub-contractor B. was not affected by A.'s separate liability in tort to the plaintiff, so that A. was entitled to recover from B. in respect of his own 25 per cent. liability to the plaintiff: *Sims* v. *Foster Wheeler* (1966).[74]

(3) Express provisions in a contract for the hire of a crane were held by the House of Lords to impose liability on the hirer for the acts or omissions of the owner's crane driver. The owner was held 40 per cent. liable to a third party injured by an accident for breach of statutory duty. A full indemnity clause apparently also existed in the case, but, as in the *Sims* case, was not proceeded with by the owner, and *Walters* v. *Whessoe* was apparently cited in that connection. *Held*, by the House of Lords, that the crane owner was entitled to be indemnified under the principal provisions in the contract that the hirer should alone be liable. *White* v. *Tarmac Civil Engineering* (1967).[75]

(4) An employee of a main contractor was injured in an accident caused by a missing cover, which was to be provided by a sub-contractor over a hole dug by the sub-contractor. The main contractor was held partly to blame and liable to the plaintiff for failure to note the sub-contractor's omission and require a replacement. Clause 22(2) of the Conditions provided that the main contractor should indemnify the sub-contractor for any act or neglect done, or committed during the currency of the contract by the main contractor, his servants or agents. *Held*, by Chapman J., that Clause 22 was intended to apply only to cases where one party or the other was solely liable, and so could afford the sub-contractor no remedy, and *Sims* v. *Foster Wheeler* was authority for saying that the sub-contractor was liable to the main contractor in respect of the main contractor's liability to the plaintiff as damages for breach of the sub-contractor's contractual duty to fence and protect the works under Clause 19 of the Conditions: *Kenney* v. *Copper Pipe Services Co.* (1968).[76]

15·050

(5) Building owners M. and main contractors T. were held liable under the Occupiers' Liability Act 1957 as to 40 per cent. and 60 per cent. respectively to A., another contractor of the building owner, whose machinery and equipment had been damaged when a building under construction was flooded in a heavy storm.[77] M. were held liable because, by their architects, they had failed to make sure that T. had got the building into a fit state to receive A.'s machinery on the date for delivery, which T. had promised the architects that they would do. The contract between M. and T. was in the RIBA (1957) revised form with quantities. By Clause 14(*b*) of the Conditions, T. had indemnified M. against damage to property arising out of the works "provided always that the same is due to any negligence omission or default of the contractor." Further, by items in the Bills, T. was required to divert stormwater to channels and drains, to protect all work and materials from injury by weather, to cover up and protect work, and to prevent water accumulating on the site. M. had sought to recover from T. in respect of their share of their liability to A. (a) under the indemnity clause and (b) as damages for breach of the provisions in

15·051

---

[73] [1895] 2 Q.B. 640, see *ante*, Chap. 8, para. 8·157.
[74] [1966] 1 W.L.R. 769.
[75] [1967] 1 W.L.R. 1508. As to the principal provision see the case illustrated *supra*, para. 15·043.
[76] (1968) 112 S.J. 47.
[77] For the facts more fully set out, see the case illustrated *ante*, Chap. 1, para. 1·335.

the Bills of Quantities. *Held*, by Mocatta J., following *Walters* v. *Whessoe & Shell Ltd.* (1960), *Canada Steamship Lines* v. *R.* (1952), and *Alderslade* v. *Hendon Laundry* (1945), that as M. had also been negligent, and as there were other claims than negligence on which the clause could operate, they could not recover under the terms of the indemnity clause; but, following *Mowbray* v. *Merryweather* (1895), M. were entitled to recover their loss from T. in full as damages for breach of the provisions in the Bills of Quantities; *AMF International Ltd.* v. *Magnet Bowling & G.P. Trentham Ltd.* (1968).[78]

15·052   (6) A sub-contractor's employee was injured due to a mains cable strung at foot height by the main contractor's workmen at a point which would be used by the sub-contractor's employees when leaving the site in darkness at the end of the day. The existence of the cable was known to the sub-contractor's supervisors, but no complaint had been made by them to the main contractor, who was in control of the site. The sub-contractor had indemnified the main contractor against "any liability loss claim or proceedings whatsoever whether arising in common law or statute in respect of personal injuries ... of any person whomsoever arising out of or happening in connection with the execution of the work ... by reason of any act, default, or omission on our part or on the part of our servants, agents or sub-contractors." The plaintiff claimed damages against both parties alleging negligence, breach of duty under the Occupiers' Liability Act, and breach of the Construction Regulations. The trial judge found both defendants guilty of negligence at common law; the main contractors to be in breach of duty under the Occupiers' Liability Act; and the sub-contractors to be in breach of the Regulations. *Held*, by McKenna J., that the sub-contractor's failure to complain was a sufficient connection with the main contractor's liability, since, but for it, the accident could have been avoided, and it was not necessary for it to be an essential element in the workman's claim against the main contractor, who was therefore entitled to an indemnity from the sub-contractor. *Per* McKenna J.: "I have not found these questions of construction easy and I have no great confidence in my answers to them": *Smith* v. *Vange Scaffolding* (1970).[79]

15·053   It is not easy to rationalise the above cases. *Walters* v. *Whessoe* was a case of 80 per cent. indemnitee negligence and so, in terms of giving sensible effect to the *Alderslade* principle and the presumed intention of the parties, presents little difficulty, it is submitted. *Smith* v. *Vange Scaffolding* was a case where neither *Walters* v. *Whessoe* nor the *AMF* cases appear to have been cited, but the judge, in enforcing the indemnity in spite of indemnitee negligence, appears to have considered that the indemnitee had only been negligent in a secondary sense from a causation point of view, and the effective "last" negligence was that of the indemnitor. *Kenney* v. *Copper Pipe* was also a case of primary indemnitee negligence, with the indemnitor only secondarily liable to the third party for supervisory negligence, so that the failure of the clause presents no real difficulty. It is cases like *AMF* v. *Magnet Bowling*, and perhaps *Smith* v. *Vange Scaffolding*, where the indemnitee's negligence is of a secondary supervisory character to the primary responsibility of the indemnitor, which appear, in

---

[78] [1968] 1 W.L.R. 1028.
[79] [1970] 1 W.L.R. 733.

context, to be difficult to explain or justify in terms of the presumed intention of the parties in regard to the failure of indemnity clause.

No attempt appears to have been made so far by the English judiciary to distinguish between categories of indemnitee negligence which, on a basis of presumed intention, might be regarded as not invalidating an indemnity under the *Alderslade* principle. In the United States, however, attempts have been made in some jurisdictions to distinguish, for the purpose of enforcing indemnification clauses, between so-called "active" and "passive" (or "primary" and "secondary") negligence, and in the Supreme Court of California examples of these latter have been suggested as including failure to detect conditions created by others, failure to inspect or order changes, or to order removal of defect work or materials which will not, if on the part of the indemnitee, deprive him of the benefit of the clause.[80]

As the cases illustrated above show, however, these difficulties will diminish if, as is very often likely to be the case in construction contract indemnity clauses, the loss at which the clause is aimed results from a *breach of contract* on the part of the indemnitor, and not from mere tortious negligence or some situation which would not, apart from the indemnity, be his *contractual* responsibility. In that event the rule in *Mowbray* v. *Merryweather*[81] will enable a partly negligent indemnitee, while defeated by the *Alderslade* principle in seeking to operate the indemnity clause itself, to obtain his full remedy by the alternative route of damages for breach of contract,[82] although the less advantageous limitation periods for simple breach of contract will apply to claims so framed.[83]

15·054

Standard forms of contract appear to have made little or no attempt at express draftsmanship to save indemnity clauses from failure in the event of purely secondary indemnitee negligence (for an exception, however, see Clause 18(3) of the Singapore S.1.A. private sector contract).[84] Moreover, in the United States some jurisdictions have even held that contractual provisions seeking to avoid the consequences of indemnitee negligence are void as being against public policy.[85]

However, a theoretical obstacle to full recovery under the *Mowbray* v. *Merryweather* principle may be encountered if statutory apportionment (contributory negligence) remedies are, or in the future become available in contract as well as in tort, thus enabling the damages recoverable to be reduced to take account of the plaintiff's negligence under (currently in England) the Law Reform (Contributory Negligence) Act of 1945.[86]

---

[80] *Rossmore Sanitation Inc.* v. *Pylon Insurance* 532 P 2nd 97, 101 (1975), and see the cases collected by Sweet, *Legal Aspects of Architecture, Engineering and the Construction Process* (2nd ed.), pp. 743 *et seq.*, and see the same subject treated more rather shortly in the third edition, pp. 849–51.

[81] [1895] 2 Q.B. 640.

[82] See the *Sims*, *Kenney* and *AMF* cases illustrated *supra*.

[83] See for the limitation advantages of indemnity clauses, *ante*, Chap. 4, paras. 4·289–4·290.

[84] Reproduced in C.C.P.P., p. 574.

[85] *E.g.* North Carolina. See *International Paper Co.* v. *Corporex Constructions Inc.* 385 S.E. 2nd 553; (1990), N.C. App.

[86] See the discussion *ante*, Chap. 1, Section 12(10) paras. 1·377–1·378.

(4) Unsuccessful Third Party Claims

15·055   Attempts have sometimes been made by indemnitees who have success-fully defended actions by third parties to recover from the indemnitor costs not recovered from unsuccessful plaintiffs in those actions. These have not generally been successful, although in the last resort this must be a matter of interpretation of the clause.

ILLUSTRATIONS

15·056   (1) A seller of teapots undertook "to protect the purchaser against all claims losses damages costs and expenses which arise from or occur as a result of the sales against any item purchased." The buyer compromised a claim by a badly burnt girl in view of the possibility of astronomical claims if the jury found for the plaintiff. *Held*, by the Ontario Court of Appeal, that despite the general words the seller had not undertaken that no-one would sue the buyer, but only to meet established liabilities to subsequent purchasers. The words should be restricted to claims arising from the implied conditions of merchan-tability and fitness, and since as a fact there were no defects in the teapot, the buyer could not recover on the indemnity: *Helfand* v. *Royal Canadian Art Pottery* (1970).[87]

     (2) A main contractor for roadworks indemnified the owner against "all claims for injury ... which may arise out of or in consequence of the works and against all claims ... damages costs whatsoever in respect thereof or in relation thereto." Similarly a sub-contractor indemnified the main contractor against "any loss liability claim or proceedings ... arising out of or in the course of or caused by the execution of the works." An injured passer-by failed in his legally aided claim against the owner and main contractor, on the ground that he had caused his own injury and had not, as he alleged, fallen into unguarded excavations. The plaintiff was legally aided and costs against him not recoverable. *Held*, by the Court of Appeal, that neither the owner nor the main contractor could recover their legal costs on the wording of their respective indemnity clauses: *Richardson* v. *Buckinghamshire County Coun-cil* (1971).[88]

15·057   However, it may be recalled that on very similar standard form wording Slade L.J. appears to have been of the opinion, when considering the application of the *Alderslade* principle, that one head of possible liability without indemnitee negligence, so invoking the principle and preventing the enforcement of the indemnity, might result from an intention that the indemnitee should be protected from all the consequences of even unsuc-cessful litigation arising from the carrying out of the works.[89]

     On the other hand, sums including costs paid under a reasonable and bona fide compromise in settlement of a third party claim, even if sub-sequently shown to be groundless, have been held to be recoverable.[90]

---

[87] 11 D.L.R. 3d 404.
[88] [1971] 1 Lloyd's Rep. 533.
[89] *Walters* v. *Whessoe*, illustrated *supra*, para. 15·048.
[90] *Comyn Ching Ltd.* v. *Oriental Tube Ltd.* (1979) 17 BLR 47, C.A., applying *Biggin* v. *Perma-nite* [1951] 2 K.B. 314, illustrated *supra*, para. 15·045.

(5) Indemnitor's Sub-contractors

It has frequently been stated judicially that indemnity clauses must be strictly construed in the same way as exemption clauses. As explained in Section 2(1) *supra*, insofar as the beneficiary of an indemnity clause may seek to contend that it will comprehend his own negligence or default, strict interpretation is obviously an entirely logical approach, indeed on an *a fortiori* basis since an indemnity clause involves positive compensation,[90a] but no such logic exists, it is submitted, for cutting down the extent of the indemnity offered by an indemnitor *in respect of his own negligence* or that of others for whom he is responsible (upon whose latter work, if he is a main contractor, he will be charging a profit as against the owner). Such a clause merely emphasises an existing contractual obligation, and is in no real sense an exemption clause—indeed the precise contrary, it is submitted. However, it seems to have been so held.

15·058

ILLUSTRATION

A contract for a municipal abattoir contained the standard RIBA/JCT indemnity Clause 14(*b*) against loss, liability, claim, etc., for damage to property, provided that the same was due "to any negligence, omission or default of the contractor, his servants or agents, or of any sub-contractor." K., the manufacturers of a patented waterproofing product, who were actually sub-sub-contractors (*i.e.* suppliers to nominated sub-contractors for the flooring of the abattoir) recommended and supplied a special sealing agent for the floors, which had to be waterproofed, and which had cracked when originally laid. The product was chemically damaging to freshly slaughtered meat, and the owners received a number of claims for spoiled meat from the users of the abattoir, and sued the main contractor on the indemnity. *Held*, by Kerr J., that the *Canada Steamship, AMF, Gillespie* and *Walters* v. *Whessose* cases were authority for the proposition that indemnity clauses should be construed strictly, analogously to an exemption clause, and insofar as a clause did not clearly have the effect of rendering the indemnitor liable, it could not be relied on. K. were not "agents" of the defendants, nor were they sub-contractors of the defendants, but of the nominated sub-contractors, and the plaintiffs' claim failed for that reason: *City of Manchester* v. *Fram Gerrard* (1974).[91]

15·059

[Note: It is submitted that the reasoning in this case is too legalistic, and gives insufficient consideration to the indifferent draftsmanship of standard forms of contract and the quite obvious commercial intention of the clause. A main contractor prices for and receives his profit upon the large and complicated network of (sub-) contracts of employment, services, work, goods and materials comprised in the project. The wording is, it is submitted, an obvious attempt to give a comprehensive indemnity, and it would be literally absurd to try and suggest some intelligible commercial reason for distinguishing between any particular category of supplier or sub-supplier when providing the indemnity. The interpretation also appears to demand an unrealistic degree of precision and of excessive repetition in the draftsmanship, or some

15·060

[90a] See, *per* Viscount Dilhorne in *Smith* v. *South Wales Switchgear* [1978] 1 W.L.R. 165, 168D quoted *supra*, para. 15·040.
[91] 6 BLR 70.

special formula of wording, in order to indicate the obviously required comprehensive result. As stated above, the reasons given by Kerr J. for subjecting the draftsmanship to this degree of semantic analysis and scrutiny do not in any case appear to be justified on a proper analysis of the principle underlying the indemnity interpretation cases. A similar tendency has also manifested itself in other construction contract interpretations in England, having the commercially subversive effect of excluding sub-contractor obligations or defaults from the expressed liabilities of the main contractor.[92] The Court of Appeal's contrary interpretation on not dissimilar wording in *Petrofina Ltd.* v. *Magnaload Ltd.*[93] seems much to be preferred.]

(6) Implied Indemnity

15·061 Some implied terms in contract may essentially involve an implied indemnity, in the sense that a breach will only occur upon some contemplated harm eventuating (as, for example, an implied term on the part of the owner of undisturbed possession).[94] However, there is also, it seems, a more general principle that if a person requests or requires another to do an act which is not obviously tortious, and that the other performs the required act without negligence on his own part, there will be an implied indemnity should the act render the other person liable to a claim by a third person.[95] An important application of this principle to construction contracts by the High Court of Australia, whereby the contractor is entitled to an indemnity if, as a necessary consequence of carrying out the work and without negligence on his part he becomes exposed to third party claims, has already been noted.[96]

---

[92] See *John Jarvis* v. *Rockdale Housing Association* (1987) 36 BLR 48, C.A., and *Scott Lithgow Ltd.* v. *Secretary of State for Defence* (1989) 45 BLR 6, illustrated *ante*, Chap. 5, paras. 5·036 and 5·037, and both the subject of critical review in (1987) 3 Const.L.J. 274, and (1991) 7 Const.L.J. 3.

[93] [1984] Q.B. 127, illustrated *supra*, para. 15·009.

[94] See *ante*, Chap. 4, paras. 4·150 *et seq.*

[95] *Sheffield Corporation* v. *Barclay* [1905] A.C. 392, 397, *per* Lord Halsbury.

[96] *The Crown* v. *Henrickson & Knutson* (1911) 13 C.L.R. 473, illustrated *ante*, Chap. 4, Section 3(6), para. 4·171, and see *supra*, para. 15·039.

CHAPTER 16

BANKRUPTCY AND LIQUIDATION

SECTION 1. INSOLVENCY GENERALLY

(1) Scope of Present Chapter

Since the last edition of this book, the English Insolvency Act 1986 has **16·001** amended and codified within one statute the law of bankruptcy of "individual insolvency" on the one hand (previously covered by the Bankruptcy Act 1914), and on the other hand company insolvency or winding-up (previously covered by the Companies Act 1948 as subsequently re-enacted in the Companies Act 1985).

The present chapter, as in the last edition, is largely confined to discussion of the practical affect of the insolvency of one contracting party on the other solvent party's position in the particular context of the two principal contracts associated with a construction project, namely the

main construction contract and the contract of employment of the owner's
A/E. Sub-contracts are not separately dealt with as such, but in the event
of the insolvency of one of the parties to a sub-contract, the discussion
in Section 4 *infra*, Insolvency of Owner, and in Section 5, Insolvency of
Contractor, will generally apply, *mutatis mutandis*, to the insolvencies of
the main contractor or sub-contractor respectively in a sub-contract
situation.

16·002   While under the Act there are a number of relatively uncommon ways
in which actual or potential insolvency will affect the other solvent party to
a contract, such as the appointment of a receiver and manager by the
Court, or by mortgagees under the Law of Property Act, or voluntary
members', creditors' or debtors' arrangements in both company and individual insolvencies,[1] the two eventualities most likely to occur in practice
will be first, in the case of a company's insolvency, the appointment of an
"administrative receiver" under the 1986 Act (that is, the old "receiver
and manager") by a debenture holder possessing a floating charge on the
company's assets (this may or may not, but often will be a precursor of full
insolvency); or secondly, the initiation of a full winding-up or bankruptcy
petition by unsecured creditors, culminating in the appointment of a liquidator or trustee in bankruptcy respectively. In addition, a further and
novel precursor to full insolvency may now be the appointment of an
administrator, as provided for by Part II of the 1986 Act; but for reasons
explained *infra*, this seems likely to occur less often in practice in construction cases.

16·003   Put very shortly, the grounds for a petition brought by an unsecured
creditor will usually be inability to pay a debt which is above the statutory
bankruptcy level and is identified in the petition, evidenced either by an
unsatisfied Court execution for the debt, or more commonly by failure of
the debtor to comply with a statutory demand requiring its payment
within the prescribed period (or in the case of a future debt to furnish
proof of ability to pay in response to the demand.)[2]

The grounds for winding-up a company are similar, with the addition of
a more general ground, not founded on compliance with a statutory
demand, that the company is shown to be unable to pay its debts as they
fall due, or taking into account its contingent and prospective liabilities.[3]
Plaintiffs seeking speedy judgment from a debtor at the present day not
infrequently resort to statutory demands and a petition as a tactical
alternative to proceedings for summary judgment. However, it has been
held that petitions based on non-compliance with a statutory demand will
fail provided there is at least a partial, even if unquantified, cross-claim.[4]
So a construction contractor's petition to wind up an owner company,
insofar as it was based on a statutory demand for sums certified by the

---

[1] Under Chaps. II to V of Part IV, and under Part VIII of the 1986 Act respectively.
[2] Sections 267 and 268 of the 1986 Act.
[3] Section 123 of the 1986 Act.
[4] See *Re A. Company* [1984] 3 All E.R. 78, applying *Re London & Paris Banking Corporation* (1874) L.R. 19 Eq 444, 445–6.

architect on interim certificates under the RIBA/JCT forms, failed in a case where the owner was disputing the standard of work by a cross-claim for an unquantified though lesser sum which, on the authority of the *Gilbert-Ash* case,[5] could be set off against the certified sum. However, the petition was upheld on the wider ground in Section 123(1)(*e*) of the 1986 Act that the accounts of the company, coupled with the fact that a larger part of the sum certified was due even after allowing for the set-off, showed that the company was insolvent and unable to pay its debts.[6]

(2) Insolvency and its Effect

In the case of an individual debtor, the effect of bankruptcy will be to vest   **16·004**
in the trustee, once appointed, all the property of the bankrupt, including both the benefit and burden of contracts, except those contracts of the debtor which are of a personal character and are still uncompleted at the date of the bankrutpcy—that is, where the personal skill of the bankrupt is regarded as essential to the contract, so that the other party is entitled to refuse to accept a vicarious performance of the contract arranged by the trustee.[7] Even in such a case, however, if the bankrupt is willing to complete the contract personally he may sue the other party on the contract or for breach of it, subject to any right the trustee may have to intervene and claim the proceeds of the action.[8]

The extent to which building contracts are personal in this sense has been discussed *ante*, Chapter 14, where it is submitted that a contractor's functions of control and co-ordination of the project may well involve the necessary personal element and so not be capable of vicarious performance.[9] This exclusion of personal contracts from a trustee's jurisdiction, incidentally, would seem to apply equally in principle to a liquidator in a winding up, at least where the liquidator is not able to offer vicarious performance by the same professional managerial or supervisory personnel.

In bankruptcy, the bankruptcy commences on the date of the bank-   **16·005**
ruptcy order,[10] and the doctrine of "relation back" to a first act of bankruptcy under the Bankruptcy Act 1914 has to that extent been discarded. However, while "dispositions of property" made between the *presentation of the petition* and the order are declared to be void if not approved and ratified by the court,[11] this does not apply if the recipient acted in good faith and for value without notice of the petition.[12] It is doubtful, therefore,

---

[5] [1974] A.C. 689. See *ante*, Chap. 7, Section 6(7)(c), paras. 6·194 *et seq.*
[6] *Re Clemence PLC* (1992) 59 BLR 56.
[7] *Knight* v. *Burgess* (1864) 33 L.J. Ch. 727, *Southway Group* v. *Wolff* (1991) 57 BLR 33. See *ante*, Chap. 14, paras. 14·004 *et seq.*
[8] *Bailey* v. *Thurston & Co. Ltd.* [1903] 1 K.B. 137.
[9] Section 1(2), paras. 14·003–14·011, and Section 2(4), paras. 14·019–14·020, and see Parker L.J.'s comments in *Southway Group* v. *Wolff* (1991) 57 BLR 33, 45–6 there cited and discussed.
[10] Section 278, 1986 Act.
[11] Section 284(1).
[12] Section 284(4).

if this represents more than a marginal practical change from the regime under the Bankruptcy Act 1914. It is unclear whether "dispositions of property" under Section 284 are apt to include entry into a construction contract by either party, but in context, and bearing in mind the trustee's subsequent right to disclaim, it probably does, it is submitted, although the section contrasts with the very different express wording of Section 45 of the 1914 Act. In addition, debts incurred by the debtor after the order itself, although set aside, will entitle the creditor at least to prove in the bankruptcy, provided he acted in good faith and for value and without notice.[13] Finally, transactions at an undervalue,[14] or more importantly in practice, preferences given by the debtor, will be liable to be set aside if, in the latter case, occurring within six months before presentation of the petition.[15]

By contrast in the case of a winding up, the company's assets, including the benefit of contracts, will normally remain vested in the company itself, and will not, as in the case of bankruptcy, vest automatically in the liquidator, once appointed, unless the latter applies for an order to that effect.[16] This the liquidator will not normally need to do, by reason of the very wide extent of his powers to act in the company's name.[17] The immediate legal and practical effect of a winding-up order is, therefore, to prevent any action or proceeding to be continued or commenced against the company without the leave of the court,[18] which will not normally be given if the matter can be dealt with conveniently and with less expense in the winding-up proceedings.

16·006   Following a winding-up order the liquidation is deemed to commence *from the presentation of the petition*, not from the order,[19] or even earlier if there has been a prior resolution passed for voluntary winding up.[20] A similar avoidance of "property dispositions" made after presentation of the petition is effected by Section 127 to that in the case of bankruptcy, but without the protection for recipients for value and without notice of the petition, it would seem. Similar provisions also exist for avoiding transactions at an undervalue,[21] or which are a preference,[22] with similar periods stipulated for their avoidance prior to presentation of the petition.[23]

Both liquidators and trustees have power to carry on the business of the company or bankrupt (but only, it may be important to note, so far as may be necessary for its beneficial winding up) under Schedules 4 and 5 of the 1986 Act respectively. As a result, entry into post-bankruptcy or post-

---

[13] Section 285(5).
[14] Section 339.
[15] Sections 340, 341. For preferences as now defined, see Section 340(3)(*b*).
[16] Section 145, 1986 Act.
[17] Under Schedule 4 of the Act.
[18] Section 130, 1986 Act.
[19] Section 129(2), 1986 Act.
[20] Section 129(1).
[21] Section 238.
[22] Section 239.
[23] Section 240, 1986 Act.

liquidation contracts by the trustee or liquidator is theoretically possible, in which event the contractee's rights under such contracts will, in the case of liquidation, rank as "expenses of the liquidation", taking precedence even over preferential creditors, while in bankruptcy the trustee will be personally liable.

By their nature, however, construction contracts will come into this last **16·007** category only very rarely, and it is much more likely that a construction contract, entered into before the petition, will be in early or mid-course at the time when the order is finally made. In the case of a liquidation, if the contract is to continue following its adoption by the liquidator when appointed, the result of the foregoing rules would seem to be that any sums due to the contractor in respect of pre-liquidation work will strictly be provable only, whereas post-liquidation work following adoption of the contract will be payable in full in priority to other creditors as "expenses of the liquidation" incurred on behalf of the general body of creditors.[24] The absence of reported cases in this area may be explained by the reluctance of trustees in bankruptcy, who will be personally liable, to adopt long-term contracts, and by the variety of remedies available to a solvent party if unwilling to continue following the bankruptcy or liquidation of the other party. Thus, apart from the express termination remedies available in many construction contracts conditioned on the substantive contractual defaults which usually accompany the other party's insolvency, it has also been seen that where there is a sufficient personal element the continuation of the contract cannot be insisted on. Moreover, contracts containing long-term obligations on the part of the insolvent party will not be capable of adoption.[25] Additionally, there is the very important discretionary entitlement to rescission available to any person who is entitled to the benefit or subject to the burden of a contract with the debtor, following a successful application to the court under Section 186 of the 1986 Act in the case of winding-up, or under Section 345(2) in the case of bankruptcy.[26]

Unlike death or illness, therefore, the bankruptcy or liquidation of a **16·008** party to a contract does not automatically have the effect of terminating the contract or constitute a breach of it, since both the liquidator and trustee have power, after obtaining leave, to carry on business of the debtor, and can, therefore, in appropriate cases not only carry on and complete contracts of the debtor, but also enter into new contracts.[26a] However, contracts under which the debtor has assumed long-term obligations in the

---

[24] See the analogous cases on post-liquidation rent paid by the company in *Re ABC Coupler and Engineering Co. Ltd.* [1970] 1 E.R. 650, and *Re Downer Enterprises Ltd.* [1974] 2 E.R. 1074.

[25] *Re Asphaltic Wood Pavement Company, Lee and Chapman's Case* (1885) 30 Ch.D. 216, illustrated *infra*.

[26] The wording in the latter case now differs fairly markedly, for some reason, from Section 54(5) of the Bankruptcy Act 1914, however, perhaps indicating a somewhat lesser entitlement by way of modification of the contract only.

[26a] If necessary for the beneficial winding up of the company.

future will be treated as impossible for the trustee or liquidator to perform, and in such a case the other party can prove at once for damages,
even though the trustee or liquidator purports to carry out the contract.

ILLUSTRATION

>A company agreed with Commissioners to pave a street and, if required, to
>keep it in repair for 15 years at a specified price. When the work of paving was
>partly done the company went into liquidation, but the liquidator completed
>the paving. *Held*, by the Court of Appeal, that on the facts the covenant to
>repair for 15 years was broken and rendered impossible and that the Com-
>missioners could prove in the liquidation for unliquidated damages for
>breach of contract, and further could set off those damages against the pay-
>ments and retention moneys due to the company for completion of the
>paving, under the mutual credits and dealing clause in Section 31 of the
>Bankruptcy Act 1914:[27] *Re Asphaltic Wood Pavement Co., Lee and Chap-
>man's Case* (1885).[28]

16·009   One further remedy, apparently exclusive to bankruptcy, and available
to either party, should be mentioned. This arose originally under Section
105 of the Bankruptcy Act 1914 and its predecessors, now re-enacted by
Section 363 of the 1986 Act. The 1914 section provided in wide terms that
the court should have full power to decide all questions of priorities and all
other questions whatsoever, whether of law or fact, which might arise in
any case of bankruptcy or which it might be necessary to decide for the
purpose of doing complete justice or making a complete distribution of
property. The 1986 wording is briefer, conferring full power to decide all
questions of priorities and all other questions, whether of law or fact, arising in the bankruptcy. Under the earlier wording, the Court of Appeal
held that, in a case where an insolvent builder's remuneration had been
made dependent upon the certificate of the architect, the Court had jurisdiction to order the architect to certify sums which he should not have
disallowed.

ILLUSTRATION

16·010   >Under a joinery contract to fit out stables there was a provisional sum of £95
>for the purchase of iron fittings from named manufacturers. Payment was to
>be on the architect's certificate only, and any dispute was to be left to the sole
>decision of the architect whose award should be final and conclusive between
>the parties. Under a power to do so, the architect instructed the contractor to
>order additional fittings to a value of £137, and these were purchased and
>installed by the builder, but had not yet been paid for when he became bank-
>rupt. At the request of the manufacturers the owners made a direct payment
>to them of £95, on receipt of an indemnity. The builder's trustee applied to the

---

[27] Now Section 323, 1986 Act (bankruptcy) and Rule 4.90, Insolvency Rules 1986 (S.I. 1986
No. 1925) (liquidation).
[28] 30 Ch.D. 216.

architect for a certificate for £137, but the architect refused to certify more than £42, namely the £137 less the sum of £95 paid direct by the owner. There was no payment direct power in the contract. The trustee, contending that the manufacturers should prove in the bankruptcy for their £137, applied to the County Court for judgment for £137 or an order that the architect should give his certificate for that amount, but the judge held he had no jurisdiction, accepting the owners' contention that the trustee was limited to his rights under the contract, and that an architect's certificate was a condition precedent to recovery. *Held*, by the Court of Appeal, that under Section 102(1) of the Bankruptcy Act 1883,[29] the bankruptcy court had jurisdiction to order the issue of the certificate for payment of the full sum to the trustee: *Re Holt, ex parte Gray* (1888).[30]

[Note: It should be noted that there was no dispute on the facts or as to the value of the work, and that the reason given by the architect for not issuing the certificate was the direct payment made by the owner to the manufacturers, which effectively gave them a preference and reduced the sum available for distribution among the creditors generally. It may be doubted whether the Court would have jurisdiction to interfere in a case where the reason for refusing the certificate was a matter within the normal jurisdiction of the architect, such as the value of the work or its compliance with the contract. In the above case the architect was indeed avowedly deciding the priorities between different creditors, thus justifying intervention by the court within the narrow wording of the section. There appears to be no comparable statutory provision in the 1986 Act in regard to company liquidations.]

SECTION 2. DISCLAIMER AND ADOPTION

As the natural corollary of their obligation to carry on the business of the debtor so far as may be necessary for its beneficial winding-up, both trustee and liquidator have power to disclaim onerous property, expressly defined as including unprofitable contracts. There now appears to be no time limit on the right to disclaim, but no doubt because uncertainty over a period can obviously be seriously prejudicial to the other party to the contract, the Act provides expressly that the right to disclaim will be lost if it has not been exercised within 28 days after an application in writing made by any person interested requiring the liquidator or trustee to decide whether to disclaim or not.[31]

16·011

If disclaimer of the contract does take place, the other party is deemed to be a creditor and can prove at once for any loss or damage caused by the disclaimer.[32] In the case of bankruptcy, where the benefit and burden of any current contracts will have vested in the trustee and he will become personally liable on contracts which are adopted by him, the effect of disclaimer can be substantial, since it first discharges the trustee from all liability as from the date when the contract vested in him (that is, upon his appointment), and secondly determines all the rights and liabilities of the bankrupt and his estate under the disclaimed contract (subject to the con-

---

[29] Re-enacted by Section 105(1) of the 1914 Act.
[30] 58 L.J. Q.B. 5.
[31] Sections 178(5) and 316(1) of the 1986 Act.
[32] Sections 178(6) and 365(5) of the 1986 Act.

tractee's entitlement to prove for damages). Moreover, in bankruptcy failure by the trustee to respond to an application under Section 316 within the requisite 28 days results in a "deemed adoption" of the contract by the trustee, which expressly cannot be subsequently withdrawn.[33] On the other hand, the effect of adoption in bankruptcy is that the trustee becomes personally liable for all breaches as from the date of his appointment, although with a right of recoupment out of the estate.[34] It has, however, been suggested that, in the case of a "deemed" adoption resulting from failure to disclaim, his liability will arise as a representative of the creditors and so only to the extent of the assets of the estate.[35]

16·012   In the case of liquidations the practical effect of the disclaimer of a current contract is minimal, since the right to prove for damages conferred by the Act following a disclaimer is no different from the damages recoverable following the company's failure to perform the contract without any overt disclaimer, and the creditor's rescission upon his acceptance of that repudiation. Since a liquidator is never personally liable when acting in that capacity, even in the case of new contracts entered into by him,[36] (and even where he has obtained a vesting order from the court[37] under which he will only become liable in his official and not his personal capacity)[38] there can be no question of adoption *by him*, and indeed the 1986 Act now makes no reference to any deemed adoption by the company of its own contract on expiry of the period following a Section 178(5) application for a decision by the liquidator (an anomalous feature of the earlier wording in Section 323(4) of the Companies Act 1948).

The liquidator will, therefore, remain free on the expiry of the period, although the right formally to disclaim will have been lost, to arrange for or permit the company to abstain from further performance of the contract, leaving it to the creditor either to rescind at common law (with precisely the same financial consequences as those following a formal disclaimer), or possibly to make an application to the Court for rescission under Section 178 of the 1986 Act.

16·013   The practical effect of adoption of a contract by the liquidator, whether actual or deemed, will be to reinforce the claim of the creditor that work done or services rendered after the adoption must be treated as "expenses of the liquidation", with recourse to the company's assets in priority to both ordinary and preferential creditors in the winding-up. Clearly this may be a less effective protection than the trustee's personal liability in bankruptcy, should there be doubt as to the extent of the company's available assets to meet the creditor's claim.

In both bankruptcy and liquidation, adoption of the contract by the trustee or liquidator will not, of course, prejudice the rights of the other

---

[33] Section 316(2).
[34] *Titterton* v. *Cooper* (1882) 9 Q.B.D. 473, C.A.
[35] *Williams & Muir Hunter on Bankruptcy* (19th ed.), 1979, pp. 394–5.
[36] *Stead Hazel & Co.* v. *Cooper* [1933] 1 K.B. 840.
[37] See *supra*, para. 16·005.
[38] *Graham* v. *Edge* (1888) 20 Q.B.D. 538, affd. 20 Q.B.D. 683, C.A.; *Re Ebsworth & Tidy's Contract* (1889) 42 Ch.D. 23.

party to the contract to terminate it for any substantive reason—for example, delay—which might have given a right of termination as against the original debtor, and whether or not before the date of adoption.

SECTION 3. RIGHT OF SET-OFF UNDER MUTUAL CREDIT AND DEALING CLAUSE

Section 323 of the 1986 Act (in the case of bankruptcy) and Rule 4.90 of **16·014** the Insolvency Rules 1986 (replacing Section 31 of the Bankruptcy Act 1914 as applied to companies by Section 317 of the Companies Act 1948) provide that where there have been "mutual credits, mutual debts or other mutual dealings" between the bankrupt or company and a creditor proving a debt, an account is to be taken of what is due from each party to the other in respect of the mutual dealings, and sums due from one party shall be set off against the sums due from the other. Debts due from the bankrupt or company cannot be taken into account in this way, however, if the creditor has notice that a bankruptcy or winding-up petition is pending at the time the debt becomes due (not, it should be noted, when the debt is incurred).[39]

This provision has been a part of English insolvency law for three centuries and has re-appeared in many statutes.[40] The right to take such an account is obviously of vital commercial importance to creditors proving in a bankruptcy or liquidation, who otherwise would find themselves liable in full for sums due to the insolvent estate while left to prove for a dividend only in respect of debts due from it. The statutory right needs to be distinguished, and differs very importantly, from the relatively narrow law of set-off as between contracting parties discussed elsewhere in this book. "The object of this clause is not to avoid cross-actions ... but to do substantial justice between the bankrupt and his creditors".[41] Moreover, while there were some restrictions in the earlier statutes on the types of debt or liability which could be taken into account (as, for example, unliquidated claims for damages in tort were excluded) and at one stage only liability in contract was thought to qualify,[42] the 1986 Act has clearly extended the definitions of a "debt" as widely as possible.[43]

Even before the new Act, the permitted set-offs under the statutory **16·015** provisions in insolvency were much wider than those available between an ordinary plaintiff and defendant, or between an assignee and debtor, in cases where insolvency had not supervened. Thus, the value of unsold goods in the possession of a self-employed salesman for sale on com-

---

[39] Section 323(3), Rule 4.90(3).
[40] See the account of its history by Brightman J., in *Re D.H. Curtis (Builders) Ltd.* [1978] Ch. 162.
[41] *Per* Parke B. in *Forster* v. *Wilson* (1843) 12 M. & W. 191, 203–4.
[42] This was finally rejected in *Re Curtis (Builders) Ltd*; see *supra*.
[43] See Section 382 and Rule 13.12.

mission, but not of tools for his use, was set off against commissions on past sales owed to him by the insolvent suppliers, notwithstanding an express term in his contract preventing any set-off by him until his employment had terminated.[44] Again, the debts did not require to be in contract, so that statutory payments due by a company to two quite different departments of the Crown were set off under the section against sums due from the Crown by way of repayment of over-paid VAT.[45] Similarly, sums due from a company to a bank on an overdrawn account were set off under the section against sums deposited by the company at the insistence of the bank in a separate current trading account for a fixed period which had not yet expired at the time of the company's insolvency.[46] Nor does the fact that the liability in question arises in the future and is of uncertain extent prevent its being set off under the statutory provisions. Thus, where payments and retention moneys were due to a bankrupt contractor, the owners were held entitled to set off unliquidated damages for the bankrupt's inability to perform a long-term maintenance obligation under the contract in question.[47] Moreover, this statutory right of set-off has recently been held, in a typical construction case, to override the normal rule that set-off will not be permitted against an action on a cheque.

ILLUSTRATION

16·016   An architect issued an interim certificate for £132,000 under a RIBA/JCT standard form contract and the owners, after deducting sums paid direct to an unpaid sub-contractor under a contractual power, sent a cheque for the balance of £102,000 to the contractors by first-class post, but stopped it the following day within an hour of the contractors' appointing a liquidator. The company sued on the cheque for summary judgment, and the owners relied on Clause 25(2) of the contract, which provided for an account to be taken following a determination of the contract by the owners, and on the statutory right of set-off under Section 31 of the Act of 1914 as applied by Section 317 of the Companies Act 1948. *Held*, by the Court of Appeal, that there was a potential liability of the contractors to make payment under Clause 25 which was provable in the winding-up as a contingent liability under Section 30 of the Act of 1914; and following *Re Asphaltic Wood Payment Co.* this was the result of mutual dealings under the building contract, so that the owners were accordingly entitled to the statutory set-off and leave to defend: *Willment Brothers Limited* v. *North West Thames Regional Health Authority* (1984).[48]

[Note: This case should not be regarded as confirming the validity of provisions determining contracts conditioned upon insolvency, which was not argued or disputed in the case, no doubt because other grounds for deter-

---

[44] *Rolls Razor Ltd.* v. *Cox* [1967] 1 Q.B. 552, C.A.
[45] *Re Curtis (Builders) Ltd.*, see *supra*; *Re Cushla Ltd.* [1979] 3 All E.R. 415.
[46] *National Westminster Bank Ltd.* v. *Halesowen Presswork and Assemblies Ltd.* [1972] A.C. 785.
[47] *Re Asphaltic Wood Pavement Company, Lee and Chapman's Case* (1985) 30 Ch.D. 216, C.A., illustrated *supra*, para. 16·008.
[48] 26 BLR 51.

mination probably also existed. For this latter difficult subject see *infra*, Section 7.]

As stated above, the 1986 Act has now been very widely worded both in **16·017** regard to the types of claim or debt which are provable, and which will also apply, as a corollary, to claims or debts qualifying as set-off, it is submitted. Thus, it is immaterial whether a debt or liability in a liquidation is present or future, certain or contingent, or capable of being ascertained by fixed rules or as a matter of opinion,[49] and "liability" is to include liability under an enactment, or for breach of trust, or in contract, tort, bailment or restitution.[50] Moreover, in the case of contingent or future debts, there is express power for the liquidator or trustee to make estimates of their quantum.[51]

On the decided cases, the reference to "mutuality" in the wording of the statutory provisions appears to mean little more than the existence of liabilities between the same debtor and creditor at the relevant time, and with no necessary implication of similarities of liability or of connected transactions, it is submitted. The key will be whether it will be just to make the creditor pay his own debts in full while proving for a dividend only in respect of those of the debtor.

However, the debts sought to be set off by the creditor against the insolvent party's claim must be owed or held *in the same right* as the insolvent party's debt. If the creditor's debt arises from a sum held by the creditor for "a special or specific purpose" which is inconsistent with the right of set-off, and which it would be unjust to ignore, it may not qualify for the statutory remedy.

> "Money is paid for a special (or specific) purpose so as to exclude mutuality of dealing within Section 31 if it is paid in such circumstances that it would be a misappropriation to use it for any other purpose than that for which it is paid; and that if in the one case, but not in the other, it would be a misappropriation so to use it, the debts are not due in the same right".[52]

ILLUSTRATION

Following the insolvency of main contractors, local authority owners were **16·018** owed some £98,000 on one contract, but owed the contractors some £11,000 for retention on another contract. The contracts incorporated conditions based on the RIBA/JCT standard forms, in which Clause 27 contemplated that nominated sub-contractors would be employed by the main contractor on terms in the sub-contracts that the main contractor's interest in any sums

---

[49] Rule 13.12(3).
[50] Rule 13.12(4).
[51] Section 322(3); Rule 4.86(1).
[52] *Per* Nourse J. in *Re Arthur Sanders Ltd.* (1981) 17 BLR 125, 133, citing *National Westminster Bank Ltd.* v. *Halesowen Presswork and Assemblies Ltd.* [1972] A.C. 758, 808 and 821, *per* Lord Simon of Glaisdale and Lord Kilbrandon.

retained under the main contract in respect of the sub-contractor's work should be fiduciary as trustee for the sub-contractors; and the nominated sub-contracts in question by Clause 11(d) did in the event so provide. Clause 30(4) (a) of the main contract provided that the owner's interest in the retention moneys should be fiduciary as trustee for the main contractor, *subject to the owner's right of recourse thereto* for the payment of *any amount which the owner might be entitled to deduct* from the sums due to the contractor. The liquidator agreed that the greater part of the £11,000 retention relating to the main contractor's own work might be set off, but not a balance of £1,374 included in that sum which was in respect of nominated sub-contract work. *Held*, by Nourse J., that since it was contemplated by Clause 27 of the main contract that the balance of £1,734 should be held on the trusts imposed by the sub-contracts, that sum was held by the owner for a "special or specific purpose" and was not held by the owners in the same right as the company's £98,000 debt to the owners, so that the statutory set-off did not apply to it: *Re Arthur Sanders Limited* (1981).[53]

[Note: As indicated *ante*,[54] Nourse J.'s interpretation of the owner's right of recourse under Clause 30(4)(a) was persuasively *not* followed by Hunter J. in Hong Kong,[55] and seems inconsistent not only with the wording itself but with the underlying philosophy of nominated sub-contracts, namely the deliberate distancing of the owner from sub-contract disputes. On Nourse J.'s view, however, the draftsmanship of this form of main contract was designed to place the nominated sub-contractor's interest in any dispute with the main contractor before and not after the owner's recourse to the main contract retention in the event of a dispute between owner and main contractor.]

16·019   It is now established that the statutory set-off of mutual debts on insolvency cannot be excluded by contract,[56] so that an express contractual exclusion or inhibition on the exercise of contractual set-off will not affect the statutory right of set-off once insolvency supervenes. Moreover, the effect of insolvency is automatically to terminate any existing rights of action by or against an insolvent person in those cases where mutual dealings exist, and to substitute the right to an account under this statutory provision.

ILLUSTRATION

Contractors went into liquidation in February 1975, with some money owing to them on two contracts, but the owners alleged a claim for the additional cost of completion and for liquidated damages for delay in excess of the claimed sum. In February 1979, the liquidator executed deeds of assignment of the full benefit of and of moneys due under the two contracts in favour of the plaintiff, and warranted to him that nothing was due to the owners. An arbitrator was appointed later in 1979, and the company itself was dissolved in July 1980. In their pleadings the owners objected to the validity of the assignment. *Held*, by Neill J. on a special case stated, that the rule as to set

---

[53] 17 BLR 125.
[54] See Chap. 8, Section 1(3)(b), para. 8·080. See also Chapter 13, Section 5(3).
[55] *Hsin Chong Construction Co. Ltd.* v. *Yaton Realty Co. Ltd.* (1986) 40 BLR 119.
[56] See the *Rolls Razor* and *Halesowen* cases *supra*.

off in insolvency applies automatically and irrespective of the wishes of the parties. Since there were claims and cross-claims under the contract, the rights of the parties *inter se*, following *Re Asphaltic Wood Pavement Co.*, became subject to Section 31 immediately in February 1975, and an account had to be taken and the balance and no more became the sum owing to or from the parties. After liquidation the only relevant chose in action owned by the contractors was the right to enforce a claim for any amount due on taking the account under Section 31, and in 1979 the liquidator was no longer in a position to assign the moneys due under the two contracts. The arbitrator was being asked in effect to take an account *ex post facto*, which under the Companies Act had to be taken at the time of the liquidation, and also on the basis that the assignments of the full sums due were valid although subject to equities, which the arbitrator had no power to do: *Farley* v. *Housing and Commercial Developments Ltd.* (1984).[57]

Section 4. Administrative Receivers

An early and in practice common precursor of the later liquidation of a **16·020** company arises on the appointment of a receiver and manager by a secured creditor. While there are other classes of receivership, such as receivers appointed by the Court, and Law of Property Act receivers of mortgage income or capital, "administrative receiver" is the new and unfortunately confusing title (particularly having regard to the major new concept of administration and administrators introduced by the Act, with which it has nothing to do) which has now been adopted by the 1986 Act for the old "receiver and manager" previously appointed by the special class of secured creditor usually known as a debenture holder. The overriding purpose of these appointments has traditionally been to get in or realise the creditor's security so as to discharge the company's obligation to the secured creditor who has made the appointment. While it is perfectly possible for a secured creditor to be given a *fixed* charge over specific and possibly very substantial identifiable assets of the company, a *floating* charge over all the company's present and future assets is clearly essential if a receiver is to be able to manage the company's affairs and continue to conduct its business while the process of realising the debenture holder's security is being carried out. The possession of a *floating* charge by the creditor, together with security over *the whole or substantially the whole* of the company's property, are now the essential statutory requirements for the appointment of an *administrative receiver*,[58] whose powers and duties are now regulated by Part III of the 1986 Act, together with its subordinate Schedules 1 and 2, and also by Part III of the 1986 Insolvency Rules. It is with this class of receiver, corresponding to the old receiver and manager, that solvent parties to construction contracts will almost invariably be required to deal, assuming that there are debenture holders in existence who choose to exercise their power of appointment.

---

[57] 26 BLR 66.
[58] Section 29(2) of the 1986 Act.

16·021 Administrative receivers, unlike liquidators, are now personally liable on new contracts made by the company when under their control, unless the contract itself provides expressly to the contrary.[59] On the other hand, except in the case of contracts of employment which the receiver has chosen to adopt,[60] he will not be personally liable for existing contracts which are continued during his management. While in law deemed to be the company's agent,[61] his overriding duty is owed to the debenture holder, so that actions which may damage the company or expose it to liability will not render him liable to the company, as would be the case with a true agent, provided he has acted in the interests of the debenture holder and has not inflicted unnecessary damage on the company.

Moreover, if he permits or procures the company to repudiate existing contracts he will, like a liquidator, be under no personal liability to the contractee whether in contract or tort. Effectively, therefore, he would appear to have an *implied* power to adopt or disclaim existing contracts but without the statutory inhibition against a later change of mind, following written application by the solvent party, which attaches to liquidators or trustees under Sections 178(5) and 316(1) of the Act.

16·022 In the absence of express terms in a contract conferring termination or other remedies on the contractee following the appointment of a receiver, the sanctions or protection available to a solvent and unwilling contracting party where an existing construction contract is continued by an administrative receiver are therefore few, if any. There will not, unless and until a winding-up commences, be any power to apply to the Court for rescission of the contract under Section 186 of the Act, notwithstanding that a construction contractor's administrative receiver may be expected, for example, to continue the contract in the interests of the debenture holder only for so long as it is considered profitable (as where a "front-loading" element is present in the pricing), and then to discontinue, with no regard to the quality of the work or to the contractor's goodwill, such as might be the case in normal trading. It is not easy to see what form an owner's objection to completion by an administrative receiver of the contractor could take in such a situation, provided the receiver does not make changes in the management and supervisory control of the contract.

Even where an express termination remedy is available, there may be doubt as to its validity if exercised solely on the ground of the receiver's appointment. However, since the receivership is in essence a procedure for realising and discharging the debenture holder's security, rather than that of the creditors as a whole, and since an owner's termination power will clearly be commercially justified for the reasons previously stated, as well as involving no overt attack on the principle of *pari passu* distribution between creditors (although there may possibly be preferential creditors with priority over a floating charge), a termination conditioned on receiv-

---

[59] Section 44(1)(*b*) of the 1986 Act.
[60] Section 44(1)(*b*) of the 1986 Act.
[61] Section 44(1)(*a*).

ership could be said to be much less offensive, from the point of view of public policy,[61a] than one conditioned on bankruptcy or liquidation itself. However, there is little or no direct authority on the point.[62]

The RIBA/JCT forms have for many years contained an owner's termination clause, providing for "automatic termination" of the contract in the event of (*inter alia*) the appointment of a receiver and manager, and now of an administrative receiver,[63] but expressly subject to its subsequent "reinstatement" by agreement, and with very substantial ancillary powers for the owner to complete by other contractors and to take assignments and make direct payments to sub-contractors failing such reinstatement.[64]

The power and importance of administrative receivers, from the point **16·023** of view of third parties in contractual relations with a potentially insolvent company, is emphasised by a perhaps surprising feature of the new concept of administration under the 1986 Act, whereby debenture holders with power to appoint an administrative receiver must be given notice of any petition for administration, and are given an absolute power to block any administration order by appointing their own receiver at any time prior to the petition being heard.[65] The only exceptions will be if the debenture is itself open to attack as a voidable transaction at an undervalue or as a preference, or if the floating charge has been recently given in respect of *previous* (not future) indebtedness within the periods stipulated by Section 245 of the Act.

Administrative receivers also have power, on application to the court, to dispose of property subject to a prior security, but this is subject to applying the net proceeds of sale to discharge of that security. This power does not, however, unlike that of an administrator, extend to property which is subject to *retention of title*, which is much more common today in the context of construction contracts. Administrative receivers also have the same new personal protection as liquidators and administrators should they seize or dispose of property which is not in fact the property of the company, provided they had reasonable grounds for believing that they were entitled to do so.[66] However, this is a purely personal protection against an action in tort by the true owner, and will not otherwise prejudice the assertion of his rights against the company or his recovery of the property.

[61a] As to which see *infra*, Section 7(7).

[62] Robert Goff J.'s judgment in *Barclays Bank Ltd.* v. *W. J. Simms Son & Cooke (Southern) Ltd.* [1980] Q.B. 677, though concerned with instructions by an owner to stop a cheque to the contractor following the "automatic termination" of the contractor's employment under the RIBA/JCT standard forms on the entry into receivership, clearly involved no ruling on the substance of the dispute or the validity of the clause as between owner and contractor. See further on this *infra*, Sections 6 and 7.

[63] Clauses 25(2) and 27.2 of the 1963 and 1980 Forms. For their effect on performance bonds see the *Perar* case (1994) 66 BLR 72, *post*, para. 17·012A.

[64] See for important amendments in 1992 to these provisions, substantially reducing the powers of owners and strengthening the position of the receiver, Mark C. McGaw "Insolvency, Project Integrity and the JCT Standard Forms" in (1994) 10 Const.L.J., and see their previous effect summarised *infra*, Section 7(3), para. 16·035.

[65] Section 9(3) of the 1986 Act (but not thereafter). [66] Section 234(3) and (4) of the 1986 Act.

SECTION 5. ADMINISTRATION AND ADMINISTRATORS

16·024   Administration, an entirely new concept in the 1985 Act, arose from the perceived need (as it has been seen, however, in the absence of any debenture holder available and willing to appoint a receiver and manager) for some procedure which will enable the business of a company unable to pay its debts to be carried on for a further period with a view to its disposal in whole or in part as a going concern, or to obtain a more advantageous realisation of its assets than would be likely on going into immediate liquidation at the suit of an unsecured creditor.[67]

While application will usually be made by the company itself, or by its directors, any class of creditor, including even contingent creditors such as sureties, can apply for an administration order. The effect of an order is to constitute the administrator as agent of the company with full management powers. Unlike an administrative receiver, the administrator will not be personally liable on new contracts or for adopted contracts of employment. On the other hand, and again unlike an administrative receiver, he may have no power to cause or permit the company to repudiate or break unprofitable contracts,[68] since it would seem that his overall responsibility is to the general body of creditors, unlike the administrative receiver, although this is not certain.

16·025   An administrator's power to carry on the company's business is not circumscribed or limited, as is a liquidator's, to the needs of beneficial winding-up. Nor is he particularly concerned with the interests of secured or preferential creditors, or of distribution to creditors of any kind, since in general he must have regard to the interests of the creditors as a whole and not of any particular class.

As previously stated, the power of the administrator to dispose of property with the approval of the Court, subject to holding the net proceeds for the benefit of its true owner, extends much more widely than that of an administrative receiver to goods subject to leasing or retention of title agreements, as well as to hire-purchase agreements.[69]

16·026   However, the main effect of an administration order, distinguishing it from all other insolvency procedures, is not only that it prevents any other procedure, such as liquidation or the appointment of an administrative receiver, being instituted so long as the original administration order remains in force, but, most importantly from the point of view of third parties, no "other proceedings" or execution or legal process can be commenced or continued against the company or its property, and no "other steps" can be taken to enforce any security, or to repossess goods in the company's possession under a wide variety of hire, leasing and retention of title agreements, *without the consent of the administrator or the leave of the Court*.[70] Section 11(3), therefore, not only imposes a freeze on pro-

---

[67] See for these purposes Section 8(3) of the 1986 Act.
[68] *Astor Chemicals Ltd.* v. *Synthetic Technology Ltd.* [1990] BCLC 1.
[69] Sections 15(2)(*b*) and 15(9) of the 1986 Act.
[70] Section 11(3) of the 1986 Act.

ceedings of virtually every kind brought against the company or its property, but by subclause (3)(c) prohibits "other steps" to enforce a security or repossess goods without the necessary consent or leave. The draftsmanship of Section 11(3)(c) seems likely to provoke difficulty in deciding precisely what "other steps" it is intended to prohibit without consent or leave.[71] In principle, an administrator refusing repossession without reasonable grounds for being entitled to do so will be personally liable for damages in conversion, and also, it seems, for their rental value if, as an officer of the Court, the administrator has made use of the goods for the purposes of the administration.[72]

In the case of construction contracts, the solvent contractee may presumably take all contractual steps, such as serving notices prior to a termination, and cease further performance in the case of a contractual termination or comon law rescission, but will require leave before actually starting proceedings by way of arbitration or litigation, it is submitted; but Section 11 will require judicial interpretation in this respect.

SECTION 6. INSOLVENCY OF CONSTRUCTION OWNER

(1) Continuation of Contract

The personality of the owner as the paying party in a construction contract **16·027** would not seem essential so as to prevent the benefit of the contract vesting in his trustee or liquidator, notwithstanding that one owner may administer a contract more severely than another.[73] Since most construction contracts will inevitably involve the giving of credit by the builder, at least to the extent of retention, before completion, as well as of the value of outstanding work from time to time prior to interim payment, contractors may well find the prospect of completing for an insolvent owner's trustee or liquidator who wishes to continue with a profitable project unattractive. There is in fact remarkably little authority in England governing this situation.

(2) Contractor's Possible Right to Security

In the case of sale of goods it has been held that, following notice of the **16·028** buyer's insolvency to the seller in circumstances which indicate that payment in full is not being offered, the seller will be entitled to refuse to

---

[71] See *Barclays Mercantile Business Finance Ltd.* v. *Sibec Developments Ltd.* [1992] 1 W.L.R. 1253.
[72] *Ibid.*, at page 1259E–F, *per* Millett J.
[73] See *ante*, Chap. 14, Section 1(2), paras. 14·003–14·011, and the comments of Staughton L.J. in *Linden Gardens Trust Ltd.* v. *Lenesta Sludge Disposals Ltd.* (1992) 57 BLR 57, 78 (not in this respect affected, indeed somewhat reinforced, by Lord Browne-Wilkinson's speech in the House of Lords), and see *Chitty on Contracts* (26th ed.), para. 14–16.

perform further without additional security,[74] and in *Re Sneezum* Mellish L.J. made a passing comment that this would also apply to contracts of employment.[75] If this is a valid independent principle, and not merely an extension of the rules of rescission for anticipatory breach, there would seem to be no reason why it should not also apply to construction contracts, it is submitted. If so, it will be a valuable support for solvent contractors in this situation.

(3) Express Termination Powers

16·029　In the normal course it would be unusual for a form of contract drafted or put forward by an owner to confer rights on the contractor in the event of the owner's insolvency, but the RIBA/JCT standard forms have contained such a provision for many years. Thus, by the 1963 standard forms the contractor was entitled to give notice determining his employment upon the owner's bankruptcy or winding-up, or on the appointment of a receiver or manager, or on certain other insolvency developments.[76] There is some doubt, however, as to the validity on policy grounds of such an express remedy, if both conditioned and exercised upon insolvency or an act of insolvency alone, since its effect (by definition taking place after the insolvency) will be to remove the benefit of the contract from the assets otherwise available for the remaining creditors, and so will arguably infringe the basic *pari passu* principle underlying the law of insolvency in most jurisdictions. Since the cases which throw doubt on the validity of termination provisions so conditioned have usually arisen in contractor insolvencies, this topic is more fully discussed *infra*, Section 7.

(4) Statutory Right of Rescission

16·030　As stated above, a statutory right for the solvent contractee to apply to the court for rescission exists under Sections 186 and 345(2) of the 1986 Act. Although the personal liability of an adopting trustee in bankruptcy[77] may be a factor, it is difficult in a case of a construction owner's company insolvency to believe that the court would refuse rescission on the contractor's application, in the absence of adequate security for the price being given. If this is correct, it may serve to explain the absence of English authority on the validity on policy grounds of contractors' termination clauses.[77a]

---

[74] *Ex p. Chalmers* (1873) L.R. 8 Ch. App. 289; *Ex p. Carnforth* (1876) 4 Ch.D. 108; and see *Williams & Muir Hunter on Bankruptcy* (19th ed.) (1979) p. 286.
[75] [1876] 3 Ch.D. 463, 473.
[76] Clause 26(1)(*d*) of the 1963 Forms.
[77] Not perhaps so clearly established by authority as some textbooks appear to assume.
[77a] See *post*, Section 7(7).

(5) Express Trust Provisions in Main Contracts

It has been seen in Chapter 8[78] that since 1963 the RIBA/JCT standard   **16·031**
forms have contained express provisions purporting to impose a trust in
favour of the main contractor on his beneficial interest in the sums
retained by the owner under that contract.[79] At a later stage the 1980 forms
additionally imposed an obligation for the retention to be paid into a joint
bank account impressed with the trust, upon the contractor's application.[79a] Since the only possible purpose of such a provision, particularly
in its original 1963 form, although not overtly mentioned, must be to confer priority on the main contractor over other creditors in the event of the
owner's insolvency, it has been submitted in Chapter 8, after examining
the numerous cases concerned with these and similar provisions in the
standard forms of sub-contract, that their validity, although now clearly
established in the Court of Appeal, may still be open to question in the
House of Lords as being contrary to public policy, particularly in the light
of the *British Eagle* case in the House of Lords,[80] which for some reason
does not appear to have been relied on in argument in several important
cases. It has also been submitted[81] that the 1980 express requirement for
opening a joint bank account might be less objectionable, and that to that
extent if such a separate fund was created and identified prior to insolvency the contractor's claim might properly prevail over that of a trustee
or liquidator. However, it seems clear that action taken after insolvency to
set up the fund will be ineffective. Thus, where a floating charge had crystallised on the appointment by the owner's bank of an administrative
receiver under a floating charge at a time when no action had been taken
to set up the fund, the receiver's claim prevailed over that of the contract-
or, the court expressing the view that any action to set up the separate fund
would be void as a preference under the insolvency legislation.[82]

SECTION 7. INSOLVENCY OF CONTRACTOR

(1) Continuation of the Contract

It is in practice unusual for trustees or liquidators of contractors to wish to   **16·032**
continue and complete existing contracts. Trustees may incur personal

---

[78] See *ante*, Section 1(3), paras. 8·081 *et seq.*

[79] Clauses 30(4) and 30.5 of the 1963 and 1980 Forms.

[79a] See *ante*, para. 8·084.

[80] *British Eagle International Airlines* v. *Cie Nationale Air France* [1975] 1 W.L.R. 758, illustrated *ante*, Chap. 8, para. 8·083, and discussed para. 8·084. See also Thean J.'s well-reasoned judgment in the sub-contractor's "pay direct" case of *Joo Yee Construction (Pte.)
Ltd.* v. *Diethelm Industries (Pte.) Ltd.* (1990) 2 M.L.J. 66, illustrated *ante*, Chap. 13, Section
5(2), para. 13·126.

[81] See *ante*, Chap. 8, para. 8·086.

[82] *MacJordan Construction Ltd.* v. *Brookmount Erostin Ltd.* (1990) 56 BLR 1, C.A., discussed *ante*, Chap. 8, para. 8·085.

liability, and it has been seen that the power of both to carry on business, unlike that of an administrator or administrative receiver, will be open to attack if it can be shown to disregard the statutory restriction that it is necessary for the beneficial winding up of the business.[83] However, it is perfectly possible that where a contract is profitable and near completion, with perhaps considerable retentions or other sums due but unpaid for work already done, a liquidator may well wish to secure these sums by completion, and also avoid the substantial proof for damages that might result from a disclaimer or repudiation of the contract before completion. Owners not wishing to continue employing the contractor in such a situation will probably be in a stronger position to object than the contractor in the reverse situation of an insolvent owner, it is submitted, since it has been seen that the personality of the contractor, at least in regard to the control and co-ordination of the project, may be essential to a construction contract, so that arrangements for vicarious performance by an assignee will not be permitted.[84]

Moreover, on an application to the court for rescission under the statutory provisions, an owner will be able to argue with considerable force, particularly where a substantial amount of important work remains to be done, that completion by a trustee or liquidator concerned only to maximise profit and wind down the business, with no regard to the considerations of reputation and future goodwill which would apply to a going concern, is likely to be prejudicial to his interest, the more so if vicarious performance by different management personnel is being offered by the trustee or liquidator.

16·033   Again, in construction contracts of any size there are almost invariably owners' termination clauses present conditioned on the contractor's failure to maintain due progress, or on other *substantive* contractual defaults which in practice are very likely to occur as a result of financial stringencies in the period leading up to the contractor's insolvency. It will be seen that, if exercised on the ground of some such substantive default and not solely of the insolvency, the cases establish that such clauses are in principle unassailable and will bind the trustee or liquidator.

This general background, with the availability of alternative remedies and sanctions to the owner, may serve to explain the lack of any clear modern authority on the question whether a termination clause conditioned solely on a contractor's insolvency infringes the basic *pari passu* principle so as to be invalid on public policy grounds, as already discussed in Subsection (2)(a) *infra*.

(2) Provisions Affected by Contractor's Insolvency

16·034   Provisions in construction contracts which may be particularly affected by the contractor's insolvency are of four main kinds, namely:

---

[83] Section 87(1) and Sched. 5, para. 1 of the 1986 Act.
[84] See the cases discussed *ante*, Chap. 14, Section 1(2), paras. 8·003 *et seq*.

(a) *provisions for termination of the contract itself, or for* the *vesting* in *or seizure* by the owner of the contractor's materials and plant, in both cases *conditioned on some default of the contractor*;
(b) *vesting provisions, not conditioned on default*, automatically transferring the ownership of plant or materials to the construction owner either immediately on being brought to the site, or sometimes on interim payment which includes their value;
(c) *provisions for direct payment* of unpaid sub-contractors; and
(d) *provisions* in either main or sub-contracts *imposing express trusts on* the contractor's beneficial interest in *retention moneys or other unpaid balances* due from the owner.

These are dealt with in the following Subsections.

(3) Termination and Seizure Provisions

Provisions for termination of the contract itself by the owner, or of the contractor's "employment under the contract" (there is no material difference in these two concepts it is submitted)[85] are frequently found in association with a seizure or sometimes a vesting power, with the objective of enabling the owner to use or sell unfixed materials or contractor's plant in order to complete the work by other contractors, or to reduce his financial loss. Termination provisions are most commonly conditioned at the present day on failure to maintain due progress or other serious defaults, although in the past there could be a considerable variety of stipulated grounds.[86] The associated seizure or vesting provisions would normally be exercisable on re-entry by the owner at the same time, and conditioned on the same defaults, as the termination provisions;[87] as where, for example, the owner is empowered to determine, to enter into possession and complete himself or appoint others to do so, and to seize and use plant and materials for this purpose, often conferring an eventual right of sale to be set off against any damages due to the owner.   **16·035**

For the purpose of the present discussion, which is concerned with the law of insolvency and its effect on the exercise of these remedies for default, the term "forfeiture clause" will be used compendiously for these various contractual powers, comprehending a clause permitting the owner to terminate the contract *simpliciter*, or a clause for entry into possession and completion by the owner, or a clause empowering the owner merely to detain, or to have a lien upon, or to seize and use, or to seize and obtain ownership of, plant, materials or other property (including the benefit of sub-contracts) of the contractor, or a clause automatically transfer-   **16·036**

---

[85] A contrary view is sometimes expressed—see *ante*, Chap. 12, Section 1(3), paras. 12·008–12·009.
[86] See *ante*, Chap. 12, Section 1(4), paras. 12·011–12·012, and 12·062–12·066.
[87] See *ante*, Chap. 12, paras. 12·013 and 12·062 and 12·064, and Chap. 11, Section 2(1), paras. 11·019 *et seq.*

ring to, or vesting such property in the owner following default, or any combination of such clauses.[88]

This classification follows the reasoning and language of the English courts, who in formulating the principles of insolvency affecting clauses of these various kinds, all of which in a greater or lesser degree pass rights of property, whether tangible or intangible, from the contractor to the owner, do not appear to have made any clear distinction between them. It is submitted that the same principles probably apply to them all, although there is an absence of clear authority in the case of forfeiture or termination of the contract as a whole.

16·037   It is submitted that the correct view in relation to forfeiture clauses of these various kinds is that, if expressed to arise or take effect on the bankruptcy or liquidation of the builder, *and if in fact invoked upon that ground alone*, they will be void as against a trustee or liquidator.[89] Conversely, if expressed to arise on some substantive default and breach of contract *or* upon insolvency, then a forfeiture will be valid if, despite supervening insolvency, the required default or breach is as a fact present so as to justify the forfeiture on that ground at the time it is exercised.[90] On the decided cases, there seems no doubt that this will apply to the seizure or vesting clauses over plant or materials associated with termination clauses of the contract as a whole, which will be void and invalid if exercised solely on the ground of insolvency.[90a] The doubt whether this is so in relation to the contract terminations *simpliciter* arises principally because there is well established authority that, in the different field of leases, a provision terminating a lease upon the insolvency of the tenant will be enforced.

While, as will be seen, the lease cases have been judicially explained on the ground of it being permissible for a landlord to limit an interest granted by him on the insolvency of the tenant grantee, this seems semantic and unconvincing, since, regarded instead from the tenant's point of view, the latter has agreed that his own interest should be terminated for the benefit of the reversion in the event of his own insolvency.[90b] It is also difficult to accept any distinction made between automatic termination of a lease and a right to terminate it upon insolvency of the lessee.

It is suggested that the true reason for the different rule in the case of leases may be that in this well developed area of property law the personality of the first tenant is of special importance to the reversioner, since, notwithstanding the assignability of the lease the first tenant will continue to remain liable by privity of contract for breach of its covenants by subsequent assignees. To invalidate a forfeiture by the landlord on the insolvency of the first tenant will deprive him of the opportunity to re-let to a

---

[88] These clauses in so far as they affect plant and materials are exhaustively examined *ante*, Chap. 11, Section 2(1), paras. 11·019 *et seq.*
[89] *Ex p. Jay, Re Harrison* (1880) 14 Ch.D. 19, illustrated *infra.*
[90] *Re Waugh, ex p. Dickin* (1876) 4 Ch.D. 524, illustrated *infra.*
[90a] *Ex p. Barter*, see *infra*, para. 16·040.
[90b] See, *per* Fry L.J. in *Ex p. Barter*, quoted *infra*, para. 16·038.

new first tenant of substance, and limit him to the rights against later assignees, thus permanently diminishing the value of the lease.

Whatever its true basis, the reason for the rule in building cases (al- **16·038** though in the immediate context of a seizure of materials) was stated as follows by Fry L.J. in *Ex p. Barter, re Walker* (1884).[91]

> "But in our opinion, a power upon bankruptcy to control the user after bankruptcy of property vested in the bankrupt at the date of the bankruptcy is invalid. The general rule on this subject was thus expressed many years ago by Mr. Swanston in language which was adopted as accurate by Lord Hatherley in *Whitmore* v. *Mason*: 'The general distinction seems to be that the owner of property may, on alienation, qualify the interest of his alienee by a condition to take effect on bankruptcy; but cannot, by contract or otherwise, qualify his own interest by a like condition, determining or controlling it in the event of his own bankruptcy, to the disappointment or delay of his creditors . . .' It was strenuously argued before us that the clause in question is clearly for the benefit and not for the detriment of the creditors because, it is said, the completion of the ship will lessen the amount for which the [shipowner] might otherwise prove against the bankrupt's estate. But this argument appears to us fallacious because, in the absence of the clause in question the trustee in bankruptcy would have had the election to complete the ship or not as might seem best for creditors, but the presence of this clause has transferred that election to the buyers . . ."

ILLUSTRATIONS

(1) Under a building contract, the owners were empowered to take pos- **16·039** session of "work already done" by the builder, in the event of his bankruptcy, subject to paying a fair proportion of the contract price. Certain sash frames had been delivered to the site for approval by the clerk of works and, after approval, returned to the builder's workshop to be fitted with iron pulleys. Three days after an act of bankruptcy they were re-delivered to the site, but were not fixed. The builder went bankrupt, and had in fact been substantially overpaid. The trustee claimed the frames or their value. *Held*, by the Court of Exchequer, that the frames were not "work already done", not having been incorporated in the work, so that they could not be taken by the owners under their power; but even if they were work done, the bankrupt had no power to make a contract which, upon his bankruptcy, would vest in other persons the property which would otherwise vest in his trustee: *Tripp* v. *Armitage* (1839).[92]

(2) An agreement for a building lease provided that in the event of certain defaults *or* the bankruptcy of the builder, all improvements, materials and effects on the land should become absolutely forfeited to the landlord, and the landlord was to be at liberty to re-enter and take possession of the ground, premises, chattels, and effects and to relet the same as if the agreement had never been made. The builder became bankrupt and the landlord went into possession. Up to the time of entry there had been no default, so the lessor could base his forfeiture only on the bankruptcy. *Held*, by the Court of Appeal, that the provision for forfeiture of materials to the landlord on the bankruptcy of the builder was void, as contrary to the policy of the bankruptcy law. *Per* Cotton L.J.: "Here the forfeiture is to take place on the hap-

---

[91] 26 Ch.D. 510 at p. 519.
[92] 4 M. & W. 687 (*per* Abinger C.B., at p. 699) followed.

pening of either of two events, which were (1) default in the performance of certain stipulations and (2) bankruptcy or insolvency ... One of the two events is not hit by the decided cases. But as to the other, though the contract is good as between the parties to it, it is on principle void in the event of the builder's bankruptcy": *Ex p. Jay, re Harrison* (1880).[93]

[Note: This was a building lease agreement, although at the time of bankruptcy no lease had as yet been executed. The validity of the lessor's re-entry itself was not in dispute between the parties, and in fact the trustee had disclaimed the agreement at a later stage. It is just possible that in the case of a building lease agreement, a re-entry conditioned on bankruptcy might be upheld on the analogy of the law relating to leases.]

16·040   (3) A *vesting* clause in a shipbuilding agreement effectively vested in the purchaser a ship and her engines and everything "bought or ordered" for them. A *seizure* clause, expressed to arise on default *or* bankruptcy, provided that it should be "lawful for the buyer to cause the ship to be completed by any person he might see fit to employ, or to contract with some other person for the completion of the work agreed to be done by the builder, and to employ such materials belonging to the builder as should then be on his premises". The buyers took formal possession on the bankruptcy, but allowed the trustee to continue the work until he suspended it, when the buyers finished the ship using the materials. *Held*, by the Court of Appeal, that the use of materials "bought or ordered" for the ship was not a conversion, as they already belonged to the buyer; but so far as the remaining materials were concerned, the clause was void as against the trustee as being an attempt to control the user after bankruptcy of the bankrupt's property, *and as depriving him of the right of election*, and the buyers were liable for their value. Nor could the seizure be supported because, subsequent to the seizure, work had later been suspended: *Ex p. Barter, re Walker* (1884).[94]

[Note: Again, the validity of the entry into possession was not in dispute between the parties, and the trustee eventually suspended work himself. However, it is submitted that the language of Fry L.J. in this case in referring to the trustee's right of election makes it clear that, where a trustee elected to complete, entry into possession and expulsion of the builder would be invalid in the same way as the ancillary right to use materials.]

16·041   Where, however, a clause of this kind is expressed to depend upon insolvency *or* upon some other event or events, it will be valid as against the trustee or liquidator if *in fact invoked* upon the other ground.[95] On the other hand, once invoked on the ground of bankruptcy, such a clause cannot be supported because subsequently other events occur upon which the clause could have been validly invoked.[96]

Prior to the 1986 Act, it was argued on numerous occasions that where a power of this kind (whether exercisable on insolvency or not) had been exercised with notice of an act of insolvency or after receiving order, the doctrine of relation back prevented the power being validly exercised against the trustee. This argument was consistently rejected by the courts,

---

[93] 14 Ch.D. 19, C.A.
[94] 26 Ch.D. 510.
[95] See, *e.g. Re Waugh, ex p. Dicken* (1876) 4 Ch.D. 524, *infra*, and, *per* Cotton L.J. in *ex p. Jay, re Harrison* (1880) 14 Ch.D. 19, *supra*.
[96] *Ex p. Barter, re Walker*, see *supra*.

who held that a power of forfeiture exercised under a building contract was a protected transaction under Section 45 of the Act of 1914 or its predecessors, and that, in effect, the transaction for the purpose of the section was the original contract, so that, provided the contract itself had been entered into before a receiving order and without notice of an act of bankruptcy, the powers under it could be exercised at any time thereafter and independently of notice of the insolvency.[97]

ILLUSTRATIONS

(1) A building contract contained a provision that, in the event *of default* or bankruptcy, the architect might, on two days' notice, appoint other persons to complete the work, and seize plant and materials.[98] On May 30, the builder filed his petition (an act of bankruptcy) and on June 2, the owners gave notice *for default*, and then entered and seized. *Held*, the evidence as to whether the owners had notice of the filing of the petition when they gave notice under the contract was obscure, but that did not matter, because the transaction for the purpose of Section 94 of the Act of 1869 really took place at the date of the contract. *Per* Bacon C.J.: "If that was a valid contract, and if the licence there granted was unimpeachable, it does not signify to what time the trustee's title related back": *Re Waugh, ex p. Dicken* (1876).[99]   **16·042**

(2) A building lease agreement contained a clause empowering the lessor, *on default only*, to re-enter, repossess and expel the lessee as if the agreement had not been made, and on such re-entry all buildings, erections, materials and things in and about the premises were to be forfeited and become the property of the lessor as and for liquidated damages. The lessor re-entered under the clause after the lessee had filed his petition. *Held*, by the Court of Appeal, that the re-entry and seizure of materials was valid against the trustee. *Per* James L.J.: "Another point taken before us was ... that the seizure was not made in sufficient time, that it was not made before the filing of the liquidation petition. To my mind it is immaterial at what particular moment the seizure was made. The broad general principle is that the trustee in bankruptcy takes all the bankrupt's property, but subject to all liabilities which affected it on the bankrupt's lands, unless the property which he takes as the ... representative of the bankrupt is added to by some express provision of the bankruptcy law": *Ex p. Newitt, re Garrud* (1881).[1]

(3) A building contract provided that, in the event of delay by the builder, the owner might serve notice, and on non-compliance with the notice, no further sums should be paid on account of the contract by the owner, and all plant and materials should be forfeited to him, and in such event it should be lawful for him to enter and take possession of the works and employ any other person to carry on and complete them. After the builder filed his petition, the owner gave notice to the builder and the receiver, and then entered and seized under the clause. *Held*, by Wright and Bigham JJ., that the contract was a protected transaction, and under it the builder's title to the goods was a   **16·043**

---

[97] In addition to the cases illustrated below, see *Re Wilkinson, ex p. Fowler* [1905] 2 K.B. 713, illustrated Chap. 13, para. 13·123.
[98] For the clause in full, see Chap. 11 *supra*, para. 11·022.
[99] L.R. 4 Ch.D. 524 (following *Krehl* v. *Great Central Gas Co.* (1870) L.R. 5 Ex. 289).
[1] 16 Ch.D. 522.

defeasible title, and the trustee could have no better title: *Re Keen, ex p. Collins* (1902).[2]

16·044   Following the discarding by the 1986 Act of the old doctrine of "relation back", the principle of the above cases may be expected to apply to contracts meeting the timing requirements under Section 284(4) of the 1986 Act in the case of bankruptcy (that is, contracts entered into bona fide after, but without notice of any earlier petition) or the rather more restrictive requirements of Sections 127 and 129(2) in the case of a winding-up (contract must be before petition).[2a] This is on the assumption that the wording of these sections "any disposition of ... property" (differing markedly from the much fuller and more explicit section 45 of the 1914 Act) will apply to the contractual liabilities undertaken by a debtor or company when entering into the construction contract.[2b]

Reverting to the question of the validity of a termination clause conditioned on insolvency, this must in the last resort be a question of policy and of the appropriate application of the *pari passu* principle.[3] Essentially, a termination clause deprives an insolvent person of what was previously his property, namely the chose in action represented by the benefit of the terminated contract. A special policy reason for permitting the termination of leases conditioned on insolvency (since otherwise lasting and irremediable damage, through loss of a solvent first lessee liable in privity of contract, will be inflicted on the lessor) has tentatively been suggested.[4]

16·045   The widely accepted validity of retention of title clauses may be thought to represent a further breach of the *pari passu* principle, but these are, it is submitted, clearly distinguishable because, first, such clauses do not bring about any transfer of the ownership of assets upon insolvency, but merely reinforce the existing rights of an unpaid seller who has agreed to part with possession only; secondly, such clauses may justifiably be regarded as a form of available credit of considerable benefit to commerce generally; and thirdly, such clauses are not either expressly or in intention targeted exclusively at the buyer's insolvency, as are the forfeiture clauses under discussion, but equally at delays in payment or other commercial defaults of a solvent buyer where repossession may be considered a more effective remedy or sanction for the unpaid seller than litigation.

In addition, there are a number of other situations where remedies have been held unenforceable following an insolvency as infringing the *pari passu* principle.[5] There are also cases where other types of contractual

---

[2] [1902] 1 K.B. 555.

[2a] See *supra*, paras. 16·005 and 16·006.

[2b] See *supra*, para. 16·005.

[3] Variously expressed in the 1986 Act in Sections 107 (voluntary winding up), 328(2) and (3) (bankruptcy) and Rule 4.181(1) of the 1986 Rules (compulsory winding up).

[4] See *supra*, para. 16·037.

[5] *British Eagle International Air Lines* v. *Cie Nationale Air France* [1975] 1 W.L.R. 758, illustrated *ante*, Chap. 8, Section 1(3), para. 8.083, and see also the "pay direct" cases in the Commonwealth including *Joo Yee Construction Ltd.* v. *Diethelm Industries Ltd.* (1990) 2 M.L.J. 66, illustrated and discussed *ante*, Chap. 13, Section 5(2), paras. 13·126–13·127.

term conditioned expressly and directly on insolvency have for long been held invalid.[6]

There is, however, a lack of modern authority on this point, some reasons for which have been suggested *supra*, and the position in the House of Lords must be regarded as open, particularly in the light of the division of opinion revealed in that House in the *British Eagle* case. Indeed there would seem to be a lack of logic in the current state of the case law which requires clarification by the Courts. Thus, in the recent "pay direct" cases and in the *British Eagle* case, contractual provisions having every commercial justification and neither conditioned nor even principally aimed at the insolvency of the other party have been held unenforceable as infringing the *pari passu* principle once insolvency has supervened.[7] By contrast, seizure and vesting provisions over plant and materials conditioned on defaults other than insolvency have for long been enforced, as the cases illustrated above show, notwithstanding that, following a subsequent insolvency, their operation involved an invasion of the *pari passu* principle. Again, while contractual rights expressly conditioned on insolvency have been invalidated on that ground alone,[8] the courts have lent every assistance to the enforcement of trusts imposed by construction contracts on retention moneys, notwithstanding that, especially in the case of the English standard form *main contract* provisions, there appears to be no possible other objective but securing financial priority in the event of the owner's insolvency.[9] An attempt to rationalise these various cases and considerations is made *infra*, Subsection (7).

16·046

As mentioned *supra*, Section 4 when discussing the position of administrative receivers, express termination clauses conditioned on a variety of related procedures of contractor insolvency, including the appointment of receivers and voluntary compositions with creditors, have long been grounds, in addition to full-scale bankruptcy or winding-up as such, of owners' termination clauses in construction contracts, including the English standard forms.[10] In the case of the RIBA/JCT termination clauses, this has taken the form of an "automatic" termination of the contract on insolvency subject to its possible "reinstatement" by agreement (possibly an attempt to secure their validity on the analogy of the judicial reasoning relating to leases discussed *supra*, Section 7(3)).[10a] However, in 1992, under the cloak of alleged delay and inconvenience said to have resulted from this particular wording, it was abandoned in favour of an owner's discretionary right to terminate in the cases only of receivership, administration or voluntary arrangements, although "automatic" termin-

16·047

---

[6] *Re Jeavons ex p. Mackay* (1873) L.R. 8 Ch.App. 643; *Re Johns, Worrell* v. *Johns* [1928] Ch. 737.

[7] These are discussed further *infra*, para. 16·054, and see further paras. 16·056 *et seq.*

[8] See *Re Jeavons* and *Re Johns*, illustrated *supra*.

[9] See Section 6 *supra*, para. 16·029, and *ante*, Chap. 8, Section 1(3), paras. 8·081 *et seq.*

[10] See Clause 63(1) of a number of eds. of the ICE Conditions, and Clauses 25(2) and 27.2 of the 1963 and 1980 RIBA/JCT forms.

[10a] See *supra*, paras. 16·037–16·038. See these clauses discussed in *Perar B.V.* v. *General Surety Ltd.* (1994) 66 BLR 72, C.A., where no point was taken as to their validity.

ation (with its alleged disadvantages) was retained for full-scale bankruptcy and liquidation. This largely cosmetic change was perhaps
designed to conceal what was significantly not revealed in the accompanying Practice Note, namely a reduction in the owner's previous powers to
take assignments of sub-contracts or to pay sub-contractors direct following *all* terminations by the owner, whether on insolvency grounds or not,
and secondly, an exposure of the owner to a possible liability to make still
further payments to a contractor *after* termination, again whether for
insolvency or for substantive default, which could not have arisen under
the previous wording. The objective appears to have been to strengthen
the tactical position of contractors' debenture holders and their administrative receivers and "insolvency practitioners" generally, and (still more
damagingly from terminating owners' point of view) of *solvent* contractors whose contracts have been determined for default.[11]

This curious spectacle of a standard form taking pains to strengthen the
position of the contractor's other creditors upon receivership or insolvency as against the owner is presumably designed to assist contractors to
raise working capital in the form of debentures or bank loans against current contracts which demonstrate weakened owner's powers in the event
of contractor default or insolvency, and is a remarkable example of the
readiness of the RIBA/JCT forms to yield to openly producer-based
pressures adverse to the owner, and indeed of deviousness in doing so.

(4) Vesting of Materials or Plant in Owner

(a) General insolvency principle

16·048   It is of course a basic principle of insolvency law that, with minor exceptions, the trustee or liquidator will only be entitled to claim or dispose of
the property of the insolvent person or company, while third persons who
are its true owners as against the debtor or company will be entitled to
reclaim it or its value, including bringing actions in tort for conversion
against a trustee or liquidator, or against receivers or administrators, subject to the limited and special protections against personal liability
afforded to the latter by Sections 234(3) and (4) of the 1986 Act, mentioned *supra*, in Sections 4 and 5. Consistently with this basic principle, it
has been shown that the Court may permit the sale by administrators (although not administrative receivers) of the property of third persons under conditional sale, chattel leasing, or retention of title agreements, but
only on payment to the true owner of the net proceeds.[12]

A question in many such cases, therefore, is whether on a true interpretation of the clauses in the construction contract a sufficient property of the
necessary extent has passed to the construction owner in the events which

---

[11] See Amendment 11 in September 1992, and the analysis by Mark C. McGaw in "Insolvency, Project Integrity, And The JCT Standard Forms" in (1994) 10 Const.L.J.
[12] Section 15 of the 1986 Act, see *supra*, Sections 4 and 5.

have happened so as to bind the contractor and so, should he subsequently become insolvent, his trustee or liquidator. Express provisions for vesting materials or plant of the contractor in the owner, not conditioned on either insolvency or substantive default, together with express seizure or vesting provisions which are so conditioned, have been exhaustively considered from this point of view, see *ante*, Chapter 11.[13] Similarly, the position where there is no express provision in the construction contract has also been there examined.[14]

(b) Retention of title

A question may also arise whether the rights of third persons, and in particular the rights of unpaid sellers or suppliers to the contractor under retention of title agreements, will prevail against any claim of the construction owner under the vesting or seizure provisions in the construction contract, or against the contractor's trustee or liquidator, who will often be in possession of the goods in question. This has also been considered in detail *ante*, Chapter 11.[15]

16·049

(c) Bills of sale, registrable charges, and Sale of Goods Act, s.25

Apart from the problems raised by provisions for retention of title in a sale or supply sub-contract with the construction contractor, there remain the further questions:

16·050

(a) whether such a clause in a supply or sale transaction constitutes a Bill of Sale and so is unenforceable unless registered; or
(b) whether it creates a charge on company assets registrable under Section 95 of the 1948 Companies Act (now Section 395 *et seq.*, of the Companies Act 1985) and so void against a liquidator or other creditor of the company unless registered; or
(c) whether it results in the contractor having been in possession with the consent of the seller under Section 25 of the Sale of Goods Act 1979 (replacing Section 25 of the 1893 Act), so conferring an indefeasible title on a bona fide owner or chargee for value to whom there has been a "sale pledge or other disposition" of the goods in question by the contractor.

Bills of Sale, and the courts' consistent refusal to extend this legislation so as to include the usual unpaid sellers' or suppliers' rights against construction contractors, are discussed *ante*, Chapter 11.[16] Registrable charges under Section 395 of the Companies Act 1985 and the effect of Section 25 of the 1979 Sale of Goods Act are also there considered.[17]

---

[13] Section 2(1) or (2), paras. 11·010 *et seq.*
[14] See *ante*, Chap. 11, Section 1.
[15] Section 2(7), paras. 11·051 *et seq.*
[16] Section 2(3), paras. 11·046–11·047.
[17] See *ante*, Chap. 11, Section 2(7), paras. 11·053–11·054 *et seq.*

16·051   In fact, there appear to have been second thoughts in regard to the wording of Section 395 of the Companies Act 1985. By its original wording, the "charge" requiring registration was defined (in so far as relevant in a construction context) as a charge "created by an instrument which if by an individual would be a bill of sale".[18] On the authorities relating to bills of sale discussed in Chapter 11, therefore, this wording served to exclude "Romalpa" clauses in supply or sale contracts to contractors. However, by Sections 93 *et seq.*, of the Companies Act 1989, which was not yet in force in 1991, a new Section 395(2) provides that "charge means any form of security interest (fixed or floating) over property other than an interest created by operation of law", and by a new Section 396(1)(*b*), a "charge" requiring registration includes "a charge on goods other than a charge under which a chargee is entitled to possession either of the goods or a title to them". This quite different wording would seem consistent, nevertheless, with the cases noted in Chapter 11,[19] and appears effective to safeguard normal retention of title cases from the need for registration.

(d) Reputed ownership

16·052   The omission from the 1986 legislation of any rule of reputed ownership comparable to the "order and disposition" Section 38 of the Bankruptcy Act 1914 should be noted, if only because of that rule's possible survival in other Commonwealth jurisdictions which may decide not to follow the English 1986 legislation.

     The broad effect of the cases involving transfers of property in plant and material to the owner which have been examined in Chapter 11 can be summarised by saying that where vesting or seizure clauses have the effect of transferring ownership or a sufficient right of detention to the owner from the contractor (either at some earlier stage before the insolvency through a vesting clause or at a later stage through a vesting or seizure provision in a termination clause conditioned on some default other than insolvency)[19a] then, subject to any prior rights of the original seller or supplier and subject to any question of an interest being void for failure of registration, the construction owner's claim will prevail over that of the contractor's trustee or liquidator.

     However, in the case of bankruptcy (but not of a company winding up) Section 38 of the Act of 1914 vested in the trustee:

> "all goods being, at the commencement of the bankruptcy, in the possession order or disposition of the bankrupt, in his trade or business, by the consent or permission of the true owner, under such circumstances that he is the reputed owner thereof".

16·053   In the context of the provisions commonly found in construction contracts, this section had the somewhat paradoxical effect that where the

---

[18] Section 396, Companies Act 1985.
[19] See *ante*, Section 2(7).
[19a] See *supra*, paras. 16·005–16·006, and 16·044.

vesting or seizure provisions had successfully transferred *ownership* to the construction owner, so that he had become the "true owner" of those goods, the trustee in a subsequent bankruptcy might now claim that the goods had vested in him under the section, since they could be regarded as having been left by the construction owner as "true owner" in the possession of the contractor (as they usually would be) at the commencement of the bankruptcy.

All of the requirements of the Section had to be strictly complied with, however. Thus, full ownership, and not a lesser right, such as a right to detain and use plant for purposes of completion but subject to ultimate return to the contractor (as was the case under many older seizure clauses), must be shown to have passed to the construction owner; if not, his lesser rights of detention and user would somewhat paradoxically, prevail over the trustee's claim.[20] Moreover, it was held in 1948 that *unfixed materials* on a construction site (as opposed to plant and equipment) carried no implication of contractor ownership, so that in such a case the "reputed owner" requirement of the section was not satisfied.[21]

As stated, this statutory rule no longer obtains in England.

(5) Power to Pay Sub-contractors Direct

This very valuable express power for owners, to be found in many main contracts, is designed to ensure the continued performance of important sub-contractors on the project in situations where the main contractor may be delaying or disputing payment without justification, or for reasons with which the owner does not agree, thereby provoking the sub-contractor's departure and imperilling the owner's commercial interest in early completion. It is important to appreciate that the power is *not* targeted at or conditioned on main contractor insolvency, although naturally the stringencies associated with an approaching main contractor insolvency might be a contributory cause to disputes with, or non-payment of a sub-contractor. The owner's right is more commonly conditioned on failure of the main contractor to pay the sub-contractor, and usually only to the extent that the main contractor has himself received payment from the owner in respect of the sub-contractor's work. In this particular type of clause the right, therefore, will involve the owner effectively paying twice for the sub-contract work, and subsequently deducting once from any later sums due to the main contractor. However, much wider powers to pay direct are understandably conferred as ancillary to the exercise of owners' termination clauses in many English standard forms. These will not be

16·054

---

[20] *Re Keen and Keen, ex p. Collins* [1902] 1 K.B. 555, illustrated on this aspect *ante*, Chap. 11, Section 2, para. 11·027.
[21] *Re Fox, ex p. Oundle and Thrapston RDC* [1948] Ch.D. 407, and see *Clarke* v. *Spence* (1836) 4 A & E 448, 472 in the case of shipbuilding contracts.

conditioned on prior payment by the owner to the main contractor, and their object will be to facilitate completion of the project by the owner following the main contractor's dismissal.

Payment direct of sub-contractors has been fully considered *ante*, Chapter 13.[22] The earlier cases there illustrated show that, provided the construction contract itself has been concluded within the timing rules prior to the contractor's insolvency, a payment direct of the sub-contractor may be made after the main contractor's insolvency and deducted as a set-off by the owner when proving in the insolvency, even though the effect of this will be effectively to constitute the sub-contractor a preferred creditor ranking ahead of all others.[23] However, these cases were not followed in South Africa in 1969, payment direct after the insolvency being held to infringe the *pari passu* principle under Sections 181 and 182 of the South African Companies Act of 1926.[24] More recently in 1990, in a highly persuasive and well-researched judgment in Singapore, Thean J., applying the principles to be derived from the 1975 *British Eagle* case,[25] again held that implementation of a direct payment following a liquidation would contravene the *pari passu* provisions of the Singapore Companies Act.[26] It is submitted that Thean J.'s judgment is to be preferred on this point to the earlier English cases, and that no payment direct, if made or contemplated under such provisions after the insolvency, will entitle an owner to set off the payment in the contractor's insolvency, even though the contract was entered into bona fide before the insolvency.[26a] In the last resort, however, this must be a question of policy for the House of Lords.

(6) Express Trust Provisions in Sub-contracts

16·055   A main contractor's insolvency may also provoke disputes between unpaid sub-contractors and the main contractor's trustee or liquidator arising from the express trusts in favour of the sub-contractor now frequently imposed by many English sub-contract forms on the main contractor's beneficial interest in the retention or other sums due from the owner to the main contractor in respect of the sub-contract work. Indeed, in one case (which seems to be questionable for other reasons) it has been seen that Nourse J. held an owner liable to the main contractor's liqui-

---

[22] Section 5, paras. 13·120 *et seq*, and see *ante*, Chap. 8, paras. 8·078–8·080.

[23] *Re Wilkinson, ex p. Fowler* [1905] 2 K.B. 713, *Re Tout and Finch Ltd.* [1954] 1 W.L.R. 178, but see the strongly contrary dicta in *Re Holt, ex p. Gray* (1888) 58 L.J.Q.B. 5, illustrated *ante*, Chap. 13, para. 13·121, and *supra*, Section 1, para. 16·010. This case was not apparently cited to Bigham J. in *Re Wilkinson*.

[24] *Administrator of Natal* v. *Magill Grant & Nell (Pty.) Ltd.* [1969] 1 S.A.L.R. 660. See *contra* in New South Wales *Re C.G. Monkhouse Pty. Ltd.* (1968) 69 S.R., N.S.W., 429 (following *Re Tout and Finch*); and in Ireland *Glow Heating Ltd.* v. *Eastern Health Board* (1988) 6 I.L.T. 237, the latter illustrated *ante*, Chap. 13, Section 5(2), para. 13·125.

[25] *British Eagle International Air Lines* v. *Cie Nationale Air France* [1975] 1 W.L.R. 758, illustrated *ante*, Chap. 8, Section 1(3)(b)(ii), paras. 8·083.

[26] *Joo Yee Construction Ltd.* v. *Diethelm Industries Ltd.* (1990) 2 M.L.J. 66, illustrated *ante*, Chap. 13, Section 5(2), para. 13·126.

[26a] See further *infra*, Subsection (7).

dator, with no right of set-off for valid cross-claims of the owner against the contractor, for retention sums of this kind and additionally refused the owner a remedy under the mutual credit and dealing statutory provisions.[27] Although such clauses have been held binding on the contractor's trustee or liquidator at the suit of the sub-contractor on numerous occasions, and although perhaps not so offensive as the similar main contract express trust provisions,[28] there must now be serious substantial doubt as to their enforceability against a trustee or liquidator on public policy grounds as contravening the *pari passu* principle, particularly in the light of the *British Eagle* case, and the ensuing *Joo Yee* decision[29] on the considerably less offensive direct payment provisions.[30]

(7) Suggested Principles of Invalidation

It is suggested that as between a trustee or liquidator and the solvent party   **16·056** to a contract, including in particular construction contracts, the cases show that provisions which have the effect of benefiting the solvent party as against the insolvent party may be invalidated on public policy grounds in the event of the latter's insolvency by two possible routes of reasoning.

The first route will be where a provision is seen to be *exclusively* aimed, whether expressly or by inference, at obtaining a preference or advantage in favour of the solvent party in the event of the other party's insolvency.[31] Moreover, it would seem to require an element of deliberate intent in the draftsmanship of the provision:

> "In my opinion a man is not allowed, by stipulation with a creditor, to provide for a different distribution of his effects in the event of bankruptcy from that which the law provides."[32]
>
> "The question is whether the provision has been created deliberately in order to provide for a different distribution of the insolvent's property on his bankruptcy from that prescribed by law".[33]

It is submitted that it is by this route that the seizure of materials provisions in the shipbuilding and construction cases, illustrated *supra*, were invalidated, and also that *main contract* provisions which purport merely to impose a trust on retention moneys or other unpaid balances in favour of the main contractor without any express provision for their setting aside in identifiable form seem open to doubt under this principle, since although there is no overt mention of the owner's insolvency, there seems

---

[27] *Re Arthur Sanders Ltd.* (1981) 17 BLR 125, illustrated and doubted on other grounds *supra*, Section 3, para. 16·018.

[28] Discussed *supra*, Section 6(3), para. 16·031.

[29] See *supra*.

[30] See the discussion and cases *ante*, Chap. 8, Section 1(3), paras. 8·076–8·086, and Chap. 13, Section 5(2), paras. 13·121–13·129.

[31] *Re Jeavons, ex p. Mckay* (1873) L.R. 8 Ch.App. 643.

[32] *Ibid.*, at page 647, *per* James L.J.

[33] *British Eagle International Air Lines* v. *Cie Nationale Air France* [1975] 1 W.L.R. 758, 780G, *per* Lord Cross of Chelsea.

to be no other possible commercial objective of such a highly technical legal provision than its operation for the benefit of the contractor in the event of the owner's insolvency. Where, however, there is express provision for a physical setting aside of separate funds subject to the trust, this may be less objectionable, it is suggested, since it offers an immediate security for the contractor provided by the owner before any question of insolvency arises, and will be clearly separated from the contractor's other funds so that creditors will not be misled as to the extent of the funds or assets of the contractor.

This first route of invalidation will also be the basis for avoiding termination clauses which are expressly conditioned on insolvency *simpliciter*, and was also the expressed basis for Thean J.'s invalidation of that part of a payment direct clause in a Singaporean contract where the power was conditioned expressly on insolvency rather than upon failure of prior payment.[34]

16·057 The second route by which a provision may be invalidated may be described as the statutory route, and applies where the effect of operating an otherwise unobjectionable contractual provision in the circumstances which have arisen will be to defeat the statutory requirement of *pari passu* distribution of an insolvent debtor's assets between his creditors, and which has been expressed in very similar wording in the insolvency legislation of most Commonwealth jurisdictions.[35] Here the contractual provision will not be inherently offensive, and may be inserted into the contract for different and fully justifiable commercial reasons, so that the element of deliberate intent to subvert the insolvency rules will be absent.[36] In such cases, while the provision's operation prior to insolvency will not be avoided, its implementation after that date will not be permitted. Invalidation by this route has been applied to defeat a contractually agreed set-off by the creditor of third parties' claims against the debtor;[37] to defeat set-off by an owner of money paid direct to unpaid sub-contractors;[38] and to defeat contractually declared trusts in retention moneys where no application had yet been made to set funds aside in a separate account, as required by the contract, by the time the main contractor had gone into liquidation.[39]

16·058 It may be added[40] that the validity of the express trusts now commonly imposed on the retention or other moneys due from the owner by the English main and sub-contract standard forms does not appear to have

---

[34] *Joo Yee Construction Ltd.* v. *Diethelm Industries* [1990] 2 M.L.J. 66, illustrated *ante*, para. 13·126. See also *Perar B.V.* v. *General Surety Ltd.* (1994) 66 BLR 72, C.A. where no point was taken on the RIBA/JCT "automatic termination" clause.

[35] For the English provisions see the reference *supra*, para. 16·044, note 3.

[36] See for this distinction between the two routes, *per* Lord Cross of Chelsea in the *British Eagle* case, [1975] 1 W.L.R. 758, 780G, *supra*, para. 16·056.

[37] *British Eagle* case *supra*.

[38] *Joo Yee Construction* case *supra*, illustrated *ante*, Chap. 13, Section 5(2), para. 13·126.

[39] *Re Jartay Developments Ltd.* (1982) 22 BLR 134 (Nourse J.); and see *MacJordan Construction Ltd.* v. *Brookmount Erostin Ltd.* (1990) 56 BLR 1.

[40] See also the discussion *supra*, Subsections (5) and (6), and *ante*, Chap. 8, Section 1(3), paras. 8·082 *et seq*, and Chap. 13, para. 13·127.

been seriously challenged under the first insolvency invalidation principle stated *supra*, notwithstanding the *British Eagle* case, and must now be regarded as having been accepted by the English Court of Appeal, albeit in default of the contrary argument suggested by that case.[41] Where plaintiffs have failed in their attempts to enforce such provisions this has been solely because of express contractual reservations of prior rights of recourse by the owner in cases where there has been contractor or subcontractor default.[42]

A broad reconsideration by the House of Lords of the validity, in the light of the *pari passu* principle in insolvency, of forfeiture provisions conditioned on insolvency (or on the appointment of both administrators and administrative receivers); of the provisions imposing express trusts on the main contractor's beneficial interest in sums due from the owner to be found in both main and sub-contracts; and of the "pay direct" provisions in main contracts, would now seem overdue, it is submitted. It seems clear that any final view must ultimately depend on policy considerations.

SECTION 8. BANKRUPTCY OF ARCHITECT OR ENGINEER

The employment of an architect or engineer to carry out professional services clearly involves his personal skill, so that the contract will not vest in or be enforceable by the trustee,[43] unless the A/E is willing to carry out and complete the contract himself.[44]   **16·059**

However, the trustee may himself sue for work done or for breach of contract prior to the bankruptcy.[45] Moreover, while it is a common law rule of bankruptcy that personal earnings or salaries will not vest in the trustee to the extent that they are reasonably necessary for the support of the bankrupt and his family,[46] this would appear to have applied principally to contracts *of service*, so that the right to remuneration of an architect and surveyor who had prepared plans and acted as architect after his bankruptcy, and to damages for breach, did vest in the trustee.[47]

Section 310 of the 1986 Act now extends the trustee's power to obtain an order of the Court attaching earnings beyond those available to him under Section 51 of the Act of 1914, by enabling him to apply for an   **16·060**

---

[41] *Rayack Construction Ltd.* v. *Lampeter Meat Co. Ltd.* (1979) 12 BLR 30 (Vinelott J.); *Re Arthur Sanders Ltd.* (1981) 17 BLR 125 (Nourse J.); *Concorde Construction Co. Ltd.* v. *Colgan Co. Ltd.* (1984) 29 BLR 120, H.K. H.C.; *Wates Construction (London) Ltd.* v. *Franthom Property Ltd.* (1991) 53 BLR 23, C.A.; *J. Finnegan Ltd.* v. *Ford Sellar Morris Developments Ltd.* (1991) 53 BLR 38.

[42] *Henry Boot Building Ltd.* v. *Croydon Hotel and Leisure Co. Ltd.* (1987) 36 BLR 41, C.A.; *Hsin Chong Construction Co. Ltd.* v. *Yaton Realty Co. Ltd.* (1986) 40 BLR 119, H.K. H.C.

[43] *Knight* v. *Burgess* (1864) 33 L.J. Ch. 727, illustrated *ante*, Chap. 14, para. 14·007.

[44] For the principle see *ante*, Chap. 14, Section 1(2), paras. 14·004 *et seq*, and see *supra*, para. 16·004.

[45] *Bailey* v. *Thurston & Co. Ltd.* [1903] 1 K.B. 137.

[46] *Re Roberts* [1900] 1 Q.B. 122, and see now Section 310(2) of the 1986 Act.

[47] *Emden* v. *Carte* (1881) 17 Ch.D. 169; affd. 17 Ch.D. 768, C.A.

"income payments order", which by Section 310(7) will extend not only to payments "in the nature of income" comparable to those covered by the 1914 Act, but also to "any payment in respect of the carrying on of any business", which will clearly apply to an A/E's professional earnings and fees in private practice, it is submitted. This subsection also serves to resolve a doubt which had existed in relation to an A/E's earnings under a partnership agreement.[48]

The general effect of the A/E's bankruptcy upon a construction contract will therefore be slight. The owner will be adequately safeguarded if, after notice of presentation of a petition, he pays all further fees due to the bankrupt either to, or in accordance with the directions of, the receiver or trustee.

SECTION 9. PRIORITY OF EARLIER ASSIGNEES OF MONEYS DUE

16·061   It frequently happens in a contractor's insolvency that he will have previously assigned moneys due or to become due under the contract to some other person. Assuming notice to have been given to the owner, the assignment will be valid as against the trustee to the extent that money has *actually been earned* by the doing of work before the insolvency, even if the money is not yet payable under the contract at that date. So in a typical construction contract the right to retention moneys and the value of work done up to the date of the bankruptcy or liquidation will effectively pass to a prior assignee for value as against the trustee or liquidator. To the extent that this will not suffice to meet the claims of the assignee under the transaction giving rise to the assignment, he will be obliged to prove in the insolvency for damages for breach of that transaction.

ILLUSTRATIONS

(1) Lessees of the Alexandra Palace made arrangements with a railway company for collection of admission money from passengers, under which the lessees were entitled to receive a certain proportion of the sums collected. Later the lessees assigned the receipts "due and hereafter becoming due" under the agreement with the railway company by way of security for a loan. The lessees subsequently went into liquidation. *Held*, by the Court of Appeal, that the assignees were entitled to the receipts until the date of the liquidation, but the trustee was entitled to the receipts after that date. *Per* Jessel M.R.: "Then it is said that the Respondents are claiming under a mortgage or assignment made to them by the bankrupts before the bankruptcy. The answer to that is, that by no assignment or charge can a bankrupt give a good title as against his trustee to profits of his business accruing after the commencement of the bankruptcy. The bankrupt cannot as against the trustee assign these profits; they are not his property." *Per* Lindley L.J.: "It is an

---

[48] See *Re Rogers, ex p. Collins* [1894] 1 Q.B. 425, 431.

agreement to assign ... not property [of the assignors], but money which would become due to them under the arrangement ... is that an equitable assignment which can prevail against the title of the trustee in the bankruptcy? It is a mere agreement, for the breach of which no doubt an action would lie, but which cannot prevail against the title of the trustee so far as regards payments received ... after his title accrued. Those payments became due to the trustee": *Ex p. Nichols, Re Jones* (1883).[49]

(2) Shipbuilders charged the final instalment due when the ship was completed with repayment of two debts owing by them. At the time they had done six-sevenths of the work but been paid only five-sevenths of the price. They went bankrupt and the ship was completed by the trustee, who was able to complete for less than the final instalment after deduction of the amounts charged, which were placed in a joint account and claimed by the trustee. *Held*, by the Divisional Court, that the ground of the decision in *Ex p. Nichols* was that the sum assigned had not been earned at the time of the charge.[50] Here the charge was upon the margin between the work done and the work paid for, which had actually been earned at the time of the charge, and was good against the trustee in bankruptcy. *Per* Mathew J.: "It was admitted in the course of argument that if the margin had been created in the way in which a margin sometimes comes into existence under a building contract, *viz.* by the reservation of a certain percentage of each instalment, if such a reservation had been made and the sum so reserved was not to be payable until some time after the completion of the work, it could not be questioned that a valid charge might be made upon that margin as a subject of property": *Ex p. Moss, Re Toward* (1884).[51]   **16·062**

(3) Builders under a contract which provided for 20 per cent. retention payable on completion, assigned a part of the retention moneys due or which might become due as security for a debt. They filed their petition at a time when the work was approximately three-quarters complete, but the retention moneys on the work done exceeded the amounts assigned. The trustee completed at a cost of approximately £4,000 using his own or the creditors' funds, and to pay for which there were no assets available except the retention monies. *Held*, by the Court of Appeal, (distinguishing *Tooth* v. *Hallett* (1869)[52] on the ground that there the contract had been determined and the trustee had completed under a new contract) that the assignment was good against the trustee: *Drew* v. *Josolyne* (1887).[53]

The above cases do not, however, state very clearly the reason for this rule, by contrast with the numerous other areas where a bona fide transaction for value before the insolvency has been given full effect, including an equitable assignment of after-acquired chattels which was apparently held valid.[54] It may be that the reason for the rule is pragmatic, on the basis that trustees or liquidators would almost never continue to perform a contract if the benefit of any further expenditure was to go to prior assignees of moneys due. However, there is no doubt as to the expressed basis of the   **16·063**

---

[49] 22 Ch.D. 782, 786, 787.
[50] The decision had actually referred to the date of the *liquidation*.
[51] 14 Q.B.D. 310.
[52] L.R. 4 Ch.App. 242, illustrated *ante*, Chap. 14, para. 14·050.
[53] 18 Q.B.D. 590, illustrated more fully *ante*, Chap. 14, para. 14·043.
[54] See, *per* Lindley L.J. in *Ex p. Nichols* (1883) 22 Ch.D. 782, 786.

cases, with Sir George Jessel M.R.'s statements of the rule cited and followed by Mathew J. in *Ex p. Moss.*

It should not be forgotten, however, that an assignee takes subject to equities, so that if the owner validly exercises a right to terminate the contract on the failure of the builder, completion of the work for the owner by a third person cannot perfect the assignee's right to the retention or other moneys, as would a completion under the contract.[55] In any event, an assignee takes subject to equities, and in such a situation would be exposed to any owner's cross-claim for damages up to, but not exceeding the amount due.[55a] Normally, however, continuing to completion by a trustee or liquidator will, in the absence of contrary indication, suggest both adoption of the contract on the trustee's part and non-exercise of any power of termination on the part of the owner, in which event the cases show that prior assignees, provided their claims relate to work done before the insolvency, will to that extent defeat a trustee's or liquidator's title to payments made by the owner.[56]

---

[55] *Tooth* v. *Hallett* (1869) L.R. 4 Ch.App. 242.
[55a] See *ante*, Chap. 14, paras. 14·049 *et seq.*
[56] *Drew* v. *Josolyne, supra.*

CHAPTER 17

BONDS AND GUARANTEES

SECTION 1. GENERALLY

This chapter is concerned with the interpretation and enforcement of the **17·001** guarantees, frequently described as and given in the form of bonds, which in the special context of construction contracts may either be provided as a result of collateral arrangements or side agreements, or which may be referred to or required to be provided by the terms of the construction contract itself. While the principal class of such guarantees or bonds will be for "due performance" of their work and of their comprehensive contractual obligations by main contractors or sub-contractors in favour of owners or main contractors respectively (usually referred to as "performance bonds") bonded owners' and main contractors' payment or repayment obligations, while less common, are by no means unusual, particularly in international contracts.

As in the case of all contracts of guarantee, in the absence of express contrary indication there will be an implied right of indemnification by the guarantor or bondsman against the principal debtor whose performance has been guaranteed, should the liability under the guarantee or bond be enforced.[1] In consequence, the only practical risk undertaken by a bondsman or guarantor is the *financial insolvency* of the principal debtor when called upon to meet the contractual obligations which have been guaranteed. Thus, in a case where a bondsman was alleging a duty on the part of the creditor obligee (that is, owner) to disclose information to the bondsman indicating the physical difficulties of a particular project, Lord Atkin said:

> "For myself, I doubt on the course of business alone whether a [commercial] guarantor looks further than the skill and experience of the contractor to guard against risk of unknown difficulties in the performance of such a contract. *The guarantors are in such a case primarily concerned with the financing ability of the contractors to complete the contract, whether it results in loss or not.*"[2]

17·002   It is this limited degree of protection which should be weighed carefully by owners or other creditors against the cost of the bond which, in the case of a contractor's obligations, must inevitably enter into the contract price payable by the owner. On the other hand, as well as against the insured himself, the guarantor's right of counter-indemnity will, other things being equal, mean that the cost of a bond or commercial guarantee should be considerably less than the cost of insurance, particularly in those cases, such as joint insurance, where rights of subrogation against another defaulting party, would not be available to an insurer.

This essentially limited protection appears to have been better understood in England and the Commonwealth, where the use of contractors' performance bonds, even in public contracts, is by no means universal, and is in any case likely to be limited to a traditionally small proportion of the contract sum, normally 10 per cent.; whereas in the United States and Canada the commercial bonding industry appears to have succeeded in persuading government and public owners into almost universal requirements of bonding of a wide number of the obligations associated with

---

[1] See *Chitty on Contracts* (26th ed.), para. 5065.
[2] *Trade Indemnity Co. Ltd.* v. *Workington Harbour & Dock Board* [1937] A.C. 1, 17–18, illustrated *infra*, para. 17·027.

construction projects, such as bid bonds and the compulsory bonding required by some owners of their main contractors' liabilities to all their sub-contractors,[3] with the owner named in some cases as obligee and trustee for the sub-contractors. (This latter type of bond no doubt a response to the risks posed to owners by unpaid sub-contractors exercising their remedies under mechanics' lien legislation). Moreover, in the case of performance bonds these are not infrequently required in North America to be bonded in larger amounts, sometimes equal to the full contract price. The earlier emergence of this substantial commercial bonding industry in North America explains the large number of English reported cases where the commercial bondsman is a United States or Canadian company.

Since the tenth edition of this book in 1970, a quite new form of "on demand" contractor's performance bond (enforceable by simple demand or "call" and without proof of default, unlike traditional performance bonds) has become widely marketed by financial institutions, particularly by banks in the international contracting field. As explained in Section 3 *infra*, due to the probable presence of a number of participating and separately charging financial institutions, though with only one effectively at risk under these arrangements (and that one with instant recourse, in the event of a call, to the bank account of the principal debtor) it again seems doubtful whether international construction owners, despite the superficial attractions of such arrangements, have made any sufficient analysis of their advantages weighed against their cost, which again must inevitably enter into the contract price and so be borne in the last resort by the owner. The historical and commercial background of both traditional and the new demand bonds is discussed in some detail in C.C.P.P.,[4] as well as in Section 3 *infra*. **17·003**

(1) Terminology

For the benefit of non-legal readers who may find the terminology used in the cases and text-books in this context difficult or confusing, the following terms may be variously used and should be regarded as largely synonymous: **17·004**

- (a) "guarantee" or "bond";
- (b) "guarantor", "surety", "bondsman", "obligor", (and in the case of some "on demand" or letter of credit situations "bank" or "issuing bank");
- (c) "(principal) creditor", "obligee" and, in some "on demand" situations, "beneficiary" (who in the case of performance as opposed to payment bonds will normally be the construction owner, or in the case of some sub-contracts the employing main contractor);

---

[3] See, for a modern example in Canada, *Citadel General Assurance Company* v. *Johns-Mansville Canada Inc.* [1983] 1 S.C.R. 513, illustrated *infra*, para. 17·032.

[4] Para. 19–16, and see paras. 19–21—19–27.

(d) "(principal) debtor", that is, the party whose obligation is guaranteed, so that in performance bonds this will be the contractor or sub-contractor; and

(e) "sight", "unconditional", "confirmed", "irrevocable", "first demand" or "on demand", which have been variously employed by commercial draftsmen outside the construction field in the past to indicate that proof of substantive default under the principal contract is not required for the enforcement of the bond obligation. Unconditional and conditional obligations or bonds are sometimes also referred to as being "single" or "double" respectively.

The expressions "unconditional" or "on demand" are generally used in this book to denote obligations of this latter kind.[5] The underlying guaranteed contract, as opposed to the contract of guarantee, is called the "principal" contract, and is often so described in the bond or guarantee, as also the "principal" creditor or debtor under that contract.

(2) Types of Obligation Guaranteed

17·005 Guarantees associated with construction contracts can be of various kinds. The commoner types include:

(a) Guarantees of the *payment* obligations of a contracting party owed by him in respect of the work or goods to be carried out or supplied by the other party. In the case of construction contracts, this will normally be the owner's obligation, but as previously stated bonds are quite commonly required from main or prime contractors in North America, with the owner as nominal obligee and trustee for due payment by the main contractor of all sub-contractors collectively, and will by various means be drafted so as to be enforceable on behalf of any individual unpaid sub-contractor.[6] Bonds may also be required to cover any *repayment* obligations of a main contractor (as, for example, of advance payments such as are quite commonly made by owners to contractors at the commencement of a project with a view to their progressive repayment by deduction from sums due as work progresses,[7] or as an alternative to retention deductions under some modern Australian contracts.[8]

---

[5] For these see *infra*, Section 3, and C.C.P.P., paras. 19–16—19–27.

[6] See, *e.g. Citadel General Assurance Co.* v. *Johns-Mansville Canada Inc.* [1983] 1 S.C.R. 513, *supra.*

[7] See, *e.g.* the recent important case in England of *Mercers Company* v. *New Hampshire Insurance Company* [1992] 1 W.L.R. 792; [1992] 3 All E.R. 57; [1992] 2 Lloyd's Rep. 365, illustrated *infra*, para. 17·013.

[8] See *Australasian Conference Association Ltd.* v. *Mainline Constructions Pty. Ltd. (in liq.)* (1979) 53 A.L.J.R. 66, *Woodfall Ltd.* v. *Pipeline Authority* (1979) 53 A.L.J.R. 487, and Dorter & Sharkey, *Building & Construction Contracts in Australia*, pp. 480–494 and a number of subsequent cases, such as *Hughes Brothers* v. *Telede Ltd.* (1989) 8 A.C.L.R. 22.

(b) Guarantees of compliance with some other specific and limited obligation (such as bid bonds, common in the United States).

(c) Guarantees of due and comprehensive performance by the contractor of all his various contractual obligations owed in return for the contract price. These include the classical *conditional* "performance bonds", enforceable against the bondsman only on sufficient proof by the owner both of default by the contractor and of damage incurred by the owner up to the amount of any limit on the bond. These have been a century-old feature of contracts in the English and Commonwealth construction field, emerging originally in civil engineering contracts, possibly because of the prevalence of public owners in such contracts. Thus, traditionally the English civil engineering standard forms have by their terms contemplated, while not positively requiring, the probable post-contract provision of such a bond by the contractor,[9] with a form of bond for this purpose available as a part of the ICE standard form documentation, for example. It is with this type of "conditional" bond that Sections 1 and 2 of the present Chapter are principally concerned.

17·006

However, as stated *supra*, unconditional or on demand bonds, enforceable without proof of default, began to emerge in commerce in the early 1970s, and while these are frequently described in the construction industry as "on demand performance bonds", this is in reality a misnomer, since the reference in their description, and indeed in the wording of the bond, to "performance" is cosmetic only and, subject only to proof of fraud, their enforceability depends only upon a demand or call, irrespective of its accuracy or justification, provided that the call itself complies with the precise terms contemplated by the bond or instrument of guarantee.[10] Thus, in cases where any breach of contract is in reality non-existent, it has been authoritatively (and justifiably) stated: "The performance guarantee then bears the colour of a discount on the price of 10 per cent. or 5 per cent. or as the case may be ... So, as one takes instance after instance, these performance guarantees are virtually promissory notes payable on demand."[11]

These latter are considered in section 3 *infra*.

(3) Form of Traditional Bond

(a) Bond effectively a guarantee

The essence of a conditional bonding obligation is a simple undertaking to be answerable for the damage suffered by the creditor if the obligations of

17·007

---

[9] See, *e.g.* Clause 10 of the older ICE Contracts.
[10] See, for two examples on each side of the line in the same case, *I.F. Contractors Ltd. (formerly GKN Contractors Ltd.)* v. *Lloyds Bank Plc.* (1990) 51 BLR 1, C.A., *infra*, para. 17.066.
[11] *Edward Owen Engineering Ltd.* v. *Barclays Bank International Ltd.* [1978] Q.B. 159, 170, *per* Lord Denning M.R.

the debtor which are to be guaranteed are not performed. The ultimate liability to pay damages arises inevitably, because the obligation guaranteed is performance of services rather than payment of money, and because it is not without more intended that the bondsman or guarantor should have the right to perform himself. All that is needed to confer the required protection on a construction owner, for example, is a single sentence: "I hereby guarantee to you Y. the due performance by X. of his contract with you dated ... [My maximum liability under this guarantee shall be £...]".

The almost universal practice of commercial bondsmen, however, is to clothe this essentially very simple legal obligation in the jargon of an eighteenth-century English bond. The form of wording purports on its face to create an immediate monetary debt binding on the bondsman in favour of the obligee in the amount of the bond, and then to provide for future release of that debt and the end of the obligation under the bond either upon payment of the bond, or upon final performance of his guaranteed obligations by the debtor. It may be speculated that this negative description of the surety's obligation was an early lawyer's device used at a time when the concept of a law of contract with a simple consensual base was undeveloped, while the concept of debt rather than contract was more easily acceptable to legal theory. It may also have had to do with avoiding the difficulties of defining precisely the consideration needed to create a binding contract as between the obligor and obligee under the bond, since the bond would be furnished at the request of, and any payment for the bond made by the principal debtor, and not by the obligee creditor.[12] A further oddity of the wording is that it states that the entire sum bonded is, or becomes due upon breach, without qualification as to the gravity or extent of that breach. This is, however, misleading, since the draftsman seems to have taken advantage of old law which held that such a provision would be a "penalty", leaving the owner to prove his actual damage, and equity restrained recovery of the full bonded sum unless damage was proved to reach or exceed that sum.[13]

17·008   There is little doubt that this continued use by commercial bondsmen of wording likely to be difficult or incomprehensible even to many lawyers is no accident.[14] Nor should it be thought that this language of bonds has the approval of lawyers or judges. Thus, as long ago as 1915 in the Court of Session, and in 1937 in the English House of Lords, its continued use was noted with strong disapproval in passages which, until their appearance in C.C.P.P. in 1986, appeared to have escaped the attention of virtually all the textbooks. So, where the surety of a construction contractor had sought to argue that the bond contract was one of insurance, thus importing a duty of disclosure to the surety of known risks by the owner obligee, one of the greatest English judges said of the traditional form of bond:

---

[12] Further discussed *infra*, Subsection (5), para. 17·017/8.
[13] See the Note by J. L. Barton in (1976) 92 L.Q.R. 20–26.
[14] See for one use in which it may have been put in order to reduce the bondsman's responsibility C.C.P.P., para. 19–17.

"I entertain no doubt that this was a guarantee, and the rights of the parties should be regulated on that footing. I may be allowed to remark that it is difficult to understand why businessmen persist in entering upon considerable obligations in old-fashioned forms of contract which do not adequately express the true transaction ... Why insurance of credits or contracts, if insurance is intended, or guarantees of the same, if guarantees are intended, should not be expressed in appropriate language, passes comprehension. It is certainly not the fault of lawyers."[15]

Similarly, as early as 1915, a Scottish judge, referring to a Canadian bond company's use of the traditional form of wording, said:

17·009

"The surety bond is in English form and is somewhat confusing to the Scottish mind, as it seems most unnecessarily involved, and instead of going straight to the point, to turn things upside down, but I have no doubt that there is some reason for its form."[16]

Again, in a modern Hong Kong Court of Appeal case, after citing the foregoing observation by Lord Atkin, Hunter J.A. said:

"We echo these words. It is lamentable that an eighteenth-century English concept should be used in this jurisdiction to confuse everybody, as we think it has confused a lot of people in this case."[17]

As it happened, the confusion caused by the "upside down" language of the traditional wording in that case enabled an ingenious point on onus of proof to be taken *against* a bondsman.

ILLUSTRATION

A traditional 10 per cent. performance bond entered into jointly and severally by the contractor and a bondsman provided, in the English form, that the condition of the bond was that if the contractor were to duly perform and observe all the conditions of the construction contract, or if on default the surety should satisfy and discharge the damage sustained by the employer up to the amount of the bond, the bond should be null and void, *but otherwise remain in full force and effect.* A dispute arose at the beginning of a contract and the owners eventually dismissed the contractor, alleging repudiatory conduct which they had accepted. The owners then proceeded for summary judgment against the bondsman for the amount of the bond and the bondsman, having failed to obtain summary judgment in third party proceedings on his indemnity against the contractor, sought leave to defend against the owner. The owner contended that by virtue of the form of the wording the onus of proof was *on the bondsman* to prove that there had been no default or dam-

---

[15] *Per* Lord Atkin in *Trade Indemnity Co. Ltd.* v. *Workington Harbour and Dock Board* [1937] A.C. 1, 17. Illustrated *infra*, para. 17·027.

[16] *Per* Lord Johnson in *Clydebank & District Water Trustees* v. *Fidelity and Deposit Co. of Maryland* 1915 S.C. 362, 372, Ct. of Sess.; 1916 S.C., H.L., 69. Illustrated *infra*, para. 17·030.

[17] *Tins Industrial* case (1987) 42 BLR 110, 120, illustrated *infra*, and citing and approving C.C.P.P. para. 19·03. See also Parker L.J.'s strictures on the archaic wording of the bond in the *Mercers'* case quoted *infra*, Subsection (6), para. 17·019.

age. *Held*, by the Hong Kong Court of Appeal, applying statements by Greer L.J. in *Workington Harbour & Dock Board* v. *Trade Indemnity (No. 2)*,[18] and by Lord Atkin in the House of Lords, that a plaintiff bringing an action on a bond in this form must, nevertheless, prove both breach by the principal debtor and damage incurred; but that since there was clearly a dispute as to this there must be leave to defend: *Tins Industrial Co. Ltd.* v. *Kono Insurance Ltd.* (1987).[19]

17·010   Since their early introduction in the industry a further common characteristic of traditional contractors' due performance bonds has been that the contractor, as principal debtor, is often made a party to the bond and accepts joint and several liability under the bond with the surety, as in the above case,[20] and in the 1937 *Trade Indemnity* case in the House of Lords from which a part of Lord Atkins speech has been quoted *supra*. Conversely, in earlier times the surety might even be joined as a party to the construction contract.[20a] It seems likely that the main objective of this practice was to facilitate the bondsman's pursuit of his indemnity against the contractor if called on to pay under bond. Having regard to the law relating to the effect and enforcement of guarantees generally, discussed in Subsection (4) *infra*, it otherwise seems otiose. The origin of the practice may also have been administrative convenience in reducing the number of documents requiring to be prepared under seal, having regard to the three different underlying contracts, and the questions of limitation and of consideration involved, as to which see further *infra* subsection 5.

Seemingly unaware that this was and remains the general practice of many if not most bonding companies at the present day, both Parker and Scott L.JJ. in a very recent case in the Court of Appeal appear to have thought that the expression of the liability of surety and principal debtor under the bond as being joint and several created a difficulty in treating the bondsman's obligation as that of a guarantor, apparently with possible substantive consequences when considering arguments for release of the bondsman following breaches of contract by the creditor or his making agreed alterations of the underlying principal contract's obligations.[21]

---

[18] [1937] 3 All E.R. 39.

[19] 42 BLR 110. Hunter J.A. at page 120 expressly approved the above analysis of the nature of a bond and explanation of the eighteenth-century wording (cited at that time from C.C.P.P., para. 19–03).

[20] Compare the ICE fourth edition form of bond dating from 1955 and repeated in 1973, the Trade Indemnity case in 1937 illustrated *infra*, para. 17·027, and see the bonds in many construction cases in Australia and in the *Tins Industrial* case in Hong Kong *supra*.

[20a] For early examples of contractor joinder to a performance bond, see *Calvert* v. *London Dock* (1838) 2 Keen 638; and *Stiff* v. *Eastbourne Local Board* (1868) 26 L.T. 339; illustrated *infra*, para. 17·026, and for a case of the bondsman being joined to the construction contract itself, see *Kingston-upon-Hull Corporation* v. *Harding* [1892] 2 Q.B. 494, illustrated *infra*, para. 17·024.

[21] See, *per* Parker and Scott L.JJ. in *Mercers Co.* v. *New Hampshire Insurance Company* [1992] 2 Lloyd's Rep. 365, 369, 375, illustrated *infra*, para. 17·013.

It is submitted that where, as is usually the case in construction contracts, the obligation to be guaranteed arises under a separate contract between the principal debtor and creditor, the fact that *the liability to pay under the bond* may be expressed to be joint and several by the surety and debtor, although discharged by unilateral due performance on the part of the debtor, is not the same thing as *joint liability under the principal contract*, and so is in no way inconsistent with the surety's true status as a guarantor. If this view is correct, no practical significance should attach to the presence of the principal debtor as an additional party liable under the bond in cases where it is the rights and liabilities *inter se* of the bondsman and obligee creditor which are in issue. The practice has been consistent from earliest times and has not previously been commented on in the courts.

17·011

(b) The *Trafalgar House* case

Subsection 3(a) *supra* was written prior to a very recent decision of the Court of Appeal in 1994 which may, if upheld, call for considerable modification of the views previously expressed.

17·011A

Notwithstanding Lord Atkin's clear statement as to a contractor's performance bond worded in the English form: "I entertain no doubt that this was a guarantee, and the rights of the parties should be regulated on that footing",[21a] and, notwithstanding nearly a century of case-law in which the English courts have invariably treated such bonds without comment as requiring proof both of default by the debtor and damage incurred by the creditor, and in the face of a clear statement by Lord Diplock (expressed, however, in relation to ordinary contracts of guarantee rather than bonds in the English form) that the creditor's cause of action against the guarantor arises at the moment of the debtor's default without need for notice or demand,[21b] what seems to be a very different view as to the meaning and effect of the traditional bond wording has recently been put forward as the basis for an interlocutory decision in the English Court of Appeal.

ILLUSTRATIONS

Major sub-contractors provided main contractors with a traditional 10 per cent. due performance bond in the usual English form, entered into jointly by the sub-contractors and the bondsman. By its terms, liability under the bond was to be null and void if all terms and conditions of the sub-contract were duly performed "or if, *on default by the sub-contractor*, the surety *shall satisfy the damages sustained by the main contractor thereby* up to the amount of the bond",[21c] but otherwise it was to remain in full force and effect. The sub-contractors went into receivership and the main contractors, after terminating the sub-contract and completing the work, claimed summary judgment for the full amount of the bond. While a valid termination was not disputed, the bondsman sought leave to defend, arguing that there were substantial cross-claims by the sub-contractors for unpaid work and loss and expense claims, and that not until the full state of accounts was ascertained could the

17·011B

[21a] In the *Trade Indemnity* case, quoted more fully, *supra*, para. 17·008.
[21b] *Moschi* v. *Lep Air Services* [1973] A.C. 331, 348, (quoted *infra*, para. 17·021).
[21c] A standard form of wording, see the *Nene* case *infra*, para. 17·012A.

extent of the main contractor's damage (if any, which was denied) be established. The trial judge gave judgment for the full amount of the bond, having satisfied himself that there was no credible evidence of cross-claims sufficient to reduce liability below the amount of the bond. *Held*, by the Court of Appeal, that it was unnecessary to go into the question whether the main contractors had sustained damage at least equal to the amount of the bond, as the trial judge had done. Having regard to the relationship between a main contractor and sub-contractor, the purpose of a bond in this form, with the sub-contractors joined as a party and provision for its release in only one of two events, was not to provide a guarantee of the financial obligations of the sub-contractors, but to create an independent obligation of the surety to pay damages for any failure of the sub-contractor to perform, and to provide a security promptly realisable in the event of extra costs being incurred by the main contractor as a result of breach by the sub-contractors. It was implicit (distinguishing *Moschi* v. *Lep Air Services*) that a demand must be made by the main contractor to the bondsman before there could be liability to pay the damages but, provided that the demand stated the amount of damages and was made bona fide, there would be immediate liability in that amount, and the presence of cross-claims of any kind was irrelevant. *Per* Saville L.J.: "The obligation under the bond is to pay up to the total amount of the bond that which the main contractors assert in good faith is the amount of the damages." *Per* Beldam L.J.: "It seems to me implicit that the demand ... should state the amount of the damages sustained by the default, but because the main contractor must state the amount of the damages, it does not follow that the surety is entitled to question the amounts claimed by arguing *that they are excessive, or have not been incurred,* provided the statement of damage is made in good faith." *Per* Sir Thomas Bingham M.R.: " ... If one infers, as one must in order to envisage a workable procedure by which the main contractor can obtain payment, that he must make a demand on the Surety for the damage he claims to have suffered as a result of the sub-contractor's breach, *it seems appropriate to assimilate this with more familiar forms of on demand performance bond.* I accordingly conclude that the Surety is bound to pay that which the main contractor asserts in good faith to be the amount of the damages he has sustained, namely the additional expenditure the main contractor has incurred or will incur as a result of the Sub-Contractor's failure to perform or complete the contract." (Emphases supplied): *Trafalgar House Construction (Regions) Ltd.* v. *General Surety & Guarantee Ltd.* (1994).[21d]

It can be seen that the *Trafalgar House* case places an "on-demand" interpretation on the wording of the bond before the Court of Appeal, certainly in regard to the *quantum of damage* allegedly suffered and the immediate obligation of the bondsman to pay the sum demanded at once, and less certainly in regard to the existence of the breach of contract itself. This can justifiably be described as a startling interpretation, and it is understood that an appeal to the House of Lords is intended. If upheld, the decision can be confidently expected to lead to the rapid abandonment of traditional bond wording used since the inception of commercial surety-ship at the end of the nineteenth century, and indeed for many formally drafted contracts of guarantee for a century before that. This latter consequence is certainly to be welcomed, but notwithstanding that com-

[21d] 66 BLR 42 C.A.

mercial bondsmen's assiduity in seeking to avoid their obligations under their bonds will have left them with few friends, and that no-one could find fault with the result on the facts of the *Trafalgar House* case itself as found and applied by the trial judge, there are, it is submitted, substantial grounds for regarding the Court of Appeal's reasoning, and its interpretation of the traditional though difficult bond wording, as mistaken.

The judgments in the *Trafalgar House* case appear to centre on the **17·011C** Court's perception of the commercial exigencies of a construction subcontract, and in particular of the main contractor's perceived needs in that situation. Support for this interpretation is also said to be found in the "puzzling and difficult",[21e] "archaic and unsatisfactory",[21f] or "archaic, difficult and ill-suited to its purpose"[21g] wording, which Sir Thomas Bingham additionally considered it was desirable to assimilate with the on-demand bonds with which the Court was more familiar.[21h]

Dealing first with the view expressed as to the exigencies of a sub-contract situation requiring an unconditional sub-contractor liability to pay damages for breach of contract on demand by the main contractor, that could have been provided for in the sub-contract itself (as indeed it has been in some recent management contracts or sub-contracts discussed *ante* in Chapter 6),[21i] although few sub-contractors with anything like reasonable negotiating power will be likely to agree to such draconian terms. Moreover, the concern expressed for the main contractor's cashflow, particularly in Saville L.J.'s judgment, overlooks the fact that the Court's interpretation must inevitably imperil a solvent sub-contractor's cashflow if unjustified or excessive calls can be made on the bondsman (who, on being obliged to pay under the bond, will immediately obtain summary judgment on his indemnity against the solvent sub-contractor). The interpretation also overlooks the fact that precisely identical bond wording, *mutatis mutandis*, is to be found in the bonds furnished to owners by main contractors.[21j] Are the same considerations to apply to the owner's cash flow? On this point, the views expressed by the Court of Appeal give the appearance of being haphazardly one-sided and speculative, and principally dictated by the facts immediately before them.

Moreover, while it is perfectly possible for any contract of guarantee, particularly of a *payment* obligation, to be expressed so as to be unconditional in the sense of not permitting any set-off,[21k] (and so to have a wider effect than a strict guarantee to answer for the debts of another) a *per*-

---

[21e] *Per* Sir Thomas Bingham.
[21f] *Per* Saville L.J.
[21g] *Per* Beldam L.J.
[21h] See *supra*.
[21i] See *ante*, para. 6·204.
[21j] See the identical wording of the main contract bonds before Hunter J.A. in *Tins Industrial Co. Ltd.* v. *Kono Insurance Ltd.* (1987) 42 BLR 110 in Hong Kong; before Mocatta J. in *Nene Housing Society Ltd.* v. *National Westminster Bank Ltd.* (1980) 16 BLR 22, and in *Northwood Development Co.* v. *Aegon Insurance Ltd.* (1994), the latter cases both illustrated *infra*.
[21k] See, *e.g. Hyundai Heavy Industries Co.* v. *Papadopoulous* [1980] 1 W.L.R. 1129, and see also letters of credit generally.

formance bond or guarantee to pay damages sustained as a result of breach of the *performance* obligations of a contractor or sub-contractor in a construction project, as in the *Trafalgar House* case itself, must usually in a case of contractor or sub-contractor default involve examination of the state of the accounts between the parties when applying the basic principles of measure of damage for breach of contract; and will require a comparison with sums due had the contract been properly performed.[211] In uncompleted contracts this will involve comparing the total cost incurred by the owner in completing, including payments already made, against what would have been incurred had the contract been properly performed. In all cases, whether or not the breach is total or partial, if a contractor or sub-contractor is very substantially underpaid at the date of the breach, or is owed considerable sums by way of retention or under compensatory provisions in the contract which exceed the particular damage resulting from the breach (perfectly possible in construction contracts), the owner or main contractor is in all these cases in a position to recover damages from moneys already in hand, and has no practical or commercial need for recourse to any bondsman in such situations, since he already has the ample security of the money in his pocket. On the Court of Appeal's interpretation, however, the bondsman is bound to pay at once on demand if there has been a breach, whether total or partial, thus possibly providing an unnecessary and excessive compensation which will subsequently need to be repaid. (It is incidentally unclear what the bondsman's remedy will be to recover any sums so paid to the owner or main contractor in a case where no damage is ultimately suffered, but the debtor contractor or sub-contractor has subsequently become insolvent, rendering the bondsman's counter-indemnity of no practical value.)

17·011D   The usual commercial reason for requiring contractors or sub-contractors to provide due performance bonds, which is well understood in the construction industry, is the need of some (but by no means all) owners or main contractors to be assured of the ultimate financial ability or a contractor or sub-contractor whose credit may be in doubt to meet its contractual obligations, it is submitted.[21m] Anything more must result in a more expensive bond with, ideally, elaborate provisional repayment obligations in the event of nothing being ultimately found due. Unconditional performance bonds payable immediately on demand are still comparatively unusual in domestic construction contracts, though occasionally to be found, and have been more common in international contracts. Nevertheless, they have in general provoked intense opposition and concern in the industry, being justifiably seen by contractors and sub-contractors alike as easily open to what is often serious tactical abuse by irresponsible or fraudulent owners of such on-demand bonds or guarantees.[21n] Thus in

---

[211] See *ante*, Chap. 8, paras. 8·109 *et seq.*

[21m] See, *per* Lord Atkin, *supra*, para. 17·001.

[21n] See *infra*, para. 17·076. The on-demand reported cases are full of examples of such abuse, including the *Edward Owen* case itself, and illustrate the almost insuperable difficulties of the innocent party in obtaining relief in cases where such wording has been used. See further on this paras. 17·067–17·077 *infra*.

1992 the ICC, in response to fully justified contractor pressures, published an elaborate cross-indemnity scheme of contractual provisions designed to give protection from the abuses seen to arise from on-demand instruments in construction projects.[21o]

Responsible owners have also been advised against their use in C.C.P.P.[21p] The industry as a whole, it is suggested, are likely to find incomprehensible the Court of Appeal's apparent advocacy of an on-demand interpretation of performance bonds as meeting some perceived commercial need, whether of owners or of main contractors in sub-contract settings, for immediate payment of damages by contractors or sub-contractors, and without any examination of the state of accounts.

Turning to the wording of the bond itself, this differed from that in the *Trade Indemnity* case (where it had been expressly held by Lord Atkin to be a "guarantee") only by the inclusion of its second limb or condition "if on default by the Sub-Contractor the Surety shall satisfy and discharge the damages sustained by the Main Contractor as a result of breach by the Sub-Contractor", which follows immediately after the generalised undertaking of due performance of all obligations by the sub-contractor in the first limb. However, this particular second limb (which it has been seen is very widely used in bonds at the present-day) does no more than spell out precisely the practical implications of the surety's obligation, similar to those of any other guarantor of performance (as opposed to payment) obligations, should a contractor or sub-contractor fail to perform; in particular the wording cannot bear the on-demand or unconditional interpretation placed upon it, it is submitted.

It is to be noted that for some 60 years since Lord Atkin's criticism of the **17·011E** use of English formal bond wording in commercial suretyship contracts in the *Trade Indemnity* case, the English judiciary (partly perhaps because the critical passage in Lord Atkin's speech about the use of this form of wording does not appear to have been noticed in any textbook dealing with the subject until C.C.P.P. in 1986)[21q] seem to have shown little or no surprise at or interest in and to have attached no interpretative significance to the use of this particular form of wording, until Hunter J.A.'s comments in Hong Kong, noting the C.C.P.P. discussion, in the *Tins Industrial* case in 1987,[21r] and the later short comment of Parker L.J. in the *Mercers'* case in 1992.[21s] However, in the *Trafalgar House* case, the Court of Appeal proceeded to draw detailed attention to a number of characteristics of the bond wording which were said to cause them difficulty. Thus, the Court:—

(a) Noted the negative language used in regard to the two "conditions" of the bond, which the Court (obviously entirely correctly, and as had all other courts in the long history of this negative wording)

[21o] See *infra*, para. 17·077.
[21p] See C.C.P.P., paras. 19·26 *et seq.*
[21q] See C.C.P.P., para. 19·03.
[21r] See *supra*, para. 17·009.
[21s] Quoted *infra*, para. 17·019.

interpreted as expressing the positive obligations of the parties to the bond.

(b) Noted but decided to disregard the absence of provision for situations where the damage may be less than the amount of the bond (this is usually explained as due to the early draftsman's taking advantage of the rules, first of equity and then at law, preventing enforcement as a penalty beyond the actual damages suffered.)[21t]

(c) Emphasised (as Parker L.J. had done in the *Mercers'* case) the presence of the debtor as a party jointly liable under the bond as being of significance, and as indicating, for some reason, a wider independent obligation than a simple guarantee on the part of the surety. This last observation is very surprising since (it may be conjectured for a number of understandable administrative and legal reasons) joinder of the debtor as a party to a commercial surety's bond, though not strictly necessary, seems to have been the rule rather than the exception, certainly in construction contracts and again without attracting attention, since earliest times.[21u] Saville L.J.'s expressed surprise at the prospect of a sub-contractor "guaranteeing his own performance" overlooks this as well as the fact that the bond is under seal, whereas the sub-contract itself might not be.

Nevertheless, the Court of Appeal, by what seems a circular process of reasoning principally dictated by the desired result, then proceeded to hold, though the bond was entirely silent on the point, that an obligation to pay damages at once could not arise until there had been a demand by the creditor, *the need for which must be implied*, and then to interpret that *implied* demand as being the over-riding condition of the bond (at least as regards quantum), in the same way as an express "on demand" or "on first demand" or other similar stipulation over-rides the nominal requirement of due performance in an unconditional commercial contract of guarantee. This seems, with respect, an excessively contrived as well as circular argument, particularly in the face of unquestionable and convincing authority that a simple conditional guarantee does *not*, in the absence of express wording, require a demand.[21v] The only case cited in support of the Court of Appeal's interpretation was *Esal (Commodities) Ltd.* v. *Oriental Credit Ltd.*,[21w] which concerned an express "on written demand" commercial guarantee of a supplier's shipment obligations under an international agreement for the sale of bulk sugar.

[21t] See J. L. Barton's Note in (1976) 92 L.Q.R. pp. 20–26.
[21u] See *supra*, para. 17·010, and see for examples the leading cases of *Calvert* v. *London Dock* (1838) 2 Keen 638, *Northampton Gas Light Co.* v. *Parnell* (1855) 24 L.J.C.P. 60, *Stiff* v. *Eastbourne Local Board* (1868) 20 L.T. 339, and the *Trade Indemnity* case itself, as well as the *Nene, Tins Industrial, Northwood Development* and *Perar* cases *supra* and *infra*, para. 17·012A.
[21v] *Moschi* v. *Lep Air Services* [1973] A.C. 331, 348, quoted *infra*, para. 17·021.
[21w] [1985] 2 Lloyd's Rep. 546, illustrated *infra*, para. 17·065.

In summary it is submitted: **17·011F**

(a) That the Court of Appeal may have been right to doubt the rather oddly-expressed explanation by Lord Diplock in the *Moschi* case that contracts of guarantee generally are to be regarded as of a "see to" character,[21x] and that it is for that reason that they are enforceable against the guarantor without any need to join the debtor (which latter is undoubtedly the case, for whatever reason) immediately upon breach of the principal contract and without notice to the guarantor; but it does not follow, it is submitted, that because a guarantee or bond may expressly (or even impliedly) require notice to the guarantor before liability arises that the obligation undertaken ceases to be a "guarantee" or in the nature of a guarantee, and becomes something more onerous. (Notice to the bondsman was in fact never in issue in the *Trafalgar House* case, as the judgments recognise.)

(b) That the Court of Appeal's observations on the commercial exigencies of sub-contracts are mistaken, and that a guarantee of the debtor's ultimate solvency in meeting his obligations has through a long history of the decided cases been treated both by the construction industry and the Courts as the object and purpose of traditional performance bond guarantees (making no distinction hitherto between wording couched in the traditional "negative condition" language of a bond and wording which in positive terms guarantees due performance of the contractor's or sub-contractor's obligations). By contrast, so-called "on-demand" performance bonds are generally regarded in the industry as novel, controversial and in general to be avoided, if possible, as potentially open to serious abuse.

(c) That bonds in the English form which are conditioned only on due performance of contractual obligations by the principal debtor (and in particular non-payment obligations) should not be interpreted as other than a simple guarantee by the surety of the damages resulting from non-performance, in the absence of express wording providing for some additional "condition" of the bond other than due performance.

(d) This additional condition of the bond may be expressed to be a demand made by the creditor against the bondsman, or some other event, and depending on the wording may be interpreted as an over-riding or independent condition of the bondsman's liability to pay—hence Lord Denning's "new creature" description of "on-demand" performance bonds.

[21x] See *infra*, para. 17·021. The view was also rejected by Mason C.J. in *Sunbird Plaza Ltd.* v. *Maloney* (1988) 166 C.L.R. 245, noted by Philips' and O'Donovan's *The Modern Contract or Guarantee* (2nd ed.), p. 8.

(e) In the absence of any such additional overriding condition the bond
     will in principle and subject to express wording be enforceable
     immediately on default and damage being sustained, but subject,
     like any other claim based on breach of contract, to defences or
     set-offs available to the debtor.
(f) On application for summary judgment against the bondsman, suf-
     ficiently credible defences or set-offs by the debtor, if exceeding the
     amount claimed, should in principle secure leave to defend, or,
     where they do not, there should in an appropriate case be final judg-
     ment for part with leave to defend as to the remainder (or possibly,
     where there are difficulties of assessment, to final judgment for
     damages to be assessed).[21y]

(4) Enforcement of Bonds

17·012 It has been seen that, except in the case of unconditional guarantees, (and
subject to the *Trafalgar House* case, if upheld, in cases where traditional
English bond forms of wording have been used), the creditor, as against
the surety, needs to prove both breach by the debtor and damage. While
the liability of a guarantor is frequently and correctly described as secondary, since it arises only upon the default of the person primarily liable, that
is, the principal debtor, this does not mean that the creditor obligee need
pursue his remedies against the debtor in the first place, or even join him as
a co-defendant. Very often the creditor will prefer to proceed directly
against the surety alone following a default,[22] leaving the latter to decide
whether or not to join the debtor as a third party defendant to the surety's
claim for an indemnity, to which he will be entitled in the vast majority of
cases where he has furnished the guarantee at the request of the debtor.[23]
In the case of some construction contracts, however, unwise language in
the express remedies available under the contract to the owner for contractor default may prevent immediate recovery of damage, as, for example, the additional cost of completion by another contractor.[24] In such
cases it may depend on the wording of the bond whether the owner's rights
under the bond are precisely co-extensive with his strictly contractual
remedies (which will normally be the presumption in interpreting a performance bond) or whether the terms of the bond may permit an earlier
claim for damages against the surety.[25]

   Generally, however, only an express term of the bond can prevent the
creditor proceeding immediately against the surety (as, for example,

---

[21y] As in the *Northwood Development* case, see *infra*, para. 17·012A.
[22] See the perhaps doubtful legal explanation for this given by Lord Diplock in *Moschi* v. *Lep Air Services Ltd.* [1973] A.C. 331, 348, cited *infra*, Subsection (7), para. 17·021, but doubted by Mason C.J. *supra*.
[23] As to this see *Chitty on Contracts* (26th ed.), para. 5065.
[24] See this defect of draftsmanship discussed *ante*, Chap. 12, para. 12·074.
[25] As, *e.g.* in *Nene Housing Society Ltd.* v. *National Westminster Bank Ltd.* (1980) 16 BLR 22, illustrated *infra*.

express notice requirements to give the debtor or surety an opportunity to remedy a default, or requiring a claim or demand before liability will arise,[26] or an express right of the bondsman to take over and complete the contract himself, or the conditioning of the bond expressly on a judgment or award). Conversely, in all United States and Commonwealth jurisdictions a surety will not, in the absence of express provision, be bound by a judgment or award against the principal debtor,[27] making it advisable to join the surety in any such proceedings as a co-defendant.

Bondsmen habitually seek to postpone meeting their obligations under a bond for as long as possible. Provided the creditor is in a position to establish that there has been a breach or default and that at least some damage must inevitably have been incurred then, in the absence of express wording, it is submitted that he will to that extent be entitled to summary judgment up to the amount of the bond.

ILLUSTRATIONS

(1) By the terms of a main contractor's performance bond the surety was **17·012A** to be released if the contractor should duly perform all his contract obligations "or if on default by the Contractor the Surety shall satisfy and discharge the damages sustained by the [owners] ... ".[27a] A receiver of the contractor was appointed, and, by Clause 25(3) of the post-1963 RIBA/JCT contract, the contract was then "automatically determined" for that reason and not subsequently reinstated by the owners under the terms of that clause. It was admitted that prior to the termination there had been defective work in breach of contract, and that expenditure on the remedial work had exceeded the amount of the bond. Clause 25(3)(d) entitled the owners to recover the additional cost of completing by another contractor following automatic termination under the clause, the final sum due to the owner to be certified by the architect on completion. The bondsman contended that until practical completion and the issue of the architect's certificate under Clause 25(3)(d), nothing was due under the bond. *Held,* by Mocatta J., that on the admitted facts there had been earlier breaches and that the damage for repairing them had exceeded the amount of the bond, so that the absence of the architect's certificate on final completion was immaterial to the owners' claim under the bond: *Nene Housing Society* v. *National Westminster Bank Ltd.* (1980).[27b]

(2) Main contractors went into liquidation and their contract was terminated under a similar provision for automatic determination, subject to agreed reinstatement, to that in the RIBA/JCT forms. There was a performance bond, to be released on full compliance by the contractor with all his obligations "or if *on default* by the Contractors the Surety shall satisfy ... *the damages* sustained by the Employer". When sued the bondsman argued that there

---

[26] See the somewhat doubtful case of *Re Brown's Estate* [1893] 2 Ch. 300.
[27] *Re Kitchen* (1881) 17 Ch.D. 668; *Bruns* v. *Colocotronis ("The Vasso")* [1979] 2 Lloyd's Rep. 412; and see *Begley* v. *A.-G. of N.S.W.* (1910) 11 C.L.R. 43; *Powell River Paper Co.* v. *Wells Construction* [1912] 2 D.L.R. 340.
[27a] Compare the identical wording in the *Trafalgar House* bond *supra*, para. 17·011B.
[27b] (1980) 22 BLR 22.

was no liability, since the automatic determination following liquidation did not depend on breach of contract, and the use of the word "damages" in the bond showed that the "default and damages" there referred to meant a breach of contract. *Held* by Judge Havery Q.C., that while the insolvency of the contractor was not by itself a breach, there had been a failure to comply with a separate contractual obligation that all the work was to be carried out in accordance with the contract, and that the word "default" in the bond was wide enough to cover a failure to comply with all obligations whether or not the failure was due to a breach of contract, while the word "damages" was also wide enough to cover a loss resulting from a failure without any breach fully to comply with all obligations. *Held* further, in reply to the bondsman's argument that liability under the bond should await the calculation and certi-fication of the additional cost of completion together with the ascertainment of any set-offs available to the contractor as provided for in the automatic determination clause, and while rejecting the owner's claim that there should be immediate payment of the full amount of the bond, since certain categories of cross-claim, though not all, would be available as a set-off in such a case, that there should be final judgment for damages to be assessed: *Northwood Development Ltd.* v. *Aegon Insurance Ltd.* (1994).[27c]

[Note: It is not entirely clear from this judgment, but presumably the trial judge was satisfied that some set-offs would be available, though not sufficient to exceed the amount of the bond.

The bondsman's argument accepted by the Court in the above case was highly opportunistic, since the bond was in a common standard form in no way influenced by the unusual automatic termination wording of the par-ticular underlying principal contract, and the event which occurred, namely contractor insolvency resulting in inability to complete, was the obvious main intended target of the bond. The judge's decision to bring the contractor's insolvency within the ambit of the bond under its first due performance limb was justice-driven and understandable. However, the case was almost immediately overruled by a decision of the Court of Appeal in another case, which held that a bond in identical terms must be interpreted as conditioned only upon breach of contract, and that on the wording of the RIBA/JCT "automatic determination" clause, notwith-standing its expressly financial remedy for the owner exactly co-extensive with damages recoverable for breach, there was on analysis no breach of contract in the strict sense which could trigger the bondsman's liability.[27d] This decision robbed the bond of all commercial value and whether on a *contra proferentem* or officious bystander or business effi-cacy basis seems open to question.

(a) Breach by creditor

17·013   Enforcement against the surety may be complicated by a breach of the principal contract by the creditor. Where this is so, the surety will be dis-charged if the breach is such as to disentitle the creditor from suing the debtor, for example, for payment; *a fortiori*, of course, if the breach is repudiatory and has been so accepted by the debtor. Non-repudiatory breaches by the creditor will not, however, discharge the surety, it seems, unless, first, they are "not unsubstantial", and, secondly, the term which

---

[27c] (1994) (Unrep.).
[27d] *Perar B.V.* v. *General Surety & Guaranty Co. Ltd.* C.A. (1994) 66 BLR 72.

has been broken can be regarded as having been "embodied in" (that is, presumably, interpreted as being an essential condition of the original bond or guarantee.[28]

ILLUSTRATION

During negotiations prior to a construction contract in the RIBA/JCT form, it was agreed by a "side letter" that for tax reasons the owners would pay virtually the entire contract sum immediately upon signing the contract as an advance payment, and that this would be repaid progressively out of sums as they became due to the contractors for interim payment under the terms of the contract. This repayment obligation of the contractors was to be secured by a bond. The bond was executed in favour of the owners by the bondsman and contractors jointly and severally, but in fact some days before the final documents for the building contract were completed. After reciting the advance, the bond, which was in the archaic traditional English form, stated that the bondsman's obligation should be void if the advance "is liquidated in accordance with the terms and conditions of said contract and is faithfully employed for the purpose of said contract, but otherwise will remain in full force and effect". When the building contract was executed an agreed starting date some six weeks later was agreed and inserted in the documents, but in the event the owner was unable to give possession for a further three weeks, when the contractor started work without objection. Some nine months later the contractor went into receivership, and the contract was terminated with substantial repayments still owing, for which the owner proceeded against the bondsman. The latter successfully argued before the trial judge that the bond had been a guarantee of due performance of the building contract, and that, following *Holme* v. *Brunskill*[29] the parties' agreement to a later commencement date without his consent released the bondsman from all liability. *Held*, by the Court of Appeal, that the bond was not a guarantee of performance of the building contract, but only of the repayment obligation in the side letter. Moreover, on the facts there had been no agreement to vary the building contract, but only a breach by the owner of a contractual obligation which was neither substantial nor a condition of the bond so that, following *National Westminster Bank* v. *Riley*, the bondsman was not released. *Held*, also (Nolan J. dissenting) that the bondsman was liable in full and not released *pro tanto* to take account of any work which the contractor might otherwise have carried out prior to the termination had he started work on time. *Per* Scott L.J.: "It is not ... necessary to consider how ... the rule in *Holme* v. *Brunskill* would have applied in the present case. [Counsel] invites us to adopt the approach of certain United States authorities and to hold that, where the surety is a professional compensated surety, the discharge of the surety brought about by a variation of the principal contract should be *pro tanto* and not absolute. I was impressed by the commonsense of this transatlantic solution and by the undesirable rigidity of *Holme* v. *Brunskill* in its application to compensated sureties. I was not convinced that binding authority stands in the way of the adoption of this sensible solution in this country, but it is not necessary for us to decide the point in the present case": *Mercers Co.* v. *New Hampshire Insurance Ltd.* (1992).[30]

[Note: Despite disagreement expressed by Parker L.J., due to the presence of a joint and several obligation, there seems little doubt that this bond was

[28] *National Westminster Bank* v. *Riley* [1986] B.C.L.C. 268, C.A., followed in the *Mercers Co.* case illustrated *infra*.
[29] (1877) 3 Q.B.D. 495. For this aspect of law see *infra*, Section 2(6).
[30] [1992] 2 Lloyd's Rep. 365, 377.

indeed a guarantee, although only of the side letter repayment obligation and not of the building contract itself (which in spite of the quoted reference to it in the bond did not mention the repayment obligation). Joint and several liability of both surety and debtor has for nearly a century been a commonplace of due performance bonds in construction cases, which seems to have escaped Parker L.J.'s notice.[30a] While it is only possible to speculate, it seems highly likely that, despite the Court of Appeal's statement to the contrary, there had indeed been a variation of the building contract, since the overwhelming majority of parties in the particular situation which arose would agree a new completion date to take account of the delayed start, particularly in view of the well-known (and, it has been suggested elsewhere, almost certainly deliberate) absence of a power to extend time for failure to give possession in the RIBA/JCT forms. However, the final result was clearly right, it is submitted, on the ground that the building contract, even if varied, had not been the bonded contract at all. For the same reason the majority were equally right, it is submitted, not to permit any *pro tanto* release of the bondsman, since on the facts it is clear from the report that a particular starting date had clearly never been a condition of the bond.]

(b) Rescission by creditor

17·014   Passing from cases of breach of contract by the creditor, while breach *by the debtor* is of course an essential part of a guarantor's obligation, in those cases where this has been followed by a rescission of the contract by the creditor, sureties have unsuccessfully sought to argue that this too should release the surety from further liability. In the case of payment guarantees, such a rescission can easily occur where the creditor terminates upon a failure of the debtor to make an instalment payment, for example. Thus, in a shipbuilding contract terminated by the builders for non-payment by the owners of an early instalment, guarantors of the owners were held liable for an instalment accrued due prior to the rescission;[31] and in a case of a guarantee of a contract to pay a debt for services which had been previously rendered by six instalments, later rescinded when the debtor had defaulted after the first instalment, the guarantors were held liable for the entire debt as damages.[32] The principle of these cases is that while upon rescission the debtor ceases to be liable to perform further, he becomes instead liable to pay damages, for which the guarantor will in turn be liable.[33]

17·015   While the normal presumption when interpreting a contract of guarantee is that the guarantor's liability is intended to be precisely co-extensive with that of the debtor under his principal contract,[34] it remains perfectly possible, particularly in the case of payment guarantees, that they may be

---

[30a] As also the Court of Appeal in the *Trafalgar House* case, *supra*, para. 17·010.

[31] *Hyundai Heavy Industries Co.* v. *Papadopoulos* [1980] 1 W.L.R. 1129.

[32] *Moschi* v. *Lep Air Services Ltd.* [1973] A.C. 331. See also, *per* Dixon J. in *Macdonald* v. *Dennys Lascelles* (1933) 48 C.L.R. 457, 476, High Court of Australia.

[33] See in particular *Moschi's* case.

[34] See *Chitty on Contracts* (26th ed.), para. 5086, but see this presumption apparently disregarded by the Court of Appeal in the *Trafalgar House* case discussed *supra*, where traditional English bond forms of wording are used.

intended to be unconditional and unqualified by disputes between creditor and debtor. Thus, in the *Hyundai* case, the House of Lords considered that even if the shipbuilders had lost the right to the accrued instalment as a result of their later rescission of the contract, the terms of the particular guarantee were nevertheless such as to entitle them to recover that unpaid instalment from the guarantors. On this point the *Hyundai* speeches in the House of Lords all approved Roskill L.J.'s observation in the Court of Appeal that the avowed object of the letter of guarantee in that case had been:

> "to enable the yard to recover from the guarantors the amount due irrespective of the position between yard and buyers, so that the yard gets its money from the guarantors without difficulty if the yard cannot get it from the buyers."[35]

Although most commercial *performance* bonds will usually take the form of defining their liability strictly in terms of the debtor's liability under the principal contract concerned, therefore, *payment* guarantees given less formally in relation to a construction project may be of this unqualified nature. In each case it will be a question of interpretation of the bond or guarantee whether it is intended to operate independently of the terms of the principal contract, in which event, if imposing greater liability than the sums strictly due under that contract, it will be more in the nature of an indemnity than a guarantee.[36]

(c) Set-off by surety

A further related and sometimes difficult problem of enforcement may arise where the surety wishes to rely on a set-off available to the debtor against the creditor's claim, so as to reduce or eliminate the surety's liability *pro tanto*. In principle this can occur in the case of both performance and payment guarantees. This subject was exhaustively considered by Isaacs J. in New South Wales in 1970, in a case where three directors had guaranteed payment for supplies of goods to a limited company, and when sued on the guarantee had sought to allege breaches of warranty of quality in reduction of their liability, and also claims for damages for loss of profit and lost goodwill. Isaacs J. considered that, except in the case of true defences, such as failure to deliver, which could be raised by the guarantors alone, claims in diminution of the price and for unliquidated damages could only be raised after joining the debtor as a co-defendant or as a third

17·016

---

[35] [1978] 2 Lloyds Rep. 502, 508.
[36] See *Chitty on Contracts* (26th ed.), para. 5050, and for a case where liability under a payment guarantee arising on completion depended on completion in fact and not on completion under the terms of the contract, see *Lewis* v. *Hoare* (1881) 44 L.T. 66, H.L., illustrated *ante*, Chap. 6, Section 7, para. 6·217.

party.[37] Opposing views have, however, been expressed in leading text-books, as indicated in Isaacs J.'s judgment, and the subject is far from clear.

Isaacs J.'s view seems correct in principle, however, since on a payment guarantee, for example, a true set-off by the debtor in principle ranks as equivalent to a payment by him, so releasing a guarantor of payment *pro tanto*, unless the guarantee can be regarded as unconditional and not co-extensive with the debtor's liability under the principal contract. Subject to this qualification, it is difficult to see how the various other liabilities of the parties *inter se* can be satisfactorily resolved without the presence of the debtor, at least as a third party if not as a co-defendant.

Apart from such procedural questions of joinder, however, it has been seen that very recently the English Court of Appeal has, in a case of a traditionally worded English due performance bond, been prepared to hold the bondsman more strictly bound than the debtor where set-offs or cross-claims of the debtor against the creditor were unsuccessfully sought to be raised by the bondsman.[37a]

(5) Writing and Consideration

17·017   By Section 4 of the Statute of Frauds 1677, a contract of guarantee, there defined as a contract "to answer for the debt default or miscarriage of another", cannot be enforced unless in writing and signed by the person to be charged thereunder. Suretyship, governed by this Act, is, as already stated, a liability secondary to the primary liability of another person. This distinguishes it from an indemnity, not caught by the Act, where the liability is a primary one and independent of the liability of the other person. The question turns upon whether the words used amount to an acceptance of unqualified liability in any event, or only to an undertaking to be responsible if the person originally liable fails to discharge his obligation. The distinctions drawn by the cases in the past could be regarded as somewhat fine, and were no doubt designed to whittle away the effect of the statute and avoid injustice.[38]

---

[37] *Cellulose Products Ltd.* v. *Truda* (1970) 2 W.N. 561, N.S.W. In the case of construction contracts, a plea of defective work will, under the terms for interim payment in many standard forms, rank as a true defence—see *Acsim (Southern) Ltd.* v. *Dancon Danish Contracting and Development Co. Ltd.* (1989) 47 BLR 55, C.A.—unless precluded by the certification provisions, as to which see *ante*, Chap. 6, Section 6(7), para. 6·186 *et seq.* To this extent this particular view of Isaac J. is not, therefore, consistent with the more modern English case law as indicated in the *Gilbert-Ash* case in the House of Lords, discussed *ante*, Chapter 6, Sections 1 and 6(7).

[37a] See the *Trafalgar House* case discussed and doubted *supra*, Subsection 3(b).

[38] See *Sutton* v. *Gray* [1894] 1 Q.B. 285, *Guild* v. *Conrad* [1894] 1 Q.B. 885, *Harburg Indiarubber Comb Company* v. *Martin* [1902] 1 K.B. 778 and *Davys* v. *Buswell* [1913] 2 K.B. 47. Of the older cases see *Dixon* v. *Hatfield* (1825) 2 Bing. 439; *Andrews* v. *Smith* (1835) 2 Cr. M & R 627; *Mallett* v. *Bakeman* (1865) L.R. 1 C.P. 163; *Lakeman* v. *Mountstephen* (1874) L.R. 7 H.L. 17; *Poucher* v. *Treahey* (1875) Up. Can. Q.B. 367; and *Petrie* v. *Hunter* (1882) 12 Ont. Rep. 233.

In English law contracts of guarantee, like any other contract, must be supported by consideration (this is no longer so by statute in some Commonwealth jurisdictions, such as Malaysia). In the case of the commercial contractors' bonds or guarantees usually required in construction projects, there are in fact usually three underlying contracts. The first is the principal contract between owner and contractor, or between a main and sub-contractor. The second will be the contract (arising often from an informal request and exchange of promises) between the contractor and the bondsman, whereby the bondsman agrees to supply the bond in favour of the owner in return for a premium to be paid by the contractor (and therefore clearly, as between them, supported by consideration). The third will be the transaction evidenced by the bond itself, under which the bondsman binds himself to the owner obligee. Since, in the case of a commercial bond, the premium consideration will almost always be supplied by the contractor, there will, therefore, often be no direct consideration or promise furnished by the owner obligee or to be found in the bond itself.

In many such contracts, however, good consideration may be implied,   **17·018**
since a *subsequent* entry of the owner into the principal contract with the contractor on the faith of the *earlier* guarantee of the bondsman can be regarded as a good consideration for the bondsman's promise. However, in many construction contracts the provision of the bond is envisaged as a *post*-contract obligation of the ultimately accepted contractor, and in such a case at the time when the bondsman makes his promise to the owner the principal contract will already have been entered into between the owner and the contractor. Since in English law past consideration is no consideration, this may well mean that the bond or guarantee will only be enforceable if under seal. However, since failure by a contractor to provide a bond, if so required by his contract, has rightly been held to be a fundamental breach or repudiation entitling the owner to rescind the contract,[39] it may even in this situation be possible to argue that, following receipt of the unsealed bond, the owner has abstained from exercising this implied contractual right against the contractor. Bondsmen of major standing have not shrunk from disclaiming liability on this ground, notwithstanding their having previously pocketed the premiums paid by the contractor, and having themselves prepared and executed a bond document without seal. In the owner's interest all bonds, therefore, and in particular all post-contract bonds, should be executed under the seal of the bonding company (or in other appropriate legal form in those jurisdictions where consideration is not a necessary ingredient of an enforceable contractual obligation). The seal will also, of course, carry substantial limitation advantages in many jurisdictions.

It is no longer, incidentally, necessary for the consideration supporting a contract of guarantee to be expressed in the contract in writing as originally required by the Statute of Frauds 1677. This was expressly provided for at a comparatively late date by section 3 of the Mercantile Law

---

[39] *Swartz* v. *Wolmaranstadt* 1960 (2) S.A. 1.

Amendment Act 1856, no doubt as a result of difficulties resulting from the unexpressed and indirect nature of the consideration moving from the obligee creditor as described above.

These previous difficulties may have been partly responsible for the very early practice, continued at the present day, of joining the principal debtor as a party to due performance bonds in the construction industry as well as the originally more common payment bonds.

(6) Interpretation

17·019   Both in England and the United States there have been frequent judicial references to the existence of a general rule requiring contracts of guarantee to be interpreted in all cases of doubt in favour of the surety. As will be seen,[40] there can be no doubt of the privileged status of guarantors in the past as "favourites of the law",[41] having regard in particular to the readiness of the Courts in all jurisdictions to discharge sureties altogether from their obligations in situations where no real, or at best only minimal or theoretical, prejudice can have in reality occurred; but it is not clear whether this apparent rule of interpretation in favour of the surety derived from the fact that the great majority of older cases related to unremunerated (often described as "accommodation") sureties, where the document relied on would in any case often be prepared by the creditor (as, for example, a bank's form of guarantee of a bank account). Whatever its true basis, the rule has been widely recognised:

> "The construction of the bond is not assisted by its archaic language or the fact that its recitals are factually inaccurate. I regard it as a most unsatisfactory document. It was put forward by New Hampshire and it must therefore in my view, in the case of ambiguity, be construed against them notwithstanding that in general contracts of suretyship are to be construed favourably to the surety."[42]

This recent comment of Parker L.J. may well represent a dawning recognition by the English Courts of the very different considerations which first principles based on the provenance of documents might suggest should have been applied long ago in England to the wholly different case of the commercial "compensated" surety,[43] as was stated more explicitly in the same case by Scott L.J. when considering the argument that an alteration of the contract had released the surety:

> "[Counsel for the creditor] invites us to adopt the approach of certain United States authorities and hold that, where the surety is a professional compen-

---

[40] See *infra* Section 2, and see C.C.P.P., pages 283–4 and para. 19–05.
[41] The expression frequently used in American cases, and see, *per* Lord Selborne L.C. in *Re Sherry* (1884) 25 Ch.D. 692, 703.
[42] *Mercers Co.* v. *New Hampshire Insurance Co.* [1992] 2 Lloyd's Rep. 365, 368, *per* Parker L.J.
[43] See the suggestions for a fundamental re-assessment by the Courts in the case of commercial bondsmen made in 1986 in C.C.P.P., pages 283–4.

sated surety, the discharge of the surety brought about by a variation of the principal contract should be *pro tanto* and not absolute. I was impressed by the commonsense of this transatlantic solution and by the undesirable rigidity of the rule of *Holme* v. *Brunskill* in its application to compensated sureties. *I was not convinced that binding authority stands in the way of the adoption of this sensible solution in this country ...*"[44] (emphasis supplied)

Reverting to the interpretation of doubtful wording in a bond, the case **17·020** of compensated sureties has been clearly distinguished by courts in the United States for many years:

"If the language of the bond is ambiguous or uncertain, it will be construed most strongly against a compensated surety and in favour of the obligee or beneficiaries under the bond ..."[45]

Thus, it was stated in the United States Supreme Court in 1955:

"The rule that the contract of a "voluntary" or "accommodation" surety is to be construed *strictissimi juris*, all doubts and technicalities being resolved in his favour, had no application to the contract of a surety company acting for compensation; as to the latter, doubts are to be resolved against a surety *and in favour of the indemnity*".[46]

Although owners commissioning construction projects in the United Kingdom are, in market terms, usually in a position to dictate the precise terms of any bond required from tendering contractors (as, for example, those forms supplied expressly in the ICE standard form documentation), and it is very much in their clients' commercial interest that owners' advisers should draft the required terms on their behalf,[47] it remains the case that a majority of construction owners appear to be permitted by their advisers to enter into bonds in printed standard forms offered by the bonding companies without question or amendment. Where this is so, it is submitted that today in England any such bond should be strictly construed in accordance with the passages from the United States authorities cited above.[48] If so this might have assisted the Court of Appeal to reach a more reasonable interpretation in the *Perar* case noted *supra*, para. 17·012.

The United States cases are further discussed *infra* sections 2(5) and (6).[48a]

(7) Notice Unnecessary: Limitation and Duration

It is frequently asserted by sureties that notice of the debtor's default is **17·021** necessary before they can become liable. In the absence of express pro-

---

[44] [1992] 2 Lloyd's Rep. 365, 377.
[45] 17 Am. Jur. 2nd, Contractors' Bonds, para. 31 (1964).
[46] *Airport Commission* v. *U.S. Fidelity & Guarantee Co.* 86 S.C. 2nd 249, 252 (1955), cited in *U.S.* v. *Algernon Blair* 329 F. Supp. 1360 (1970).
[47] For the provisions of well-drafted performance bonds in construction contracts see C.C.P.P., para. 19–20.
[48] See, *e.g.* the cases on notice requirements, *infra*, Section 2(5), paras. 17·032 and 17·033.
[48a] Paras. 17·032–17·033 and 17·039–17·040 and 17·047–17·048, and 17·053.

vision requiring notice or a demand as a condition of liability under bond or guarantee,[49] the liability of the surety arises *immediately* upon the default of the debtor.

> "By the beginning of the nineteenth century it appears to have been taken for granted ... that the contractual promise of a guarantor to guarantee the performance by a debtor of his obligations to a creditor arising out of a contract gave rise to an obligation on the part of the guarantor to see to it that the debtor performed his own obligations to the creditor ... It is because the obligation of the guarantor is to see to it that the debtor performs his own obligations to the creditor that the guarantor is not entitled to notice from the creditor of the debtor's failure to perform an obligation which is the subject of the guarantee, and that the creditor's cause of action against the guarantor arises at the moment of the debtor's default and the limitation period then starts to run."[50]

In fact Lord Diplock's "see to it" explanation of the undoubted immediate liability of the surety seems open to criticism in that it fails to describe accurately the true nature of a guarantor's obligation, namely to answer for the default of another, and has been persuasively rejected in the High Court of Australia.[50a] The rule seems more likely to be pragmatic and consensually based.

While, therefore, this basis of the surety's liability emphasises the immediate recourse available to the creditor in the event of a default, it also has the incidental effect of starting the running of the limitation period under the bond, providing a further reason why a performance bond should, in the interest of the owner, be under seal so as to obtain the benefit of its extended limitation period.

17·022   Turning to the duration of the surety's liability under the bond, traditionally no termination date was provided in the past for the liability under construction contract performance bonds. For example, the form of bond provided with the English ICE standard forms in 1973 was expressed to be discharged "on due performance of all the contractor's obligations" under his contract or upon payment of damages for any default. This wording had the effect of continuing the surety's liability (for example, in regard to undetected defective work) until the expiry of whatever period of limitation might be applicable to such a breach of contract by the contractor (subject only to any certification or other provisions in the construction contract which might have the effect of shortening that period). The traditional bond, therefore, had a duration equivalent to the limitation period applicable to a default under the principal contract or arguably, if that contract was not under seal whereas the bond was, for the longer period of the bond.

---

[49] The mere use of the words "on-demand" in a conditional bond will not have this effect, it is submitted, in spite of *Re Brown's Estate* [1893] 2 Ch. 300, which was concerned with liability for the principal sum under a mortgage. See for a more convincing example the need for the surety to be "called on to pay" before the counter-indemnitor became liable in *General Surety and Guarantee Co. Ltd.* v. *Francis Parker Ltd.* (1977) 6 BLR 16 *infra*, para. 17·061.

[50] *Moschi* v. *Lep Air Services Ltd.* [1973] A.C. 331, 348, *per* Lord Diplock.

[50a] Per Mason C.J. in *Sunbird Plaza Ltd.* v. *Maloney* (1988) 166 C.L.R. 245, noted by Philips' and O'Donovan's *The Modern Contract of Guarantee* (2nd ed.), p. 8.

Of recent years, however, by a little noticed change (unsurprisingly unaccomplished by any alterations in premium rates) in the wording of the forms of bond made available in the market, the provision for "release" or discharge of the bond is made to take effect *upon completion of the work* rather than upon due performance of the contract, in some other cases with specific reference to a maintenance or other completion certificate, or to the earlier expiry of the extended contract period (for instance, practical completion). This has the effect of eliminating a large and very important element of the commercial protection afforded to owners by the previous wording (in respect of undetected defects) while at the same time accompanied by premium payment arrangements which can now be plausibly based on time, so that if the original contract period is exceeded and the bondsman's new "release" postponed as a result of extensions of time, still further premiums can then seem justified in respect of the project.[51]

SECTION 2. DISCHARGE OF SURETY

(1) Generally

Sureties may obviously be discharged in a number of ways, such as by release of the principal debtor, or even of a co-surety; by supervening illegality (although a contract capable of being operated by the parties so as to avoid the illegality, for example, by varying the work, may not discharge the surety)[52]; or in some cases by a statutory change in the identity of a creditor local authority.[53] However, the present Section is principally concerned with discharge as a result of acts or conduct of the creditor (for instance, in the case of due performance bonds the owner, or in sub-contract cases the main contractor) which can be said to prejudice the surety and so, under case law almost entirely developed in relation to non-commercial "accommodation" sureties, held to release the surety either wholly (in almost all the English cases) or *pro tanto* (that is, to the monetary extent that the surety can show damage or loss, of which there have been very few examples in English case law). United States law has, however, diverged strongly, in the case of "compensated" commercial sureties and over a period of many years, by rejecting any theory of wholesale release and, in many situations, even of *pro tanto* release if the default is not substantial.[54]

17·023

---

[51] For these developments discussed in more detail see C.C.P.P., para. 19–17.

[52] *One Hundred Simcoe Street Ltd.* v. *Frank Burger Contractors Ltd.* [1968] 1 Ont. R 452, illustrated *ante*, Chap. 4, Section 3(6), para. 4·281.

[53] *Provident Accident* v. *Dahne & White* [1937] 2 E.R. 255; but see *Town of Truro* v. *Toronto General Insurance* [1974] S.C.R. 1129.

[54] See *supra*, Section 1(6), "Interpretation", paras. 17·019–17·020, and see *infra*, Subsection (6), "Acts to the Prejudice of the Surety", paras. 17·034 *et seq.*.

(2) Discharge by Full Performance

17·024   It is a question of construction of a guarantee or bond as to what constitutes sufficient performance so as to release the surety. In the case of payment guarantees, a payment made in full, if subsequently set aside by process of law for any reason, will generally not discharge the surety, as in the case of a payment subsequently invalidated and set aside as a preference over other creditors in a bankruptcy.[55] In the case of performance guarantees conditioned on due performance *simpliciter*, the surety's liability, as already indicated in Section 2 *supra*, will only finally terminate on expiry of the limitation date applicable to breach of the principal contract or to the bond itself, in the absence of express provision. Where some earlier date is stipulated for release of the surety, such as completion of the work or the issue of a particular certificate, release may not always be automatic, as a matter of construction, particularly in cases where the principal debtor has not been similarly released.

ILLUSTRATION

Sureties who were made parties to a construction contract between contractors and the owner undertook that the contractors would "well and truly" perform the contract. Under the contract the work was to be to the satisfaction of the Engineer, and was also to be conducted and completed under his superintendence and to his satisfaction, with provision for a certificate of completion followed by a final certificate releasing the last 10 per cent. of the price six months later. The sureties were expressly not to be released until six months after the certificate of completion. Widespread defective work was discovered after the completion and final certificates had both been given and the final 10 per cent. payment made, and when the sureties were sued the jury found that the defective work had been deliberate and concealed by the fraud of the contractors, but also that the owners had failed to supervise properly, which had led to the scamping of the work. The sureties contended that they had been released by the certificates and payment and, if not, that the owner, nevertheless owed them a duty to supervise carefully, and that they should be released for that reason. *Held*, by the Court of Appeal, that on the true construction of the contract the stipulated release of the sureties was not to follow automatically on the expiry of the six months, but only if that also had the effect of releasing the contractors. Since the certificates had been obtained by fraud they had not released the contractors, and the sureties remained liable. *Held* also, that under the contract the owners had the right, but owed no duty to the contractors or to the sureties, to supervise the work: *Kingston-upon-Hull* v. *Harding* (1892).[56]

[Note: The second limb of the judgment in this case is also of importance in the context of the "prejudicial conduct" cases in Subsection (6), see *infra*, and also in the more modern context of the A/E's duty of care to persons other than his client, discussed *ante*, Chapter 1 and Chapter 2.][57]

---

[55] *Petty* v. *Cooke* (1871) L.R. 6 Q.B. 790.
[56] [1892] 2 Q.B. 494.
[57] Chap. 1, Section 12(2)(d), paras. 1·297 *et seq*, Section 12(10), paras. 1·383 *et seq* and Chap. 2, Section 6(2), para. 2·138 *et seq* and 2·196 *et seq*.

(3) Non-disclosure

Sureties have frequently attempted to argue that contracts of guarantee   **17·025**
should, like insurance contracts, be treated as contracts *uberrimae fidei*,
with a consequential duty to disclose any material facts on the part of the
obligee, or even sometimes of the principal debtor, and, comparably with
the case of insurance, a consequential total discharge rather than a *pro
tanto* reduction in liability.

It is generally accepted that contracts of suretyship are not as a class in
the *uberrimae fidei* category,[58] but, nevertheless there do appear to be
some areas of suretyship, such as fidelity bonds for due performance of
their duties by employees or officials, where a duty to disclose has
occasionally been upheld.[59]

However, Lord Atkin's percipient observation in the *Trade Indemnity*
v. *Workington* case in regard to a compensated bondsman for a construction project, to the effect that in such cases the bondsman would be concerned primarily with the financial standing of the contractor rather than
the physical risks or difficulties or correct pricing of a particular project,
has already been cited in Section 1,[60] and it is submitted, despite some
earlier judicial comments, that in the construction field today compensated bondsmen, bearing in mind that they have ample resources at their
disposal for ascertaining the financial standing of contractors, and also
that doubts as to the financial viability of the contractor are the only justifiable reason for an owner to require a bond in the first place, are owed no
such duty by the creditor.

ILLUSTRATIONS

(1) Sureties bound themselves jointly with the contractor as principal debt-   **17·026**
or for due performance of a sewerage contract for a drainage Board. The
contract was to be carried out under the Board's surveyor, but unknown to
the contractors or sureties the Board had previously agreed to share the
expense of the project with a local landowner, whose surveyor was to supervise jointly with their own. When the contractor failed to complete and the
Board sued on their bond, the sureties obtained an interim injunction staying
the proceedings, alleging non-disclosure of the earlier agreement. *Held*, by
the Court of Appeal, that since non-disclosure could be raised as a defence,
the injunction should be discharged: *Stiff* v. *Eastbourne Local Board* (1868).[61]

[Note: On a close reading this case does not, however, establish that such a
defence would have been successful, it is submitted.]

(2) A contractor's bid of $85,000, which was $10,000 below the next, but
very considerably less than the higher bids, was accepted, and he placed
materials on the site. Four days later, however, he notified the owners that he
had made two substantial omissions of $6,000 and $7,000 when estimating his
costs, and required release from the contract or a higher price. Not surpris-

---

[58] *London General Omnibus Co.* v. *Holloway* [1912] 2 K.B. 72; *Trade Indemnity Co. Ltd.* v.
Workington Harbour and Dock Board [1937] A.C. 1.
[59] See *Chitty on Contracts* (26th ed.), para. 5024.
[60] See *supra*, para. 17·001.
[61] 20 L.T. 339.

ingly,[62] the owners refused and threatened forfeiture of his deposit should he withdraw, and the contractor decided to proceed. A bond was subsequently provided to the owners without disclosure to the bondsman of these facts. *Held*, by the Supreme Court of Canada, (Kerwin J. dissenting) that an amendment should have been allowed alleging non-disclosure of the pre-contract events, and that, but for the release of the sureties on other grounds,[63] a new trial would have had to be ordered: *Reverend E.G. Doe (trustee)* v. *Canadian Surety Co.* (1937).[64]

[Note: Again, this case does not establish that the defence would have been successful, although the very nearly contemporaneous *Trade Indemnity* case, next illustrated *infra*, was cited to the Supreme Court.]

17·027   (3) Clauses 2 and 5 of a civil engineering contract contained the usual provisions that the contractors were to make their own investigations and satisfy themselves as to risks and contingencies; and by clauses 6 and 7 that no claim was to be made on the ground of any representation, save only replies in writing by the Clerk to enquiries, and the engineers were expressly to have no authority so to bind the Board. The contractors' tender of £284,000 was far the lowest, but the engineers warned them that their excavation prices were too low for ground with high water levels, and gave them an opportunity to withdraw. The contractors maintained their tender price, however, and on the advice of the engineers the tender was then accepted by the Board, but on the condition that a £50,000 bond due performance was provided. Before the bond was issued the contractors met an assistant of the engineer to discuss groundwater levels, and subsequently a partner of the engineers again gave the contractors an opportunity to withdraw. A week later the contract was signed and a due performance bond provided which had been entered into jointly and severally by the contractors and the surety. The latter sought to avoid liability under the bond, arguing that the traditionally worded bond was in reality a contract of insurance, and that the existence of excessive groundwater, the inadequacy of the estimates of abnormal expenditure and the inadequacy of the price, together with the offers permitting withdrawal, should have been communicated to the bondsman beforehand. *Held*, by the House of Lords, affirming Scrutton L.J.'s dissenting judgment in the Court of Appeal, that the construction contract clearly showed that the Board was not to be liable for adverse ground conditions; there was no evidence of fraud; and in the circumstances no duty to disclose to the bondsman. *Per* Lord Atkin: "There may be a question whether in the formation of a contract of guarantee there is an obligation ... to make a disclosure of material facts which would not exist in the formation of an ordinary contract ... the duty to [disclose material facts] or the implied representation (that the guaranteed transaction has no unusual or abnormal characteristics) will depend upon the particular circumstances of each transaction. In this case the one outstanding feature is that the Dock Board took every care to make it plain that they left it to the proposed contractors to ascertain for themselves all material facts relating to the conditions ... and guarded themselves in precise terms against liability for any representations made otherwise than in accordance with clause 7 ... This intimation was plainly made to [the guarantors], for all the relevant documents were incorporated in the contract of guarantee. For myself, I doubt on the course of business alone whether a guarantor looks

---

[62] For some reason Canadian and North American law reports contain many cases where successful public tenderers very shortly afterwards allege errors in their bids and seek higher prices; see *ante*, Chap. 1, Section 2(3), paras. 1·025 and 1·027, and Section 5(2), paras. 1·108. This is a practice virtually unknown in England.

[63] See for these *infra*, Subsection (6), para. 17·037.

[64] [1937] S.C.R. 1.

further than the skill and experience of the Contractor to guard against risk of unknown difficulties in the performance of such a contract. *The guarantors are in such a case primarily concerned with the financing ability of the contractors to complete this contract, whether it results in a loss or not."* (emphasis supplied): *Trade Indemnity Co. Ltd.* v. *Workington Harbour and Dock Board* (1937).[65]

While it may be conceded that situations may exist where, depending on the situation or dealings between a particular creditor and a bondsman, it is possible to imply a warranty by the creditor that no unusual risks exist (the obverse of a duty to disclose such risk), that will be, on analysis, a case of an implied representation arising from the special factual matrix of a particular contracting situation. It is submitted that the *Trade Indemnity* case rightly shows that in the case of a due performance bond or guarantee of a construction contract this can only happen on very unusual facts, and that the reality of construction contracts in particular is that eventualities such as unfavourable physical conditions or hazards, or instances of under-pricing by bidders, are such a commonplace as to call for no special duty by owners to warn a guarantor.

(4) Laches

In the context of suretyship, this expression means more than simple lack **17·028** of care by the creditor in protecting his own interests under the principal contract:

> "If there be an omission to do something *which the employer has contracted with the surety to do,* [emphasis supplied], or to preserve some security, to the benefit of which the surety is entitled, the case is different. There the omission would be one inconsistent with the relation between the surety and the person with whom he has contracted to be surety."[66]

ILLUSTRATION

A contract to instal fittings in a warehouse for £3,450, with payment by instalments, contained a stipulation that the owner "shall and may insure the fittings from destruction by fire at such time and for such amounts as the architects may consider necessary and deduct the costs of such insurance for the time during which such works are unfinished from the amount of the contract". The owner had paid £1,800 by instalments at a time when fittings to the value of £2,300, which the owner had neglected to insure, were destroyed by fire in the contractor's workshop. Later the contractor became insolvent, and the owner completed and claimed the additional completion cost over the original contract price from a due performance surety under a guarantee which had recited the installation contract. The owner argued that even if the surety was to be released because of the owner's omission, it should only be to

---

[65] [1937] A.C. 1, 17–18.
[66] *Per* Bowen L.J. in *Kingston-upon-Hull Corporation* v. *Harding* [1892] 2 Q.B. 494, 508, a construction contract case.

the extent of the part of the loss claimed caused by the failure to insure. *Held*, by the Exchequer Chamber, affirming the decision below, that the owner had been contractually bound to insure the fittings, and that on the analogy of the *Calvert* and *Rolt* cases[67] the creditor had altered the situation of the surety, who was entitled to be discharged *in toto*: *Watts* v. *Shuttleworth* (1861).[68]

[Note: It is not easy to follow the reasoning in this case. The cases referred to by Williams J., involving increased or advanced instalment payments by the creditor were clearly based on removal or reduction of the debtor's incentive to complete, and seem to offer no useful analogy. The decision could in modern terms perhaps be regarded as a case of a "not unsubstantial" creditor breach "embodied" in the guarantee agreement,[69]—in other words insurance by the owner was regarded as a condition of the guarantee given—but even then it remains difficult to see on what principle a total as opposed to *pro tanto* reduction of liability can be explained.]

It has been seen that a failure to supervise diligently will not discharge a due performance guarantor of the contractor.[70] So, too, a failure to exercise close financial control by a main contractor resulting in unintended interim overpayment of a sub-contractor who was known to be likely to be overbilling was held not to discharge the sub-contractor's surety, in a valuable and persuasive judgment in Ontario.[71]

(5) Express Notice Requirements

17·029 It has been seen in Section 1(7) *supra*, that in the absence of express provision notice to the bondsman of a default by the principal debtor is not necessary as a condition of the bondsman's liability.[71a] However, bonds very frequently do contain express provisions requiring notice of one kind or another. In the law of contract generally, failure to comply with a notice requirement will not in the absence of sufficiently explicit language be treated as a condition precedent to liability, so depriving a party of his rights altogether,[72] although where a bondsman is expressly given power to take over the work from a defaulting contractor (in practical terms an extremely unwise provision for owners to accept, but very common in North America) it may be speculated that a more strict interpretation might for this reason be placed on a notice requirement in the bond.

ILLUSTRATIONS

(1) A bondsman took over completion of a project from a defaulting contractor, but during the course of the work discovered that there had been a

---

[67] Illustrated *infra*, Subsection (6).　　[68] 7 H & N 353.

[69] See *supra*, Section 1(4)(a), para. 17·103.

[70] The *Kingston-upon-Hull* case, illustrated *supra*, para. 17·024.

[71] *Thomas Fuller Construction Ltd.* v. *Continental Insurance* (1973) 36 D.L.R. 3d. 336, (Houlden J.), illustrated *infra*, Subsection (5), para. 17·031.

[71a] *Moschi's* case *supra*, para. 17·021. The contrary was, however, held as part of the Court of Appeal's reasoning in the *Trafalgar House* case *supra*, paras. 17·011 *et seq*.

[72] Compare the similar presumption in relation to the binding character of certificates formulated by Lord Diplock in the *Gilbert-Ash* case, see *ante*, Chap. 6, Section 1(1), para. 6·005.

number of instances where, at the request of the owner and in response to complaints from the contractor, the architect had agreed to a relaxation of strict compliance with the specification, in the most important instance permitting a less rich mix of cement mortar.[73] Later the bondsman abandoned the contract after disputing the extent of the work required to complete and, after failing on that issue when sued on the bond, obtained leave to amend and claimed to be released by reason of a provision in the bond requiring immediate notice to the bondsman of "any changes or alterations in the plans or specifications of the work". *Held*, by the Supreme Court of Canada, overruling unanimous lower decisions, that the provision did not apply to alterations in the work resulting from omissions or reduced quality tacitly acquiesced in by the owner or his architect. "There is certainly danger if we adopt too strict a construction of the duties of the obligee in such transactions that there will always be some technical error or omission of his part which will render the bond void, thus destroying the whole object of entering into such bonds": *Ferrara* v. *National Surety Co.* (1917).[74]

(2) A bond, using explicit condition precedent language, provided: "The **17·030** surety shall be notified in writing of any non-performance ... on the part of the Contractor of any of the stipulations or conditions contained in the contract ... which may involve a loss for which the surety is responsible within one month after such non-performance ... (and which) shall have come to the knowledge of the employer or his representatives having supervision of the contract ... and the employer shall insofar as it may be lawful permit the surety to perform the stipulations of the said contract which the Contractor shall have failed to perform ...". The project was a seasonal pipe-laying contract due to start in February and finish by November of the same year before the onset of winter, with a particular area to be passed through by April, and other intermediate completion stages. The contractor started work three months late, for disputed reasons, and only half the work had been done by November. In September the owners informed the bondsman that there was two months' delay, which was in fact an underestimate. Work then stopped for the winter, and was to restart at the end of March in the following year, but in January the contractors went into liquidation, and the owners then gave prompt notice to the bondsman, who did not, however, complete. The owners sued for the additional cost of completion by another contractor, but not for liquidated damages for delay, but the bondsman relied on lack of any notice given in the previous year. *Held*, by the Scottish Court of Session, and upheld by the House of Lords, that even in a controversial situation where an extension of time might or might not be due, there had been, on the wording of the bond, a duty to notify the bondsman of a potential likelihood of late completion and of a possible claim for liquidated damages early in the previous year, and, notwithstanding that the claim was for the abandonment of the project and not for damages for delay, the sureties were released from all liability: *Clydebank and District Water Trustees* v. *Fidelity and Deposit Co. of Maryland* (1915).[75]

[Note: This case is of considerable potential importance in the construction field, because the exact wording of the notice requirement, after a disappearance of some 60 years, appears to have re-emerged recently in a number of international performance bonds. It is hard to conceive of any construction project resulting in a claim against the bondsman where a minute examin-

---

[73] For a fuller account see C.C.P.P., para. 19–06.

[74] [1917] 1 W.W.R. 719. Compare the alterations of the specification acquiesced in but not invalidating the bond in *Hayes* v. *City of Regina* [1959] S.C.R. 801, illustrated *infra*, Subsection (6).

[75] 1915 S.C. 36 (Ct. of Sess.); 1916 S.C. 69, H.L.

ation of its history would not supply sufficient material for invalidation of the bond if interpreted as in this case. The case is examined critically and exhaustively (and indeed was first noticed in textbooks on this point) in C.C.P.P., paragraph 19–10, where it is suggested that the powerful dissenting judgment in the Court of Session of the Lord President (Lord Strathclyde) is to be preferred. It should be compared with the next following case where, however, the more explicit wording of the *Clydebank* notice requirement was absent.]

17·031   (3) A plumbing sub-contractor's performance bond in Ontario in favour of the main contractor undertook responsibility for proper completion "whenever Principal shall be, and declared by Obligee to be, in default under [the sub-contract]". The sub-contractor started work in May, but his labour force was inadequate, and he failed to provide a competent project manager or to expedite shop drawings. From August onwards he was overbilling for his work, and in October the main contractor wrote to the sub-contractor threatening to inform the bondsman if his complaints as to progress and supervision were not remedied within two weeks. By November the delays were such that heating would not now be available for the project as a whole during the winter. In early February of the following year certain of the sub-contractor's sub-sub-contractors were unpaid and withdrew labour, and his own unpaid workmen went on strike. At this stage the main contractor notified the bondsman that it might be necessary to declare the sub-contractor in default. Finally, in March the sub-contractor abandoned work altogether. When sued, the bondsman contended that he should be released from his obligations, arguing that the cumulative defaults required notice to be given at least by the time of the main contractor's letter to the sub-contractor in October threatening to inform the bondsman. *Held*, by Houlden J., that the wording of the bond requiring a declaration of default did not apply unless the default was so serious that the obligee deemed it proper to declare the default and call on the bonding company to perform its obligations: "A bond for a large construction project which required that the bonding company be kept informed of defaults by its sub-contractor would have been of little use to a general contractor. On this particular contract there were performance bonds in respect of other sub-contractors, and if the bonding company's position were the correct one, the policing of the bonds would impose a heavy burden on the contractor ... the only practical and sensible basis on which bonding can be done on large construction projects is by permitting the general contractor to be the judge of when the default by a sub-contractor is sufficiently serious that the bonding company should be called in with resultant disruption of the [main contractor's] contract": *Thomas Fuller Construction* v. *Continental Insurance* (1973).[76]

17·032   (4) A main contractor for a government project was required to furnish a bond to the Minister as trustee for payment by the main contractor within 90 days of the accounts properly due to all sub-contractors. The notice requirement in the bond provided that no suit or action should be commenced thereunder by any individual claimant sub-contractor unless he should have given written notice by registered mail within certain time limits to the Principal (main contractor), the surety, and the Obligee (the Minister). The sub-contractor in the event gave notice to the surety by registered mail within the period, and by ordinary mail to the Minister within the period, but no written notice was given to the contractor, who was however aware of the proceedings, and who it was found had suffered no prejudice. The bondsman, relying on the cases where sureties had been released by any alteration of the contract terms as indicating a rule of *strictissimi juris* construction of surety con-

---

[76] 36 D.L.R. 3d 336, 350.

tracts, contended that the requirements for giving notice must be strictly complied with, and that the claimant could not succeed. The claimant contended that a mere technical breach of the terms of a bond should not permit a compensated surety to escape liability where there had been no prejudice, and here there had been none since the full objectives of the notice provisions had as a fact been achieved. *Held*, by the Supreme Court of Canada, that the rules hitherto applicable to accommodation sureties were in many ways inapplicable as being unrealistic to professional sureties undertaking surety contracts for profit. Such a surety could not escape liability merely because of a minor variation in the guaranteed contract or because of a trivial failure to meet the bond's conditions. Here the object of the notice provision in the bond had been fully achieved within the time limits imposed, there was no prejudice, and the whole object of the bond would be defeated if the surety were to be discharged: *Citadel Assurance v. Johns-Manville Canada* (1983).[77]

[Note: This important case reviews the American authorities on compensated securities, and appears to accept that, in the absence of proven prejudice, even express provisions using condition precedent language or its equivalent will not be permitted to defeat the object of the bond by releasing the surety *in toto*. McIntyre J. pointed out that a number of English authorities cited all appeared to relate to accommodation sureties. The judgment holds only that the more liberal interpretation in favour of claimants in the case of compensated sureties to be derived from the American authorities will in Canada permit departures from the strict terms of notice requirements in the bonds provided by compensated sureties, but the case is clearly also implicit authority for the extension to Canada of the American approach of *pro tanto* release for the various alterations in the situation of the parties to the principal contract which have hitherto been held to release sureties *in toto* under the earlier case law in England and Canada.]

The United States have explicitly abandoned old *strictissimi juris* rules **17·033** as to notice requirements in the case of compensated sureties.

ILLUSTRATION

A contract gave the owner company the absolute right to terminate the employment of the contractor at any time, and complete by itself on seven days' notice. In the event, the owner by agreement with the contractor, and with his active co-operation, took assignments of the various sub-contracts and completed the work, but did not give the required notice, although the contractor's surety was kept informed of events on a daily basis. The surety claimed to be discharged. *Held*, by the U.S. 6th Circuit Court of Appeals, following *Waldon v. Maryland Casualty Co.* (1923), that under modern American surety law with regard to compensated sureties, mere technical breach of a surety contract not resulting in damage or prejudice to the surety would not release it from its obligations. Here, the owner had only exercised his contractual entitlement, but even if there had been a change of the contracting arrangements it was not material: *Winston Corporation v. Continental Casualty Co.* (1975).[78]

---

[77] [1983] 1 S.C.R. 513.
[78] 508 F 2nd 1299, citing *Waldon v. Maryland Casualty Co.* 116 S.C. 828 (1923) as authority for not construing notice requirements strictly in compensated surety cases.

As noted in the next succeeding Subsection, the American relaxation of strict interpretation rules in compensated surety cases has been applied much more widely and not merely to notice requirements, where it had been of long standing,[79] including particularly the other principal grounds for full discharge of accommodation sureties, such as acts or alterations which might prejudice sureties, which the earlier cases had so willingly permitted.[79a] Thus, in the *Winston Corporation* case in 1975 the Court said:

> "The obligation of a surety was considered *stricti juris*, and even a slight devi-
> ation from the contract terms discharged the surety. The result of applying
> this rule was often harsh and unjust especially when compensated sureties
> were relieved of their obligations because of technical breaches of the assured
> contract. Consequently most Courts departed from the rule of *stricti juris* in
> cases in which a surety had been compensated for its undertaking and devel-
> oped the rule that a compensated surety is discharged only if the change is
> material and causes some injury loss or prejudice to it."[80]

(6) Acts to the Prejudice of the Surety

(a) Generally

17·034   The broad principle which emerged from the nineteenth-century case law, notably from the leading Court of Appeal case in England of *Holme* v. *Brunskill*,[81] was that no subsequent alteration of the debtor's obligations agreed to by the creditor would bind a guarantor of those obli-
gations without his prior consent, unless it was either wholly trivial and insubstantial, or, if not, self-evidently could not in any conceivable circumstances prejudice the surety:

> "... in cases where it is *without enquiry evident* that the alteration is insubstan-
> tial, or that *it cannot be otherwise than beneficial* to the surety ... if it is not
> self-evident that the alteration is insubstantial, or one which cannot be preju-
> dicial to the surety, the Court will not ... go into an enquiry as to the effect of
> the alteration ... the surety himself must be the sole judge of whether or not
> he will consent to remain liable."[82] (Emphases supplied.)

However, the cases do show that alterations in the debtor's obligations must be the subject of a binding agreement to that effect, or an irretrievable step such as payment in advance, and mere passive acquiescence by an owner or his advisers in departures from the contract will generally not discharge a surety.[83]

---

[79] The *Waldon* v. *Maryland Casualty* case, see *supra*, was decided as early as 1923.
[79a] See *supra*, para. 17·019 and 17·020.
[80] 508 F 2nd 1298, 1302.
[81] (1877) 3 Q.B.D. 495.
[82] *Ibid.* at p. 505, *per* Cotton L.J.
[83] This is the general result of the authorities, but see also, *per* Idington J. in *Ferrara* v.
   National Surety Co. [1917] 1 W.W.R. 719, 726–727, illustrated *supra*, Subsection (5), para.
   17·029 and *infra* para. 17·050.

The general principle has been followed throughout the Common-   **17·035**
wealth.[84] The principle as such is unexceptionable and fully justified, since
in many cases where some concession is made by a creditor to a debtor,
which superficially might be thought to benefit the surety also, this may
well not be so because, depending on its nature, it may relieve the pressure
on the debtor to perform his immediate obligations on the guaranteed
contract, which would have released the guarantor. Instead, by serving to
postpone performance of the debtor's obligations until supervening insolvency arises from liabilities incurred elsewhere, it may result in a default
on a guaranteed contract which otherwise might have been fully performed.[84a] As pointed out by Coleridge J. in 1857, and reiterated by Lord
Diplock in 1973, the effect of a binding agreement between creditor and
debtor to postpone or forego an entitlement against the debtor also has
the effect of depriving the surety of his right to compel prompt enforcement of the creditor's rights against the debtor which, for precisely these
reasons, is understandably accorded to sureties under the general law.[85]

What, however, has certainly justified the description of sureties as   **17·036**
"favoured by the law",[86] has been the use made of this principle by the
earlier courts, since instead of treating alterations of the principal contract
without consent as a breach of the suretyship contract *sounding in damages,* no enquiry was permitted to ascertain whether there had as a fact
been prejudice which a concession of this kind might have caused to the
surety, or whether on the other hand it might not have been positively
beneficial, in the events which happened, to him and the surety. Instead,
provided prejudice was theoretically possible, the surety was automatically released by the courts *in toto*, and little use made of the exceptions
envisaged by the *Holme* v. *Brunskill* principle. In *Holme* v. *Brunskill* itself,
an agricultural tenant provided a surety to his landlord for the return of a
flock in good condition at the end of the tenancy. The surety was released
in toto because during the lease one field had been surrendered by the
tenant in return for a reduction of the rent. As the above quotation shows,
no enquiry was permitted as to the fact or extent of the prejudice, if any, to
the tenant's or surety's interest.

In the special case of construction contracts, it can be confidently   **17·037**
expected that circumstances will often arise on a day-to-day basis where
the elements of compromise, indulgence, premature payment, granting of
time, or alteration of contract terms may all be present in varying degrees;
often this will be in the context of the compromise of a dispute with the
contractor where at the time the true facts may not be certain, or where an
owner may have decided to make the best of an unsatisfactory situation in

---

[84] See, *e.g.* in Canada the law as stated by the Supreme Court in *Reverend E.G. Doe (trustee)*
v. *Canadian Surety Co.* [1937] 1 S.C.R. 1, and later in *Hayes* v. *City of Regina* [1959] S.C.R.
1; (1959) 20 D.L.R. 2nd 256.

[84a] See further on this in the case of construction contracts, *infra*, para. 17·046,

[85] See *Frazer* v. *Jordan* (1857) E&B 303, 310; *Moschi* v. *Lep Air Services Ltd.* [1973] A.C. 331,
398.

[86] See *supra*, Section 1(6), para. 17·019.

the interest of obtaining early completion. In the absence of suitably worded bonds, the dangers to owners arising in such situations are well illustrated by a leading Canadian case.

ILLUSTRATION

A contractor finished late and with some difficulty. Rainwater penetration through the brickwork had been noticed during construction and was still a continuing and disputed problem, since the contractor was blaming the architect's design. The contract provided that the final payment certificate should discharge the contractor from all liability for defects, save in regard to defects appearing within one year after completion due to bad workmanship. The final payment certificate was issued, and in the following month the owners agreed to pay the certified balance directly to certain unpaid sub-contractors in return for the contractor's unqualified undertaking to carry out free of charge whatever remedial works the architect should require. *Held*, by the Supreme Court of Canada (Kerwin J. dissenting), (a) that the agreement concluded with the contractor to do whatever the architect required was an alteration of the contract; (b) that the agreement for direct payment to sub-contractors rather than to the main contractor also constituted an alteration; and (c) that the payment was in any event made in advance of the contract obligation, so that the sureties were entitled to be discharged separately on all three grounds: *Reverend E.G. Doe (trustee)* v. *Canadian Surety Co.* (1937).[87]

17·038   In the context of construction contracts, it seems doubtful if from this point of view, there is any difference in principle between payment and performance guarantees. Thus, in the former case concessions made in regard to the discharge of the payment obligation, such as an agreement to accept delayed payment, will invoke the principle and release the surety.[88] In the case of performance guarantees, the commoner alterations likely to occur will be excessive or advanced payment during construction to a faltering contractor, alterations of the work itself, or alterations of some other obligation, perhaps as a result of a compromise in a matter of disputed interpretation.

Well-drafted bonds in the owner's interest will expressly permit alterations of the contract or of the work, allowances of time, indulgences, forbearances or concessions, including additional or advance payment and compromises of disputes.[89]

17·039   It has already been seen that in the United States a now long-established line of authority has dispensed with any notion of *in toto* release of a compensated surety in the context of both interpretation and notice requirements.[90] While the law with regard to *accommodation*

---

[87] [1937] 1 S.C.R. 1.

[88] See *infra.*

[89] For these and a number of other requirements of a competently drafted bond in the owner's interest see C.C.P.P., para. 19–20. See also the forms of bond supplied by the ICE with their standard forms in England.

[90] See *supra*, Section 1(6), paras. 17·019 and 17·020, and Subsection (5), para. 17·053.

sureties is stated in American Jurisprudence with perhaps even greater severity than under the *Holme* v. *Brunskill* English and Commonwealth formulation, the *compensated* surety or bondsman is a very different case:

> "Absent an agreement in the contract or bond allowing the parties to make alterations in the work to be done, a material alteration made without the consent of the surety on the contractor's bond will discharge a non-compensated surety *irrespective of whether it is prejudicial.* This rule applies even where the alterations actually benefit the surety and do not increase the expense to the owner, or even though the contract as altered is not carried out. A compensated surety, however, cannot be discharged from its obligation when there is an alteration or modification in the contract unless it was prejudiced or injured by the variance. If a change in the construction contract una-greed to by the surety results in injury to the surety, the surety will be discharged *only to the extent of the injury.*"[91] (Emphases supplied).

Moreover, in the context of a surety remaining silent when aware of a departure from the contract, compensated securities have been held to owe a duty of good faith to the creditor.[92]

It seems that the general United States position is now likely to be adopted by the Supreme Court of Canada: **17·040**

> "It is clear that, while Canadian authority to date has tended to favour a more liberal approach to the consideration of the rights of claimants under bonds of this nature, it has not gone as far as the American Courts in distinguishing the compensated from the accommodation surety. It is my view, however, that the rules which have been applied to accommodation sureties are in many ways unrealistic and inapplicable to cases where professional sureties, in the course of their ordinary business, undertake surety contracts for profit and thereby approach very closely the rôle of the insurer. The basis of the surety's liability must, of course, be found in the bond into which it has entered, but in the case of the compensated surety it cannot be every variation in the guaran-teed contract, however minor, or every failure of a claimant to meet the con-ditions imposed by the bond, however trivial, which will enable the surety to escape liability."[93]

(b) Payment guarantees

Mere acquiescence or failure to take action by a contractor or other creditor following late payment will not release a surety, whose right to compel a prompt enforcement of the creditor's rights will not have been prejudiced in such a case.[94] What will be required to release the surety will   **17·041**

[91] 17 Am. Jur. 2d, para. 31. See also for *pro tanto* release only in the case of premature pay-ments, etc., *ibid.* at para. 41.

[92] *Trinity Universal Insurance Co.* v. *Gould* 258 F 2nd 883 (1958).

[93] *Per* McIntyre J., delivering the judgment of the Court in *Citadel Assurance* v. *Johns-Man-ville Canada* [1983] 1 S.C.R. 513, 524. See also the earlier passages in the judgment (al-though this was strictly a notice requirement case where *pro tanto* release was not applicable) pointing out that the earlier contrary authorities related to accommodation sureties. See also the extracts from the judgments cited and the case illustrated *supra*, Section 1(5), para. 17·032.

[94] See as to this latter *supra*, paras. 17·034 and 17·035.

be a *binding* agreement *made with the debtor* without the surety's consent which defers the time of payment (an agreement to *reduce* the payment must self-evidently benefit the surety *pro tanto* and so not release him as to the balance). A binding agreement to defer payment of even one instalment of a single overall price will discharge the entire guarantee, so that where hire-purchase owners agreed with the debtor to accept a third person's cheque on a deferred date in respect of an instalment already in arrears the surety was released *in toto*.[95] If, however, the binding agreement to defer payment is made by the creditor *with a third person*, the surety will not be discharged, since while an action brought against the debtor in breach of the agreement might expose the creditor to damages at the hands of the third person, it cannot afford the debtor any defence, and so will not prejudice the surety's right to compel prompt enforcement by the creditor.[96]

17·042   In the case of a deferred instalment payment, the instalment may sometimes relate to separable goods or work, and if so the surety's release may be severable and *pro tanto* and relate only to that particular instalment.

ILLUSTRATION

A purchaser agreed to take tar from a gas company and pay for each month's supply within 14 days of the following month. The gas company agreed to take a promissory note for July, but not for August or September. *Held*, by the Court of Appeal, the surety was released in respect of the payment for the July delivery, but not for the rest. *Croydon Commercial Gas Company* v. *Dickinson* (1876).[97]

A further example of severability may occur in the case of payment guarantees where extra or additional work has been ordered without the knowledge or consent of the surety. Thus, in a case where a very substantial amount of additional work, not included in the original contract, had been agreed and carried out, the High Court of Australia considered that the first question to be decided was whether the work was covered by the variation clause in the guaranteed contract, in which case the guarantor would be liable; secondly, the work might have been done as the result of a separate agreement, so that the surety's liability would continue unaltered, but only for the payments due in respect of the original contract work; thirdly, there might have been a variation of the original agreement by the parties to the effect that the new work should be included under it, and if so the question might arise whether it had been agreed to by the surety.[98]

---

[95] *Midland Motor Showrooms* v. *Newman* [1929] 2 K.B. 256.
[96] *Frazer* v. *Jordan* (1857) 8 E&B 303.
[97] 2 C.P.D. 46. See for a case of severability of a performance guarantee, but where instalments were not involved and the work only was severable, *Harrison* v. *Seymour* (1866) L.R. 1 C.P. 518, illustrated *infra*, para. 17·051.
[98] *Wren* v. *Emmetts Contractors Pty. Ltd.* (1969) 43 A.L.J.R. 213.

(c) Performance guarantees

(i) *Increased or advanced payments*

For good commercial reasons it is very common in a construction con- **17·043** text for owners, faced with a contractor in apparent difficulties, or in a controversial situation where the merits of a dispute may be uncertain, to agree to relax the contract provisions relating to interim payment when the overriding commercial interest is to secure early completion. This may take the form of allowing payment in full, notwithstanding work known or suspected to be defective[99]; advancing more money than is properly due on valuation to assist a contractor in difficulties[1]; or paying in advance of the due date for instalments.[2]

While it has been seen that inadvertent overpayment will not release a surety, and that there is no duty of care owed to the surety in this regard by the creditor,[3] payment concessions of these kinds made by a creditor with eyes open, even though in the expectation of avoiding the contractor's failure and securing completion, and so superficially seeming to benefit the surety, have been held by the Courts to release the surety *in toto* on numerous occasions.

ILLUSTRATIONS

(1) Payment for the construction of a dock entrance was to be by instalments of 75 per cent. of the price during the progress of work, with a 25 per cent. balance payable one month after completion. The contractor jointly with two sureties executed a due performance bond in favour of the owners. The owners, without informing a due performance surety, knowingly advanced some £13,000 in excess of the £36,000 then due on a 75 per cent. basis at the time when the contractor failed. The owners completed themselves, in fact for less than the contract price, and would have suffered no loss had they paid in accordance with the contract. The Court of King's Bench awarded nominal damages against the surety, holding that the loss had been caused by the advances made and not by the failure of performance,[4] but upon the owners refusing a full release the surety applied in Chancery for a permanent injunction. *Held*, by Lord Langdale M.R., that the advances made by the creditor without the surety's consent had released the surety, and any further proceedings to enforce the guarantee should be permanently stayed: *Calvert* v. *London Dock* (1838).[5]

(2) Payment under a shipbuilding contract was to be by fixed stage instal- **17·044** ments. The owner had allowed the builder, who became bankrupt before the

---

[99] *Reverend E.G. Doe (trustee)* v. *Canadian Surety Co.*, illustrated *supra*, para. (a), para. 17·037, and see *Town of Mulgrave* v. *Simcoe & Erie General Insurance Co.* (1977) 73 D.L.R. 3(d) 272 illustrated immediately *infra.*
[1] *Calvert* v. *London Dock Co.* (1838) 2 Keen 638.
[2] *General Steam Navigation Co.* v. *Rolt* (1858) 6 C.B., N.S., 550.
[3] *Fuller Construction* v. *Continental Insurance* (1973) 36 D.L.R. 3d 336, see *supra*, para. 17·031.
[4] *Warre* v. *Calvert* (1837) 7 A & D 143.
[5] 2 Keen 638.

ship was finished, to anticipate the last two instalments. In an action against a surety for due performance for the additional cost of completion and for delay penalties, the surety pleaded that the payments had been made without his knowledge and consent and had prejudiced his position. *Held*, by the Court of Exchequer Chamber, that unless the owner could prove that the advances had been made with the knowledge and assent of the surety and at his request, the surety must be released: *General Steam Navigation Co.* v. *Rolt.*[6]

(3) At the conclusion of a Canadian construction contract the owner contended that there were defects amounting to $650 in the main contractor's work, and some $1650 in certain sub-contractors' work. There was also $2800 uncompleted work by one other sub-contractor. The owner paid the contractor the $650 and $1650 in full, on the contractor's promise to see that the various deficiencies represented by those sums would be rectified, but withheld the $2800 in respect of the last sub-contractor (who, probably for this reason, did ultimately return and complete his work). The main contractor defaulted, and the other sub-contractors did not return to complete. *Held*, by the Nova Scotia Appellate Division, that the two knowing overpayments by the owner had discharged due performance sureties. *Town of Mulgrave* v. *Simcoe & Erie General Insurance Co.* (1977).[7]

17·045   Two principal considerations tend to be judicially emphasised in support of this rule. First, in cases where overpayment is involved, the effect will be to deprive the owner, and hence the surety, of the benefit of any retention or balance otherwise available as a security against any failure of performance. Secondly, the effect in all cases can be to remove or reduce the incentive or spur for the contractor to complete the guaranteed contract expeditiously. Thus, in the earlier *Calvert* case, referring to the provision for interim payment at 75 per cent. of the value, Lord Longdale M.R. said:[7a]

> "The effect of this stipulation was at the same time to urge [the contractor] to perform the work and to leave in the hands of [the owner] a fund wherewith to complete the work, if it did not; and thus it materially tended to protect sureties. What the [owner] did was perhaps calculated to make it easier for [the contractor] to complete the work, *if he acted with prudence and good faith*; but it also took away that particular sort of pressure which by the contract was intended to be applied to him." (Emphasis supplied.)

In the later *Rolt* case Cockburn L.J. said of the anticipatory payments there made to the builder, that the owners had:

> "thereby prejudiced the position of the surety, who loses, by that anticipatory payment to the principal, the strong inducement which would otherwise have operated on his [the principal's] mind to induce him to finish the work in due time."[8]

---

[6] (1858) 6 C.B., N.S., 550.
[7] (1977) 73 D.L.R. (3d) 272. See also *Reverend E.G. Doe (trustee)* v. *Canadian Surety Co.* [1937] 1 S.C.R. 1, illustrated *supra*, para. (a), para. 17·037.
[7a] 2 Keen 638, 644–5 (1837).
[8] *General Steam Navigation Co.* v. *Rolt* (1858) 6 C.B., N.S., 550, 595.

Again in the *Rolt* case, Pollock C.B. said:

> "... prima facie, the withdrawal of a fund which is a security for the thing in respect of the not doing of which he is now called upon to pay damages is a prejudice to the surety. He is not in the same situation with regard to his principal, in which he ought to be placed; he is deprived of the security of the fund out of which the [creditors] might in the first instance have indemnified themselves."[9]

The considerations mentioned in these passages are in fact powerful ones in a construction contract threatened by insolvency. The first argument (the reduction in the owner's security resulting from such payments) can be re-stated by pointing out that to the extent that overpayment has taken place it must directly and measurably increase the creditor's ultimate claim against both debtor and surety (even in some cases, constituting the only element of claim, as in the *Calvert* case). The second argument (removal of the incentive to complete) is in fact perhaps more powerful, in the special context of construction contracts, than the early judiciary may have realised. Disregarding altogether situations of financial stringency or approaching insolvency, it is a not uncommon practice for perfectly solvent contractors to "front-load" prices so that early work on a project will be more profitable than the finishing stages, with a resulting tendency for the premature transfer of resources to new contracts entered into before completion of the old in order to maintain both a high level of current profitability and cash flow, and a "bank" of future work. With many contractors, therefore, there is in any case a tendency towards the end of a project for resources to be deployed elsewhere and wherever owner pressures are at their strongest.[10] In a situation of financial stringency and approaching insolvency, therefore, relaxation of pressure, *a fortiori* sums overpaid, can paradoxically result in the diversion of resources to other contracts where pressures are felt to be more intense, thereby increasing the chance that, if insolvency does supervene, it will be the guaranteed contract which will suffer. Proof of this having happened is obviously more controversial and difficult to establish than the straightforward loss resulting directly from an overpayment, and may tend to explain the doctrine of release *in toto* evolved in the early cases,[11] but it is nevertheless clear from the reasoning in the *Calvert* and *Rolt* judgments, as in the case of alterations of the contract under the *Holme* v. *Brunskill* principle,[12] that generally no enquiry will be permitted to ascertain whether in fact prejudice of the kind described has occurred.

17·046

---

[9] *Ibid.* at pp. 605–6.
[10] See this explained in more detail, when advocating interim payment by suitably calculated fixed rather than valuation-based instalments as a more efficient inducement to progress than traditional liquidated damages remedies, in *Construction Contract Policy* published by Centre of Construction Law, King's College London (1989), pp. 225–7.
[11] See particularly the language of Lord Langdale M.R. quoted *supra*, referring to the contractors' treating the sums overpaid with prudence and good faith.
[12] Quoted *supra*, para. 17·034.

17·047   Such an enquiry would obviously involve examination of the use actually made by the contractor of any overpaid funds, since to the extent that the funds could be shown to have been used for the carrying out of work under the guaranteed contract, and not diverted elsewhere, there could be no loss and only benefit to both creditor and surety. This latter point was clearly taken by a United States court in a compensated surety case.

ILLUSTRATION

A general contractor knowingly advanced payments which were not yet due to a sub-contractor, in the belief that the sub-contractor would be able to complete the work if enabled to meet its payroll and to pay for supplies, and the advance payments were in fact used by the sub-contractor to pay its employees on the project. Later the sub-contractor failed, and the main contractor proceeded against the sub-contractor's surety for the additional cost of completing the work. The district judge awarded the additional cost of completion, but released the surety *pro tanto* to the extent of the advance payments. *Held*, by the U.S. 6th Circuit Court of Appeal, that the Court below had overlooked the development of the rule in many jurisdictions requiring proof of loss or prejudice to a compensated surety following a departure from the terms of the contract. Since the advance payments had in fact been used for the further completion of the contract they had benefited the surety, and the general contractor was entitled to recover in full. *Ramada Development Co.* v. *U.S. Fidelity and Guaranty Co.* (1980).[13]

17·048
In the case of compensated sureties the principle in relation to advanced payment was stated as long ago as 1911 by an American authority cited in the above case in the following terms:

"If money is given to a contractor or for his benefit by an owner in advance of a payment becoming due upon a contract as a temporary loan, or for a special purpose, the amount thereof and the circumstances of the payment should be considered in connection with the obligation of the surety. The rule of strict construction is liable at times to work a practical injustice, and it ought not to be extended beyond the reason for the rule, particularly when the surety is engaged in the business of becoming a surety for pay and presumably for profit ... [the money given in this case] was in the nature of a temporary loan for the express purpose of preventing an abandonment of the contract by the contractors and to avoid labour troubles ... the payments made cannot, under any view that can be taken of them, be said to remove in any degree the incentive that the contractors had prior thereto for completing the contract. If the rule invoked by the [surety] is applied in this case, it will be both harsh and unjust."[14]

It is submitted that in cases of advanced or overpayment there is today everything to be said for the adoption in the Commonwealth of the United

---

[13] 626 F2(d) 517 (1980). See also *Maryland Casualty Co.* v. *Eagle River Union High School District* 205 N.W. 926 (1925). For a similar decision where payments had been made without required Architect's certificates and the money used for completion of the work.

[14] *St. John's College* v. *Aetna Indemnity Co.* 94 N.E. 994; 201 N.Y. 335 (1911). For the general position of *pro tanto* release only following overpayment, see Am.Jur. 2nd, Vol. 17, para. 40.

States position, at least where compensated sureties are involved, and perhaps more widely. Meanwhile, however, it remains important for bonds to be drafted so as expressly to permit advanced or additional payments at the owner's discretion.

(ii) *Alterations of the work*

A very common incident of construction contracts will be alterations of the work itself, usually of course as a result of an express power in the construction contract. In less formal contracts without a variation clause this is usually achieved by collateral agreement.

17·049

Where a variation clause is present, no alteration of the contract itself, as opposed to the work under it, is involved, and it is submitted that, even in the absence of an express power in the bond, and provided that the principal construction contract documentation has been sufficiently identified or cited by reference or otherwise in the bond, it will not be possible, at the very least in the case of commercial due performance bonds, for the security to obtain a release by reason of the exercise of the variation power,[15] unless some express limit on the power to vary has been imposed by the bond. In addition the Courts have understandably been reluctant to treat alterations in or departures from the work as originally specified as releasing the surety in cases where this has not resulted from positive instructions or action on the part of the owner, but rather from his acquiescence in the face of contractor initiatives or pressures. They have also been reluctant to interpret alterations of the work authorised in such circumstances as infringing any express limitations on the power to vary which may be imposed in a bond.

ILLUSTRATIONS

(1) After complaints from the contractor an owner instructed his architect not to interpret the specification too strictly, and as a result the architect accepted a leaner mix of cement than he would otherwise have required under the contract description "of the best quality". There was no evidence that this contributed to the subsequent failure of the contractor. *Held*, by the Supreme Court of Canada, that this was not a "change or alteration in the plant or specification for the work" requiring immediate notice under an express provision in the bond. *Ferrara* v. *National Surety Co.* (1917).[16]

17·050

(2) Specialist manufacturers of pre-cast concrete pipes persuaded owners to use them as an economical substitute for steel pipes, and contracted to manufacture and supply them. Their surety's due performance bond provided, first, that the surety should not be released by "any arrangements made for ... variation of the work" but subject to written notice and consent, and, secondly, that the surety would be bound by all the decisions orders and directions of the engineer as if a principal party to the contract. When difficulties in

---

[15] *Wren* v. *Emmetts Contractors Pty. Ltd.* (1969) 43 A.L.J.R. 213 see *supra*, para. 17·042, and see for an early U.S. case *U.S.* v. *Walsh* 115 F. 697 (1902).
[16] [1917] 1 W.W.R. 719, illustrated more fully *supra*, Subsection (5), para. 17·029.

manufacture occurred the engineer acquiesced in proposals by the suppliers to use calcium chloride in the mix, which was not mentioned in the detailed specification, and also to use hot water rather than the specified steam heating for the curing of the pipes. When the pipes failed to pass tests following manufacture, which it was later found was due to the use of calcium chloride in the mix, the owners determined the contract. When they sued the sureties, the latter claimed to be released, alleging variations and that notice of and consent to them had not been given as required by the bond. *Held*, by the Supreme Court of Canada, that the use of calcium chloride where the specifications were silent did not involve a variation, but was simply a method of manufacture agreed to by the engineer in reliance on the suppliers; and that while the use of hot water proposed by the supplier was a change from the specification, it was not a variation within the intent of the first provision in the bond, but was covered by the second provision requiring compliance with the decisions orders and directions of the engineer, so that the surety was not released. *Hayes* v. *City of Regina* (1959).[17]

17·051   Although not very likely to occur in a normal construction context, there can be cases where the work or project may be regarded as severable, and a due performance surety remain liable for the remainder, notwithstanding that he has been released in relation to one part of the work.

ILLUSTRATION

Shipbuilders sold a ship in return for a payment down plus a second ship in part exchange, on which latter, however, the buyers retained a mortgage for £6,000. As part of the transaction, the shipbuilders agreed to put the ship they had sold into good order within two weeks of its arrival in port, and to repair the part exchange ship up to Lloyds A1 standard, and the sureties guaranteed due performance of the shipbuilders' work on both ships. Without informing the sureties the shipbuilders later agreed with the buyers both to increase the work, and shorten the time for carrying it out, on the ship which they had sold. *Held*, by the Court of Common Pleas, that the sureties had been released in relation to the ship sold, but not in relation to the work on the part-exchange ship. *Harrison* v. *Seymour* (1866).[18]

(iii) *Extensions of time*

17·052   It has been seen[19] that in the case of payment guarantees a binding agreement between the creditor and debtor to extend the time for payment will release a surety if without his consent, for the same reasons as overpayment in the case of a performance guarantee,[20] namely removal of an incentive to early performance by the debtor, and taking away the surety's right to compel a prompt exercise of the creditor's remedies against the debtor.[21]

---

[17] [1959] S.C.R. 801.
[18] L.R. 1 C.P. 518.
[19] See para. (b), para. 17·041.
[20] See *supra*, para. (c)(i), para. 17·043 *et seq.*
[21] See *supra*, para. (a), para. 17·035.

Similarly in the case of a performance guarantee, a binding contract to extend the debtor's time for performance would under the older law serve to release the surety, notwithstanding that in most cases the only consequence would be to reduce the liquidated or other damages recoverable by the owner for delay, to that extent benefit the surety. However, it is submitted that on general principle such an agreement can only have this effect where to the knowledge of the owner there is no entitlement of the contractor to an extension. Agreement to extend time where the contractor is so entitled will not generally be an alteration of the contract, and any agreement to extend time as a consequence of a breach by the owner could not, unless excessive, prejudice the surety, but would merely recognise the consequences of the breach, leaving the surety to seek a possible release on the different ground of a "not unsubstantial" breach by the owner of an obligation "embodied" in the bond or guarantee.[22]

(iv) *Other alterations to the contract*

It seems very arguable that, apart from questions of release of the surety **17·053** *in toto* and in the absence of express provision, an alteration knowingly made by a creditor in the debtor's obligations without a surety's consent will be a breach of any contract there may be between creditor and surety, and if so that this should sound in damages, or go to causation, so as to result in an apparent *pro tanto* release of the surety. This may be the explanation of a very shortly reported Court of Appeal case in England where a construction owner, who had agreed to an independent arbitrator rather than require the contractor to submit to the binding decision of the owner's own surveyor as required by the contract, was held unable to recover the greater costs of the reference from the contractor's sureties. Superficially this was an apparent case of *pro tanto* release, but the fact that the sureties had conceded liability for the sum awarded by the arbitrator may perhaps have meant that otherwise there would have been a full release.[23]

However, it is of the essence of the principle laid down in *Holme* v. *Brunskill*, and of Cotton L.J.'s dictum in that case,[24] that in the absence of purely trivial alterations or ones which could not on any possible view prejudice the surety,[25] first, no enquiry is permitted as to the extent or even existence of prejudice, and, secondly, the release of the surety will be *in toto* and not *pro tanto*. The American cases, on the other hand, which the Commonwealth Courts may well now be disposed to follow, require to be satisfied, in the case of compensated sureties, both as to the existence and the extent of any prejudice suffered, and will only accord *pro tanto* release for any damage so established.

---

[22] Compare the somewhat unclear facts in *Mercers Co.* v. *New Hampshire Insurance Co.* [1992] 2 Lloyd's Rep. 365, illustrated *supra*, Section 1(4), para. 17·013.
[23] *Hoole UDC* v. *Fidelity and Deposit Co. of Maryland* [1916] 2 K.B. 568.
[24] See *supra*, Subsection (6)(a), paras. 17·034 and 17·035.
[25] See, *e.g.* the alteration of wording agreed to in *Andrews* v. *Lawrence* (1865) 19 C.B., N.S., 768.

SECTION 3. UNCONDITIONAL OR "ON DEMAND" BONDS

(1) Generally

(a) Recent emergence

17·054   "On demand" or unconditional "performance" bonds, nominally purporting to secure due performance of a contracting party's obligations other than payment, have only recently emerged in commerce. This seems to have started in international commercial contracts where sellers or suppliers were increasingly required to provide unconditional guarantees of performance of their obligations, usually to balance the letters of credit guaranteeing the buyer's payment obligations, including advance payment, which had for long been an essential lifeline of international commerce. It was of these bonds securing performance of sellers' or manufacturers' obligations that the Court of Appeal said in 1978:

> "A performance bond is a new creature so far as we are concerned. It has many similarities to a letter of credit, with which of course we are very familiar. It has been long established that when a letter of credit is issued and confirmed by a bank, the bank must pay it if the documents are in order and the terms of the credit are satisfied. Any dispute between buyer and seller must be settled between themselves. The bank must honour the credit."[26]

17·055   In construction projects, *conditional* due performance bonds covering all the contractors' various obligations under the contract have been a familiar feature for well over a century, but a new class of "on demand" or *unconditional* bonds came into use in the international field in the 1970s similar to the trend in international sale or supply contracts. These "on demand" bonds in construction contracts have already been mentioned *supra*,[27] and have been extensively discussed in C.C.P.P.[28] While the new unconditional sellers' or suppliers' obligations in international commerce have more recently been described judicially on a number of occasions as "performance bonds" or "performance guarantees"[29] therefore, confusion will be avoided if it is appreciated that the identical description has been used for decades in the construction industry for *conditional* contractors' due performance guarantees requiring proof of contractor default. Lord Denning M.R.'s analysis in the *Edward Owen* case shows clearly that all *unconditional* performance bonds, whatever their subject

---

[26] *Edward Owen Engineering Ltd.* v. *Barclays Bank International Ltd.* [1978] 1 Q.B. 159, 169, *per* Lord Denning M.R.
[27] See Section 1, para. 17·003, and Section 1(2), para. 17·006.
[28] See paras. 19–21—27.
[29] Notably by Lord Denning M.R. in *Edward Owen Engineering Ltd.* v. *Barclays Bank International Ltd.* [1978] 1 Q.B. 159, 165–9, and see the same usage adopted by Young J. in *Hortico (Australia) Pty. Ltd.* v. *Energy Equipment (Australia) Pty. Ltd.* [1985] 1 N.S.W.L.R. 545.

matter, are, first, *primary* obligations of the bondsman or issuing bank equivalent to an indemnity given to the owner or other obligee, and, secondly, despite their description, operate entirely dependently of the degree of performance or non-performance of the principal contract, and are effectively the equivalent of a promissory note payable upon demand.[30] So in an Australian case it has rightly been said of the contractual description "Bank Guarantee" there given to an *unconditional* document available in place of retention moneys as security for a construction contractor's "due and faithful performance of the work":

> "... the description 'guarantee' commercially applied to the bank documents in this case is, in my opinion, a complete misnomer. The relationship of the bank to the owner or the contractor has, in my opinion, none of the elements of suretyship ... there is no basis whatever upon which the unconditional nature of the bank's promise to pay on demand can be qualified by reference to the terms of the contract between the contractor and the owner."[31]

(b) Nature of unconditional or "on demand" undertaking

The essence of an on demand bond or guarantee derives from express   **17·056**
wording which "triggers" the surety's liability upon some event, document or certificate, or more often a mere demand or "call" by the creditor (provided the call is expressed in accordance with any requirements of form which are to be inferred from the wording of the bond).[32] In such cases the occurrence of the event or document or the making of the demand in appropriate form will override any need to establish the accuracy or justification of any facts or alleged facts, such as failure of due performance, under the principal contract on which the bond or guarantee may have been nominally conditioned. In the case of construction contracts the nominal or cosmetic basis for the creditor's calling of such an unconditional bond is usually stated to be failure of "due performance" of the contractor's obligations (although "guarantees" or bonds for *due payment* by construction owners, where the contractor is in a position to require them, are now not infrequently required to be expressed unconditionally as well). In fact, the attributes of the modern unconditional performance bond in both commercial and construction contracts, and its intended consequences, have clearly been derived from the letters of credit used to secure the *payment* obligations in international commercial contracts. Classically, these guarantee an automatic consequence (payment) at a particular stage of the transaction (for example, delivery on board ship evidenced by a bill of lading or other carrier's receipt), usually well in advance of receipt or acceptance and examination of goods by the purchaser in his own country. Being payment obligations, these letters of

---

[30] See, *per* Lord Denning M.R., in the *Edward Owen* case, cited *supra*, on this point Section 1(2), para. 17·006.

[31] *Wood Hall Ltd.* v. *Pipeline Authority* (1979) 141 C.L.R. 443, 445, *per* Barwick C.J.

[32] *I.F. Contractors Ltd.* v. *Lloyd's Bank Plc* (1990) 51 BLR 1, C.A., illustrated *infra*, para. 17·066.

credit became negotiable to third parties, introducing an additional commercial reason why an acceptor or issuing bank should not be concerned with the merits of any dispute between debtor or creditor in the absence of established fraud.[33] They are also frequently exchanged against documents giving title to the goods in question. Neither of these two attributes are a consideration with contractors' performance bonds, however, where any expressed payment obligation in the bond only indicates the upper limit of liability under the bond.[34]

17·057   While letters of credit are accordingly likely to be conditioned on relatively simple and easily ascertained and documented or certified events, such as the arrival of a named date, or delivery of goods on board or to a warehouse, it will be apparent that due performance by a manufacturer or supplier or by a construction contractor of many different obligations over a lengthy contract period will be a far less precise and much more controversial requirement. The following early case illustrates the emergence of the unconditional "due performance" guarantee in a commercial manufacture and supply contract setting.

ILLUSTRATION

£25,000 was payable by the buyer as an initial advance "on presentation of the seller bank guarantee" against a total price of £500,000 for manufacture and delivery of equipment over a two year period. The seller's bank provided the guarantee to refund the initial advance payment in favour of the buyers "on their first demand in case of non-delivery of the ordered goods". The sellers completed manufacture of much if not all of the equipment, and had received over £300,000 against a final instalment due of £425,000, when there was a dispute as to whether there had been satisfactory delivery on time, and the sellers sought an injunction to prevent the buyers recovering the initial £25,000 from the bank by calling on the guarantee. *Held*, by the Court of Appeal, that the Bank was in a similar position to having opened an irrevocable letter of credit, and its obligation to pay did not depend on a correct resolution of the dispute as to the sufficiency of the seller's performance. *Howe Richardson Scale Co. Ltd.* v. *Polimex–Cekop* (1978).[35]

Whether a bond or guarantee is unconditional or not will depend, therefore, on whether, as a matter of interpretation and expressed intention, and, notwithstanding any references to "due performance", the requirement of a demand or call by the obligee or beneficiary, or the provision of some other document or certificate, is seen to override any questions of contract compliance as between the debtor and creditor. Examples near the borderline are discussed in Subsection (2), "Interpretation" *infra*.

---

[33] See *Discount Records Ltd.* v. *Barclays Bank Ltd.* [1975] 1 W.L.R. 315, 319, *per* Megarry J.
[34] For the similarities see Lord Diplock in *United City Merchants (Investments) Ltd.* v. *Royal Bank of Canada* [1983] A.C. 168, 183H–184A.
[35] [1978] 1 Lloyd's Rep. 161.

Where a bond or "guarantee" is construed as being unconditional or on **17·058** demand, it is not only, therefore, not a guarantee in the properly defined sense of a liability arising on the default of another, but any reference in the document indicating that due performance of obligations in the principal contract is the purpose or objective of the bond or "guarantee"—for example, "due performance" wording—must be treated as cosmetic and of no practical or legal effect as between the beneficiary and the issuing bank or bondsman. However, such wording may have one consequence *as between the parties to the principal contract*, since if it is possible to establish positively that the beneficiary has no honest belief in the existence of any default in respect of which the bond has been nominally conditioned, this may be treated as fraud, and may afford remedies by injunction or otherwise to the debtor against the calling of the bond by the beneficiary, or against payment by the issuing bank against the call, or against that bank's subsequent exercise of any counter-indemnities, provided always that the bank itself had knowledge of the fraud.[36] Such wording may also in some cases serve to support an implied term of the principal contract, or of any side agreement to provide the unconditional bond, having the effect of restricting the exercise of the beneficiary's right to call the bond, with attendant remedies by way of injunction, as between debtor and creditor, even in the absence of fraud. These defences against the calling of the bond, which it should be emphasised are likely to be available only in very rare cases, are discussed in Subsection (4) *infra*.

(c) Counter-indemnities and the "indemnity string"

In international contracts the practice has grown up, originally fostered **17·059** by a number of Third World countries, where in their capacity as purchasers of goods or as construction owners their governments or public entities require the provision of unconditional due performance bonds by foreign suppliers or contractors through a local issuing or confirming bank, itself often a government or government-influenced entity. No doubt this is with the twin objectives, first, of producing premium income for that institution and, secondly, of ensuring rapid and unquestioning compliance with any call which the public or government beneficiary of the bond might decide to make. The local bank in turn avoids any ultimate substantive liability, and so any need to have recourse to its own funds in the event of a call, by refusing to issue or confirm the bond without an unconditional counter-indemnity from an international bank of standing, usually, but not always, in the contractor's country. That bank in turn will require a counter-indemnity, and it or the last of any intermediate banks will do so from the contractor's own domestic retail bank. By this means payment of the initial call by the original issuing or confirming bank in the country of the project, and activation of its own and any later counter-indemnities by telex will result in virtually immediate debiting of the con-

---

[36] See Subsection (4), *infra*.

tractor's domestic bank account by its own banker following the call made on the original issuing bank.

Apart from the effect of such a system on the cost of unconditional bonding, with only one participating bank (the last) at effective financial risk, no direct legal consequences flow from this practice, and many if not most of the cases discussed in the next subsections are concerned as much with the interpretation and enforcement of one or other of the later counter-indemnities as with the original bond or guarantee. For example, where fraud, in the sense defined above, is suspected as between the original beneficiary caller and the original issuing or confirming bank, this may result in proceedings brought by the supplier or contractor with the object of preventing payment by a later counter-indemnifying bank, which, if successful, would break the chain and safeguard the contractor's own funds.[37]

(2) Interpretation

17·060   Whether a bond or guarantee is unconditional will depend on whether it contemplates that some event, such as the issue of a document or certificate like a bill of lading, or the arrival of a date, or a mere written demand by the beneficiary, is to "trigger" liability under the bond irrespective of the rights of the parties *inter se* under the principal "guaranteed" contract. Since the words "on demand" can be used merely to indicate the timing of an obligation and as an additional requirement to a proven default under the principal contract, they will not by themselves necessarily indicate an unconditional bond obligation. The words "on first demand" usually will.[38]

While some remarks of Lord Denning M.R. in *Edward Owen* case have occasionally been taken out of context as suggesting that contractors' performance bonds generally, including those in the construction industry, are all *prima facie* liable to be regarded as of an "on demand" character,[39] it should be emphasised that this is not so, and that there is no presumption (indeed the reverse having regard to the long history in the construction industry of contractors' conditional performance bonds dependent on proof of default) that such a bond is intended or likely to be unconditional in the case of a normal construction contract performance bond. In the *Edward Owen* case, Lord Denning M.R. was dealing with an obviously unconditional performance bond payable "*on demand without proof or conditions*" and issued to the buyer to cover the seller's obligations in an international "supply and install" contract, and balanced by an earlier

---

[37] See particularly the cases referred to in Subsection (3) *infra*, and see the English and U.S. cases discussed in greater detail in C.C.P.P., paras. 19–22—25.

[38] See, *e.g.* the guarantee in *Howe Richardson Scale Co. Ltd.* v. *Polimex–Cepok* [1978] 1 Lloyd's Rep. 161, illustrated *supra*, para. 17·057.

[39] See [1978] 1 Q.B. 159, 170H, 171AB, and see the *Syarikat* case illustrated *infra*, para. 17·063, which appears to have adopted this view of the *Edward Owen* judgment.

unconditional letter of credit in favour of the seller for the price. Thus Lord Denning acknowledged openly that these were only recently introduced creatures in commerce,[39a] whereas conditional contractors' performance bonds have been common in the construction industry for well over a century. Similarly, Staughton L.J. was again dealing with an obviously unconditional bond, of the new kind: "We undertake to pay you *unconditionally the said amount on demand* being your claim for damages", and speaking only in the context of these new unconditional bonds, when he said:

"I take this to show that there is a bias or presumption in favour of the construction which holds a performance bond to be conditioned on documents rather than facts..."

and again:

"The first principle which the cases establish is that a performance bond, like a letter of credit, will generally be found to be conditioned upon the production of one or more documents rather than upon the existence of facts which these documents assert."[40]

No such presumption, it is submitted, applies to construction industry performance bonds.

ILLUSTRATIONS

(1) Sureties, who had entered into traditional *conditional* performance "guarantee bonds" on behalf of building contractors and in favour of the City of Liverpool, obtained a counter-guarantee from the contractors' parent company as follows: "The guarantor hereby undertakes that the contractor will duly perform and observe all its obligations under the contracts and that if [the surety] *is called upon* to make any payments ... under any of the said Guarantee Bonds the Guarantor will forthwith *on demand* pay to [the surety] the full amount of such payment..." Following termination of the contract in disputed circumstances, the City did "call upon" the sureties to pay the amount of the bond, and they in turn brought proceedings on the counter-guarantee, arguing that it was conditioned simply on a call, whether right or wrong, by the City. *Held*, by Donaldson J., that the surety's claim against the parent company failed. The words "is called upon" meant no more than that actual payment by the surety was not necessary, but they only applied where the sureties would be liable to pay. Proof of liability was required, as otherwise the opening undertaking that the contractor would duly perform would be otiose. *General Surety & Guarantee Co. Ltd.* v. *Francis Parker Limited* (1977).[41]

[Note: Interestingly, counsel (Staughton Q.C.) apparently advanced no argument in this relatively early due performance case based on the "on-demand" wording used. No doubt the background of the undoubted conditional liability under the primary bond was an important factor in the decision, but Donaldson J. also stressed the need for clear draftsmanship such as "conclusive evidence" wording.]

17·061

[39a] See *supra*, para. 17·054, and see (1978) 1 Q.B. 159, 169.
[40] *I.F. Contractors Ltd.* v. *Lloyd's Bank Plc* (1990) 51 BLR 1, 7–8, 9, illustrated *infra*, para. 17·066.
[41] 6 BLR 18.

(2) English suppliers contracted to supply and erect greenhouses in Libya for Libyan Government buyers. The contract provided that an irrevocable letter of credit for the price should be opened at the suppliers' English bank, and that the suppliers should provide a performance bond for some £50,000, which was to be given to the Libyan buyers by a local Libyan bank, which in turn was to be given a performance bond by the suppliers' English bank against the suppliers' counter-guarantee to that bank. The English bank's performance bond to the Libyan bank was expressed to be payable "*on demand without proof or conditions*". The Libyan buyers in breach of contract never provided the letter of credit, and the English suppliers accepted their conduct as a repudiation of the contract and, after informing the English bank, obtained an interim injunction restraining them from paying the Libyan bank. *Held,* by the Court of Appeal, affirming Kerr J., that a performance bond using this wording stood on a similar footing to a letter of credit and, unless the English bank had notice of clear fraud on the part of the Libyan buyers or the Libyan bank,[41a] and in the absence of sufficient evidence of fraud before the Court, that the injunction must be discharged: *Edward Owen Engineering Ltd.* v. *Barclay's Bank International Ltd.* (1977).[41b]

17·062   (3) Suppliers who were successful bidders for a contract for the sale of sugar to a public authority in Egypt were required to provide a performance bond in place of an earlier bid bond. The bond, issued by an Egyptian bank to the buyers, undertook to pay the buyer the amount of the bond "on your written demand in the event that the supplier fails to execute the contract in perfect performance". In a dispute between the Egyptian bank and counter-indemnifying banks who had refused to pay on the ground that there had been no breach of the supply contract. *Held,* by the Court of Appeal, that the objective of the bond would be defeated if the Egyptian bank was required to satisfy itself as to the existence of a breach; the bond was unconditional and proof of breach unnecessary. *Esal (Commodities) Ltd.* v. *Oriental Credit Ltd.* (1985).[42]

(4) A bank guaranteed payment by the owners of the contract sum for the design, manufacture, installation and commissioning of a boiler in New South Wales. The guarantee given to the manufacturer stated: "The ... Bank ... hereby undertakes to hold itself responsible to you on behalf of [the owners] for the sum of $570,000 with regard to design, supply, installation and commissioning of one ... boiler and housing to be installed at .... The Bank will be responsible for the said sum until a notification has been received from you ... that you desire payment to be made to you ... Should you notify the Bank that you desire payment to be made to you ... such payment ... will ... be made forthwith to you without reference to [the owners] and, notwithstanding any notice given by them to the Bank not to pay same." The order was cancelled by the owners, and when the manufacturers called on the guarantors for their damages, the owners applied for an injunction against them and the bank to prevent payment to the contractors, contending that the owners had validly rescinded the contract for late delivery. *Held,* by Young J., that the only possible construction of the document was that it was an unconditional promise to pay intended as security for the manufacturers; that an interlocutory injunction should be discharged, and a Mareva injunction attaching the sums paid by the bank should also be refused, notwithstanding that the manufacturers' accounts showed them to be technically insolvent. *Hortico (Australia) Pty. Ltd.* v. *Energy Equipment (Australia) Pty. Ltd.* (1985).[43]

[41a] For avoidance of such bonds by fraud see *infra,* Subsection (4), paras. 17·067 *et seq.*
[41b] [1978] 1 Q.B. 159.
[42] [1985] 2 Lloyd's Rep. 546. Further illustrated *infra,* para. 17·065.
[43] [1985] 1 N.S.W.L.R. 545.

(5) A bank's guarantee of a building contract in Malaysia headed "Bank **17·063**
Guarantee for the Performance Bond" read: "If the Contractor (unless
relieved from the performance by any clause of the Contract...) shall in any
respect fail to execute the Contract or commit any breach of his obligations
thereunder then the Guarantor will indemnify and pay the principal
[M$————] provided that the principal...has made a claim...not later than
six months after the expiry date of the Contract". The contractors ceased
work on the site in disputed circumstances, alleging a wrongful termination
and claiming damages. When called on by the owners the bank refused to
honour the guarantee. In an action by the owners against the bank they contended that the bank was in the same position as if it had opened an irrevocable letter of credit, relying on the *Howe Richardson* case.[44] *Held*, by Lim J.,
relying on statements by Lord Denning M.R. in the *Edward Owen* case,[45] that
performance guarantees given by banks must be honoured unless there was
clear fraud of which the bank had notice. *Syarikat Perumahan Sdn.* v. *Bank
Bumiputra* (1991).[46]

[Note: Lord Denning M.R.'s remarks relied upon by Lim J. must, it is submitted, be taken in context as referring to cases where letter of credit or "on
first demand" or other appropriate wording has been used.[47] So, too, the
Howe Richardson case makes the comparison with letters of credit only in the
context of cases where the wording justifies an unconditional interpretation,
it is submitted. Nothing in the wording of the guarantee in the above case, at
least as reported in I.C.L.R., appears to justify an unconditional interpretation, the reference to making a claim merely indicating the duration of the
obligation under the bond.]

It has been seen that in a very recent case, in 1994, where traditional
bond wording had been used, with no reference to a demand and no other
express indication, a sub-contractor's due performance bond in respect of
damages sustained by the main contractor as a result of breach of the sub-
contract was held, by the Court of Appeal to be unconditional, requiring
only a bona fide demand by the main contractor, see the *Trafalgar House*
case, discussed and doubted *supra* section 1(3)(*b*).

(3) Call must Conform to Bond Requirements

Where the event which is to trigger liability under an unconditional bond **17·064**
is the written or other demand of the beneficiary, but the bond nevertheless also indicates as is usually the case in construction contract performance bonds, the nature or subject matter of the demand to be made, the
demand or call must be worded to conform with that requirement, although it would seem that a doctrine of strict compliance which has
evolved in relation to letters of credit will not be applied so rigorously in
the case of performance bonds. Thus, it has been said of an on-demand
bond of this kind that a beneficiary's "need to inform the bank of the true
basis upon which he is making his demand may be very salutary", where

---

[44] [1978] 1 Lloyd's Rep. 161, illustrated *supra*, para. 17·057.
[45] [1978] 1 Q.B. 159, 171.
[46] [1991] 2 M.L.J. 565.
[47] See the discussion *supra*, para. 17·060.

the beneficiary was seeking the surety's agreement to an extension of the period of such a bond as an alternative to making an immediate call; and again:

> "The requirement that he must, when making his request for an extension, also commit himself to claiming that the contract has not been complied with, may prevent some of the many abuses of the performance bond procedure that understandably occur."[48]

ILLUSTRATIONS

17·065   (1) A bank originally guaranteed: "We undertake to pay the said amount on your written demand in the event that the supplier fails to ship the agreed quantity in accordance with the terms of their contract with you". This was later amended to "... on your written demand in the event that the supplier fails to execute the contract in perfect performance". The buyers wrote requesting payment of the amount of the bond or alternatively an extension of its date which was about to expire, but giving no reasons. *Held*, by the Court of Appeal, that in addition to the beneficiary making the demand he must also inform the bank that he does so on the basis provided for in the performance bond itself. *Esal (Commodities) Ltd.* v. *Oriental Credit Ltd.* (1985).[49]

17·066   (2) (a) An unconditional performance bond in favour of owners of poultry slaughter houses being built in Iraq was expressed "to indemnify you against any damages that you may sustain ... covering performance of contract guarantee *covering damages which you claim are duly and properly owing by [the contractors]* ... we undertake to pay you unconditionally the said amount on demand being your claim for damages..." The owners' subsequent written demand to the issuing local bank was: "In view of the non-discharge by the company of its contractual obligations in making good the deficiencies of the slaughter-houses ... we request ... transference of [the amounts guaranteed]." The contractors brought proceedings for injunctions and declarations that the demands had been defective and, the bonds having now lapsed, that there was no liability. *Held*, by the Court of Appeal, overruling Leggatt J. and following *Siporex Trade S.A.* v. *Banque Indosuez*,[50] that there was less need for a doctrine of strict compliance in the case of performance bonds than in the case of letters of credit; that the demand need not follow the exact wording of the bond; and that since the demand in substance, although it did not in terms mention damages, did imply that what it claimed was damages for breach of contract, the owners were entitled to be paid on the bond.

       (b) On two of the three sites in Iraq the issuing local bank had obtained counter-indemnities from an English bank to pay "on demand any sum or sums *which you may be obliged to pay*". On the third site the counter-indemnity was to pay "any amount *you state* you are obliged to pay". The Iraqi bank's actual demand was: "At the beneficiaries' demand please credit full amount ... due to shortages not finished yet". *Held*, by the Court of Appeal, overruling Leggatt J., that although there was a presumption that an

---

[48] *Per* Ackner L.J. in *Esal (Commodities) Ltd.* v. *Oriental Credit Ltd.* [1985] 2 Lloyd's Rep. 546, 550.
[49] [1975] 2 Lloyd's Rep. 546. Illustrated more fully *supra*, para. 17·062.
[50] [1986] 2 Lloyd's Rep. 146.

unconditional bond would be conditioned on a document rather than a fact, in the case of the first two sites the demand, since the local bank was as a fact obliged to pay under its bond, was valid; but not on the third site, which required a statement of the obligation to pay: *I.F. Contractors Ltd.* v. *Lloyds Bank Plc and Rafidain Bank* (1990).[51]

[Note: As explained *supra*,[52] the statements of principle in Staughton L.J.'s judgment should not be treated as raising any presumption that performance bonds in normal construction contracts, as opposed to bonds for due performance of sellers' and suppliers' obligations in international commercial contracts, are to be regarded as unconditional or on demand rather than conditional and requiring proof of default.]

(4) Fraud as a Ground of Avoidance

The essence of an unconditional performance bond will be that the issuing bank or guarantor is obliged to pay the beneficiary without investigation of the contractual position as between the beneficiary and the principal debtor, and that the issuing bank will then be prima facie entitled to enforce any counter-indemnity. The English Courts have repeatedly stated, however, that a general exception to this will be where there is fraud.[53] Apparently, fraud for this purpose will be on the part of a beneficiary who knows that there is no right to payment, but expressly or impliedly represents his claim to be valid,[54] provided that this is known to the issuing bank at the time of paying or passing on the demand,[55] although later knowledge, if the bond has not yet been paid, will probably also suffice.[56] The so-called "fraud exception" will also apparently apply where the beneficiary claims payment in good faith, but the bank is aware of an invalidity.[57] The basis of this "fraud exception" is not a breach of the particular contract between the ultimate debtor and the issuing bank, but an equitable jurisdiction to prevent the defrauding of the ultimate debtor.[58] However, despite considerable lip service to this apparent exception, it cannot be said that it has proved of much practical benefit to debtors in the English courts, however strong the facts might seem.

17·067

Thus, in the *Edward Owen* case Lord Denning M.R. observed:

"On the facts so far known, it appears that the English suppliers had not been in default at all. The only person in default were the Libyan customers. They

---

[51] 51 BLR 1.
[52] See para. 17·060.
[53] *R.D. Harbottle (Mercantile) Ltd.* v. *National Westminster Bank Ltd.* [1978] Q.B. 146; *Edward Owen Engineering Ltd.* v. *Barclays Bank* [1978] 1 Q.B. 159; *United City Merchants (Investments) Ltd.* v. *Royal Bank of Canada* [1983] A.C. 168; *Bolivinter Oil S.A.* v. *Chase Manhattan Bank N.A.* [1984] 1 Lloyd's Rep. 251, C.A.; *G.K.N. Contractors Ltd.* v. *Lloyds Bank Plc* (1985) 30 BLR 53, C.A.
[54] The *Edward Owen* case [1978] Q.B. 159 at 169, see *supra, per* Lord Denning M.R.
[55] The *United City Merchants* case [1983] A.C. 168 at 183–184, see *supra, per* Lord Diplock.
[56] See, *per* Sir John Donaldson M.R. in the *Bolivinter* case [1984] 1 Lloyd's Rep. 251, 256.
[57] *G.K.N. Contractors Ltd.* v. *Lloyds Bank Plc* (1985) 30 BLR 53, 63, *per* Parker L.J.
[58] The *Bolivinter* case.

had not issued the confirmed letter of credit as they should have done. Yet the
Libyan customers appear to have demanded payment from the Union Bank
on their guarantee ... The long and short of it is that although prima facie the
Libyan customers were in default in not providing the letter of credit nevertheless they appear to have claimed against Union Bank on the performance
bond issued by them ..."[59]

17·068   It is clear that on the facts before the Court the Libyan customers had
repudiated the contract, but the English bank were, nevertheless held
liable to pay the Libyan bank, on the counter-indemnity, *fraud not having
been alleged*. Again, in the *Bolivinter* case, Syrian cargo owners, who had
been in default, agreed to release an unconditional performance guarantee given by shipowners, provided they would agree to complete a third
voyage, but on completion of that voyage the cargo owners immediately
claimed under the guarantee from the local bank, who were held entitled
to recover on their counter-indemnity from the shipowners' bank.[60]
Again, where goods were shipped after a letter of credit had expired, but
the documents had been fraudulently altered to conceal this by the carriers without the knowledge of the seller beneficiaries, the bank was held
liable to pay the sellers under the letter of credit.[61] Again, the courts have
upheld a claim on a counter-indemnity against an English bank arising
from an unconditional due performance bond paid by an issuing Iraqi
bank to a different Iraqi Government entity from that named in the
bond, and with no clear Iraqi legislation authorising the new entity as
successors.[62]

17·069   On the other hand, the American courts appear to have been much
readier to give relief where fraud is alleged. Thus, in a straightforward case
of a letter of credit in a New York court the defence was permitted against
a seller alleged to have loaded 50 cases with rubbish, and to have provided
false documentation to conceal his default.[63] Although this case was
approved in the English Court of Appeal in the *Edward Owen* case,
Megarry J. had previously refused to apply it on very similar facts, pointing out that in the *Sztejn* case fraud had been formally conceded for the
purpose of the argument, and also that no third person to whom the letter
of credit might have been negotiated had been involved.[64]

     In addition, the American courts appear to have been readier to draw
realistic conclusions and inferences of collusion and fraud from the facts
and to injunct foreign local paying banks from pursuing unconditional
counter-indemnities against domestic United States banks, where examination of the principal contract and of the record shows that no colour-

---

[59] [1978] Q.B. 159, 167–8.
[60] For the facts of these cases, pointing to local collusion, see C.C.P.P., paras. 19–22.
[61] The *United City Merchants* case *supra*.
[62] *G.K.N. Contractors Ltd.* v. *Lloyd's Bank Plc* (1985) 30 BLR 53. See also the facts in *Esal
(Commodities) Ltd.* v. *Oriental Credit Ltd.* [1985] 2 Lloyds Rep. 546, where the performance bond would seem to have expired, though upheld in a foreign arbitration, and no
reasons had been given for calling it.
[63] *Sztejn* v. *J. Henry Schroder Banking Corporation* 31 N.Y.S. 2d 631 (1941), New York Court
of Appeals.
[64] *Discount Records Ltd.* v. *Barclays Bank Ltd.* [1975] 1 W.L.R. 315.

able breach has occurred and where there is a reasonable doubt as to the independence of the local paying bank.[65] In one of these cases a United States Court of Appeals found that the attempt to call, which required a written representation that the debtor manufacturer had not performed his contract, had been made in circumstances where the principal contract explicitly provided for termination of the contract and release of the guarantee following *force majeure*, and where only a very small part of the total shipment to Iran had been prevented by United States regulations, but the call was, nevertheless, for the entire contract sum. The Court held that this was sufficiently suggestive of fraud to grant an injunction, noting that both the beneficiary and the issuing bank were government enterprises.[66] In another unusual case, where the foreign beneficiary was already the defendant in arbitration proceedings brought by the contractor under the principal contract in New York, the United States Court of Appeals granted an injunction against a domestic bank placing in escrow the sums payable under an unconditional guarantee (which had been conditioned on a certificate given by the beneficiary owner asserting "clear and substantial breach" on the part of the contractor) to await the outcome of the substantive arbitration.[67]

Bearing in mind that contractors' performance bonds in typical construction contracts are frequently not part of a transaction balanced by countervailing letters of credit for payment by the purchaser, as in many international manufacturing and supply or sale contracts, and also the fact that no negotiation of the instrument to third party holders will be involved, unlike the case of letters of credit covering payment obligations, it is submitted that the attitude of the English Courts in construction cases has been unduly rigorous in refusing to draw inferences of fraud, or to grant at least temporary relief in performance bond cases where there is no evidence before the Court of a colourable breach of contract by the guaranteed party or of a bona fide claim by the beneficiary.   **17·070**

Moreover, while the English cases contain many judicial references to the importance of safeguarding the status of letters of credit and of the reputation of issuing or confirming banks in honouring such documents,[68] it is difficult to see any real analogy between letters of credit and unconditional contractors' performance bonds in construction projects, nor how the reputation of a bank can suffer if prevented by an order of the Court from making a payment in a case where the bond obligation itself is, however nominally or cosmetically, expressed to secure due performance and to arise on contractor default.   **17·071**

This is not to say that a bank which has met its obligation to pay without any reason for suspicion and in bona fide circumstances will not clearly be

---

[65] *Harris Corporation* v. *National Iranian Radio* 691 F 2d 1344, 1982. U.S. C.A. 11th Circuit; *Itek Corporation* v. *First National Bank of Boston* 730 F 2d 19 (1984), U.S. C.A. 1st Circuit.

[66] *Harris Corporation* case, see *supra.*

[67] *Sperry* v. *Government of Israel* 689 F 2d 30 (1982).

[68] See, *e.g. Bolivinter Oil S.A.* v. *Chase Manhattan Bank N.A.* [1984] 1 Lloyd's Rep. 251, 257, *per* Sir John Donaldson M.R.

entitled to enforce counter-indemnities, without which it would not itself have entered into the transaction. There are also obvious difficulties where the issuing bank is outside the jurisdiction, and possibly constrained to pay by its own domestic courts or law. Nevertheless, if the reasoning of the United States Court of Appeals in the *Harris Corporation* case (not cited to the English Court of Appeal in the *Bolivinter* case) were to be followed, both the *Bolivinter* and the earlier *Edward Owen* cases might have been differently decided, it is submitted, on the ground that "the fraud exception" applied; and, but for the complication of a binding foreign arbitration award the facts in the *Esal (Commodities)* case might also well have justified a similar different result, it is submitted.

The position remains that there are few if any reported cases in England or the Commonwealth where enforcement of an unconditional performance bond in a construction contract has been prevented on the ground of "the fraud exception", despite the frequently expressed acknowledgment of the principle of such an exception by the courts.

(5) Contractual Restrictions on Call

17·072 Subsection (4) *supra*, has been concerned with possible remedies or relief preventing payment by an issuing or confirming bank or guarantor to the beneficiary, or by a counter-indemnifying bank or guarantor to an earlier surety or bank. However, the principal contract between the parties, or any relevant side contract, may on its proper interpretation control or restrict, whether by express or implied terms, the circumstances in which a beneficiary is entitled, as between the parties, to call on an unconditional bond or guarantee.[69] If so, there is in principle no reason why the beneficiary should not be injuncted from making the call, or if he has already done so and been paid, why a *Mareva* injunction should not be granted or other order made affecting the proceeds. Obviously, however, neither remedy is likely to be as effective in an international context, for practical reasons, as in purely domestic contracts, where both beneficiary and principal debtor will be in the same jurisdiction. There is no doubt that jurisdiction exists for the English Courts to issue a *Mareva* injunction in respect of sums paid under an unconditional bond or guarantee.[70] It will be seen that the Australian Courts, due to the presence in a number of their building standard forms of provisions requiring or permitting security to be provided by the contractor in the form of unconditional guarantees, as an alternative to retention moneys or in other events, have to some extent anticipated the English Courts in injuncting owner beneficiaries from making calls

---

[69] See, *per* Stephen J. in *Wood Hall Ltd.* v. *Pipeline Authority* (1979) 141 C.L.R. 443, 459. Followed by Yeldham J. in New South Wales when granting an injunction in the *Pearson Bridge* case, illustrated *supra*.

[70] *Intraco Ltd.* v. *Notis Shipping Corporation, The Bhoja Trader* [1981] 2 Lloyd's Rep. 256; *Potton Homes Ltd.* v. *Coleman Contractors (Overseas) Ltd.* (1984) 28 BLR 19, illustrated *infra*.

where a restriction on doing so can be inferred from the wording of the principal contract.

ILLUSTRATIONS

(1) Clause 5 of a New South Wales contract, after requiring security to be **17·073** given by the Contractor in various alternative forms if required, provided by clause 5·05 that "If the Principal becomes entitled to exercise all or any of his rights under the contract in respect of the security the Principal may convert into money the security that does not consist of money". The contractor was required to and did provide an *unconditional* bank guarantee. Following a termination by the owners and during proceedings in which the validity of the termination was in dispute, the owners notified the contractor of their intention to call on the guarantee and the contractor obtained an *ex parte* injunction preventing the call. *Held*, by Yeldham J., that clause 5.05 on its true interpretation defined and limited the circumstances under which the owner could convert any security into money to cases where he was entitled to exercise his contractual remedy and, following Stephen J.'s dictum in the *Wood Hall* case, the injunction should be confirmed pending the determination of that issue: *Pearson Bridge (N.S.W.) Ltd.* v. *State Rail Authority of New South Wales* (1982).[71]

(2) English suppliers of pre-fabricated building units in Libya received advance payments from English buyers, and in turn provided a bank unconditional performance guarantee bond for £68,000. The suppliers later claimed moneys due under their contracts, of which £89,000 was admittedly due and £140,000 disputed. The buyers defended alleging defects, and called on the bond. The trial judge gave judgment with a stay of execution for £89,000; and while holding that he had no power to restrain a call on the bank or to issue a *Mareva* injunction, ordered the sums paid by the bank to be placed in a joint account. *Held*, by the Court of Appeal, that, while there was power to grant a *Mareva* injunction, the facts did not justify such an order, and there was no other power, since the proceeds of the bond in this case were the equivalent of cash in hand and must be paid to the defendants. *Per* Eveleigh L.J., after considering the position between the seller and the bank: "As between buyer and seller the underlying contract cannot be disregarded so readily ... Moreover, in principle I do not think it possible to say that in no circumstances whatsoever, apart from fraud, will the Court restrain the buyer ... I do not see why, as between seller and buyer, the seller should not be able to prevent a call upon the bond by the mere assertion [of the buyer] that the bond is to be treated as cash in hand ... For a large construction project the employer may agree to provide finance (perhaps by way of advance payments) to enable the contractor to undertake the works. The contractor will almost certainly be asked to provide a performance bond. If the contractor were unable to perform because the employer failed to provide the finance, it would seem wrong to me if the Court was not entitled to have regard to the terms of the underlying contract and could be prevented from considering the question whether or not to restrain the employer by the mere assertion that a performance bond is like a letter of credit ... I would wish at least to leave it open for consideration how far the bond is to be treated as cash in hand as

---

[71] (1982) 1 A.C.L.R. 81. The interpretation of the contract in this case seems doubtful, however.

between buyer and seller.": *Potton Homes Ltd.* v. *Coleman Contractors (Overseas) Ltd.* (1984).[72]

[Note: Eveleigh L.J.'s illustration of a construction contract in the above passage is particularly significant, since the facts postulated by him are effectively those in the *Edward Owen* case. The quoted passage is likely to be of seminal importance in supporting a potential remedy for debtors where beneficiaries have abused their rights under unconditional bonds.]

17·074   (3) Construction owners in Singapore terminated a contract on the ground of delay by the contractor, at a time when they had considerable funds in hand under the contract, as well as a S$1 million personal guarantee, and in addition an *unconditional* bank guarantee of S$120,000 for due performance by the contractor. The validity of the termination was disputed by the contractors, who obtained an *ex parte* injunction preventing the calling of the bond. *Held*, by Thean J., after considering the principal English authorities, and following the views expressed by Eveleigh L.J. in the *Potton Homes* case, that none of the English cases were concerned with disputes between the contracting parties to the underlying contracts; and that merely because the bond was like a letter of credit should not inhibit the Court from exercising its equitable jurisdiction to grant an injunction where it was proper to maintain the *status quo*: *Royal Design Studio Ltd.* v. *Chang Development Ltd.* (1991).[73]

17·075   However, insofar as a construction contract may make clear provision for the furnishing of an *unconditional* guarantee as security for due performance, the normal interpretation, as in the *Potton Homes* case, will be that, in response to the stipulated demand, an unqualified transfer of the sums in question is intended, provided only that there is a bona fide dispute or claim on the secured party's part, and any further investigation of its merits or extent is not usually intended by the contract. In this regard the *Pearson Bridge* case *supra*, does not seem entirely convincing.

As previously stated, some standard forms of both main building contract and sub-contract in Australia contain provisions requiring unconditional due performance guarantees to be provided as security by the contractor or sub-contractor.[74] Given the common domestic jurisdiction available to the parties, there have not surprisingly been a number of attempts in Australia to obtain injunctions preventing the calling of the bond, but the courts appear to have been relatively conservative, it is submitted rightly, in refusing such injunctions in practice, notwithstanding the *Pearson Bridge* case illustrated *supra*, which depended on the particular wording of that contract. Thus, in one case a *Mareva* injunction attaching to the sums paid by the bank was refused, notwithstanding evidence of the technical insolvency of a contractor beneficiary.[75] In another, it was held that an injunction preventing a call under a standard form by owner beneficiaries should be refused notwithstanding that the allegations of

---

[72] 28 BLR 19.
[73] [1991] 2 M.L.J. 229.
[74] See, *e.g.* clause 10.25 of JCCA 1985, considered in *Hughes Bros. Ltd.* v. *Telede Ltd.* (1989) 8 A.C.L.R. 22.
[75] *Hortico (Australia) Pty. Ltd.* v. *Energy Equipment (Australia) Pty. Ltd.* [1985] 1 N.S.W.L.R. 545 (Young J.), see *supra*, para. 17·062.

owner default were found to be "serious and not fanciful".[76] In each case, it is submitted, the contract requires to be examined to determine the circumstances in which it is envisaged that the rights under the unconditional bond or guarantee will be exercised. Only if satisfied by evidence that no bona fide and arguable claim or complaint of the kind envisaged by the contract exists will the Court usually be justified in overriding the contractual intention to be inferred from the unconditional description or intention of the guarantee, namely that the sum claimed under the bond is to be treated as effectively cash in hand without regard to the degree or extent of the beneficiary's complaint, provided it is colourable and bona fide.

(6) Abuse of On Demand Bonds

While a relatively severe attitude by construction owner beneficiaries to the calling of performance bonds is to be expected in those cases where there is a corresponding contractual liability on their part to make advance payments to contractors, there have been many reports of abuse by construction owners of their right to call unconditional bonds nominally conditioned on due performance by the contractor in cases where no such countervailing right of the contractor to advance payment exists, and where no colourable breach by the contractor has occurred. Indeed it is not uncommon to find the right to call used as a tactical weapon by owners to discourage the contractor from pursuing interim remedies, and the only real evidence of default available on the record is of breach of contract by the owner beneficiary. Governments or owners with this reputation can expect to find tendered contract prices increased against themselves by the full financing cost of an anticipated early and unjustified call of the bond, as explicitly recommended by Lord Denning M.R. in the *Edward Owen* case. Added to the direct cost of the original bond and of its accompanying counter-indemnities in the "indemnity string", this would seem to make an unconditional bond a less attractive option from the owner's point of view than a straightforward equivalent addition to the sums to be retained on interim payment under the principal contract.

17·076

(7) ICC Counter-guarantee Scheme

In an endeavour to avoid the imbalance created by the unconditional performance bonds demanded by international owners, the International Chamber of Commerce published proposals in 1992, no doubt for use in association with the rules of arbitration of that body, for a combined "Guarantee and Counter-Guarantee" for use in international construction projects. These proposals envisage the appointment of a "Pre-arbitral Referee"; and payment of the bond by the bank unconditionally

17·077

---

[76] *Hughes Bros.* v. *Telede* (1989) 8 A.C.L.R. 22 (Cole J.).

on the owner's demand *only in exchange for* a repayment counter-guarantee bond given by the owner. The counter-guarantee becomes activated in the event that the Referee's decision on the substantive validity of the original call proves to be adverse to the owner. Failing provision of such a counter-guarantee by the owner, no liability to pay will arise under the original contractor's guarantee until a decision of the Referee favourable to the owner. Finally, any payments made as a result of the Referee's decisions will be subject to ultimate review by the arbitrators appointed under the principal contract.

While this is an ingenious, if not elegant, scheme which reduces the maximum loss from an unjustified call of the original performance bond to whatever period may be necessary for the Referee to reach a decision, the scheme cannot, of course, be fully effective unless the liability of the bank or other guarantors to make payments under the two guarantee documents is expressed to arise in terms exactly conforming to the scheme.

(8) Debtor's Rights when Bond is Paid

17·078   It is generally assumed, and there is no real reason to doubt, that the Courts will provide a remedy by way of repayment to the other contracting party if a beneficiary who has been paid under an unconditional bond is ultimately shown to have called on it without justification: "I do not doubt that in such an event the money would be repayable, but it is not so certain it would be repayable with interest".[77]

In cases where an owner or buyer is claiming damages against the seller or contractor which exceed the amount of the bond there is little difficulty in holding that he must give credit for the "cash in hand" received by him if he has made a call under any unconditional guarantee arrangements. Where, however, there is no defence or counterclaim to the contractor's claim for moneys due, other than sufficient payment in full, or where the sum already received from the bank or guarantor exceeds the set-off or damages ultimately awarded, the contractor's or seller's claim for repayment of the whole or any balance of the sums called and paid can be put, it is submitted, in two ways. First, the payment by the bank or guarantor, being required in most cases under the principal construction contract itself, or sometimes by a side-contract, must be regarded as being made by the bank as agent for the contractor and subject, it is submitted, to an implied term for repayment if not in fact due. Secondly, it has been seen that in the case of a *conditional* bond, equity would not permit recovery of a sum in excess of the true debt or damages, as being a penalty,[78] so that by analogy in a case where the payment under the bond was obligatory and unavoidable, and indeed brought about by the owner's own act in making the call, it would be only logical to order repayment for the same reasons.

---

[77] *General Surety and Guarantee Co. Ltd.* v. *Francis Parker Ltd.* (1977) 6 BLR 16, 21, *per* Donaldson J.
[78] See *supra*, Section 1(3), para. 17·007.

Such a claim could also be based in quasi-contract on wider principles of unjust enrichment and unconscionability, it is submitted. In cases where there has been no default at all on the part of the contractor, there would additionally be a total failure of consideration for the payment. Questions of interest and costs pose considerable difficulties, however.

SECTION 4. CO-SURETIES

If there is more than one surety, the sureties may be co-sureties jointly and **17·079** severally liable, usually as a result of one transaction, or they may be separately and severally liable only. Release of the principal debtor by the creditor, or of one of a number of sureties who are jointly and severally liable, will release all or the remainder of the sureties.[79]

There is a very substantial case law on the rights *inter se* between sureties, including rules for assessing the proportion to be contributed by each surety if some are insolvent, and for bringing into hotchpot for the benefit of co-sureties any security given to a surety by the principal debtor. This subject was discussed shortly in the tenth edition, but has only incidental application to construction contracts and seems more appropriate to a specialist work on the subject.

---

[79] *Ward* v. *National Bank of New Zealand* (1883) 8 App. Cas. 755; *Commercial Bank of Tasmania* v. *Jones* [1893] A.C. 313.

CHAPTER 18

ARBITRATION

Section 1. General Principles

(1) Submissions and Agreements to Refer

Some special forms of arbitration are permitted or compulsorily required **18·001** by statute, but the present Chapter is concerned only with consensually based arbitration arising out of an agreement voluntarily entered into between the parties, under which defined disputes are agreed to be referred to and decided by an arbitrator or arbitrators (and not, therefore, as would otherwise be the case, by the courts). These agreements may be designed to govern a known and pre-existing dispute between the parties which has already occurred, which are sometimes referred to as "submissions", or they may be directed to a defined class or type of dispute, should it arise between the parties in the future. These latter are very often expressly described or defined in the arbitration agreement as disputes arising out of a single identified substantive contract or transaction between the parties, although in some cases they may relate to a wider group of contracts or transactions or course of dealing. They are normally described, in contrast to submissions of pre-existing specific disputes, as "agreements to refer" and their commonest form in commerce is the "arbitration clause", itself forming a part of the substantive transaction or contract between the parties.

In practice, specific submissions, which by definition will be separately entered into at some date later than the underlying contract or transaction giving rise to the dispute, are relatively rare; whereas agreements to refer, in the shape of arbitration clauses in the substantive agreements or commercial documentation between the parties, are extremely common in commerce generally, and not least are almost invariably to be found in the standard forms of construction contract in most developed countries. In the English Arbitration Acts themselves, an arbitration agreement is defined as "a written agreement to submit present or future disputes to arbitration, whether an arbitrator is named in the agreement or not."[1]

This distinction between specific submissions on the one hand and agreements to refer future disputes on the other can be overlooked when examining the case law relating to the procedural aspects of arbitration, since the degree of enthusiasm for or genuine consent to arbitration by private persons may obviously be far less in the case of arbitration clauses, particularly in the case of the many "contracts of adhesion" which contain them so often found in commercial and business life.[2] This important distinction is in fact only occasionally explicitly recognised in the English arbitration legislation,[3] but it may often be important in understanding the English procedural case-law of arbitration in situations where the exercise of the court's discretion when permitting arbitration in the first place, or in setting aside arbitration agreements or removing or revoking the authority of abritrators, is involved.[4]

(2) Principal Characteristics of English Arbitration

(a) Control by the courts

18·002   The fundamental basis of arbitration law in England, whatever the position in other and particularly civil law countries, is that English arbitrators, although in consensual cases they can only derive their original jurisdiction and authority from the parties themselves, are nevertheless at all stages subject to and dependent upon the overriding control and approval of the courts, both in their original assumption of jurisdiction as

---

[1] s.32 of the 1950 Act. See also s.7(1), 1975 Act.

[2] See Lord Mustill's perceptive comments on the lukewarm attitude even of many businessmen, to arbitration in the International Business Law Journal ("Contemporary Problems in International Commercial Arbitration" (1989) 17 I.B.L. 145), noted and discussed by the Editor in (1990) 6 Arb. Int. 253, 256.

[3] For an example see s.24(2), 1950 Act (in cases where fraud is alleged). The distinction is also recognised in the definition of an arbitration agreement in s.32, 1950 Act *supra.*

[4] *e.g.*, the cases on refusal to order a case stated under the old procedure where a point of law had been specifically referred to a legal arbitrator.

well as in the later exercise of their arbitral powers. Thus, in domestic arbitrations the English courts enjoy the widest of discretions (extending, for example, to considerations of convenience) to refuse a stay for arbitration at the request of a plaintiff who has preferred to bring proceedings in the courts, notwithstanding the presence of an arbitration clause,[5] thereby permitting the dispute to be dealt with by the courts, and effectively defeating both the arbitration agreement and the defendant's expectation of arbitration under that agreement.

Conversely, should arbitration proceedings be initiated by a party in advance of later court proceedings brought by the other party, the courts have a similar general and unfettered power[6] both to revoke the appointment of any arbitrator and to declare an arbitration agreement to be of no effect.[7] Moreover, should such an arbitrator purport to make an award after court proceedings have commenced in regard to the same dispute it will be void as an attempt to oust the jurisdiction of the court,[8] although it would seem that if the court proceedings are abandoned or withdrawn the arbitrator's jurisdiction may revive.[9]

However, in the case of international "non-domestic" arbitrations (that **18·003** is, contracts providing for a foreign *locus arbitrii* or where one or more of the parties is foreign),[10] the situation is different since there, by virtue of section 1 of the 1975 Act, no discretionary power exists to refuse a stay under section 4 of the 1950 Act, provided a valid arbitration agreement exists (and so by implication, presumably, no possible parallel exercise on discretionary grounds, in the absence of specific misconduct or an undisclosed interest, of any more general discretion to revoke under section 1 of the 1950 Act).[11]

Furthermore, arbitration clauses in so-called "*Scott* v. *Avery*" form[12] (that is, clauses which expressly make an arbitration award under the clause a condition precedent to bringing any action on the contract) have long been recognised and accepted as valid by the courts, although in one sense they could certainly be said to constitute an ouster of the court's jurisdiction. The validity of such clauses is expressly recognised by section

---

[5] See for cases on refusals of a stay *infra*, paras. 18·088 and 18·104 *et seq.*

[6] Although possibly of less wide extent —see *City Centre Properties (I.T.C. Pensions) Ltd.* v. *Matthew Hall & Co. Ltd.* [1969] 1 W.L.R. 772, *per* Harman L.J., who considered it might be limited to cases of misconduct, and that a stronger case might be needed in revocation cases. See further *infra*, Section 3(2)(g), paras. 18·113 *et seq.*

[7] ss.1 and 25(2)(*b*) of the Arbitration Act 1950; (quite apart from the special powers of removal for misconduct, or for revocation of authority where the arbitrator is not impartial, or where fraud is alleged, under ss.23 and 24 of the Act).

[8] *Doleman & Sons* v. *Ossett Corporation* [1912] 3 K.B. 257. Contrast the contrary interpretation of a *certifier's* powers and jurisdiction under the final certificate provision in clause 30(7) of the RIBA/JCT standard forms in *P & M Kaye Limited* v. *Hosier & Dickinson Ltd.* [1972] 1 W.L.R. 146, see *ante*, Chap. 6, Section 4(3), para. 6·085.

[9] *Concrete Developments Ltd.* v. *Queensland Housing Commission* [1961] Qd.R. 356.

[10] See for the precise definition *infra*, s.1(4) of the Arbitration Act 1975.

[11] See s.1(1) of the Arbitration Act 1975, replacing the very similar regime under s.4(2) of the 1950 Act in regard to the (somewhat differently defined) foreign arbitration agreements to which the Geneva Convention and Part II of the 1950 Act applied.

[12] From the case of that name, (1856) 5 H.L. Cas. 811.

24(2) of the 1950 Arbitration Act, which provides that, where an order has been made by the court under section 25(2)(*b*), so that the arbitration agreement ceases to have effect (that is, in cases of an undisclosed interest or misconduct or where fraud has been alleged in the arbitration) it may also order that the *Scott* v. *Avery* provision should cease to have effect. Again, by section 34(2) of the Limitation Act 1980, the cause of action in contracts with a *Scott* v. *Avery* provision is expressly deemed to commence at the usual date when it would otherwise have arisen under the principal substantive contract, and not at the later date when the award expressly said to found the cause of action is finally obtained.

(b) Appeal to the courts on points of law

18·004 A further characteristic of English arbitration law for more than a century has been the right of appeal to the courts on a point of law, whether from the award itself or on a preliminary point during the course of the reference and prior to any award. This was available to the parties under the earlier "case stated" procedures, most recently regulated by section 21 of the 1950 Arbitration Act, but now replaced by a new and quite different regime under sections 1 and 2 of the 1979 Act. Although leave of the court was required in the event of an arbitrator refusing to state a case at the request of a party under the old law, not only did arbitrators very rarely so refuse (and without doubt in construction disputes such refusals were virtually unheard of immediately prior to the 1979 Act) but the courts would in any case themselves freely give leave following such a refusal, provided that a bona fide point of law materially affecting the rights of the aggrieved party was involved and the application was not an obvious abuse of the appeal process. There was, therefore, an effective and wide-ranging right of appeal on a point of law either from an arbitrator's preliminary decisions or from his final award. This has always in the past distinguished English and Commonwealth arbitration law from most other legal systems, and has in the past contributed greatly to respect for arbitration in England and for English commercial law.

However, the 1979 Act (and subsequent amending legislation) not only imposed extremely severe restrictions on any *second stage* appeal to the Court of Appeal by requiring both leave and certification of a point of law of importance by the first instance appellate judge, but, much more seriously, it now not only required either leave of the court or agreement by both parties before an appeal from the arbitrator could be made at all, but also in 1981 imposed special restrictions on appeals from a first instance judge's refusal of leave to appeal from the arbitrator.[13] Subsequently, in two remarkable examples of judicial interpretation (if not judicial legislation), the House of Lords in *The Nema*[14] and *The Antaios*[15] unexpectedly evolved what have become universally known as the *"Nema Guidelines"*. These severely restricted the occasions on which the judge of first instance

---

[13] See ss.1(7) and 2(3) of the 1979 Act, and ss.1(6A) and 2(2A) respectively, the latter introduced in 1981.
[14] *Pioneer Shipping* v. *BTP Tioxide, The Nema* [1982] A.C. 724.
[15] *Antaios Cia Naviera S.A.* v. *Salen Rederierna A.B., The Antaios* [1985] A.C. 191.

would now be permitted to grant leave to review an award on a question of law under section 1(3)(*d*) of the Act, although little or no express indication of any such restrictions was to be found in the wording of the 1979 Act itself.[16] Coupled with the Act's severe restrictions on an appeal from a judge's refusal of leave to appeal from the arbitrator,[17] the guidelines represented a massive judicial intervention restricting still further the earlier liberally available right of appeal.[18]

The asserted justification for the *Nema* interpretation and guidelines in the House of Lords was that the old case stated procedure had been abused by unmeritorious litigants with the principal object of securing delay, and that "businessmen" as a class desired a speedy and final result in preference to the delays involved in an appeal.[19] As a result, the guidelines now avowedly serve to deny leave to many bona fide applicants, particularly in the case of so-called "one-off" contracts, unless it can be established *within 10 to 15 minutes* both that a point of wide application to other disputes is involved and that there is an exceptionally high degree of probability, *amounting to a near certainty*, that the award is wrong.[20]

18·005

Since the *Nema* guidelines, at least one standard form of contract in England[21] has endeavoured to circumvent the serious anomalies perceived as resulting from the guidelines by taking advantage of the wording of section 1(3)(*a*) of the 1979 Act (which expressly permits appeals "with the consent of all the other parties to the reference") by making *express provision in the arbitration clause itself* giving the advance consent by the parties to the exercise by either party of the right of appeal under both sections 1 and 2 of the 1979 Act. "One-off" contracts are also emerging in the reports where the parties have used the same technique so as to avoid the guidelines.[21a]

---

[16] See the vigorously expressed and persuasive views of Robert Goff J. in *Schiffahrtsagentur Hamburg Middle East Line G.m.b.H. Hamburg* v. *Virtue Shipping Corporation Monrovia, The Oinioussian Virtue* [1981] 1 Lloyd's Rep. 533, 538.

[17] Sections 1(6A) and 2(2A), introduced by s.148 of the Supreme Court Act 1981.

[18] For the *Nema* guidelines, see the definitive and comprehensive discussion in *Mustill and Boyd, Commercial Arbitration* (2nd ed., 1989), pp. 602 *et seq.*, and see also the Editor's "Control by the Courts: a plea for more, not less" in (1990) 6 Arb. Int. 253. The guidelines are discussed in greater detail *infra*, paras. 18·175 *et seq.*

[19] These theories seem to have been first openly put forward (in advance of the Act) by Donaldson J.—see his statements as early as 1977 in *Tramountana Armadora S.A.* v. *Atlantic Shipping Co. S.A.* [1978] 1 Lloyd's Rep. 391, 394, quoted *infra*, para. 18·194.

[20] The last (time for argument) restriction was too much for the Australian Courts even where their legislation had expressly sought to replicate the guidelines—see *Promenade Investments* v. *State of New South Wales* (1992) 26 N.S.W.L.R. 203 discussed *infra*, para. 18·174. This subject is discussed further *infra*, Section 5(6), paras. 18·173 *et seq.*, but see for the inappropriateness and injustice of the guidelines in construction cases, and the absence of the alleged abuses of the old procedure in construction litigation at least, the commentary of the BLR Editors in (1990) 43 BLR 98, 100–101; the discussion in C.C.P.P., pp. 267–9; and in (1990) 6 Arb. Int., pp. 253 *et seq.*, where the asserted justifications for the guidelines are questioned as being unrealistic and unfounded in fact, at least in non-commodity arbitrations and in particular in construction arbitrations.

[21] See the RIBA/JCT Intermediate Form of Contract, Article 5.3, discussed by the editor in (1990) 6 Arb. Int. 253, 258.

[21a] See, *e.g.* the contract in *Balfour Beaty Building Ltd.* v. *Chestermount Properties Ltd.* (1993) 62 BLR 12.

In addition, section 3 of the 1979 Act now expressly permits "exclusion agreements" in *non-domestic* arbitration agreements or clauses, and similar exclusion agreements (but only if made *after the commencement of an arbitration* and not in the arbitration agreement or clause itself) in the case of domestic agreements (thereby ensuring that only a party entering into such an agreement with eyes open will, in a domestic contract, be bound by it). These are agreements whereby the parties renounce in advance or "contract out" of their rights of appeal under sections 1 and 2 of the 1979 Act altogether (previously such an agreement would have been void as against public policy, or as ousting the jurisdiction of the courts).[22] This section was apparently inserted in response to representations from interested bodies in the working parties under the Act to the effect that the United Kingdom, and London in particular, had been losing valuable international "arbitration business" as a result of the known availability of rights of appeal to the courts on points of law should the arbitration take place in England.[23]

Nevertheless, it remains the case that a structured, although now much more limited, process for appeal on a point of law, both in regard to preliminary points of law and errors in the arbitrator's award itself, still survives in principle under English arbitration legislation in both domestic and foreign cases, subject to the very considerable current obstacle to obtaining leave resulting from the *Nema* guidelines and the 1981 Amendments to the 1979 Act, as well as to valid express exclusion agreements. The subject is considered in more detail *infra*, Sections 5(6) and 6.[23a]

(c) Arbitrator may not decide his own jurisdiction

18·006   Objections by parties to the jurisdiction conferred by an apparent arbitration agreement can go to its very root—for example, denial of entry into any contract at all, or of capacity or authority to contract, or the invalidity of the substantive contract for lack of consideration, or its avoidance for fraud or misrepresentation, or for mistake or illegality rendering it void *ab initio*. Other objections can be less fundamental, namely that a dispute or part of a dispute is not within the ambit of an otherwise admittedly valid arbitration clause, or that it is premature by reason of provisions prohibiting early arbitration before completion.

While arbitrators undoubtedly have power to investigate and give a *provisional* ruling on their own jurisdiction should it be questioned[24] (since any other view would enable a party to bring arbitration proceedings to a halt simply by raising a challenge of this kind), it is nevertheless, a basic and widely recognised principle of English law that an arbitrator

---

[22] *Czarnikow* v. *Roth Schmidt & Co.* [1922] 2 K.B. 478.

[23] Whether these representations were other than self-serving is discussed and doubted by the editor in C.C.P.P., pp. 267–9, and in (1990) 6 Arb. Int., pp. 253, 255–6.

[23a] Paras. 18·172 *et seq.*, and 18·194–18·195.

[24] See particularly, *per* Devlin J. in *Christopher Brown Ltd.* v. *Genossenschaft Ostereichischer Waldbesitzer Holzwirtschaftsbertriebe Registrierte G.m.b.H.* [1954] 1 Q.B. 8, 12–13, and see Peter Gross Q.C. (in 1992) 8 Arb. Int. 205. See also *Mustill and Boyd* (2nd ed.), pp. 574–6.

cannot finally determine his own jurisdiction so as to bind the parties. Thus there are a number of alternatives, including an action for a declaration or for an injunction, or resistance to enforcement of an award, which are available to a party who denies the arbitrator's jurisdiction. So, in a construction case where the contract had been terminated, but arbitration was expressly not permitted until after completion, enforcement of an award was refused on the ground that the arbitrator had not had jurisdiction to rule finally on an objection that the arbitration was premature.[25] Consistently with this view, a provision in an arbitration agreement or in the rules of an arbitral body purporting to enable an arbitrator to decide finally on his own jurisdiction will not be effective.[26] (However, it should be noted that by concurring in the appointment of an arbitrator or in the conduct of the arbitration, a party may effectively confer jurisdiction where, previously to this "ad hoc submission", jurisdiction did not exist.)[27]

Following the House of Lords decision in *Heyman* v. *Darwins Ltd.*,[28] it **18·007** has become widely accepted that an arbitration clause will, for many purposes, be regarded as separable from, or what has been described as "collateral or ancillary" to, the substantive contract or transaction between the parties of which it forms part,[29] so that it may have a continued existence, notwithstanding events which may have had the effect in law of terminating or avoiding the "parent", or substantive agreement. The importance of this in the context of an arbitrator's jurisdiction will be that under the commonly used wording of many if not most arbitration clauses which expressly or impliedly refer to disputes "arising out of", "under", "concerning" or "in connection with" the substantive contract, the clause may often be interpreted as clothing the arbitrator with authority to make an award giving effect to the rights and liabilities of the parties in a case where a contract has been rescinded or avoided in accordance with the relevant law. The only qualification to this will be if the invalidating circumstances should be regarded as impeaching the arbitration agreement as well as the parent substantive agreement.[30]

Thus arbitrators under the wording of most contractual arbitration clauses will have jurisdiction to make awards giving full effect to the parties' rights, notwithstanding that the substantive contract has been validly rescinded as a result of repudiation.[31] Similarly, a plea that the contract has been frustrated by supervening events will be a dispute "arising under

---

[25] *Smith* v. *Martin* [1925] 1 K.B. 745.

[26] See *Dalmia Dairy Industries Ltd.* v. *National Bank of Pakistan* [1978] 2 Lloyd's Rep. 223, 292–3.

[27] *Westminster Chemicals and Produce Ltd.* v. *Eichholz and Loeser* [1954] 1 Lloyd's Rep. 99, and see *Higgs & Hill Building Ltd.* v. *Campbell Denis Ltd.* (1982) 28 BLR 47.

[28] [1942] A.C. 356.

[29] See, *per* Lord Diplock in *Bremer Vulkan Schiffbau und Maschinenfabrik* v. *South India Shipping Corporation Limited* [1981] A.C. 909, and in *Paul Wilson & Co. A/S* v. *Partenreederei Hannah Blumenthal, The Hannah Blumenthal* [1983] A.C. 854, 917F. See also the *Dalmia Dairy Industries* case *supra*.

[30] *Harbour Assurance Co. (U.K.) Ltd.* v. *Kansa General International Insurance Co. Ltd.* [1993] Q.B. 701, discussed *infra*, para. 18·008.

[31] *Heyman* v. *Darwins Ltd.*, see *supra*.

this contract" so as to clothe the arbitrator with jurisdiction to hear it,[32] as also a plea of *supervening* illegality.[33] On the other hand "arising under this contract" wording has been held not to give jurisdiction over disputes arising from a collateral agreement, or from a negligent misstatement under the *Hedley Byrne* principle, or from an innocent misrepresentation under the 1967 Misrepresentation Act[34] (or where the contract permitted arbitration before completion of the work and the contractor had terminated for non-payment).[35] By contrast, "in connection with" wording has been said to be sufficient to cover issues of misrepresentation, and has been held to give jurisdiction to the arbitrator to rectify the substantive contract itself[36]; and "arising during the execution of this charterparty" has permitted damages to be awarded *in tort* for wrongful detention of a ship.[37]

18·008   In the cases of both illegality and mistake there were clear *obiter dicta* in *Heyman* v. *Darwins* to the effect that while issues of *supervening* illegality would be within the scope of the usual arbitration clause, cases, whether of mistake or illegality, rendering the substantive contract void *ab initio* would be outside the arbitrator's jurisdiction, and this view was accepted until recently in all the principal textbooks. However, in a persuasive and highly important and innovative decision in the Court of Appeal in 1993, (where the arbitration clause contained "arising out of this agreement" wording, and where the allegation was one of unlicensed trading which it was assumed might render a reinsurance contract void *ab initio*) the court, distinguishing earlier authorities and after considering the contrary *Heyman* v. *Darwins* dicta, overruled Steyn J. and granted a stay, holding that only if the initial illegality was such as to impeach *the arbitration agreement itself* would the arbitrator be without jurisdiction.[38] In that case Hoffman L.J. said:

> "There will obviously be cases in which a claim that no contract came into existence necessarily entails a denial that there was any agreement to arbitrate. Cases of *non est factum* or denial that there was a concluded agreement, or mistake as to the identity of the other contracting party suggest themselves as examples. But there is no reason why every case of initial invalidity should have this consequence ... In every case it seems to me that the logical question is not whether the issue goes to the validity of the contract but whether it goes to the validity of the arbitration clause. The one may entail the other but, as we have seen, it may not. When one comes to voidness for illegality, it is particularly necessary to have regard to the purpose and policy for the rule which

---

[32] *Kruse* v. *Questier & Co. Limited* [1953] 1 Q.B. 669; *Government of Gibralter* v. *Kenney* [1956] 2 Q.B. 410. See also *Codelfa Construction Ltd.* v. *State Rail Authority of New South Wales* (1982) 149 C.L.R. 337.
[33] *Mackender* v. *Feldia A.G.* [1967] 2 Q.B. 590, C.A.
[34] *Fillite (Runcorn) Limited* v. *Aqua-Lift* (1989) 45 BLR 27, C.A.
[35] *Smith* v. *Martin*, see *supra*.
[36] *Ashville Investments Ltd.* v. *Elmer Contractors Ltd.* [1989] Q.B. 488.
[37] *Astro Vencedor Cia Naviera S.A. of Panama* v. *Mabanaft G.m.b.H., The Damianos* [1971] 2 Q.B. 588, and see the cases noted *infra*, para. 18·096.
[38] *Harbour Assurance Co. Ltd.* v. *Kansa General International Insurance Co. Ltd.* [1993] Q.B. 701, distinguishing *David Taylor & Son Ltd.* v. *Barnett Trading Co.* [1953] 1 W.L.R. 562.

invalidates the contract and to ask, as the House of Lords did in *Heyman* v. *Darwins Ltd.*, whether the rule strikes down the arbitration clause as well. There may be cases in which the policy of the rule is such that it would be liable to be defeated by allowing the issue to be determined by a tribunal chosen by the parties ... Thus to say that arbitration clauses, because separable, are never affected by the illegality of the principal contract is as much a case of false logic as saying that they must be."[39]

In the context of arbitrators' power to determine their own jurisdiction, **18·009** two points should be noted. In the first place, while there have been numerous decisions in the courts suggesting somewhat fine distinctions in determining jurisdiction, depending, for example, on whether the form of words used in the arbitration clause referred to disputes "arising out of", "under", or "concerning" the substantive contract or agreement,[40] it is submitted that these differences are generally unlikely to represent any considered view of the draftsman, and in most cases the use of the words "this contract" or "this Agreement" are primarily directed, in default of some alternative convenient description, at the *commercial transaction or project* in contemplation between the parties rather than at their written contract or document in that limited sense.[41] If this view is correct, it should widen the class of disputes which are intended to be included in the arbitrator's jurisdiction by the use of such wording.

The consequence of holding, as in the above examples, that determination of a particular dispute going to his jurisdiction is within the jurisdiction conferred on the arbitrator under the terms of the arbitration clause means that any later challenge to the arbitrator's determination of the matter in the English courts will be limited to such rights of appeal as are available on a preliminary point of law under section 2 of the Arbitration Act 1979, or on appeal from the award itself under section 1 of that Act.

(d) Arbitrator must apply the law

While permitted a considerable degree of latitude in regard to pro- **18·010** cedural law and the conduct of the arbitration, it is regarded as axiomatic that in English law an arbitrator is under a duty to apply the existing substantive law[42] (which may sometimes of course involve applying foreign law under choice of law principles). An English arbitrator may not knowingly depart from the law should he consider it to be unfair or inappropriate in the circumstances before him.

---

[39] *Ibid.* at p. 723G.
[40] See, *e.g. Fillite (Runcorn) Ltd.* v. *Aqua-Lift* (1989) 45 BLR 27, C.A.
[41] See this also suggested by Ralph Gibson L.J. in the *Harbour Assurance* case [1993] Q.B. 701, and see also the cautions expressed by *Mustill and Boyd* (2nd ed.), pp. 117–8, against overemphasis on particular wording.
[42] See for recent examples of the principle *Techno-Impex* v. *Gebr van Weelde Scheepvaartkantoor B.V.* [1981] 1 Lloyd's Rep. 587, C.A.; and *President of India* v. *La Pintada Cia Navigacion S.A.* [1985] A.C. 104, 119.

ILLUSTRATION

A contract for the sale of canned meat was illegal under price control legislation. In arbitration proceedings brought by the buyers the umpire awarded
damages for non-delivery, although the illegality of the transaction was
pointed out to him. It was argued that an arbitrator could award what he
thought was fair, despite the illegality. *Held*, by the Court of Appeal, overruling Goddard C.J., that although the award was not bad on its face, the umpire
had misconducted himself in law in failing to take account of the illegality of
the contract, and that the award should be set aside. *Per* Denning L.J.: "If a
contract is illegal then arbitrators must decline to award upon it, just as the
Court would do". *David Taylor & Son Ltd.* v. *Barnet Trading Co.* (1953).[43]

18·011   Were this not so, the old law enabling an award to be set aside for error
of law on its face (now in fact abolished by the 1979 Act) and the case
stated procedures previously available under section 21 of the 1950 Act,
would both have been based on a false premiss. Nor can it make any difference that under the 1979 Act (or the *Nema* guidelines if they are to be
regarded, as presumably they must be, as an interpretation of that Act)
leave to appeal on a point of law will now be much less frequently given.
Again, the fact that exclusion agreements removing the right of appeal on
a point of law are now for the first time permitted in certain cases under
section 3 of the 1979 Act carries no implication that in such cases the parties will be authorising the arbitrators to apply some private discretion or
principles differing from the applicable law when deciding the dispute.

Thus, it is submitted that if arbitrators can be shown knowingly to
depart, or to intend to depart, from the law when making the award, they
will have misconducted themselves, and whether or not there is an
exclusion agreement present, or leave to appeal on a point of law is
unlikely to be available under the *Nema* guidelines, the court will nevertheless be able to remove the arbitrators, and if necessary set aside any
award on grounds of misconduct under section 23 of the 1950 Act.

18·012   While in one sense arbitrators can be regarded as subject to restraint in
this regard, the same principle can also have the effect, in certain cases, of
extending an arbitrator's powers. Thus, under legislation in both England
and Australia specifically conferring powers on the courts to award interest, but apparently only in terms applying where court proceedings had
been commenced, the present principle has been invoked by the courts so
as to confer the same powers on arbitrators, and an arbitrator refusing to
award interest without justifiable reasons when requested to do so has
been held guilty of misconduct.[44]

One further apparent exception or qualification to this basic principle
of English law needs to be noted in the particular context of construction

---

[43] [1953] 1 W.L.R. 562. See the case discussed and analysed by the Court of Appeal in *Harbour Assurance Co. Ltd.* v. *Kansa General International Insurance Co. Ltd.* [1993] Q.B.
701.
[44] See the *Wildhandel* case illustrated *infra*, para. 18·134.

contracts. In a controversial and difficult decision in 1984 in *Northern Regional Health Authority* v. *Derek Crouch Construction Co. Ltd.*,[45] the Court of Appeal, and in particular Lord Donaldson M.R., appeared to hold that, in those construction contracts which confer the long-standing express "open up review and revise" power on the arbitrator in relation to previous certificates or rulings of the owner's architect, the intention and effect of such a clause is to confer a special and particular discretion *on the arbitrator* to investigate the facts and review or revise such rulings, which would not be open *to the courts* should for any reason they, and not an arbitrator, be seised of the dispute. It is not the least of the various grounds for doubting the *Crouch* decision or interpretation, it is submitted, that it attempts to clothe the arbitrator with some special power or discretion to decide a dispute in a manner not open to the courts, envisaging the application of undefined but different principles by an arbitrator to those which the courts would themselves apply when deciding the dispute, and so is in contravention of the present basic principle.

(3) The English Legislation

(a) The current arbitration Acts

Three principal Acts govern the general law of private consensual arbitration in England at the present day, namely the Arbitration Acts 1950, 1975 and 1979 (with certain relatively minor amendments to the 1950 and 1979 Acts effected by the Administration of Justice Acts 1970 and 1985, and by the Supreme Court Act 1981). Minor amendments to the 1950 Act were also effected by section 6 of the 1979 Act (which made minor changes in the terms to be implied in arbitration agreements providing for two or more arbitrators). **18·013**

The 1975 and 1979 Acts are directed at two special subjects: the former with foreign "non-domestic" arbitrations and the enforcement of their awards under the New York Convention on the Recognition and Enforcement of Foreign Arbitral Awards 1958 (Cmnd. 6419), and the latter with a new procedure for appeals from arbitrators on a point of law, in place of the previous "case-stated" procedure for such appeals then under section 21 of the 1950 Act (although in fact first introduced into English legislation by section 5 of the Common Law Procedure Act 1854). The 1979 Act also abolished the alternative and much more limited common law remedy of setting aside an award for error of law on its face, which had evolved much earlier under the common law. These of course represented major amendments of the greatest importance to the 1950 Act.

The Arbitration Act 1950, the principal Act, with a total of 44 sections as amended, is concerned mainly to define the courts' powers of inter-

---

[45] [1984] Q.B. 644, considered *ante*, Chap. 6, Section 4, paras. 6·063. Examined *in extenso*, and doubted in C.C.P.P., Chap. 17.

vention, and the consequential remedies available to the parties, in relation to an arbitration agreement or award, together with the interpretation and effect of certain types of arbitration agreement. It also deals expressly with the powers of arbitrators to award costs and interest, and with the enforcement of awards in general. Part II of the 1950 Act re-enacts the older regime for foreign awards and their enforcement under the Geneva Convention on the Execution of Foreign Arbitral Awards 1927, originally contained in the Arbitration (Foreign Awards) Act 1930, but this Part will today be in practice replaced by the 1975 Act, to the extent that a "non-domestic" arbitration, as defined in the 1975 Act, will be governed by the New York Convention, so producing a "Convention award" as defined in the 1975 Act.

The majority of the substantive provisions of Part I of the 1950 Act are, however, not new, and either re-enact, or have their origins in a long line of English legislation, commencing with the Arbitration Act 1697 (9 Will 3 c. 15), followed by the Civil Procedure Act 1833, the Common Law Procedure Act 1854, and the Arbitration Acts 1889 and 1934.

(b) Historical background

18·014   None of the English Acts, including the three current statutes, have purported or been designed to create a comprehensive code of arbitration law, and in particular to define or regulate in any detail the powers or responsibilities of arbitrators themselves. Even in relation to the statutory powers of intervention by the courts, these appear to have been evolved piecemeal by past and present legislators to deal with perceived deficiencies arising from time to time in then existing statute or common law; while their characteristic and continuing drafting technique has been to create or re-state as shortly as possible wide discretionary powers of the courts, leaving the development of the occasions for, and principles underlying their exercise of the discretionary powers, to be developed through case law.

Thus, the core distinguishing feature of English domestic private arbitration law (namely that an apparently binding arbitration agreement in law only confers a *discretionary* entitlement to arbitration, while subject thereafter to the continuing control, approval and leave of the courts) finds its modern expression in only the briefest of wording contained in the two crucial sections 1 and 4 of the 1950 Act. The key to understanding the effect of those sections lies in the fact that in the seventeenth and eighteenth centuries the courts felt unable to provide remedies by way of specific performance or injunction in order to enforce a private arbitration agreement made out of court against a party choosing to repudiate the agreement. This could either happen by a party resorting to the courts in defiance of the agreement, or by his withdrawing his authority to the appointed arbitrator at any time prior to the making of the award.[46] Thus,

---

[46] See for an instance, upheld by Dowse B. in the Irish Exchequer Division, *Moyers* v. *Soady* (1886) 18 L.R. Ir. 499, 507.

there was no power to order a stay if proceedings were started in breach of a private arbitration agreement made out of court. While theoretically either a stipulated penalty or damages for breach of contract would be available to the aggrieved party in all these cases, there would be obvious difficulties in establishing more than nominal damage, beyond any abortive costs thrown away, so devaluing either form of monetary remedy. Furthermore, no powers existed for the courts to intervene in cases of error or misconduct by a private arbitrator appointed out of court.

It had early been found, however, that many of these objections could **18·015** be met by the device of formally starting proceedings in court and then securing an order for reference of the dispute to arbitration. Once court proceedings had been stayed effectively by the court's own motion, the remedies for contempt of court were available if any attempt was made by a party to revoke the arbitrator's authority, and powers to intervene and correct errors or misconduct by the arbitrator were much easier to justify and exercise through the court. The perceived advantages of this device led to the Arbitration Act 1697, which provided a more convenient and less costly summary procedure by which private arbitration agreements could, by agreement, be made rules of court and later, by section 25 of the Civil Procedure Act 1833, the contempt power was reinforced by providing that arbitration agreements which had been made rules of court were to be irrevocable without the leave of the court.

By the middle of the nineteenth century it was considered desirable to extend these procedural advantages to all private arbitration agreements arrived at out of court. This was achieved by section 11 of the Common Law Procedure Act 1854, which enabled *any* submission to arbitration to be made a rule of court *unilaterally*, notwithstanding the absence of consent by both parties, which had previously been essential. This section also conferred a discretion on the court to stay an action (now effectively in all cases, therefore) if brought in breach of a written arbitration agreement. Finally, by section 1 of the 1889 Arbitration Act, extending section 25 of the Civil Procedure Act 1833, *all* arbitration agreements *in writing* were made irrevocable without the leave of the court. These two last provisions, now represented by sections 1 and 4(1) of the 1950 Act, therefore indirectly do enable domestic arbitration agreements to be enforced, provided they are in writing, either by staying actions brought in breach of the agreement, or by preventing a party's revocation of an appointed arbitrator's authority. In each case, however, the statutes are careful to confer a discretion through their requirement of leave of the court, which if refused in the one case or given in the other, will mean that an action in court will be permitted either to continue or be started, notwithstanding the existence of an arbitration agreement. As will be seen, the discretion to refuse a stay, so retaining the matter in court, is a very wide one, including grounds of convenience, such as the dispute involving a third party not subject to arbitration.[47] The logic of the legislation's history suggests,

---

[47] *Taunton-Collins* v. *Cromie* [1964] 1 W.L.R. 633. See generally *infra*, paras. 18·104 *et seq.*, and see para. 18·111.

therefore, that the discretionary grounds for permitting revocation under section 1 should be precisely co-terminous with those for refusing a stay under section 4. However, this view appears to have been rejected relatively recently in the Court of Appeal, where it was stated that a stronger case was needed for permitting revocation than for refusing a stay.[48]

(c) Deficiencies in the present law

18·016   The evolution of the various common law, equitable and statutory sources of arbitration law in England has been comprehensively and authoritatively discussed elsewhere.[49] Its importance lies in the fact that the sources of the law are various, that the statutory elements are piecemeal and not comprehensive, and that the statutory interventions themselves not infrequently raise as many questions as they answer, or fail to deal with known and commonly encountered everyday problems.

Thus, the relatively simple questions whether an arbitrator has power to strike out a claim for want of prosecution, or whether, and if so by what statutory or common law route, the court has power to grant a *quia timet* injunction to a party while an arbitration is pending, have both provoked difficult House of Lords' discussions and speeches, often involving considerable historical erudition.[50] Again, not only is the 1950 Act, together with its predecessors, notoriously lacking in defining the available powers of the arbitrator should a party fail or refuse to comply with his interlocutory orders, or to require if not pleadings then at least a proper particularisation of a party's case, (with section 12 of the 1950 Act giving no indication of available powers or sanctions in such situations), but the effect and intentions of section 5 of the 1979 Act, apparently directed specifically to the problem of non-compliance, are extremely difficult to deduce from the draftsmanship.[51] Moreover, the legislation makes no attempt to provide for a procedural matter as important as payment into court, leaving the parties to invent and develop their own inevitably much less satisfactory "sealed offer" procedures.[52] Again, while the Acts have, since 1934, recognised the existence of arbitrators' interim awards,[53] no indication is given as to their possible content, or the circumstances in

---

[48] See, *per* Harman L.J. in *City Centre Properties (I.T.C. Pensions) Ltd.* v. *Matthew Hall & Co. Ltd.* [1969] 1 W.L.R. 772, noted *supra*, Section 2(1)(a), para. 18·113, when considering a situation precisely similar to that in the *Taunton-Collins* case, see *supra*.

[49] *Mustill and Boyd* (2nd ed.), pp. 432 *et seq.*

[50] See *Bremer Vulkan Schiffbau und Maschinenfabrik* v. *South India Shipping Corporation Ltd.* [1981] A.C. 909 (now resolved by statutory provision in a new Section 13a of the 1950 Act introduced in 1990), and *Channel Tunnel Group* v. *Balfour Beatty Construction* [1993] A.C. 334 respectively. See also the doubts as to the jurisdictional source of the courts' readiness to receive appeals from awards as to costs, *infra*, Section 5(6)(c), para. 18·178, and of the extent of the remedy of remitter in such cases, discussed *infra*, Section 5(6)(c).

[51] See *Mustill and Boyd* (2nd ed.), pp. 536–543 for a lengthy discussion of this difficult practical problem.

[52] See *infra*, Section 5(7), paras. 18·182 *et seq.*

[53] See now s.14 of the 1950 Act.

which such awards should be given. Nor do the Acts make any attempt to deal with the difficult question of multi-party disputes, where either different or no arbitration agreements exist between all the parties to a dispute such as (in the construction field) sub-contractors, or the owner's A/E, or other contractors, in those circumstances where in the courts third party procedures would be available to bring such disputes under one roof.

Attention has been drawn to this general background and the particular **18·017** history of the English law of arbitration because the legislation in most Commonwealth countries has followed the developments in the English statute and case law of arbitration very closely in the past, up to and including the passing of the 1950 Act. The inadequate nature of much of the present statute law now seems to be provoking attempts overseas to modernise and rationalise their statutory law of arbitration, sometimes in advance of the law in England,[54] although there is still a tendency in some jurisdictions to follow English developments.[55]

It may be helpful to list shortly what appear to be certain *lacunae* in the present law:

(a) The precise purpose and scope of interim awards under section 14 of the 1950 Act is not defined or explained, and remains obscure.

(b) While a number of the more important High Court procedural and interlocutory powers are made available in support of an arbitration under section 12 of the 1950 Act, this is by no means comprehensive. The absence of any machinery for payment into court has been noted *supra*. The arbitrator's powers and responsibilities in regard to the proper particularisation of the parties' cases against each other, whether in the form of pleadings or not, has also been noted, and is considered in more detail *infra*.[55a] The extent or otherwise of other interlocutory powers, such as the new interlocutory powers to order a payment on account, or to strike out for want of prosecution, has also been noted.

(c) The arbitrator's powers to enforce interlocutory orders and direc- **18·018** tions against a recalcitrant party are not defined and may be inadequate, and little of clarification or improvement has been achieved in this regard by section 5 of the 1979 Act.

(d) While for limitation purposes a notice requiring arbitration is the equivalent of issuing a writ, no statutory provision is made for the very common situation where an action is started by writ but subsequently stayed—if so the plaintiff loses the benefit of the date of the writ, which seems anomalous.[56]

---

[54] See, *e.g.* the Hong Kong arbitration legislation making special provision for multi-partite or third party arbitration.

[55] See, *e.g.* the Australian legislation designed to give effect to the House of Lords' *Nema* Guidelines, noted *infra*, Section 5(6), para. 18·174.

[55a] See paras. 18·159 *et seq.*

[56] See, for a striking example, *County and District Properties* v. *Jenner* [1976] 2 Lloyd's Rep. 728, illustrated *infra*, Section 3, para. 18·106.

(e) Third party proceedings are not available in arbitrations, except by agreement, and the present case law in regard to staying an action or revoking an arbitrator's authority and setting aside arbitration agreements in such situations in order to achieve a single tribunal seems inconsistent and unsatisfactory.[56a]

(4) Comparative Law of Arbitration

18·019 It may be helpful to give some very general indication of the law under other legal systems. It is not perhaps sufficiently appreciated that the form of the English Arbitration Acts is dictated by the fact, already mentioned, that prior to statutory intervention the early law of contract meant that any arbitration agreement was, for practical purposes, unenforceable. As noted *supra*, at any time before publication of the award (when an effective contractual right to damages would undoubtedly arise), either party could unilaterally repudiate the agreement and revoke the arbitrator's authority, thereby depriving any subsequent award of contractual or other force. On such a repudiation the other party would, of course, be left with a remedy in damages but, in the absence of sufficiently compelling (and frank) evidence as to the superiority, from the complaining party's point of view, of an arbitrator as a tribunal by comparison with the courts (of which, not surprisingly, there is little or no suggestion in the cases) such an action could only give rise to nominal damages in English law. The fundamental statutory interventions in the nineteenth century were, therefore, designed, while very importantly leaving room for a discretion through the requirement of leave, to render arbitration agreements in practical terms specifically enforceable by indirect means against an unwilling party. As has been seen, this was achieved by the two intimately connected sections 1 and 4 of the 1950 Act, and their corresponding sections in the earlier nineteenth-century legislation.[57]

18·020 At the end of the Second World War, the Anglo-Saxon view of arbitrators as in all cases obliged to decide according to the law appeared to be limited to the English and certain Commonwealth or ex-Commonwealth jurisdictions, and to some states in the United States. A second, and larger group of nations appeared to have treated arbitration as subject to varying degrees of control by the courts to ensure that arbitrators' decisions accorded with the law, but only if the parties expressly so required in their arbitration agreement, and these nations permitted a further category of arbitration or conciliation, not subject to such control, should the parties so desire. Arbitrators of this latter kind are often described as "*amiables compositeurs*". Finally, a third group of nations treated all arbitration as being in this latter class, with arbitrators under no obligation to decide according to law. The foregoing summary of the comparative position

---

[56a] See *infra*, paras. 18·113 *et seq.*
[57] See the discussion of the historical background to these sections *supra*, paras. 18·014–18·015.

in different countries at the outbreak of the Second World War was regarded as authoritatively expounded in 1941.[58]

Following the Second World War, while there was a tendency for a number of jurisdictions within the second and third groups above to move toward a greater degree of control by the courts, there was also an independent movement by some contracting parties to provide expressly for arbitrators to decide disputes as *"amiables compositeurs"*, while a number of nations continued to maintain policies of abstention from intervention.[59]

It has been seen that for over a century the right of appeal to the courts   **18·021**
from an arbitrator's award on a point of law has been a special feature of English arbitration law—originally this arose under a practice of the parties to state a case for the opinion of the court, which was at that time dependent upon agreement between them. That practice was adopted and confirmed by the legislature in section 5 of the 1854 Act, but widened and made mandatory and independent of the other party's consent by sections 19 and 9 of the 1889 and 1934 Acts respectively.

Following the Second World War, however, and with the support of bodies such as the World Bank, there has been a vast increase in the number and value of international construction projects, particularly in the Third World, where for both technical and political reasons international arbitration has in many cases been seen as a virtual necessity by the parties, in the absence of sufficiently reliable and sophisticated local courts. As a result, a massive increase in international construction arbitration has occurred. Very substantial professional interests have become involved specialising in international arbitration, whether as arbitrators, expert witnesses or consultants and advisers. These new post-war professional arbitration interests, embracing the various categories of construction professional and a few academic and other lawyers likely to be appointed as arbitrators, appear for some reason to have conceived a strong antipathy to any form of control by the courts, and in particular to any rights of appeal on points of law or review of their awards. In this they have been consistently and strongly supported not only by domestic as well as international professional and arbitration institutions, but particularly by the contracting side of the construction industry, who have seen arbitration primarily as a vehicle for the advancement of financial claims for additional payment, and who have perceived a considerably less critical and more liberal approach to such claims from both domestic and international arbitrators, whether on liability or *quantum*, than in courts of law.

These differing vested interests appear to have exerted an overriding   **18·022**
international influence of recent years, both in the United Nations in the project leading up to the drafting of the UNCITRAL Model Law, as also in the various bodies concerned with providing international arbitration

---

[58] By Cohn in (1941) 4 Univ. of Toronto L.J. 1.
[59] See F. A. Mann, *Arbitration Extra Legem* (1978) 94 L.Q.R. 486.

facilities, such as the ICC in Paris and the London Court of Arbitration (together with, more recently, arbitration centres in Hong Kong, Kuala Lumpur, Australia and elsewhere). The same interests were clearly strongly influential in the working parties leading up to the Arbitration Act 1979, in England (and later, for example, to the Australian Commercial Arbitration Act 1990).

It may be speculated that in England the exclusionary agreements now permitted by section 3 of the 1979 Act, and the highly restrictive *Nema* guidelines laid down shortly thereafter by the House of Lords in regard to leave to appeal, reflect the influence of these same interests in the working parties prior to the 1979 Act,[60] which appear to have attracted the early and influential support of Donaldson J. even before the 1979 Act was passed[60a]; and in the case of the later 1990 Australian Act, similar influences in the Australian working parties appear to have succeeded in obtaining provisions in express statutory form designed to reproduce and give effect to the English House of Lords *Nema* guidelines.[61]

Again, parties to arbitration agreements under the articles and rules of the ICC will find that they have subscribed to the widest possible exclusionary rule preventing access to the courts following an award, since they are "deemed . . . to have waived the right to any form of appeal insofar as such waiver can validly be made".[62] Moreover, decisions of the Court (that is, of the International Chamber itself) as to the appointment, confirmation, challenge or replacement of an arbitrator on any ground appear to be final, and the reasons for such decisions are not to be communicated.[63]

18-023   In the case of the UNCITRAL Model Law, no court is to intervene except where provided in the Law,[64] and while under Article 16(3) resort to the identified court is permitted from a decision of the arbitral tribunal ruling that it has jurisdiction against objection by a party, the tribunal is given a discretion as to whether to give its ruling in its final award rather than as a preliminary question, thereby, in the former case, placing an objecting party in a position of extreme tactical difficulty.[65]

---

[60] See C.C.P.P., para. 17–47(b) and the editor in (1990) Arbitration International 253, 256 and see *supra*, Section 1(2)(b), paras. 18·004–18·005.

[60a] See *supra*, para. 18·005 and *infra*, para. 18·194.

[61] See this influence discussed in the New South Wales Court of Appeal in *Promenade Investments* v. *State of New South Wales* (1992) 26 N.S.W.L.R. 203, and see a powerful, if implied protest by Kirby P. at the consequences of curtailing rights of appeal in *Warley Ltd.* v. *Adco Constructions Ltd.* (1988) 8 A.C.L.R. 73, 80, *infra*, para. 18·024.

[62] Article 24.2.

[63] Article 2.13. Contrast in Australia *Hooper Bailie Ltd.* v. *President M.B.A.* (1988) 8 A.C.L.R. 83, illustrated *infra*, para. 18·077, where an appointing body's unfair appointment was declared void in the A.C.T. Supreme Court.

[64] Art. 5.

[65] Moreover, even if the matter is decided as a preliminary question, and the matter has then been referred to the identified court, the tribunal is permitted to continue the proceedings and make an award. These seem extraordinary powers in the face of a bona fide objection to jurisdiction, but may perhaps be explained as necessary in cases where resort to the courts is not bona fide and designed to secure delay, as can happen in some international situations. But preventing immediate resort to the courts at, in effect, the discretion of the

It would seem, therefore, that there has been a widespread movement by influential interests involved in the arbitration process against control by the courts, supported by the many modern governments who perceive a public financial advantage in diverting litigation away from the publicly funded judiciary into the privatised sector which arbitration represents. It remains to be seen whether users of arbitration, and in particular consumers or other private interests enjoying genuine freedom of contract and bargaining power, will find arbitration unaccompanied by judicial control an acceptable substitute for access as of right to the courts.

It is inescapable that the price which must be paid for such advantages **18·024** as are thought by legislatures or judiciaries to attend the abandonment or reduction of judicial appellate powers of control over arbitrators will be borne by the justice of the individual case. As has been eloquently observed in a dissenting judgment in the Court of Appeal of New South Wales in the analogous situation where there is no evidence to support an arbitrator's award:

> "... The result of this appeal will be to reserve to arbitrators a substantial measure of immunity from appellate review in the Supreme Court. This will occur in a jurisdiction where the Court has no power to order further reasons; simply a power to find that purported reasons given are so inadequate as to amount to an error of law. This immunity will doubtless gladden those who believe that, typically, curial intervention in arbitration has not, on the whole been happy or useful. Such observers will doubtless regard this decision as an important victory for the finality of arbitration and of the right of arbitrators to find facts without any effective danger of appellate review. Such a conclusion may well enhance the efficiency of arbitration. This is itself a laudable objective, but it may do so at too high a price. It may place too great a store on the objective of finality. As the Law Reform Commission pointed out, there is a competing consideration. It is the justice of the particular case. By the present approach, that consideration may be neglected, no matter how unreasonable and perverse is the decision of the arbitrator. I do not consider that conclusion necessary, I do not think it is desirable, but it is required by the authority of this Court's decision ..."[66]

It may perhaps be added that not only uncorrected errors of law, but elements of over-confidence, unfairness and inquisitorial and domineering attitudes can be expected to increase with the withdrawal of appellate powers and sheltered by the lack of publicity provided by arbitration, not least, it would seem, in construction arbitrations.[67]

---

arbitrator(s) by permitting the ruling to be delayed until final award seems anomalous and possibly an error of draftsmanship.

[66] *Per* Kirby P., dissenting, in *Warley Limited* v. *Adco Constructions Ltd.* (1988) 8 A.C.L.R. 73, 80. For no evidence as a ground of appeal, see *infra*, Section 5(6), paras. 18·175.

[67] See a number of the more modern misconduct cases illustrated *infra*, Section 4(3), paras. 18·132 *et seq.*, and see also (1990) 6 Arbitration International 253, 266 and 627, and C.C.P.P., para. 17–47(h).

SECTION 2. THE ARBITRATION AGREEMENT

(1) Formal Requirements

18·025   The English Arbitration Acts, including in particular the key sections 1 and 4 of the 1950 Act in regard to irrevocability and indirect enforcement by means of a stay respectively, apply in terms only to an arbitration agreement in writing, defined by section 32 of the 1950 Act as "a written agreement to submit present or future differences to arbitration, whether an arbitrator is named or not".

Apart from some very special cases, for example, under the Law of Property Act 1925, there is no requirement that the written agreement should be signed.[68] The necessary agreement may be made by duly authorised agents, and an endorsement on counsel's brief has been held to be a good agreement.[69]

However, arbitration agreements may be implied in certain cases, as where, after the original contract containing an arbitration clause has expired, parties have gone on dealing on the same terms[70]; or where a contract was intended to be construed with and as supplemental to a previous contract containing an agreement for arbitration.

ILLUSTRATIONS

18·026   (1) A commission agreement relating to a single voyage contained an arbitration clause conforming to the requirements of the Common Law Procedure Act 1854. Two more voyages in successive years were undertaken with the same terms indorsed on the agreements. Prior to a fourth voyage, a letter was written that it should be "on the same terms as the former one". *Held*, by Keating J., that a dispute relating to the fourth voyage should be stayed under the Act: *Hattersley* v. *Hatton* (1862).[71]

(2) Parties to a lease by deed which contained an arbitration clause executed a supplemental deed, of even date, whereby the lessee was released from certain restrictive covenants contained in the lease. When the landlord brought an action for breach of covenant and the lessee applied for a stay, it was objected that there was no arbitration clause in the supplemental agreement, on which the lessee was relying. *Held*, by Bacon V.C., that the action should be stayed. *Wade-Gery* v. *Morrison* (1877).[72]

(3) A partnership agreement for one year contained usual provisions for accounts following the termination of the partnership, and an arbitration clause for all differences arising under the agreement. The partnership was in

---

[68] *Baker* v. *Yorkshire Assurance Company* [1892] 1 Q.B. 144; *Hickman* v. *Kent & Romney Marsh Sheep Breeders' Association* [1915] 1 Ch. 881; *Excomm Ltd.* v. *Bamaodah, The St. Raphael* [1985] 1 Lloyd's Rep. 403, C.A.
[69] *Aitken* v. *Batchelor* (1893) 62 L.J.Q.B. 193.
[70] *Gillett* v. *Thornton*, see *infra*.
[71] 3 F. & F. 116.
[72] 37 L.T. 270.

fact continued for a further three years before being terminated by agreement. It was contended that, in respect of the work done after the first year,
there was no agreement in writing. *Held*, by Hall V.C., that the parties must be
taken to have adopted the terms of the old partnership when they prolonged
it, and that an action brought for an account following its termination should
be stayed: *Gillett* v. *Thornton* (1875).[73]

However, it is very common in commerce, and construction contracts   **18·027**
are no exception, for contracts to be concluded by reference to or incorporation of the terms of some other document, such as the terms of a parent charter party incorporated into a bill of lading, and in the construction
field of some standard form of contract into a sub-contract,[74] or of some
other specific contract, such as a main or superior sub-contract entered
into between different parties engaged on the same project. Such references or incorporations are often informally concluded, either orally at
meetings, or in partly oral and partly written form. In such cases, there
may often be two questions: first, whether the particular arbitration provision or clause has been successfully incorporated by a generally worded
reference to its parent document[75]; and secondly, if so, whether the reference to arbitration so achieved can be regarded as a written one satisfying
the statutory requirement of writing. In such a case not only must the
incorporated arbitration agreement or clause itself be in writing, but it
would seem that the reference to, or incorporation of that agreement must
itself be in sufficiently explicit documentary form to satisfy the requirements of the Act.[76] Cases on incorporation of arbitration clauses are considered *infra*, Subsection (3).

(2) Terms of the Agreement

Beyond the very short statutory definition in section 32 of the 1950 Act   **18·028**
supra, there are no other stipulated requirements as to the content of an
arbitration agreement. Generally speaking this does not give rise to difficulty, and it can be assumed that the courts will give a liberal interpretation where an intention to submit differences to arbitration can be
reasonably inferred from the wording used. Thus, in the analogous and
possibly stricter situation where it is necessary to determine whether the
limitation period has expired by reference to the terminal date when
proceedings commence, and to interpret the statutory requirement for
this purpose of a notice of arbitration under section 30(3)(*a*) of the

---

[73] L.R. 19 E.Q. 599.
[74] See, *e.g. Modern Buildings Wales Ltd.* v. *Limmer and Trinidad Co. Ltd.* [1975] 1 W.L.R.
1281, C.A.
[75] See, *e.g.* the bill of lading cases of *Thomas & Co. Ltd.* v. *Portsea S.S. Co. Ltd.* [1912] A.C. 1,
and *Annefield (owners)* v. *Annefield (cargo owners), The Annefield* [1971] P. 168, C.A.
[76] See, *per* Ralph Gibson L.J. in *Aughton Ltd. (formerly Aughton Group Ltd.)* v. *M.F. Kent
Services Ltd.* (1991) 57 BLR 1, illustrated *infra*, para. 18·033, discussing *Modern Buildings
Wales*, *supra*, and *The St. Raphael* [1985] 1 Lloyd's Rep. 403.

Limitation Act 1980 (which requires the other party "to appoint an arbitrator or to agree to the appointment of an arbitrator") Lord Denning M.R. said:

> "It seems to me that a notice which says 'I require the difference between us to be submitted to arbitration' is sufficient to commence the arbitration, because it is by implication a request to concur in the appointment of an arbitrator".[77]

However, in construction contracts it will often be necessary to distinguish between a clause providing for a *certifier* (once actually described judicially as "a preventer of disputes")[78] or a *valuer* on the one hand, or for an *arbitrator* in the full sense on the other. In the former two cases a full arbitral hearing or investigation may not be the intention (so that in certain circumstances, paradoxically, depending on the contract wording, their decisions may be less open to review or challenge than those of a full arbitrator). The question may be complicated by finding both types of provision in the same contract, sometimes naming the same person (usually the owner's A/E) as both certifier and arbitrator. This distinction is discussed and cases cited *infra*, Subsection (4)(e), and see also *ante*, Chapter 6 Section 4(3) and Section 9.

18·029   In some cases it has also been held that wording using permissive rather than mandatory language, which is occasionally encountered in arbitration clauses and which may appear only to suggest, but not sufficiently positively to require arbitration, will fail to take effect as an arbitration clause, even in a case where other clauses in the contract seem only consistent with a normal mandatory arbitration intention.

ILLUSTRATION

Clause 10 of a Canadian contract made the engineer's decisions as to the contract documents binding "subject always to arbitration". Clause 21 gave a right to determine the contract on failure to pay "any sum certified by the engineer or awarded by arbitrators". Clause 22 was an indemnity clause, and provided that claims under it "shall be adjusted by agreement or arbitration". Clause 28 then provided that in the event of a dispute either party "*shall be entitled to give* ... notice of such dispute *and to request* arbitration thereof ... and the parties *may* ... *agree* to submit the same to arbitration". *Held*, by the Saskatchewan Court of Appeal (Hall J.A. dissenting) and following a majority of the Ontario Court of Appeal in *Re McNamara Construction of Ontario Ltd.* v. *Brook University*,[79] that this was not a binding submission to arbitration within the Saskatchewan Arbitration Act 1965: *Re Fischbach & Moore of Canada* v. *Noranda Mines* (1971).[80]

---

[77] *Nea Agrex S.A.* v. *Baltic Shipping Co. Ltd., The Agios Lazaros* [1976] Q.B. 933, 944 D.
[78] See *ante*, Chap. 6, Section 4(3), paras. 6·065 *et seq.*, and Section 9, para. 6·220 for a discussion of the special status of certifiers in construction contracts, and see *infra*, Subsection (4), paras. 18·061 *et seq.*
[79] (1970) 11 D.L.R. 3d 513.
[80] 19 D.L.R. 3d 329.

[Note: It is difficult not to feel sympathy with Hall J.A.'s and King J.'s respective dissenting judgments in the above cases. Hall J.A. agreed with King J. in the Ontario case that the words "request" and "may" were "nothing more than a polite way of indicating the steps to be taken", besides pointing out that the contrary view meant that the other references to arbitration in the Saskatchewan contract became meaningless. In the Ontario case, which was on clause 44 of the RAIC CCA standard form, the other references to arbitration in that contract were not so compelling.]

In addition to confused draftsmanship in construction contracts which   **18·030**
fails to distinguish sufficiently clearly between the roles of certifier and arbitrator,[81] arbitration clauses in construction contracts frequently contain a number of special provisions which can give rise to complication and difficulty. These include particularly:

(a) Express *inhibitions against early arbitration* of disputes before completion of the work (usually described in this book as "early arbitration" provisions).[82]

(b) Whether or not associated with (a) above, *earlier preliminary reference* of disputes to the owner or his A/E, usually to be found in civil engineering contracts, required as a first step before, and as a condition of, any later arbitration (usually described in this book as "prior reference" provisions).[83]

(c) Time-bar provisions, whereby the right to claim or arbitrate will be lost unless notice of the claim or of arbitration has been given within a stipulated period.[83a]

These various special types of arbitration clause in construction contracts are considered *infra*, Subsection (4).

(3) Incorporation of Arbitration Clauses

The subject of incorporation of contractual documents by reference has   **18·031**
been considered in general terms in Chapter 3,[84] and in the case of subcontracts in Chapter 13,[85] although this often takes place in a loose or general sense not targeted specifically at particular terms of the contract or the arbitration clause itself.

Such references to other external documents, and hence a possible incorporation of the arbitration clause contained in such documents, may take the form of a reference, sometimes informal or inaccurate in its

---

[81] See also *ante*, Chap. 6, Section 4(3), paras. 6·065 *et seq.* for a number of examples.
[82] For these, see also *ante*, Chap. 6, Section 6(7)(f), paras. 6·209 et seq.
[83] See *infra*, paras. 18·045 *et seq.*
[83a] See *infra*, paras. 18·048 *et seq.*
[84] See *ante*, Chap. 3, Section 2, paras. 3·048 *et seq.*
[85] See *ante*, Chap. 13, Section 4(3), paras. 13·099 *et seq.*

description, to a standard form of contract or sub-contract,[86] or a reference to another and possibly not in all respects appropriate contract already in use on the same project but made between different parties (as, for example, references in a sub-contract or a sub-sub-contract to the terms of a superior main or sub-contract).[87] References may also be made to another existing contract between the same parties, but obviously these will create less difficulty in arriving at an interpretation which incorporates the earlier arbitration clause.

18·032   Thus, it has been seen that in a case where reference was made in correspondence to the RIBA Conditions of Engagement, which might well have been intended to regulate the amount of and entitlement to remuneration only, the Court of Appeal held that this did successfully incorporate the arbitration clause into an architect's contract of employment.[88] In that case the document to be incorporated was accurately identified, but the difficult question to be decided was the precise extent of its intended incorporation.

It will frequently happen that the parties may refer to a document which cannot be used to fit the parties' own contractual relationship or description without some necessary modifications. In the case of an arbitration clause in a main contract, for example, it may or may not be worded so as to be applicable to sub-contracting parties without modification of at least some parts of the clause. In the analogous field of marine contracts of affreightment, a substantial case law has built up as a result of the practice whereby bills of lading incorporate by reference the terms of the principal charterparty.[89] Relatively rigid rules of interpretation have been developed by the English Commercial Court in bill of lading cases, to the effect that where the terms of the charterparty's arbitration clause are not applicable without some modification of its provisions to suit the bill of lading relationship or transaction, a general incorporating reference to the charterparty without some more specific reference to the arbitration clause itself will not suffice.[90] However, it would be wrong, it is submitted, for any such rigid rule to apply in the quite different commercial relationship between construction contracts and sub-contracts, although the following recent case in the Court of Appeal shows a difference of opinion on the point.

---

[86] See, *e.g. Geary Walker & Co. Ltd.* v. *Lawrence & Son* (1906) Hudson, *Building Contracts* (4th ed.), Vol. 2, 382, *Modern Buildings Wales Ltd.* v. *Limmer and Trinidad Co. Ltd.* [1975] 1 W.L.R. 1281, C.A.; *Brightside Kilpatrick Engineering Services* v. *Mitchell Construction (1973) Ltd.* [1975] 2 Lloyd's Rep. 493, for all see *ante*, Chap. 13, Section 4(6), paras. 13·101 *et seq.*

[87] See the cases collected *ante*, Chap. 13, Section 4(3), paras. 13·100–13·104.

[88] *Kaye* v. *Bronesky* (1973) 4 BLR 1, C.A., illustrated *ante*, Chap. 2, Section 3(1), para. 2·043.

[89] *Thomas & Co. Ltd.* v. *Portsea S.S. Co. Ltd.* [1912] A.C. 1, as explained in *Skips A/S Nordheim* v. *Syrian Petroleum Company Ltd., The Varenna* [1984] Q.B. 599, where incorporation of the charterparty's arbitration clause was rejected.

[90] See, *per* Brandon J. in *The Annefield* [1971] P. 168, 173, cited by Ralph Gibson L.J. in *Aughton Ltd.* v. *M.F. Kent Services Ltd.* (1991) 57 BLR 1, 16–17. See also *per* Lord Denning M.R. in *The Annefield* [1971] P. 168, 183, C.A., and, *per* Bingham L.J. in *Federal Bulk Carriers Inc.* v. *C. Itoh & Co. Ltd., The Federal Bulker* [1989] 1 Lloyd's Rep. 103, 105.

ILLUSTRATION

Sub-contractors entered into a sub-sub-contract by an order letter stating **18·033**
"(7) You will enter into a sub-sub-contract with us based on GC Works 1 *as discussed at our meeting*; (11) Our previous correspondence and the documents . . . in our enquiry form part of our agreement". GC/Works/1 was in fact the standard form which had been used for the main contract, with an arbitration clause which was not relied on by the sub-contractors when sued by the sub-sub-contractors for sums allegedly due; but the "previous correspondence and documentation" referred to in the sub-sub-contract, when analysed, contained main contractor/sub-contractor documentation, by clause 61 of which all disputes *between the parties to the sub-contract and relating to the sub-contract*, other than certain matters in which the decision of the *main contractor* was to be conclusive, were to be referred to arbitration. The sub-contractors relied on clause 61 as entitling them to a stay against the sub-sub-contractor's claim. *Held*, by the Court of Appeal, that a stay should be refused. *Per* Ralph Gibson L.J.: It would be illogical to incorporate documents requiring necessary modifications at many points to govern the sub-sub-contract, but to refuse to incorporate the arbitration clause because it, too, required necessary modifications, and the bills of lading cases to that effect do not apply to a construction contract; but here the contract was partly oral as well as partly in writing, as evidenced by clause (7) of the order letter, and depended on the oral part in order to incorporate clause 61 of the sub-contract, so that it was not an arbitration agreement *in writing* satisfying clause 32 of the Arbitration Act 1950, and the stay should be refused for that reason. *Per* Sir John Megaw: There was no sufficiently precise reference to the arbitration clause, which required modifications to suit the sub-sub-contract within the *Thomas* v. *Portsea* principle, so that the arbitration clause had not been incorporated at all: *Aughton Ltd. (formerly Aughton Group Ltd.) v. M.F. Kent Services Ltd.* (1991).[91]

It is submitted that Ralph Gibson L.J.'s reasoning in the above case, at least in regard to the incorporation intention, is to be preferred. The presence of arbitration clauses is currently so near universal in the producer dominated English construction industry standard forms, since it is perceived as highly advantageous on the contracting side of the industry (whatever its disadvantages for informed owners), that an intention to incorporate an arbitration clause, once an intention to adopt a particular set of contract conditions *as a whole* is established, usually seems inescapable. This situation can be compared, in a different context, with the reasoning of the Court of Appeal, and particularly of Edmund Davies L.J., when holding that the arbitration clause in the RIBA's conditions of engagement had been incorporated by reference into the contract of employment of an architect.[92]

On the other hand, it has been submitted[93] that in many circumstances **18·034**
"loose incorporation" or references in a sub-contract to a superior con-

---

[91] 57 BLR 1.
[92] *Kaye* v. *Bronesky* (1976) 4 BLR 4, see *ante*, Chap. 2, para. 2·043.
[93] See *ante*, Chap. 13, para. 13·103.

tractor's head-contract obligations may often only be intended to mean that *the physical work* under the inferior contract is to comply with all the superior contractor's obligations in that regard to his own employer—that is to say, only the specifications or descriptions of the work, or of its mode and manner of carrying out, in the superior contract are intended for incorporation into the inferior contract. Once, however, the intention is shown to go beyond that point and adopt another contract's terms or conditions generally, the onus may well shift to the party seeking to avoid incorporation of the arbitration clause, even if some necessary modification of the other contract may be required, it is submitted. The fact that in the *Aughton* case there were two different superior contracts and arbitration clauses, and that it was the least easily applicable one which was apparently more directly referred to in the sub-sub-contract order letter and at meetings, clearly made it difficult for the Court of Appeal to give effect to what had almost certainly been the intention, as had in fact been evidenced by the claimant sub-contractor's own earlier conduct in that case.

There may, however, be an intermediate class of case where, while not actually justifying a stay, it may be intended that a decision or award under the main contract arbitration clause will bind a sub-contractor.

ILLUSTRATION

18·035   Clause 2 of a plumbing sub-contract provided that "the main contract conditions shall apply equally to the sub-contract works *insofar as they are applicable to those works* and the sub-contractor shall comply with and perform its obligations on the same conditions as the main contractors". By clause 6 the terms of payment under the sub-contract were to be as laid down for the main contractor and certified by the architect or engineer as being due under the sub-contract. Clause 61 of GC/Works/1, which was the main contract arbitration clause, was in general terms, but would require modification by substitution of the defendant main contractors for the Authority and the removal of a section relating to matters which would be final and conclusive as against the main contractor. The sub-contractor brought an action in the courts for breach of contract for failure to give due access, and relied on various provisions of GC/Works/1 for this purpose, while the main contractors applied for a stay relying on that contract's arbitration clause. *Held*, by Judge Fox-Andrews, following *Goodwin Jardine & Co.* v. *Brand*,[94] that while the GC/Wks/1 conditions were to apply to the sub-contract *so far as applicable*, and while the bill of lading cases did not apply, the sub-contractors' claim for damages did not relate to any matter on which the main contract architect was required to rule, nor was there anything in it to which the arbitration clause in the main contract could apply, so that the clause had not been incorporated and a stay would be refused: *Lakers Mechanical Services Ltd.* v. *Boskalis Westminster Construction Ltd.* (1986).[95]

[Note: There was actually another party interposed between the main con-

---

[94] Illustrated *ante*, Chap. 13, para. 13·100.
[95] 5 Const. L.J. 139.

tractor and the owner in this case, so that strictly this was a sub-sub-contract, but the judgment makes it clear that nothing turned on this.]

(4) Special Provisions in Construction Contracts

(a) *"Scott v. Avery"* clauses

It has been seen that without express authorisation from the parties an   **18·036**
arbitrator cannot finally decide matters which go to his own jurisdiction.[96]
Nor can the parties to an arbitration agreement agree that the courts shall
have no jurisdiction whatsoever.[97] They can, however, agree that no right
of action shall accrue in respect of any disputes between them until after
those disputes have been decided and awarded upon by an arbitrator. The
fact that such provisions were acceptable and could be enforced, notwithstanding their apparent displacement of the jurisdiction of the courts, was
first established when terms of this kind began to be introduced into
insurance policies, which provided that no claim might be made under the
policy until either liability or the amount of the claim (or both) had first
been settled by arbitration.[98] Such provisions are almost invariably
referred to by the name of the House of Lords decision on this point in
1856, as *"Scott v. Avery"* clauses.

In construction contracts, many of which in the past provided for
interim and final certification by the owner's A/E of payments due to
contractors, combined with separate provisions for arbitration of disputes
either by the A/E or by a fully independent arbitrator, their application to
perhaps the commonest of all construction disputes, namely a contractor's
claim for moneys due resisted by the owner's set-off or cross-claim for
defective work (or for excessive valuation or for delay), has occasionally
caused difficulty.

ILLUSTRATIONS

(1) An Australian building contract provided for payment upon the certifi-   **18·037**
cates of the architect, and that if any disputes should arise the dissatisfied
party should give the architect seven days' notice requiring the matter to be
referred to arbitration. Neither party was to be entitled to commence an
action upon any such matter in dispute until it had been determined by arbitration. The contractor sued for moneys due on an interim certificate, but the
owner counterclaimed for defective work, and also pleaded that, as a dispute
had arisen, the contractor could not sue without an award. The contractor
replied that it was the owner who was disputing the interim certificate, and
that as the dissatisfied party it was for the owner to require arbitration, which

---

[96] See *supra*, paras. 18·006–18·009.
[97] See, *per* Warrington L.J. in *Re Bjornstad and Ouse Shipping Co.* [1924] 2 K.B. 673.
[98] *Scott* v. *Avery* (1856) 5 H.L.C. 811; *Viney* v. *Bignold* (1888) 20 Q.B.D. 172.

he had failed to do. With regard to the owner's counterclaim, the contractor similarly pleaded that it could not be prosecuted in the absence of an award. *Held*, by a majority of the High Court of Australia (Latham C.J. & McTiernan J. dissenting), that the builder was entitled to recover on the interim certificate; and by the whole Court, that the owner could not pursue his cross action. *Per* Latham C.J. dissenting, when the owner refused to pay alleging defective work there was a dispute entitling the contractor to require arbitration, so that without an award the contractor could not recover: *John Grant & Sons Ltd.* v. *Trocadero Building Ltd.* (1938).[99]

18·038
(2) An arbitration clause in an Australian contract required notice of dispute to be served and reference to arbitration within seven days thereafter, and that "neither party shall be entitled to commence or maintain any action upon any such dispute or difference until such matters shall be referred or determined ..." When the contractor requested payment of sums certified by the architect, the owner's solicitor wrote a letter in reply which, while not requiring arbitration, alleged defective work and that the cost of making good exceeded the sums certified. In an action for the amount of the certificate, the owner denied the existence of a contract, which was rejected, but also sought to set off against the claim amounts for faulty workmanship in the building. *Held*, by the High Court of Australia, that while a mere refusal to pay an unchallenged progress certificate was not a dispute arising "under or in connection with the contract" within the terms of the arbitration clause, the refusal to pay for allegedly defective work was a dispute which, distinguishing *Grant* v. *Trocadero* on the wording of that contract,[99a] prevented commencement of an action without an award, whether or not notice was given, so that the contractor's claim must fail: *Plucis* v. *Fryer* (1967).[1]

18·039
(3) A contractor brought an action for wrongful termination of his contract, claiming damages for breach of contract, the release of a guarantee or bond, and the return of substantial plant and materials seized and detained by the owner or, alternatively, damages for their detention and conversion. By clause 32 of the contract disputes of every kind were to be referred to the Chief Engineer for Railways to be settled and decided finally and conclusively by him, subject to a limited right of appeal (in relation to the measurement of the work and the prices paid for it) to an arbitrator appointed by the Minister of Works. By clause 35, no suit or action was to be brought by the contractor or the owner against the other to recover money for breach of contract or for any other matter arising out of the contract unless the contractor or owner should have obtained a certificate order or award of the Chief Engineer for Railways for the amount sued for. The owners alleged that the contract had been validly determined by them, and that the contractor had not obtained a certificate as required by clause 35. The contractor alleged that the owner was precluded from relying on the absence of a certificate, order or award by reason of waiver, and also because the Chief Engineer had not acted independently. *Held*, by the High Court of Australia, that clause 35 was a "*Scott* v. *Avery*" clause; that the allegations of waiver and lack of independence failed on the facts; and that the contractor was prevented from bringing the action for damages for breach of contract, but not the action for release of the guarantee, or for the return of the plant and materials or damages for their detention or conversion: *South Australian Railways Commissioner* v. *Egan* (1973).[2]

[99] 60 C.L.R. 1.
[99a] See *infra*, para. 18·041.
[1] 41 A.L.J.R. 192.
[2] 130 C.L.R. 506.

"*Scott* v. *Avery*" clauses have not of recent years been commonly found   **18·040**
in English construction contracts or standard forms, although, as the
above illustrations show, they are still retained in a number of public contracts in Australia. In their practical effect they will only differ in principle
from the large number of construction contracts where a certificate of the
owner's A/E has been made a condition precedent to recovery[3] by reason
of the fact that it is an *arbitrator's award*, rather than a certifier's certificate
or decision, which must be obtained before there can be a cause of action.
The effect of the "*Scott* v. *Avery*" clause is, therefore, that until the award
is obtained there is no cause of action at all, and it is this view of the clauses
which has enabled the courts to hold that they do not represent an ouster
of the court's jurisdiction.

As in the case of certification provisions, however, the cardinal *Gilbert-*   **18·041**
Ash principle of interpretation applies, namely that the parties will not in
the absence of sufficiently clear language be treated as abandoning remedies available to them at common law for the enforcement of their
rights.[4] Thus, a "*Scott* v. *Avery*" provision will, in the absence of sufficiently clear wording, be restricted in its operation only to those types of
claim or defence which are clearly identified by the clause as being within
its scope. This is the explanation for the apparent inconsistency between
the two *Grant* and *Plucis* cases in the High Court of Australia illustrated
above. In the latter case, the High Court emphasised a relatively subtle
difference in the wording used in the two clauses, and expressed the opinion that the *Plucis* wording had been altered in order to avoid the *Grant*
result (where the contractor suing in the courts on a certificate had not
been defeated by the clause while the owner's set-off and cross-claim had
been). There seems little doubt that the *Egan* wording of the clause, still
more widely expressed, had indeed been designed in the owner's favour to
avoid the earlier *Grant* result, although the High Court did succeed in
holding that at least some of the contractor's heads of damage were not
within the scope of the clause in the later case.

It has been seen that in those cases where the courts exercise their
power under the Arbitration Acts to order that an arbitration agreement
shall cease to have effect on grounds of fraud or the arbitrator's undisclosed interest or misconduct, they are given the additional power to
declare a "*Scott* v. *Avery*" provision to be of no further effect.[5] Additionally, special provision has been made in the English limitation legislation
to modify what would otherwise have been the effect of the English
accrual-based limitation period in the case of a "*Scott* v. *Avery*" clause.[6]

---

[3] See *ante*, Chap. 6, Sections 3(1) and (2), paras. 6·036 *et seq.*, and Section 6(7)(b), paras.
6·190 *et seq.*
[4] See, *per* Lord Diplock in *Modern Engineering (Bristol) Ltd.* v. *Gilbert-Ash (Northern) Ltd.*
[1974] A.C. 689, 717–8, cited and discussed *ante*, Chap. 6, Section 1(1), paras. 6·005, and
Section 6(7)(c), paras. 6·195 *et seq.*
[5] s.25(2)(*b*) of the Arbitration Act 1950, mentioned *supra*, Section 1(2)(a), para. 18·003.
[6] Limitation Act 1980, Section 34(2), see *supra*, Section 1(2)(a), para. 18·003.

On the same principles as arbitration clauses generally, a "*Scott* v. *Avery*" provision may survive the rescission or avoidance of the substantive contract of which it forms part.[7]

(b) "Early arbitration" provisions

18·042   These provisions, designed to prevent commencement of the arbitration of disputes or differences under the terms of the arbitration clause prior to completion of the work, are a commonplace of English construction contracts, and their interpretation has been discussed *ante*, Chapter 6.[8] They are often ineptly drafted, posing a number of questions of interpretation including:

    (a) Precisely what is intended by "commencement of the arbitration" in this context?

    (b) Precisely what degree or stage of "completion" is contemplated before the arbitration can be "commenced"?

    (c) Precisely what is the ambit of certain commonly expressed exceptions to the prohibition, in particular exceptions directed at disputes over "certificates" or "the withholding of certificates"?[9]

    (d) What is to be the position if the contract has been terminated or abandoned or frustrated, or in cases where, after a termination, the owner does not wish to complete the project, but there is no express term qualifying the prohibition in such situations?

18·043   Apart from the difficulties created by ambiguous wording stipulating that, with some specified exceptions, a "reference to arbitration shall not be opened" before completion (for example, in the case of the RIBA/JCT forms), some of the other difficulties mentioned in (b) above are met in those forms by the later words "until Practical Completion or alleged Practical Completion of the Works or termination or alleged termination of the Contractor's employment under this Contract or abandonment of the Works".[10] The corresponding words in the ICE conditions are that "no steps shall be taken in the reference to the arbitrator"[11] until "completion or alleged completion of the Works". The RIBA/JCT wording, which is typically ambiguous, will probably only inhibit the opening of the arbitration *hearing*, it is submitted, whereas the ICE wording would seem to prevent steps such as delivery of written statements of case or pleadings, although not the original initial reference itself. On the other hand words used, as is the case in some contracts, which forbid "commencement of

---

[7] *Heyman* v. *Darwins* [1942] A.C. 356, and see the cases and discussion *supra*, Section 1(2) (c), paras. 18·007 *et seq*.

[8] See Section 6(7)(f), paras. 6.209–6·213.

[9] See the cases cited *ante*, Chap. 6, Section (6)(7)(f), paras. 6·210–6·212.

[10] See Article 5.2 of the 1980 Forms.

[11] See, *e.g.* Clause 66(1) of the fifth edition. Compare the wording that "the arbitrators are not to enter on the reference" in the FIDIC second edition (later FIDIC editions have dropped the "early arbitration" prohibitions altogether).

arbitration" before completion may mean that, consistent with the definition of that expression in section 34(3) of the English Limitation Act 1980, not even notice of arbitration can be given until the stipulated stage of completion.[12]

Where an "early arbitration" clause is silent, the Court of Appeal in **18·044** 1925 appeared to accept that, in a case where a contract had been terminated by the contractor for non-payment, arbitration of his claim must nevertheless await completion of the work by the owner, no doubt using another contractor.[13] Should an owner decide not to complete the project at all, as can quite often happen for commercial reasons in some termination situations, no doubt the prevention principle[14] can be invoked to overcome any objection that the arbitration is premature. The Court of Appeal in the *Smith* v. *Martin* case decided that an arbitrator with the usual jurisdiction over disputes "arising under" the contract would not have jurisdiction to decide *finally* whether a sufficient completion had been achieved so as to found his jurisdiction under such an "early arbitration" inhibition. It is submitted, in the light of more recent case-law in which arbitrators have been held to have jurisdiction to decide objections that the contract was void *ab initio*,[15] that *Smith* v. *Martin* requires reconsideration in this respect. The point is now even more important, since if jurisdiction does exist to decide an "early arbitration" objection, the aggrieved party's only remedy will be by way of appeal on a point of law under the 1979 Act, now much more restricted than before by the *Nema* guidelines, and he will in any case be bound by any relevant findings of fact reached by the arbitrator when deciding the matter.

(c) "Prior reference" provisions

Arbitration is not infrequently, particularly in traditional English style **18·045** civil engineering forms of contract, made conditional upon prior reference of the dispute to the owner's engineer or other certifier for an initial decision by him. This result is often achieved by providing that the prior decision will become permanently binding upon both parties unless notice, (either of dissatisfaction with the decision, or requiring arbitration, or both) is given within a stipulated period. If so, there is a time-bar element[16] present as well. Failure to submit a dispute for prior decision in this way may, therefore, act as a temporary or even permanent bar to arbitration or litigation, depending on the wording, in much the same way as an "early arbitration" provision (which may also be found in association

---

[12] Compare the reasoning in *Blackpool B.C.* v. *Parkinson Ltd.* (1991) 58 BLR 85, where the wording of the RIBA/JCT time-bar provision following issue of the final certificate was under consideration.

[13] *Smith* v. *Martin* [1925] 1 K.B. 745, and see in the case of an owner's termination, *Pethick Bros.* v. *Metropolitan Water Board,* Hudson, *Building Contracts* (4th ed., 1911), Vol. 2, p. 456, C.A.

[14] See *ante*, Chap. 1, Section 6(2), paras. 1·186 *et seq.*

[15] See *supra*, Section 1(2), paras. 18·007–18·008.

[16] These are discussed separately in para. (d) *infra*.

with a prior reference clause), while failure to meet any subsequent time requirement for giving notice of dissatisfaction or of arbitration will usually act as a permanent bar not only to arbitration itself but to litigation as well.[17]

Prior reference clauses, of which clauses 66 of the ICE Conditions and clause 67 of the International FIDIC Conditions are the best known examples, appear to be highly valued by the consulting engineering profession and their professional institutions, and are constantly inserted in their standard form contracts. They can easily, however, cause great tactical difficulties and injustice, particularly to contractors, and particularly if in conjunction, as they usually are, with time-bar clauses. This leads to unmeritorious arguments by owners that the right to arbitrate, and hence to claim at all, has been lost as a result of an earlier rejection of the claim by the A/E, later said to have constituted a decision settling the dispute under the prior reference clause.[18]

18·046   Informal references of disputes to A/Es by contractors, together with negotiation or compromise of claims, continually take place in any event on construction projects without the assistance of contractual structures of this kind, which appear to fulfil little practical function except to delay the settlement and resolution of justified claims. The clauses are, in fact, notoriously full of ambiguities, and in practice appear to raise more questions and create more anomalies and procedural difficulties than any perceivable advantage to be derived from them.[19] Their popularity with engineering institutions appears to be due to the fact that they are seen as giving official sanction to a delay mechanism which avoids the necessity for immediate or early provisional decisions by the A/E and facilitates a process of negotiation or "horse trading" which it is hoped will avoid an ultimate confrontation.

This type of clause can also lead to complicated and unmeritorious procedural arguments to the effect that while some issues between the parties before an arbitrator may be disputed by reason of a prior reference to the Engineer, others raised by way of cross-claim or set-off by the opposing party cannot, in the absence of prior reference on his part.[20]

A further form of prior reference provision, which has very recently emerged in larger or international construction projects, involves the reference of disputes to an intermediate level of independent adjudicators or conciliators before full arbitration is permitted. These new provisions rarely give careful consideration to the precise use which may be made of any findings or reports which result at this intermediate level in any later

---

[17] See *infra*, para. (d).

[18] Compare the use made of a rather similar provision by the owners in *Commonwealth of Australia* v. *Jennings Construction* [1985] V.L.R. 586 *infra*, para 18·054.

[19] See, *e.g.* the detailed analysis of these clauses by the editor in *ICE Conditions of Contract fifth edition: A Commentary* (1978), pp. 266–272 and his commentary on the FIDIC International Contract in *The International Civil Engineering Contract* (1974), pp. 169–172. See also "The Time Bar in FIDIC Clause 67", in C.C.P.P., Chap. 18.

[20] See, *e.g. Mid-Glamorgan C.C.* v. *Land Authority of Wales* (1990) 6 Const. L.J. 234, 49 BLR 61.

full arbitration, or of the precise status, whether as assessors or as experts capable of giving evidence in a later arbitration, of the earlier adjudicators.

Moreover, under the English Arbitration Acts and their statutory requirements for a stay of arbitration, which include a statement of readiness to proceed to arbitration forthwith on the part of the applicant, an action may well be commenced by a plaintiff at a time when, due to the presence either of an "early arbitration" inhibition or of a prior reference requirement, the time to initiate arbitration proper has not yet arrived under the terms of the contract. It has now been held that these considerations will not prevent the courts from making an order staying the proceedings where a prior reference under clause 66 of the ICE Conditions is not yet complete,[21] or where the matter is still currently before an intermediate panel of adjudicators.[22]

18·047

In the classic prior reference clause exemplified by clauses 66 and 67 of the ICE and FIDIC contracts, and indeed in nearly all such clauses, the position of the Engineer as prior referee in the earlier reference will be that of a certifier and not of an arbitrator, and so under considerably less onerous obligations of an *audi alteram partem* kind than would be the case with a full arbitrator.[23] The prior referee giving his decision under such clauses also owes no duty of care in tort to the contractor under the *Hedley Byrne* principle.[24]

(d) Time-bar provisions

(i) *Generally*

In many other types of commercial contract it is common to find clauses requiring claims or particular classes of claims under the contract to be brought within a limited period, whether or not the contract provides for arbitration. For example, notice of claim objecting to the quality of goods delivered may need to be given, or the claim itself made, within so many days or weeks of delivery. English Commercial Court judges have, generally speaking, lent their support to the principle of such exclusionary clauses, almost invariably interpreting them as conditions precedent to making a claim, rather than as contractual obligations for breach of which damages, if provable, could at best be recovered. In particular, it will make no difference that the time provided for is very short, sometimes so much so that it may be difficult, if not actually impossible in the events which have happened, for an aggrieved party to comply with the time requirement at all.[25] Today such time limits will presumably attract the provisions

18·048

[21] *Enco Civil Engineering* v. *Zeus International* (1991) 56 BLR 43.
[22] *Channel Tunnel Group Ltd.* v. *Balfour Beatty Construction Ltd.* [1993] A.C. 334.
[23] See *Kollberg* v. *Capetown Municipality* [1967] 3 S.A. 472, illustrated with other cases *ante*, Chap. 6, Section 5(4), para. 6·124.
[24] *Pacific Associates Inc.* v. *Baxter* [1990] 1 Q.B. 993, but see the later Canadian cases cited *ante*, Chap. 1, Section 12(2)(d), paras. 1·293 *et seq.*, and the U.S. cases *ante*, paras. 1·305 and 1·306.
[25] See *Mustill and Boyd* (2nd ed.), p. 204, and the cases there cited, see also C.C.P.P., para. 18–18.

of the English Unfair Contract Term legislation or its equivalent elsewhere, if applicable to the contract in question, but subject to that the English Commercial Court cases show that such clauses will be strictly interpreted and enforced to the letter.

Where an arbitration clause is present, the time-bar may or may not take the form of providing that *arbitration* will not be permitted if notice is not given within the stipulated period. Despite doubts expressed in the earlier editions of *Russell* and elsewhere, it is submitted that where this is so, and whether or not the arbitration clause itself is in "*Scott* v. *Avery*" form, on the decided English cases such provisions will also be interpreted so as to defeat action in the courts as well as by way of arbitration.[26]

Clauses imposing a time limit *for arbitration* are, however, subject to a discretion of the courts to extend the time in cases of "undue hardship" under section 27 of the 1950 Act. The court's exercise of the discretion under that section has, however, been relatively conservative and is considered *infra*.[27]

(ii) *Time-bars in construction contracts*

18-049 In the case of construction contracts, there are, in fact, justifiable commercial reasons why the contractor should be required to give notice of claims, whether for additional payment or for extensions of time, within a stipulated reasonable period of time. This will enable owners to maintain closer budgetary control over the project and, if necessary, to vary the work or withdraw previous instructions before it is too late in the interests of economical or timeous completion. In construction contracts, time-bar provisions may on their wording be found to date from the event giving rise to the claim, or from the time of first presentation of a claim, or more often, from the date when a "dispute" or difference between the parties has arisen in regard to the claim.

Given the propensity for contractors to make tentative informal efforts to lay the ground for a claim in early correspondence, or to persuade the A/E to agree to it, and particularly where the time-bar operates in conjunction with arbitration or prior reference provisions, owners seeking to exploit the advantages of such provisions can often find themselves in a position to argue, however unmeritoriously, that a claim has been put forward too late; or conversely that the claim has already been advanced previously or disputed at an earlier date than that contended for by the contractor, so that a later notice becomes out of time. As with all

---

[26] See *Metalimex Foreign Trade Corporation* v. *Eugenie Maritime Co. Ltd.* [1962] 1 Lloyd's Rep. 378, *per* McNair J. citing *Pompe* v. *Fuchs* (1876) 34 L.T. 800 and doubting *Pinnock Bros.* v. *Lewis & Peat Ltd.* [1923] 1 K.B. 690. See also *Bruce* v. *Strong* [1951] 2 K.B. 447, where a stay was granted, notwithstanding that the applicant was proposing to argue before the arbitrator that the arbitration would be out of time. See also the analysis in C.C.P.P., para. 18–18.

[27] See *infra*, Subparagraph (iii).

exclusionary provisions, however, the courts, while supporting the principle that failure to comply with such a time-bar provision will be fatal to any claim, will seek to restrict their application strictly within the letter of the clause.

ILLUSTRATIONS

(1) A Scottish arbitration clause referred disputes and differences to arbitration, with a proviso that no dispute or difference should be referred "unless one party has given notice in writing to the other *of the existence of such dispute or difference* within seven days after it arises". The contract was for the supply of turbine machinery by manufacturers to a coal company. Following delivery of some of the machinery, the company's engineer wrote a letter giving notice that the machinery was defective and did not comply with the agreement, and formally rejected it under a clause in the contract. 13 days later the manufacturers replied that the condition of the machinery was due to damage caused by the coal company, and that they could not accept their right or power to reject the machinery under the conditions of the contract. The manufacturers brought an action for the price, and contended that the buyers' right to arbitration had been lost due to their failure to give notice of arbitration in writing within seven days of the letter rejecting the machinery. Their own letter had not been a notice of arbitration, but a challenge to the buyers to invoke arbitration. The buyers in turn argued that as the manufacturers had not given a notice to invoke arbitration, their only remedy was gone, so that the rejection by the engineer was final. Alternatively the buyers argued that the questions raised should be decided by arbitration. *Held*, by the Court of Session, that the proviso to the arbitration clause did not require a notice *of arbitration* within the seven days, but notice *of the existence of a dispute*. A dispute between two parties could not arise unless there was disagreement. Until the manufacturers disagreed with the engineer's rejection, there was no dispute. Their letter of refusal to accept the rejection itself constituted notice of the existence of a dispute, and the action should be stayed: *Howden & Co.* v. *Powell Duffryn Steam Coal Company* (1912).[28]

18·050

(2) Clause 50 of an engineering contract provided that the decisions and directions of the engineer with respect to a number of matters were to be final and without appeal, but that any other decision or direction, etc., should be subject to arbitration and review in all respects as if it were a decision under clause 51. Clause 51 was an arbitration clause referring all disputes and differences to the Engineer, who should state his decision in writing in the form of a final certificate or otherwise. His decision was to be final and without appeal, unless either party if dissatisfied with the decision required arbitration within 28 days of receiving notice of the decision. During the course of the contract the resident engineer required the use of timbering or other forms of sheeting, which the contractor disputed as being unnecessary, and which he also contended were variations of the contract; but the Engineer refused either to change the instructions or to sanction any additional payment or issue a variation order, considering that he was contractually entitled by the specification to impose such methods of work. At the end of the contract the contractor submitted a claim and formally requested the Engineer's decision. *Held*, by Diplock J., no notice requiring arbitration having been given within 28 days of

18·051

---

[28] 1912 S.C. 920.

the disputed decisions or directions of the Engineer, the contractors were out of time and their claim must fail: *Neodox Ltd.* v. *Swinton and Pendlebury Borough Council* (1958).[29]

18·052   (3) Clause 37 of a Queensland building contract required notice of "any claim or question" to be given before 14 days "after the making or arising thereof". Clause 40 barred any right to require such claim dispute or question to be referred to arbitration if the party failed to give written notice of claim, dispute or question within the time limited. By clause 45, which was in "*Scott* v. *Avery*" form, no action was permitted in respect of a claim until an award had been made. On April 15, 1953, a contractor who had carried out remedial works submitted a quotation for the work, alleging it was a variation. On May 15, 1953, the Commissioner himself replied, rejecting the claim and saying the work would be at the contractor's cost. After submitting an invoice at the end of 1953, the contractor wrote on May 15, 1954, alleging that there had been prior agreement by the Chief Technical Officer to pay for the work in the 1953 quotation. This was replied to on June 18, 1954, in a letter denying any such agreement. On July 13, 1954, the contractor made a demand for payment within 14 days, and a further demand on July 19. On July 23, 1954, the Commissioner refused to pay in any circumstances, and on August 6, 1954, the contractor gave notice in writing requiring arbitration. The Commission refused to take part in the arbitration, and the contractor obtained an award on which the contractor sued the Commission. *Held*, by Philip J., following *Howden* v. *Powell Duffryn*, and affirmed by the Full Court, that a dispute arises when one party claims something and the other notifies him that he rejects the claim. Here the dispute had arisen on receipt of the letter of May 15, 1953, so that the arbitration was out of time, and the award could not be enforced. Even if there could be said to be an alternative later dispute as to the alleged authorisation of the invoice, that occurred at latest on the receipt of the contractor's letter of July 13, 1954, which had refuted the contents of the letter of June 18, 1954, and demanded payment within 14 days failing which action would be taken to recover the amount. That letter was received by the owner on July 19, 1954, more than 14 days before the letter requiring arbitration. The terminus for the 14 days' notice under the arbitration clause was the arising of the dispute and not the refusal to pay money demanded following a dispute: *Concrete Developments Ltd.* v. *Queensland Housing Commission* (1960).[30]

18·053   (4) Clause 66 of the ICE standard form of contract provided that if *any dispute* should arise it should be referred to and settled by the Engineer who should state his decision in writing. If either party was dissatisfied with the decision, then they might within three calendar months of receiving notice of the decision require the matter to be referred to an arbitrator. In April 1960, the contractor had put forward a number of claims which had been disputed by the Engineer in correspondence, and the contractor wrote on April 11: "Our claims are now well in course of preparation and will be submitted to you with our Semi-Final Certificate. Upon receipt of the claims you can, of course, give your decision under the relevant clauses of the contract, and we in due course will have to notify you of our intention to go to arbitration". In March 1961, the contractor wrote enclosing 11 claims, some of which were new and some of which had been previously advanced but rejected, and requested the Engineer's comments. The Engineer replied by letter on April 7, 1961, enclosing "my observations and comments on your claims", and at the end of his detailed comments on each claim, wrote "I cannot agree with or

[29] 5 BLR 38.
[30] [1961] Qd. R. 356.

consider this claim". The contractor failed to give notice requiring arbitration of his various claims within three months of this letter. The owners contended that the right to arbitration had been lost in all cases: *Held*, by Mocatta J., that under clause 66(1) the decision of the Engineer settling a dispute was final, and prevented any action or arbitration being brought unless notice requiring arbitration was given within the requisite period; (2) before the Engineer could give a decision having this effect, there must be a *dispute*, that is to say a rejection by the Engineer or the employer of the claim in question; (3) no special words were necessary for the statement of the decision, which need not specifically purport to be a decision; (4) in so far as he was dealing with claims previously rejected by him, the Engineer in his letter of April 7, 1961, had given decisions, and the right to litigate those claims had been lost. *Held*, by the Court of Appeal, that the Engineer's statement must make it quite clear that it was intended as a decision under the clause. The contractor's letter of March 8, 1961, had merely requested comments. There was no express reference to a decision under the terms of the clause to be found in the Engineer's letter of April 7, 1961, and no distinction between the wording used on claims previously rejected and those received for the first time. On the facts, the letter was not a decision under the clause on any of the claims. *Per* Harman L.J., words of this kind needed to be construed strictly, since they could have the effect of shutting out the right to go to the courts. *Monmouth County Council* v. *Costelloe and Kemple Ltd.* (1965).[31]

(5) By clause 44 of a building contract in Victoria, disputes or differences **18·054** during construction or after completion were to be submitted by the Contractor *to the Director of Works* for decision not later than 14 days after the dispute or difference arose. If the Contractor was dissatisfied with the decision, he might, *not later than 14 days thereafter*, submit the matter *to the Director-General* for investigation and decision. If dissatisfied with the *Director-General's* decision, the Contractor might within 28 days give notice requiring arbitration. In 1978, the Contractor put forward a claim for alleged breach of contract, based upon the ordering of excessive variations, in a letter to the Director of Works, who rejected it in his letter of reply. In 1980, the Contractor made a further claim, now based on a valuation of the variations ordered under the terms of the contract and not on breach of contract, and which in part duplicated the prolongation costs in the 1978 claim. The Director of Works refused to consider or give any decision on the 1980 claim, on the ground that it was the same claim as that presented in 1978, and contended that the Contractor was unable to take the claim to arbitration. The Contractor claimed a declaration that the Director of Works was required to give his decision on the matters in dispute. *Held*, by the Full Court of Victoria, that the 1980 claim was not the same as the 1978 claim and that the Director of Works was bound to give a decision upon it, so as to enable the Contractor to proceed further to arbitration. In any event the contract did not take away rights for failure to submit claims to the Director of Works or to the Director-General, but only for the final step, following the Director-General's decision, requiring arbitration: *Commonwealth of Australia* v. *Jennings Construction Ltd.* (1985).[32]

[Note: The court in the above case followed the *Concrete Development* case in Queensland in holding that there had, as yet, been no *decision* by the Director of Works in relation to the 1978 claim, and that the Director's letter merely caused a dispute to arise at that stage.[33] The court also seems to have

---

[31] 63 L.G.R. 429.
[32] [1985] V.R. 586.
[33] *Ibid.* at p. 591.

thought, noting that there was an express prohibition against *legal proceedings* in the absence of the final notice *to the Director General* requiring arbitration in the earlier case, that failure to take the onward step *to the Director-General* within the time limited did in that case necessarily involve loss of rights.][34]

18·055   Clause 66 of the ICE Conditions has for some years been still further complicated by new incorporating references made in that clause to the ICE Arbitration Procedure Rules of 1983 or subsequently. Moreover, as stated *supra*, in regard to prior reference clauses generally and the ICE clause 66 in particular, considerable difficulties for arbitrators can arise from legalistic tactical objections that some, although not all, of the individual items eventually shown to be in dispute on the pleadings should be excluded from any final arbitration on the ground of there having been no prior reference to the engineer with regard to those particular items.[35]

The above cases show that what exactly constitutes a "dispute" or a "decision" can be of crucial practical importance in interpreting not only time-bar provisions but also contractual provisions according finality to the decisions or certificates of an A/E.

Some arbitration clauses in English construction contracts refer to disputes which are described as being "between the employer or the A/E on his behalf and the contractor". This has led some contractors to argue that, on this or similar wording, differences where it is *the owner* who disputes his A/E's decision or certificate are not to be referred to arbitration and that the owner has been bound, since in such a case there is no dispute between the contractor and the A/E. Such an interpretation ignores the fact that there can never be a dispute *under the building contract* between the contractor and the A/E to go to arbitration, who are not in contractual relations with each other. The true view is that any dispute by the owner with an A/E's decision or certificate on which the contractor is relying *ipso facto* constitutes a dispute with the contractor, it is submitted.[36]

(iii) *"Undue hardship" under section 27 of the Arbitration Act 1950*

18·056   Notwithstanding that a time-bar preventing arbitration has expired, the court has power under section 27 of the 1950 Act to extend the time limited by the contract if in its opinion "undue hardship" would otherwise be caused. The section expressly only applies, however, to time requirements whereby "notice to appoint an arbitrator is given or an arbitrator is appointed or some other step to commence arbitration proceedings is taken" within a stipulated period. Thus, where a charterparty contained a

---

[34] *Ibid.* at p. 595.
[35] *Wigan Metropolitan Borough Council* v. *Sharkey Bros. Ltd.* (1987) 4 Const. L.J. 162; *Mid-Glamorgan County Council* v. *Land Authority for Wales* (1990) 49 BLR 61.
[36] *Modern Engineering (Bristol) Ltd.* v. *Gilbert-Ash (Northern) Ltd.* [1974] A.C. 689, 709, *per* Viscount Dilhorne, and see *F.H. Compton & Sons Ltd.* v. *Umpty Ltd.* (1989) 7 A.C.L.R. 38, S.C. of N.S.W., Smart J.

provision excluding any liability of the charterers to the owners unless *a claim* by the owners was presented in writing with all available supporting documents within 90 days from completion of discharge of the cargo, and the charterparty also contained an arbitration clause, the Court of Appeal affirmed Bingham J. in holding that the jurisdiction under section 27 could not extend to such a generally expressed time limit excluding claims of this kind, since the limit did not relate specifically to the appointment of an arbitrator or a step to commence arbitration proceedings.[37] So also in the case of section 48(1) of the Australian Commercial Arbitration Act 1984, which gave a similar power to extend the time fixed by an arbitration agreement for "doing any act in relation to an arbitration," Smart J. in New South Wales held that there was no power to extend time, for the same reason, where a sub-contract provided that the contractor should not be liable for "any claim" by the sub-contractor unless "the claim" with full particulars was lodged in writing with the main contractor not later than 14 days after the events or circumstances on which it was based, or at least a *written notice of intention to claim* was lodged within that period of time with full particulars before final certificate.[38]

However, the *Babanaft* case has been distinguished in the case of an **18·057** English building contract using the 1980 RIBA/JCT standard form, and jurisdiction to extend time under section 27 has been exercised on the particular wording of the final certificate clause in that form of contract.

ILLUSTRATION

Article 5.3, part of the arbitration clause in the 1980 RIBA/JCT standard forms, gave powers to the arbitrator to direct measurements and to review and revise the architect's decisions, "subject to Clause 30.9". Clause 30.9.1 provided that the Final Certificate should have effect *in proceedings whether by arbitration or otherwise* as conclusive evidence (*inter alia*) that necessary effect had been given to terms of the contract requiring amounts to be added to the Contract Sum. However, clause 30.9.3 provided that if arbitration proceedings were commenced within 14 days of the Final Certificate it should not have such conclusive effect as regards to matters raised in those proceedings. Contractors disputed the Final Certificate, alleging that certain additional sums were due to them under the contract, but served their notice requiring arbitration one day outside the stipulated period. *Held*, by Gatehouse J., that the link between clause 30.9 and the arbitration clause, exemplified by Article 5.3, meant that if the contractor did not commence arbitration proceedings within 14 days of the issue of the Final Certificate, he would be bound by its effect as conclusive evidence. This served to distinguish the *Babanaft* case, where there was no reference at all to the arbitration clause. Notwithstanding that the wording did not preclude arbitration as such, there was no dispute that the four heads of claim put forward were all covered by the final certificate, and the reality was that the arbitration proceedings were out of time, and

[37] *Babanaft International Co. S.A.* v. *Avant Petroleum Inc., The Oltenia* [1982] 1 W.L.R. 871, C.A.
[38] *Jennings Construction Ltd.* v. *Q.M. Birt Ltd.* (1986) 8 N.S.W.L.R. 18.

if so the whole claim must inevitably fail. It would be no comfort for the plaintiffs to know that they had begun a valid arbitration when their whole claim must inevitably fail on being presented to the arbitrator, and there was for this reason jurisdiction to extend time under section 27: *McLaughlin & Harvey plc* v. *P & O Developments Ltd. (formerly Town & City Properties (Developments) Ltd.)* (1991).[39]

[Note: In this case there was no theoretical time limit for arbitration as such, and indeed there were other possible bases for substantial claims by a contractor in an arbitration after the Final Certificate (*e.g.* claims for damages for breach of contract), which does not appear to have been noticed by Gatehouse J. On the other hand, the particular claims being advanced undoubtedly required reference to arbitration within the stipulated period in order to be viable. The decision, while obviously to be welcomed on the merits as mitigating the effect of an exclusionary and unattractive contract provision (from both parties' point of view) is not an easy one to reconcile with the reasoning in the *Babanaft* case, and it is clear that Gatehouse J. did not reach this decision without feeling some difficulty.]

So far as the discretion under section 27 is concerned, the principles for its exercise have been comprehensively analysed by the Court of Appeal and approved in the House of Lords.[40] There are a number of examples of their application in construction cases.[41]

(iv) *The FIDIC time-bar*

18·058   A serious problem of interpretation, or rather of misinterpretation, has arisen over recent years in regard to the time-bars in clause 67 of the Second (1969) and Third (1977) FIDIC International Civil Engineering Contracts respectively. Fortunately, the problem has been avoided by the change of wording in clause 67 of the fourth (1987) edition, but a considerable majority of international civil engineering disputes will continue for many years to be governed by contracts using or adapted from the two earlier forms. The problem goes to the heart of the jurisdiction of arbitrators appointed under these forms, and its resolution is rendered particularly intractable in the light of article 24 of the Rules of Conciliation and Arbitration of the ICC, which are expressly incorporated by this clause in both these FIDIC editions. That article expressly precludes and waives "any form of appeal insofar as such waiver can validly be made" from an ICC arbitration award, and has been held in England, not surprisingly, to qualify as a valid exclusionary provision under section 3 of the 1979 Act, thus preventing resort to the courts on a point of law (in that case under section 2 of that Act in the case of a "non-domestic" arbitration as defined in the Act).[42]

---

[39] 55 BLR 101.
[40] *Libra Shipping and Trading Corp. Ltd.* v. *Northern Sales Ltd., The Aspen Trader* [1981] 1 Lloyd's Rep. 273, CA, *per* Brandon L.J.; approved by the H.L. in *Comdel Commodities Ltd.* v. *Siporex Trade S.A. (No. 2)* [1991] 1 A.C. 148. See the full discussion in *Mustill and Boyd* (2nd ed.), pp. 212–18.
[41] See, *e.g. International Tank & Pipe S.A.K.* v. *Kuwait Aviation Fuelling Co. K.S.C.* [1975] Q.B. 224, C.A.; *Emson Contractors Ltd.* v. *Protea Estates Ltd.* (1987) 39 BLR 126.
[42] *Marine Contractors Inc.* v. *Shell Petroleum Development Co. of Nigeria Ltd.* [1984] 2

This particular problem associated with the FIDIC Clause 67 wording is dealt with *in extenso* in C.C.P.P.,[43] and affords powerful support to critics of exclusionary provisions similar to article 24 to be found in the rules of many other arbitration institutions. It arises because in both FIDIC editions the time-bar on arbitration under clause 67 is expressed to operate (so that the Engineer's decision given in the prior reference "shall remain final and binding upon the Employer and the Contractor") if within a stipulated period following the decision "no *claim to arbitration* has been communicated" to the Engineer or (in a case where no decision has been given by the Engineer when requested) if the party requesting the decision does not, within a stipulated further period, "require that the matter in dispute be referred to arbitration as hereinafter provided".

It has been seen[44] that the commencement of proceedings for limitation **18·059** purposes is, in the case of arbitration, defined by section 34(3)(*a*) of the Limitation Act 1980, replacing section 27(3) of the Limitation Act 1939, as occurring when *a notice* is served *requiring the other party to agree* to the appointment of an arbitrator (not upon the appointment of such an arbitrator), and that that requirement has itself been interpreted liberally by the court to include any generally worded requirement of arbitration.[45] The concept of "notice requiring arbitration" is not only, therefore, one dictated by the practical exigencies of commerce, but also one very familiar to English arbitration law, and, therefore, to those responsible in the past for drafting the FIDIC contracts (which are self-evidently closely modelled on the English domestic civil engineering forms, and do not hesitate to use English legal terminology).[46] Thus, the words "if any arbitration proceedings *have been commenced* within fourteen days after the Final Certificate" in Clause 30.9.3 of the RIBA/JCT forms of contract have been held to have the same meaning as that in section 34(3)(*a*) of the Limitation Act 1980 quoted above.[47]

Against this background there seems no possible reason to doubt that the two expressions "no claim to arbitration has been communicated" or "require that the matter in dispute be referred to arbitration as hereinafter provided," in each case within a stipulated period of time under clause 67 of the two FIDIC editions, refer, at most, to a simple letter or notice requiring arbitration or the appointment of an arbitrator to be sent or given within those periods (or possibly even a mere statement of intention to arbitrate made within the period).[48] However, the remarkable (and unmeritorious) argument has been advanced to international arbitrators under these forms of contract, in a number of cases apparently successfully, that clause 67 requires *delivery to the ICC* of the formal ICC docu-

---

Lloyd's Rep. 77, C.A., where both parties had requested the arbitrator to give his reasons for an interim award, but it was held that the reasons so given could not be challenged.

[43] Chap. 18.
[44] See *supra*, para. 18·028.
[45] See *supra*, para. 18·028.
[46] See C.C.P.P., para. 18–03.
[47] *Blackpool Borough Council* v. *F. Parkinson Ltd.* (1991) 58 BLR 85.
[48] See C.C.P.P., para. 18–09—17, and 18–20—22.

ment called a "Request for Arbitration" (that is, a request for the ICC Court to accept jurisdiction accompanied by a full statement of the Claimant's case) which is required by article 3 of the ICC Rules of Conciliation and Arbitration, and in response to which the respondent is required by the rules to deliver his own formal defence pleading.

18·060   The very serious practical anomalies and extreme injustice, effectively disfranchising many contractor claimants, which such an interpretation of clause 67 involves are more fully explained in C.C.P.P.,[49] and it is there submitted that this interpretation is in any event clearly wrong.[50] However, the difficulty is further compounded by the fact that the ICC has of recent years commenced an arguably unwise practice of publishing the awards of its arbitrators (in what is called "sanitised" form).[51] These now include a number of precisely contrary awards in favour of each side of this particular argument, between which there is no available means of distinguishing in terms of the weight to be attached to them,[52] while at the same time the ICC has done everything possible, through the medium of article 24 of its Rules, to impede any attempt to obtain any authoritative judicial ruling on the point.[53]

It seems likely, in the case of an ICC "non-domestic" arbitration held in England (that is, one caught by section 3 of the Arbitration Act 1979) that the only possible remedy for a party faced with this objection, in spite of having given a normal written notice of arbitration in time, will be an action in the courts for a declaration that the arbitrators are entitled to exercise jurisdiction, initiated the moment that any such objection is taken on the pleadings, and before any award has been made which could activate article 24 of the Rules.

(e) Arbitration agreements distinguished from agreements for valuation or certification

18·061   It is important to distinguish between arbitration agreements on the one hand, and contractual provisions for valuation, appraisement or certification on the other, since in the latter cases it has long been held that the provisions of the Arbitration Acts are not applicable.[54]

Certification provisions are, of course, extremely common in construction contracts. If a person is appointed, owing to his skill and knowledge of the particular subject, to decide any questions, whether of fact or of value, by the use of his skill and knowledge and without taking any evidence or hearing the parties, he is not, prima facie, an arbitrator.

> "It has been held that if a man is, on account of his skill in such matters, appointed to make a valuation, in such manner that in making it he may, in

---

[49] See C.C.P.P., para. 18–14.
[50] *Ibid.* at paras. 18–13, 18–15—18, 18–20—22.
[51] *i.e.* removing references to the names of the parties.
[52] See "Control by the Courts: A Plea for More, Not Less" in (1990) 6 Arb. Int. 253, 264–5.
[53] *Ibid.*, criticising the policy of article 24.
[54] *Collins* v. *Collins* (1858) 26 Beav. 306.

accordance with the appointment, decide solely by the use of his eyes, his knowledge and his skill, he is not acting judicially: he is using the skill of a valuer, not of a judge. In the same way, if two persons are appointed for a similar purpose, they are not arbitrators but only valuers. They have to determine the matter by using solely their own eyes and knowledge and skill."[55]

If, on the other hand, a person is appointed with the intention that he should hear the parties and their evidence and decide in a judicial manner, then he is an arbitrator, although mere absence of a hearing, provided it does not result in any unfairness to the parties, will not necessarily invalidate an award.[56] Obviously this must depend on the subject-matter of the dispute and the terms of any written pleadings or submissions to the arbitrator.

Lord Esher M.R., in *Re Carus-Wilson and Greene* (1886),[57] described **18·062** the position as follows:

"If it appears, from the terms of the agreement by which a matter is submitted to a person's decision, that the intention of the parties was that he should hold an inquiry in the nature of a judicial inquiry, and hear the respective cases of the parties, and decide upon evidence laid before him, then the case is one of arbitration. The intention in such cases is that there shall be a judicial inquiry worked out in a judicial manner. On the other hand there are cases in which a person is appointed to ascertain some matter for the purpose of preventing differences from arising, not of settling them when they have arisen, and where the case is not one of arbitration but of a mere valuation. There may be cases of an intermediate kind[58] where, though a person is appointed to settle disputes that have arisen, still it is not intended that he shall be bound to hear evidence and arguments."

The last sentence of this passage was probably directed at certifiers acting under "prior reference" provisions[59] in construction contracts, where conditional finality is attached to the certifier's decision unless arbitration is required within a stipulated period under a time-bar provision.[60] Thus, even though such a certifier's decision may be expressed to become binding upon the parties, and even though the certifier may be expressly required to settle disputes or differences, a separate provision for arbitration elsewhere in the contract will almost always mean that the certifier *under the certification clause* is not intended to be an arbitrator in the full sense, or subject to the control of the Arbitration Acts.[61] Consequently, a certifier's decisions cannot be set aside or remitted under the 1950 Act,[62] or his appointment revoked, as would be the case with an arbitrator, nor

---

[55] *Per* Lord Esher M.R. in *Re Dawdy & Hartcup* (1885) 15 Q.B.D. 426.
[56] *Star International* v. *Bergbau-Handel* [1966] 2 Lloyd's Rep. 16.
[57] 18 Q.B.D. 7.
[58] *Cf.* the engineer under the ICE arbitration clause, and the clause in *Pierce* v. *Dyke*, illustrated *infra*, para. 18·069.
[59] See *supra*, Subsection (4)(c), paras. 18·045–18·047.
[60] See *supra*, Subsection (4)(d), paras. 6·060 *et seq.*
[61] See, *per* Lord Morris in *Sutcliffe* v. *Thackrah* [1974] A.C. 727, 774B, and see Lord Reid's comprehensive and persuasive analysis of the position of certifiers, *ibid.* at pp. 736–7.
[62] The grounds upon which a certifier's decisions can be disregarded or invalidated are discussed fully, *ante*, Chap. 6, Section 5.

can an appeal lie from his decisions on a point of law.[63] Paradoxically, therefore, the lesser status of the certifier or valuer might, prior to the *Nema* guidelines, result in his decisions being more difficult to circumvent (unless, of course, subject to review by an arbitrator).[64] It can therefore be of considerable practical importance to determine whether a particular clause confers the jurisdiction of a true arbitrator, on the one hand, or of a valuer or a certifier on the other, on the person named in the clause.

18·063   To avoid confusion, it should not be assumed that a valuer cannot also be an arbitrator.[65] Disputes about valuation can be formulated between two parties and submitted to a valuer in terms which require him to give a decision resolving the dispute.[66] But it will not be enough that the parties affected by the decision have essentially opposed interests and that the decision is on a matter that is not agreed between them[67]—the terms of the reference or contractual clause must show that he is being required to exercise a judicial function in relation to an actual or prospective dispute.[68]

In some old-fashioned construction contracts this could give rise to particular difficulty, since in some cases both certification and arbitration were provided for in terms which suggested an overlap or conflict of jurisdictions.[69]

The precise status of the certifier in construction contracts has been extensively discussed *ante*, Chapter 6.[70] Additionally, it has been seen *supra*,[71] that in many civil engineering forms of contract the engineer's decisions settling a dispute under a prior reference clause like clause 66 of the ICE Conditions is a necessary preliminary to arbitration, and that his obligation to hear the parties is not that of an arbitrator, even though his decision may become permanently binding on the parties if arbitration is not invoked within the stipulated period.[72]

ILLUSTRATIONS

18·064   (1) H. agreed to purchase from L. lands and shares in certain mines at a price to be determined by A. and B., who were to make their award before a

---

[63] But see the possibilities of disregarding a certificate or decision where wrong matters are taken into consideration discussed *ante*, Chap. 6, Section 5(6)(g), paras. 6·149–6·151.
[64] See *ante*, Chap. 6, Section 4, paras. 6·065 *et seq.*
[65] *Sutcliffe* v. *Thackrah* [1974] A.C. 727, 736 G, *per* Lord Reid. *Re Hopper*, illustrated *infra*.
[66] *Arenson* v. *Arenson* [1977] A.C. 405, 424 E–F, *per* Lord Simon of Glaisdale and Lord Wheatley.
[67] *Ibid.* at p. 424F.
[68] *Ibid.* at p. 428F.
[69] See *ante*, Chap. 6, Section 4, paras. 6·065 *et seq.*, and the cases there cited; in particular *Lloyd Bros.* v. *Milward* (1895) Hudson, *Building Contracts* (4th ed.), Vol. 2, p. 262, and *Clemence* v. *Clark* (1880) *ibid.* at Vol. 2, p. 54. See also *ante*, Chap. 6, Section 9, para. 6·226. See now, however, *infra*, para. 18·070.
[70] Sections 1(1), para. 6·009; 3(1), paras. 6·031 *et seq.*; 4(3), paras. 6·065 *et seq.*; 5(1), paras. 6·096 *et seq.*; and 9, paras. 6·220 *et seq.*
[71] See paras. 18·045–18·047.
[72] *Kollberg* v. *Cape Town Municipality*, illustrated *ante*, Chap. 6, Section 5(4), para. 6·124.

certain time. They duly made their award as to the price, but H. refused to pay upon L. tendering a conveyance. The original agreement had been made a rule of court, and L. sought to enforce it by attachment under the Arbitration Act 1698. *Held*, by the Court of King's Bench, that the agreement was not a reference to arbitration within the Act, and the plaintiff's remedy was to sue for the price under the covenant in the agreement: *Re Lee & Hemmingway* (1834).[73]

(2) Sureties for a contractor, who had agreed to build a gasholder tank, entered into a deed with the contractor and the owners in which they covenanted to pay such sum to the owners as their Engineer should adjudge to be recoverable should the contractor default in completing the work. When sued for the sum adjudged by the Engineer, the sureties pleaded that, before the adjudication, any submission to arbitration contained in the deed had been revoked. *Held*, by the Court of Common Pleas, that the adjudication by the Engineer was an appraisement, and not an arbitration award as to a matter in dispute, so that the plea was bad and the defendants bound by the Engineer's decision: *Northampton Gas Light Co.* v. *Parnell* (1855).[74]

(3) Contracts for making waterworks for the city of Liverpool contained a **18·065** clause giving power of forfeiture for default, which provided that on such termination of the contract "the engineer shall fix and determine what amount, if any, is then reasonably earned by the contractor in respect of work actually done, and in respect to the value of any materials, implements, or tools provided by the contractor and taken by the corporation ... and the said engineer shall be at liberty to authorise by his certificate the said corporation to deduct the damages, losses, costs, charges and expenses in his opinion incurred by them in consequence of the premises, or to which they may be put or liable, together with the forfeiture, if any, incurred by the said contractor, from any sum which would become due to the said contractor." There was also a clause of considerable length referring all disputes generally to arbitration *by the engineer*. The contractor disputed the engineer's decision and suggested independent arbitration. After refusing an offer of arbitration by the engineer, the contractor filed a bill in equity for an account of moneys due. *Held*, by Lord Chelmsford L.C., that in the absence of arbitration the contractor was bound by the engineer's decision under the forfeiture clause, which was not a provision for an arbitration: *Scott* v. *Liverpool Corporation* (1858).[75]

(4) An agreement for the sale of a number of properties provided that reasonable compensation for any errors in quantities or description was to be given, "such compensation to be settled" by two referees, one to be appointed by either party, or an umpire named by the referees. The plaintiffs claimed compensation, and the defendants having failed to appoint a referee, the plaintiffs, acting under the provisions of the Common Law Procedure Act 1854, section 13,[76] appointed their referee to act as sole arbitrator, and a sum of money was awarded by him to them by way of compensation. *Held*, by the Court of Exchequer, following *Collins* v. *Collins* (1858),[77] that the agreement was not a reference to arbitration of an existing or future difference within the meaning of the Common Law Procedure Act 1854, section 11, and that the plaintiffs had therefore no power under section 13 of that Act to appoint their referee as sole arbitrator: *Bos* v. *Helsham* (1866).[78]

---

[73] 15 Q.B. 305 n. For the effect of a rule of court see *supra*, Section 1, para. 18·015.
[74] 24 L.J.C.P. 60.
[75] 28 L.J.Ch. 230; distinguishing (at p. 237) *Scott* v. *Avery* (1856) 5 H.L.C. 811.
[76] Now s.7 of the 1950 Act.
[77] 28 L.J.Ch. 184; 26 Beav. 306.
[78] L.R. 2 Ex. 72.

18·066

(5) A lease of a farm stipulated that, in the event of a sale of the premises during the term, the tenant, upon notice, should quit, and that in such case each party should appoint a valuer to estimate the compensation to be given to the tenant for so quitting. The premises having been sold, the amount of compensation to be paid to the tenant was, *by deed between the parties*, submitted to the award of A. and B. or such third person as they should appoint as umpire under their hands, to be endorsed on the submission before proceeding to value, *with power to examine witnesses*, etc. *Held*, by the Court of Exchequer, distinguishing *Collins* v. *Collins* and *Bos* v. *Helsham* that not every provision for compensation and value necessarily precluded arbitration. If agreement requires the parties' cases to be heard and the decision to be arrived at upon the evidence of witnesses, it was a submission to arbitration. Here the deed of submission was not merely to ascertain the amount of compensation or value to be paid to the tenant in the nature of an appraisement, but was an arbitration within section 17 of the Common Law Procedure Act 1854: *Re Hopper* (1867).[79]

(6) A contract for the sale of land contained a stipulation that each party should appoint a valuer, and give notice thereof by writing to the other party within 14 days from the date of the sale, and that the valuers thus appointed should, before they proceeded to act, appoint an umpire in writing, and that the two valuers, or, if they disagreed, their umpire, should make the valuation. The valuers disagreed and the umpire made the valuation. *Held*, by the Court of Appeal, that this was not a provision for arbitration: *Re Carus-Wilson and Greene* (1886).[80]

18·067

(7) A building contract provided for payments on account of the price of the works during their progress, and for payment of the balance after their completion, upon certificates of the architect, and that a certificate of the architect showing the final balance due to the contractor should be conclusive evidence of the works having been duly completed and that the contractor was entitled to receive payment of the final balance. The Court of Appeal (Romer L.J. dissenting) held that the architect, in ascertaining the amount due to the contractor, and certifying the same under the contract, occupied a position similar to that of an arbitrator and could not be sued for negligence in certifying: *Chambers* v. *Goldthorpe* (1901).[81]

(8) Where by the terms of a contract it was provided that the engineer "shall be the exclusive judge upon all matters relating to the construction, incidents and consequences of these presents, and of the tender, specifications, schedule and drawings of the contract, and in regard to the execution of the works or otherwise arising out of or in connection with the contract, and also as regards all matters of account, including the final balance payable to the contractor, and the certificate of the engineer for the time being, given under his hand, shall be binding and conclusive on both parties": *Held*, that such clause was not an arbitration clause, and that the duties of the engineer were administrative and not judicial: *Kennedy Ltd.* v. *Barrow-in-Furness (Mayor of)* (1909).[82]

18·068

(9) W. undertook to pay to a railway company the cost of labour and interest on the value of materials employed upon the construction of work. By the

---

[79] L.R. 2 Q.B. 367.
[80] 18 Q.B.D. 7.
[81] [1901] 1 K.B. 624. This case was overruled, and Romer L.J.'s dissenting judgment preferred, in *Sutcliffe* v. *Thackrah* [1974] A.C. 727.
[82] Hudson, *Building Contracts* (4th ed.), Vol. 2, p. 411 (*cf.* the very similar wording in *Hickman* v. *Roberts* [1913] A.C. 229 quoted *infra*).

contract, the engineer of the company had to fix the amount of the cost and value. *Held*, that he was to do this as a skilled person, and could arrive at this determination as he chose and need not hear the parties or take evidence: *North British Railway* v. *Wilson* (1911).[83]

(10) A clause in a contract for the construction of water mains provided that "all...disputes...on any matter arising whatsoever arising out of or connected with this contract, and also as regards to the final balance due to the Contractor, shall be referred to and settled by the Engineer *with or without formal reference or notice to the parties*[84]...and the certificate of the Engineer...shall be binding and conclusive on both parties...The certificate of the Engineer shall have the force and effect of an award." The owners applied to stay an action brought by the contractor for a balance alleged to be due. *Held*, by Lord Coleridge J. (in Chambers), that this was not a submission to arbitration and that a stay under section 4 of the Arbitration Act 1889 should be refused: *Jowett* v. *Neath Rural District Council* (1916).[85]

(11) The plaintiff contracted to build a house for the defendant, for which he was to be paid by instalments when a certificate was given by the architect. By clause 8 of the contract, in case of dispute arising out of the contract the decision of the architect was to be binding upon the parties. The builder disputed the architect's certificate, and the architect suggested that a different architect should arbitrate and was unwilling to act under clause 8 himself. *Held*, by the Court of Appeal, that the architect should have acted as the arbitrator, and that the builder was free to pursue his claim in the courts: *Neale* v. *Richardson* (1938).[86]   **18·069**

(12) A clause in a Jamaican contract provided "If...any dispute shall arise...as to whether the works have been properly executed or completed or as to delay in such completion or as to extras to or deviations from the works either the owner or the builder may apply to X. to appoint an architect to decide the same and such architect *after such investigations as he may consider proper* may by his certificate in writing decide such dispute and declare what payment or deduction is to be made...and such decision and declaration shall be conclusive and binding on both the owner and contractor." *Held*, by McGregor C.J., following *Jowett* v. *Neath R.D.C.* that as there was no indication of a judicial hearing or inquiry this was not an arbitration clause: *Pierce* v. *Dyke* (1952).[87]

In considering the above cases, it should be borne in mind that the appointment of an owner's A/E as arbitrator under a construction contract could never, prior to 1934, be the subject of objection on the ground of partiality or a disqualifying interest arising *ipso facto* from his status, where that fact was known to the contractor at the time of contracting.[88]   **18·070**

---

[83] 1911 S.C. 730.

[84] Identical emphasised words did not appear to attract the attention of the Court of Appeal or counsel in *Doleman* v. *Ossett Corporation* [1912] 3 K.B. 257, discussed *supra*, Section 1(2)(a), para. 18·002. They are in fact commonly found in many nineteenth-century construction contracts.

[85] 80 J.P. 207.

[86] [1938] 1 All E.R. 753. See the case also illustrated *ante*, Chap. 6, para. 6·131.

[87] [1952] 2 W.I.R. 30, Jamaica.

[88] See *ante*, Chap. 6, Section 5(2), paras. 6·099 *et seq.* on the disqualification of certifiers.

No doubt because it was thought that an element of oppression might be involved in such contracts, however, section 14 of the Arbitration Act 1934, now section 24 of the 1950 Act, enabled objection to be taken on the ground of partiality, notwithstanding that the facts relied on were known to the party objecting at the time of entering into an agreement for arbitration of future disputes. The section was clearly aimed at construction contracts, where such clauses were then common. In such cases, the agreement can now be set aside, as an alternative to appointing a new arbitrator, under section 25 of the Act. In consequence such clauses are rarely, if ever, found in England at the present day.

18·071   The distinction between a valuer or certifier and an arbitrator is of additional importance, since it is now clear that an immunity from suit for negligence, whether in contract or tort, is almost certainly enjoyed by arbitrators deciding a formulated dispute, for fairly obvious policy reasons; whereas certifiers will be liable in contract to their clients,[89] and valuers may also be liable in tort to parties who are not their clients under the *Hedley Byrne* principle.[90] Certifiers in construction contracts will generally not, however, owe any duty of care to contractors in tort provided they do not step outside their required function.[91]

It has been seen that an essential feature of arbitration in construction contracts, unlike some of the "commodity" or "quality" arbitrations in other fields of commerce, is that the sense of the contract, however short the wording, requires a dispute or difference to be heard in a judicial manner after receiving full statements and representations of their case from the parties, as well as any relevant evidence, before a decision can be reached.[92] On the other hand, in the case of those certifiers or valuers who are not intended to be arbitrators, the contract contemplates a relatively summary and administrative function and procedure, even if the subject of certification is described as a dispute and even if, as in many construction disputes, it necessarily involves questions of interpretation of the contract or of substantive law.

(f) Two or three arbitrator provisions

18·072   In the absence of express provision, the Acts deem arbitration agreements to be submissions to a single arbitrator.[93] However, there are frequently express references of disputes in arbitration clauses to two or to three arbitrators. In the case of construction contracts, much the commonest arrangement, if more than one arbitrator is desired, is to provide

---

[89] *Sutcliffe* v. *Thackrah* [1974] A.C. 727.
[90] *Arenson* v. *Arenson* [1977] A.C. 405.
[91] *Pacific Associates Inc.* v. *Baxter*, see *ante*, Chap. 1, Section 12(2)(d), paras. 1·302–1·303; and see Chap. 2, Section 6(4), paras. 2·218 *et seq.*, and see the editor in (1990) 6 Const. L.J. 207.
[92] The judgments in the Court of Exchequer in *Re Hopper*, see *supra*, although short, are of considerable value, as also the speech of Lord Reid in *Sutcliffe* v. *Thackrah*, see *supra*. See also *Fox* v. *Wellfair Ltd.* (1981) 19 BLR 52, C.A., and the other cases illustrated and discussed *infra*, Section 4(3), paras. 18·137 *et seq.*
[93] s.6 of the 1950 Act.

for each party to appoint one arbitrator, and for the third to be appointed by the two party-appointed arbitrators (or sometimes, whether failing agreement or not, by an external professional arbitration institution, such as the ICC or, in English domestic contracts, the RIBA, ICE or RICS).

In the case of agreements for two arbitrators, the Acts intervene to support these agreements in a number of ways. First, since 1854, refusal by one party to appoint his "own" arbitrator under such a clause cannot stultify the agreement, and confers a statutory power on the other party, after notice, to appoint a single arbitrator for the dispute.[94] Secondly, in the absence of contrary provision, the two arbitrators are entitled to appoint an umpire at any time, and since 1979, must do so forthwith, if and when they disagree.[95] Wherever an umpire is appointed, the court may order that he act as a single arbitrator.[96]

It should be appreciated that it is of the essence of an umpire arrange- **18·073** ment that his jurisdiction and decisions replace those of the two arbitrators, so that no question of majority voting arises.[97] In complicated and difficult disputes, such as construction litigation undoubtedly provokes, with often numerous items of dispute including issues of cross-claim and set-off as well as of claim, and with the possibility of intermediate findings of fact or conclusions of law on both liability and *quantum* on many issues, the concept of majority voting by three arbitrators can be extraordinarily difficult, if not virtually impossible, to apply in practice; this leads inevitably in many cases to a process of negotiation and compromise between the arbitrators in order to reach an ascertainable and acceptable "majority" view on all the various matters in dispute. By contrast, the overriding jurisdiction of an umpire enables him to reach clear-cut decisions in detail after giving full weight to the views put to him by the other two (usually party-appointed) arbitrators.[98] Indeed this role of the umpire accords with the realities of the role of party-appointed arbitrators, not only where there are two arbitrator clauses or references, but also those three arbitrator references where the third arbitrator is to be appointed by two party-appointed arbitrators. Thus, by the unamended section 9(1) of the 1950 Act, dating from the 1934 Act, arbitration agreements for three arbitrators of this kind took effect, in the absence of contrary provision, as if they provided for the appointment of an umpire, and not of a third arbitrator.

However, for reasons which are not clear (particularly since the umpire **18·074** principle is left intact and undisturbed in two arbitrator references) the 1979 Act removed the old section 9(1) of the 1950 Act and substituted a requirement of majority awards in *every* reference to three arbitrators.

---

[94] Now s.7 of the 1950 Act.
[95] s.8(1) of the 1950 Act (as amended).
[96] s.8(3) of the 1950 Act.
[97] See also s.8(2), 1950 Act.
[98] See the remarks of Denman J. in first instance in *Re Hohenzollern Actien Gesellschaft Für Locomotivban* (1886) Hudson, *Building Contracts* (4th ed.), Vol. 2, p. 100, 102, on the acceptable practice of umpires sitting with the arbitrators to hear the evidence.

While this may be appropriate for simple single issue arbitrations which are perhaps common in other fields of commerce, or in so-called quality or commodity arbitrations, the difficulties which this new policy creates in more complicated and difficult arbitrations such as construction contract disputes do not appear to have been considered. It may be doubted whether the serious disadvantages of this policy are balanced by any increased attraction or advantage for arbitrating parties of majority voting.[98a] However, majority voting appears for some reason to be popular among the vested interests associated with arbitration, and it is currently expressly provided for both in the ICC and UNCITRAL Rules, together with those of most international arbitration institutions.

There appear, from the comparative law aspect, to be differing views as to the role and status of party-appointed arbitrators and of their relationship with the third "independent" arbitrator or chairman. In some countries the party-appointed arbitrators are regarded as little more than discreet high-level advocates acting for their respective parties, and prior to appointment are not infrequently requested to confirm their support for any particular propositions of law, interpretation or the merits of the case which it is proposed to advance by the party in question. In addition, in many countries, frequent access to and communication with a party's own arbitrator appears to be the norm during the course of the reference. In English law a much higher degree of independence and neutrality, similar to that of a single arbitrator, appears to be expected of party-appointed arbitrators, and the conduct mentioned above, although there is a lack of authority on the point, would in the English courts almost certainly result in the revocation of the arbitrator's appointment on application by the other party. In international arbitration, where the parties' arbitrators and the appointing parties can be expected to derive from very different jurisdictions and systems of law, this can have the effect of placing an English or Commonwealth party and his arbitrator at a tactical disadvantage if their opposing party and his arbitrator feel free to regard their internal relationship during the course of the arbitration as a less independent one. This is a real problem which calls for more open recognition and greater clarification in the articles and rules of arbitration institutions such as the ICC and in the UNCITRAL Model Law and Rules.

It should be mentioned that in some trades there is a tradition or practice of appointing "advocate arbitrators", whose role *vis-à-vis* the umpire is quite different.[99] These are not, however, found in the construction industry, and are not discussed in this Chapter.

(g) Court's powers of appointment of arbitrators

18·075   Whether the arbitration reference is to one, two or three arbitrators, the Acts have intervened in support of arbitration agreements in cases where

---

[98a] A D.T.I. consultation paper in February 1994 for a new draft Arbitration Bill now reverts to the old rule.

[99] See *Mustill and Boyd* (2nd ed.), Chap. 19, and see for this particular role *Société Franco-Tunisienne d'Armement-Tunis* v. *Government of Ceylon* [1959] W.L.R. 787, commented on by Donaldson J. in *Fox* v. *Wellfair Ltd.* (1981) 19 BLR 53, 76.

the machinery of appointment breaks down by conferring power on the court to supply vacancies, where these occur due to the death, incapacity or refusal to act of an arbitrator or umpire or third arbitrator, or where contemplated appointments of such arbitrators are not agreed or made.[1] The 1979 Act has also supplied a lacuna in the 1950 Act[2] by enabling the court to fill a vacancy where an appointing body named in an arbitration agreement refuses or fails to appoint an arbitrator when requested to do so.[3] A further lacuna, in three arbitrator cases where a party fails to appoint his own arbitrator, has also been recently remedied.[4]

(h) Named arbitrators and appointing bodies

Individual arbitrators named in an arbitration agreement are naturally **18·076** much more likely to be found in the case of ad hoc submissions of existing disputes than in arbitration clauses governing future disputes, since the latter will usually be entered into at a time when the future availability of a particular arbitrator, perhaps long after the end of the construction period, cannot be relied on. Single arbitrator arbitration clauses, therefore, usually contemplate future agreement by the parties on the selection of the arbitrator, and as explained *supra*, failing such agreement the courts have, since 1854, had power to appoint an arbitrator on application.[5] However, the parties frequently deal with the problem themselves, as do most standard forms, by providing expressly for appointment by some related professional or arbitration institution in default of the parties' agreement.

Thus, prior to 1963 the RIBA/JCT standard arbitration clause combined these possibilities by providing for:

> "the arbitration and final decision of _____ , and in the event of his death or unwillingness or inability to act [to] a person to be appointed by the President of the RIBA".

It was not uncommon for owners, by inadvertence or for other reasons, to fail to insert a name in the blank space provided, in which event it was strongly arguable that there was no enforceable arbitration agreement at all. However, in a case where a schedule forming part of the contract modified or deleted several of the other RIBA/JCT contract conditions, but not the incomplete arbitration clause, the Court of Appeal held that there was an overriding intention to arbitrate, and the parties themselves appeared to assume, as did the court without argument, that the court could appoint an arbitrator in these circumstances under section 10(1)(*a*) of the 1950 Act (which then applied where "all the parties do not, after

---

[1] s.10, 1950 Act as amended.
[2] Exposed by the Court of Appeal in *National Enterprises* v. *Racal Communications* [1975] Ch. 397.
[3] s.10(2), 1950 Act as now amended.
[4] s.10(3), 1950 Act (as amended in 1985).
[5] Now s. 10(1)(*a*), 1950 Act.

differences have arisen, concur in the appointment of an arbitrator").[6] However, in a later Court of Appeal case (where Russell L.J. was once more a member of the court) the reference in the arbitration clause was a direct one to an appointee of an outside body, in that case of the CBI. The latter body had subsequently refused to appoint, and the court held that section 10(1)(*a*) of the 1950 Act as then drafted was not apt to cover cases where the failure to appoint was that of the appointing person or body, and that the assumption made in the *Davies* case had in fact been wrong.[7] As stated *supra*, this lacuna in the court's powers of appointment was subsequently remedied by the 1979 Act.[8]

18·077   It has been held in Australia that an appointor or appointing body must proceed fairly, and that an appointment not made with procedural fairness will be void. An implied term of the arbitration agreement was put forward, it is submitted entirely correctly, as the juridical basis for this necessary qualification of the power to appoint.

ILLUSTRATION

Failing agreement under an arbitration clause in an Australian building contract in the ACT, a single arbitrator was to be appointed by the President of the MBA. The owners had initially assigned the contract to an associated company, and had taken the view that as assignors they were not bound by the agreement; but later, when asked by the builders to agree to one of two proposed names, the assignees' managing director wrote on February 15, 1988, to the Executive Director of the MBA, confirming that the builders had proposed the two names, and indicating acceptance of one of them. The other name (Morrissey) was in fact objectionable to the owners, since he had acted as an arbitrator in three arbitrations concerning them or associated companies, but this was not communicated to the MBA. A member of the MBA staff then sent a list of five names to both parties, commencing with the name of Morrissey, but not containing the name which had been accepted by the owners, and incorrectly stating that she understood that Morrissey had been agreed to by the assignor owners. The assignees replied putting forward and repeating the agreed name, and asking if he was available. The staff member replied that the agreed name was unknown to the MBA but would be checked. Another company in the owner's group also wrote to the MBA confirming their agreement to the agreed name. The staff member then wrote to the builder's solicitors, who orally, in the absence of the relevant partner, denied that they or their clients had ever agreed the name (which they had in fact proposed originally) and criticising the owners for "stalling", and trying to transfer the debt to a "straw" company. This was followed by a letter to the MBA formally denying any agreement on a name, again not mentioning that they had originally put forward the agreed name. The staff member then reported to her superior that the builders were sick of stalling by the owners

[6] *Davies Middleton & Davies Ltd.* v. *Cardiff Corporation* (1963) 62 L.G.R. 134, C.A.
[7] *National Enterprises Ltd.* v. *Racal Communications Ltd.* [1975] Ch. 397, C.A.
[8] s.10(2), 1950 Act as then amended.

who would not accept a name independently put forward by the builders. As a result, and without apparently consulting his own file, which would have shown the owner's position, the Executive Director of the MBA orally transmitted the same five names, without the agreed name, to the President, who appointed Morrissey. On an application for a declaration that the appointment was void, the President of the MBA contended that the power of appointment was a bare power imposing no duty in the absence of fraud, if exercised bona fide, and that he was not responsible for the staff member or the Executive Director, who were not his servants.[8a] Counsel for the builders, however, contended that there was an implied duty to proceed in a manner which was procedurally fair to the parties. *Held*, by Davies J., that while there might be no duty, following *Palgrave Gold Mining Co.* v. *McMillan*,[9] compelling an appointor to give the parties a hearing, it could not be doubted that the parties did not agree to be bound by an appointment if it was not made in a manner procedurally fair to both of them. Here the owners' letters had not been answered; they had not been informed of the later letters to the MBA from the builders; nor of the decision not to place their desired name on the list. The President must take responsibility for the procedural aspects of the matter handled by the staff member and Executive Director, whose duty was to process the application for his decision, and the appointment was void and should be remitted to the President to reconsider his nomination: *Hooper Bailie* v. *President MBA* of the ACT (1988).[10]

(5) International Arbitration

The main problems arising from international arbitration concern, first, the jurisdiction of the English courts in such cases, including the extent to which the courts can be resorted to by the parties in relation to such arbitration; and, secondly, problems of choice of law as between competing legal systems in relation to the substantive law and interpretation of any parent or substantive contract or transaction, or of the arbitration agreement itself, or the law governing the procedure of the arbitration (the curial law).[11]   **18·078**

(a) Jurisdiction of the English courts

First, English courts will always have jurisdiction, and be available to a plaintiff as a right, if the defendant is *resident within the jurisdiction.*   **18·079**

Secondly, even if a defendant is not resident within the jurisdiction, acceptance of jurisdiction and service outside the jurisdiction, subject to leave, will be available provided the arbitration has been, is being or is to be held in the jurisdiction,[12] whether or not what is called "the arbitration" is governed by English law. This latter wording would seem to mean the law of the substantive parent agreement or transaction, or of its arbitration agreement component, but not the curial law.[13] There are, how-

---

[8a] A surprising attitude in such a situation, perhaps.

[9] [1892] A.C. 420.

[10] 8 A.C.L.R. 83. See also for an unsatisfactory role played by an appointing body *Pratt* v. *Swanmore Builders Ltd.*, illustrated *infra*, para. 18·135.

[11] This subdivision may not be exhaustive—see *infra*, and also *Mustill and Boyd* (2nd ed.), p. 61.

[12] R.S.C. Ord. 73, r. 7.

[13] See *Mustill and Boyd* (2nd ed.), p. 90.

ever, a number of quite important exceptions, which exclude applications for certain types of relief, under R.S.C. Order 73, rule 7.[14]

Thirdly, service with leave outside the jurisdiction will be permitted in the usual way under R.S.C. Order 11—that is, where a defendant is *domiciled, but not resident* in the jurisdiction; where *injunctions* within the jurisdiction, are sought; or where the substantive contract or transaction has been made within the jurisdiction, or through an agent trading or resident within the jurisdiction; or has been broken within the jurisdiction, or is governed by English law.

Finally, the jurisdiction of the English court in regard to arbitrations is not affected by the European Judgments Convention, which expressly does not apply to arbitrations.

18·080 However, notwithstanding their having jurisdiction, the exercise of the English courts' *discretion*, which it has been seen is a characteristic of nearly all their powers in relation to arbitration, may be substantially inhibited or affected by the international character of an arbitration agreement. As a generalisation, it can be said that there will be a strong inclination to abstain from intervention in cases with an international element if the background to the principal transaction is thought to be against intervention.

It has been seen that this philosophy has, in important instances, even taken statutory form. Thus, under section 1 of the 1975 Act, in the case of "non-domestic" arbitration agreements (defined as arbitration agreements which provide expressly or by implication for arbitration outside the United Kingdom, or where *one* party is a foreign national or not "habitually resident", or in the case of a company is centrally managed or controlled outside the United Kingdom[15]) the court has no power to refuse, but must grant a stay.[16]

Again, by section 3 of the 1979 Act, clauses referring future disputes which expressly exclude the rights of appeal under section 1 of that Act are permitted to take effect in the case of non-domestic agreements; but this is not the case in domestic contracts, where such an exclusionary agreement will only be effective if entered into after the dispute has been referred to arbitration.

The following are cases which show this philosophy of the courts when interpreting agreements or exercising a discretion in an international setting.

ILLUSTRATIONS

18·081 (1) An international commercial contract under the heading "General Terms" provided: "INCO Terms 1980: English law—arbitration, if any, Lon-

---

[14] See *Mustill and Boyd* (2nd ed.), p. 88.
[15] s.1(4), 1975 Act.
[16] Subject to the fairly self-evident exceptions defined in Section 5.

don according ICC Rules". *Held*, by Leggatt J., when refusing leave to appeal from an award on a point of law, that section 3 of the 1979 Act did not require an overt demonstration of an intention to exclude the right of appeal. The wording used was sufficient to incorporate article 24 of the ICC Rules, under which the parties were deemed to have waived the right to any form of appeal, and this constituted a valid "agreement in writing ... which excluded the right of appeal" under section 3(1) of the Act: *Arab African Energy Corporation Ltd.* v. *Olieprodukten Nederland BV* (1983).[17]

(2) Under a pipe-line contract it was provided: "Arbitration shall be conducted in London under the Rules of the ICC. The governing law shall be that of Nigeria". The parties requested the arbitrator to make an interim award on certain preliminary points which would not finally dispose of the matter, and when the arbitrator asked if he should give his reasons they agreed that he should do so. *Held*, by the Court of Appeal, that rule 24 of the ICC Rules was not on its wording limited to final awards; that the agreement by the parties to the arbitrator giving reasons had not been a variation or waiver of the Rules; and that there was still, therefore, a valid exclusionary agreement under section 3 of the 1979 Act, so that leave to appeal had been correctly refused: *Marine Contractors Inc.* v. *Shell Petroleum Development Co. of Nigeria Ltd.* (1984).[18]

(3) A contract between foreign parties was to be governed by the law of **18·082** Iran, but provided for arbitration in London in accordance with the ICC Rules. The respondents in the arbitration applied to the court for security for costs, on the grounds of the claimants' residence abroad and of the likelihood of their inability to pay the respondents' costs if the latter succeeded in the arbitration. The ICC Rules contained a number of specific provisions with regard to costs, as well as for security of the *costs of the arbitration*, but none with regard to security for a *party's legal costs*. *Held*, by the Court of Appeal, that while the curial law of the arbitration was English law, and while the ICC Rules did not expressly or impliedly exclude the present application, the parties themselves had no connection with the English legal system, and the application was sufficiently inconsistent with the scheme and spirit of the ICC Rules to make it inappropriate for the court to exercise its discretion in favour of the order: *Bank Mellatt* v. *Helliniki Techniki S.A.* (1984).[19]

(4) The Channel Tunnel principal construction contract was expressly to be governed by an amalgam of English and French law, with provision for disputes to be heard at a preliminary stage by a panel of experts, subject to final arbitration by arbitrators in Brussels. A running dispute developed over the sums properly due for interim payment, and the contractors eventually threatened by letter to suspend work alleging breach of contract, whereupon the owners brought proceedings in the English courts for an injunction to restrain the contractors from doing so. In those proceedings the contractors applied for a stay under section 1 of the 1975 Act, notwithstanding that the dispute was currently before the panel of experts and so could not yet be referred to arbitration. The Court of Appeal, overruling the trial judge, granted a stay of the injunction proceedings under the 1975 Act. *Held*, by the House of Lords, (1) that the courts had an inherent jurisdiction to stay any action brought in breach of an agreement to decide a dispute by alternative means, whether or not it was an arbitration agreement; (2) that in any event,

---

[17] [1983] 2 Lloyd's Rep. 419.
[18] [1984] 2 Lloyd's Rep. 77.
[19] [1984] Q.B. 291, C.A.

affirming the Court of Appeal, the contractors were entitled to a stay under section 1 of the 1975 Act, notwithstanding that arbitration could not be immediately resorted to under clause 67; (3) that the court had no power under section 12(6)(*h*) of the 1950 Act to grant an interim injunction in a foreign arbitration; but (4) that there was a general power by virtue of section 37(1) of the Supreme Court Act 1981 to issue an interlocutory injunction in association with a mandatory order for a stay; however, (5) that since the grant of such an injunction would in effect pre-empt a decision of the panel of experts or of the arbitrators under clause 67 of the contract, it would not be appropriate to grant this relief at this stage of the dispute. *Channel Tunnel Group* v. *Balfour Beatty Construction* (1993).[20]

18·082A   (5) Contracts between a Kenyan public company with a substantial government shareholding and Austrian and Belgian suppliers provided for arbitration in London in accordance with the ICC Rules, and that the proper law of the contract should be Belgian law. The Kenyan company, which had gone into liquidation, commenced an arbitration alleging conspiracy and breach of contract against the suppliers, and was being supported and maintained in doing so by the State of Kenya as part shareholders and principal creditors of the company. The suppliers applied for security for their legal costs. *Held*, by the House of Lords, overruling the Count of Appeal's majority reasoning in the *Bank Mellatt* case, that there was nothing in the ICC Rules or its general scheme of arbitration which was inconsistent with such an application to the Court, nor was there any principle, where the only connection of the arbitration or its parties with English law was, as here, the seat of the arbitration in England, that even if special circumstances existed security should not be ordered in such a case. While the mere fact that claimants were foreign would not by itself be sufficient to invoke the Court's discretion in the case of an international arbitration held in England, the fact that here the claimants were insolvent and supported by a party which would not be legally liable to pay the suppliers's costs should the claimants fail in their action was a sufficient reason (Lords Mustill and Browne-Wilkinson dissenting) for exercising the Court's discretion and making an order for security under section 12(6)(*a*) of the 1950 Act: *Coppée Lavaline SA/NV* v. *Ken-Ren Chemicals and Fertilisers Ltd.* (1994).[20a]

Lord Mustill's speech in the last of the above cases contains an authoritative account of the emergence and status of the ICC and of its Court of Arbitration, and a discussion of its important Article 8(5) (which expressly provides that the parties are to be at liberty to apply to any competent judicial authority for "interim or conservatory measures", and that by doing so they will not be held to infringe their agreement to arbitrate or affect the arbitrator's powers).

(b) Choice of law

18·083   There would appear to be at least three and possibly four different aspects of an arbitration dispute which may be governed by different systems of law. These are, first, the proper law of the parent transaction or contract, according to which it will be interpreted and on which the par-

---

[20] [1993] A.C. 334.

[20a] House of Lords, May 5, 1994. For a further case distinguishing the *Bank Mellatt* case, see *K/S A/S* v. *Korea Shipbuilding and Engineering Corporation Ltd.* [1987] 2 Lloyd's Rep. 445. See also *Badger Chiyoda* v. *CBI NZ* [1986] 2 N.Z.L.R. 599 for another case involving the ICC Rules in this context.

ties' substantive rights will depend. Secondly, there will be the law governing the arbitration agreement itself, whether a reference of future disputes in the shape of an (ancillary) arbitration clause[21] or an ad hoc submission of a pre-existing dispute, which may be different from the proper law of the parent contract or transaction. Thirdly, there will be the curial (procedural) law governing the procedures to be followed in the arbitration. Fourthly, there may be an agreement between the parties specifically regulating the procedure to be followed, so that the proper law of that agreement may also need to be determined.[22]

As a very general principle, and in the absence of express or implied agreement to the contrary, the curial law will be that of the *lex loci* or "seat" of the arbitration (that is, its principal location, since modern arbitrations may involve hearings in more than one country). There is at least no doubt that this curial law of the arbitration agreement may differ from the proper law governing the parent contract or transaction.

ILLUSTRATION

A Scottish contractor undertook to construct a factory in Scotland for an **18·084** owner who was English. The contract was in the 1963 English RIBA standard form last available before the 1965 version (which latter contained express alternative provisions for Scottish contracts for the first time). The architect was English, but the agreement was made in Scotland. A Scottish arbitrator had commenced an arbitration, but when requested to state a case for the opinion of the English courts refused to do so, being of the opinion that Scottish law governed the procedure of the arbitration. He had himself been appointed by the President of the English RIBA, following the commencement of proceedings in the English courts by the Scottish contractor, and the granting by those courts of a stay on the application of the English owner. Following the stay, the Scottish contractor had applied to the President of the RIBA for the appointment of an arbitrator, specifically mentioning the English Arbitration Act 1950. *Held*, by the Court of Appeal, and by a majority of the House of Lords, that while the general facts and place of performance of the contract might point to Scottish law as the proper law of the parent transaction, the use of the English RIBA form of contract, with its many references to and dependence on English substantive and procedural law pointed to a contrary intention, even though the subsequent conduct of the parties could not be taken into account[23]; but *held* also, by the House of Lords, overruling the Court of Appeal, that the *procedural* law could be different from the proper law, and that the latest conduct of the parties after the appointment, notwithstanding the contractor's reference to the 1950 Act in his letter asking for the appointment, showed agreement that the proceedings should be governed by the law of Scotland, and consequently that the arbitrator's award was final: *Whitworth Street Estates (Manchester) Ltd.* v. *James Miller & Partners Ltd.* (1970).[24]

---

[21] See *supra*, Section 1(2)(c), paras. 18·006–18·009.
[22] This fourth distinction is not very clear, but is suggested in *Mustill and Boyd* (2nd ed.), p. 61.
[23] As to this last point see, *per contra*, *Wickman Sales* v. *Schuyler* [1974] A.C. 235.
[24] [1970] A.C. 583.

18·085   The subjects of choice of law and of the private international law of
arbitrations are extraordinarily complicated, and effectively beyond the
scope of the present book. The expression itself is usually used in relation
to the proper law of the parent transaction, but it is presumably equally
applicable to the possibly different law of the arbitration agreement. The
subject becomes still more complicated because not all legal systems agree
as to which subjects or remedies are to be regarded as governed by the
proper law of the contract and which by the curial law,[25] or indeed on the
rules for determining the proper law. Additionally, some systems accord
overriding effect to the expressed wishes of the parties in regard to procedural matters, while others do not. English law, for example, regards the
power to extend time on ground of undue hardship under section 27 of the
1950 Act as a matter involving the interpretation of the arbitration clause,
and so governed by the proper law of the contract (or presumably of the
arbitration agreement itself, if different) and not as a procedural matter
governed by the *lex loci*.[26] Questions of the proper law can be very finely
balanced and difficult to decide.

ILLUSTRATION

18·086   English main contractors had a contract with the Iraqi state for a project in
Iraq governed by Iraqi law, but with the conditions of contract in the FIDIC
second edition standard form. Northern Irish sub-contractors negotiated in
Iraq with the main contractor and concluded an agreement for part of the
works. The sub-contract was in the standard FCEC English domestic form of
sub-contract, and contained no choice of law clause. In default of agreement,
disputes under the sub-contract were to be decided by an arbitrator
appointed by the President of the English ICE. The sub-contract price was
payable as to 75 per cent. in sterling; all the documents were in English; and in
the course of negotiations the parties had agreed that in case of disputes they
would try to avoid the courts of Iraq and resolve matters in England. *Held*, by
Mervyn Davies J., that viewed from the point of view of the parties, since the
sub-contractor was expressly undertaking "the like obligations" to those in
the main contract, and since the main contract was governed by Iraqi law, the
proper law of the sub-contract was the law of Iraq. Viewed objectively, the
system of law with which the transaction had its closest and most real connection was the law of Iraq, notwithstanding the expressed hope that litigation
would be in England, that the parties were British, and that the sub-contract
was in English form: *J&J Contractors Ltd.* v. *Marples Ridgeway Ltd.* (1985).[27]

18·087   Since 1990 the complex rules governing choice of law, notwithstanding
their provenance from a very substantial and well-tried case law and jurisprudence evolved over a period of centuries, appear to have been aban-

---

[25] *e.g.* the question of entitlement to interest.
[26] *International Tank & Pipe S.A.K.* v. *Kuwait Aviation Fuelling Co. K.S.C.* [1975] 1 Lloyd's
Rep. 8. See also *Consolidated Investment and Contracting Co.* v. *Saponaria Shipping Co.
Ltd., The Virgo* [1978] 3 All E.R. 988.
[27] 31 BLR 100. The decision itself seems open to doubt on an "officious bystander" basis.

doned altogether and replaced by statutory intervention in England in the form of the Contracts (Applicable Law) Act 1990. That Act was passed in order to bring into force the 33 comparatively short articles of the 1980 Rome Convention and its attendant Brussels Protocol which, apparently in response to no particular demand or need, set out to harmonise and provide a uniform and comprehensive code for determining choice of law in the legal systems of all the parties to the Convention. Both the purpose of this enterprise and the detail of its implementation have attracted widespread, authoritative and indeed withering criticism by (among many others) Lord Wilberforce, Lord Goff of Chieveley and Dr. F. A. Mann.[28] As pointed out by C. G. J. Morse, and even accepting the desirability of its overall purpose:

> "It is not easy to accept the view that settling disputes through the [Convention's] rules will involve the same law being applied irrespective of the Member State in which the decision is given. This is because, as will be seen, the rules of the Convention tend towards an open-ended, flexible or 'soft' character, a feature which will not ensure that their *application* to a given set of facts will not vary according to the particular perception of the Court in whichever country the decision is given."[29]

This latter factor may in the long run prove advantageous for the English courts when faced with this comparatively short and highly generalised series of Articles, which nevertheless, are of the widest possible application, since they are required to apply "to contractual obligations in any situation involving a choice *between the laws of different countries*",[30] and so not merely to questions of choice of law as between the laws of the members to the Convention, but also to choice of law questions in contracts involving foreign parties and the legal systems of countries *which are not members of the Convention.* The Convention may also be applied as between different legal systems within one country, as, for example, the different States of the United States; thus, the United Kingdom has for some reason chosen to apply the Convention to conflicts between the laws of the different parts of the United Kingdom.[31]

It can confidently be predicted that the Convention and the 1990 Act will create uncertainty and provoke tactically motivated and unmeritorious and unnecessary jurisprudence in the English courts (and quite probably in the courts of other member states).

---

[28] See the illuminating Introduction to the Act and General Note by C. G. J. Morse in 1990, Vol. 3, Current Law Statutes Annotated.

[29] *Ibid.* at 36–3.

[30] See Sched. 1, Art. 1.

[31] Section 2(3) of the Act.

SECTION 3. EFFECT OF THE ARBITRATION AGREEMENT

(1) Enforceability Generally

18·088   It has been seen in Section 1 *supra*, that the cardinal feature of the English law of arbitration, balancing the substantial support for and enforcement of arbitration agreements provided by the Arbitration Acts, is that the right of a party to arbitration under a validly concluded arbitration agreement, in the case of domestic arbitrations at least, is only discretionary and not as of right. This position results from the two crucial sections 1 and 4 of the 1950 Act which, it has been suggested in Section 1 *supra*, are in their historical origins closely linked and effectively the opposite sides of the same coin.

In cases where one party to an arbitration agreement later considers litigation more appropriate than arbitration, it can happen that an arbitrator is sometimes successfully appointed, notwithstanding his objections and before he has himself commenced proceedings. Where this is so, an application under section 1 of the Act to revoke the appointment of the arbitrator would seem to be the only available remedy, other than an injunction application, to bring the matter before the courts and invoke their discretion to reverse the arbitrators appointment. However, in the much more common situation where the party now desiring litigation has initiated proceedings in breach of an applicable arbitration agreement, an application by the other party under section 4 to stay those proceedings provides the obvious basis for the court's decision. It has been submitted in Section 1 *supra*, that in principle the same considerations should apply in both cases, but there is relatively modern authority to the contrary.[32]

It should also be borne in mind when considering the cases that an application for a stay under section 4, apart from involving the discretion of the courts whether to grant or refuse the stay, may also provide the forum for the plaintiff in the proceedings to argue either that there is no entitlement to arbitrate at all, and, therefore, no jurisdiction to grant a stay (for example, on the ground that there is no valid arbitration agreement at all, or no dispute to be referred, or no dispute coming within the terms of the arbitration agreement in question, or that the arbitrator does not have power to grant the relief being sought, or that a time-bar has expired or that a binding certificate has been given). On the other hand it may be conceded that an applicable arbitration agreement does exist, but argued that the stay should, nevertheless, be refused and the dispute retained in the courts in the exercise of the court's discretion.

This last category of general discretion is considered *infra*, Subsection (2)(g).

---

[32] See *supra*, paras. 18·002 and 18·005, and see the cases reviewed *infra*, paras. 18·113–18·115.

(2) Grant and Refusal of Stay

Section 4 of the 1950 Act, which applies in all *domestic* arbitrations,[33] is as **18·089**
follows:

> "If any party to an arbitration agreement, or any person claiming through or under him, commences any legal proceedings in any court against any other party to the agreement, or any person claiming through or under him, in respect of any matter agreed to be referred, any party to these legal proceedings may at any time after appearance, *and before delivering any pleadings or taking any other step in the proceedings*, apply to that court to stay the proceedings, and that court . . . , *if satisfied that there is no sufficient reason why the matter should not be referred* in accordance with the agreement, and that the applicant *was, at the time when the proceedings were commenced, and still remains ready and willing to do all things necessary to the proper conduct of the arbitration*, may make an order staying the proceedings."

Thus, plaintiffs in the courts opposing the grant of a stay in practice may contend variously:

(a) That no dispute between the parties exists either at all, or, in some cases, "at the time of commencing proceedings" (that is, of the writ).
(b) That the party applying for the stay is not in fact able or permitted, and so was not "ready and willing", to arbitrate "at the time of commencing proceedings".
(c) That the dispute, or a part of it, is not within the terms of the arbitration clause.
(d) That the relief sought is not within the terms of the clause or is outside the arbitrator's powers (for example, cases of misrepresentation, mistake, frustration, illegality or where rectification of the contract is required).
(e) That arbitration should be rejected on general discretionary grounds, including grounds of justice or convenience.

It can be seen that grounds (a)–(c) *supra*, are based, at least in part, on the express wording of section 4 of the 1950 Act quoted above. Grounds (c) and (d) are essentially grounds of objection going to the jurisdiction of the arbitrator. Only ground (e) exclusively involves the discretion of the court. These grounds will be considered in turn.

(a) "No dispute" cases

Relying perhaps on some of the "prior reference" and "time bar" cases, **18·090**
which in the different context of interpreting those particular clauses have held that a dispute or difference requires rejection by one side of a claim or

---

[33] For the quite different statutory rule in "non-domestic" arbitrations under section 1 of the 1975 Act see *supra*, paras. 18·080–18·082, and see also para. 18·003.

position taken by the other,[34] it has been contended by plaintiffs disputing applications to stay that section 4 cannot be invoked where a dispute or difference has not crystallised in this manner prior to commencement of proceedings. Thus, the argument has been advanced where a number of claims for "despatch moneys" by charterers were simply ignored by shipowners prior to proceedings being commenced[35]; or where, following many requests, no accounts were supplied by a film distributor to the owners of a film[36]; or where it was alleged that prior to action the defendant had given no indication of his reasons for disputing an account for services performed by a railway company.[37]

These arguments have all failed, but where a defendant can be shown to have agreed with a plaintiff's demand but subsequently has refused or failed to pay without good reason, it may be possible to argue successfully that there is no dispute within section 4.[38] Even where there are demonstrably no sufficient reasons for disputing liability, there may still be a dispute technically justifying a stay under section 4,[39] although in such a case an application for summary judgment by the plaintiff may be given priority.[40]

(b) "No dispute" as to part

18·091   A common situation can occur, particularly in construction disputes, where a plaintiff may be able to demonstrate on affidavit that there is no possible defence as to at least a part of his claim. The practice in such cases was to give judgment for the part of the claim which was indisputably due, and to grant a stay as to the remainder.[41] However, the Court of Appeal in 1977 (Lord Denning M.R. dissenting), in a "non-domestic" case where a stay was mandatory under section 1 of the Arbitration Act 1975, held that judgment could only be given in this way if there was a "definable or quantified part of the claim" not in dispute, so that, notwithstanding that it was evident that the plaintiffs in that case must be entitled to very substantial damages for an admitted wrongful repudiation of the contract, a stay of the whole claim must be granted in the absence of any such identifiable or quantifiable part of the claim for damages.[42] The court pointed out the absence, at that date, of any power for the court to order payments on account. The new Order 29 conferring a power to order interim payments

---

[34] See *supra*, paras. 18·045–18·055.
[35] *Tradax Internacional S.A.* v. *Cerrahogullari T.A.S., The M. Eregli* [1981] 2 Lloyd's Rep. 169.
[36] *Ellerine Bros. (Pty.) Ltd.* v. *Klinger* [1982] 1 W.L.R. 1375, C.A.
[37] *London and North Western Rly. Co.* v. *Jones* [1915] 2 K.B. 35.
[38] See all three cases *supra*.
[39] *The Eregli supra*.
[40] A somewhat philosophical distinction perhaps—see *Mustill and Boyd* (2nd ed.), pp. 123–4.
[41] *Ellis Mechanical Services Ltd.* v. *Wates Construction Ltd.* [1978] 1 Lloyd's Rep. n. 33.
[42] *Associated Bulk Carriers Ltd.* v. *Koch Shipping Inc.* [1978] 1 Lloyd's Rep. 24, distinguishing the *Ellis* case. See also *S. L. Sethia Liners Ltd.* v. *Naviagro Maritime Corp., The Kostas Melas* [1986] 1 Lloyd's Rep. 18 and *Modern Trading Ltd.* v. *Swale Building Ltd.* (1990) 6 Const.L.J. 251.

on account was introduced shortly thereafter. Despite language in the Order which seems appropriate only to proceedings in court rather than an arbitration, the Court of Appeal has now held that a court which intends to grant a stay under section 4 of the 1950 Act has power to make such an order for interim payment prior to granting the stay.[43]

In some cases plaintiffs resisting a stay may argue, as stated *supra*, that **18·092** although a dispute may have arisen since the date of the writ, at that time there was as yet no dispute. These arguments have seldom met with success. Thus, where an architect authorised deduction of liquidated damages from a final certificate, but had omitted to issue the required "reasonable completion" certificate under clause 22 of the 1963 RIBA/JCT condition until after the contractor had commenced proceedings for the full sum certified, Forbes J. held that the dispute had arisen at the moment the contractor refused to accept the deduction made in the certificate, and that a stay should be granted.[44]

"No dispute" arguments designed to avoid arbitration are, rightly, likely to be treated sceptically. They are usually unrealistic, since the mere fact of there being a sufficient need to initiate proceedings will be strongly indicative of the existence of a dispute.

(c) Defendant not ready and willing to arbitrate

It has been seen that in cases where the contract machinery requires **18·093** prior reference of disputes to certifiers or adjudicators, or notices or other intermediate steps before arbitration can be commenced, or where there are inhibitions on early arbitration, it is sometimes argued that the fact that arbitration cannot be immediately invoked at the time when proceedings are commenced justifies the refusal of a stay. Provided the defendant is prepared to take whatever preliminary or current steps as are then contractually permitted with a view to ultimate arbitration, these arguments are also unlikely to be successful.[45] But if he has been denying the existence of any contract at all at the time proceedings commence a stay will be refused on this ground,[46] (at least in domestic proceedings, it may be surmised).

ILLUSTRATION

Sub-contractors carried out work for main contractors on an informal **18·094** order documentation which appeared to incorporate the "Green Form" standard form of sub-contracts, Clause 24 of which provided for arbitration. Fol-

---

[43] *Imodco Ltd.* v. *Wimpey Major Projects Ltd.* (1987) 40 BLR 1.
[44] *Ramac Construction Co. Ltd.* v. *J. E. Lesser (Properties) Ltd.* [1975] 2 Lloyd's Rep. 430, illustrated *ante*, Chap. 6, para. 6·075.
[45] *Enco Civil Engineering Ltd.* v. *Zeus International Development Ltd.* (1991) 56 BLR 43; *Turner Corporation* v. *Austotel Ltd.* (1992) 11 A.C.L.R. 156; *Channel Tunnel Group* v. *Balfour Beatty Construction* [1993] A.C. 334, and see *supra*, Section 2(4)(c), para. 18·047.
[46] See *Dew & Co. Ltd.* v. *Tarmac Construction Ltd.* (1978) 15 BLR 22, C.A.

lowing conclusion of the work, the sub-contractors submitted an account for work done, which was disputed, and also claimed damages for lack of possession of the site. The main contractors refused to pay, denying the existence of any contract at all, and in a final letter in April 1976, the main contractors wrote pointing out that they had not replied to the last pre-contract offer letter of the sub-contractors, nor returned the form of sub-contract signed to the sub-contractors. The last words of the letter stated: "There is no contract containing an arbitration clause which binds us". After further inconclusive negotiations the sub-contractors issued a writ in February 1977, followed by a statement of claim. The main contractors then finally applied for a stay, relying on the terms of the arbitration clause in the "Green Form". *Held*, by the Court of Appeal, affirming the judge, that "at the time when the proceedings were commenced" the main contractors had not been ready and willing to do all things necessary for the conduct of the arbitration within section 4(1) of the 1950 Act, and that a stay should accordingly be refused: *Dew & Co. Ltd.* v. *Tarmac Construction* (1978).[46a]

(d) Dispute not within the clause

18·095   In the nineteenth century the courts were often ready to construe relatively strictly that part of the wording of an arbitration clause which endeavoured to define the disputes to be referred to arbitration. Thus, in a construction case (which would almost certainly not be decided in the same way on this point today, it is submitted) the Divisional Court held that there had been an implied obligation of the owner to remove certain staging (which was not specifically mentioned in the contract, but which until removal would prevent the contractor from starting work) "within a reasonable time." When the contractor claimed greater sums in an arbitration than those allowed by the Engineer as damages for breach of this implied term of the contract, the court held this was not a difference "concerning the work contracted for or concerning anything in connection with the contract."[47] Again, in an Irish public contract with a widely-framed arbitration clause and an extensive power to order variations, it was conceded by the parties that compensation for suspension of a small part of the work which had been ordered by the owner was not within the clause.[48]

18·096   While of course it is open to the parties to exclude expressly particular categories of future disputes from the ambit of an arbitration clause,[49] the most likely intention of the parties in a modern construction context, and of their draftsman if they have decided to have an arbitration clause, will be to refer all disputes between the parties arising out of or connected with *the work or the project*, it is submitted. Since the House of Lords' decision in *Heyman* v. *Darwins* that disputes "arising out of" a contract will include

---

[46a] (1978) 15 BLR 22. This case might also, perhaps, have been decided on grounds of estoppel.

[47] *Lawson* v. *Wallasey Local Board* (1882) 11 Q.B.D. 229; affd. (1883) 48 L.T. 507, C.A.

[48] *Moyers* v. *Soady* (1886) 18 L.R. Ir. 499. See also *McAlpine* v. *Lanarkshire and Ayrshire Rly. Co.* (1889) 17 R. 113.

[49] As, *e.g.* liability as opposed to *quantum*, *O'Connor* v. *Norge Union Insurance* (1894) 2 Ir. R. 723.

disputes following its repudiation and rescission, there has evidently been a greater and justifiable readiness to interpret arbitration clauses more liberally and not to restrict their scope unnecessarily. It has been suggested *supra*, that the word "contract" in this part of an arbitration clause will often be used to refer *to the project or transaction as a whole* and not as a narrow reference to the written contract between the parties.[50] It is submitted that against the background in the construction industry of today only clear language should be permitted to exclude from the ambit of a generally worded arbitration clause using these or similar words any of the more usual disputes or claims likely to arise on a construction project, whether as a result of carrying out original or varied contract work or as a result of express or implied terms, and including claims for contractual compensation on the one hand and damages for breach of contract on the other, as well as matters of repudiation, termination or frustration, and not excluding quasi-contractual claims arising in the event of successful avoidance of the "parent" contract. Even tort claims, if sufficiently closely connected with the transaction or contract, can come within "arising out of" wording.[51]

Nevertheless, there are sometimes cases, not usually involving construction contracts, where part of a claim may be outside the terms of the arbitration clause. Thus, where in a lease the lessor covenanted to supply water to the lessee, and there was an arbitration clause under the terms of the lease, but some years later a dispute was settled by entering into a new agreement without an arbitration clause which involved additional obligations of the lessor and varied the old ones, the court refused a stay of proceedings brought by the lessee, since an important part of the claim arose out of the later agreement.[52]

(e) Arbitrator without power to decide dispute

As stated above, objections to a stay on these grounds usually concern   **18·097**
the arbitrator's jurisdiction as such, rather than the exercise of any discretion of the court with regard to a stay. The subject of objections to jurisdiction on a number of such grounds has already been considered at some length, see *supra*,[53] and is also relevant to the present discussion.

(i) *Contract void ab initio*

The leading case of *Heyman* v. *Darwins* in 1942 decided that under gen-   **18·098**
erally worded references of future disputes under the contract to arbi-

---

[50] See the discussion *supra*, Section 1(2)(c), paras. 18·008–18·009, and see for a discussion of the Australian cases related to the various types of wording used, Pryle in (1993) 67 Aust. L.J. 503, 506–9.
[51] *Astro Vencedor Cia Naviera S.A. of Panama* v. *Mabanaft G.m.b.H., The Damianos* [1971] 2 Q.B. 588; *Empresa Exportadora de Azucar* v. *Industria Azucarera Nacional S.A., The Playa Larga* [1983] 2 Lloyd's Rep. 171; *Ulysses Cia Naviera S.A.* v. *Huntingdon Petroleum Services Ltd., The Ermoupolis* [1990] 1 Lloyd's Rep. 160.
[52] *Turnock* v. *Sartoris* [1889] 43 Ch.D. 150.
[53] Section 1(2)(c), paras. 18·006–18·009.

tration, arbitrators would have jurisdiction to hear disputes where it was contended that a repudiation of the contract had been accepted and the contract rescinded by one of the parties. The reasoning was based partly on the analysis that the true nature of a rescission following a repudiation was not to produce a total avoidance of the contract, either *ab initio* or at all, but merely a release of the parties from the performance of any further obligations under the contract, leaving other parts of the contract still viable; and to a lesser extent on the interpretation to be given to "arising out the contract" wording in the arbitration clause.

Despite specific House of Lords dicta in the *Heyman* case to the effect that an arbitrator would not have jurisdiction to decide disputes which involved the contention that the contract had been void *ab initio*, whether due to mistake or illegality (as opposed to supervening events which might avoid the contract at a later stage), a later and authoritative analysis of the *Heyman* case indicates that its true basis was that the arbitration agreement represented by its arbitration clause should be treated as having a separate and independent existence from the "parent" contract or transaction of which it formed part. On this analysis, the arbitration agreement did not necessarily fall with the parent contract, even in a case where the latter was held to have been void *ab initio*, unless the invalidating factor could be seen to apply to the arbitration agreement as well as to the remainder of the parent transaction. In consequence, a mistake or illegality which does not relate to the arbitration agreement or clause itself will not affect it, and the arbitrator will have jurisdiction to decide the dispute according to the law governing the parties' rights, whether quasi-contractual or otherwise, in a situation where their substantive parent contract is void *ab initio* for any such reason—*a fortiori*, of course, where *supervening* events occur which *subsequently* render the contract illegal, void or unenforceable. This follows from the important and welcome decision of the Court of Appeal in 1993 in the *Harbour Assurance* case,[54] which has been considered in Section 1 *supra*.[55] A future case law may, of course, develop in which it is contended, depending on the facts, that particular instances of mistake or illegality do indeed attach to and affect the arbitration clause, so invalidating it, as well as the parent transaction of which it forms part.

(ii) *Rectification*

18·099   This contractual remedy, which, it is submitted, is on analysis only a rule of evidence to enable the true contractual intention to be established where there has been a mistake in preparing contract documents, has been considered *ante*, Chapter 1.[56]

---

[54] *Harbour Assurance Co. Ltd.* v. *Kansa General International Insurance Company Ltd.* [1993] Q.B. 701.
[55] Section 1(2)(c), paras. 18·008–18·009.
[56] Section 5(3), paras. 1·104 *et seq.*

It has been stated in the past that an arbitrator has no jurisdiction to rectify the contract out of which his jurisdiction springs. Thus, in a dispute between architect and client where an award had been made under "arising out of the said agreement *or the subject-matter thereof*" arbitration clause wording, the losing party in the arbitration resisted enforcement of the award and applied for rectification of the parent contract. It was objected that this was too late, and that the matter should have been raised before the arbitrator, but the Court of Appeal held that rectification should be allowed, and in the course of his judgment Sir Wilfred Greene M.R. observed that rectification *could not have been obtained* from an arbitrator.[57] Again where an arbitration in a lease was to settle disputes "touching the construction, meaning or effect of the lease, or the right of the parties under or in relation to the lease", the court refused to stay an action on the lease, in so far as it claimed rectification of the lease.[58]

The *Printing Machinery* case may be explained by the narrow terms of its arbitration clause, and, also, no doubt, by the consideration that on final exchange at the conclusion of the often lengthy negotiations preceding agreement on the exact wording of a lease, a party might be willing to arbitrate interpretation of the agreed wording, but not arguments that the finally agreed terms should be modified or altered to accord with an alleged prior and less formal agreement such as a claim for rectification will involve. Nevertheless, it is submitted, that in essence rectification is little more than a rule of evidence permitting a departure from the parol evidence rule in certain special circumstances, so that under the generalised wording defining the disputes to be referred which is to be found in typical arbitration clauses in construction contracts, and by parity of reasoning with the *Harbour Assurance* case mentioned *supra*, only rectification *of the arbitration clause itself* will be outside an arbitrator's jurisdiction. This more rational view was clearly adopted by a relatively early and persuasive South African decision, and appears to be the basis of a recent decision in the English Court of Appeal.

ILLUSTRATIONS

(1) Clause 33 of a lease in South Africa provided that "any dispute . . . as to the rights, duties or obligations hereunder or as to the meaning . . . of any of the terms and provisions hereof or *as to any matter arising out of or concerning this agreement*" should be referred to arbitration. The tenant claimed rectification of a clause regulating the adjustment of the rent by the insertion of certain words alleged to have been omitted under a common mistake. *Held*, by the Appellate Division, granting a stay and not following the *Printing Machinery* and *Crane* cases, that when the parties signed the lease they must have believed that it contained what had in fact been agreed upon, *i.e.* their real agreement, and when in clause 33 they used the words "this Agreement",   **18·100**

[57] *Crane* v. *Hegeman-Harris Inc.* [1939] 4 All E.R. 68, 72 A–E, C.A.
[58] *Printing Machinery Co.* v. *Linotype & Machinery Ltd.* [1912] 1 Ch. 566.

"rights, duties and obligations hereunder" and "provisions hereof" they intended to refer to the agreement which they thought had been embodied in the document. It followed, that a dispute about what any term of that agreement was arose out of or concerned the agreement. To hold otherwise would mean that a dispute about subsequent verbal or separate written variations of the agreement, or about a subsequent release or estoppel or waiver or set-off, would also have to be considered a dispute outside the document, and therefore not referable to arbitration: *Kathmer Investments* v. *Woolworth* (1970).[59]

18·101   (2) In a dispute between owners and contractors as to what precisely was the governing specification for the work to be done, the contractors claimed rectification of the agreement on the ground of mistake, and damages for innocent and negligent misrepresentation. The arbitration clause was to govern disputes "as to the construction of this contract or as to any matter or thing arising thereunder *or in connection therewith*". *Held*, by the Court of Appeal, that the claim for rectification alleging mistake, and also the claim for misrepresentation and negligent misstatement, were disputes "in connection with" the contract, so that the arbitrator would have jurisdiction both to grant rectification and to award damages on the basis claimed: *Ashville Investments Ltd.* v. *Elmer Contractors Ltd.* (1989).[60]

It will be seen that the *Ashville* case was decided on the relatively narrow ground of the particular wording used in that contract's arbitration clause. It is submitted that, particularly in construction arbitration clauses, the word "contract" used in the course of a generalised description of the disputes to be arbitrated is often only intended to refer to the *project* rather than its governing written documents. Even if it does refer to "the contract" in its legal context, it will normally be to the true contract as proved in evidence (appropriately rectified if necessary), and not to documents which do not represent the parties' agreed intentions at the time of contracting (the required basis in law for granting rectification).[61] On either view of the use or meaning of the word "contract", even such narrower wording as "under" or "arising out of" the contract in an arbitration clause should imply a jurisdiction to rectify, it is submitted.

(f) Fraud or serious personal charges

18·102   The word "fraud" is often used loosely to denote dishonesty in the course of a transaction. In so far as it usually involves a fraudulent misrepresentation by a contracting party which induces the other party to enter into the contract, and which is not itself a term of the contract, there are in any case clear consensual difficulties, it is submitted, in regarding such conduct as coming within the ambit of most arbitration clauses, since there are obvious reasons why a party might be regarded as willing to arbitrate bona fide commercial differences with an opposing party, however wide

---

[59] [1970] 2 S.A. 498.
[60] [1989] Q.B. 488, C.A.
[61] This is the reasoning in the *Kathmer Investments* case *supra*.

the wording of the arbitration clause, but not necessarily if it was later to emerge that the other party had been fraudulent in either his pre-contract or post-contract conduct.

Whether or not impelled by this consideration, the Court of Appeal in 1915 held that a dispute concerning alleged fraudulent pre-contract misrepresentations as to the nature of the sub-soil in a construction contract did not "arise upon or in relation to *or in connection with* the contract" under the terms of the arbitration clause.[62]

Since 1934, however, the legislature has intervened directly in the case of arbitration clauses or agreements *as to future disputes* (not, it would seem, specific or ad hoc submissions, although such an issue could possibly arise after such a submission) where the dispute "involves the question whether any such party has been guilty of fraud". Under (now) section 24(3) of the 1950 Act, the court is expressly permitted to refuse a stay in such a case, and by section 24(2) to revoke the authority of any arbitrator and also order that the arbitration agreement itself shall cease to have effect (and if necessary under section 25(4) that any "*Scott* v. *Avery*" provision[63] will also cease to have effect).

The ordinary rule established by the case law in 1880, prior to the 1934   **18·103** legislation, is that the party *against whom* fraud is alleged can have arbitration if he wishes or the High Court if he wishes,[64] unless there are special reasons present, such as the unsuitability of arbitration or the public interest.[65]

Obviously a party should not be able to avoid arbitration by the mere expedient of alleging fraud by the other party. On the other hand the preference for compromise shown by many arbitrators, the fact that in many industries the arbitrator will have had or may expect to have future dealings with a party involved, and the relative inexperience of arbitrators in assessing the credibility of witnesses, may well mean that in cases where it is imperative for a party to establish fraud the greater independence and experience of the judiciary should properly also be available to the party alleging fraud, it is submitted. There may also be cases where the privacy of arbitration may be thought inappropriate to the justice of the case having regard to the nature of the fraud alleged. In deciding whether to refuse a stay, however, it may be conceded that much will depend on the strength and bona fide character of the fraud allegation if it is the party making the allegation who is resisting the stay.

In the unlikely event of there being express stipulation in an arbitration   **18·104** clause that questions involving fraud of the parties should be submitted to

---

[62] *Monro* v. *Bognor Urban District Council* [1915] 3 K.B. 167. Compare the "in connection with" wording in relation to *non-fraudulent* misrepresentation in *Fillite (Runcorn) Ltd.* v. *Aqua-Lift* (1989) 45 BLR 27, C.A., and in a case of rectification *Ashville Investments Ltd.* v. *Elmer Contractors Ltd.* [1989] Q.B. 488, see *supra*, para. 18·100.

[63] See *supra*, para. 18·036 *et seq.*

[64] See, *per* Sir George Jessel M.R. in *Russell* v. *Russell* (1880) 14 Ch.D. 471.

[65] See particularly Bingham L.J. in *Cunningham-Reed* v. *Buchanan-Jardine* [1988] 1 W.L.R. 678, 688 H, and see also, *per* Lord Wilberforce in *Camilla Cotton Oil Co.* v. *Granadex S.A.* [1976] 2 Lloyd's Rep. 10, 16.

arbitration, the court will probably not refuse to stay the action,[66] *a fortiori*, of course, where the dispute in question has been the subject of an ad hoc submission. In addition, section 3(3) of the 1979 Act expressly requires a stay to be granted in cases involving fraud, in the case of non-domestic agreements only, if an exclusion agreement under section 3 of the 1979 Act is present.

When substantial personal charges other than fraud are alleged, the court may allow the party against whom they are made to have them investigated in open court, but the mere fact that a dispute will involve questions of credit is not sufficient.[67] The principle is that the court will hesitate before depriving a party against whom serious personal charges are made of his right of appeal upon questions of fact, which must occur if arbitration takes place. This same principle was formerly applied by the courts in the different context of referring cases involving professional negligence to Official Referees.[68] There seems little doubt that as a general principle there are "charges which are too serious to be tried by an arbitrator".[69]

However, where the arbitration agreement clearly contemplates the possibility of the type of dispute in question (as will usually be the case, of course where a dispute is the subject of a specific submission, and will also be the case, for example, where contracts of employment of architects or engineers contain an arbitration clause and negligence is alleged) there is in principle no reason for refusing a stay.[70]

(g) General discretion to grant or refuse stay

(i) *Generally*

18·105   Quite apart from questions going to jurisdiction, or the special cases of fraud and serious personal charges, the court has the widest of discretions as to whether or not it will stay an action (and also, it is submitted, to revoke the appointment of an arbitrator, but only after taking into account in the latter case any waiver or collaboration by the plaintiff in the appointment of the arbitrator or in the later conduct of the arbitration). "There is no limitation to the cases in which a judge may exercise his discretion by refusing to stay".[71]

---

[66] *Heyman* v. *Darwins Ltd.* [1942] A.C. 356, 392.
[67] *Minifie* v. *Railway Passengers Assurance Co.* (1881) 44 L.T. 552.
[68] *Charles Osenton & Co.* v. *Johnston* [1942] A.C. 130. But see now O. 58 r.5; and for such a case involving a professional engineer's liability and a hearing of six weeks, see *Scarborough Rural District Council* v. *Moore* (1968) 112 L.J. 986.
[69] *Vawdrey* v. *Simpson* [1896] 1 Ch. 166.
[70] This is perhaps the best explanation of the two Hong Kong cases of *Binnie & Partners International* v. *Swire Chemsyn Ltd.* (1982) 23 BLR 92 and *A.-G. of Hong Kong* v. *Aoki Construction Co. Ltd.* (1981) 23 BLR 81.
[71] *Per* Vaughan Williams L.J. in *Kennedy Ltd.* v. *Barrow-In-Furness* (1909) Hudson, *Building Contracts* (4th ed.), Vol. 2, 411, 414.

ILLUSTRATIONS

(1) A civil engineering contract referred all disputes to the arbitration of the owner's named engineer. One dispute related to a verbal agreement made with the Engineer for the conversion of the weight of material for rubble filling into its volume for pricing purposes, and the other to a verbal agreement by the Engineer to allow both an agreed price for pumping and a further sum to be ascertained for the cost of a dimensional alteration which he had ordered. The owners refused to appoint an independent arbitrator in place of the named arbitrator, and applied for a stay. *Held*, by the House of Lords, affirming the Master, the judge and the Court of Appeal, that a stay should be refused. Although in general a party must be held to arbitration by an engineer, notwithstanding the possibility of previously formed views or decisions while exercising that function, in a case where he will be required to be both judge and witness as to the existence and interpretation of verbal agreements made by him on behalf of the owner, a stay should be refused: *Bristol Corporation* v. *Aird Ltd.* (1913).[72]

(2) Sellers gave buyers two letters of indemnity in England, as a result of which the buyers paid certain invoiced amounts to third party suppliers. The buyers issued a writ in England claiming damages under the indemnity letters, and later amended to allege breach of the contract of sale as well. The sale notes had provided that all disputes were to be arbitrated in Pakistan and subject to Pakistani law. The sellers applied for a stay. *Held*, by Mocatta J., refusing a stay, that there was a danger of inconsistent findings of fact and holdings in law if the issues were split between the English action on the indemnities and the arbitration in Pakistan. It was unlikely that Pakistani law would differ substantially from English law, and on the balance of convenience all issues should be decided in the English courts: *Brazendale & Co. Ltd.* v. *St. Freres S.A.* (1970).[73]

18·106

(3) A holiday maker sued a travel agency for the return of £200 moneys paid in respect of a package holiday cruise as damages for breach of contract. The documentation contained an arbitration clause, and the defendants applied for a stay. The County Court judge refused a stay on the ground that the costs of the arbitration would exceed those likely to be incurred in the County Court for such a small claim. *Held*, by the Court of Appeal, that, notwithstanding that this was a contract of adhesion and the plaintiff had not himself required the arbitration clause, the prima facie leaning of the court should be to stay the action and leave the plaintiff to the tribunal which he had agreed, and a stay should be granted: *Ford* v. *Clarkson's Holidays Ltd.* (1971).[74]

(4) Main contractors employed the plaintiff, who was a plumber, as a sub-contractor under a number of sub-contracts using the main contractor's usual form of sub-contract, which contained an arbitration clause. The plaintiff brought a claim on a number of the contracts totalling over £80,000, and had obtained legal aid to bring the action. On a summons to stay, he alleged that he was impoverished as a result of the defendants' default and was unable to finance proceedings, and that legal aid would not be obtainable and his proceedings would have to be discontinued if an arbitration was ordered. *Held*,

18·107

---

[72] [1913] A.C. 241. Since 1934 there has, however, been power to revoke the appointment of such an arbitrator; see now s.24(1), 1950 Act, discussed *ante*, para. 18·070.
[73] [1970] 2 Lloyd's Rep. 34.
[74] [1971] 1 W.L.R. 1412.

by the Court of Appeal (Megaw L.J. dissenting), and overruling Griffiths J., justice required that since there was a reasonable probability in the plaintiff's charge that his poverty was directly induced by the defendants' breaches, that in the exceptional circumstances a stay should be refused: *Fakes* v. *Taylor Woodrow Construction Ltd.* (1973).[75]

(5) An owner claimed damages for defects against a builder in the courts. The writ was just in time from the point of view of limitation. The builder applied for a stay. The owner objected that the effect of a stay would be to deprive him of his remedy, since the limitation period had now expired and for purposes of limitation, the arbitration would date from the day of the stay being granted.[76] The builder replied that by reason of the late issue of the writ he himself was in danger of having limitation successfully pleaded against him by a number of the sub-contractors who had actually done the work, while being himself liable to the owner. *Held*, by Bean J., that a stay should be refused, so as to allow the owner the advantage of his writ, but on terms that the builder issued third party proceedings against the sub-contractors, and if limitation was raised successfully on a preliminary issue in any of those proceedings (with the plaintiff participating in those proceedings on that issue) then the plaintiff should to that extent discontinue his own proceedings against the defendant: *County and District Properties Ltd.* v. *C. Jenner & Son Ltd.* (1976).[77]

(ii) *Some issues only within clause*

18·108   In addition to the *Brazendale* case illustrated *supra*, there are a number of cases where arbitration clauses in earlier construction contracts have been held to apply to some, but not all, of the issues between the parties, although this is increasingly less likely on the wording of most modern contracts, and in the light of the more recent case law since *Heyman* v. *Darwins* on the interpretation of arbitration clauses. In these earlier cases, as in the *Brazendale* case, stays were refused.[78]

(iii) *"Scott* v. *Avery" clauses*

18·109   It has been seen that the fact that a party may lose a contractual or other remedy if a stay is granted or refused may be an important factor in the court's decision. Thus, where a clause is in *"Scott* v. *Avery"* form, a stay will only be refused in the most exceptional circumstances, since by so doing a defendant may be deprived of his remedies altogether.[79]

---

[75] [1973] Q.B. 436.

[76] A lacuna in the English limitation legislation—see *supra*, Section 1, para. 18·018, despite the many amending statutes, this long-standing anomaly still remains unaddressed.

[77] [1976] 2 Lloyd's Rep. 728. Bean J.'s judgment was unreported, but the facts in this illustration are disclosed in Swanwick J.'s judgment on the limitation issue which developed later, and which is the principal subject of the report. For the case on limitation and indemnities, see the discussion *ante*, Chap. 4, paras. 4·289–4·290.

[78] See *Young* v. *Buckett* (1882) 51 L.J. Ch. 504, Fry J.; *Moyers* v. *Soady* (1886) 18 L.R. Ir. 499; *Turnock* v. *Sartoris* (1889) 43 Ch.D. 150, C.A., and the discussion *supra*, Subsection (2)(d), paras. 18·094–18·095.

[79] *Smith Coney & Barrett* v. *Becker Gray & Co.* [1916] 2 Ch. 86, 95, 101, *per* Lord Cozens-Hardy M.R. and Phillimore L.J.; *Bruce* v. *Strong* [1951] 2 K.B. 447, 453, *per* Somervell L.J.

On the other hand, if it is argued that the right to arbitration has been lost due, for example, to the operation of a time-bar, the courts will nevertheless grant a stay, notwithstanding that the applicant for the stay proposes to contend that the arbitrator will be bound to reject the claim as being out of time (or as a result of a prior reference decision not appealed against in time, or of an A/E's binding certificate, as further examples).

ILLUSTRATION

Importer-sellers sold a cargo of figs to a purchaser. The contract contained a clause that any claim for arbitration must be made within two months of arrival of the goods, and also a clause in "*Scott* v. *Avery*" form that no action should be brought before an award had been obtained. There were three subsequent sub-sales, and by the time the last sub-purchaser brought an action to recover for underweight goods, the time for making a claim by the purchaser under the original contract had expired. Parker J. refused a stay, on the ground that there would otherwise have to be separate sets of High Court and arbitration proceedings in which the same points as to shortweight and damages would have to be decided. *Held*, by the Court of Appeal, that the sellers were entitled to have the dispute settled by arbitration, and the more so because of the "*Scott* v. *Avery*" clause. The fact that they would contend that the arbitration was out of time did not mean that they were not ready and willing to do all things necessary to the proper conduct of the arbitration within the terms of section 4(1) of the Arbitration Act 1950: *Bruce* v. *Strong* (1951).[80-81]

18·110

(iv) *Multiplicity of proceedings*

Where special provisions of a "*Scott* v. *Avery*" or time-bar kind, such as were present in *Bruce* v. *Strong*, are absent, the existence of a present or potential dispute arising out of the same facts between one of the prospective parties to the arbitration and a third party may, in view of the absence of any available third party procedures in the case of arbitration, be a ground for refusing a stay, so as to bring all the disputes before one tribunal. This will ensure that, with these procedures available in the courts, the greater expense and delay of separate proceedings can be avoided, as well as the real possibility of inconsistent findings by different tribunals.

18·111

ILLUSTRATIONS

(1) A house owner brought an action against his architect for negligent design and supervision, and in his defence the architect alleged that the defects in the building were caused by the bad work of the contractor. The owner then joined the contractors as co-defendants, but they applied for a

---

[80-81] [1951] 2 K.B. 447.

stay under the arbitration clause in their contract. *Held*, by the Court of Appeal, affirming the Official Referee, and following and approving the "Pine Hill,"[82] that a stay should be refused. *Per* Lord Denning M.R., *Bruce* v. *Strong* was a special case. If the two proceedings here should go on independently, there might be inconsistent findings. There would also be extra cost involved in having two separate proceedings going on side-by-side and more delay, including procedural difficulties and manoeuvres. *Per* Pearson L.J., the most sensible solution would be to have a tripartite arbitration, but that depends upon the consent of the parties. There is a conflict of two well-established and important principles. One is that parties should normally be held to their contractual agreement to have the dispute referred to arbitration. The other is that a multiplicity of proceedings is highly undesirable. There might be different decisions on the same questions, and confusion and procedural difficulties, if there was an arbitration and action side-by-side between different parties, including the question which side might call the third party as a witness in either proceeding. This was not the case of an owner really wishing to sue the contractor and adding the architect as a second defendant in order to avoid the arbitration clause. Here the primary action was against the architect. Once the defence was received, the only reasonable course for the owner was to add the contractor as a second defendant: *Taunton-Collins* v. *Cromie* (1964).[83]

18·112   (2) Owners of a block of flats brought an action in respect of serious defects in the building against contractors as first defendants and their architects as second defendants. Both the contract of employment of the architects and the construction contract contained arbitration clauses. The contractors alone made an application to stay, while the architects indicated that their case would be that the defects had been caused by the fault of the owner's consulting engineers. The judge granted a stay to the contractors. *Held*, by the Court of Appeal, that since the architects had made no application to stay, no doubt so as to preserve their third party rights against the engineers, there was no power to force them to arbitrate; consequently if a stay was granted to the contractors, there would be one action and one arbitration proceeding side-by-side, and possibly third party proceedings, with a risk of differing conclusions on the same facts. Applying *Taunton-Collins* v. *Cromie*, a stay would be refused and the appeal allowed: *Berkshire Senior Citizens Housing Association* v. *McCarthy & Fitt Ltd.* (1979).[84]

As noted by Lord Denning M.R. in the *Taunton-Collins* case, this problem is one of great importance in the construction industry, having regard to the differing and often overlapping contractual obligations of a number of the parties concerned with a construction project, together with the likelihood that their individual contracts may or may not contain arbitration clauses, or may contain different arbitration clauses of different scope or with different appointing bodies. The *Taunton-Collins* decision was greatly to be welcomed, therefore, particularly since tactical manoeuvres by unmeritorious defendants to obstruct and embarrass a

---

[82] [1958] 2 Lloyd's Rep. 146.
[83] [1964] 1 W.L.R. 633.
[84] 15 BLR 27. On the other hand, a parallel action and arbitration did not disturb the court in *Northern Regional Health Authority* v. *Derek Crouch Construction Ltd.* [1984] Q.B. 644; illustrated on this point *ante*, Chap. 13, para. 13·051, with the facts set out in greater detail in C.C.P.P., para. 17–39.

plaintiff by opting for the difficulties and expense and the risk of inconsistent findings involved in having separate tribunals are today commonly used in construction litigation. Unfortunately, the value of the decision has been diminished by what is essentially, it is submitted, an inconsistent Court of Appeal decision.

ILLUSTRATION

Developers of a hotel contracted in 1964, with prospective lessees for the latter to pay its building costs in excess of £3,000,000 under an earlier building contract made between the developers and builders in November 1962, and to complete the remainder of the building in accordance with the lessees' requirements. The builders had sub-contracted the mechanical and heating services to nominated specialist sub-contractors in 1963. A dispute arose between the sub-contractors and the architect over the amount of their account, and in December 1967, the sub-contractors applied for the appointment of an arbitrator to decide their claim, which they brought under a "name-borrowing" provision in the name of the builders against the developers under clause 11(d) of a standard form of sub-contract. In January 1968, the lessees brought an action against the developers under the 1964 agreement, and also against the sub-contractors (against whom they alleged a number of direct warranties as to design and workmanship) for damages for breach of contract caused by defects in the sub-contractors' work, and for a declaration as to sums properly due to the sub-contractors under the main contract and to the developers under their 1964 contract with the lessees. In February 1968, an arbitrator was appointed in the sub-contractor's proceedings against the developers. One day later the developers issued third party notices in the lessees' action claiming indemnities and contribution from the sub-contractors', as well as from the architects and quantity surveyors, and eight days later the developers applied to revoke the arbitrator's appointment under section 1 of the 1950 Act. *Held*, by the Court of Appeal, that the sub-contractor's claim for money due was relatively simple, whereas the lessee's proceedings would be very complicated and lengthy, and since the sub-contractor could not in those proceedings counter-claim for remuneration by arbitrating in the name of the builder, which on its face seemed their only remedy under the sub-contract, it would be a hardship to deprive them of their right. Moreover, distinguishing *Taunton-Collins* v. *Cromie*, a much stronger case must be made out to induce the court to act under section 1 of the 1950 Act than under section 4, since the effect of an order under section 1 was to deprive a party of his contractual right to go to arbitration, whereas an order under section 4 confirmed the parties' contractual rights to do so. Section 1 should only be used in very exceptional circumstances, such as misconduct by an arbitrator. On the whole, the applicants had not made out the very strong case which alone would justify the court's interfering under section 1: *City Centre Properties (I.T.C. Pensions) Ltd.* v. *Matthew Hall & Co. Ltd.* (1969).[85]

18·113

With respect, this important decision, while admittedly on complicated facts, seems open to question at a number of points, not least in regard to

18·114

[85] [1969] 1 W.L.R. 772.

the view expressed as to a section 1 application. In the first place, it is submitted that the court was exaggerating the difficulties and wrong in expressing the view that the sub-contractor's only and exclusive remedy under the sub-contract was to claim in the name of the main contractor against the owner. Even if this were so, in the action the sub-contractor would have been free to bring in the main contractor (not yet a defendant). Moreover, the terms of the declaration sought would have enabled the sub-contractor to establish the sums properly due. It is submitted that either the sub-contractors' work was or was not defective. That issue would clearly have taken priority in the action, since all other liabilities depended on it. However, this only goes to the exercise of the court's discretion on the facts.

Much more importantly, the distinction made by the judgment between the section 1 and section 4 applications under the 1950 Act is with respect not, even disregarding the historical connection between the two sections,[86] a logical one. Revocation of an arbitrator's appointment deprives a party of his contractual right to go to arbitration. But so, too, does refusal of a stay. If convenience or other considerations justify one, there seems no reason why they should not justify the other, subject to the special circumstance, in revocation cases, that conduct by way of participation in the arbitrator's appointment, or later on in the process of the arbitration, may be relevant as a waiver when considering the application to revoke. Moreover, in a later (and for quite different reasons controversial) decision in the Court of Appeal, where arbitration proceedings involving sub-contractors and an action involving the main contractors were both in being against the owners, and where the application to the Court was for injunctions preventing continuance of the arbitration proceedings, so that the court could deal with any disputes, the entire discussion and reasoning in the Court of Appeal related to considerations of justice, convenience and delay, and also to the expressed view that the Court might not have the full powers enabling it to deal with the merits, should an injunction be granted, which an arbitrator would have under the terms of the arbitration clause in question. No mention was there made that the applications for injunctions were only a procedural alternative to an application to revoke, and that they could not be entertained in the absence of serious matters such as misconduct by the arbitrator.[87] The *City Centre* case, if correct, also encourages premature initiation of arbitration (for example, by application to an appointing body) as a tactical and obstructionist manoeuvre when an action is anticipated in a multipartite dispute.

18·115   However, similar views have again been expressed in relation to revocation applications under section 1.

---

[86] Discussed *supra*, paras. 18·014–18·015.
[87] *Northern Regional Health Authority* v. *Derek Crouch Construction Co. Ltd.* [1984] Q.B. 644. For its rather complicated facts, see C.C.P.P., paras. 17–39 *et seq.*, and see the case illustrated *ante*, Chap. 13, para. 13·051.

ILLUSTRATION

Hotel owners placed three contracts, two for an "extension project", which were in the RIBA/JCT 1963 standard form with appropriate arbitration clauses. The third "entrance project" contract was not subject to the RIBA/JCT contract conditions, and contained no arbitration clause. The contractors issued arbitration notices in respect of the two "extension" contracts for sums due, against which the owners counter-claimed damages for defective work, and a writ in respect of the "entrance" contract, where the owner counter-claimed for delay and defective work. The owners consistently opposed any arbitration proceedings on jurisdictional grounds, and when the arbitrator ruled provisionally against them applied for revocation of his authority; first, on the ground that there would be two separate proceedings in existence in regard to the same building, workforce and witnesses; and secondly, because in the case of the two "extension" contracts, an important defect would involve a specialist supplier of windows, who could not be joined if the proceedings were by way of arbitration. *Held*, by Steyn J. applying *City Centre Properties* v. *Matthew Hall*, that the court ought only to revoke an arbitrator's authority in wholly exceptional circumstances, which fundamentally imperil the fair and proper functioning of the arbitral process, and the application to revoke should be refused. *Per* Steyn J., section 1 must be construed as a provision which was intended to make it more difficult to remove arbitrators. ... The statement in *Mustill and Boyd* that revocation is appropriate in situations where "justice demands that the arbitration proceedings shall be temporarily halted or permanently brought to an end, and no other method of doing so is available to the court" appears to be too widely stated. ... In my judgment the application is squarely based on grounds of convenience only, *and this will never warrant an order under section 1*. ... Plainly, when two parties enter into a commercial contract containing an arbitration clause, they know, or ought to know, that in multi-party disputes they will be unable to join other parties. This is a risk of future inconvenience which they assume in the interests of the perceived benefits of arbitration": *Property Investments Ltd.* v. *Byefield Building Services Ltd.* (1985).[88]

[Note: It is clear that in this case there was no adequate case for revocation on the facts, since the judgment shows that there was virtually no connection between the complaints made on the different contracts, and in consequence the possibility of conflicting decisions did not exist; at worst only some additional expense could result from the separation of the proceedings. Steyn J.'s view that inability to take advantage of third party proceedings in the event of arbitration disputes with sub-contractors, for example, is a normal feature of commercial contracts, while true and possibly known to informed advisers familiar with the construction industry, appears to give insufficient weight to the fact that most of the types of owner persuaded to use standard forms are unlikely to be aware of these particular deficiencies of arbitration law and procedure, any more than of the now much more limited rights of appeal available to them to correct arbitrators' errors of law resulting from the *Nema* guidelines. The strongly negative views expressed as to the availability of the revocation remedy would not seem necessary to the decision, and appear to result from an uncritical acceptance of Harman L.J.'s statement in the *City Centre* case, and to ignore the historical connection between the two sections.[88a]]

---

[88] 31 BLR 47.
[88a] See *supra*, paras. 18·014–18·015.

18·116   This difficult area, which is of every-day occurrence in construction disputes, is one of the many which English arbitration legislation has left
unaddressed. A distinction needs to be made, of course, between those
tripartite or multi-partite cases where only one of the disputes is subject to
an arbitration agreement (where there are obvious difficulties about making procedures for the addition of defendants or for joining third parties
available) and those cases where, on the other hand, two or more of such
disputes involving the same subject matter are governed by separate, but
possibly differently organised arbitration clauses. In the latter case some
statutory machinery designed to ensure a single arbitration, with the arbitrators exercising a similar jurisdiction and powers to those of a judge
when dealing with more than one defendant or with third or fourth parties, seems feasible with only minor invasion of consensually based
rights.[89]

Given the absence of any statutory remedies or procedures, various
attempts have been made in English standard forms, in the special case of
nominated sub-contracts, to provide for "name borrowing" powers where
owners and sub-contractors may be expressly empowered to initiate arbitration or legal proceedings against each other in the name of the main
contractor.[90] There is little authority on these provisions, and this particular device is in fact not usually likely to be an effective remedy, since it is
only rarely that a sub-contractor's entitlement or liability will correspond
exactly with the main contractor's corresponding rights or liabilities in the
main contract. Additionally, standard or other forms of main and sub-
contract designed for use on the same project may contain attempts in
their respective arbitration clauses to secure a single arbitration or the
same arbitrator in cases where the disputes under the two contracts
involve the same facts, but the task of evolving a satisfactory practical
solution for these situations can be a difficult challenge to the draftsman.[91]

18·117   A further difficulty is that provisions designed to secure the same arbitrator for disputes between different parties (as, for example, for main
contract and sub-contract disputes) is that, without power to hold a single
arbitration and hearing with all parties represented, sequential arbitrations, even though before the same arbitrator, become necessary. This
can lead to real and understandable objections by a party to the second
arbitration only, since the arbitrator's views may inevitably be affected by
evidence in the previous arbitration where the later party has no right to
be present or to adduce evidence or cross-examine.[92] There can also be
other difficulties with such clauses.

---

[89] Compare the recent arbitration legislation in Hong Kong which has attempted this task,
and see for a contractual attempt under the Singapore S.I.A. contract C.C.P.P., pp. 614–15.
[90] See *ante*, Chap. 13, Section 2(4), paras. 13.046 *et seq.*
[91] See the attempt at this made by the Singapore private sector S.I.A. contract in Clause 37(9)
and (11) set out in C.C.P.P., pp. 614–15.
[92] See the Court of Appeal's attempted response to this difficulty when appointing a single
arbitrator in *Abu Dhabi Gas Liquefaction Company Ltd.* v. *Eastern Bechtel Corporation*
[1982] 2 Lloyd's Rep. 425.

ILLUSTRATION

Clause 24 of a standard form of sub-contract provided for arbitration of disputes and ended with a proviso "that if the dispute or difference between the contractor and sub-contractor is substantially the same as a matter which is a dispute or difference between the Contractor and Employer under the main contract, the Contractor and sub-contractor hereby agree that such dispute or difference shall be referred to an arbitrator appointed or to be appointed pursuant to the terms of the main contract ...". The sub-contractors asked the main contractors to agree to the appointment of an arbitrator of a claim which they proposed to make and, agreement not being forthcoming, secured the appointment of an arbitrator under the first part of the clause. The main contractors challenged his jurisdiction, invoking clause 24, but he decided that he had jurisdiction and ordered pleadings to be served, which was done, and the hearing date was then fixed. Prior to the hearing the main contractors reached agreement with the owners for the nomination of an arbitrator to determine disputes under the main contract, and the main contractors then applied once more to the arbitrator challenging his jurisdiction, and he once more ruled that he did have jurisdiction. At that time the arbitrator under the main contract had not been formally appointed and had not given directions. The main contractors then issued a summons claiming a declaration that the arbitrator had no jurisdiction in view of the later appointment, contending that they could invoke the proviso to clause 24 at any time, while the sub-contractors contended that objection under clause 24 could only be taken at the time of the original appointment of the sub-contract arbitrator. *Held*, by Boreham J., that the main contractor, as a party to both contracts, was best placed to know whether there were matters in dispute in the two contracts which were substantially the same at the time of the proposed appointment of the sub-contract arbitrator. If at that time (i) a dispute existed which was the same in the two contracts and (ii) an arbitrator had been or was to be appointed under the main contract, the reference must be to the main contract arbitrator. If neither of those conditions were present, the appointment under clause 24 must proceed. On the facts, the first arbitrator had been properly appointed as an arbitrator in respect of the sub-contract disputes. Clause 24 made no provision for any subsequent revocation of his appointment.[93] *Held*, further, that on the facts there had been an ad hoc submission of the issue of jurisdiction to the first arbitrator on the second of the two occasions when his jurisdiction had been challenged and, applying *Westminster Chemicals & Produce Ltd.* v. *Eichholz and Loeser*,[94] the main contractors were bound by the first arbitrator's decision on jurisdiction: *Higgs & Hill Building Ltd.* v. *Campbell Denis Ltd.* (1982).[95]

(v) *Where questions of law are involved*

Specific submissions of known and disputed questions of law are obviously a case by themselves, where it is evident that a stay will rarely be in issue and if so almost always granted.[96] In the case of agreements to refer   **18·118**

---

[93] Contrast clause 37(8), and see also clause 37(9), of the Singapore S.I.A. private sector contract, reproduced in C.C.P.P., p. 614.

[94] [1954] 1 Lloyd's Rep. 99. See also *supra*, Section 1(2)(c), paras. 18·006 *et seq*.

[95] 28 BLR 47.

[96] Compare *F. R. Absalom Ltd.* v. *Great Western (London) Garden Village Society Ltd.* [1933] A.C. 592, 607–8, where the distinction is emphasised in the analogous case of setting aside an award for error of law on its face.

future disputes, that is, the typical arbitration clause, there will equally be little difficulty in obtaining a stay if a point of law is involved which is of a class constantly dealt with by arbitrators, or where the question of law requires findings of fact.[97]

ILLUSTRATION

A civil engineering contract provided that disputes should be referred to an arbitrator, who was to be an engineer. A party to the contract took out a summons for construction of a clause in the contract. It appeared that evidence would be needed, both as to custom in such matters and as to the meaning of technical terms used, before the clause could be construed. *Held*, by the Court of Appeal, (overruling the judge) that the proceedings should be stayed: *Metropolitan Tunnel Ltd.* v. *London Electric Railway* (1926).[98]

18·119   No doubt the same principle will apply where the question of law is one likely to arise in a transaction of the kind in question should a future dispute arise, whether or not it is of a class constantly dealt with by arbitrators. Where, however, the dispute relates to one or more isolated points of law, for example on admitted facts, or even one of considerable importance which is almost certain to return to the courts notwithstanding the necessity for some findings of fact (disregarding for the moment the impact of section 2 of the 1979 Act), the Courts in the past have had little hesitation in refusing a stay:

"Everybody knows that with regard to the construction of an agreement, it is absolutely useless to stay the action, because it will only come back to the court on a case stated."[99]

"Where in such a document as a building contract or a partnership agreement, you have an all-embracing arbitration clause, it may often be bad practice to permit matters of law or construction to go to arbitration for, though such matters are strictly covered by the agreement, they are questions not appropriate to be dealt with by arbitration, and it may be futile to allow them so to be."[1]

However, there may have been a shift in judicial attitudes in favour of granting a stay where the question referred is one of law, even prior to such inferences as are to be drawn from the philosophy of the Arbitration Act 1979 itself,[2] and of the current climate of pressure to reduce the demands made on the courts of which the *Nema* guidelines are a reflec-

---

[97] *Heyman* v. *Darwins Ltd.* [1942] A.C. 356, 369, *per* Viscount Simon L.C.
[98] [1926] Ch. 371.
[99] *Per* Lord Parker in *Bristol Corporation* v. *John Aird & Co.* [1913] A.C. 241, 261.
[1] *Per* Evershed M.R. in *Milas-Martin Pen Co. Ltd.* v. *Selsdon Fountain Pen Co. Ltd. (No. 2)* (1950) 67 R.P.C. 64, 69.
[2] See Lord Wright's comment on Lord Parker's dictum in the *Bristol* case in *Heyman* v. *Darwins Ltd.* [1942] A.C. 356, 389.

tion. The modern tendency in England is probably against refusing a stay, and the onus will be on the party opposing the stay to show, for example, that the point is of sufficient substance for it to be likely that it will come to the courts whatever the arbitrator decides.[3]

The present state of the authorities in this very important area is not, therefore, entirely clear. Moreover, it is not apparent what the effect on the exercise of the discretion to refuse a stay where a point of law is involved ought to be of the much greater difficulty of securing leave to appeal from arbitrators on a point of law in domestic contracts as a result of the 1979 Act and the *Nema* guidelines. The following is a recent and interesting example of a stay being refused in a construction case.

18·120

ILLUSTRATION

> Condition 2 of a standard form sub-contract provided that "The Main contract conditions shall apply equally to the sub-contract works in so far as they are applicable to those works and the sub-contractor shall comply with and perform their obligations on the same conditions as the main contractors." The main contract was in the GC/Wks 1 standard form with an arbitration clause which, if incorporated, would need some amendment to suit a sub-contract relationship. The sub-contractors brought an action claiming damages for delay and disruption, and the defendant main contractors contended that the GC/Wks 1 arbitration clause had been incorporated in the sub-contract and applied for a stay. *Held*, by Judge Fox Andrews, that in his view the arbitration clause did not apply to the particular claims being advanced by the sub-contractors and had not been incorporated; *but that, if it did*, difficult questions of fact and law would arise as to the precise nature and effect of the arbitration clause upon the sub-contract and on the arbitrator's powers. Unlike other main contract standard forms, GC/Wks 1 had not yet been considered by the courts in this particular context. For these reasons a stay would be refused in the exercise of the court's discretion: *Lakers Mechanical Services Ltd.* v. *Boskalis Westminster Construction Ltd.* (1986).[4]

It is hardly necessary to point out that the foregoing Subparagraphs (i)–(v) relate to *domestic* arbitration agreements. By virtue of section 1 of the 1975 Act, applications for a stay *must* be granted in the case of *non-domestic* arbitrations as there defined, subject only to the requirements that the arbitration agreement is not null and void, inoperative or incapable of being performed, and that there is a sufficient dispute between the parties with regard to the matters agreed to be referred.[5] A considerably wider list of exceptions, however, prevents the enforcement of awards in those cases[6] and could presumably be invoked by way of an

---

[3] Compare in Australia *Goodwin Ltd.* v. *Stephenson & Watt* [1967] 2 N.S.W.R. 637, *per* Macfarlan J.

[4] 5 Const.L.J. 139, also illustrated *supra*, para. 18·035.

[5] s.1(1), 1975 Act.

[6] See s.5, 1975 Act.

action for a declaration or injunction by the party resisting a stay under that Act.

(h) Step in the action

18·121 Both section 4(1) of the 1950 Act and section 1(1) of the 1975 Act expressly permit applications to stay, in the case of both domestic and foreign arbitrations respectively, "at any time after appearance, and before delivering any pleadings or taking any other steps in the proceedings". These long-standing words have recently been interpreted by the courts, by contrast with the earlier cases since the inception of the legislation a century ago, in an increasingly artificial and restrictive way. Thus, today it will apparently make no difference that a "step" may have been taken when a party was in ignorance of an arbitration agreement.[7] Moreover, in the case of applications for summary judgment under R.S.C. Order 14, the defendant will lose his right to arbitration if, when seeking leave to defend, he has not *simultaneously* issued a summons to stay.[8]

Thus, it is eminently possible for a party to lose his right to arbitration in situations where there is no conscious intention to abandon the right to arbitration; no possible prejudice or delay caused to the other side; and even where the other side has been made fully aware not only that the claim is disputed but that arbitration is desired or intended. Anomalies and injustices of this kind are most likely to occur in the haste and urgency imposed on defendants by applications to the courts for summary judgment—paradoxically all the more so if these are oppressive or premature, unjustified or in clear breach of contract and, therefore, unexpected.

ILLUSTRATION

18·122 Plaintiff contractors issued a writ for a balance due and applied for summary judgment under R.S.C. Ord. 14. The defendant's solicitor filed an unusual and obviously inexperienced affidavit alleging delay, overcharging, defective work, and disagreements by the owner with his own architect; offering on behalf of the owner to bring the sums claimed into court if so desired; identifying the contract arbitration clause; and at two points in the affidavit inviting consideration to be given to the question whether the claim should be arbitrated. *Held*, by the Court of Appeal, overruling *Zalinoff* v. *Hammond*[9] and following *Pitchers Ltd.* v. *Plaza (Queensbury) Ltd.*[10] that the filing of the affidavit without taking out a summons to stay was a step in the action, and that the right to arbitration had been lost: *Turner and Goudy* v. *McConnell* (1985).[11]

---

[7] *Parker Gaines & Co. Ltd.* v. *Turpin* [1918] 1 K.B. 358.
[8] *Pitcher Ltd.* v. *Plaza (Queensbury) Ltd.* [1940] 1 E.R. 151.
[9] [1898] 2 Ch. 92.
[10] See *supra*.
[11] [1985] 1 W.L.R. 898.

Not surprisingly, there is a long and substantial case law as to what does or does not constitute a step in the action.[12]

This attitude of the courts, whereby the right to arbitration can so easily be lost inadvertently in situations where no possible prejudice to the other party is involved, seems the more odd at the present day in the light of the openly avowed changes in attitude displayed by the judiciary in other parts of the modern case law of arbitration. It is difficult to reconcile a decision like the *Turner and Goudy* case illustrated *supra*, for example, with the zeal in holding parties to an arbitration agreement in spite of great practical difficulties, additional expense, and the possibility of inconsistent findings, shown by the Court of Appeal and Steyn J. respectively in their decisions in the *City Centre* and *Property Investment* cases illustrated *supra*, as also with the Court of Appeal's openly stated desire to force parties towards arbitration in order to reduce pressure on the courts, notwithstanding that parallel, and possibly inconsistent proceedings might result, in the *Crouch* case.[13]

Nor is it easy to see how this policy can be reconciled with the spirit of the 1975 Act, where non-domestic arbitrations are clearly intended by the legislature, for understandable reasons of international comity and treaty obligation, to be the subject of virtually mandatory stays. The possibility of so-called "steps in the action" being taken inadvertently on behalf of foreign parties finding themselves sued in England without appreciation of the consequences is in practice likely to be even greater, it might be thought. Yet the 1975 Act uses *identical* wording in regard to steps in the action, to section 4 of the 1950 Act, even though, in non-domestic cases, the clear objective of the later Act is to require a stay to be refused effectively in every case where there is a valid arbitration agreement. **18·123**

As it happens there are a number of examples in the earlier case-law of a more rational and less legalistic approach, even in domestic disputes, which required some conduct demonstrating a deliberate intention to abandon the right to arbitration and in favour of the action proceedings before a stay would be refused.[14] It is submitted that reconsideration by the House of Lords of this line of over-legalistic case-law is overdue.

(3) Succession and Assignment

(a) Succession

Questions of succession will arise on the death of a party to an arbitration agreement, or on his personal bankruptcy. In the former case, sec- **18·124**

---

[12] See *Mustill and Boyd*, (2nd ed.), pp. 472–3. See also for a more recent case *Rumput (Panama) S.A.* v. *Islamic Republic of Iran Shipping Lines, The Leage* [1984] 2 Lloyd's Rep.

[13] *Northern Regional Health Authority* v. *Derek Crouch Construction Co. Ltd.* [1984] Q.B. 644. See particularly the closing remarks in Lord Donaldson M.R.'s judgment discussed in C.C.P.P., para. 17–49 at p. 271.

[14] See the cases referred to in *Mustill and Boyd* (2nd ed.), p. 472.

tion 2(1) of the 1950 Act provides expressly that the agreement shall be enforceable by or against the deceased's personal representatives. The Act also provides, perhaps unnecessarily, that the death of a party will not revoke an arbitrator's appointment previously made by the deceased.[15]

In the case of bankruptcy, claims for the arbitration of future disputes are expressly enforceable by or against a trustee in bankruptcy if he adopts the contract[16] (in which event the trustee under both past and present insolvency legislation is personally liable on the agreement).[17] Where the trustee does not adopt the contract, the other party, (or indeed the trustee himself provided he obtains the consent of the Committee of Inspection) can apply to the court for an order for the dispute to be determined by arbitration.[18]

In a case of company insolvency, where the liquidator will normally never be personally liable, the 1950 Act makes no express provision and the situation seems unclear.

Statutory succession can obviously occur in different situations in different jurisdictions. Thus, under French law a demerger of companies ("traité de scission") has the effect that the transferor company ceases to exist, and its assets and liabilities are thereupon transferred automatically to two or more transferee companies. Thus, where this occurred to a claimant buyer company comparatively early in an arbitration against sellers, but without this being appreciated by the persons engaged in the arbitration, and an award was made and a subsequent appeal to a Board of Appeal dismissed some two and a half years later, the transferee company finally gave notice of the transfer of the assets to the parties and the Board shortly before the Board's decision dismissing the appeal. It was held by the Court of Appeal that the statutory transfer had ranked as an equitable assignment of the buyer's rights, but that it did not render the assignees a party to the continuing arbitration, and that their minimum obligation had been to give notice to the other side and to submit formally to the arbitrator's jurisdiction. Not having done so, the arbitration had lapsed, and could not be resurrected by the later notice, so that the award of the arbitrators and the decision of the Board had been void.[19]

(b) Assignment

18·125   Assignment of contractual rights with particular reference to rights under an arbitration clause has already been considered in Chapter 14.[20] Notwithstanding a difficult decision of Wright J. in 1928,[21] where the view

---

[15] s.2(2), 1950 Act.
[16] s.3, Arbitration Act 1950.
[17] See *ante*, Chap. 16, Section 2, para. 16·011.
[18] s.3(2), Arbitration Act 1950.
[19] *Baytur S.A.* v. *Finagro Holdings S.A.* [1992] 1 Q.B. 610, C.A. See, however, the possible right of an assignor in certain situations to sue on behalf of the assignee adumbrated by the House of Lords in *Linden Gardens Trust Ltd.* v. *Lenesta Sludge Disposals Ltd.* [1993] 3 W.L.R. 408, see *ante*, Chap. 14, paras. 14·027–14·029 or possibly as a constructive trustee.
[20] See *ante*, Chap. 14, Section 4(3), paras. 14·038–14·039.
[21] *Cottage Estates Ltd.* v. *Woodside Estates Ltd.* [1928] 2 K.B. 453.

was expressed that arbitration rights were not assignable, it now seems clear that an assignee of rights under a normal commercial transaction or contract takes subject to the other party's right to a stay for arbitration should there be an arbitration clause,[22] and is also entitled to enforce his assignor's rights to and in an arbitration,[23] provided notice of the assignment is given both to the other party and to any arbitrators.[24]

It may be necessary in some cases to distinguish between the substantive agreement itself and its "ancillary" arbitration clause or agreement.[25] In some contracts of a family or personal nature, no doubt, the arbitration element of a transaction may be regarded as personal to the contracting parties, and so not assignable even though the benefit of the remainder of the transaction may be, but in the great majority of commercial transactions arbitration, rightly or wrongly, is likely to be regarded by one side or the other (and certainly in construction contracts) as a genuinely advantageous remedy for commercial reasons,[25a] it is submitted, and not as a remedy dependent on any special relationship of trust in the opposing party which would render it less acceptable if available to the other party's assignee. In such a case, the arbitration clause will follow the assignment of the subject matter of the contract.[26] It is difficult, moreover, to see how a party can be deprived of the benefit of an arbitration agreement as a consequence of a unilateral assignment of rights by the other party.

Possibly, too, a distinction may need to be made in this context between an assignment of the "fruits" or benefit of a contract and an assignment of *the right to have the contract performed.*[27]

Section 4. Disqualification and Misconduct of Arbitrators

(1) Generally

An improper interest or bias, if unknown at the time of the arbitration **18·126** agreement, or the subsequent misconduct of an arbitrator after his appointment, may be grounds for refusing a stay, or for the arbitrator's removal and the revocation of his authority,[28] or for setting aside an award if already made,[29] or for setting aside the arbitration agreement itself,[30] or

---

[22] *The Leage* [1984] 2 Lloyd's Rep. 259, Bingham J.
[23] *Montedipu S.p.A.* v. *JTP-RO Jugotanker, The Jordan Nicolov* [1990] 2 Lloyd's Rep. 11, Gatehouse J.
[24] *Ibid.*, and see also the *Baytur* case *supra.*
[25] See *Heyman* v. *Darwins Ltd.* and the discussion *supra*, Section 1, paras. 18·007 *et seq.*
[25a] See, *e.g.* the Court of Appeal's reasoning in *Bruce* v. *Strong*, illustrated *supra*, para. 18·109.
[26] See, *per* Lord Greene M.R. in *Shayler* v. *Woolf* [1946] Ch. 320, 323.
[27] See generally *ante*, Chap. 14, Section 4(1), para. 14·057, and for this more recent distinction *Linden Gardens Trust Ltd.* v. *Lenesta Sludge Disposals Ltd.* [1991] 57 BLR 47, C.A., and the editor's "Assignment of Rights to Sue for Breach of Construction Contract" in (1993) 109 L.Q.R. 82, 87–88, but see now the above case in the H.L., [1994] 1 A.C. 85 and the editor's "Assignment of Rights to sue: Half a Loaf" in (1994) 110 L.Q.R. 42.
[28] s.23(1), 1950 Act.
[29] s.23(2), 1950 Act.
[30] s.25(2)(*b*), 1950 Act.

for the appointment of a new arbitrator.[31] Failure to use reasonable despatch is also a separate ground for removal of an arbitrator.[32]

A detailed examination of these various alternative remedies is outside the scope of this book, but some account of the circumstances which will or will not justify intervention on these various grounds may be of assistance to both arbitrators and parties in construction disputes.

(2) Interest and Bias

18·127 Cases indicating the difference in this context between valuation or certifying provisions in a contract on the one hand and arbitration clauses or agreements on the other have been illustrated both *supra*, and *ante*, Chapter 6.[33] Invalidating interest, or bias, or misconduct in relation to certifiers has also been considered *ante*, Chapter 6.[34]

It is clear that in the nineteenth century a fairly close connection between the owner and his A/E (particularly in the case of the company's engineer in railway cases) was regarded as to be expected, and this extended to contracts where the A/E was also the named arbitrator. The climate of opinion in this respect has clearly changed considerably, as evidenced by section 14 of the Arbitration Act 1934, now clause 24(1) of the 1950 Act. These enable an arbitrator's authority to be revoked, notwithstanding an interest known at the time of contracting. The following cases of interest and bias need to be considered with this later legislation in mind, for which reason many would not cause a problem at the present day. It will be seen that these earlier cases are not entirely consistent. More modern cases will be found *infra*, Subsection (3), Misconduct.

ILLUSTRATIONS

(1) An arbitrator was held not to be disqualified by being owed or paid money by one of the parties in the ordinary course of business, such as the debt due from an owner to his architect: *Morgan* v. *Morgan* (1832).[35]

(2) The circumstances of the engineer who was arbitrator under a contract for constructing a railway subsequently being appointed manager of the company was held not to be, *per se*, a sufficient ground to disqualify him from acting as such arbitrator: *Phipps* v. *Edinburgh, etc., Railway* (1843).[36]

18·128   (3) A. acted as agent for the S. Railway Company, and as such made an offer to E. of a price for a certain piece of land which the company wished to purchase under their compulsory powers. The company and E. not agreeing,

---

[31] s.25(2)(*a*), 1950 Act.
[32] s.13(3), 1950 Act.
[33] See *supra*, paras. 18·061 *et seq.*, and see *ante*, Chap. 6, paras. 6·065 *et seq.*, and see paras. 6·220 *et seq.*
[34] Section 5(2), paras. 6·099 *et seq.* (interest) and Subsections 5(3) and (5), paras. 6·106 *et seq.* (invalidating conduct).
[35] 2 L.J.Ex. 56: see also *Stevenson* v. *Watson* (1879) 4 C.P.D. 148, para. 6·110, *ante*.
[36] 5 D. Ct. of Sess., 1025.

the price was to be settled by arbitration. The company appointed A. as their arbitrator: E. appointed B. as his arbitrator; and an umpire, C., was chosen by B. from a list supplied to him by A. B. was, unknown to E., a surveyor of, and a shareholder in the G. Company, who were interested in the success of the undertaking of the S. Company. C. was also, unknown to E., a surveyor employed by the G. Company. *Held*, that E. by appointing his own arbitrator had waived any objection to the appointment of A., and that the facts as to B. and C. did not afford any judicial grounds for setting aside the award: *Re Elliott, ex p. South Devon Railway* (1848).[37]

(4) An engineer was held not to be disqualified from acting as arbitrator under a railway building contract from the personal interest natural to his position, nor by holding shares in the company for which he was acting: *Ranger* v. *G. W. Railway* (1854).[38]

(5) A., one party to an arbitration, raised an action to declare the arbitrator disqualified before final award, because he had been connected with B., the other party, as his law agent, and because he had a personal interest in B.'s solvency. *Held*, that these averments were not relevant to support an action, which was not to set aside an award, but to stop the proceedings under the submission: *Drew* v. *Drew* (1855).[39]

(6) Accepting hospitality from a party was held to be an improper act on the part of an arbitrator, but unless it could be shown that he had been influenced thereby, his award should not be set aside: *Re Hopper* (1867).[40]

(7) If in the course of an arbitration the arbitrator is found to have a large interest in the award, a party may move to have him removed, and an injunction may issue: *Beddow* v. *Beddow* (1878).[41]

18·129

(8) A strong report by the engineer to the owner complaining of the way in which the work had been done by the contractor under the contract, in which the engineer was also arbitrator, did not disqualify him from acting as arbitrator: *Scott* v. *Carluke Local Authority* (1879).[42]

(9) M. contracted to do engineering work for the B. Parochial Board. All matters, claims, and obligations whatever arising out of the contract were to be referred to A., who was, in fact, the engineer of the board. A. had, as engineer, complained of some of M.'s work, and had measured the work and brought out as due to M. less than he claimed. *Held*, that A. was not disqualified from acting as arbitrator: *Mackay* v. *Barry Parochial Board* (1883).[43]

(10) An arbitrator was held not to be disqualified by the fact of his having previously made a valuation for third persons for a mortgage of the property, the building of which was the subject of the arbitration: *Botterill* v. *Ware Guardians* (1886).[44]

(11) The arbitration clause in a contract for building a railway provided that the arbitrator should not be disqualified from acting by being or becoming consulting engineer to the railway company. *Held*, that he was not barred

---

[37] 12 Jur.(o.s.) 445.

[38] 5 H.L.Cas. 72, for this case in more detail, see Chap. 6, para. 6·102, *ante*.

[39] 14 D. Ct. of Sess., 559; affirmed by, H.L., *The Times*, March 12, 1855.

[40] L.R. 2 Q.B. 367.

[41] 9 Ch.D. 89.

[42] 6 R. Ct. of Sess., 616.

[43] 10 R. (Ct. of Sess.) 1046.

[44] 2 T.L.R. 621, C.A.; where *Kemp* v. *Rose* (1858) 1 Giff. 258. Illustrated *ante*, Chap. 6, para. 6·102, was distinguished. The case is further illustrated *ante*, Chap. 6, para. 6·127.

from acting as arbitrator by the fact that he had revised the specifications and schedules upon which the work which formed the subject of the arbitration was performed: *Adams* v. *Great North of Scotland Railway Co.* (1889).[45]

18·130   (12) An award was set aside on discovery that the plaintiff had assigned to his arbitrator for value his claim under a fire policy, the subject of the dispute: *Blanchard* v. *Sun Fire Office* (1890).[46]

(13) Where a dispute arose as to timbering a trench, because the contractors wished to leave the timber *in situ* and contended that it would not be safe to remove it, while the engineer ordered its removal and refused to certify for payment for it if left: *Held*, that the contractors must not be compelled to submit to the arbitrament of the engineer, whose professional capacity and reputation were at stake: *Nuttall* v. *Manchester Corporation* (1892).[47]

(14) By an engineering contract disputes were to be referred to the engineer as arbitrator. A dispute arose as to whether certain work was an extra. The dispute was then referred to the engineer. After the reference, and on the day for which the first appointment had been made, the engineer wrote to the contractor repeating his former view. *Held*, that as the engineer must necessarily, in his position as agent of the company, have already expressed his opinion on the point in dispute, his repeating that opinion after the arbitration had commenced did not disqualify him unless, on the fair construction of the letter, it appeared that he had so made up his mind as not to be open to change it upon argument: *Jackson* v. *Barry Railway* (1893).[48]

18·131   (15) Disputes under an engineering contract were by its terms referred to the engineer. At the end of the work the contractor put in claims, of which somewhat less than half involved the allegation that there had been radical and extensive alterations, and that there had been delay in supplying the plans. He further complained that some items of the other claims had been disallowed at this time without any reasons being given. The employers required the contractor's claims to be referred to the engineer under the arbitration clause, whereupon the contractor applied to revoke the submission to the arbitrator. *Held*, the allegation of delay when carefully examined did not show any misconduct or negligence by the engineer as in *Nuttall's* case, but only an allegation of delay arising from the necessity to alter the work. Consequently the appointment would not be revoked: *Re Donkin and Leeds and Liverpool Canal Co.* (1893).[49]

(16) The fact that one of the main questions in dispute was as to the care and competence and skill of the arbitrator's son, who had acted as assistant engineer, and might hope to succeed to his father's position, was held not to be a sufficient ground for refusing to enforce the arbitration clause: *Eckersley* v. *Mersey Docks and Harbour Board* (1894).[50]

(17) A building contract contained an arbitration clause referring disputes in the widest possible terms to the engineer. The contractors brought an action involving first, the proper construction of a verbal contract made with the engineer, and secondly, whether the engineer had accepted the owner's liability for certain varied work. *Held*, by the House of Lords, that where a

---

[45] 26 S.L.R. 765 at p. 772; [1891] A.C. 31.
[46] 6 T.L.R. 365.
[47] Hudson, *Building Contracts* (4th ed.), Vol. 2, p. 203.
[48] [1893] 1 Ch. 238. See the fuller illustration and quotation from Bowen L.J. in this case, *ante*, Chap. 6, paras. 6·135 and 6·138.
[49] Hudson, *Building Contracts* (4th ed.), Vol. 2, p. 239.
[50] [1894] 2 Q.B. 667, C.A.

dispute involved a probable conflict of evidence between the contractor and the engineer, the fact that the engineer, without any fault of his own, must necessarily be placed in the position of judge and witness was a sufficient reason why the matter should not be referred: *Bristol Corporation* v. *Aird* (1913).[51]

(3) Misconduct

It has been stated *supra*, that an arbitrator's appointment can be revoked or an arbitrator's agreement set aside on the ground of an arbitrator's misconduct. This may involve a wide range of matters, varying from unfair and unjudicial behaviour to mistaken actions or decisions where no moral turpitude or professional incompetence is involved, but where in the interests of justice the arbitration should not continue. It will be seen that examples of unfair and unjudicial behaviour have been reaching the reports more frequently in recent times.

18·132

ILLUSTRATIONS

(1) An arbitrator appointed by one of the parties asked the solicitor for that party, after the close of the hearing, but before the umpire made his award, whether the company would not undertake to take up the award in any event; to this an affirmative answer was given. It was argued that an undertaking by a solvent company to take up the award amounted practically to the same thing as payment of money, and was a ground for setting aside the award for misconduct of the arbitrator. *Held*, by the Queen's Bench Divisional Court, that the award should be upheld. The fact that one party would take up the award and pay the fees, even if it was against him, was no inducement to an arbitrator to find in favour of that party: *Re Kenworthy & Queen Insurance Co.* (1893).[52]

(2) A dispute arose as to whether buyers of textile goods were entitled to reject them as not being of merchantable quality. The dispute was referred to arbitration under the Rules of the Manchester Chamber of Commerce, which appointed a sole arbitrator. The Chamber's rules provided expressly for arbitration by commercial men of experience with special knowledge of the subject matter of the dispute. The arbitrator found that the goods were of merchantable quality, but disregarding the seller's claim for the price of the goods (which was the wrong basis of a claim in such a situation) substituted a sum as damages for loss of profit, (which was the correct basis), although neither side had led any evidence as to the amount of such damages. The buyers moved for the award to be set aside for misconduct. *Held*, by Lord Goddard C.J., that the principle that an arbitrator who was appointed because of his knowledge and experience of the trade might act on his own experience and knowledge was not limited to disputes of quality, and could extend to *quantum* as well, and that there was no reason to interfere with the award: *Mediterranean and Eastern Export Co. Ltd.* v. *Fortress Fabrics (Manchester) Ltd.* (1948).[53]

---

[51] [1913] A.C. 241, illustrated more fully *supra*, para. 18·104.
[52] 9 T.L.R. 181.
[53] 81 Lloyd's Rep. 146.

[Note: While an understandable result on its facts, the principle was probably stated too widely in this case in regard to more complex disputes, and construction arbitrations in particular, as to which see *Fox* v. *Wellfair Ltd.* and *Town City Properties (Development) Ltd.* v. *Wiltshier* illustrated *infra*.]

18·133

(3) A county court judge in an industrial accident case inspected the place of work and saw a demonstration of the system of working. By a mistake the plaintiff workman was not informed of the appointment and was not present, although the defendants' representatives were. *Held*, by the Court of Appeal, that whether or not an inspection amounted to receiving evidence (*per* Denning L.J. it did, *per* Hodson L.J. it did not) a new trial before a different judge should be ordered: *Goold* v. *Evans & Co.* (1951).[54]

(4) An arbitrator appointed under an Irish statute to determine the amount of compensation for works executed by a local authority under certain land informed the parties at the end of the hearing that he would view the land himself. Unknown to the landowner, he in fact viewed the land in the company of the local authority's engineer. *Held*, by the Irish Supreme Court, that while accepting the arbitrator's statement that nothing related to the case was discussed, and whether or not the view amounted to receiving evidence in the technical sense, the arbitrator's award should be set aside on the ground of misconduct, since justice must not only be done but be seen to be done: *The State* v. *Winters* (1953).[55]

18·134

(5) An arbitrator awarded damages to buyers for non-delivery of goods, notwithstanding that it was pointed out to him, and not challenged, that the price was in excess of the maximum price under emergency legislation, and the contract consequently illegal. On a motion to set aside the award as bad on its face or for misconduct, it was argued that an arbitrator could do what he considered to be fair and award damages in this situation, whatever the strict position at law might be. *Held*, by the Court of Appeal, that the award, which gave no reasons, was not bad on its face; but since the arbitrator's duty was to apply the law, once apprised of the illegality he had been guilty of misconduct in awarding damages and the award must be set aside: *David Taylor & Son Ltd.* v. *Barnett Trading Co.* (1953).[56]

(6) An arbitrator wrote that he would view before the hearing. The claimant conducted his case on the basis that there would be a view, calling no expert evidence. The arbitrator did not in fact view before his award. *Held*, by Park J., that there had been misconduct within section 23(2) of the Act, and the award should be set aside. *Micklethwait* v. *Mullock* (1974).[57]

(7) An arbitrator refused to award interest, although asked to do so. *Held*, by Kerr J., that it was technical misconduct to do so where sufficient facts were before the arbitrator for the purpose: *P.J. Van Der Zijden Wildhandel N.V.* v. *Tucker & Cross Ltd.* (1976).[58]

(8) An arbitrator who was a professor of engineering accepted an appointment to settle a dispute over a pipe-line contract in Victoria after intimating that he could not be available before December 1977. At the preliminary meeting in January 1978, he intimated that he would not be available between the end of March and August 1978, and the owners, who thought that a major

---

[54] [1951] 2 T.L.R. 1189.
[55] 92 I.L.T.R. 66.
[56] [1953] 1 W.L.R. 562. See further *supra*, para. 18·010.
[57] 232 E.G. 337.
[58] [1976] 1 Lloyd's Rep. 341. See also for a case of inadvertence the *Marples Ridgeway* case discussed *infra*, para. 18·168.

item in dispute only involved a relatively short point of law as to whether or not work was a variation, and that no serious issues of fact or quantum were involved, agreed to a hearing date commencing on March 8 and ending on March 23 sitting six days a week until 5.00 p.m. in Sydney, New South Wales, and that the arbitration could recommence in August to deal with remaining issues. However, the Points of Claim and extensive documentation delivered by the contractors in February 1978, made it clear that there were major issues of fact and quantum involved, and on the first day of the hearing the contractors provided a written witness statement which with annexed documents totalled several hundred pages, and would take many hours to peruse and absorb. On the second day of the hearing the owners applied for the hearings to conclude at 4.00 p.m. each day to enable them to prepare their case for cross-examination on factual issues in the light of the material they had received. The arbitrator refused this application.

The owners then applied for the person making the witness statement, who had only been personally involved with the project for a very short time at the end, to be examined on oath in accordance with the normal rules of evidence and without reference to his written statement, having regard to his apparent lack of direct factual knowledge of the project and the possible absence of any other direct witnesses. When eventually agreeing to this application, though after considerable resistance, the arbitrator said: "If you want it conducted that way, then I am afraid I am bound to do it, otherwise you are going to object to the evidence and dash off to the Supreme Court and get an award or this arbitration stayed".

Counsel for the contractors, who had given no indication in the pleadings or in his opening as to how it was contended that the disputed work was a variation, then called an employee of the owners and put to him a single sentence in "rough notes" which that employee had prepared of a conversation which he had had with the contractors, and which by itself might have suggested that the owners were calling for the disputed work as a variation; but the rest of the "rough notes" made it clear beyond doubt that the owners were requiring the work as included in the contract. When the owners' counsel requested that the remainder of the notes should be put and considered in context, the arbitrator stated that he did not wish to see them, and though finally agreeing under pressure to admit them, clearly did not understand the point and continued to consider the document as being adverse to the owners' case, which it plainly was not.

On a rather more difficult point of the admissibility of certain pre-contract discussions with all tenderers regarding the extent of the contractors' required work under the contract, the arbitrator stated that he regarded the matter as concluded by an express provision in the contract excluding implied terms and other agreements, and interrupted the owners' counsels' argument with a ruling adverse to the owners before their argument was completed.

Held, by Marks J., (a) that unless expressly absolved by the parties, arbitrators in a normal type of reference are required to conduct the hearing in accordance with the ordinary rules applicable to legal proceedings and to apply the rules of evidence; (b) the principles of natural justice required the arbitrator to be impartial and unbiased, and to give each party a full and fair opportunity to present its case; (c) mistakes of law or fact, or misunderstanding a party's arguments, though not amounting to misconduct, might in certain circumstances arouse a reasonable suspicion of bias or might include a trend or pattern unfairly disadvantaging a party. In this case the failure to grant the request for shorter sittings put unfair pressure on the owners and disadvantaged them, and was a denial of natural justice. It might also be reasonably suspected that considerations of his own personal convenience had influenced the arbitrator's ruling. The owners' application for the witness to be examined on oath without his written statement was a proper one, but

18·134A

the arbitrator had criticised the owners for taking the point rather than ruling upon it, and his comments on it were unjudicial and adverse to the owners. Though the arbitrator had eventually admitted the entire "rough note", his remarks showed that he had not understood the relevance of the remainder of the note, which should have been obvious, and still regarded it as adverse to the owners' case. While not in itself misconduct, his remarks indicated a degree of pre-judgment on that issue. On the more difficult question of the admissibility of the pre-contract meetings, the arbitrator had heard the contractor's arguments without interruption, but had interrupted the owners' counsel and then prematurely ruled against their argument before they had completed their submissions. That was a breach of natural justice. In all the circumstances a fair observer could reasonably suspect that the arbitrator would not bring a fair and impartial mind to the questions before him, and there had been misconduct justifying his removal: *Gas and Fuel Corporation of Victoria* v. *Woodhall Limited* (1978).[58a]

[Note: This judgment contains a valuable and thorough review of the English and Australian authorities on misconduct involving breach of the principles of natural justice. It also merits reading *in extenso*, since there are a number of detailed examples of unjudicial actions or language which clearly contributed to the final result. It is also clear from the judgment that the arbitrator's standing as an educated man might in itself be a relevant factor in suspecting bias in areas of apparent misunderstanding or error of fact or law. The elements of the arbitrator's convenience, and the distortion of programmes to suit the arbitrator's convenience and availability rather than the justice of the case, represents an increasing feature of modern arbitration. The arbitrator's non-availability for an important period does not appear to have been brought to the attention of the parties prior to his acceptance of his appointment, another common feature, though this is not expressly noted in the judgment. See also *per* Marks J. "Further, it might reasonably have been suspected that the arbitrator had it in mind that his own convenience was a matter of some importance in dealing with the application, and further that he had, tentatively at least, set a time limit on the total duration of the arbitration and that tentative fixation of time limit bore some influence on his ruling. It was not proper for the arbitrator to allow matters of personal convenience to have influenced his ruling.".][58b]

18·135   (9) An owner contracted for work to be done to her house, with an arbitration clause in general terms providing for the appointment, failing agreement, of a single arbitrator by the President of the (English) Chartered Institute of Arbitrators. A dispute arose with the builders, during which they informed her that if she pressed her claim they would go into liquidation and she would have wasted her costs. Failing agreement on an arbitrator, she made a unilateral application to the President, who agreed to nominate an arbitrator, subject to her agreement that the reasonable fees and expenses of the arbitrator should be paid; that the proceedings would be governed by the Institute's regulations; and that she would provide adequate security for the arbitrator's fees. In response to an initial letter from the arbitrator, she indicated her agreement that the regulations should apply, but in view of the builder's earlier threat, she made it a condition that the arbitrator would make orders for security under two of the Regulations, namely regulation 4.6 which empowered the arbitrator to order security or payment of the whole sum in dispute, and regulation 6.3 for the arbitrator's and parties' costs. The builder in a letter merely agreed to the arbitrator's proposed fees.

[58a] [1978] V.R. 385.
[58b] *Ibid.* at p. 407.

Following an initial hearing where the arbitrator took no steps to ascertain the builder's acceptance of the other conditions, he made a first order that both parties pay into a solicitor's joint account £3,000 in respect of the sum in dispute, and £500 in respect of costs. The owner paid these sums promptly, but the builder's solicitors challenged the arbitrator's authority to make the order, and intimated that in any case their clients did not have funds available. Correspondence then took place which indicated that the arbitrator was now not sure what course he or the owner ought to take, but meanwhile pleadings were exchanged. The owner brought matters to a head, when ordered to deliver further particulars of her claim, by refusing to do so until the builder complied with the arbitrator's order. The arbitrator then issued a second post-dated order (to give the builder an opportunity to consent, which he did not in fact take) providing now for only £500 security for costs, and effectively cancelling his previous order. The builder then wrote offering a bond for this sum, provided that the arbitration could be concluded within one month, but the arbitrator did not act on this suggestion, or forward it to the owner. Later he refused to supply a copy to the owner when she heard about the builders' letter, although eventually she did obtain a copy from the builder's solicitors.

The owner now applied to the President of the Institute under a provision in the Regulations for an order revoking the arbitrator's appointment, but before the application was heard the arbitrator, after consultations with officers of the Institute, made a third order, effectively cancelling both his previous orders, and returning to the owner the deposits previously paid by her with interest, but ordering immediate delivery of the further particulars. At the subsequent hearing before the Vice-President of the Institute the owner's application to revoke the arbitrator's appointment was then rejected. At that hearing, the arbitrator made the untrue allegation that the owner had required confirmation from him that her claim would be successful before agreeing to his fees on appointment. The owner immediately protested and denied this, and now applied to the Court for revocation of the arbitrator's authority under Section 13(3) of the 1950 Act (failure to use reasonable despatch) and Section 23(1) (misconduct of the arbitrator or of the proceedings).

Held, by Pain J., that by including his name in the Institute's Panel, the arbitrator had held himself out as a skilled arbitrator. Although he could not be liable for negligence, it could be misconduct to fail in important respects to show the elementary skill of an arbitrator. There had been a fundamental error on his part at the outset in failing to establish just what the arbitration agreement between the parties was. Later, when the builder refused to comply with the first order, various and quite tricky points of law arose as to how the order should be enforced.[59] At that stage the arbitrator could have taken proper legal advice as to his own position, and he could have indicated that he could not proceed further in the absence of agreement. In making his second order, the arbitrator may not have been deliberately unfair and was probably very muddled at the time, but in the circumstances, with his own knowledge that the builders lacked funds, it was grossly unfair to the owner to continue with the arbitration without the full security she had originally required as a condition of his appointment. The letter he had sent to the owner refusing to supply a copy of his letter from the builder was quite extraordinary. As to his third order requiring the arbitration to proceed with no security whatever, which had been said by him to have been advised by the Institute's officers, it was difficult to believe that he could be given advice to act so unfairly, and

---

[59] See the discussion *supra* as to this lacuna in the Acts in Section 1(3)(c), paras. 18·016–18·018, and for various suggested possible courses of action see *Mustill and Boyd* (2nd ed.), pp. 535 *et seq.*

there was nothing in writing confirming this advice. Finally, it would have been obvious to any fair minded person, following receipt of the owner's immediate letter of protest about his submissions to the Vice-President as to what she was alleged to have told him, that he had misunderstood her, and that it would have been easy for him to withdraw the allegation as he had been invited to do; but instead he had persisted in it at the oral hearing before the Vice-President of the Institute, and now by bringing evidence before the Court. In so doing he had further misconducted himself, and the right course was to remove him and order that the arbitration agreement should cease to have effect: *Pratt* v. *Swanmore Builders Ltd. and Baker* (1980).[60]

18·136   [Note: this case and judgment has been set out at unusual length because it affords illustrations of a number of successive examples of misconduct by an arbitrator in handling the proceedings; nor was the role played by the appointing body a particularly happy one.[60a] In one respect only, the arbitrator's position was a difficult one for which some sympathy can be felt. That arose from the lack of any clear indication or guidelines in section 12 of the 1950 Act, as supplemented on this point by section 5 of the 1979 Act, as to the powers of an arbitrator or the methods of enforcement or remedies available to the opposing party when a party fails to comply with an arbitrator's interlocutory orders.[61] The case also indicates the difficulties which can arise from incorporating the rules of arbitration bodies, unless these are very well drafted with the difficulties and lacunae in the arbitration legislation well understood. Thus, the draftsmen of rules conferring a power to order security or interim payments, as in this case, face the daunting task of specifying practical but fair machinery for their enforcement in the event of default. Otherwise attempts to use the powers are likely to be little more than cosmetic, if not a source of added difficulty for the parties, as they were in this case.]

18·137   (10) A dispute arose between electronics main contractor purchasers and engineering sub-contractor suppliers, who were to supply 10 vehicles suitably modified for conversion by the main contractors into mobile radio stations for a foreign government. The purchasers were dissatisfied with the standard of the vehicles delivered, and the dispute was the subject of a specific submission to an arbitrator to be appointed by the President of the (English) Chartered Institute of Arbitrators. The latter appointed a practicing barrister who was also a qualified engineer. The parties agreed with the barrister that he should act as arbitrator and not as conciliator; but that they would dispense with legal representation, and exchange written statements of their case and bundles of relevant documents prior to an oral hearing. They also agreed that relatively informal procedures could be used, including visits of the arbitrator to the supplier's works with freedom for him to make private inquiries of engineering personnel. Following the first meeting with the arbitrator, a written document was delivered by the suppliers to the arbitrator which presented the purchaser's performance and commercial behaviour in a very damaging light. No copy of this was made available to the purchasers, but during a subsequent oral hearing its existence became known, and the purchasers requested a copy of it; but when the suppliers objected that it also contained confidential pricing information the arbitrator ruled that it need not be disclosed, and the supplier, being without legal representation, accepted the ruling and continued the hearing. The arbitrator then made a first interim award, and following agreement that a second award should take account of all outstanding

---

[60] [1980] 2 Lloyd's Rep. 504.

[60a] Compare the Australian *Hooper Balie* case, see *ante*, para. 18·077.

[61] See this discussed *supra*, Section 1(3)(c), paras. 18·016 *et seq.*, and see *Mustill and Boyd* (2nd ed.), pp. 536 *et seq.* See also Peter Pain J.'s acknowledgement of these difficulties in [1980] 2 Lloyd's Rep. 504, 509.

matters of claim and counter-claim in one sum of money, his second award was for a round figure due to the supplier to take account of taxed costs, interest, and all claims and counter-claims (except for a liquidated damages delay claim which had been agreed would not be covered by the award). When asked for a breakdown of the overall figure, the arbitrator refused to supply it. The purchaser applied to set aside the award. *Held*, by Bingham J., applying statements of principle by Lord Langdale M.R. in *Harvey* v. *Shelton*[62]; by Lord Denman C.J. in *Dobson and Sutton* v. *Groves*[63]; and by Megaw J. in *Government of Ceylon* v. *Chandris*,[64] that to receive material representations without permitting the opposing party to have a copy was such a serious breach of a fundamental obligation ordinarily binding on any arbitrator that neither interim award could stand. The informal nature of the arbitration could not justify it. "A party who seeks, for understandable reasons, to dispense with the formalities of ordinary litigation should not without more be treated as wishing to dispense with the fundamental rules underlying the administration of all justice, however informal; and while the court should be slow to intermeddle with the procedural conduct of arbitrations, it has a responsibility to safeguard the ultimate integrity of the arbitration process."[65] No doubt many, but probably not all, the matters in the supplier's document had been canvassed before the arbitrator. But even if all of them had been, that would not have been the same as their notification in a coherent and effective document. Nor could the purchasers be said to have waived their rights because they had not made a formal protest and had accepted the arbitrator's ruling. They were without legal representation and believed that he was entitled to give the ruling. But *held* also, that the arbitrator could not be criticised for failing to give reasons for the details of his second award, since the parties had agreed that an overall sum should be awarded. However, on the main issue the proper order was not to remit the matter to the arbitrator, but to set the awards aside: *C.M.A. Maltin Engineering Ltd.* v. *J. Donne Holdings Ltd.* (1980).[66]

[Note: This judgment makes clear that neither the suppliers nor the arbitrator had acted in anything but good faith, and it was quite possible that all the matters contained in the document had been fully canvassed during the hearing before the arbitrator. However, from the point of view of the purchasers, there would be a real advantage in seeing the documents and complaints in advance in order to prepare their counter-arguments and case, and it is this factor, quite as much as a perceived breach of natural justice, which calls for the disclosure requirement to be stringently applied in all arbitrations, however informal.]

(11) Main contractors brought a claim for delay and defective work against sub-contractors under the FASS "Green Form" nominated sub-contract. A surveyor arbitrator was appointed by the President of the RICS under the terms of the sub-contract arbitration clause. On the issue of delay the architect had given a certificate under clause 8(*a*) of the sub-contract, and counsel for the main contractors in his opening address on the first day of the hearing deployed in detail his arguments why the arbitrator would not be bound by that architect's certificate, while counsel for the sub-contractors briefly confirmed that the matter was indeed in issue and gave a short outline of his prospective counter-arguments. After a day devoted to other matters, and

18·138

[62] (1844) 7 Beav. 455, 462.
[63] (1844) 6 A&E N.S. 637, 697.
[64] [1963] 1 Lloyd's Rep. 214, 225.
[65] *Per* Bingham J., (1980) 15 BLR, 61, 75.
[66] 15 BLR 61.

following an intervening adjournment, the arbitrator without any warning issued a signed document deciding that he did have jurisdiction to disregard the architect's certificate. The sub-contractors applied under section 23(1) for his removal, on the ground that he had misconducted the proceedings by arriving at a decision without having heard the sub-contractor's full arguments on the point. The arbitrator never at any time gave any reason or explanation of his action to the parties or to the Court, or any undertaking to reconsider the matter after full argument. The main contractors conceded that the arbitrator's decision in their favour was a breach of the rules of natural justice and that the interim award must be set aside, but the issue before the court was whether the arbitrator should be removed altogether, or whether the case should be remitted to him for his reconsideration under section 22 of the 1950 Act. Robert Goff J. had held that, applying the test whether the arbitrator had been shown not to be a fit and proper person to continue the proceedings, the question should be remitted to him. *Held*, by the Court of Appeal, allowing the appeal, that the test was whether the arbitrator's conduct was such as to destroy the confidence of the parties, or either of them, in his ability to come to a fair and just conclusion. Applying that test, the arbitrator should be removed, and the President of the RICS asked to appoint a new arbitrator: *Modern Engineering (Bristol) Ltd.* v. *C. Miskin & Sons Ltd.* (1980).[67]

[Note: As Lord Denning M.R. pointed out, this was not a case of the arbitrator misconducting himself in any moral sense, but of *misconduct of the proceedings*.[68] The factors weighing with the Court were, no doubt, the impression of inexperience amounting to incompetence created by the nature of the error made.[69] It is also clear that the fact that the arbitrator had not seen fit (it was said to the Court on advice, but if so on bad advice) to state or explain his position or his readiness to reconsider the matter, at least in a letter to the parties' solicitors, if not on affidavit, was clearly an important factor in the Court's decision not to remit. The Court made it clear that in cases such as this it was a useful practice for arbitrators to inform the Court by one means or another of their reasons for their actions.]

18·139   (12) An association of long leaseholders in a block of flats had serious complaints about the structure. Their contracts were with the builders, but under the English NHBC arrangements (whereby a degree of insurance was available), the Presidents of the RIBA and RICS jointly appointed an arbitrator under the terms of the arbitration clause who was a licensed architect and qualified surveyor and who had practised at the Bar for over 30 years after two years as a local authority Assistant Valuer. He had conducted over 200 arbitration disputes. The arbitration then continued with leave of the Court after the builders had gone into liquidation, but neither the liquidator nor the NHBC chose to be represented before the arbitrator, and the builders did not attend.

There was one "main arbitration" involving the leaseholders association as claimants, and certain "individual" arbitrations by individual lessees. Six witnesses were called for the claimants in the arbitrations, including four experts, namely a civil engineer, chartered surveyor, chartered quantity surveyor and chartered surveyor and valuer. The arbitrator first made an interim award as

---

[67] [1981] 1 Lloyd's Rep. 135.
[68] See s.23(1) 1950 Act.
[69] Premature decisions or awards of this kind are, in fact, quite common in construction arbitrations, however distinguished in other fields arbitrators may be—see, *e.g.* for a case of inadvertence *Marples Ridgeway & Partners* v. *C.E.G.B.* [1964] Q.B.D. (Special Paper) discussed *infra*, para. 18·168, and see *The Elissar* and *Asia Construction* cases illustrated *infra*.

to the precise extent of the builder's liability for the defects in the building, and it was intimated by the claimants that no case stated would be requested as to that award. The arbitrator then published a further interim award, in which he awarded £12,471 in the main arbitration (against £93,000 claimed), and £1,212 in one of the individual arbitrations (against £3,817 claimed). To reach such reductions there must have been major matters of criticism of the presentation of the claims, or the arbitrator must have had some scheme in mind for the necessary remedial works which differed from the experts', but the arbitrator had given no indication to the witnesses or counsel that he was rejecting the evidence or his reasons for doing so.

On receipt of the awards, the lessees in the main arbitration and individual arbitrations applied for the removal of the arbitrator on the ground of misconduct, or for the awards to be set aside, on the ground that the arbitrator had decided against the evidence, and had taken into account facts and matters contradicting the evidence without giving the claimants notice of or an opportunity of dealing with the same, so that he had failed to conduct the proceedings in accordance with the principles of natural justice. On this motion the NHBC now chose to appear and support the award on behalf of the builders.

In an affidavit to the Court, the arbitrator stated that he considered it was his duty where a party was unrepresented to protect their interests, and that he did not think it was his duty to indicate at the hearing that he did or did not accept particular evidence. In his opinion the claims were grossly exaggerated and a large part of them was a "try-on." *Held*, by the Court of Appeal, affirming the trial judge, that even though the arbitrator was clearly an expert, in arbitrations such as building contracts the arbitrator was not appointed to form his own opinion and act on his own knowledge without recourse to evidence given by witnesses on either side, and without the submission and guidance of advocates. *Per* Lord Denning M.R. the NHBC in choosing not to appear in the arbitration were the real authors of all the trouble. This had led the arbitrator into making a mistake. It was not the duty of the arbitrator to protect the interests of the unrepresented party or use his own knowledge to derogate from the evidence, at any rate without putting his own knowledge to them and giving them an opportunity to answer it. *Per* Dunn L.J., in order to reach the figures awarded the arbitrator must have had in mind a different scheme for the necessary remedial works; and, if so, natural justice required him to put his alternative scheme and costings to the experts to give them an opportunity for dealing with them. *Per* Lord Denning M.R., the arbitrator had misconducted the proceedings; *Per* Dunn and O'Connell L.JJ., the arbitrator had misconducted himself; and, *per* the whole Court, he should be removed: *Fox* v. *Wellfair Ltd.* (1981).[70]

[Note: There was much to be said for the arbitrator's view of his function, it is submitted, which would certainly have been that of a judge in a case where a party was not represented. His error, and a serious one, lay in remaining deliberately silent and not making clear to the experts his reasons for questioning their evidence. Had he done so, and then made an award disagreeing with their explanations, there could have been no complaint, it is submitted (particularly, as Lord Denning M.R. pointed out, since the NHBC as insurers had a legitimate interest entitling them to conduct the case in the builder's name but had chosen not to do so).]

(13) An arbitrator was required to decide between ship owners and charterers whether a delay to the ship had been caused by its inability to join a convoy in the Persian Gulf due to its low speed, or whether the cause was   **18·140**

---

[70] [1981] 2 Lloyd's Rep. 514.

mechanical defects and crew incompetence. By an agreement concluded by telex between the parties, a third argument by the shipowners, namely that the nominated port was not an accessible and safe port, was reserved for later evidence and was not dealt with at the hearing. The arbitrator forgot this, and made a monetary award in favour of the charterers, expressed to be final, although subject to a later award as to costs, but then added that if the decision had depended on whether or not the port was accessible or safe he would have found that it was. The ship owners applied to set aside the award and remove the arbitrator. The trial judge held that this was only a preliminary and tentative view, and that in the light of the Court's knowledge of the arbitrator himself the award should merely be remitted for reconsideration. *Held*, by the Court of Appeal, that in deciding whether to remit or remove, the proper test was the objective one, whether a reasonable person would think there was a real likelihood that the arbitrator would not fairly determine the safe port issue on the basis of the evidence. The trial judge had been wrong in thinking that the arbitrator's statement had been no more than a preliminary or tentative view. However, the arbitrator in a later telex had stated that he would determine the safe ports issue on the submissions and evidence, and the Court of Appeal would exercise its own discretion in favour of remitter and against removal in the same way as the judge had done: *Arda-halian* v. *Unifert International S.A., The Elissar* (1984).[71]

18·141   (14) Main contractors had terminated their contract for non-payment, and commenced proceedings against the owners in which the first substantive hearing was about to start. Most of the sub-contractors had agreed to defer claims until after the main contract arbitration had ended, but one of the sub-contractors brought proceedings against the main contractors which were then stayed, and failing agreement an arbitrator was subsequently appointed by the Singapore High Court in June 1987 for the sub-contract dispute. The arbitrator was a chartered surveyor and an ex-chairman of the (English) Chartered Institute of Arbitrators.

Before the arbitrator formally accepted his appointment, the main contractors' Singapore solicitors raised objection that the sub-contractors were represented by American attorneys, contrary to the Singapore Legal Profession Act. The arbitrator replied, without hearing the parties, that, while unfamiliar with the Act, it seemed to him very strange if such a submission was well-founded. During July 1987, when dates for a preliminary hearing were under discussion, the arbitrator made adverse comments about the sincerity of the main contractors' American lawyers' desire to be present, and responded acrimoniously when the main contractors' Singapore lawyers wrote formally reserving their client's position on the matter of the sub-contractors' Singapore representation. On July 27, the arbitrator wrote indicating a continuing difficulty in accepting the contractor's argument about Singapore representation, and intimated that if it proved unsuccessful, he would take this into account both in regard to fixing dates and awarding costs. On August 3, 1987, the arbitrator wrote a letter stating that the main contractor's Singapore solicitors "would appear to be consciously attempting to misrepresent the true position" about previous correspondence relating to the date of the preliminary hearing. He later apologised for this letter in writing, but made a number of points detracting from the apology in his letter.

On August 17, 1987, the contractors made an application to the High Court on the issue of Singapore representation (which was ultimately successful) and also for the removal of the arbitrator. Following the application for his removal, further events occurred. The arbitrator wrote a letter to the parties'

---

[71] [1984] 2 Lloyd's Rep. 84. Compare the *Marples Ridgeway* case, discussed *infra*, para. 18·168.

solicitors, commenting on the contractors' affidavit in support of their application to remove the arbitrator in terms of ridicule and using the epithet "stupid", and describing a purportedly hypothetical situation of a party's lawyer seeking to delay or postpone or abort a reference which closely resembled assertions by the sub-contractors against the main contractors made to him in the instant case. Later, when the main contractors delivered a defence in draft and at that stage took the point under the terms of the sub-contract that the arbitration was premature by virtue of an "early arbitration" inhibition in the contract,[72] it was agreed that the parties would make their submissions about this to the arbitrator, who would rule upon it. The arbitrator then took upon himself to write directly to the parties themselves, over the heads of their solicitors, stating that "there seems to be a risk of a possible denial of justice" and that the main contractors' lawyers' actions "are without doubt intended to delay, postpone, thwart, or prevent an arbitration taking place. This would defeat the provision in the [early arbitration] Clause 22 of the sub-contract for the procedure to be followed ..." Eventually on December 15, 1987, following receipt of the parties' submissions on the Clause 22 point, the arbitrator now declined to make any ruling "as in so doing I could not avoid ruling on my own jurisdiction." He then described the contractor's arguments as "persuasive but not overwhelmingly so", and stated that he proposed to leave the matter to the High Court to decide, but meanwhile proposed to continue the substantive arbitration, on the assumption that he had jurisdiction, until ordered not to do so. Despite these statements, at a further preliminary hearing on January 13, 1988, the arbitrator refused to give his consent, which was necessary under the Singapore Arbitration legislation, to an application to the Court for a ruling on the clause 22 early arbitration point which he had previously declined to decide.

Following this, when fixing a date for the substantive hearing itself, the arbitrator suggested three sets of dates, two of which he knew conflicted with the main contractors' arbitration against the owner, when the same counsel and witnesses could not possibly be available in both places at once. Finally there was an acrimonious exchange of correspondence in which the contractor's solicitors asked him to refrain from further unpleasant remarks and the arbitrator replied refusing to accede to this request.

On the main contractors' application for his removal: *Held*, by Chao Hick Tin J.C., that the test to be applied on such an application was the "reasonable suspicion" test—would a reasonable fair minded person have a reasonable suspicion that a fair trial for the applicant was not possible—rather than the so-called "real likelihood" test[72a]; and that in relation to the events up to the time of the application to revoke in August 1987, there was a reasonable suspicion of bias. The arbitrator did not seem able to restrain himself from entering the fray. He seemed prone to make premature utterances without hearing the parties. His language was far from measured and sarcastic to the point of being hostile. Even without the later events after the motion to remove, he had misconducted himself and the proceedings. In his letter to the parties' solicitors commenting on the contractors' affidavit, the arbitrator had resorted to ridicule and taken points unbefitting to an arbitrator, and his "hypothetical situation" really referred to the present case. Despite the earlier issue by the Singapore High Court of an interim injunction on the question of Singapore representation, he had continued to suggest that it was an unmeritorious attempt to delay proceedings. His subsequent correspondence, and in particular his letter to the parties themselves, showed hostility,

---

[72] See *supra*, Section 2(4)(b), para. 18·044, and the case of *Smith* v. *Martin* [1925] 1 K.B. 745 there discussed.

[72a] As to this see *infra*, para. 18·147.

and was probably targeted at the sub-contractors' solicitors for not taking a sufficiently strong stand against the main contractors, particularly on the early arbitration point. Later the arbitrator, having agreed to receive submissions on this point himself, misconducted the proceedings when he declined to decide himself while at the same time refusing consent to its being referred to the High Court. This was also evidence that he was not acting fairly. Offering two out of three sets of dates which conflicted with the main arbitration, and the refusal to refrain from further unpleasant remarks, also prevented faith in his impartiality. On both the issues raised by the contractors, namely the Singapore representation issue and the early arbitration issue, his approach gave the impression of being adversarial. Not only had it been amply established that there was reasonable suspicion of bias, it had been shown there was a real likelihood of bias. Besides bias, two separate grounds for his removal were his conclusion that there were no merits in the clause 22 early arbitration issue in the early stages before hearing the parties, and his refusal to consent to the clause 22 issue being referred to the Court: *Turner (East Asia) Pte. Ltd.* v. *Builders Federal (Hong Kong) Ltd.* (1988).[73]

18·142   (15) At a meeting in Hong Kong, five days before the hearing of the arbitration of a contractor's claim for extensions of time was due to commence, the owner asked for a preliminary issue to be ordered, which the contractors objected to, on the ground that the issue would take 12 days to decide. The arbitrator obtained further information from the parties on the following day, when the contractors stated that if the preliminary issue was ordered a three-day adjournment would be needed to prepare for the issue. Two days before the hearing the arbitrator purported to issue an interim award deciding the issue. He also declined to adjourn the hearing on the first day of the hearing though he did do so on the second day. Before the Court, the arbitrator offered to reconsider the matter and reopen his award, but stated that he did not consider that there had been any breach of the rules of natural justice: *Held*, by Bokhary Deputy J. that there had been a serious violation of a basic rule of natural justice, and the arbitrator should be removed and the award set aside. Applying the "real likelihood" test formulated by Ackner L.J. in *The Elissar*,[74] a reasonable man might have been less apprehensive that the question would be fairly determined on the evidence and arguments had the arbitrator fully recognised his error immediately: *Asia Construction Co.* v. *Crown Pacific Ltd.* (1988).[75]

18·143   (16) An arbitrator who was an architect and quantity surveyor and Fellow of the (English) Chartered Institute of Arbitrators was nominated by the President of the RIBA to settle a dispute between contractors and developers over the alleged inadequacy of three interim certificates. On receipt of points of claim, the arbitrator wrote to the parties that in his view the involvement of counsel was not justifiable, and that the dispute related to quantity surveying practice and procedure. Later he suggested that the hearing should consist of meetings between himself and the parties' technical representatives, particularly their quantity surveyors; but the developers protested and required a hearing with oral evidence, cross-examination and speeches. The arbitrator then directed a technical meeting, with lawyers attending only as observers, apparently in order to form a preliminary view. He held four of such meetings, while the developer's solicitors repeated their requirement that there eventually be a formal hearing. He then published a detailed and substantial 70 page document entitled "Provisional Findings Not an Award", which

[73] 42 BLR 128.
[74] [1984] 2 Lloyd's Rep. 84, 89.
[75] 44 BLR 135.

referred to specific findings he had made, and asked the parties "if they wished to make any further submissions before I make my award." The developers then applied for his removal. *Held*, by Sir William Stabb Q.C., adopting statements of principle in *Mustill and Boyd*,[76] that an arbitrator is required to adopt an adversarial rather than inquisitorial procedure, and that the arbitrator should be removed. There had never been a proper hearing, and the arbitrator had adopted an inquisitorial procedure. The parties agreed that he would find it almost impossible to retreat from his "Preliminary View" document in the light of his express findings, and he had virtually reached a final conclusion without resorting to a proper hearing. The principles in arbitrations of a domestic nature or in quality arbitrations which the arbitrator appeared to have followed had no application to the present case. The parties had never agreed to them, and the developers had constantly protested, expecting that he would allow a full hearing, and could not be said to have waived their rights: *Town & City Properties (Development) Ltd.* v. *Wiltshier Southern Ltd.* (1988).[77]

(17) An arbitrator in New South Wales exercised a power under section 20 **18·144** of the Australian Commercial Arbitration Act to order no legal representation in a building dispute. The owner, who had no technical knowledge, took a building consultant and expert with him to the hearing, but the arbitrator refused to allow him to be present to advise the owner until he gave evidence as an expert witness, and in reply to objections said he would himself explain technical matters to the owner in the expert's absence. Several adjournments were needed to enable the owner to consult his advisers, which he had some difficulty in doing due to his lack of understanding. After the owner's expert had given evidence the arbitrator permitted him to stay in the hearing room, but when seen to be taking notes he was ordered, following an application by the builder, to move away from the owner and not to speak to him. At the conclusion of the hearing the owner asked, as he was entitled to do under the statute, for reasons for the award to be stated, to which the arbitrator replied that, if the owner insisted on this, the builder would have to be given the opportunity to give still more evidence. On an application to remove the arbitrator for misconduct, reliance was placed first on the exclusion of the owner's expert from the hearing room, secondly on the separation of the owner from his expert preventing him for consulting him, and thirdly on the arbitrator's reply to the request for reasons, which it was contended showed both bias and that the proceedings had been improperly conducted to date. *Held*, by Hunt J. that with legal representatives excluded it was all the more important that a layman pitted against a builder should have the assistance of an expert. In courts of law experts were permitted to assist solicitors at a hearing. On that basis alone, there had been misconduct. Additionally, there was no innocent explanation for the reply to the owner's request for reasons to be given, since there was no possible reason why different evidence should have been given when it was not anticipated that reasons would be requested. Taken in combination, the arbitrator had misconducted himself in a pejorative sense, and had done so disgracefully, and he should be removed and the amount of his fees refunded to the parties: *Traynor* v. *Panan Contractors Ltd.* (1988).[78]

(18) Main contractors proceeded by way of arbitration against developers **18·145** (Laings) for loss and expense due to delay. Laings, if liable, wished to join their architects ("D.L.G.") and claim an indemnity or damages for breach of

---

[76] (2nd ed.) p. 299.
[77] 44 BLR 114.
[78] 7 A.C.L.R. 47.

contract or negligence. The main contract contained an arbitration clause
providing for appointment of an arbitrator, failing agreement, by the President of the RIBA. The architect's contract contained an arbitration clause
with appointment by the Vice-President of the Chartered Institute of Arbitrators. The president of the RIBA had already appointed the main contract
arbitrator. Laings then brought proceedings in the courts against the main
contractors (for a declaration that they had no right to an extension of time or
to loss and expense) and against the architects, but both defendants applied to
stay the action, which Laings resisted in an endeavour to secure tri-partite
litigation before one tribunal, but Laings were unsuccessful.[79] Laings then
applied to the Institute of Arbitrators to appoint the same arbitrator, and the
Institute, *without consulting D.L.G.'s solicitors, though the Institute knew that
they had objected*, on the following day did appoint the same arbitrator as in
the main contract.

At an initial meeting of the parties in the architect arbitration in February
1991, before points of claim had been received by Laings in the contractors'
arbitration, the arbitrator intimated there would be a further meeting to
decide on procedure when points of claim were received. However, on March
8 without warning, he ordered delivery of the points of claim by Laings
against D.L.G. by April 15, with points of defence four weeks thereafter in
May, and points of reply four weeks thereafter in June. On March 20,
D.L.G.'s new solicitors confirmed that they were taking counsel's opinion on
the question of the arbitrator's jurisdiction. On March 27, points of claim in
the contractors' arbitration were received by Laings, and on April 15, they
served their own points of claim in the architect arbitration. The points of
claim against the architects were seriously deficient and required massive particularisation in order to make clear the allegations against D.L.G.[80] On April
23, D.L.G.'s solicitors notified the arbitrator that counsel's opinion on the
arbitrator's jurisdiction had not yet been received, but on May 10, D.L.G.'s
solicitors wrote again, now accepting his appointment.

Both the contractors and the architects had throughout taken the position
that they would not agree to one arbitration, but required separate sequential
arbitrations. D.L.G.'s Points of Defence were delivered only four days late on
May 21, with a request for further particulars. D.L.G. pointed out that the
points of claim were wholly unparticularised. The arbitrator immediately
wrote a letter to Laing's solicitors saying he expected them to furnish the
particulars within 14 days "because of the considerable delays occasioned by
D.L.G.", and emphasised the importance of adhering to the original timetable. (The judge held that this statement blaming D.L.G. had no foundation
and in fact there had been very little delay.) On May 22, D.L.G.'s solicitors
wrote to the arbitrator explaining the difficulties created for D.L.G. by two
consecutive arbitrations with the same arbitrator as being the reasons why
they had objected to the arbitrator's jurisdiction originally. On June 4, the
arbitrator wrote suggesting that by consent the issues should be dealt with at
one hearing, and repeated a previous observation that difficulties within the
building industry required an award as soon as possible. (The judge held that
there had now developed a continuing obsession on the part of the arbitrator
to adhere to the rigid and compressed timetable he had originally imposed on
the parties.)[80a]

---

[79] It may be surmised on the basis of the *City Centre Properties* and other cases illustrated and
doubted *supra*, para. 18·113–18·115.
[80] Compare the facts in *Wharf Properties Ltd.* v. *Eric Cumine Associates (No. 2)* (1991) 52
BLR 1; *McAlpine Humberoak Ltd.* v. *McDermott International Inc.* (1992) 58 BLR 1.,
illustrated *ante*, paras. 8·207 and 8·210, and see *infra*, 18·159–18·160.
[80a] Compare the *Gas and Fuel Corporation of Victoria* case *supra*.

When D.L.G. agreed without objection to a request by Laings for a further 14 days for the delivery of further particulars the arbitrators sharply rebuked Laings, citing the contractor's arbitration as a reason "why it was essential for all parties to rigorously adhere to the strict timetable." Obviously incomplete further particulars were then supplied on June 20 by Laings, but the arbitrator, without referring to the parties, then ordered delivery of D.L.G.'s defence and counter-claim by July 11, in accordance with his original order for directions. D.L.G.'s solicitors replied pointing out, correctly, that the original directions had been sent out unilaterally and without consent, despite a previous indication from the arbitrator that there would be a further meeting before any such order. They now requested that meeting, and pointed out that the further and better particulars supplied by Laings added nothing of significance to the original defective points of claim. The arbitrator replied (wrongly as the judge found) that "adequate time had been provided through many weeks" and that the pleadings were to proceed as ordered. He again referred to "unnecessarily high costs" likely to be incurred "by your continued choice of inactivity" (described by the judge as "quite unfair and a most unfortunate expression for an arbitrator") and that "such delays in the present national conditions of the building industry are inexcusable." There was no indication that the arbitrator had given any consideration to the adequacy of the further particulars.

The solicitors protested in moderate language on July 3, and repeated their request for an urgent meeting (for which counsel on both sides were available on July 11). The arbitrator ignored the convenience of the July 11 date, and without explanation instead ordered a meeting for the first week of August. Laing's solicitors then suggested to D.L.G.'s solicitors that lists should be exchanged by July 26, that inspection should take place during August, and that there should be a meeting in September, copying this letter to the arbitrator. On July 16, the arbitrator, without any communication with D.L.G.'s solicitors, abandoned the August meeting and adopted Laings' proposals, ordering lists by July 26, and inspection by August 9. D.L.G. again protested. On August 14, without inquiring whether counsel were available, the arbitrator ordered details of lists by August 23, and completion of the defence by the same date, and with no regard to the justifiable complaint as to the total inadequacy of Laings' pleaded case.

In September, at a further meeting, the arbitrator again suggested a single arbitration, notwithstanding the contractors' and architects' continued refusals of this, and also a hearing in late December with a duration of six weeks, noting that the contractor's arbitration had been fixed for early December. In October he ordered a timetable leading to a hearing date in early February 1992, which implicitly rejected D.L.G.'s fully justified request for further particulars. However, on December 17, the contractors' arbitration was settled, and on December 18, Laing's amended their points of claim to sue, now, for an indemnity in the amount of that settlement in place of damages. They then on January 8 and 24 furnished lists, in addition to their first list of 7,000 documents in the previous August, of a further 30,000 documents.

The settlement of the main contract arbitration of course meant, as pointed out by the judge, that all considerations of building industry cash flow urgency, even if they had ever been relevant, had now been removed. By letter of December 11, Laing's requested mid-February 1992, against a later date requested by D.L.G., for an expert's report; put forward January 1992 as an *agreed date* for witness statements, and June 1992 as an *agreed hearing date*. The arbitrator in his reply on January 3, 1992, rejected these dates, ordering experts' reports by January 17, witness statements by January 20, and mid-February for the hearing. Later the arbitrator, without reference to D.L.G., for the second time adopted a series of slightly modified dates proposed by Laings. The arbitrator then refused a meeting to discuss the discovery problems resulting from the additional 30,000 documents. On January 24, D.L.G. wrote a formal letter asking for a meeting and adjournment of the now fixed hearing date of March 2; for additional time to deal with discovery; for an order for specific discovery of missing documents not supplied; and for the order for further and better particulars. All these were rejected by the arbitrator, who stated that the discovery difficulties were due to D.L.G.'s unwillingness to comply with his orders or directions, and that the points of claim was sufficiently explicit. D.L.G. then applied for his removal under section 21. In a letter to the Court the arbitrator repeated his charges that D.L.G.'s legal advisers had "continually sought to disrupt and delay the preparation and submissions of particulars, and also referring to "many months of non-co-operation by the architect's agents." He added that "arbitration, as with the law, is seriously suffering from unnecessarily high costs and delays not disconnected at times with legal contrivance. My orders had been deliberately not carried out and ignored by the legal advisers."

Held, by Gatehouse J. that to assert that D.L.G.'s solicitors or counsel, in pressing for proper particulars, declining to plead positively in the absence of those particulars, and in asking for more time to complete the discovery process and proper preparation of their case, were guilty of contumacious legal contrivance was unjustified and unfair. The history showed that proper consideration had not been given to the architects in the preparations for the arbitration. On the whole history, D.L.G.'s attitude had been reasonable. The latest and perhaps most serious complaint was the arbitrator's refusal to postpone the hearing date despite the fact that D.L.G. was simply not ready for a hearing. The arbitrator had unjustifiably pointed the finger at the architects and repeatedly accused them unfairly of deliberate delay, and had paid no proper regard to their objections. Applying Ackner L.J.'s test in *The Elissar*, there were grounds for a reasonable person to think that there was a real likelihood that the arbitrator could or would not fairly determine the issues in the arbitration on the basis of the evidence and the documents adduced before him, and he must be removed: *Damond Lock Grabowski* v. *Laing Investments (Bracknell) Ltd.* (1992).[81]

18·146

[Note: The facts of this case, which in many respects are very similar to those in the *Gas and Fuel Corporation of Victoria* and *Turner (East Asia)* cases, afford a startlingly close illustration of the attitudes which it has been suggested elsewhere are being increasingly shown by arbitrators in construction disputes.[82] Their principal characteristics are: (a) a readiness of arbitrators to override the wishes and convenience of *both* parties in regard to procedural matters, including particularly the dates of meetings or adjournment; (b) the fixing of wholly inadequate and unrealistic short timetables for various interlocutory steps, including particularly delivery of defence documents; (c) the constantly reiterated pressure for an early hearing date; (d) repeated decisions taken without giving sufficient opportunity for representations to be made by the party affected; (e) the failure to detect or understand the vital significance of inadequately particularised claims or defences, and the difficulties in which this can place an opposing party with a good case; (f) the reaching of hasty and unjustified and often quite wrong conclusions as to the merits from the pleadings or from the course of events during the interlocutory process; and (g) an almost total inability to understand the practical difficulties involved in the preparation of his case which

---

[81] 60 BLR 112.
[82] See the editor's "Deficiencies in Current International Arbitration Practice in Construction Cases," (1991) 7 Arb. Int. 149.

can be inflicted on a party in the right by such attitudes. To this may be added, as in the *Turner* and *Pratt* cases, and the *Gas and Fuel* case in Australia, a surprising readiness to make unfounded charges, and to draw adverse inferences without any adequate evidence to support them, and the use of intemperate language. With regard to the above case, it should be borne in mind that it was one where the allegations were serious ones of professional negligence against a firm of architects where, as in the *Cumine* case, claims by contractors had been settled and precise and quite different particularisation of the negligence alleged against the architects would be needed if indemnification was to be obtained. It is interesting to note from the cases that the conduct of appointing bodies has often been unhelpful (see also *supra*, para. 18·077) and that the bias shown is almost invariably against defendants, and in particular owners disputing payment.]

The above cases have been illustrated in much more than usual detail in the belief that they afford useful guidance at many points as to the attitudes and conduct which arbitrators should either avoid or display. The reports themselves will repay careful re-reading *in extenso*. They show that conduct, viewed as a whole and with perhaps no particular incident by itself amounting to outright misconduct, can reach a point where a reasonable suspicion of lack of impartiality or bias, and sometimes of incompetence, will justify removal. Alternatively, a single specific act or omission may be so fundamentally flawed as to justify setting aside an award and removal of the arbitrator rather than remitter. Such acts or omissions of an arbitrator may either be "misconduct of himself" or "misconduct of the proceedings" within the meaning of section 23(1) of the 1950 Act. The latter expression no doubt applies to many situations where no personal criticism of the arbitrator is justified, but where the nature of his error is such that an award cannot stand, so that faced with a choice between removal and remitter, sufficient confidence has been lost to justify the former and more drastic remedy.   **18·147**

The well researched and careful Singapore judgment of Chao J.C. in the *Turner (East Asia)* case illustrated *supra*, which contains a full review of the authorities, shows, despite the language of some of the English cases, that in recent years the acid test for removal has been re-defined in favour of a "reasonable suspicion" rather than "real likelihood" basis, if so making removal somewhat easier for an applicant to justify. There had in fact been earlier authority in 1976 in the High Court of Australia (where a judge's conduct was under review) to the same effect: "The question is whether it has been established that it *might reasonably be suspected by fair minded persons* that [he] might not resolve the question before him with a fair and unprejudiced mind."[83] The *Turner* and *Gas & Fuel* judgments are also useful in identifying at a number of points indiscreet language and conduct by an arbitrator, and in indicating by contrast what a more correct approach would have been.

---

[83] *Per* Barwick C.J., giving a joint judgment in *R.* v. *Watson* (1976) 9 A.L.R. 551. See also Cozens-Hardy M.R.'s statements, on facts not dissimilar to those in the *Turner East Asia* case, in *Re Enoch and Zaretzky, Bock & Co.'s Arbitration* [1910] 1 K.B. 327, cited in both the *Turner (East Asia)* and *Pratt* cases *supra*. For a full discussion of the Australian authorities see also *Gas Fuel Corporation of Victoria* v. *Wood Hall Ltd.* [1978] V.R. 385 (Marks J.).

18·148   The cases establish, it is submitted, the following propositions namely:

   (a) That perhaps the most cardinal error an arbitrator can commit is to
       receive communications, in whatever form, from one side which
       are not communicated to the other,[84] or to defeat a party's expec-
       tations by depriving him of the opportunity to make his sub-
       missions or to deal with an adverse opinion or criticism.[85]
       An opportunity to make representations before all interlocu-
       tory decisions must be afforded, and the more recent reported
       cases show arbitrators constantly ignoring this fundamental
       requirement.
   (b) That construction disputes as a class rarely if ever justify a "quality"
       or "commodities" arbitration approach, so that the arbitrator, how-
       ever experienced or qualified, must be prepared to hold a proper
       hearing with both parties present, to receive submissions, and to
       hear witnesses and to apply the law,[86] unless there is agreement to
       the contrary.

18·149   (c) That the arbitrator must be prepared to leave the broad conduct of
       the proceedings to the parties themselves, (assuming that they are
       adequately represented), and it will be for them to consider and
       choose their opposing positions on any matter, whether pro-
       cedural, or substantive, or of law, or of fact. This "adversarial"
       philosophy of the dispute process is all the more essential in the
       case of an arbitrator as opposed to a judge, since the entire basis of
       an arbitrator's jurisdiction is essentially consensual. Aggressively
       taking command or initiating investigative inquiries unilaterally—
       that is, an inquisitorial attitude—will always involve a risk of re-
       moval, as will excessive pressure for haste or to shorten a hearing.[87]
       These tendencies are commonly encountered in arbitrators in con-
       struction disputes at the present day, not least amongst those
       appointed from the panels of arbitration institutions.[88]
   (e) The cases also show that straightforward errors, due to failure to
       keep a proper note of developments during the proceedings or of
       the submissions of the parties, appear to be comparatively common
       in all fields of arbitration.[89] Where such mistakes occur, conscien-
       tious arbitrators should admit them at once to the parties and

---

[84] For a further Australian case on this see *McInnes* v. *Hall* (1988) 7 A.C.L.R. 37, illustrated
   infra, Section 5(3)(c), para. 18·164.
[85] *Micklethwait* v. *Mullock*, see *supra*; *Maltin Engineering Ltd.* v. *J. Donne Holdings Ltd.*; and
   see the reasoning in *Fox* v. *P.G. Wellfair Ltd.*
[86] *Fox* v. *Wellfair Ltd.*; *Town & City Properties (Development) Ltd.* v. *Wiltshier.*
[87] *Turner (East Asia) Pte. Ltd.* v. *Builders Federal (Hong Kong) Ltd. Town & City Properties
   (Development) Ltd.* v. *Wiltshier*; and see *Fox* v. *Wellfair Ltd.* This is now an increasing fault
   of construction arbitrators—see (1991) 7 Arb. Int. 149.
[88] *Ibid.*
[89] Compare the *Miskin, Elissar,* and *Asia Construction* cases, see *supra*.

seek their co-operation and agreement, wherever possible, as to the best method of dealing with them. They should never seek to obstruct and indeed should facilitate and adjourn to await the result of any bona fide applications to the court, unless satisfied that delay will seriously prejudice a party who expresses a desire to continue, or that the application is either not bona fide or has little or no prospect of success.[90]

SECTION 5. PROCEDURE IN ARBITRATIONS

(1) Generally

Undoubtedly the main reason for the popularity of arbitration in the past has been the fact that parties may have had greater confidence in a tribunal, when the subject matter of the dispute is almost entirely technical, if the tribunal itself is technically qualified and experienced in the same field. There is no doubt that in principle the fact that a tribunal may be technically qualified can restrain the exuberance of the parties and of their expert witnesses and induce a greater degree of caution in their evidence than a tribunal perceived to be less qualified. This applies particularly in quality or commodity arbitrations. On the other hand, in those construction disputes which do involve technical expert evidence, the degree of specialisation in the industry is such that A/E arbitrators will often not have direct specialist expertise themselves in the area of technical dispute. **18·150**

However, in building and engineering disputes the relevant documentation can often be massive,[91] both on liability or *quantum*, and the relative informality of arbitration proceedings can sometimes, although not perhaps so often as is thought, reduce the expense of copying and preparing documentary evidence in the form usually required by the courts, although short cuts will usually require the co-operation and agreement of the parties' legal advisers if an award is not to be imperilled.

On the other hand, the inexperience of technical arbitrators in sifting and weighing evidence can be a much more serious disadvantage, even in reaching findings of fact, than laymen usually realise, and in the absence of a high degree of restraint and fairness by the parties' legal or other representatives (regrettably not always present), an arbitrator who is not an experienced lawyer can be placed in a very difficult position if the rules of evidence or procedure are flouted by the parties' representatives during the hearing, since inevitably he will be in no position to judge with real confidence between legal submissions or objections in procedural matters, and may be quite unaware of the failures or omissions of a party to comply with proper evidentiary or procedural requirements, or of their

---

[90] Compare the *Turner (East Asia)* case. See also the *Carlisle Place Investments* case, *infra*, para. 18·163.
[91] See, *e.g. The Fuel and Gas Corporation* and *Damond Lock Grabowski* cases *supra*, paras. 18·134 and 18·145.

significance and the valuable inferences of fact or credit which can properly be drawn from them.

18·151   Arbitrators of great note in their own field can also have understandable difficulty in analysing the underlying reasons for rules of substantive
or procedural law, and can give way to impulses of sympathy or compromise producing anomalous and sometimes startling results. This instinct
for compromise, and a reluctance to hold a claim wholly valid or invalid, is
one of the most serious faults of non-legal arbitrators; it can work great
injustice, and is perhaps the greatest single factor encouraging a policy or
unrealistically low competitive tendering by contractors in order to secure
a construction contract balanced by the subsequent presentation of exaggerated or unjustified claims. By contrast with this tendency to make
compromise awards or findings, a surprisingly overbearing attitude in the
conduct of their proceedings has become noticeable of recent years, particularly among a class of English arbitrators in the construction field, in
which even the agreed submissions or positions of both parties can be
ignored and overridden—for example, in regard to the timetable for
pleadings and for adjournments and hearing dates, as some of the cases
illustrated in Section 4 *supra*, have shown. This, coupled with the inexperience of non-legal arbitrators in regard to pleadings and the interlocutory
stages of litigation, can lead to quite wrong conclusions being drawn from
submissions made by the parties at that stage, and to disastrously wrong
and premature assessments of the merits and then to unfair and unreasonable interlocutory decisions prejudicing the justice of the dispute.[92]

Undoubtedly arbitration proceedings have what is sometimes the
extremely important advantage from the point of view of at least one and
sometimes both of the parties, of privacy. Against this, some classes of
litigant will undoubtedly find arbitration much less attractive than in the
past since the 1979 Act and the subsequent Nema guidelines, and of the
obstacles so created against even well founded and meritorious appeals on
a point of law.

18·152   It should also be borne in mind that owing to the practice of the High
Court for many years of referring nearly all building and civil engineering
disputes to an Official Referee for trial, the English Official Referees possess a very considerable knowledge and expertise in building and civil
engineering problems and practice. Moreover, trial by an Official Referee
or judge is usually a cheaper means of settling disputes than arbitration
proceedings (since the arbitrator's fees have to be paid for and accommodation rented for the arbitration), while, as in the case of arbitrations, the
only appeal allowed is upon a point of law, except in cases of fraud or
professional negligence. Overseas equally experienced construction judiciaries are to be found or are now coming into existence in response to

---

[92] See particularly the recent misconduct cases of *Turner (East Asia)* v. *Builders Federal*,
   Town & City Properties v. *Wiltshier*, and *Damond Lock Grabowski* v. *Laing Investments*,
   illustrated *supra*, Section 4(3), and the somewhat earlier, but closely comparable *Fuel and
   Gas Corporation of Victoria* case in Australia.

demand. In the United States, of course, the Court of Claims is a jurisdiction of long standing and great experience,[93] and specialist judiciaries of high quality are now to be found in New South Wales, for example, and in Hong Kong and Canada.

A discussion of the advantages and disadvantages of arbitration in 1986, prior to some of the later reported misconduct cases, is to be found in C.C.P.P.,[94] and of emerging difficulties in the conduct of construction arbitrations in 1991 in Arbitration International,[95] for which considerable support is apparent, it is submitted, in the later misconduct cases illustrated in Section 4(3) *supra*.

(2) Nature of Construction Disputes

It does not seem to be appreciated by many arbitrators that construction **18·153** contracts give rise to disputes of unusual difficulty and complexity even by comparison with other types of litigation. The contracts themselves are, like so many commercial contracts, lengthy and often badly drafted, and fail to address with clarity problems and disputes of the most everyday character. In some cases the contract terms represent compromise between opposing interests reconciled to ambiguous wording designed to give each interest some argument in support of its position. In other cases the draftsmanship is excessively archaic or legalistic, or seeks to conceal unattractive objectives in deliberately obscure wording. All this makes for contested interpretations even on everyday and mundane matters.

Moreover, performance of the contracts runs over much longer periods than most other forms of commercial contract, with potential scope for argument and financial disagreement arising constantly during the construction period, and with large sums of money and cash flow pressures involved on both sides (and not, as is so often suggested, on one side alone).

In major projects a massive contemporary documentation, with many letters written by both sides daily on numerous different topics, is quite normal. Thus, in one misconduct case where the arbitrator was later held by the judge to have been obsessed with adherence to his originally fixed hearing date, no less than 30,000 documents were disclosed by one side at a very late stage in addition to an earlier 7,000.[96] Examination of the entire history of the contract, virtually on a day-to-day basis, is very frequently essential in order to determine liability (for example, whether drawings have been delivered on time, or whether interruption of possession has caused disruption of progress, or where extensions of time are in dispute),

---

[93] With a far more developed jurisprudence in regard to the *quantum* of construction claims than the English or Commonwealth judiciaries, for example.

[94] Paras. 7–47—48.

[95] See the editor's "Deficiencies of Current International Arbitration Practice in Construction Cases" (1991) 7 Arb. Int. 149.

[96] *Damond Lock Grabowski* v. *Laing Investments* (1992) 60 BLR 112, illustrated *supra*, Section 4(3), para. 18·145.

and almost always in determining *quantum* (where delay or disturbance causing loss to the contractor is frequently in issue) whether under compensatory provisions such as variation clauses, or as damages for breach of contract.

18·154   Added to this, the industry is highly litigious, with little apparent regard for long-term goodwill, and contemporary correspondence on both sides and over long periods may need to be cross-examined to in detail against other contemporary records in order to determine whether it should be discounted as specious and unreliable. It is also of the nature of the industry that claims are often only finally pressed to arbitration after disputes on the final account at the end of the project cannot be resolved, at a time when witnesses have dispersed elsewhere and may be difficult to trace or interest in the dispute.

All these factors combine to make the task of advisers in dealing with an exaggerated or unjustified claim, or in rebutting a specious and unjustified defence, exceptionally difficult and time consuming by comparison with other types of litigation. Many arbitrators seem totally unaware of these exigencies, and order unrealistic dates for delivery of defence statements, or for replies to a defence or counter-claim (often arrived at by uncritical adoption of judicial pronouncements made in the context of far simpler types of dispute, such as personal injuries claims), and in preparing time-tables for the various interlocutory stages of a construction dispute. Again, the massive and often very difficult task of legal advisers in the later interlocutory stages when exchanging documents, where experience shows that almost every contemporary document in the parties' possession may be potentially relevant on liability or *quantum*, does not seem to be understood by technically qualified arbitrators (and even by some judges), nor the very great value of patient and thorough discovery in arriving at the truth in a construction dispute.[97]

(3) Conduct of the Arbitration

(a) Prior to acceptance of appointment

(i) *Jurisdiction*

18·155   It is of cardinal importance that, at the earliest possible stage after receiving an invitation to act, an arbitrator should take steps to ascertain and record exactly what his jurisdiction is intended by the parties to be, and in particular precisely what areas of dispute are being referred to him. Most importantly, he should ascertain whether there are agreed areas for

---

[97] See "Deficiencies of Current International Arbitration Practice," (1991) 7 Arb. Int. 149, and see Gatehouse J.'s interesting comparison of the periods of time assessed by official reports on litigation in the County Court in England with the periods of time being allowed by the arbitrator in the far more complex professional negligence dispute in the *Damond Lock Grabowski* case (1992) 60 BLR 112, 128–9.

dispute or whether, notwithstanding his appointment, there are any disputed areas of jurisdiction, or any such areas on the extent of which he will
be requested to rule. Mere perusal or interpretation of an original arbitration clause or subsequent submission may not be the end of the matter,
since the parties can and often do expressly or impliedly extend any original jurisdiction under an arbitration clause on an ad hoc basis.[98] Many
arbitrators frequently fail to recognise the need for a careful and meticulous approach at this stage, with sometimes disastrous results.[99]

(ii) *Remuneration*

A more mundane but necessary matter is to secure agreement on the   **18·156**
arbitrator's fees. Construction arbitrations can be of unpredictable
length, and the massive detail often involved can call for long periods of
professional and other time to be committed to a major arbitration, if the
arbitrator's duty is to be conscientiously performed, and for the necessary
amount of professional time to be allocated and set aside in advance for
this purpose. Thus, arbitrators have been held entitled in such cases to
require substantial commitment fees.[1]

The remuneration of arbitrators is virtually a subject in itself, and
beyond the scope of the present book.[2] However, it may be relevant to
point out that the ICC has recently adopted a policy of paying a fixed fee to
arbitrators irrespective of the length of the hearing. In the context of construction litigation, this seems unwise, and indeed to militate against the
interests of whichever party is in the right and assist the party in the wrong.
This is because it is a more difficult and demanding task for advisers to
refute and expose in detail an unmeritorious or exaggerated claim or
defence, often expressed in an insufficiently particularised statement of
case, than it is simply to advance and assert such unparticularised claims or
defences in the mouths of interested witnesses or parties.[3] Whether or not
as a result, there have recently been quite extraordinary restrictions
placed upon the length of hearings and on the time available for presenting evidence or cross examination of witnesses by some ICC arbitrators,
which if English law were to apply would certainly warrant their removal
for misconduct, with denial of justice further clouded by suspicion of
self-interest.[3a]

At the stage of appointment, therefore, the parties should, wherever
this is possible (which in the case of many institutionally appointed arbi-

---

[98] For implied "ad hoc" submissions, see, *per* Devlin J. in *Westminsters Chemicals Produce
Ltd.* v. *Eichholz and Loeser* [1954] 1 Lloyd's Rep. 99, followed in *Higgs & Hill Building
Ltd.* v. *Campbell Dennis Ltd.* illustrated *supra*, para. 18·117.

[99] See, *e.g. Pratt* v. *Swanmore Builders Ltd.* [1980] 2 Lloyd's Rep. 504, illustrated *supra*, Section 3, paras. 18·135.

[1] *Norjarl K/S A/S* v. *Hyundai Heavy Industries Co. Ltd.* [1991] 1 Lloyd's Rep. 524, C.A.

[2] See *Mustill and Boyd* (2nd ed.), p. 233 *et seq.*

[3] See this subject developed in (1991) 7 Arb. Int. *op. cit.*, and the valuable Australian cases
discussed *infra*, paras. 18·159–18·160.

[3a] Compare *Gas & Fuel Corporation of Victoria* v. *Woodhall Ltd.* [1978] V.R. 385, illustrated
supra, para. 18·134.

trators under contracts of adhesion it may not be) obtain express under-takings as to an arbitrator's availability before agreeing to an appointment. Unfortunately there are many examples of arbitrators who, even against the expressed wishes of both parties, let alone in disputed situations where it is necessary to balance the interests of the parties, are nevertheless prepared to inflict not only premature interlocutory or hear-ing dates,[4] but also undesired adjournments of considerable length and, on grounds of availability, hearing dates long in the future. It is difficult to avoid the conclusion that in some cases the convenience and other engagements of arbitrators take precedence over the needs of the dispute itself, and without regard to the parties' agreement.[4a]

(iii) *Availability of arbitrator*

18·157   Availability to meet the reasonable requirements of the parties and the justice of the case in regard to the length and dates of hearings is, it is submitted, a moral and professional duty of arbitrators, and those parties with a justified interest in a proper rate of progress will as already pointed out, be well advised, where they are in a position to do so, to obtain explicit assurances about this prior to an arbitrator's appointment. This is particu-larly desirable since there is obviously a serious risk of still further preju-dicing the chance of a fair hearing should an application for an arbitrator's removal after his appointment on the ground of premature or restricted hearings on the one hand or excessively delayed or extended hearings on the other, or indeed any other kind of misconduct, prove unsuccessful. In a very large number of cases, both domestic and international, the parties will find themselves involuntarily committed to unknown arbitrators appointed by arbitration institutions or appointing bodies failing agree-ment, and whose availability may not in the event coincide with the par-ties' wishes, or the needs of the justice of the case where the parties differ. The practical remedies for a party finding himself in this increasingly com-mon situation are almost non-existent, and arbitration institutions are fre-quently unhelpful and unwilling to intervene or take steps to assist a party in such a situation, usually proclaiming themselves as *functus officio* once the appointment has been made.

(b) Interlocutory matters after appointment

(i) *Generally*

18·158   It has been previously pointed out (see *supra*, Section 1) that the English Acts are by no means comprehensive in scope, and in particular give little precise guidance as to the day-to-day conduct of arbitrations. Thus, subsections 12(1), (2), (3), (4) and (5) of the 1950 Act, while giving

---

[4] See for at least three examples the cases illustrated *supra*, Section 4.
[4a] See, *e.g.* the *Gas & Fuel Corporation of Victoria* case, *supra*, para. 18·134A.

the arbitrator *power* to compel evidence from the parties themselves and to call for documents in their possession or power, as well as to examine witnesses on oath, does not expressly impose any *obligation* on him to do so. Again, while the powers of the High Court are made available to compel the attendance of witnesses, and in regard to a considerable number of other matters in support of the arbitration, including discovery and interrogatories (both of which pre-suppose the existence of pleadings, or at least some definition or outline of the relevant issues, without which these remedies would be inoperable) there is no mention in the Acts of pleadings as such, or even of a written statement of the parties' cases.

Nor is there any statutory indication of those matters on which the arbitrator has power to give interlocutory orders or directions, such as delivery of adequate written statements of case or pleadings, or, very importantly in construction disputes, of further particulars where the original pleadings are inadequate; or of his powers in default of compliance with such orders. Section 5(1) of the 1979 Act would seem to require that the arbitrator himself should apply to the Court for assistance in this latter situation, assuming that the opposing party is not himself prepared to do so. The difficulties which this situation can create are well illustrated by one of the misconduct cases illustrated in Section 4 *supra*,[5] and the very limited value and scope of the special power to continue with the reference conferred by section 5(2) of the 1979 Act should be appreciated.[6]

(ii) *Pleadings*

It has been said of the general corpus of Australian arbitration legislation, which on the whole has followed the English legislation fairly closely: "The policy of the Act is, in my opinion, clear. It is to keep a tight hold upon arbitrators in the course of their pre-trial procedures in those cases where the exigencies of the arbitration call for strict compliance with court rules while leaving arbitrators free to use whatever procedures "they think fit" in uncomplicated, informal arbitrations".[6a] So, too, while it has been said that an arbitrator is master of the procedure to be followed in an arbitration[6b], a number of judgments in England have recently and rightly emphasised that arbitrations in typical construction contract disputes are *not* in the same category as "commodity" or "quality" arbitrations, or other classes of arbitration where the arbitrator is selected for his skill and judgment in a particular trade, and where pleadings and formal hearings can sometimes be properly dispensed with.[7] These cases, by

18·159

---

[5] *Pratt* v. *Swanmore Builders* [1980] 2 Lloyd's 504, commented on *supra*, para. 18·136.
[6] See also *Kontek* v. *Daveyduke Industries* (1987) 6 A.C.L.R. 36, S.C. of Victoria, Gobbo J., discussing a comparable section 18(3) of the Australian Commercial Arbitration Act 1984.
[6a] *Per* White, J. in the Full Court of South Australia in *South Australian Superannuation Fund* v. *Leighton Contractors* (1990) 55 S.A.S.R. 327, 331.
[6b] See *infra*, para. 18·162.
[7] *Fox* v. *Wellfair Ltd.* (1981) 19 BLR 52, C.A.; see particularly *per* Denning L.J. at pages 61–62. See also *Town & City Properties* v. *Wiltshier* (1988) 44 BLR 114. Both cases are illustrated *supra*, paras. 18·139, 18·143. See also *infra*, para. 18·161.

implication, therefore, emphasise the need, if not for pleadings in any formal sense, at least for a precise and properly particularised written statement in advance of the respective parties' cases sufficient to satisfy the requirements of natural justice. Thus, the statement of Bingham J., in a case where the parties had in fact expressly agreed to dispense with formal pleadings—"Whether and to what extent an arbitrator insists on the parties serving pleadings is a matter for his judgment in the circumstances of the particular arbitration"[8] needs to be read in context.

In a typical construction contract dispute an arbitrator who, against the wishes of a party, dispenses, as a minimum, with written statements of the parties' cases equivalent to pleadings will be in danger of removal for breach of the principles of natural justice, and any award subsequently made by him imperilled, it is submitted, subject only to contrary agreement or waiver. Equally, an arbitrator of a construction dispute who does not apply the principles of natural justice by requiring further particulars of an inadequate statement of a party's case[9] will equally risk removal.[10] If in any doubt an arbitrator in England should give his consent for determination of a preliminary point of law under section 2 of the 1979 Act, it is submitted.

18·159A An unsatisfactory aspect of construction contract disputes in the past, not confined to arbitration, has been that until relatively recently there has been some laxity in enforcing proper particularisation of claims by the courts themselves.[10a] Thus "total cost" has been increasingly employed in the quantification of monetary claims, even where separate individual grounds of claim are being advanced, and this has been combined with unwillingness to plead or explain the precise causation *nexus* between an alleged event or breach and the resulting loss or damage. These techniques help to conceal claims lacking in any real substance or degree of preparation, and can place defendants in great difficulties both in knowing with sufficient precision the case they have to meet and so in the preparation of their own case. The recent Privy Council and English Court of Appeal decisions in *Wharf Properties Ltd.* v. *Eric Cumine Associates* and *McAlpine Humberoak Ltd.* v. *McDermott International Inc.*[10b] represent, it is submitted, a welcome and overdue reaction, basically grounded on the principles of natural justice, against this increasingly widespread practice.

The tenth edition of this book contained two major passages[10c] where it was suggested that, in view of the considerable complexity of most mod-

---

[8] *Maltin Engineering Ltd.* v. *J. Donne Holdings Ltd.* (1980) 15 BLR 61, 79.

[9] For these principles, see particularly *Wharf Properties Ltd.* v. *Eric Cumine & Associates (No. 2)* (1991) 52 BLR 3, P.C. and *McAlpine Humberoak Ltd.* v. *McDermott International Inc.* (1992) 58 BLR 1, illustrated *ante*, Chap. 8, Section 2(3)(1), paras. 8·207 and 8·120.

[10] In addition to the *South Australian Superannuation Fund* case illustrated *infra*, see the *Damond Lock Grabowski* and *Town & City* cases illustrated *supra*, Section 4, paras. 18·145 and 18·143, respectively.

[10a] See *ante*, Chap. 8, paras. 8·200 *et seq.*, and see C.C.P.P., paras. 8–40—43.

[10b] Illustrated *ante*, Chap. 8, paras. 8·210 and 8·211.

[10c] Tenth edition, pp. 858–861, reproduced in full when citing from White J.'s judgment in the Full Court of South Australia, see *infra*.

ern construction contract disputes, arbitrators should, as a matter of natural justice, normally apply the same principles and require the same degree of particularisation of the parties' written cases as in the case of litigation in the Courts, and that the pleadings rules as to particularisation themselves represented no more than a refined application of the principles of natural justice. This view has recently received support in the Full Court of South Australia.

ILLUSTRATION

Owners in South Australia received six binders of written material in response to an order by arbitrators for delivery of Points of Claim. The owners argued that the documents were not remotely like Points of Claim; that they could not understand them so as to prepare the Points of Defence, which had also been ordered, or to prepare their own case; and they applied for an order that properly prepared Points of Claim be served. The arbitrators refused the application, saying that they understood most of the material. The owners then applied to the Court for an order directing the arbitrators to require delivery of properly pleaded Points of Claim. The contractors objected that by virtue of section 14 of the South Australian Commercial Arbitration Act 1986 (which provided that arbitrators might conduct proceedings as they thought fit) the Court had no jurisdiction to consider the arbitrators' pre-trial procedures, and the Master upheld that objection. *Held*, by the Full Court (Bollen J. dissenting), that section 14 was expressly made subject to the remainder of the Act, and in particular to section 22 (which provided that questions in the course of proceedings should be determined according to law); to section 4 (which provided that breach of natural justice was to be misconduct); and to sections 43 and 47 (which provided for remitting matters to arbitrators, and conferred power on the Court to make interlocutory orders). Accordingly the case should be referred back to the Master for him to examine the Points of Claim which had been filed and, if in his opinion they were not appropriate, to remit them to the arbitrators for reconsideration of their ruling: *South Australian Superannuation Fund Investment Trust* v. *Leighton Contractors Ltd.* (1990).[10d]

[Note: In regard to its interpretation of the Act and the question of jurisdiction, this judgment has been heavily criticised by Rogers C.J. in New South Wales[10e] on the ground that, in the light of recent legislation in Australia and of the *Nema* and other cases in England, and of a corresponding new Australian legislative attitude to arbitration, the Court now had no supervisory power to intervene in matters of procedural injustice. However, it is submitted that, properly understood, White J.'s judgment was expressly based upon a potential breach of the principles of natural justice, in the special context of a complex construction dispute, which the Full Court considered it was free to investigate, and that this does not seem to have been appreciated in Rogers C.J.'s judgment. The importance of the case in other jurisdictions, it is suggested, lies in its valuable substantive discussion of the proper degree of particularisation required in the arbitration of a typical complex construction dispute and of the requirements of natural justice in such a case, whatever the

---

[10d] (1990) 55 S.A.S.R. 327.
[10e] *Imperial Leatherware Ltd.* v. *Macri and Marcellino Ltd.* (1991) 22 N.S.W.L.R. 653.

position about statutory remedies may have been under later Australian legislation.]

18·159B   Thus, giving the judgment of the majority, White J. in the above case said:

> "Counsel for the builder conceded from the Bar table that procedural justice requires that arbitrators should, in long complex arbitrations, follow as nearly as reasonably practicable the pre-trial pleading, discovery and other procedures of the Court. This concession was correctly made in my opinion. It has long been universally recognised in the authorities and in the text-books, at least in relation to arbitrations under prior Acts in the other States and the United Kingdom, that arbitrators should, in appropriate cases, set a programme at the outset for the exchange of Points of Claim and Points of Defence (and Counterclaim), followed by discovery and inspection ... [authorities cited]
>
> The same obligations apply to both pre-trial and trial procedures, as to the great importance of arbitrators requiring full compliance with pre-trial pleadings: see *Hudson*. At all stages of long, expensive arbitration proceedings, including the pleading stage, the dictates of procedural justice require full notice to the other party of the case being made out against it and a full opportunity to prepare for and answer that case.
>
> These arbitrators recognised these principles and they orderd at the start the exchange of pleadings in the form of Points of Claim and Points of Defence; they also set a time-table for the pleadings and for discovery and inspection and the like. To my mind, the use of the words "Points of Claim" and of "Statement of Claim" makes no difference.
>
> By their conduct the arbitrators properly recognised that, whatever might be the situation in smaller less formal arbitrations, the exigencies of this major arbitration (involving a dispute over $10m for work done and forecasts of a long hearing lasting from 6 to 12 months together with a vast amount of oral, documentary and technical evidence as to complex issues) require that they ought to follow as closely as reasonably practicable the pleading practice of the Supreme Court. *It is not suggested that every aspect of every pleading rule should be followed to the letter, only the substance and spirit of those rules.*"[10f] *(Emphasis supplied.)*

White J. then proceeded to adopt the two passages from the tenth edition[10g] mentioned above and said:

> "Since the matter should, in my opinion go back to the Master with a direction that he has jurisdiction, it is important, I think, for his information that he should consider the Points of Claim in the light of the following passage from *Hudson*. And if he does remit the points of claim back to the arbitrators for their reconsideration, it is important that they, too, should take these passages "on board". I gratefully adopt the following passage from *Hudson* at pages 858–860):."
>
> "(3) Preparation of hearing
>
> The general purpose of the preliminary meeting before the arbitrator is equivalent to that of proceedings on a summons for directions in the High

---

[10f] (1990) 55 S.A.S.R. 327, 329–330.
[10g] At pp. 858–860. The emphases in the following cited passages are those of White J. himself.

Court. It is a curiosity of the Act that no specific reference to written pleadings is made, but Section 12(1) requires the parties to "do all other things which, during the proceedings or the reference, the arbitrator may require", and arbitrators in practice in cases of any substance or complexity almost invariably order delivery of pleadings in the same way as the High Court. There is no doubt that once the parties have delivered pleadings, the arbitrator has power to allow amendments and control them in the same way as the Courts (*Re Creighton* v. *Law Car and General Insurance Corporation Ltd.* [1919] 2 K.B. 738). Arbitrators, unless they are given express power by the terms of their submission to dispense with the procedural techniques of the Courts, *should endeavour to model their control of the proceedings at the interlocutory stage*, as it is called in the Courts, and indeed at all stages, *as closely as possible upon the correct legal procedure and rules as to pleadings*, which, while refined in detail, are in the last analysis based on principles of natural justice designed to give parties *adequate warning of the case they will have to meet*, and to assist in securing all available evidence for that purpose".[10h] (Emphases those of White J.)

White J. then cited a further passage from the tenth edition (at pages **18·159C** 860–861):

> "*Arbitrators should realise that pleadings are of the greatest importance in narrowing the issues between the parties and reducing ultimate cost*, and in building and engineering disputes the time needed for completing the pleadings is often far greater than in ordinary litigation, by reason of the multiplicity of issues and the necessity of obtaining instructions in detail from professional and technical witnesses ... The sheer bulk of the pleadings and documents, and the frequent multiplicity of issues, also mean that the periods of time provisionally allowed in the High Court for the pleading stages of ordinary litigation are wholly inappropriate. In fact, even with punctilious attention and immediate availability by all concerned, pleadings in a complicated building or engineering matter can rarely take less than 12 to 18 months, and frequently more than that. The parties who are most vociferous in complaining of and seeking to shorten the time available to their opponents are frequently those whose pleadings are the most defective and lacking precision. *Arbitrators should appreciate that none of this delay, and the great expense of such interlocutory work*, *is wasted*, since building and engineering litigation is concerned with a careful assessment of the monetary value of claims. Very frequently it is not until the parties reach their legal advisers that this type of assessment even begins to be made, and the course of patient and thorough investigation of all aspects of claim and defence *during the pleading stages* will in many cases produce a different attitude and will enhance the likelihood of a settlement before the hearing takes place. *Arbitrators should remember that a weak or unjustified claim can be put forward in a comparatively short time but its rebuttal may require long and careful preparation* and patient probing in the form of a request for particulars."[10i] (Emphases those of White J.)

The above passages from the tenth edition of this book have been repeated in the present edition in the form of citation in White J.'s judgment since it may be of value to identify the parts chosen for emphasis by White J. While not of course binding in any jurisdiction, they represent the

---

[10h] (1990) 55 S.A.S.R. 327, 338–339.
[10i] (1990) 55 S.A.S.R. 327, 339.

view that even in 1970 there had been an increasing abuse of process of this kind by claimants in construction contract disputes. Whether in arbitration or the courts, but particularly the former, this can place defendants at a serious disadvantage and represent a substantial procedural injustice, which it has been seen in the case of litigation has recently and rightly led to insufficiently particularised claims being struck out as embarrassing and an abuse of process.[10] As indicated *ante*, Chapter 8 there may be special difficulty in affording adequate protection to defendants in the case of arbitrations, since not only is the question whether or not a claim represents an abuse of process or is embarrassing often a matter of degree depending upon the facts of the particular case (as also in the case of actions brought in the courts), but in addition an arbitrator may make "convenient" findings of fact, in an area of apparent expertise on his own part, to the effect that particularisation is impracticable or impossible, as in the *Crosby* case, or state that he at least is able to understand bulky documentation put forward as a claim document, as in the above case, which a court may understandably feel reluctant to disregard. Thus in the following not all too familiar case the court was not prepared to assist the defendant.

ILLUSTRATION

18·159D   Contractors in Victoria first delivered Points of Claim against owners in August 1991, alleging disturbance and delay caused by other contractors of the owners, failure to give instructions, and failure to give possession, and claiming some $1.5 million, based on a comparison of total hours worked and a total of reasonable hours *allegedly derived from the prices quoted by other tenderers*. After delivery of Points of Defence and a Request for Particulars by the owners in September 1991, the contractors submitted Amended Schedules and Points of Reply in October 1991, in which they substituted a reduced claim for prolongation and disruption costs of $1.2m. The hearing date was fixed for February 17, 1992, but in December 1991, and later still in February 1992, the contractors twice informed the arbitrator that they would be amending their claim, but without giving details. Amended Schedules were then served on the morning of the hearing on February 17. These bore no relation to the original schedules, and there was a complete re-casting of the claim, with the number of specific events relied on significantly reduced, and instead a number of broad allegations with a few specific instances stated to be given by way of example. When the owners objected to the total cost basis of claim and the reduced number of specific examples, counsel for the contractors submitted to the arbitrator that the case "was put on the basis of overall impression", and that "that was the way that loss of productivity claims were often put." The arbitrator then directed that the owners deliver any requests for particulars within two days, and that the hearing be resumed on March 2. On March 10, 1992, the contractors supplied "an extremely lengthy document" of costings, to which the owners objected on the ground of the total cost nature of the claim, and that no particulars had been supplied, as previously requested, showing precisely how and in what manner

---

[10] See *ante*, Chap. 8, paras. 8·200 *et seq.*, where the *Leighton Contractors* and *Nauru* cases are referred to, and the *Wharf* and *Humberoak* cases illustrated in paras. 8·210–8·211.

and what types of damage resulted from the specific instances relied on. On
March 13, 1992, the arbitrator rejected the owners' complaint as to the total
cost basis of claim, and out of 81 events now referred to in the revised schedules ordered particulars in only seven cases, and fixed a hearing date for April
6, 1992. The owners then applied to the Court to remove the arbitrator;
alternatively to strike out the claim for disruption as an abuse of process; and
finally and alternatively for an order remitting the matter to the arbitrator and
directing him to order particulars of the loss of productivity claim. *Held*, by
Smith J., that counsel for the contractors had asserted before the arbitrator
that it was not possible to provide a further detailed breakdown. As the arbitration was not governed by the rules of evidence it was open to the arbitrator
to accept that statement, which he appeared to have done, although he had
required particulars of the broad nature of the disruption in a few instances
without requiring more detailed particulars. On the case pleaded there was a
complex interaction between alleged disruptive events and the way they
affected progress, and the Court was justified in proceeding on the basis that
the contractors, as was put to the arbitrator, could not supply particulars of
the *nexus*. The contractors had the right, like any litigant in an adversary system, to choose the way that they would present their case. Subject to the
requirements of natural justice and understanding the case to be met, they
were not obliged to give particulars of "nexus" when it was not part of their
case to establish a "nexus" between each disrupting event and particular dis-
ruptions and loss. The arguments against total loss claims had been overstated, and highlighted the risks a plaintiff, as opposed to a defendant, might
run in putting its case on such a global basis. The conduct of the arbitrator had
not resulted in a denial of natural justice to the owners, so that had been no
misconduct, nor had there been an abuse of process. On balance, however,
particulars as to how the owners had been responsible for the events and of
the nature and extent of the alleged disruption of the works should have been
ordered in the arbitration, but following Rogers C.J. in the Imperial Leatherware case *supra*, section 47 of the uniform legislation in Australia did not set
up a supervisory jurisdiction for dealing with procedural errors, whether in
complex arbitrations or simple ones, and the powers conferred by that section
should not be exercised to direct further particulars or to direct the arbitrator
so to direct: *Nauru Phosphate Royalties Trust* v. *Matthew Hall Mechanical &
Electrical Engineers Ltd.* [1992].[10k]

[Note: Disregarding the jurisdiction element in this case, this was a careful   **18·159E**
judgment which shows a history with which defendants' advisers in construc-
tion disputes have become depressingly familiar. However, on the substantive question whether the defendants' presentation of their case was being
unfairly prejudiced so as to be a breach of natural justice, the judgment, with
respect, seems ambivalent and unpersuasive. At a number of points it clearly
recognises the dangers of permitting total cost claims, and exposes with precision the lack of specificity that developed in the claimants' frequently
amended and re-cast claims, as evidenced by the Court's ultimate conclusion
that particulars should have been ordered. Elsewhere, however, the objections to total cost claims are for no explained reason said to be overstated. The
judgment at one important point relies heavily on what seems to be only the
slenderest evidence that separation of the individual items of claim was
impossible, but elsewhere apparently takes the view that, whether or not this
is so, a claimant is in any event entitled *as of right, should he so wish*, to put
forward a delay and disturbance claim arising from a number of matters
on a total cost and unparticularised and unitemised basis (attended,

---

[10k] (1993) 12 A.C.L.R. 99. See the case not followed and distinguished by Moynihan J. in the
Ralph M. Lee Ltd. case in Queensland, discussed *ante*, Chap. 8, para. 8·211A.

so it is said, by unexplained risks for the plaintiff rather than the defendant). What is not mentioned in the judgment is the feature, so common at the present day, of the extraordinarily short periods imposed by many arbitrators on defendants in their time-tables and when fixing hearing dates.[101] Thus in this case, as the judge found, while the plaintiffs were given complete latitude to re-cast (for the second time) their entire claim on the morning of the first hearing date on February 17, and still further substantial amendments were apparently made in their later particulars on March 10, the claim itself was based on an obviously highly theoretical form of total cost; there had been no written complaint ever made by the contractors during the course of the contract; and on the basis of particulars so far delivered the only alleged instructions relied upon were oral. Nevertheless the defendants were ordered to deliver requests for particulars within only 48 hours of receiving the wholly re-cast claim on the morning of the hearing on February 17, and when inadequate particulars were supplied and objected to on March 10 (which the judge later found to be inadequate) the arbitrator nevertheless on March 13, ordered the hearing to commence on April 6.

The case is illustrated as being on its apparent facts typical of a trend in construction arbitrations in which inadequately particularised and inherently improbable claims are accepted at face value by arbitrators, but of early hearing dates insisted upon which can only be oppressive and unfair to defendants, and a standing encouragement to the speculative presentation of unjustified or exaggerated claims.]

18·160 Arbitrators, with far more excuse than some English and Commonwealth judiciaries in the past,[11] can all too easily be persuaded that the often lengthy and bulky documents submitted as statements of their case or of their defence and counter-claim by the parties to construction disputes are in fact a sufficient explanation of their case to enable the opposing party to plead in reply and to prepare his case for the hearing. In fact, on close analysis these documents often show that the party concerned is either not pleading specific incidents or facts upon which he relies at all (which could then be easily refuted), or more often is pleading a whole mass of facts or assertions but not showing any necessary logical linkage or chain of events or identifying and separating specific facts which lead to the conclusions of liability or *quantum* which he is asserting.[12] In other words there is, again, a breach of the principles of natural justice, in that the opposing party is not being informed in advance with sufficient precision of the case he has to meet. This leaves the party in default free to shift his ground at the hearing within the generalised mass of claims or assertions which he has been allowed to put forward, and makes it difficult, or impossible for his opponent to assemble evidence and marshal his counter-arguments in advance. Such pleadings are described by lawyers

---

[101] See the misconduct cases *supra*, para. 18·146, and in particular the *Gas and Fuel Corporation of Victoria* case, see *supra*, para. 18·134; the *Asia Construction* case see *supra*, para. 18·142; and the *Damond* case see *supra*, para. 18·145. See also these same tendencies noted in (1991) 7 *Arb. Int.* 149.

[11] See *ante*, Chap. 8, Section 2(3)(i), paras. 8·200 *et seq.*, and see C.C.P.P., paras. 8–40—47.

[12] See for this particularly the Privy Council case of *Wharf Properties Ltd.* v. *Eric Cumine*, illustrated *ante*, para. 8·207.

as "embarrassing", and in the courts will warrant striking out or dismissal of a claim no less than pleadings which fail to disclose sufficient facts.[13]

Notwithstanding that this practice of pleading generalities or large numbers of facts without sufficient specifics is extremely common in construction disputes,[14] and is a clear indication to the informed eye of a weak or non-existent or exaggerated case, it has been seen that parties seeking further particulars of apparently bulky pleading documents, or indeed taking any legitimate procedural objection, tend to be treated by many if not most technical arbitrators with considerable suspicion as attempting to obstruct the arbitral process and the arbitrator's desire to achieve rapid progress in accordance with his own pre-determined and frequently unrealistic programme for the dispute.[15]

(c) The hearing

An arbitrator is sometimes said to be "the master of his own proceed-   **18·161**
ings". Like many generalisations this can be misleading. While the courts have accepted that there may be some "commodity" or "quality" arbitrations where pleadings or formal hearings can be dispensed with, this will almost always be on the basis of custom and practice in that trade, and so, on analysis, based on at least implied consent. Moreover, when an arbitrator can be shown to have been selected for his special experience and skill in a particular trade, it has been seen that he may supplant a lacuna in the evidence put before him by the parties by assessing damages on the basis of the value and profitability of supply contracts for certain goods with which he is commercially familiar without specific evidence on that point from the parties.[16] However, subsequent cases have rightly made it clear beyond doubt that the great majority of construction contract disputes are not in any of these categories. For example, in a case where the arbitrator was also a surveyor and architect, it was held that he must not act on his own knowledge without recourse to witnesses on either side and the submissions and guidance of advocates.[17] In another case where an arbitrator was an architect and quantity surveyor and required meetings and discussions with the quantity surveyors on each side without counsel and in the presence of solicitors acting only as observers, and later made a provisional finding in what he said was a purely quantity surveying matter, he was removed.[18]

Arbitrators in normal construction disputes should never, therefore, dispense with a written statement of both parties' cases, and should restrict the evidence called at the hearing within the limits imposed by those

---

[13] See the *Wharf* case.
[14] See the position in the U.K. and U.S. compared in C.C.P.P., paras. 8—40—47.
[15] Note the similarity in this respect of the *Gas & Fuel Corporation, Turner (East Asia)* and *Damond Lock Grabowski* cases *supra*, paras. 18·134, 18·141 and 18·145.
[16] *Mediterranean & Eastern Export Co.* v. *Fortress Fabrics* [1948] 2 All E.R. 186, illustrated *supra*, para. 18·132.
[17] *Fox* v. *Wellfair* [1981] 19 BLR 59, C.A., see *supra*, para. 18·139.
[18] *Town & City Properties* v. *Wiltshier* (1988) 44 BLR 114, see *supra*, para. 18·143.

documents, unless prepared to give leave to amend. If so, this will in many cases fully justify an adjournment to enable the opposing party to reconstitute his own case or call new evidence. In general, bona fide amendments should be allowed freely, unless the arbitrator is satisfied beyond doubt that the amendment is not bona fide (for example, designed to secure delay) and that an adjournment must inevitably seriously prejudice the other party in some way which cannot be met by an award of costs thrown away, or in appropriate cases by an award of interest on any eventual sum awarded.

18·162   In regard to the conduct of the hearing itself, it is sometimes suggested that an arbitrator has an extremely free hand, and reliance is often placed on a passage in a speech of Lord Diplock, when noting the lack of specific guidance and generalised wording in section 12(1) of the 1950 Act:

> "By appointing a sole arbitrator ... the parties make the arbitrator the master of the procedure to be followed in the arbitration. Apart from a few statutory requirements under the Arbitration Act 1950, ... he has a complete direction to determine how the arbitration is to be conducted from the time of his appointment to the time of his award, *so long as the procedure he adopts does not offend the rules of natural justice.*"[19]

These words were, however, spoken in the quite different context of deciding on the extent of the interlocutory powers of an arbitrator to strike out a claim for delay in its prosecution, and the emphasised wording is all important. In a normal construction case it will be clear misconduct, it is submitted, for an arbitrator to refuse to allow representation by solicitors and counsel.[20] Again, in normal construction cases an arbitrator must only act on admissible evidence, in the absence of contrary agreement or waiver, and he is not, as is frequently thought, free to disregard the rules of evidence.[21] Finally, natural justice will usually require the exchange of points of claim or statements of case and of reply differing only in form, but not in substance, from conventional pleadings, it is submitted.

It follows that an arbitrator must leave it to the parties to decide on the case which they wish to present, and his award will be imperilled if he attempts to exclude or prevent them from putting forward any part of their case. The following case should not be regarded as authority to the contrary.

ILLUSTRATION

18·163   A dispute arose as to the liability for and extent of defects in 83 roofs forming part of two office blocks. On the application of the contractor, the arbi-

---

[19] *Bremer Vulkan Schiffbau und Maschinenfabrik* v. *South India Shipping Corporation Ltd.* [1981] A.C. 909, 985.
[20] *Town & City Properties* v. *Wiltshier* (1988) 44 BLR 109, sup.
[21] See *Mustill and Boyd* (2nd ed.), p. 352 *et seq.*

trator made an opposed order, subject to a case being stated as to whether he had jurisdiction to make the order, that the issue of liability should be determined by reference to a maximum number of 25 roofs to be selected or agreed by the parties, or if not to be referred to him. A month later the arbitrator, now aware that the matter would be taken further to the Court, wrote to the parties stating that in his opinion his order "in no way inhibited or limited either party from raising issues concerning roofs where any additional defects requiring consideration, over and above the agreed number of inspected roofs, could not (*sic*) be dealt with under an application from either party under a 'liberty to apply'." *Held*, by Robert Goff J., that the arbitrator had by his letter left the door open for further application by the parties, and the evidence before him might in due course lead him to accede to a different order. Given that set of circumstances, the arbitrator could not be said to be refusing to decide a case submitted to him, or to allow either party a fair opportunity to present his case, or to be acting unfairly. The matter was within the discretion of the arbitrator as to how to conduct the arbitration, and did not raise any question of law where it would be proper to order the arbitrator to state a case for the court's decision: *Carlisle Place Investments Ltd.* v. *Wimpey Construction (U.K.) Ltd.* (1980).[22]

[Note: But for the belated action of the arbitrator in sending his later letter, it seems clear that the decision in the above case might have been very different. Additionally, the judgment expresses doubt as to the use of the appellate procedure on a point of law under section 2 of the 1979 Act in such a situation, and suggests that an application for removal or remitter under sections 22 and 23 of the 1979 Act would be more appropriate.]

During the hearing, sometimes in relatively informal and perhaps not   **18·164**
entirely appropriate types of accommodation, arbitrators should be particularly careful to avoid communications or association with one side without the full knowledge or consent of the other, and to avoid creating the slightest impression of intimacy or of favouring or assisting one party at the expense of the other.

ILLUSTRATION

  During a morning tea-break in a building arbitration in New South Wales the builder, who was under cross-examination as to certain plans, remained seated at the same table with the plans. All parties were present in the room at the time, when the arbitrator approached the builder and exchanged some remarks during which a money valuation was thought by a witness to have been stated by the builder. The witness also thought that the plans had been referred to. The owner applied for a permanent stay alleging a reasonable suspicion of bias. The arbitrator, who had been joined as a second defendant, supplied an affidavit to the court stating that the conversation had had nothing to do with the case but related to the profitability of local clubs in the area. It also appeared, however, that the arbitrator's affidavit had been typed in the builder's counsel's chambers, which the owner also relied on as indicating a closeness with the builder which increased her apprehension of bias. *Held*, by Newman J., that as a matter of probability the case had not been

---

[22] 15 BLR 109.

discussed at all; but applying the test of reasonable apprehension of bias in *Regina* v. *Watson*,[23] that the arbitrator should not act further as arbitrator between the parties: *McInnes* v. *Hall* (1988).[24]

18·165   While there are many potential situations where an arbitrator can properly intervene of his own volition in relation to the conduct of an arbitration,[25] it has been said that no intervention is to be preferred to too much.[26] In such a case it has been said that "he descends into the arena and is liable to have his vision clouded by the dust of conflict."[27]

The Acts and the law of arbitration generally lay down no principles for the proper conduct of arbitrations by arbitrators, while the case-law tends merely to afford examples of negative conduct whereby the validity of an award has been affected or the removal of an arbitrator justified. The misconduct cases illustrated *supra*, Section 4 afford a number of examples of conduct to be avoided. The principles of natural justice, namely that no party should be taken by surprise and that a party is entitled to know the full case brought against him, are, however, basic and not dependent on the use of any particular type of arbitration.[28] Thus, the receipt by an arbitrator of information not made available to both parties, or his reaching a decision prematurely before full argument has been put to him by the affected party, will almost automatically invalidate an award, whatever the type of arbitration.[29]

However, it should be borne in mind by arbitrators that virtually any departures from the norm in the conduct of proceedings, whether interlocutory or at the hearing, will be cured and free of any possible objection if freely agreed to whether beforehand or retrospectively, by both parties, or if this can reasonably be implied from continuing with the arbitration. Only in the event of objection by a party in disagreement will any serious question of misconduct usually arise (other, of course, than a matter of which the party is unaware at the time). On the other hand, failure to object will not usually prejudice a party who is not professionally represented.[29a]

18·166   In some cases a reluctant party may seek to frustrate arbitration proceedings by refusing or failing to attend the hearing. While section 5(2) of the 1979 Act (which, however, requires a High Court order) does refer to "default of appearance", that section, which expressly authorises continuance of the reference, appears to be primarily aimed at failure to comply

---

[23] (1976) 136 C.L.R. 248, 258–263, cited *supra*, Section 4, para. 18·147.

[24] (1988) 7 A.C.L.R. 37.

[25] See, *e.g. Mustill and Boyd* (2nd ed.), pages 348–9.

[26] *Ibid.*

[27] *Yuill* v. *Yuill* [1945] P. 15, 20, *per* Lord Greene M.R. The reference there was to a judge who had intervened to examine a witness himself.

[28] *Maltin Engineering Ltd.* v. *J. Donne Holdings Ltd.* (1980) 15 BLR 61, illustrated *supra.*

[29] *Ibid.*, and for premature decisions reached before concluded argument, see *Modern Engineering (Bristol) Ltd.* v. *Miskin & Sons Ltd.* [1981] 1 Lloyd's Rep. 135 and the other cases illustrated *supra*, Section 4.

[29a] See the *Maltin Engineering* and *Traynor* cases, illustrated *supra* paras. 18·137 and 18·145.

with interlocutory orders generally rather than a party's simply absenting himself from a hearing. In Victoria a rather similar, although not identical, section 18(3) in the Australian Commercial Arbitration Act was so construed, and it is submitted that the view there expressed was correct, namely that on ordinary principles of natural justice an arbitrator can proceed with a hearing *sui motu* in the absence of a party, provided, of course, that adequate notice has been given, and will not be guilty of misconduct in so acting:

> "[The section] is directed to the more specific question of the powers of an arbitrator to compel attendance for examination or compliance with a requirement, such as production of documents. The more general question of the power of the arbitrator to proceed in the absence of a party is to be dealt with as a matter of principle resting essentially on considerations of natural justice. It is axiomatic that an arbitrator cannot proceed *ex parte* unless notice of the hearing has been given to the absent party. It is equally clear that a party cannot frustrate an arbitration by merely absenting himself from the hearing. In the present case, notice of hearing was given, together with a warning that the arbitrator would proceed *ex parte* if only one party was present ... There was no breach of any relevant requirement of natural justice or any basis or finding misconduct in this matter."[30]

(4) Interim Awards

The Acts at no point indicate when or in what circumstances interim   **18·167** awards may be made, though an express power to do so has been expressly conferred by the Acts, in the absence of contrary agreement, since 1889.[31] In practice, arbitrators may make interim awards of different kinds. They may deal with some or all matters of liability, but not *quantum*; they may deal with preliminary points of law only; they may deal with some claims but not others; or they may order an interim payment where at least some moneys are due.

By definition, it would seem that any award which does not finally conclude all matters in dispute will be an interim award, although in the special case of a substantive "final" award which only omits to deal with costs (which can be a useful device, if done deliberately, in order to enable argument on costs to take place after, and not before the substantive content of the award is known) there is a special right under section 18(4) of the Act for either party to apply to the arbitrator for an order of costs within a limited period.

In cases where the award is for an interim payment, while there is undoubtedly power to make such an award, the arbitrator must give full effect to any bona fide set-off or counter-claim available to a respondent, as, for example, where sums have been certified as due for interim payment under provisions like those in the pre-1980 RIBA/JCT standard

---

[30] *Kontek* v. *Daveyduke Industries* (1987) 6 A.C.L.R. 34, 36, *per* Gobbo J.
[31] Now s.14, 1950 Act.

forms, and the owner raises a defence or cross-claim.[32] In such a case the award should, however, only be for such sums as are indisputably due.[33]

It remains an open question whether an arbitrator can award sums on account on the same principles as a judge may now do so under the recent RSC Order 29, although a court may itself make such an order immediately prior to granting a stay for arbitration.[34] In view of many other statutory remedies which have been held to be available to arbitrators, although on their face apparently available only to courts (for example, statutory powers to award interest), there seems no reason in principle why an arbitrator should not have the same power as a judge in this respect. However, arbitrators would be well advised to use such powers circumspectly and only where there is the clearest evidence that the sum awarded represents a minimum due and that some further sums must undoubtedly be due on the final award.

A valid exclusion agreement under section 3 of the 1979 Act preventing appeal on a point of law will apply equally to interim awards.[35]

18·168   One disadvantage of arbitration procedure, particularly in the case of disputes where a number of issues both factual and financial may be determined in different ways, is that at the conclusion of the hearing, if cost submissions are to be made at that stage, they will require to be made by the parties in ignorance of the arbitrator's ultimate findings. This can be a very real disadvantage to all concerned. In this, of course, the situation is completely different from proceedings in court, where submissions on costs are not made until after judgment has been delivered. A useful device, first suggested in the tenth edition of this book (where an unreported judgment of Wynn J. in *Marples Ridgeway & Partners Ltd.* v. *C.E.G.B.*[36] was referred to) was for the arbitrator to be requested to issue a substantive award only, expressly describing it as an interim award, thus enabling the parties to address him on costs and secure the final award thereafter. This has since 1970 become a relatively common practice, and has now received formal judicial approval.[37] It is submitted that an arbitrator who chooses to adopt it, notwithstanding objection by one party, cannot be regarded as having misconducted himself, since he will have modelled his own procedure more closely upon that of the courts, quite apart from the intrinsic justice and advantage of the procedure.

Interim awards determining a preliminary issue, which will enable an arbitrator to find relevant facts and give reasons for his award, may be a useful alternative, in some situations, to an application made by a party

---

[32] *Modern Trading Co. Ltd.* v. *Swale Building and Construction Ltd.* (1990) 6 Const.L.J. 251, Waller J.

[33] *The Kostas Melas* [1981] 1 Lloyd's Rep. 18, Robert Goff J.

[34] *Imodco Ltd.* v. *Wimpey Major Projects Ltd.* (1987) 40 BLR 1, C.A.

[35] *Marine Contractors Inc.* v. *Shell Petroleum Development Co. of Nigeria Ltd.* [1984] 2 Lloyd's Rep. 77.

[36] [1964] Q.B.D. (Special Paper) in (1970) Hudson, *Building Contracts* tenth edition pp. 867–868.

[37] See, *per* Lord Donaldson in *King* v. *Thomas McKenna Ltd.* [1991] 2 QB 480, 482, cited *infra*, Subsection (7), para. 18·184.

under section 2 of the 1979 Act for determination of a preliminary point of law.[37a] If the arbitrator feels that he needs guidance and would in any case be minded to support such an application, he should canvass the alternatives with the parties, since the two procedures are different, and his consent will be an important factor in the one case,[38] while it will be irrelevant in the other; moreover, the conditions for obtaining leave from the High Court may be different in the two cases.

(5) Final Awards

(a) Costs

The practice whereby a "final" substantive award may deliberately abstain from dealing with the question of costs, so as to enable further argument to be addressed on costs once the full substantive elements of the award are known, has been discussed *supra*, in the context of interim awards. In such a case, of course, the award only becomes formally "final" on the making of the award as to costs. This is further discussed *infra*, Subsection 7.[38a]   **18·169**

Since construction disputes frequently consist of claim and counter-claim, it is very desirable, if not absolutely necessary in the interests of clarity and also in the context of costs and possible appeals, that these two elements should be dealt with separately in the award, followed by a final statement of the net sum awarded to one party or the other. Since construction disputes also frequently consist of a series of claims, it is equally desirable that the award should deal with each claim separately as well as any final total. If the award does deal finally with the question of costs, and if the award differs in any way in this respect from the usual principle that costs should follow the event, there are so many decisions of the High Court emphasising the desirability of the arbitrator stating his reasons for any such departure,[39] that the time must be approaching, (and despite earlier decisions to the contrary in the courts)[40] for it to be not only incompetent but actual misconduct to fail to do so, it is submitted. Appeals from orders as to costs are considered *infra*, Subsection 6(c).

(b) Reasoned awards

A further question facing an arbitrator is whether or not to make his award, whether interim or final, a reasoned one. The 1979 Act makes it   **18·170**

[37a] For this latter, see *infra*, Subsection 6(b).
[38] See s. 2(1)(*a*), 1979 Act.
[38a] See para. 18·183.
[39] *Lewis* v. *Haverfordwest R.D.C.* [1953] 1 W.L.R. 1486; *Dineen* v. *Walpole* [1969] 1 Lloyd's Rep. 261; *The Eric Schroeder* [1974] 1 Lloyd's Rep. 192; and see the protest of Megaw J. at the then stage of the law in *Matheson & Co. Ltd.* v. *A. Tabah & Sons* [1963] 2 Lloyd's Rep. 270, 274–275.
[40] *e.g. Perry* v. *Stopher* [1959] 1 W.L.R. 415.

clear by inference that there is no immediate obligation to state reasons, since the court is expressly empowered by section 1(5) to order an arbitrator to state or supplement his reasons for the award. However section 1(6) also provides that such an order may only be made if a party to the reference has given notice to the arbitrator requiring a reasoned award prior to the award being made.

On the other hand, there is nothing to prevent, and everything to be said for an arbitrator giving reasons for his award of his own volition. Indeed, *Mustill and Boyd* suggest that in the general interest of arbitration he should always do so.[41] In the rare event that he should be asked by all parties not to do so, or in the perhaps rather more likely event that both parties, while wishing to avoid the possibility of an appeal, desire to know his reasons, this can be achieved by the device of stating the reasons in a separate document which states expressly that they are not to form part of the award and are not to be used in legal proceedings for any purpose without the arbitrator's consent. If one party requests reasons and the other objects an arbitrator cannot possibly be faulted for doing so and, consistently with *Mustill* and *Boyd's* views, should do so, it is submitted.

(c) Where the award is made

18·171   Wherever international considerations are present, care needs to be taken with regard to the place where an award is "made". Thus, in a case where the arbitrator was a resident of Paris, but had professional chambers in London at which his awards were collected by the parties' representatives following an arbitration which had taken place in London, the awards were expressed to be dated and signed and witnessed in Paris. The Court of Appeal held that the awards had been "made" in France, so that the award became a "Convention award" under section 7(1) of the 1975 Act, notwithstanding that the arbitration had been between English parties and was governed by English law. As a consequence an application for leave to appeal under section 1(3) of the 1979 Act only in the event succeeded in surviving the barrier created by section 3(2) of the 1975 Act as the result of an estoppel arising on the particular facts from the parties' conduct.[42]

(6) Appeals from Arbitrators

18·172   This subject has already been shortly discussed in Section 1.[43] As there indicated, the 1979 Act not only abolished the early and rather restricted

---

[41] (2nd ed.), p. 381.

[42] *Hiscox* v. *Outhwaite* [1991] 2 W.L.R. 1321, C.A.; (affirmed in the H.L. ([1992] 1 A.C. 562) on the different ground that section 3(2) of the 1975 Act did not after all create a barrier to an application under section 1(3) of the 1979 Act).

[43] See *supra*, Subsection (2)(b), para. 18·004 *et seq*. See also the short discussion *infra*, paras. 18·194–18·195.

case-law permitting the setting aside of awards for errors on their face, but also the far more important century-old "case stated" procedures for appeals on points of law, whose statutory origins have been examined *supra*. In their place there are now three possible avenues in England for judicial intervention based on errors of law, namely:

(a) appeals from an arbitrator's *award* on a point of law under section 1(3) of the 1979 Act;
(b) determinations of *a preliminary point of law* under section 2(1) of the 1979 Act (that is during the pendency of the arbitration, before any final award); and
(c) appeals from an arbitrator's awards as to costs.

(a) Appeals on a point of law

(i) *The requirement of leave and the* Nema *guidelines*

Appeals on a point of law under section 1(2) of the 1979 Act require the **18·173** consent of all the parties to the arbitration or, if not, the leave of the court. The subsequent *Nema* and *Antaiaos* guidelines, however, not only greatly reduced the occasions upon which the court would give leave itself, but very greatly increased the procedural difficulties for a party seeking to obtain leave. As a result the right of appeal is today far more circumscribed than under the old "case stated" procedures and case law. It remains to be seen whether these policies, resulting from judicial interpretation rather than express wording in the 1979 Act itself,[44] will be sustained by the House of Lords in future years, or by subsequent legislation once their full consequences become more apparent. The current state of the law under the guidelines can be shortly summarised by stating that in the case of "one-off" contract provisions, leave will not be granted unless the arbitrator's decision can be seen to be "obviously wrong on mere perusal of the reasoned award". In the case of more standard and widely used terms, the appeal must be "seen to add to the clarity and certainty of English law", but even then only if there is "a strong prima facie case" that the arbitrator is wrong. All this is to be established on an application for leave lasting not more than 10 to 15 minutes.[45]

In Australia the *Nema* guidelines were considered to be inappropriate **18·174** under pre-1990 Australian arbitration legislation in a number of cases, notwithstanding that section 38 of the Australia 1984 Commercial Arbitration Act had substantially repeated sections 1(1)–(4) of the English

---

[44] See Robert Goff J.'s forthright views on the absence of any indication of *Nema* style restrictions in the Act itself in *The Oinoussian Virtue* [1981] Lloyd's Rep. 533, 538, when considering Lord Denning M.R.'s early adumbration of the guideline principles in the Court of Appeal in *The Nema* [1980] 1 Q.B. 547, 564B, 565C.

[45] See the discussion of the law as at 1989 in *Mustill and Boyd* (2nd ed.), pp. 602–608, and see the editor's "Control by the Courts: A Plea for More, Not Less" in (1990) 6 Arb. Int. 253; and for further discussion of this rationale in the context of domestic construction contracts, *ibid.* at pp. 255–9. The guidelines themselves are not further discussed in this Chapter, but see the further comments *infra*, paras. 18·194–18·195.

1979 Act.[46] However, the Commercial Arbitration (Amendment) Act 1990 amended section 38(5) of the Commercial Arbitration Act 1984 so as to incorporate a statutory version of the *Nema* guidelines, by requiring either "a manifest error of law on the face of the award", or "*strong* evidence" that the arbitrator had made an error of law, and "that the determination of the question may add or be likely to add *substantially* to the certainty of commercial law". Even under this later wording the New South Wales Court of Appeal, could not agree that the wording "manifest error of law" in section 38(5) implied a mere perusal without benefit of adversarial argument.[47] Moreover it was held in the same csve that the statutory "strong evidence" wording did not necessarily require an obvious error on the face of the award, *but one demonstrable by evidence.*[47a] Even after the passage of amending legislation, therefore, it would seem that the Australian judiciary have not accepted the more extreme procedural aspects of the *Antaiaos* judicial interpretations of the English Act.

(ii) *No evidence as a point of law*

18·175   Both statute and case law are, of course, clear that the right of appeal to the High Court is to be only "on any *question of law* arising out of an award".[48] This makes it necessary to define precisely the borderline between law and fact. Straightforward questions of law, such as the proper interpretation of a contract, raise no problem; but it has long been recognised that some questions of law depend upon applying what have been called primary facts to a legal proposition itself containing a factual element (or conversely expressed, to secondary facts containing a legal element), sometimes described as a question of mixed law and fact, or simply as a secondary finding of fact.[49] Classical examples would be a finding that, on primary facts found, a contract had been frustrated[50]; or that a particular period constituted a reasonable time within which service of a required notice was to take place.[51]

In these latter cases, an arbitrator's secondary finding will be open to review and treated as an error of law if "no person acting judicially and properly instructed as to the relevant law could have come to the determination",[52] or "the decision was such that no reasonable arbitrator could reach".[53] Thus, in *Edwards* v. *Bairstow* Lord Radcliffe said:

---

[46] See *Quantas Airways Ltd.* v. *Joseland* (1986) 6 N.S.W.L.R. 327 C.A.; *Leighton Contractors Ltd.* v. *Kilpatrick Green Pty. Ltd.*, [1992] 2 V.R. 505, the latter case, illustrated *ante*, para. 8·097, containing an extensive review of the Australian cases in different states.

[47] *Promenade Investments* v. *State of New South Wales* (1992) 26 N.S.W.L.R. 203, N.S.W. C.A.

[47a] *Ibid.*, at p. 226 DEF, *per* Sheller J.A.

[48] 1979 Act s. 1(2).

[49] *Mustill & Boyd* (2nd ed. p. 592) appear to use this latter expression in a rather different sense as meaning an inferential finding of fact without legal content.

[50] *Tsakiroglou and Co. Ltd.* v. *Noblee Thorl G.m.b.H.* [1962] A.C. 93; *BTP Tioxide Ltd.* v. *Pioneer Shipping Ltd., The Nema* [1982] A.C. 724.

[51] See *Mustill and Boyd* (2nd ed.), p. 591.

[52] *Per* Lord Radcliffe in *Edwards* v. *Bairstow* [1956] A.C. 14, 36.

[53] *Per* Lord Denning M.R. in the C.A. in *The Nema, supra.*

"If the case contains anything *ex facie* which is bad law and which bears upon the determination, it is, obviously, erroneous in point of law. But, without any misconception appearing *ex facie*, it may be that the facts found are such that no person acting judicially and properly instructed as to the relevant law could have come to the determination under appeal. In those circumstances, too, the court must intervene. It has no option but to assume that there has been some misconception of the law and that this has been responsible for the determination. So there, too, there has been error in point of law. I do not think that it much matters whether this state of affairs is described as one in which there is no evidence to support the determination, or as one in which the evidence is inconsistent with and contradictory of the determination, or as one in which the true and only reasonable conclusion contradicts the determination".[54]

The above propositions relate to "secondary" findings by an arbitrator **18·176** with an inherent legal implication or content. The further and quite different question arises, however, where an arbitrator's primary (or indeed secondary)[55] findings of fact by themselves involve no legal content, whether the findings may be reviewed on the grounds of their being *no evidence* to support them—in other words a perverse, demonstrably wrong, finding of fact unsupported by evidence and in the face of contrary evidence.

There have in any event always been very considerable *procedural* difficulties facing parties seeking to appeal from an arbitrator's findings on this last ground—for example, the considered refusal of the courts to examine a transcript of the evidence before an arbitrator for this purpose.[56] Disregarding this factor, however, the Court of Appeal of New South Wales unanimously considered that the speeches in *Edwards* v. *Bairstow* did indeed permit an appeal on this ground, in a case where an Australian arbitrator had placed a minimal monetary value on what was obviously seriously defective building work (although the majority of the Court also held that this right of appeal did not represent the law of Australia)[57] and there are undoubtedly passages in the speech of Lord Simmonds in *Edwards* v. *Bairstow* which appear to support this view.[58]

On this point, *Mustill and Boyd* take a contrary view,[59] but in any event, as stated, the evidentiary and procedural difficulties in the face of a party seeking to put forward such a contention appear formidable. In the first place, a reasoned award is unlikely to be worded in such a way as to provide evidentiary assistance; and, secondly, there will almost certainly be an additional difficulty, in view of the later *Nema* guidelines, in obtaining the leave of the court for any such appeal.

---

[54] [1956] A.C. 14.
[55] In the sense used by *Mustill and Boyd*, see n. 49.
[56] *Tersons* v. *Stevenage Development Corporation* [1965] 1 Q.B. 37.
[57] *Warley Ltd.* v. *Adco Construction Ltd.* (1988) 8 A.C.L.R. 73, applying *Azzopardi* v. *Tasman UEB Industries Ltd.* [1985] 4 N.S.W. L.R. 139—but see Kirby P.'s powerful and justice-driven dissenting judgment, quoted *supra*, para. 18·024.
[58] See [1956] A.C. 14, 29.
[59] See (2nd ed.), p. 596.

(b) Determination of preliminary points of law

18·177   This quite different procedure under section 2 of the 1979 Act relates to questions of law "arising during the course of the reference" (that is, prior to any award) and requires either the consent of the parties *or of the arbitrator*, although the application itself must be made by a party. However, the High Court must also be satisfied that substantial savings in costs will be produced, *and the application must also be one for which leave would be granted under section 1(3)(b)*.[60] On the wording of the Act, this last requirement would seem to refer to section 1(4), which requires that the determination will substantially affect the rights of a party to the arbitration, but it is of course equally arguable that the requirements of the *Nema* guidelines are also imported by this provision. Since an application under this section must either be supported by the other party or have the support of the arbitrator, the *Nema* guidelines hardly seem necessary in the circumstances of such an application, regarded from a purely policy point of view.

(c) Appeals from awards of costs

18·178   While section 18(1) of the 1950 Act provides that costs shall be in the discretion of the arbitrator, it has long been held that this discretion must be exercised judicially.[61] However, the precise juridical basis for appeals from arbitrators' awards of costs has led to judicial debate, since no specific provision is made for it in the Acts, notwithstanding the express provision with regard to costs in section 18. Until comparatively recently it was considered that no appeal could lie at all unless the arbitrator was prepared to give reasons either in the award or subsequently.[62] This may have had to do with the old "error on the face of the award" remedies abolished by the 1979 Act, however, probably on a juridical basis of misconduct,[63] it now seems clear that in appropriate cases an appeal will lie.

ILLUSTRATIONS

(1) A builder sued for about £75 worth of defects pleaded in his defence: (a) lateness of a notice under the defects clause, (b) his agreement to make good the defects, but the owner's refusal to allow remedial work when a workman attended, (c) later dates for access offered by the owner which gave too short notice or were not practicable, (d) refusal of the owner to suggest later

---

[60] s. 2(2), 1979 Act.
[61] *Smeaton Hanscombe & Co. Ltd.* v. *Sassoon Setty Son & Co. (No. 2)* [1953] 1 W.L.R. 1481.
[62] *Heaven & Kesterton* v. *Sven Widaeus A/B* [1958] 1 W.L.R. 248; *Perry* v. *Stopher* [1959] 1 W.L.R. 415; and see *Matheson & Co. Ltd.* v. *Tabah & Sons* [1963] 2 Lloyd's Rep. 270.
[63] See *Mustill and Boyd* (2nd ed.), p. 398, n. 12. But see the recent view that the appeal can only lie under s. 1(3) of the 1979 Act expressed by the Court of Appeal on two occasions in 1990 in *Blexen* v. *G. Percy Trentham Ltd.* (1990) 54 BLR 37 and *King* v. *Thomas McKenna* [1991] 2 W.L.R. 1234, illustrated *infra*, paras. 18·185 and 18·191.

dates for access, and (e) his own readiness at all material times to remedy the defects. He denied the owner's entitlement to an award of damages, and specifically asked for his own costs to be paid by the owner. The arbitrator awarded £45, but costs against the owner. *Held*, by the Court of Appeal, after reading the correspondence between the parties and the affidavits of the solicitor advocates: (a) that there is a settled practice of the courts that in the absence of special circumstances a successful litigant should receive his costs, (b) that it was for the party seeking to justify an order which departed from this principle to show that there was material justifying such a departure, (c) on the facts no such material existed in the present case. Dictum of Lord Goddard C.J. in *Lewis* v. *Haverford West R.D.C.* (1953)[64] (to the effect that it is necessary to show grounds why an order of this kind should be made) approved, and of Diplock J. in *Heaven & Kesterton Ltd.* v. *Sven Widaeus* (1958) (to the effect that unless reasons were given interference with the award was not possible) disapproved; and (d) that the award should be set aside and the builder ordered to pay the owner's costs: *Dineen* v. *Walpole* (1969).[65]

(2) Contractors failed in a claim against a Council for £20,000 for an alleged variation under a building contract, but recovered somewhat under £3,000 against a claim for a further £7,000 for delay and breach of contract. After hearing argument, the arbitrator ordered each side to bear their own costs (*i.e.* made no order). The Council applied to the court for the case to be remitted to the arbitrator for his reconsideration under section 22 of the 1950 Act. They argued that the arbitrator should have considered each claim separately, and that his award should have reflected their having won on the main claim. *Held*, by the Court of Appeal, that although the order was not one which the Court might have made, there was no universal principle that costs on different issues should be considered separately, and the fact that the order made lay between the extremes of one side or the other being awarded their costs against the other made it impossible to interfere with the arbitrator's discretion: *Thyssen Ltd.* v. *Borough Council of Afan* (1978).[66]

    18·179

(3) A marine arbitration was held on two successive days, at the end of which a claim for rectification of the contract by the plaintiff shipowners was indicated by them for the first time. The arbitration was then adjourned for over a year. During the adjournment the defendant charterers increased an earlier offer of settlement to $6,000, and confirmed that this sum was inclusive of both interest and costs. The arbitration then proceeded for two further days, during which the rectification claim was pursued. The arbitrator awarded a net sum to the shipowners after allowing for a counter-claim by the charterers, of $2,710.00; but he awarded the costs of *both* hearings to the respondent charterers. In an affidavit to the court he said that he did so because of the much larger sum offered, and also because the claim for rectification, which had ultimately been successful, should have been made at the beginning and in any case had made no difference to the sums finally awarded. He also stated that each party had recovered less than they had originally claimed, but that the proportion finally allowed had been greater in the case of the charterers' counter-claim than it had been in the shipowners' claim. On the shipowners' appeal, *held*, by Donaldson J.: (a) following Mocatta J. in *The Erich Schroeder* that the discretion as to costs must be exercised judicially; (b) that the offer, not being an offer to pay a particular sum plus costs, could

    18·180

---

[64] [1953] 1 W.L.R. 1486, 1487 followed in West Australia in *Harper Davidson Ltd.* v. *Keywest Building Ltd.* (1988) 7 A.C.L.R. 54, (Kennedy J.).
[65] [1969] 1 Lloyd's Rep. 261. See also *The Erich Schroeder* [1974] 1 Lloyd's Rep. 192.
[66] 15 BLR 98.

not rank as a sealed offer equivalent to a payment into court, and should be disregarded for purposes of costs, since without knowing what the amount of costs would be the arbitrator would have no means of comparing the sum awarded against the sum offered; (c) however, that the award could be justified in regard to the last two days, since the rectification claim, although successful, had gained nothing for the shipowners; but (d) that the differing proportions of recovery on claim and counter-claim did not warrant a departure from the primary rule that costs follow the event or the disallowance of the shipowners' costs of the first two days, and that the award should be remitted to the arbitrator for reconsideration: *Tramountana Armadora S.A.* v. *Atlantic Shipping Co. S.A.* (1978).[67]

[Note: Donaldson J.'s explanation in the above case for the exceptional readiness of the courts to review arbitrators' awards of costs was that an award shows by its form the arbitrator's substantive decisions on the claim and also his decision on costs. A patent departure from the prima facie rule that costs follow the event raises a rebuttable presumption that the arbitrator has erred in law or acted unjudicially.[68] This judgment also gives a number of useful examples of situations where departures from the prima facie rule that costs follow the event will be justified.]

18·181   *Dineen* v. *Walpole supra*, appeared to have satisfactorily resolved the difficulties for parties appealing against unusual or erratic orders as to costs (which are very frequently experienced in all fields of arbitration). However, later observations of the Court of Appeal in two "sealed offer" decisions in 1990,[69] stating that the juridical basis for reviewing inappropriate awards as to costs, at least in the case of reasoned awards, could now only be as an appeal under section 1(3) of the 1979 Act on a point of law from the award, seem certain to cause confusion and recreate the earlier difficulties of access to the courts for aggrieved parties in such cases, since it is difficult to see how any appeal on costs alone can survive the *Nema* guidelines as at present formulated.

However, if due to what has been described as a "procedural mishap", an unexpected award of costs is made which takes the parties by surprise, and deprives them of the opportunity to address the arbitrator on costs, the award can be remitted to the arbitrator for reconsideration.[70]

(7) Sealed Offers

18·182   One of the serious lacunae in successive English Arbitration Acts has been their failure to extend one of the most important and valuable of the procedural features of English common law litigation to arbitrations, namely the procedures for payment into court, which provide a powerful safeguard for defendants against abuse of their rights by plaintiffs. In

---

[67] [1978] 1 Lloyd's Rep. 391.
[68] *Ibid.* at p. 394.
[69] See the *King* and *Blexen* cases, see *infra*, paras. 18·185 and 18·191.
[70] *Harrison* v. *Thompson* [1989] 1 W.L.R. 1325, Knox J. See also the sealed offer case of *King* v. *Thomas McKenna Ltd.* [1991] 2 Q.B. 480, illustrated *infra*, para. 18·191.

consequence, parties to arbitrations evolved an informal procedure, fundamentally based on consent, which was designed to achieve the same result in regard to the costs as a payment into court, (namely that a party who persists in his action after receiving an offer in appropriate form, and who subsequently obtains judgment for a lesser sum than that offered, is treated as having lost the action as from the date when he could reasonably have accepted the earlier and higher offer). Unavoidably the procedure in arbitrations differs from that in the High Court in one very important respect, namely that cash is not actually paid out by the respondent, who instead makes an open contractual offer capable of a binding acceptance.

At the time of the ninth edition of this book, the device used by legal advisers for this purpose, bearing in mind the rule that an unaccepted "without prejudice" offer could never be put before a court in any circumstances, was for the respondent to make the offer in an "open" letter to the other side. By convention and consent, these letters, however, were not placed in the arbitrator's bundle of open party-and-party correspondence, but instead a copy of the letter was handed to the arbitrator in a sealed envelope at the close of counsel's submissions in the arbitration, with the request that the arbitrator should not read the contents until after he had decided on his substantive award, and before deciding the question of costs.

This procedure had a number of serious disadvantages by comparison   **18·183**
with payment into court. First, the arbitrator, unlike a judge, would be aware that *some* offer had been made, although he would not know how much. Secondly, nothing but his own personal integrity could prevent the arbitrator from reading the letter prematurely before reaching a decision on his award, and tailoring his award appropriately in a marginal case. Thirdly, its exclusion from the arbitrator's bundle, and so from his knowledge, was dependent on the co-operation and consent of the other party or his advisers (although this seems invariably to have been accorded by advisers).

Quite apart from these problems of the sealed offer, it had always been an unsatisfactory, but unavoidable feature of arbitration procedures that, if a final award was to be given which dealt with all matters including costs, the parties' representatives would be compelled to make their submissions as to costs without knowing what the substantive award of the arbitrator had been, and in the light of many possible combinations of circumstance, for example, where there were a number of different claims, or cross-claims as well as claims, or where claims might prove to have been very exaggerated, or substantially unsuccessful in the light of the final award. These were grave disadvantages for all concerned, including the arbitrator, and mention has already been made *supra*,[71] of the recent, and now relatively common device of requesting the arbitrator to give his substantive decisions in an interim award leaving costs for his final award,

---

[71] See Subsection (4), para. 18·168.

thus enabling submissions as to costs to be made, after the "interim" substantive award, and with knowledge of its contents, in the same way as before a judge. This interim award device could also be extremely useful in the past by enabling the parties to postpone any request for a case to be stated under the pre-1979 legislation until such time as the parties had been able to consider the details of the substantive award, thus often saving the quite substantial abortive costs of preparing a case stated which was later found to be unnecessary. An unreported decision of Wynn J. enforcing an agreed arrangement of this kind with regard to case stated where an arbitrator had inadvertently made a final award in breach of the arrangement, was illustrated in this book in the tenth edition.[72]

18·184   The interim award device was also, of course, ideally suited to overcome virtually all the disadvantages of the traditional sealed offer procedures listed above. It is interesting to note that in 1978 Donaldson J. had not apparently encountered it, since his then suggested solution for avoiding the arbitrator's knowledge of the fact of an offer being made (but not the remaining disadvantages) was that arbitrators could themselves spontaneously make a practice in all cases of themselves inviting the submission by the parties of sealed envelopes which would, in due course, inform them whether or not a sealed offer had been made at all (and, if so, of course, of its precise contents), so that no inference of an offer having been paid could now be drawn from the handing in of a sealed envelope.[73] It is now, however, clear that the different device of requesting an interim award in sealed offer cases has spread rapidly and is to be regarded as the "standard solution": Thus in 1991 Lord Donaldson M.R. said:

> "The standard solution to this dilemma is:
> (a) to give the arbitrator the sealed offer, inviting him to open and consider it only after he has decided upon a substantive award; or
> (b) to invite the arbitrator to make an interim award on the substance of the dispute and then to hold a further hearing on costs leading to a final award disposing of that aspect.
> Course (a) avoids the expense of a second hearing, but is only appropriate if there is no reason to believe that the arbitrator might be embarrassed in, for example, assessing damages if he knew that *some* offer had been made, even if he did not know its amount. Course (b) involves the need for, and the cost of, a further hearing, but may be justified *independently of the existence of an offer of settlement* if there are complex arguments on costs which may not arise if the arbitrator's decision goes one way and/or cannot sensibly be deployed unless and until it is known what view the arbitrator has taken on particular claims or parts of claims. It follows that no arbitrator should assume that an offer has been made just because he is invited to postpone a decision on costs until after he has reached a decision upon the substantive claim or claims."[74]

When making a sealed offer it should preferably be addressed to the overall balance as between claims and counter-claims, although every-

---

[72] *Marples Ridgeway and Partners Ltd.* v. *C.E.G.B.* [1964] Q.B. (Special Paper) (unrep.), illustrated in the tenth edition, pp. 867–8.
[73] *Tramountana Armadora S.A.* v. *Atlantic Shipping Co. S.A.* [1978] 1 Lloyd's Rep. 391, 397.
[74] *Per* Lord Donaldson in *King* v. *Thomas McKenna Ltd.* [1991] 2 Q.B. 480, 492.

thing will of course yield to the precise terms of the offer, and there is no absolute reason in principle why it should not be limited to specific claims or issues, it is submitted, provided their costs can be clearly segregated (which latter may, however, often prove difficult).

The guiding principle has been expressed as follows: **18·185**

> "How should an arbitrator deal with costs where there has been a 'sealed offer'? I think that he should ask himself the question: 'Has the claimant achieved more by rejecting the offer and going on with the arbitration than he would have achieved if he had accepted the offer'?"[75]

While there will usually be little room for argument as to the consequences in costs when a sealed offer exceeds the amount awarded, there may nevertheless be situations where, in the proper exercise of the judicial discretion, a sufficient sealed offer may nevertheless fail in its effect. Thus, in a case of payment into court in legal proceedings, a payment in will fail to take effect if it is only because of a wholly new cause of action resulting from a later amendment that the final overall judgment exceeds the payment in.[76] Difficulties can also arise in applying the principle where later *amendments of the defence*, or other later developments following the offer, falsify the assumptions upon which the offer was originally based.

ILLUSTRATIONS

(1) Sub-contractors claimed £221,000, and the main contractors made a sealed offer of £77,000 including interest. Later, just before the hearing, the main contractors amended, pleading a quite new defence showing a mistake in the calculation of the claim. This was successful, and reduced the claim by £34,000. The sub-contractors were eventually awarded £27,000 less than the contractors' sealed offer—*i.e.* but for the new defence they would have recovered more than the offer. The arbitrator found that, even if they had known of the new defence at the time of the offer, the sub-contractors would have rejected the offer, and awarded the contractors their costs after the offer. *Held*, by the Court of Appeal, that it was not desirable to lay down any general rule when a defendant amended to plead a new defence, although normally a plaintiff should recover his costs in such a case; but in view of the arbitrator's finding it was clear that he had considered whether it was reasonable for the plaintiffs to continue after the offer, and the award should stand: *Blexen Ltd.* v. *Percy Trentham Ltd.* (1990).[77]

(2) Main contractor claimants claimed £93,000 from sub-contractor   **18·186**
respondents for damages, for delay and bad work, and in the event recovered £8,000. The sub-contractors counter-claimed some £17,000 for a final balance due, and £28,700 damages for breach. In the event £1,954 was recovered as damages. Five months before the hearing the sub-contractors wrote offering to accept a figure in satisfaction of all their own claims of £17,000, which after

---

[75] *Per* Donaldson J. in *The Tramountana* case, [1978] 1 Lloyd's Rep. 391, 397–8.
[76] *Tingay* v. *Harris* [1967] 2 Q.B. 327, C.A. See also *Cheeseman* v. *Bowaters U.K. Paper Mills Ltd.* [1971] 1 W.L.R. 1773.
[77] 54 BLR 37, C.A.

allowing a sum of £12,000 against the contractors' claim would produce a net payment to themselves in full satisfaction of their claims of £5,000. They also proposed that there should be "no order as to costs". The letter contained the usual terms for its ultimate disclosure to the arbitrator on the issue of costs. After a lengthy and expensive hearing where the balance due to the sub-contractors had been agreed at the outset at a sum in excess of £15,000 and occupied no time, the arbitrators greatly reduced both parties' claims for damages, producing a net figure due to the sub-contractors of £9,829. On costs the arbitrator ordered the sub-contractors to pay the main contractors' full costs until the date of the hearing, including brief fees; but ordered the contractors to pay 7/8 of the sub-contractor's remaining costs of the hearing. The arbitrator stated that, but for the sum due to the sub-contractors on their account, which had occupied no time, £8,000 of damages had been awarded to the main contractors against £1,954 to the sub-contractors, and that this was the reason for his order. On appeal, the main contractors argued that the sealed offer, since it did not contain an offer to pay costs separately, was not a valid sealed offer and should be disregarded, relying on the *Tramountana* case.[78] *Held*, by the Court of Appeal, (a) as to the costs up to the date of the hearing, that while some recognition to the partial success of the main contractor's claim might be given so as to disallow some part of the sub-contractor's costs, it could not be a proper exercise of the discretion to order the sub-contractors to pay the main contractor's costs, or any part of them, up to that date, and the award should be remitted to the arbitrator for that reason; (b) as to the costs of the hearing, it was clearly wrong in principle not to give effect to the offer until a date five months after it was made, so as to entitle the main contractors to their brief fees; moreover, distinguishing the *Tramountana* case, that the offer made by the sub-contractors had been a valid sealed offer, notwithstanding the use of the phrase "No order as to costs", and beyond doubt the main contractors had not achieved any advantage by rejecting it. This was an offer by a creditor, not by a debtor, effectively offering to forego expected costs. At the date of the offer there was a likelihood at best of costs on claim and counter-claim, which were likely to balance each other, and in any case the costs were relatively very small at that stage. The offer was an adequate and clear provision for any costs which might be due to the contractors. In view of the additional sums recovered of nearly £5,000 over their offer, there was only one answer which could be given to the question whether the contractors had gained by continuing the proceedings, and the sub-contractors were entitled to be paid all their costs by the contractors, including the brief fees, incurred after the date of the offer: *Archital Luxfer Ltd.* v. *Henry Boor Construction Ltd.* (1980).[79]

18-187   (3) Shipowners claimed $73,000 balance of hire under a charter party. A month before the hearing the charterers offered $15,000 plus interest and costs. The arbitrators subsequently awarded $16,215 excluding interest. But for the sealed offer, the arbitrators stated that they would have ordered each party to bear their own costs, in spite of the recovery of $16,215, due to false allegations, and other rejected evidence which had taken up much time, given by the shipowners. Since the owners would not be able to recover their own costs for these reasons, they considered that, applying Donaldson J.'s test in the *Tramountana* case, the shipowners, who had been originally offered $15,000 plus their costs, which would be much more than $1,215, had in the event by continuing their action recovered less in total, including costs, than they had been offered; so that in addition to depriving the shipowners of their

---

[78] Illustrated *supra*, para. 18·180.
[79] [1981] 1 Lloyd's Rep. 642.

own costs, the arbitrators ordered the shipowners to pay the charterers' costs after the offer. *Held*, by the Court of Appeal, (Sir Thomas Bingham M.R. dissenting), affirming the judge, that the charterers could not be permitted to say that an offer of $15,000 should be treated as being an offer for more than $16,215, because the offer of costs had been proved to be unnecessary by subsequent events. The offer to pay costs could not be treated as if it was a supplementary offer to pay more than $15,000 in respect of the claim. Based on the arbitrators' own view of the shipowners' conduct, and applying the principle that costs should follow the event, the proper order would be that each side should bear its own costs of the reference, and the award should be remitted to the arbitrators for their further consideration: *Everglade Maritime Inc.* v. *Schiffahrtsgesellschaft Datlaf Von Appen m.b.H.*, (*The Maria*) (1993).[80]

The above cases illustrate the importance rightly attached by the courts   **18·188** to enforcing the primary principle that costs should follow the event. This recognises the strong public interest in the prevention of wasteful litigation which the principle enforces, not only in the case of ordinary cost orders but also in giving effect to sealed offers. Arbitrators as a class, no doubt influenced by their characteristic inclinations toward compromise, tend to depart from this basic principle in their awards far more frequently than judges in the courts.[81]

Finally, mention should be made of a new device, recently deployed in litigation, but in principle applicable to arbitration, designed to secure protection against an order for costs. This consists of an offer expressly described as being "without prejudice", but also expressly reserving the right to place it before a court or arbitrator in the future in the context of costs, and has become eponymously known as a *Calderbank* offer.[82] While offers of this type, evolved in the Family Division of the High Court, are probably not appropriate to the discharge of an obligation to pay moneys due, or damages for breach of contract, and to this extent will not supplant the sealed offer procedure, one real advantage of the courts' approval of the *Calderbank* formula will be that sealed offers in arbitrations can now be formally designated as being "without prejudice", (thus dispensing with convention or the consent of the other party to their exclusion from the open correspondence and from the arbitrator and without affecting their intrinsic value when cost submissions are made). Combined with the interim award device, or the device of a final award making no mention of costs, these constitute real improvements on the earlier forms of sealed offer in use at the time of the tenth edition in 1970.

Summarising the effect of the above cases, the following appeared to be   **18·189** guiding principles when using sealed offers:

---

[80] [1993] Q.B. 780.
[81] For collected examples justifying, or not justifying a departure from the primary principle, see *Mustill and Boyd* (2nd ed.), pp. 396–8, and see, *per* Donaldson J. in the *Tramountana* case *supra*.
[82] *Calderbank* v. *Calderbank* [1976] Fam. 93; *Cutts* v. *Head* [1984] Ch. 290.

(a) the basic test of the adequacy of the offer is whether an offeree rejecting the offer has failed to recover as much as the offer by continuing with the arbitration[83];

(b) sealed offers ideally, but not necessarily, should deal with *interest* separately (since the arbitrator is in a position to assess interest himself, and so to compare an offer which does not deal separately with interest with any sums finally awarded). Nevertheless, defendants will receive greater and more precise protection if interest is separately provided for in the offer;

18·190 (c) sealed offers should *invariably* deal with *costs* separately and clearly, so as to enable the arbitrator to compare the substantive sums offered and awarded on a like-to-like basis at a time when he can almost certainly have no sufficiently accurate knowledge of what the amount of the costs will be. Some offers which do not make such separate provision may, however, achieve their overall purpose if the disparity between offer and award is so great as to show that, on the facts, the costs could have made no difference to the overall outcome[84];

(d) where there are events subsequent to the offer which could not be foreseen at the time and which result in the party who has rejected the offer recovering less by continuing with the arbitration, he may nevertheless, be entitled to disregard the offer (despite its adequacy) if in the particular circumstances it was reasonable for him to continue[85]; and

(e) conversely, the making of a sufficient offer may not entitle an offeror to receive his costs from the other party if other valid reasons exist for depriving him of his costs.[86]

18·191 It has been seen that, as an accidental by-product of the contractual basis of arbitration, final awards which deal with costs require submissions on costs to be made prior to award and without knowledge of its contents, but that a self-styled "interim award" not dealing with costs, or a "final award" in fact making no mention of costs (and so invoking section 18(4) of the 1950 Act) both represent variations of a device which will enable the parties to make their submissions as to costs at the more appropriate time after the substantive contents of the award are known.[87] Procedural mistakes can occur, however, as a result of which an arbitrator does in fact deal with costs inconsistently with an agreed or intended arrangement, and in such cases these "final" awards have been set aside.[88]

A procedural mishap of this kind can obviously also happen in the case of sealed offers. Notwithstanding that the mishap may have been the fault

---

[83] The *Tramountana* case illustrated *supra*, para. 18·180.

[84] See, *per* Ralph Gibson L.J. in the *Archital Luxfer* case, illustrated *supra*, para. 18·186.

[85] The *Blexen* case illustrated *supra*.

[86] *The Maria*, illustrated *supra*.

[87] See *supra*, Subsections (4) and (7), paras. 18·168 and 18·183.

[88] *Marples Ridgeway & Partners Ltd.* v. *C.E.G.B.* (1964) unrep., tenth edition, pp. 867–868; *Harrison* v. *Thompson* [1989] 1 W.L.R. 1325, Knox J., noted *supra*, para. 18·181.

of the offeror, in a case where there has been a genuine and adequate sealed offer as a fact received by the opposing party and of which the arbitrator is unaware when making his award the courts have given effect to the justice of the case by remitting the award for reconsideration.

ILLUSTRATION

A sealed offer of £5,000 and costs in settlement of a claim and counterclaim was followed by a final award on the same basis of £4,743 net, together with costs to the claimant. Counsel for the offeror had deliberately not placed the sealed offer before the arbitrator in the course of final speeches, in the mistaken belief that the arbitrator was intending to hold a further hearing to consider costs. *Held*, by the Court of Appeal, that, notwithstanding that the arbitrator had been in no way at fault himself and that the misunderstanding had been the fault of the offeror, the procedural mishap was within the scope of a remitter under section 22 of the 1950 Act, and the arbitrator should reconsider his award: *King* v. *Thomas McKenna Ltd.* (1991).[89]

SECTION 6. CURRENT OUTLOOK FOR ENGLISH ARBITRATION LAW

The previous Sections in this Chapter reveal, it is submitted, a divided and sometimes confused series of attitudes both by the judiciary and the legislature of recent years towards the role of arbitration.   **18·192**

One school of thought, evident in the immediate post-war era, is exemplified by an unreported decision of Diplock J. in 1960.[90] There, a small respondent builder had been wholly successful in defending a claim for the cost of reinstating post-completion movements in the foundations, which it was found had been due exclusively to the architect's design failing to take sufficient account of a buried mediaeval land drain nearby, but had been ordered to bear his own costs. Diplock J. expressed the view that if parties chose arbitration they did so in the knowledge that their rights of appeal were limited to those conferred by the case stated procedures or errors on the face of the award, and that the parties must also accept that arbitrators are entitled to make mistakes whether of fact or law.[91] At that time, Diplock J.'s earlier dictum in the *Heaven & Kesterton* case in 1958 (to the effect that unless an arbitrator gave reasons in his award or supplied reasons by way of affidavit or otherwise an award of costs could not be questioned)[92] had been expressly approved by the Court of Appeal in the following year.[93]

During the same post-war period there has also been a much greater overall tendency for the judiciary to encourage arbitration by granting   **18·193**

---

[90] *Lashmar* v. *Phillips & Cooper Ltd.* (1960) Q.B.D., Special Paper, unrep., but noted in the tenth edition, p. 869.
[91] *Heaven & Kesterton Ltd.* v. *Sven Widaeus A/B* [1958] 1 W.L.R. 248, 254–5.
[92] *Ibid.* at p. 257.
[93] *Perry* v. *Stopher* [1959] 1 W.L.R. 415.

stays more freely than in earlier periods, when scepticism as to the value of arbitration in all situations, and a greater willingness to refuse a stay, had previously been more evident.[94] More recently, positive pressures to force parties to arbitration, or to exclude them from the courts when endeavouring to appeal from arbitrators awards, have been evident, perhaps due to governmental budgetary influences, and what might be described as a "privatisation" school of thought. In the case of the judiciary, this reached its apogee, perhaps, in the judgment of Sir John Donaldson M.R. in the Court of Appeal in 1984, when he suggested that, in view of the current state of the lists in the Official Referee's Courts, consideration should be given to legislation requiring compulsory arbitration of construction disputes by arbitrators even where there was no arbitration agreement.[95] The Court in that case also put forward a startling new interpretation of a century old form of wording used in English arbitration clauses. This effectively disfranchised contractors from making any claim in High Court proceedings if it was not supported by the owner's architect's opinion or certificate, thereby forcing contractors (or indeed owners who differed from their architects) to use arbitration even in "no dispute" or summary judgment situations, in case leave to defend might be granted and so leave them stranded in the courts without remedy. It also provided unmeritorious defendants, particularly owners and employing main contractors, with invaluable tactical and procedural opportunities to disrupt and embarrass proceedings brought against them by contractors or sub-contractors.[96]

18·194   The same school of thought clearly provided the background both to the legislative barriers against obtaining leave from a judge to the Court of Appeal in arbitration appeal cases expressly imposed by the 1979 Act, and to the much more important and severe restrictions on appeals to the judge from an arbitrator resulting from the *Nema* guidelines and interpretation of the 1979 Act as enunciated by Lord Diplock in the House of Lords in that case. A significant early indication of the reasons said to support the *Nema* guidelines is to be found in a judgment of Donaldson J. in 1977 when, well before the 1979 Act had become law, he expressed the view that businessmen preferred speed and finality in arbitration as a higher priority than legal correctness of the award, and also suggested the desirability of legislation restricting the availability of case stated procedures, which he stated had been abused in recessionary times in order to secure delay in meeting commitments:

> "When I say that a foreign lawyer would find the English law on arbitration very odd, I do not refer to the unappealable status of an award. That he would find quite understandable and, indeed, in accordance with the practice in his own country. There parties to a dispute can, if

[94] See *supra* Subsection (3)(2)(g), paras. 18·104 and 18·118 *et seq.*
[95] *Northern Regional Health Authority* v. *Derek Crouch Construction Co. Ltd.* [1984] Q.B. 644, 674–675.
[96] See *ante*, Chap. 6, paras. 6·063–7·064; and see the full analysis of the directly contrary preceding case-law and criticism of the *Crouch* view in C.C.P.P. Chap. 17.

they wish, *agree to have a quick decision which may be wrong* rather than one which is subject to several appeals with all the associated delay and expense, even if the result is, perhaps, more likely to be right ... If, therefore, it is desirable to restrict the right of appeal from an arbitral award, *as it undoubtedly is*, it would be much better to do so *by statutory restrictions on the right of appeal*, while encouraging or even requiring the giving of reasons ... If the same approach were adopted in relation to arbitral awards, it would be possible to abolish the special case procedure *which is widely misunderstood and lends itself to misuse by those who, in times of economic stress, wish to achieve extended credit.*"[97] (Emphasis supplied)

This may be contrasted with Robert Goff J.'s powerful response to Lord Denning's early adumbration of the *Nema* guidelines in *The Oinoussian Virtue*,[97a] and with a very different (extrajudicial) assessment of businessmen's real attitudes to arbitration by Lord Mustill in 1990.[97b]

18·195

However, there are even some legislative indications which are apparently contrary to the guidelines and philosophy exhibited by the *Nema* protagonists, and which seem to recognise the need to safeguard and reinforce the right to appeal from an arbitrator, and which also recognise that arbitration may not be an unmixed blessing unless freely entered into. Thus, section 3(6) of the 1979 Act significantly requires that exclusion agreements (whereby the right of appeal under the Act will be lost) must be concluded on an ad hoc basis *after an arbitration has commenced* in the case of domestic contracts, only permitting such provisions to take effect *in arbitration clauses or agreements regulating future disputes* in the case of non-domestic contracts. Similarly, the Consumer Arbitration Agreements Act 1988 *actually nullifies* arbitration agreements in all cases where a party contracts "as a consumer",[98] in the absence of *post-dispute* consent to the arbitration by the consumer party.

There has also been a school of thought in the judiciary much more prepared to intervene where justice requires it. Thus, it has been seen that in the case of inappropriate awards of costs, a whole new philosophy of intervention, initiated originally by Goddard C.J., was developed in the Court of Appeal in 1969 in *Dineen* v. *Walpole*,[99] and further explained and rationalised by Mocatta J. in 1974,[1] which over-turned the *Heaven and Kesterton* doctrine. (Very recently in 1990, however, a Court of Appeal presided over by Lord Donaldson M.R. supported an earlier view of the Court of Appeal that an appeal from a reasoned award as to what might be

---

[97] *Tramountana Armadora S.A.* v. *Atlantic Shipping S.A.* [1978] 1 Lloyd's Rep. 391, 393–4. *Mustill and Boyd* do, however, state that appeals had become a problem in *commodity* arbitrations prior to the 1979 Act—see (2nd ed.), p. 604, but this hardly seems to warrant cutting down rights of appeal in more complicated and sophisticated types of dispute.

[97a] [1981] 1 Lloyd's Rep. 533, 538.

[97b] Quoted in (1990) 6 *Arbitration International* 253, 256.

[98] The definitions are the same as in the Unfair Contract Terms Act 1977, see *ante* Chap. 1, Section 9(7), paras. 1·238–1·240.

[99] [1969] 1 Lloyd's Rep. 261, see *supra*, para. 18·178.

[1] In *The Erich Schroeder* [1974] 1 Lloyd's Rep. 192. See *supra* Section 5(6), paras. 18·178 and 18·180.

justifiably regarded as costs could only be pursued through the inhospitable thickets of section 1(3) of the 1979 Act.)[2] If correct, this effectively subverts the justice-driven effects of the *Dineen* case.[2a]

18·196   A further example of a more justice-driven approach was the readiness of a Court of Appeal in 1964 to confirm the refusal of a stay so as to secure a single tribunal in the courts with their third party procedures available to deal with a case of multiple proceedings.[3] But it has been seen that another Court of Appeal, in very similar circumstances, refused its assistance in 1969 when revocation of a prematurely appointed arbitrator's authority was the only means available for achieving the same object, apparently taking the view that this would be outside the historical scope of the revocation remedy under section 1 of the 1950 Act.[4] That unhelpful reasoning was even more firmly and comprehensively restated by Steyn J. in 1985,[5] and on analysis must lead to proliferation of proceedings, with additional expense and the possibility of inconsistent findings, as well as assisting unmeritorious defendants to delay and embarrass proceedings brought against them.

A further area of inconsistent or confused judicial activity is to be found in the case law as to "steps in the proceedings". Here, quite inconsistently with the many pressures and tendencies in favour of arbitration and against access to the courts already noted, there appears to have been a shift from an early and reasonable approach, based on estoppel and prejudice, to an extraordinarily legalistic approach which has the effect of denying arbitration to a party in circumstances where it is entirely appropriate, and where no possible prejudice could have been suffered by the opposing party.[6] There is also the potential embarrassment that precisely identical "steps in the proceedings" wording is to be found in the 1975 Act in non-domestic cases, where for understandable reasons the statutory policy is clearly that stays should virtually always be granted.[7]

18·197   By contrast, as in the case of appeals from awards of costs, the judiciary have been extremely helpful in intervening so as to ensure a proper judicial exercise of an arbitrator's discretion where the parties have made use of sealed offer procedures.[7a] More recently still, the courts have shown much greater readiness to investigate carefully, and if necessary to act decisively, upon allegations of incompetent or unfair conduct by arbitrators.[8]

---

[2] *King* v. *Thomas McKenna Ltd.* [1992] 2 Q.B. 480 approving *Blexen* v. *Percy Trentham* (1990) 54 BLR 48.

[2a] See *supra*, para. 18·181.

[3] *Taunton-Collins* v. *Cromie* [1964] 1 W.L.R. 633, see *supra*, para. 18·111.

[4] *City Centre Properties* v. *Matthew Hall* [1969] 1 W.L.R. 772 illustrated and doubted *supra*, para. 18·113.

[5] *Property Investments (Developments) Ltd.* v. *Byefield Building Services Ltd.* (1985) 31 BLR 47, illustrated *supra*, para. 18·115.

[6] *Turner & Goudy* v. *McConnell* [1985] 1 W.L.R. 898, illustrated *supra*, Section 3(2)(h), para. 18·122.

[7] See *supra*, Section 3(2)(h).

[7a] See paras. 18·182 *et seq.*

[8] See the more modern misconduct cases, illustrated *supra*, Section 4(3), paras. 18·135 *et seq.*

So far as the legislature is concerned, in contrast to its "privatisation policies" of encouraging arbitration and discouraging access to the courts, little or no interest seems to have been shown in legislating to improve or assist arbitration or to deal with recognised problems. A number of *lacunae* have already been noted *supra*, in Section 1.[9] It is noteworthy that nothing whatever has been done, for example, to make the court's payment in machinery available. Nor is anything being done to asssist with the problems of multi-partite proceedings. Nothing has been done to clarify or regulate the arbitrator's powers in regard to pleadings (while it may be conceded that there are clearly some classes of arbitration where pleadings or written statements of case are not contemplated), and the only intervention in regard to the enforcement of interlocutory orders seems hardly to have shed much light in that area.[10]

Moreover, it seems extraordinary that lengthy debate and historical examination should still be needed at the present day in order to determine, for example, whether arbitration proceedings can be struck out for want of prosecution[11]; whether, and if so what jurisdiction exists to issue an injunction during the pendency of an arbitration[12]; from what source the jurisdiction is derived to entertain an appeal on costs when the award is silent as to reasons; or what precisely is the court's power of remitter following an inappropriate order of costs.[13]   **18·198**

A relatively short statute supplying the known existing lacunae and defining more clearly at points of doubt both the court's powers of intervention in support of arbitration and the extent of an arbitrator's interlocutory powers and their enforcement by interlocutory orders, would seem valuable. In addition, a critical re-examination of the policies and effect of the *Nema* interpretation and guidelines, either by the legislature or by the House of Lords itself, may ultimately prove unavoidable, it can be predicted, if arbitration is to retain its appeal for the minority of informed parties who have hitherto chosen it voluntarily, or the majority who have been led into it involuntarily through contracts of adhesion. The price of such policies in denial of justice and the reduced appeal and standing of arbitrators and arbitration may be found to be too high.[14]   **18·199**

However, the view that a justice-driven judicial intervention can only improve the quality and so the attraction of arbitration, whereas removal of judicial control can only lead to a decline in its use, certainly in the construction industry as owners become better informed. More recently, following publication of the UNCITRAL Model Law in 1985, which could   **18·200**

---

[9] See para. 18·018.
[10] See s.5, 1979 Act.
[11] *Bremer Vulkan Schiffban und Maschinenfabrik* v. *South India Shipping Corporation Ltd.* [1981] A.C. 909. Now the subject of recent statutory intervention, see s.102 of the Courts and Legal Services Act 1990.
[12] *Channel Tunnel Group* v. *Balfour Beatty Construction* [1993] A.C. 334.
[13] *King* v. *Thomas McKenna* [1991] 2 Q.B. 480.
[14] See Kirby P.'s dissenting remarks, in an analogous appellate context, in the New South Wales C.A., in *Warley Ltd.* v. *ADCO Constructions Ltd.* (1988) 8 A.C.L.R. 73, 80, quoted *supra*, Section 1, para. 18·024.

be said broadly to adopt the opposing philosophy of conferring greater freedom from restraint and reducing judicial control over arbitrators both in regard to procedural and evidentiary matters as well as to questions of substantive law, the English Departmental Advisory Committee under Mustill L.J. in 1989 recommended against adoption of the Model Law, while at the same time suggesting that there should be a new arbitration statute following as closely as possible the same structure and language as the Model Law "so as to enhance its accessibility to persons familiar with the Model Law".[15] This was followed by a privately funded attempt, with apparent DAC or other official encouragement, at what appeared to be a consolidating Act with the expressed intention of making no recommendations or changes which could be regarded as controversial.[16] This latter draft was subsequently rendered abortive by a change of departmental policy, and in February 1994, the Departmental Committee published a new draft Bill for consultative purposes.

This latter draft Bill appears to follow the form suggested by the 1989 Committee. Consideration of its detailed contents is clearly outside the purview of this book, but while the opportunity has been taken to correct a few anomalies (for example the unwise 1979 alteration requiring an unqualified majority decision in umpire-type provisions for three arbitrators),[17] on a preliminary perusal of the draft bill it does not appear to initiate any but minor changes in the existing corpus of English arbitration law, although consolidating the statutory element, and in places making some minor gestures facilitating voluntary adoption of model law procedures.

---

[15] See for an authoritative account of this history Steyn L.J. in (1994) 10 *Arb. Int.* 1, 2–3.
[16] Under the auspices of what became known as "The Marriot Group", Op. cit. pp. 3–4.
[17] Draft Bill, Clause 22.

INDEX

Abandonment. *See also* **Non-completion; Repudiation.**
architect/engineer's employment, of, 2·260–2·264
common law freedom to, 12·010
contractor, by, damages for, 8·119–8·155
damages for, 8·119–8·155
liquidated damages, effect on, 10·047–10·053
owner, by, damages for, 8·119–8·155
remedies, 4·205–4·231
repudiation is, 4·209
substantial performance, doctrine of, and, 4·019

Acceptance. *See also* **Offer; Tender.**
binding, when, 3·054
commencement of work, relation to, 1·037, 3·069–3·070
conditional, 1·033, 3·055–3·065
conditions, subject to, 3·062–3·065
death, effect of, 1·030
defects of. *See* **Acceptance of work.**
letters of intent, 3·071
nature of, 1·032–1·033
new term, introducing, 1·033
post, by, 1·040
pricing, mistake in, and, 3·072
reasonable time for, 3·068
retrospective effect, 1·041, 3·067
silence not, 1·033
"subject to contract", 1·057–1·060, 3·056
tender, of. *See* **Tender.**
time for, 3·068

Acceptance of work, 5·001–5·024. *See also* **Defects.**
approval required, where
architect/engineer, of, 5·014–5·019, 5·052–5·058
owner, of, 5·012–5·013
third person, of, 5·014–5·019
damages, effect on, 5·007–5·011, 5·052–5·058, 8·116–8·117
occupation, and, 5·003–5·006
substantial performance, doctrine of, 5·001–5·002

Accord and satisfaction, 1·071–1·078, 4·232
Accounts,
architect, special employment of, for settling, 2·268
checking of, certificate, 6·162–6·166
final, 8·215
Act of God, 4·265–4·266, 10·042
Additions. *See* **Variations.**

Adjoining owners,
architect, duty of, as to, 2·152–2·153
Adjoining property insurance, 15·006, 15·023–15·025
Administration and administrators, 16·024–16·026. *See also* **Bankruptcy and liquidation.**
Administrative receivers, 16·020–16·023. *See also* **Bankruptcy and liquidation.**
Advances. *See* **Interim certificates; Payment by instalments.**
Advertisement,
deceit and, 1·020
offer, does not constitute, 1·020
Agent,
architect as. *See* **Architect/engineer.**
commission or discount of, 2·235, 3·079
fraud of, principal's liability for, 2·232, 3·077–3·078
secret dealings with, 2·233–2·236, 3·079
Agreements to refer, 18·001. *See also* **Arbitration.**
submissions distinguished, 18·001
Air,
right to, architect's duty as to, 2·152
Alterations. *See* **Variations.**
Anns principle,
anticipatory repairs, 1·346, 1·351, 1·364, 2·152
application of, 1·357
not applicable, where, 1·352
to whom duty owed, 1·350
D. & F. Estates case, 1·354–1·356, 14·002A
"complex structure theory", 1·355, 1·358
disclaimers, effect of, 1·324–1·326
generally, 1·276, 1·277, 1·292, 1·345–1·346
Heyman case, 1·353, 1·356
housing authorities, negligent inspection or supervision, 1·346
limitation of action, 1·307, 1·347–1·349, 1·351, 1·361, 2·222, 4·284, 4·285
Murphy, effect of, 1·357–1·360, 2·152, 13·044, 14·002A
repair of defective chattel or building, 1·346
sub-contractors, liability of, under, 13·044
Appointment,
architect/engineer, of, 2·042–2·053, 4·197–4·201, 6·145, 6·173–6·175
condition precedent, as, 4·197–4·199
contractor could require, 6·175
certifier, of, contractor could require, 6·175